Excel Business Applications: IBM® Version

John Annaloro with Patrick Burns

QUE® CORPORATION
LEADING COMPUTER KNOWLEDGE

Excel Business Applications: IBM® Version

Copyright © 1990 by Que® Corporation.

All rights reserved. Printed in the United States of America. No part of this book may be used or reproduced in any form or by any means, or stored in a database or retrieval system, without prior written permission of the publisher except in the case of brief quotations embodied in critical articles and reviews. Making copies of any part of this book for any purpose other than your own personal use is a violation of United States copyright laws. For information, address Que Corporation, 11711 N. College Ave., Carmel, IN 46032.

Library of Congress Catalog No.: 89-62002

ISBN No.: 0-88022-495-9

This book is sold *as is*, without warranty of any kind, either express or implied, respecting the contents of this book, including but not limited to implied warranties for the book's quality, performance, merchantability, or fitness for any particular purpose. Neither Que Corporation nor its dealers or distributors shall be liable to the purchaser or any other person or entity with respect to any liability, loss, or damage caused or alleged to be caused directly or indirectly by this book.

93 92 91 90   8 7 6 5 4 3 2 1

Interpretation of the printing code: the rightmost double-digit number is the year of the book's printing; the rightmost single-digit number, the number of the book's printing. For example, a printing code of 90-1 shows that the first printing of the book occurred in 1990.

Excel Business Applications: IBM® Version is based on Version 2.1 of Microsoft® Excel.

DEDICATION

For Sheryl Ann

Your passion for life and your dedication to family survive through Timothy and Taryn.

— *P. J. B.*

ACKNOWLEDGMENTS

As I reflect on the period of time that has passed during the making of this book, I realize that the contributions of three people have made this dream a reality.

To Terrie Lynn Solomon:

My sincere thanks for your patience, compassion, support, and good humor in the face of personal losses, natural disasters, and general chaos.

To Elna Tymes:

My admiration for your perseverance and counsel over the last four months.

To Lisa Hunt:

My gratefulness for your enduring professionalism and fanatical attention to detail.

— P. J. B.

Publishing Director
   David P. Ewing

Acquisitions Editor
   Terrie Lynn Solomon

Product Director and Technical Editor
   Steven R. Sogge

Editors
   Lisa Hunt
   Tim Huddleston

Technical Support
   Tim Stanley
   Jerry Ellis

Indexed by
   Joelynn Gifford

Book Production
   William Hartman
   Corinne Harmon
   Jodi Jensen
   David Kline
   Lori A. Lyons
   Jennifer Matthews
   Dennis Sheehan
   Bruce Steed
   Nora Westlake

Composed in Times by
   William Hartman, Hartman Publishing.

Table of Contents

Introduction 1
   Who Will Benefit from This Book? 2
   How To Use This Book 3

1   Understanding Excel and the Ideal Computer Environment .. 7

   Understanding the Excel Concept 8
      Envisioning Your Individual Business Needs 9
      Planning the Specific Application Goals 11
      Developing the Appropriate Tools 13
   Creating the Ideal Computer Environment 21
      Microsoft Windows 22
      Microprocessor Chips and Math Coprocessor Chips 23
      Video Displays 23
      Printers 23
      Memory Management 23
   Summary 25

2   Designing Spreadsheets and Financial Statements 27

   Designing the Income Statement 28
      The Service-Oriented Income Statement 28
      The Product-Oriented Income Statement 32
   Designing the Balance Sheet 38
   Designing the Financial-Ratio Report 44
   Using What-If Analysis 50
   Enhancing the Financial Worksheet Model (INCBALRA.XLS) 53
      The Monthly Income Statement 54
      The Monthly Balance Sheet 56
      The Financial-Ratio Report 58
   Summary 60

3   Managing a Business Checkbook 61

   Building the Check Register 62
   Building the Reconciliation Sheet 72
   Building the Check Register Accounting Summary: A Linked Worksheet Model 77

Testing the Entire Checkbook Management System 81
Automating the Checkbook Management System 83
Safeguarding Your Sensitive Data 84
    Protecting Cells in the Accounting Summary Worksheet 84
    Password-Protecting the Accounting Summary Worksheet 88
Summary 89

4 Using Financial Spreadsheets To Promote Your Standing 93

Using the Cash Budget Forecast (CASHBUDG.XLS) 94
    The Sales Forecast 98
    The Charge vs. Cash Sales Analysis 99
    The Cash Receipts Forecast 10
    Base-Period Purchases and the Charge vs. Cash Purchases Analysis 103
    The Cash Disbursements Forecast 104
    The Completion of the Cash Budget Model 105
    A Review of the Cash Budget 107
Using Pro Forma Financial Statements (PROFORMA.XLS) 108
    The Historical and Pro Forma Income Statement 110
    The Historical and Pro Forma Balance Sheet 112
    The Historical and Pro Forma Ratio Analysis 116
Maintaining Your Historical Records (HISTORY.XLS) 117
Using Breakeven Analysis (BREAKEVN.XLW) 120
    Creating a Data Table 121
    Using a Chart-Creating Macro 123
    Using Excel Workspaces 125
Summary 125

5 Performing Accurate Asset and Investment Analysis 127

Understanding Asset Management 129
    Model 1: The DuPont Method (DUPONT.XLS) 129
        Using the DUPONT.XLS Model 130
        Modifying the DUPONT.XLS Model 132
    Model 2: The Depreciation Analyzer (DEPRECI8.XLS) 133
        Using the DEPRECI8.XLS Model 134
        Modifying the DEPRECI8.XLS Model 137
Understanding the Time Value of Money 137
    Model 1: Future Value Investment Analysis (FV.XLS) 138
        Using the FV.XLS Model 138
        Modifying the FV.XLS Model 141
    Model 2: The Present Value Investment Analysis Model (PV.XLS) 142
        Using the PV.XLS Model 142
        Modifying the PV.XLS Model 145
Evaluating Risk and Return 146
    Model 1: Single-Asset Risk Evaluation (RSK&RTN.XLS) 146
    Model 2: The Capital-Asset Pricing Model (RSK&RTN.XLS) 149

Using Valuation Techniques 152
    Model 1: Stock Analyzer (STOCKS.XLS) 153
    Model 2: Bond Analyzer (BONDS.XLS) 155
    Model 3: Discounted-Cash-Flow Analyzer (DCFA.XLS) 161
Summary 164

6 Achieving General Ledger Accounting Success 165

An Overview of the GLAS Model 166
Understanding the GLAS Model Components 168
    GL.XLW: The GLAS Workspace File 168
    GENMENU.XLS: The GLAS Main Menu Worksheet File 168
    GL.XLS: The GLAS General Ledger/Journal Worksheet File 169
    GL.XLM: The GLAS Application Macros File 169
    REPMENU.XLS: The GLAS Print Reports Menu File 169
    TMP.XLS: The GLAS Report Worksheet File 170
    PROTOCOL.XLS: The Model Company's General Ledger/
        Journal Worksheet File 170
Preparing the GLAS Model for First-Time Use 171
    Entering the New Chart of Accounts 171
    Manually Entering Account Descriptions and Balances 174
Using the Options on GLAS's Main Menu and Print Reports Menu 176
    Adding a New G/L Account 177
    Entering and Editing Journal Transactions 177
    Posting Transactions 179
    Printing Reports 181
    Closing and Clearing the Journal 181
    Quitting GLAS and Returning to Excel 183
    Printing the Chart of Accounts 184
    Printing the Trial Balance Sheet 185
    Printing the Budget Summary and Variance 185
    Printing the Period-to-Date Summary 185
    Returning to the Main Menu from the Print Reports Menu 185
A GLAS Case Study: Protocol Services, Int'l 186
Expanding the GLAS Database 194
Summary 195

7 Controlling Your Accounts Receivable and Accounts Payable 197

Using the Credit-Application Generator (CREDAPP.XLS) 198
Using Simple Accounts Receivable and Accounts Payable Worksheets
    (AR10_89.XLS, AP10_89.XLS, AR4_90.XLS, AP4_90.XLS) 200
Using an Invoice Register (INVCREG1.XLS) 204
Sharing Information between Files (INVCREG.XLW) 209
    The Sales Summary (INVSALES.XLS) 212
    The Aging Report (INVAGING.XLS) 213
    Accounts Receivable Summaries (INVARCUS.XLS, INVARDAT.XLS) 215

       The Collections Worksheet (COLWKSHT.XLW, COLWKSHT.XLS) 216
       The Accounts Payable Tickler File (TICKLER.XLS) 217
  Creating Workspaces 219
  Modifying Existing Worksheets (INVFREG.XLS) 220
  Summary 222

8   Using Marketing, Sales, and Financing Applications 225

  Developing Market Projections 227
       Understanding Unit Costs 228
       Gathering Unit Costs 229
       Analyzing Unit Costs 230
  Creating a Market Projection for Ford's Pan-Galactic Bar & Grill 230
       The Equivalent Units Conversion Worksheet (MN-CNVRT.XLS) 232
       The Costs and Sales Forecast Worksheet (MN-FRCST.XLS) 234
       The Pro Forma Monthly Sales Worksheet (MN-PROFM.XLS) 235
  What-Iffing under Different Scenarios 236
  Using the Cost Data Elsewhere (MN-INCST.XLS) 240
  Dealing with the Impact of Financing 242
       Building In the Effects of Financing 242
       Business Borrowing (AMORTIZE.XLS, DAILYINT.XLS) 243
       Investor Financing 247
  Summary 248

9   Managing Databases 249

  Setting Up the Database 249
  Conducting a Search (SLSCONTC.XLS) 253
  Extracting Records (EMPPHONE.XLS) 256
  Plotting Trends with a Database (PR89COND.XLC,
      PR89HOME.XLC, SLSPR89.XLS) 258
  Using Database Functions To Verify Reliability (SVLHSJUN.XLS) 267
  Sorting Records (PROJECTS.XLS) 270
  Making It Pretty: Formatting Hints for Your Reports (PROJECTS.XLS) 272
  Printing Your Report (PROJB89.XLS, PROJECTS.XLS) 273
  Summary 278

10   Creating Business-Presentation Charts 281

  Understanding Excel's Chart Types 282
       Area Charts 283
       Bar Charts 284
       Column Charts 284
       Line Charts 284
       Pie Charts 285
       Scatter Charts 286
       Combination Charts 287

Selecting and Organizing Your Numerical Data 287
Understanding the Evolution of the Excel Chart 289
Using Existing Models To Create Fully Formatted Charts 293
    Reviewing the Basics of Chart-Making 293
    Using Models To Create Charts 298
Printing Excel Charts 301
Enhancing and Modifying Charts 302
    Building Charts from Noncontinuous Ranges 305
    Adding Enhancements to Graph Data Blocks 309
Summary 311

A   How To Use the Applications Disk 313

What You Need To Get Started 313
How To Make Backup and Working Copies 314
How To Use the Applications 315
How To Troubleshoot Problems 316
How To Get Help 317
Copy Restrictions 317

B   Using Excel's Worksheet Functions and Macro Language Library 319

Worksheet Functions 320
    Database Functions 321
    Date and Time Functions 322
    Financial Functions 323
    Information Functions 324
    Logical Functions 326
    Lookup Functions 327
    Mathematical Functions 328
    Matrix Functions 329
    Statistical Functions 330
    Text Functions 331
    Trigonometric Functions 333
Macro Language Library 334
    Command-Equivalent Functions 334
    Action-Equivalent Functions 344
    Customizing Functions 347
    Macro Language Control Functions 352
    Value-Returning Functions 353

About the Authors

John Annaloro has developed many accounting programs and income-tax-preparation programs that are sold worldwide, including the best-selling J.K. Lassers's *Your Income Tax*. His educational software that teaches business, finance, economics, and accounting is used in a fair percentage of all colleges and universities. He is a part-time college professor in both the arts and computer science. Currently he is a senior executive at a large financial institution, overseeing electronic banking operations.

Patrick J. Burns has a B.S. in finance and economics. A native of Pennsylvania, he has traveled worldwide, having spent much time living in both Europe and Asia. He is a founder and principal of B.K. Global, a Pacific Rim import-export concern. His work in the computer field includes the beta-site testing and confidential review of software packages for major publishers.

Trademark Acknowledgments

Que Corporation has made every attempt to supply trademark information about company names, products, and services mentioned in this book. Trademarks indicated below were derived from various sources. Que Corporation cannot attest to the accuracy of this information.

Apple LaserWriter® is a registered trademark of Apple Computer, Inc.

AT&T® is a registered trademark of AT&T.

Hewlett-Packard® LaserJet is a registered trademark of Hewlett-Packard Company.

PS/2™ is a trademark of, and IBM® and OS/2® are registered trademarks of, International Business Machines Corporation.

Lotus® 1-2-3® is a registered trademark of Lotus Development Corporation.

Microsoft® Corporation, Microsoft® Excel, Microsoft® Mouse, and Microsoft® Windows/386 are registered trademarks of Microsoft Corporation.

Unisys™ is a trademark of Unisys Corporation.

Introduction

Over the past months, the computer trade press has begun to call Excel the premier productivity software for the IBM computer. Why? Excel surpasses all other similar products in both its breadth of features and ease of use. Offering a simple-to-use pull-down menu structure, a built-in database builder, the macro recorder, and extensive, high-quality graphics, Excel is clearly the best spreadsheet product on the market, defining the look of the new generation of spreadsheets.

Excel has more features, more graphics, and the capability to make use of today's (and tomorrow's) more powerful computers. It has the capability to produce and print complicated charts and graphs, create elaborate reports, and build entire databases.

Excel can even be programmed into automated templates—with their own title screens that load from a disk like a stand-alone applications program—and continue to perform specialized business-management tasks.

Sophisticated applications can be designed through Excel's extensive mathematical and programming functions. Excel automatically handles many computational tasks at one time, controlling every operation perfectly. *Excel Business Applications: IBM Version* makes it easier than ever for you to use these features to build applications that yield elegant computer solutions to specific business needs. And this book will ease your journey in pursuit of logical, interactive applications to manage your personal or business productivity goals.

Yet no real computer-programming background is needed to make Excel work, your way. By following the simple step-by-step instructions, you can create powerful, automated operations that use the IBM-style 286 and 386 machines (and clones), DOS, and OS/2 to their fullest extent.

Excel Business Applications: IBM Version shows you how to conceive, then automate, spreadsheets that you will use often—and how to make an applications program that will produce logical, well-organized, up-to-the-minute reports. You will learn how to make the computer easier to use and easier to command in the business environment. You will even learn how to safely delegate to others simple tasks such as data input, without the worry of compromising the integrity of the program and the information held in a database.

Who Will Benefit from This Book?

Excel Business Applications: IBM Version goes beyond beginning books about Excel and beyond the program documentation. This book will benefit first-time Excel learners who are already familiar with other spreadsheet software packages and who don't need to start at the absolute "let's turn on the computer now" beginning. Not only does Excel offer the entire range of features found in Lotus 1-2-3, but it goes far beyond. If you are a Lotus devotee, this book will help you learn the working features of Excel (and of the next generation of spreadsheets) not found in 1-2-3.

Finally, this book is written for those who may have used Excel or Lotus 1-2-3 templates—who know the "look" of a spreadsheet product yet have never actually created business applications themselves.

Although *Excel Business Applications: IBM Version* may not truly be for the beginner, the beginning user will still find instructional help in this book. Chapters 1 through 5 provide information in an easy-to-follow, one-step-at-a-time format. These chapters also serve as a review for experienced Excel users—reinforcing what they may already know—and provide a "jumping in" point for learning more about Excel.

More experienced Excel users, as well as experienced Lotus 1-2-3 users, will benefit from being able to expand their functional library of computer solutions with the examples provided in this book. Although the book is organized by programs that produce specific results, information on building spreadsheets, creating charts, producing reports, designing Excel databases, and developing Excel macros will teach you to turn an idea into a working reality—for personal use or for advancement in the corporate environment.

Advanced Excel users and experienced programmers will learn about the concepts involved in developing complicated applications and customizing business solutions. And everyone, advanced user or novice, will find Appendix B a useful, day-to-day guide to Excel operations.

How To Use This Book

Excel Business Applications: IBM Version offers an orderly approach to learning Excel. This "what to do first, second, third..." approach prevents you from suffering through trial-and-error learning. All the important functions, concepts, rules of business, and programming procedures are emphasized throughout the book, helping you to develop an efficient, self-paced curriculum that will prepare you to create Excel business applications successfully.

The features of the program unique to Excel are covered extensively at the beginning of each chapter to help teach you "power user" skills. And all the figures—including screen pictures—show you the look of the "new generation" of spreadsheets.

Chapter 1, "Understanding Excel and the Ideal Computer Environment," provides an overview designed to familiarize the reader with the "Excel concept." This nontechnical introduction, which contains actual examples of working programs, will help you envision uses for Excel applications and plan specific application goals. The chapter teaches new Excel users (and refreshes the memory of experienced users) about the best way to configure a computer used with expanded memory, a math coprocessor chip, advanced color graphics, and hard disk drives. Also included are tips on using Excel's excellent on-line help tutorial. This basic information will teach you how to "load and go" and use the system at its maximum potential.

Chapter 2, "Designing Spreadsheets and Financial Statements," guides you through the construction of simple financial statements and simple Excel programs to reinforce how to build electronic spreadsheets that mirror the characteristics and features found in all business reports. The chapter uses important business terminology and provides simple shells to be used in exercises. Skip-ahead readers who feel lost in later chapters will be referred to these exercises for quick help and assistance.

Chapter 3, "Managing a Business Checkbook," teaches the fundamentals of check-register reconciliation and accounting summaries for the business checkbook. This chapter discusses Excel-specific functions that enable you you to protect your work with locks or passwords. Finally, the procedures for saving, retrieving, combining, and linking spreadsheets are reviewed so that the checkbook can become a working model and so that the check register—complete with general ledger reference numbers—can be made fully operative.

Chapter 4, "Using Financial Spreadsheets To Promote Your Standing," examines the many different ways to present the standing of your business or the condition of another organization. This chapter's main thrust is the basics of portraying financial health and well-being. Here, special attention is placed on format, composition, and design; the use of Excel's fonts and borders; and the use of lines and shadow outlines to highlight important information.

Chapter 5, "Performing Accurate Asset and Investment Analysis," offers solution-oriented investment planning and analysis methods for situations in which money needs to be used and invested wisely. You can use this group of 10 related spreadsheets to plan, budget, save, and invest capital and reserves—or to determine what your assets are worth now or will be worth later.

Chapter 6, "Achieving General Ledger Accounting Success," outlines ways to make a complete general ledger accounting system that can be customized to keep track of your business, your way. The model shells in the text include spreadsheets for accurately tracking all your financial activity. This chapter also reviews budget forecasting so that you can compare actual expenses with budgeted expenses.

Chapter 7, "Controlling Your Accounts Receivable and Accounts Payable," discusses A/R and A/P management techniques and helps you produce a valid cash forecast. From credit applications to final account write-offs from a delinquency report, Excel can help with receivables management. Evaluating your business's cash cycle will help you know when to disburse your payables so that you can hold your money as long as possible, thus maximizing the accrued interest and dividends.

Chapter 8, "Using Marketing, Sales, and Financing Applications," shows the link between Excel spreadsheets and the automatic processing of information for a variety of business needs. The emphasis is on establishing a link among marketing, sales, and lending and then building the Excel worksheet models, which enable you to analyze unit costs, forecast unit sales, and gather the critical data together for investors, creditors, and lenders. The chapter also shows you how to build stand-alone computer solutions that have the "Excel look."

Chapter 9, "Managing Databases," puts Excel's database functions to work. The chapter illustrates Excel's capability to save a group of financial entries from *any* worksheet and then translate those records into a fully functional database that you can sort, search, query, merge, and use to produce meaningful reports. Examples in this chapter teach how to use database query methods to create seasonal indexes, sales histories, and trend-analysis worksheets. Report functions include how-to's for creating headers and footers, hiding information, adding borders, numbering pages, and managing your printer.

Chapter 10, "Creating Business-Presentation Charts," demonstrates how to automatically generate attractive formatted charts and graphs that give visual impact to processed data and how to convert numerical analysis to a pictorial display. Excel's extensive graphics library is applied to many of the major examples used in previous chapters to illustrate the practice of making a picture worth a thousand words. Topics cover adjusting the size of charts and graphs for inclusion in written reports; adding text, color, and font selections; and controlling graphic printing.

Appendix A, "How To Use the Applications Disk," covers such information as what kind of equipment you need in order to use the Excel applications and how to make working copies of the disk.

Appendix B, "Using Excel's Worksheet Functions and Macro Library," offers the complete list of Excel commands. Each command description includes the operational syntax.

6

Excel Business Applications: IBM Version

1
Understanding Excel and the Ideal Computer Environment

This chapter introduces the "Excel concept." A brief, ideological review, the chapter emphasizes the benefits that you as a user of Excel in business receive when you do the following:

- Envision your own business uses for an Excel application
- Plan specific application goals
- Develop the appropriate macro tools to be used by the application

This three-part spreadsheet-creating method will bring you "power user" skills, and with these skills you will quickly build your own "concept library"—a collection of concepts that you pick up as you become a power user. In short, the "Excel concept" will help you understand what is, and isn't, pertinent when you use Excel in your business.

You also will learn about creating the ideal computer environment in which to use Excel. The discussion covers such topics as math coprocessor chips, expanded memory, advanced color graphics, hard-disk-drive organization, and the use of Excel in the Windows environment. As you read the discussion, reevaluate your current system setup in light of the recommended ideal environment and make the necessary improvements wherever possible. As a result of making these improvements, you may find it necessary to edit your current program configuration or to reinstall your personal copy of Excel. Then you'll be ready to "load and go," prepared to use the system at its maximum potential.

Understanding the Excel Concept

Undoubtedly you have already experimented with Excel, having used its capability to add, subtract, multiply, and divide the contents of worksheet cells. That's fine. If you have been using Excel for a longer period of time, you're probably even building linked worksheets, small databases, and your own macro sheets. That's fine, too. If at first it seems that the topics covered in this section are too basic, just be patient for a while: you will soon blast forward. If the presentation seems somewhat complex, then grab your Excel reference guides, take full advantage of Excel's on-line help mode, and refresh your Excel vocabulary while reading this first chapter.

You see, you already know how to use Excel to one degree or another. But in the process of honing your user skills, you may have lost sight of the fact that just like any successful business venture, the continued successful use of Excel requires *planning* and *development*. And within the scope of the "Excel concept," planning and development are the second and third most critical steps that you will follow in the process; the first critical step requires only that you be able to envision your individual business needs.

Envisioning Your Individual Business Needs

Always be prepared to unleash your artistic flair. Even though Excel is the preeminent high-powered, multiapplication number cruncher, envisioning your application gives you the opportunity to create an application uniquely your own. Everyone adds and subtracts in roughly the same manner, but no two people create a painting with the exact same brushstrokes.

For example, a "weekend" sailor would surely be interested in knowing the heights and times of high and low tides for the local bay. Using the tide calculator in figure 1.1, an Excel sailor could determine just that.

As a diplomat who frequently travels around the world on business, wouldn't you be interested in a macro-driven flight log that enables you to store the date, mileage, bonus miles, destination, origin, and cost of each individual trip? The macro program in figure 1.2 meets this need perfectly.

Do you know the accurate composition of the fixed and variable operating costs in your company? Your vice president of finance could surely use a reporting tool that automatically segments fixed, variable, and other expenses; performs a linear regression of each monthly expense detailed in the general ledger; and then spits out a forecast for the coming fiscal year (see fig. 1.3).

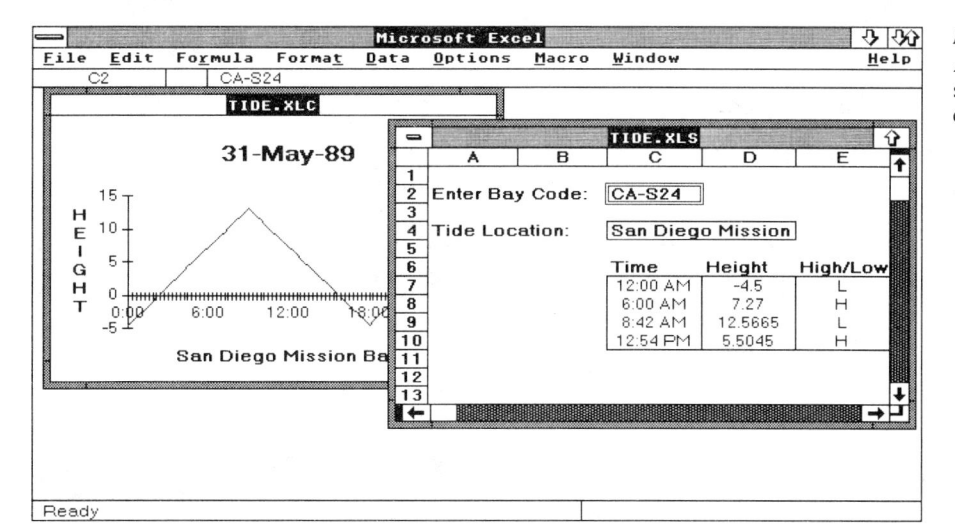

Understanding Excel and the Ideal Computer Environment 9

Fig. 1.1.
A worksheet showing a tide calculator.

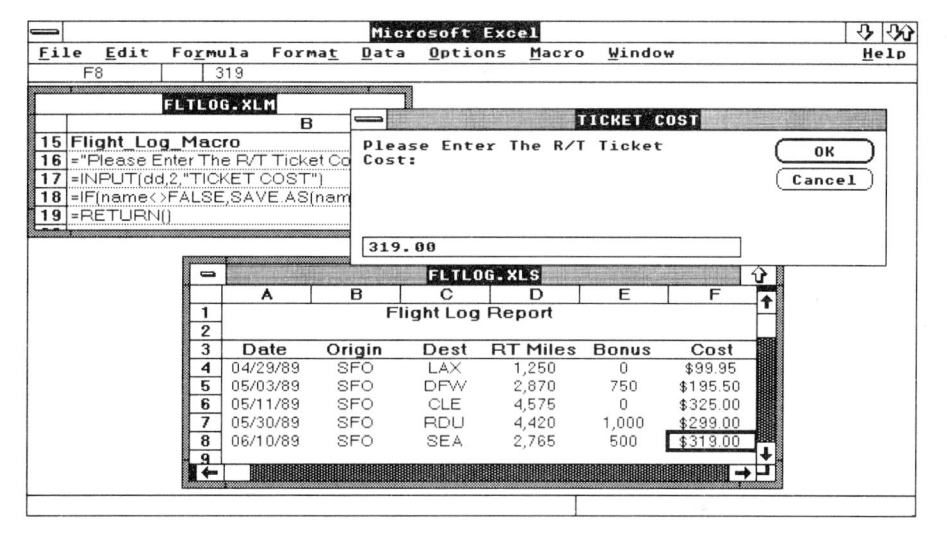

Fig. 1.2.
A macro showing a frequent-flier log.

Once you have envisioned the Excel application, you can be tempted to plunge into Excel in an attempt to develop that application. Doing so rarely produces a desirable result, but there are exceptions to the rule.

If the application involves converting Celsius temperatures to Fahrenheit, eliminating the planning stage from the process is logical. Why? In this application, the tool is a simple formula that calculates and converts the user's input value, sending the answer as output to the screen. Meeting this objective is easy enough. Simply enter the well-known conversion formula directly into cells A1 through C4, as shown in figure 1.4.

10   Excel Business Applications: IBM Version

Fig. 1.3.
A forecast showing fixed versus variable expenses.

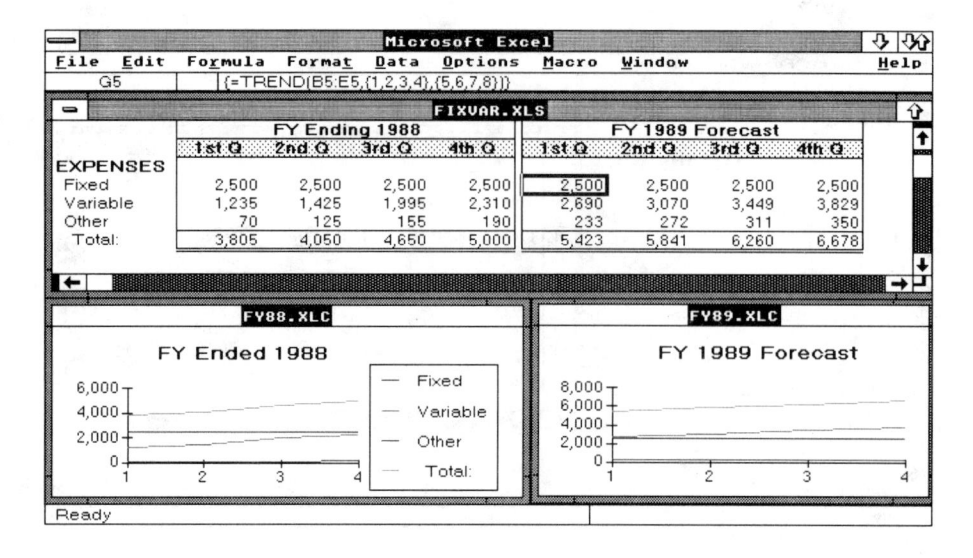

Fig. 1.4.
A temperature-conversion spreadsheet.

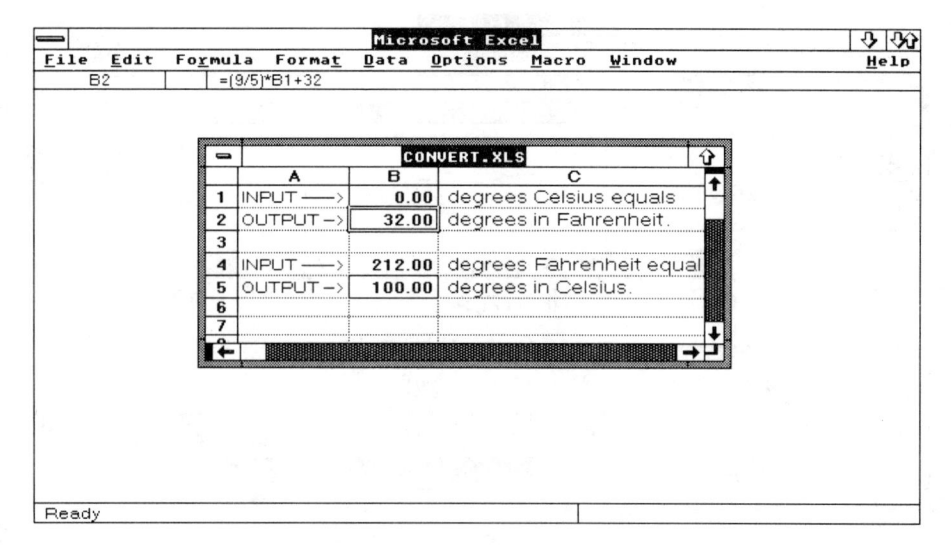

If, however, the application requires that the conversion formula's output also act as input for another Excel application—such as a formula that predicts the failure-frequency trends of NASA shuttle metals subjected to user-selected temperature fluctuations—you should first mull over the necessary inputs, the ideal structure of the worksheet area, and an appropriate format for the output *before* running to the computer. And that mesmerizing prospect brings us to the next topic.

Planning the Specific Application Goals

There are two ways to work with Excel: the first involves *using* Excel as a program; the second involves *programming* with Excel (see fig. 1.5). To clarify:

- When you choose an Excel menu, select a menu option, or call a macro sheet and tell it to execute, you are *using* Excel.

- When you invoke Excel's macro recorder to store commonly used worksheet formats or to accept input for calculation, or when you create or replicate macro language code, you are *programming* with Excel.

```
              USING EXCEL

      ▫ Click-select the File menu, select New,
        choose Worksheet, and click OK.
      ▫ Click-select the Macro menu, select Run,
        choose a macro name, and click OK.
      ▫ Enter the formula "=A1+A2" into cell A3.

         PROGRAMMING WITH EXCEL

      ▫ With the Macro Recorder on, click-select
        the Format menu, select Font, and choose
        Courier-10-Bold.
      ▫ In cell B1 of a blank Macro sheet, enter
        the formula "=FORMAT.NUMBER("mm/dd/yy")".
```

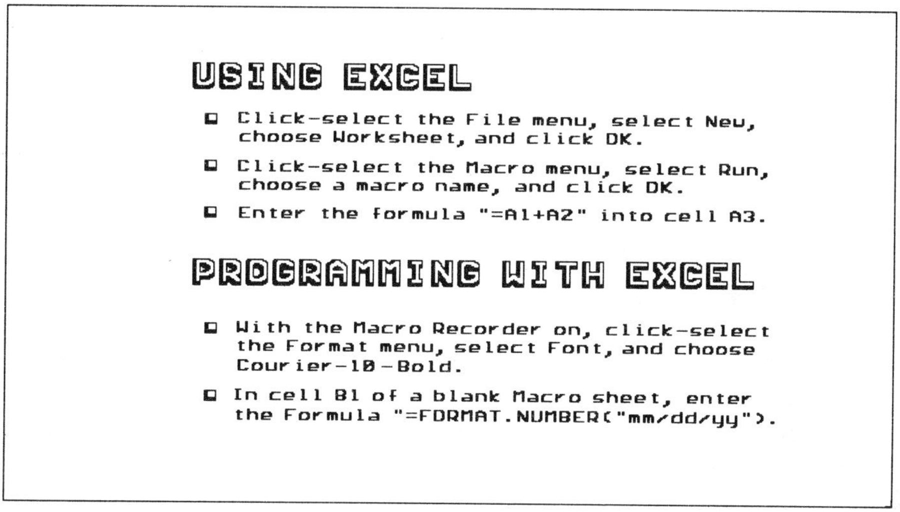

Fig. 1.5. Using Excel versus programming with Excel.

The distinction between *using* and *programming* is important for two reasons: First, because business-reporting needs differ from company to company—and often change over time within one company—a certain amount of Excel programming will always be necessary.

Second, and for the purposes of this book, both these approaches will be demonstrated because of the importance of knowing one (using) before attempting the other (programming).

You may decide that programming in Excel is not for you. In fact, it's likely that you will eventually delegate all programming chores, content with the responsibility of endorsing the final product. As published macro libraries become more readily available, you will often find that it's easier to amend a prewritten macro to your own specifications.

Beware, though. You should become familiar with the logic behind Excel macro programming if only because you must be able to evaluate the worth of someone else's macro program before determining its merit and suitability for use in your own business.

Whenever you begin thinking about your specific application goals, consider the information required to meet your envisioned objective. Specifically, begin by considering the following questions:

User Issues

- What job task does this macro enable me to fulfill?
- Who will use the macro program most often?
- Should the macro control all worksheet activity, or should the macro user have control of certain macro operations?
- Should I employ password protection to safeguard sensitive data?

Programming Issues

- What Excel worksheets will I need for this macro?
- How do I want the macro to select data?
- How do I want the macro to manipulate data?
- Are there other macros that perform some of the functions that this one will include?
- Will some of the same steps be repeated several times during the operation of this macro?
- Have I taken full advantage of the workspace autoexecute and Ctrl-key features?

Cosmetic Issues

- What is the best output format for my data? Which font and stylistic options provide the most aesthetic result?
- Should I use a chart, or is data-table output sufficient?

Documentation Issues

- Do the worksheet, macro, and chart file names conform to a well-organized, recognizable coding system?
- Are the macro subroutines aptly documented with descriptions that appear at the beginning of each new code section?

In the next few chapters, you will actually be able to build macros that create various reports. As you follow the macro-building steps, such as those in figure 1.6, think about the particular issues that each step addresses. Doing so reinforces your concept of how to create Excel applications.

> Step 1. Open the Personnel worksheet.
> Step 2. Select the column containing the dates of the employees' last performance review.
> Step 3. On the Edit menu, select Insert.
> Step 4. On the title line of the new column, enter "Anniversary Date".
> Step 5. Select the entire column.
> Step 6. On the Format menu, select Number, and choose "mm/dd/yy".
> Step 7. Enter each employee's hire date.

Fig. 1.6. Macro-building instructions.

For the most part, though, the book is devoted to equipping you with finished macros capable of producing report-quality output and attractive, meaningful graphics. Also, these chapters are sprinkled with tips and shortcuts for better macro programming and program modification. Once you've added your personal design touch to the prewritten macro programs, they'll be ready to "load and go" (see fig. 1.7).

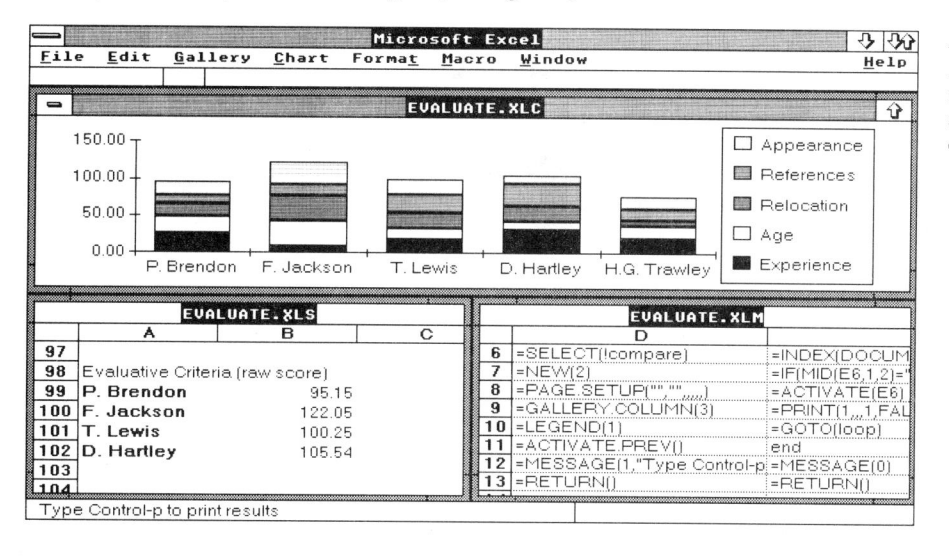

Fig. 1.7. A ready-to-use macro with the accompanying output.

Developing the Appropriate Tools

The final ingredient in the "Excel concept" recipe—developing the tools used by the application—can be the most exciting one, but programming of any kind is often a frustrating experience. Fortunately, Excel eliminates most of the frustrations involved in programming, and this book should eradicate the rest.

Developing an Excel macro application without vision and proper planning is like building a house of cards on a windy day: you know roughly what it is that you want to do, but the elements just won't let you succeed. Successful macro development begins with clearly pictured application goals and concludes with the provision of concrete answers to the various user, programming, documentation, and cosmetic issues. Only then can you construct a finished product that accomplishes all your specific tasks.

Consider a case in which two people follow quite different paths to productivity nirvana:

The Nu-Klear, Inc., Case Study: Frank Goldwaith, sales manager for Nu-Klear, Inc., reflects on the one task that exhausts him most: tallying the sales totals, by salesperson, for the month-end sales meeting.

"I need something that will quickly add a lot of numbers together and store the total for future review," he ponders, staring idly at his computer screen, "and I think I know how to do it: I'll use Excel—that spreadsheet program that the accountants seem to love so much." Soon Frank has typed all the appropriate data into an Excel worksheet, organizing it in the manner that seems most logical to him (see fig. 1.8).

Fig. 1.8.
Frank's month-end sales report, by salesperson.

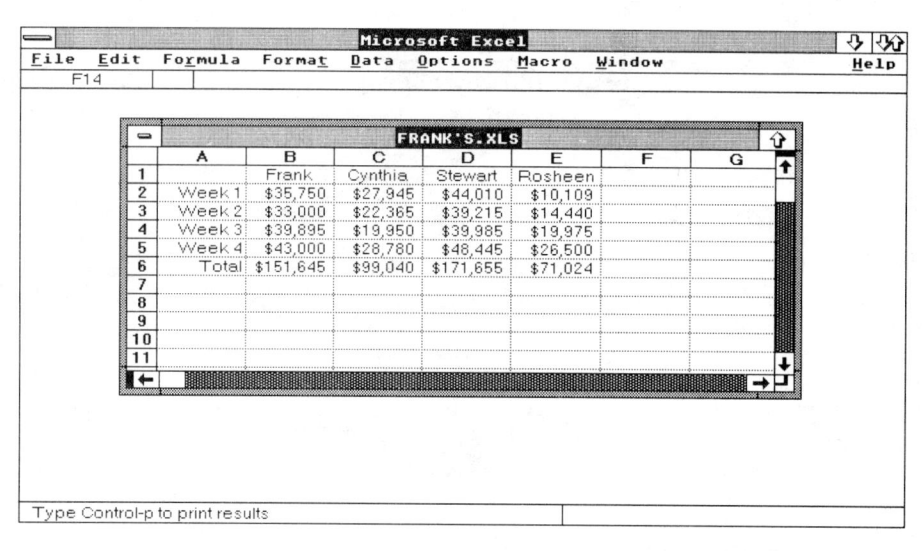

	A	B	C	D	E
1		Frank	Cynthia	Stewart	Rosheen
2	Week 1	$35,750	$27,945	$44,010	$10,109
3	Week 2	$33,000	$22,365	$39,215	$14,440
4	Week 3	$39,895	$19,950	$39,985	$19,975
5	Week 4	$43,000	$28,780	$48,445	$26,500
6	Total	$151,645	$99,040	$171,655	$71,024

Bypassing the first two steps in the process, our sales manager has proceeded directly to the development stage. Granted, Frank isn't designing a worksheet for NASA's metallurgical research division, but by using a little foresight, he could have produced dramatically better results. His problem? Without vision and proper planning, Frank missed an excellent opportunity to capitalize on Excel's inherent flexibility and tremendous power. He's certainly produced a computer-generated report that meets a stated objective, but couldn't he have accomplished the same task with a hand calculator?

Suzy Hillen, assistant sales manager and self-avowed Excel "power user," chuckles under her breath at the conclusion of Frank's presentation during June's month-end sales meeting. "Frank," she asks innocently, "would you mind if I added a few things to your Excel progra...er...worksheet? I think I envision this report differently." Begrudgingly, Frank mutters an "okay" as Suzy disappears through the conference-room doorway.

Sitting at her desk, Suzy maps out her strategy to make Frank's report worth more than the paper it was printed on (see fig. 1.9).

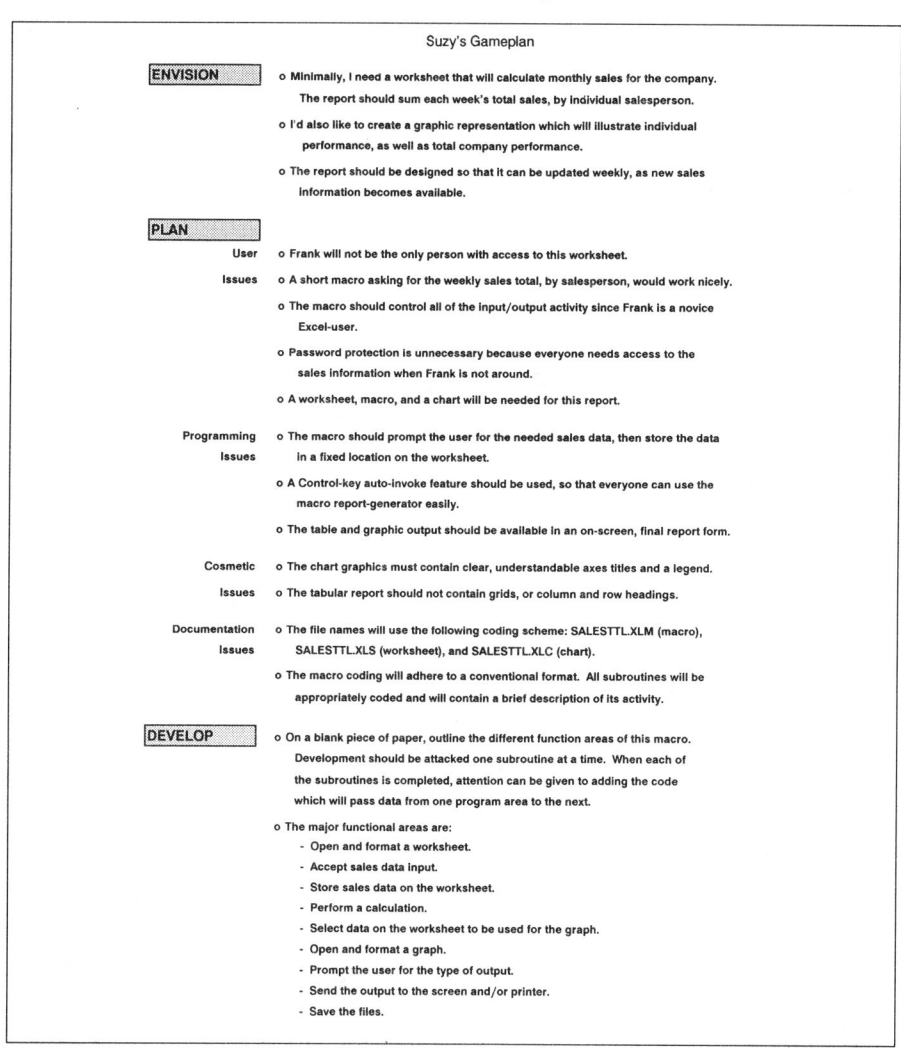

Suzy's Gameplan

ENVISION

- Minimally, I need a worksheet that will calculate monthly sales for the company. The report should sum each week's total sales, by individual salesperson.
- I'd also like to create a graphic representation which will illustrate individual performance, as well as total company performance.
- The report should be designed so that it can be updated weekly, as new sales information becomes available.

PLAN

User Issues
- Frank will not be the only person with access to this worksheet.
- A short macro asking for the weekly sales total, by salesperson, would work nicely.
- The macro should control all of the input/output activity since Frank is a novice Excel-user.
- Password protection is unnecessary because everyone needs access to the sales information when Frank is not around.
- A worksheet, macro, and a chart will be needed for this report.

Programming Issues
- The macro should prompt the user for the needed sales data, then store the data in a fixed location on the worksheet.
- A Control-key auto-invoke feature should be used, so that everyone can use the macro report-generator easily.
- The table and graphic output should be available in an on-screen, final report form.

Cosmetic Issues
- The chart graphics must contain clear, understandable axes titles and a legend.
- The tabular report should not contain grids, or column and row headings.

Documentation Issues
- The file names will use the following coding scheme: SALESTTL.XLM (macro), SALESTTL.XLS (worksheet), and SALESTTL.XLC (chart).
- The macro coding will adhere to a conventional format. All subroutines will be appropriately coded and will contain a brief description of its activity.

DEVELOP

- On a blank piece of paper, outline the different function areas of this macro. Development should be attacked one subroutine at a time. When each of the subroutines is completed, attention can be given to adding the code which will pass data from one program area to the next.
- The major functional areas are:
    - Open and format a worksheet.
    - Accept sales data input.
    - Store sales data on the worksheet.
    - Perform a calculation.
    - Select data on the worksheet to be used for the graph.
    - Open and format a graph.
    - Prompt the user for the type of output.
    - Send the output to the screen and/or printer.
    - Save the files.

Fig. 1.9. Suzy's three-tiered strategy.

After developing her version of the worksheet, Suzy proudly hands the new, improved report to Frank's immediate superior (see figs. 1.10 and 1.11). Consider the individual pieces of the macro program that created these professional results for Suzy.

Fig. 1.10. Suzy's month-end sales report for June 1989.

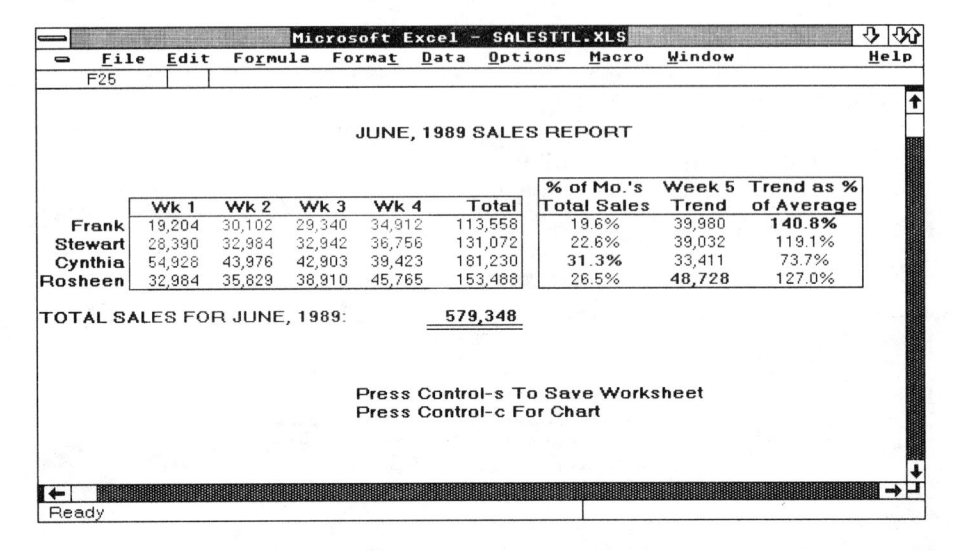

```
                    JUNE, 1989 SALES REPORT

              Wk 1    Wk 2    Wk 3    Wk 4    Total    % of Mo.'s   Week 5   Trend as %
                                                       Total Sales  Trend    of Average
    Frank    19,204  30,102  29,340  34,912  113,558     19.6%      39,980    140.8%
    Stewart  28,390  32,984  32,942  36,756  131,072     22.6%      39,032    119.1%
    Cynthia  54,928  43,976  42,903  39,423  181,230     31.3%      33,411     73.7%
    Rosheen  32,984  35,829  38,910  45,765  153,488     26.5%      48,728    127.0%

    TOTAL SALES FOR JUNE, 1989:         579,348

                    Press Control-s To Save Worksheet
                    Press Control-c For Chart
```

Fig. 1.11. Suzy's sales-performance chart.

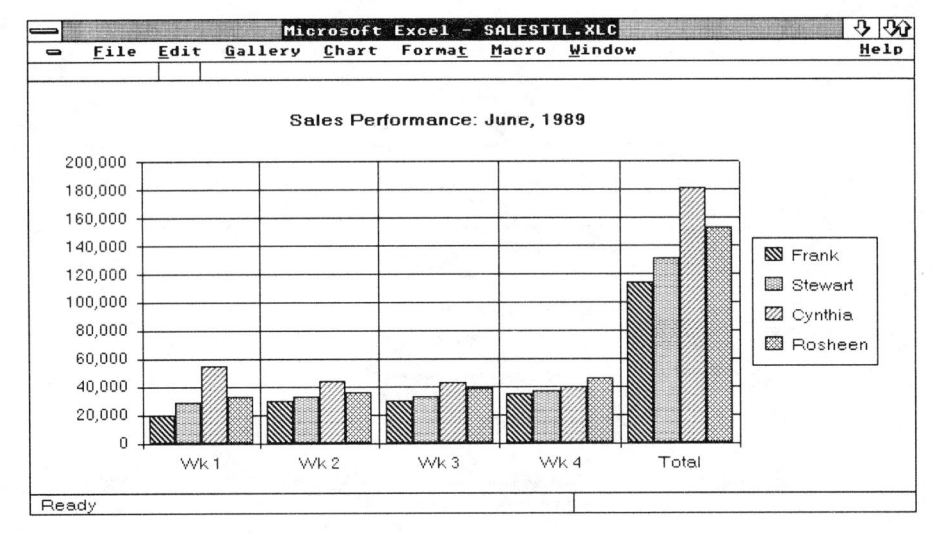

[Bar chart: Sales Performance: June, 1989 — showing Wk 1, Wk 2, Wk 3, Wk 4, and Total for Frank, Stewart, Cynthia, Rosheen]

While mapping out her three-tiered game plan, Suzy realized that much of the work required to prepare this report could be accomplished through Excel's powerful auto-macro programmer, the Recorder. Remember that the Recorder, once turned on, will copy onto a blank macro sheet every keystroke and click selection made. Using Define Name from the Formula menu, Suzy created a Ctrl-key command that, when executed, reproduces all the steps required to re-create her worksheet.

Understanding Excel and the Ideal Computer Environment

Suzy also realized that the best way to produce this macro program was to first create on a worksheet the actual design of her final report. She paid careful attention to designing formulas, identifying which cells the formulas would affect and which worksheet design created the finest report-quality format. Then, with the Recorder turned on, Suzy simply retraced the steps necessary to produce the sales report.

The macro shown in figure 1.12 opens a new worksheet, formats the column widths and row heights, and adds the report heading and titles. Notice that the types of numeric data that will appear in the cells have yet to be identified. So far, only the framework of the report—the spreadsheet *shell*, in other words—is designed.

	A	B
1	Format Worksheet Macro	
2	=NEW(1)	Open a new worksheet
3	=FULL(TRUE)	
4	=SELECT("C1,C6,C9","R1C9")	Format column widths
5	=COLUMN.WIDTH(9)	
6	=SELECT("C2:C5")	
7	=COLUMN.WIDTH(7)	
8	=SELECT("C7")	
9	=COLUMN.WIDTH(1)	
10	=SELECT("C8,C10","R1C10")	
11	=COLUMN.WIDTH(11)	
12	=SELECT("R14")	
13	=ROW.HEIGHT(3)	Format row height
14	=SELECT("R3C5")	
15	=FORMULA("JUNE, 1989 SALES REPORT")	Report title
16	=SELECT("R8C1:R11C1")	
17	=FORMULA("Frank")	Column headings
18	=SELECT("R8C1:R11C1","R9C1")	
19	=FORMULA("Stewart")	
20	=SELECT("R8C1:R11C1","R10C1")	
21	=FORMULA("Cynthia")	
22	=SELECT("R8C1:R11C1","R11C1")	
23	=FORMULA("Rosheen")	
24	=SELECT("R7C2:R7C6")	
25	=FORMULA("Wk 1")	
26	=SELECT("R7C2:R7C6","R7C3")	
27	=FORMULA("Wk 2")	
28	=SELECT("R7C2:R7C6","R7C4")	
29	=FORMULA("Wk 3")	
30	=SELECT("R7C2:R7C6","R7C5")	
31	=FORMULA("Wk 4")	
32	=SELECT("R7C2:R7C6","R7C6")	
33	=FORMULA("Total")	
34	=SELECT("R6C8:R7C10")	
35	=FORMULA("% of Mo.'s")	
36	=SELECT("R6C8:R7C10","R7C8")	
37	=FORMULA("Total Sales")	
38	=SELECT("R6C8:R7C10","R6C9")	
39	=FORMULA("Week 5")	
40	=SELECT("R6C8:R7C10","R7C9")	
41	=FORMULA("Trend")	
42	=SELECT("R6C8:R7C10","R6C10")	
43	=FORMULA("Trend as %")	
44	=SELECT("R6C8:R7C10","R7C10")	
45	=FORMULA("of Average")	
46	=SELECT("R13C1")	
47	=FORMULA("TOTAL SALES FOR JUNE, 1989:")	"Total" row title
48	=SELECT("R18C5:R19C5")	
49	=FORMULA("Press Control-S To Save Worksheet")	Save worksheet macro call
50	=SELECT("R18C5:R19C5","R19C5")	
51	=FORMULA("Press Control-C For Chart")	Chart macro call

Fig. 1.12.
A macro that formats an Excel worksheet.

18   Excel Business Applications: IBM Version

The Create Cell Formulas macro in figure 1.13 contains formulas that total row and column values and then calculate percentages, as shown. One of Excel's built-in functions—the TREND() function—appears in cell A69. TREND() uses the sales data from the prior four weeks to calculate week 5's trend. Consider this function's syntax:

$$\{=TREND(B8:E8,\{1,2,3,4\},\{5\})\}$$

Fig. 1.13.
A macro that creates cell formulas.

	A	B
53	Create Cell Formulas Macro	
54	=SELECT("R8C6")	
55	=FORMULA("=SUM(RC[-4]:RC[-1])")	Formulas to sum rows, and
56	=COPY()	then sum the total column
57	=SELECT("R9C6:R11C6")	
58	=PASTE()	
59	=SELECT("R13C6")	
60	=CANCEL.COPY()	
61	=FORMULA("=SUM(R[-5]C:R[-2]C)")	
62	=SELECT("R8C8")	
63	=FORMULA("=RC[-2]/R13C6")	Formula to compute %
64	=COPY()	
65	=SELECT("R9C8:R11C8")	
66	=PASTE()	
67	=SELECT("R8C9")	
68	=CANCEL.COPY()	
69	=FORMULA.ARRAY("=TREND(RC[-7]:RC[-4],{1,2,3,4},{5})")	Formula to compute trend
70	=COPY()	
71	=SELECT("R9C9:R11C9")	
72	=PASTE()	
73	=SELECT("R8C10")	
74	=CANCEL.COPY()	
75	=FORMULA("=RC[-1]/(RC[-4]/4)")	Formula to calculate sales
76	=COPY()	improvement over average
77	=SELECT("R9C10:R11C10")	
78	=PASTE()	
79	=CANCEL.COPY()	

Notice that this formula appears as an array formula, which means that the creator of the formula entered it by holding down the Ctrl and Shift keys while pressing Return.

> **Tip:** When successfully entered, an array formula appears in the formula bar, surrounded by braces. If these braces do not appear, simply press F2 to edit the current cell, and repeat the procedure. Remember that even though you don't see the braces on your macro sheet, they really are there. Make A69 the active cell to verify this.

You can enhance the performance of certain Excel functions by making them array formulas. In this example, Excel uses the values in cells B8 through E8 as the input array {1,2,3,4}. Using this input array, Excel computes a "historical pattern" and then extrapolates the month {5} trend, which it returns as the value appearing in cell A69.

The macro in figure 1.14 tells Excel which cells will appear as numbers and which cells will appear as percentages. The Format Cells macro aligns all

the report data in the respective cells and then constructs a border around
the data-input and -output blocks.

	A	B
81	Format Cells Macro	
82	=SELECT("R8C2:R11C6,R13C6,R8C9:R11C9","R8C9")	Designate cell format
83	=FORMAT.NUMBER("#,##0")	
84	=SELECT("R8C8:R11C8,R8C10:R11C10","R8C10")	
85	=FORMAT.NUMBER("0.0%")	
86	=SELECT("R7C1:R11C6,R13C6","R13C6")	
87	=ALIGNMENT(4)	Designate cell alignment
88	=SELECT("R6C8:R11C10")	
89	=ALIGNMENT(3)	
90	=SELECT("R3C5,R7C2:R7C6,R6C8:R7C10,R8C1:R11C1,R13C1,R13C6,R	
91	=FORMAT.FONT("Helv",10,TRUE,FALSE,FALSE,FALSE)	Designate font type
92	=SELECT("R1C1")	
93	=DISPLAY(FALSE,FALSE,FALSE,TRUE,0)	
94	=SELECT("R7C2:R11C6,R6C8:R11C10","R6C8")	
95	=BORDER(TRUE,,,,,FALSE)	Designate border format
96	=SELECT("R7C2:R7C6,R7C8:R7C10","R7C8")	
97	=BORDER(FALSE,,,,TRUE,FALSE)	
98	=SELECT("R14C6")	
99	=BORDER(FALSE,FALSE,FALSE,TRUE,TRUE,FALSE)	

Fig. 1.14.
A macro that formats cells to accept different types of input.

> Tip: Always enter a number into a cell before using the Format
> Number command. For example, if you formatted a cell by using the
> date format and then entered a whole-number value, Excel attempts to
> convert the whole number into a date—definitely not the desired
> result.

The short macro in figure 1.15 selects and highlights the sales-data block.
The SELECT() command serves two purposes: First, it signifies the area
into which the user should enter the sales data. The second purpose is a bit
more subtle.

	A	B
101	Highlight Input Cells Macro	
102	=SELECT("R8C2:R11C5")	
103	=ALERT("Please Enter the Week's Sales Figures:",2)	Cue user to enter data.
104	=RETURN()	Macro end

Fig. 1.15.
A macro that highlights the sales-data block, preparing it for input.

Had the data block not been highlighted, the user would have found the
sales-input area anyway. But in a large, multipage worksheet containing
several input blocks, losing track of the worksheet chronology is quite easy.

What is *worksheet chronology*? When you design a worksheet, you typically
program in a top-to-bottom fashion. Formulas appearing in the middle of a
worksheet often rely on data that was entered (or calculated) in earlier
worksheet areas and sometimes pass their value to another area on the
worksheet. By using SELECT to select the data-input areas in your macro
program, you eliminate any doubt about what goes where, and in what
order.

> Tip: Use cell protection to prevent a macro user from accidentally erasing worksheet titles, headings, and cell formats. This technique improves worksheet chronology because only unprotected cells can be selected and highlighted.

In the Nu-Klear, Inc., case study, Suzy included an ALERT() function to notify the user that the worksheet is fully formatted and ready for data entry.

The macros in figures 1.16 and 1.17 perform two precise operations. The first macro saves the worksheet as SALESTTL.XLS. The second macro creates the chart that displays June's sales totals by salesperson.

Fig. 1.16.
A macro that saves the new sales report.

	D
1	Save Report Macro
2	=SAVE.AS("salesttl.xls")
3	=RETURN()

Fig. 1.17.
A macro that creates the sales-performance chart.

	F
1	Performance Chart Macro
2	=SELECT("R7C1:R11C6")
3	=NEW(2)
4	=LEGEND(TRUE)
5	=GRIDLINES(TRUE,FALSE,TRUE,FALSE)
6	=ATTACH.TEXT(1)
7	=FORMULA("=""""Sales Performance: June, 1989"""""")
8	=FORMAT.FONT(0,1,FALSE,"Helv",10,TRUE,FALSE,FALSE,FALSE)
9	=SELECT("")
10	=SAVE.AS("salesttl.xlc",1,"",FALSE)
11	=RETURN()

In review, Suzy used three documents to create her month-end sales report: a worksheet, a macro, and a chart (see fig. 1.18). Although there is no fixed prescription indicating when to use these document types, the most attractive and professional reports use some combination of all three. Can you guess what happened at Suzy's and Frank's next job-performance interview?

The following are five ways to enhance Suzy's sales-report macro:

1. Add a print routine to the macro. This new macro could automatically print a copy of the report and the chart. Or if you use the INPUT() and IF() functions, the macro could ask the user which report to print.

2. Use the INPUT() function to prompt the user and to then store the salesperson names that are to appear in the report.

3. If the user wants to add additional names to this report, use the DATA.SERIES() function to extend the number of rows needed to store the sales and statistical formula data.

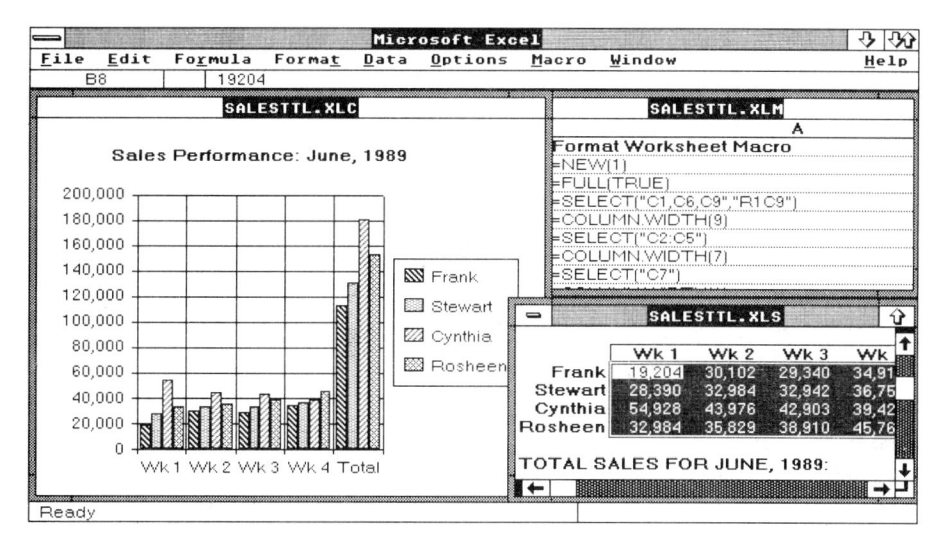

Fig. 1.18.
The three documents used to create Suzy's month-end sales report.

4. Design another chart that depicts which salesperson enjoys the greatest improvement in sales over the course of the month. To do this, graph *Week 5 Trend* versus *% Increase of Trend over Average*, using the Combination graph option found in Excel's Chart Gallery.

5. Add an "accumulator block" below the sales-data-report area of SALESTTL.XLS. This block would total new monthly sales data each time the report is rerun.

As you can see, you can improve the value of this report in many ways. In fact, the only limitation in enhancing any Excel tool is your own imagination.

Creating the Ideal Computer Environment

To take full advantage of Excel's operating power, you must first take stock of the equipment at your disposal. Excel requires that you have the following minimum hardware and operating system configuration:

Hardware: IBM AT-286, PS/2, or compatible
            5M of free hard disk storage space
            640K of random-access memory (RAM)
            Hercules, VGA, or EGA compatible graphics display card
Operating system: DOS 3.0 or a later version

If you are fortunate enough to own more advanced hardware and operating system software, Excel's performance will surely exceed your expectations.

The following configuration is an example of an "ideal" operating environment that lets you take full advantage of Excel's computing power:

    Hardware: IBM AT-386 or compatible
                  80387 math coprocessor chip
                  2M to 4M of random-access memory (RAM)
                  VGA graphics display card
                  Microsoft Mouse
    Operating system: OS/2 2.0 or a later version
    Microsoft Windows/386

Excel's performance improves markedly when you can create this ideal configuration. However, unless you have the means to buy an 80386-based system loaded with RAM, an 80387 math coprocessor chip, a VGA display, and so on, then you're in the same boat as most current Excel users. Even so, perfect system configuration is attainable if you use the computer hardware discussed in the following sections.

Microsoft Windows

Microsoft Corporation designed Excel as a windows-environment software program; it's clear that Excel has the "windows look" found in Apple Computer's software products. Although you don't have to have Microsoft Windows in order to use Excel, Microsoft Windows greatly enhances the use of the program.

If you don't own Windows 2.0 or later versions, you've installed your copy of Excel by using the run-time Windows utility provided with your distribution disks. If that is the case, you don't know what you're missing.

When you operate Excel with Windows, you can run more than one application at a time. The benefit of this capability may be somewhat obscure, so consider a hypothetical situation. How many times have you had to exit from Excel so that you could run a DOS operation or file-management utility? More times than you care to remember, if you're like most people. With Windows you can access DOS commands while running Excel. Or you can transfer data between your word processor and database (assuming that they also operate under Windows).

If you own an 80386-based system and choose to buy Microsoft Windows, consider getting Windows/386. Although Windows 2.0 or later versions will work on your machine, Windows/386 takes advantage of special memory-management features that are built into the 80386 chip.

Microprocessor Chips and Math Coprocessor Chips

The microprocessor clock speed regulates how fast Excel processes commands. Early AT systems use an 80286 chip whose clock speed ranges from 8mhz to 20mhz. The new 80386 chips process data at a rate of 16mhz to 35mhz. If you are using an 80286-based system and don't want to upgrade your microprocessor chip, there are only two things that you can do to improve Excel's processing efficiency. First, if your current chip has a switchable clock speed (as many do), make sure that it is on the highest setting. Second, invest in a math coprocessing chip. Such an add-on chip (Excel supports the 8087, 80287, and 80387 chips) decreases your main coprocessor's workload by assuming many of the number-crunching responsibilities. Best of all, math chips are relatively inexpensive, saving you the cost of buying a completely new system.

Video Displays

Excel can display extremely high-resolution color graphics. Although there is no recommended or "ideal" video display for Excel, you can best take advantage of Excel's wide range of graphic presentations by using an EGA- or VGA-compatible display. Suffice it to say that when you use a higher-quality display, you more fully appreciate the results of your work sessions.

Printers

Excel supports all IBM- and Epson-compatible dot-matrix printers. You also can configure Excel to use the popular Hewlett-Packard LaserJet and Apple LaserWriter laser printers, as well as any plotter compatible with Microsoft Windows 2.0 or later. You can control the print quality and reconfigure the printer settings for your printer by choosing Printer Setup from Excel's File menu.

Memory Management

If you have less than 1M of RAM, you must learn how to use that memory efficiently. Microsoft suggests that you limit worksheet models to 100K when your system's RAM size lies in the range between 640K and 1M. This suggestion makes good sense because your available system memory is affected by activities both external and internal to Excel operations. For example, operating systems, memory-resident programs, and applications drivers are examples of operations external to Excel that reserve certain amounts of your system's memory.

You can increase the amount of memory available to Excel by deleting all nonessential memory-resident utilities (such as disk-caching programs and RAM disks) and peripheral driver programs. These programs are generally executed in CONFIG.SYS and AUTOEXEC.BAT files. To delete a memory-resident utility, remove its program name from the CONFIG.SYS or AUTOEXEC.BAT file. After deleting such a utility from CONFIG.SYS, you must reboot in order to remove the utility from memory.

Another way to maximize the amount of memory available to your system is to build efficient worksheets. Excel's internal operations—such as the creation and formatting of worksheets and the holding of multiple worksheets in memory—all use system memory.

Also, check to see whether you have an expanded-memory card. Expanded-memory cards increase your system's memory beyond the 640K that resides on your computer's motherboard. An expanded-memory card enables you to build worksheets larger than 100K, makes possible a quicker execution of Excel operations, and expedites the execution of multiple applications when you are using Windows.

The following list specifies actions that you can take to reduce the memory Excel dedicates to internal and external system activities:

1. Periodically review the number of open files in Excel's memory. Close files that are not essential to the current Excel work session. When you close unneeded documents, Excel regains system memory.

2. Excel reserves memory for each font that you use in your worksheets. Reduce the number of fonts used in each worksheet and thus keep memory available to Excel for other operations.

3. Excel uses system memory in blocks. The larger the active area of a worksheet, the more memory Excel needs. Excel automatically regains memory blocks when you erase column and row data on your worksheets. However, large blocks of unused space residing between data on your worksheets use space—and thus use memory. Whenever possible, delete these "gaps" to regain system memory.

4. Build streamlined worksheets. Instead of creating huge worksheets to assimilate large volumes of data, try using several smaller, linked worksheets. The process of recalling and updating several smaller worksheets is much faster—and uses less memory—than struggling with large worksheets.

5. Eliminate nonessential memory-resident programs. Instead of erasing or altering your current AUTOEXEC.BAT file (from which most memory-resident programs are loaded), create a separate AUTOEXEC.BAT file just for running Excel, one that loads only those programs crucial to Excel's reliable performance.

Summary

This chapter has laid the foundation for using Excel in the business environment. Its broad approach is intended to stimulate your thoughts about how you can use Excel to build personalized business applications. The "Excel concept" is the springboard that will propel you into deeper and more remarkable waters.

After reading this chapter, you're also abreast of the latest tricks for structuring the ideal operating environment for Excel. To construct this environment, you will probably have to reconsider the limits of your hardware and software tools. Fortunately, Excel is fully operable straight from the package—even if you use it in a minimum configuration. Additional performance-enhancing tools (such as coprocessing chips and Microsoft Windows) are icing on the cake.

Chapter 2 discusses how to build spreadsheets and financial statements and is full of tips and shortcuts that will refresh your memory about Excel operations. Once you finish reading Chapter 2, you will be prepared to create original applications.

2

Designing Spreadsheets and Financial Statements

Chapter 1 explained the "Excel concept" and showed you the proper way to employ this concept when designing an Excel spreadsheet. The Nu-Klear, Inc., case study demonstrated two ways to approach the task of molding your ideas into fully working business productivity tools. This conceptual approach has shed some light, it is hoped, on the strengths and weaknesses inherent in your own spreadsheet-building techniques. In any case, this book's goal is to help you develop and enhance your own creative process as you begin to tackle more complicated business-reporting tasks.

Now you will turn to the issue of building a well-designed spreadsheet. This chapter uses simple financial-statement shells to reinforce the "Excel concept" discussed in Chapter 1. This chapter also offers tips and shortcuts that will help streamline the entire process. The statements you will build during the course of the chapter can actually be used in your own business; all you need to do is add your personal design stamp to these statements. As you proceed further into this book, you will learn more tricks and techniques for improving the reports already in use at your business.

The financial statements covered in this chapter are essential to any going concern. You will build basic working versions of an income statement, a balance sheet, and a financial-ratio report. Don't worry if the sample reports you build in this chapter are condensed. Content is sacrificed for form here, because it would be impossible to anticipate all the accounts and formats you want to appear in your own reporting system. As your knowledge of Excel operations grows, you will find it a minor task to mold these simple shells into full-blown, personalized financial reports; the tips and shortcuts are applicable whether an income statement contains 13 or 30 accounts. Commit these tactics to memory, because as you progress through later examples and chapters, you will be expected to employ these tactics without being told to do so. Why? Because you will benefit most when concentrating on how to mold and implement your own strategies for making that perfect spreadsheet.

Designing the Income Statement

As you already know, the income statement describes revenues and expenses for the duration of one period of time. Small-business concerns usually find quarterly or even yearly income-statement preparation sufficient to meet their financial-management needs. Medium- to large-size concerns generally require a monthly accounting of their profitability. Either way, the important issue is that the income statement be logically organized, use fitting descriptions for the revenue and expense accounts, and adhere to generally accepted accounting methods.

Even so, each business does have different internal-reporting requirements. Some businesses earn their revenues solely from service-oriented actions (consulting, real estate, secretarial services), whereas others incur purchasing costs for the goods they sell (wholesale, retail, manufacturing). Total revenues for the former type of business require only a single line to report, for example, consulting revenues. In addition to a section for total revenues, the latter type of business needs to report the cost of goods sold, which when deducted from total revenues provides a gross-profit figure.

The grouping of the income-statement accounts is significant because it can provide easy-to-read summary totals or departmentalized, segmented figures that help management identify each division's profitability.

In the following example, you will learn the basics of producing both types of reports. It's up to you to determine which report offers the best information.

The Service-Oriented Income Statement

Whitney Productions represents young, budding theater actors. Its revenues are earned solely on a commission basis. Every time one of its stars wins a part in a play, Whitney Productions earns a commission equal to 10 percent of the star's contract.

To create the income statement for Whitney Productions, follow these steps:

Step 1. Choose the File menu and select New.

Step 2. When the New Worksheet dialog box appears, click OK.

Step 3. Select the range D1:D3. In D1, type **Whitney Productions**. In D2, type **Income Statement**, and in D3, type **For the Month Ended June 30, 1989**.

Step 4. Select the range A5:A14. Enter the account descriptions as the following (see fig. 2.1):

- A5: **Sales Commissions Earned:**
- A7: **Expenses:**
- A8: <space>**Advertising expense**
- A9: <space>**Office Salaries expense**
- A10: <space>**Telephone expense**
- A11: <space>**Depreciation expense: Equipment**
- A12: <space>**Depreciation expense: Automobile**
- A14: **Net Income:**

> Tip: When you select a continuous range, such as cells A5:A14 in figure 2.1, you can skip over cells not requiring input (A6 and A13) by simply pressing Return or Enter.

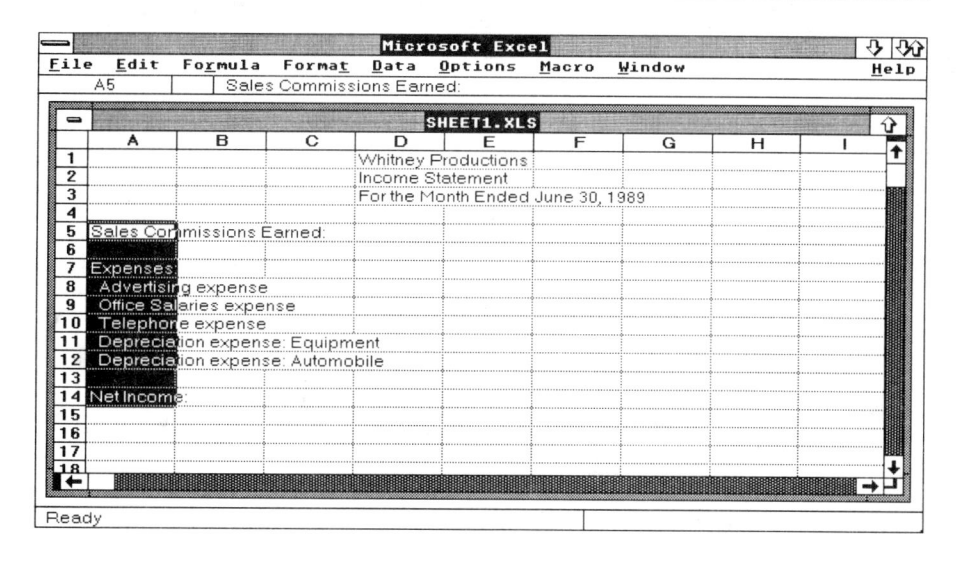

Fig. 2.1. A continuous selection range with alpha input.

Step 5. Select the range H5:H12. Enter the account values as the following (see fig. 2.2):

        H5: **32000**
        H8: **1000**
        H9: **3400**
        H10: **1750**
        H11: **360**
        H12: **150**

Fig. 2.2.
A continuous selection range with numeric input.

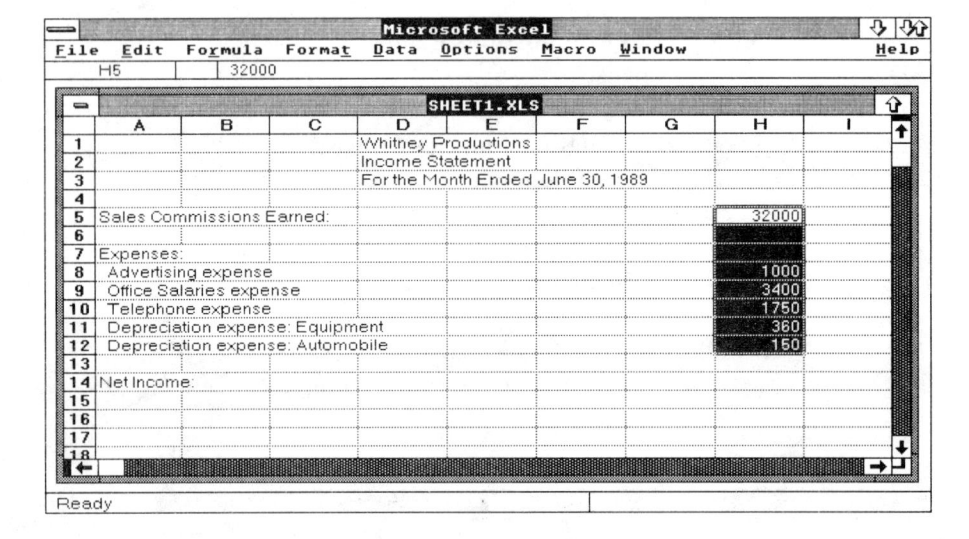

	A	B	C	D	E	F	G	H	I
1					Whitney Productions				
2					Income Statement				
3					For the Month Ended June 30, 1989				
4									
5	Sales Commissions Earned:							32000	
6									
7	Expenses:								
8	Advertising expense							1000	
9	Office Salaries expense							3400	
10	Telephone expense							1750	
11	Depreciation expense: Equipment							360	
12	Depreciation expense: Automobile							150	
13									
14	Net Income:								

Step 6. Select cell H14. In H14, enter the formula that deducts the sum of the expenses from the commission revenues.

> Tip: Several formulas will work in H14. For example, the formula =H5-H8-H9-H10-H11-H12 computes the correct answer: 25340. A better formula, which makes use of Excel's built-in SUM() function, is =H5-SUM(H8:H13), shown in figure 2.3. Notice that H13 is included in the range. Whenever possible, extend a formula range by one blank cell. That way, when you add a new account later (by selecting Insert from the Edit menu), the new row will automatically be included in the computed formula range.

Designing Spreadsheets and Financial Statements 31

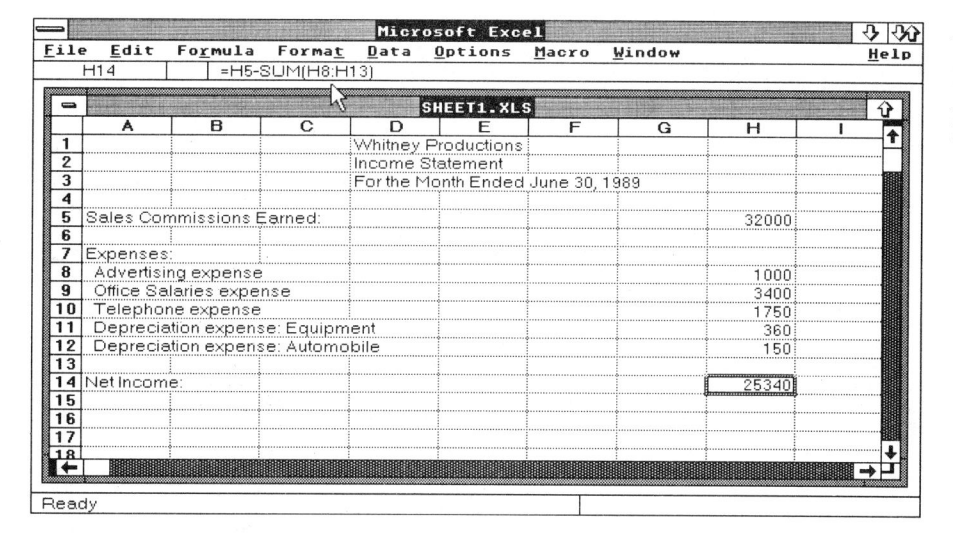

Fig. 2.3.
An alternative formula that produces the same result.

> Shortcut: Another method for entering any of Excel's built-in functions is available from the Formula menu. In cell H14, enter **=H5-** and then select Paste Function from the Formula menu. Scroll down the function menu, click-select SUM(), and then click OK (see fig. 2.4).

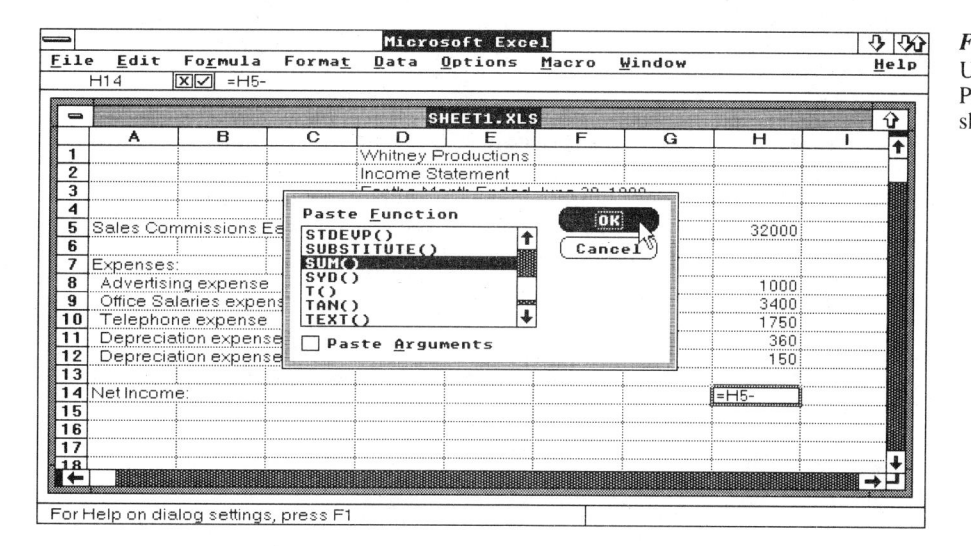

Fig. 2.4.
Using the Paste Function shortcut.

Step 7. Notice that the formula-bar cursor appears between the parentheses of the newly entered SUM() function (see fig. 2.5). With your mouse, select the range H8:H13. A *marquee* (a moving dashed line) surrounds the selected range.

Fig. 2.5.
The Excel marquee, surrounding a selected range.

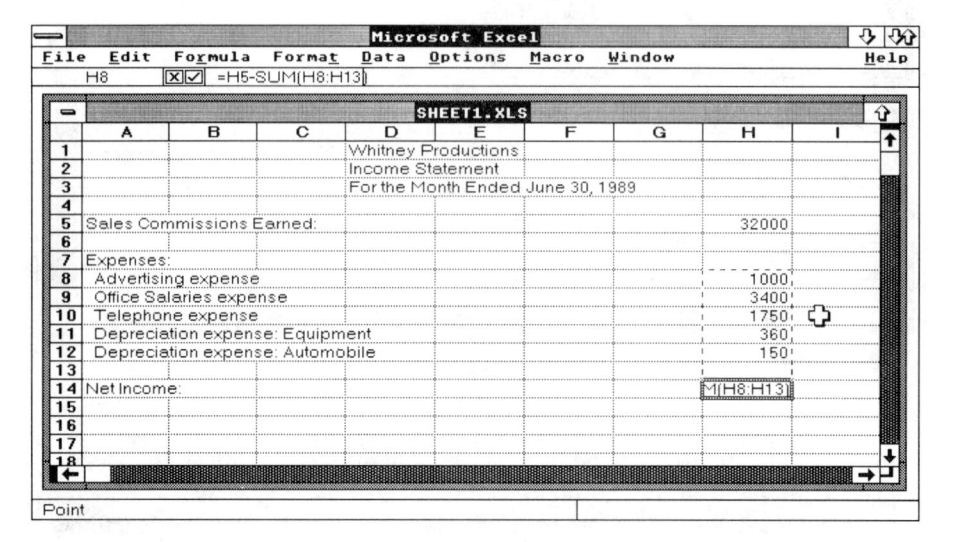

Now press Return; the same, correct net-income number, 25340, appears.

Step 8. Choose the File menu and select Save As. Type **WHITNEY**; Excel will save your work under the file name WHITNEY.XLS.

The Product-Oriented Income Statement

Now modify Whitney Productions' income statement and create a similar financial statement for Blaire & Cory's Wholesale Flowers. Remember that often the best way to build a new business spreadsheet is to modify an existing report. Why do the work twice?

Before you begin, remember that if you modify an existing Excel worksheet, you *must* rename it by selecting Save As from the File menu. Don't use the Save command! If you accidentally select Save, Excel will save the modifications by using the existing default name. This action effectively saves your modifications but, unfortunately, erases the initial worksheet's structure from disk. Your best bet is to always begin any new modification by giving the worksheet a new name. In this book, you'll always be reminded to rename your modified worksheets, but in your future spreadsheet-building endeavors, you must remember this critical task.

Create the Blaire & Cory's Wholesale Flowers income statement by following these steps:

Step 1. Rename the active worksheet, using the name BLARCORY.

Step 2. Click the maximize icon to fully enlarge your worksheet area; you'll need the extra space.

Step 3. Select the range D1:D3. In D1, type **Blaire & Cory's Wholesale Flowers** and then skip D2 by pressing Return once.

> Shortcut: When you modify an existing worksheet, use Excel's F2 edit key to quickly change a title or a number. In some cases, it's easier to retype the entire title or number; however, using F2 to edit a cell's contents is generally easier and faster.

Step 4. While in cell D3, press F2. Using the left-arrow key, change the description to **Fiscal Year Ending July 31, 1989**.

Step 5. Highlight the range of rows, 6:9, and select Insert from the Edit menu. This action adds four more rows to your worksheet.

> Tip: Be sure to select the row numbers 6:9 and not the range A6:A9. If you choose the range A6:A9 and click OK, Excel inserts cells rather than rows.

Step 6. Select the range A5:A9. Enter the account descriptions as the following:

    A5: **Revenues:**
    A6: **Gross Flower Sales**
    A7: <space>**Less: COG Sold**
    A8: <space>**Less: Returns & Allowances**
    A9: **Gross Profit on Sales**

Step 7. Highlight row 15. Choose Insert from the Edit menu. Enter the new account additions as the following:

    A15: <space>**Auto expense**
    A16: <space>**Insurance expense**
    A17: <space>**Depreciation expense: Equipment & Automobile**

> Tip: Use the F2 shortcut to change the existing text in A17.

Step 8. Now select the range H5:H19. Choose the Edit menu and select Cut. Select the range G5:G19. Choose the Edit menu once more and select Paste (see fig. 2.6).

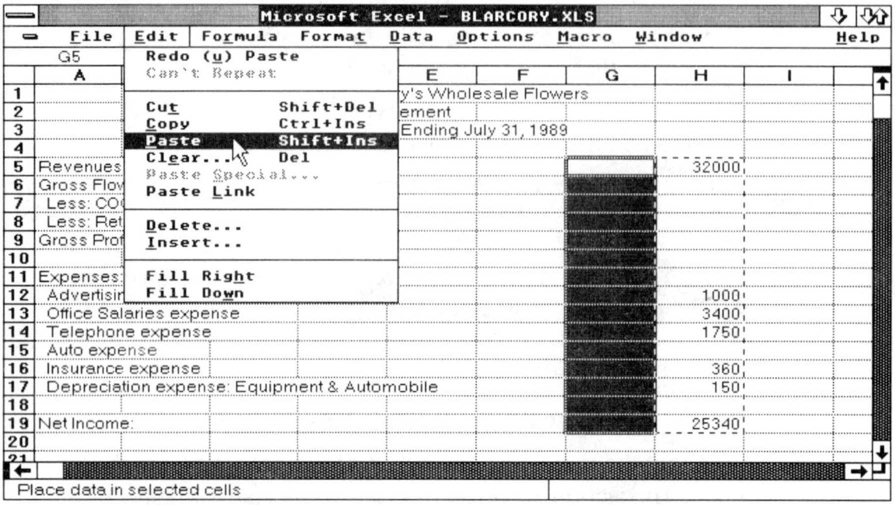

Fig. 2.6.
Using the Cut and Paste commands to move column H.

> **Shortcut:** There's a quicker way to move an entire column, such as the one you moved in Step 8 above. To test this shortcut, first select Undo Paste from the Edit menu. Then highlight column G and select Delete from the Edit menu (see fig. 2.7). This command shifts the data from column H to column G. Make sure that the column you delete is an empty column, or you'll also delete any data appearing in other parts of the column.

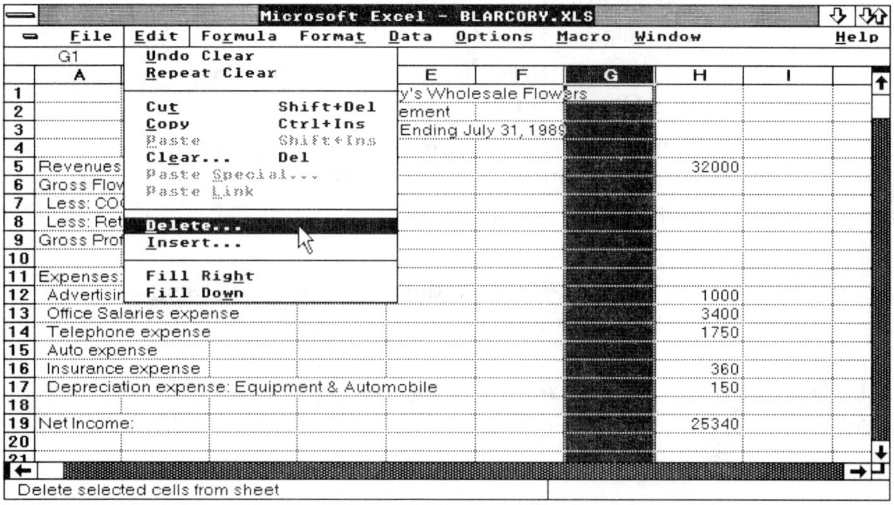

Fig. 2.7.
A shortcut method to move column H.

Step 9. Select cell G5. Choose the Edit menu, select Clear, and then click OK.

Step 10. Select the range G6:G8. Enter the revenue-account values as the following:

> G6: **195000**
> G7: **117000**
> G8: **3900**

Step 11. In cell G9, enter the formula that computes the gross profit on sales. This formula subtracts the values in cells G7 and G8 from the value in G6. If necessary, refer to the two methods for entering formulas, discussed in the first example (Steps 6 and 7).

Step 12. Select the range G12:G17 and enter the expense-account values as the following:

> G12: **8200**
> G13: **8000**
> G14: **4500**
> G15: **1750**
> G16: **600**
> G17: **600**

Step 13. Enter into cell G19 the formula that calculates the net-income figure by deducting from the gross profit on sales the sum value of the expenses.

Step 14. In cell H7, enter the formula **=G7/$G$6**. This formula computes the cost of goods sold as a percentage of gross sales (in this case, gross flower sales)—an important financial ratio.

Step 15. While still in H7, choose the Edit menu and select Copy. Highlight the range H8:H9, choose the Edit menu once more, and select Paste.

Step 16. Highlight the range H12:H17, choose the Edit menu, and reselect the Paste command.

Step 17. Move your cursor to cell H19. Again, select Paste from the Edit menu.

Tip: The dollar signs in the term $G$6 designate it as an *absolute reference* (see fig. 2.8). The dollar signs tell Excel to reproduce the reference in its exact, original form if this value is copied to another location on the worksheet. Without the dollar signs, a cell value appears in a *relative-reference* format.

> Shortcut: Excel offers you an easy, one-step method for placing into a cell a numeric value in an absolute-reference format. Go back to Step 17 and reenter the formula, this time typing the cell reference **G6** into the formula. Now press F4 once. Notice that Excel automatically inserts the dollar signs for you. Experiment with this shortcut key by pressing it several times consecutively. Notice how the absolute-reference format changes each time.

Fig. 2.8.
The result of using the correct reference format.

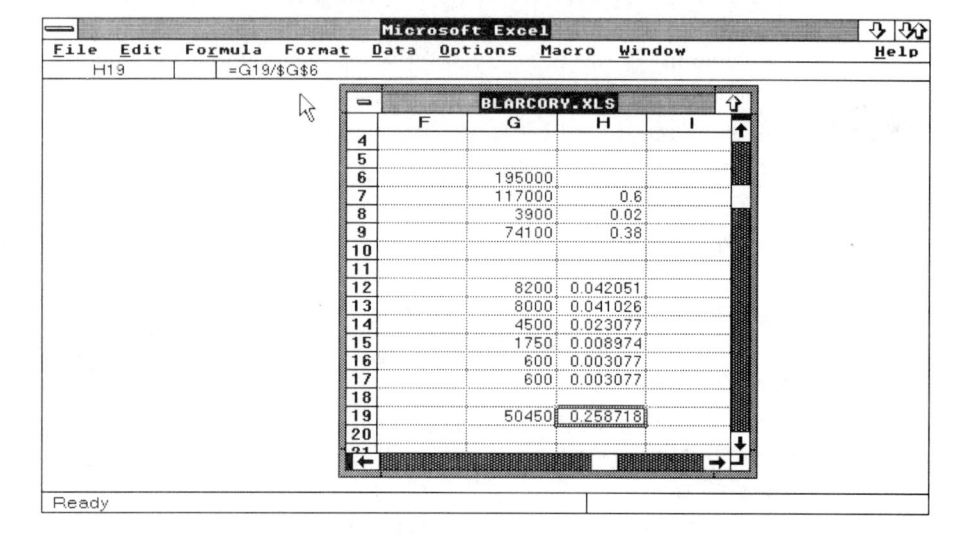

If the rationale behind this strategy is unclear, consider the results of the same case when the absolute-reference format is not used. You will always encounter the absolute- versus relative-reference decision when you copy the contents of one cell to another cell or to a range of cells. This type of operation occurs frequently when you create business applications with Excel; it's an important, powerful feature that you'll want to remember.

Figure 2.9 demonstrates how the failure to use the appropriate reference format produces an erroneous result. Notice that when a relative-reference formula is copied to a different cell (from H7 to H8), Excel adjusts the destination cell formula in a relative fashion. That is, when the formula =G7/G6 is copied into the cell one row down, the destination cell formula becomes =G8/G7. Each cell referred to in the formula was adjusted by one row—the exact distance between the origin cell and the destination cell.

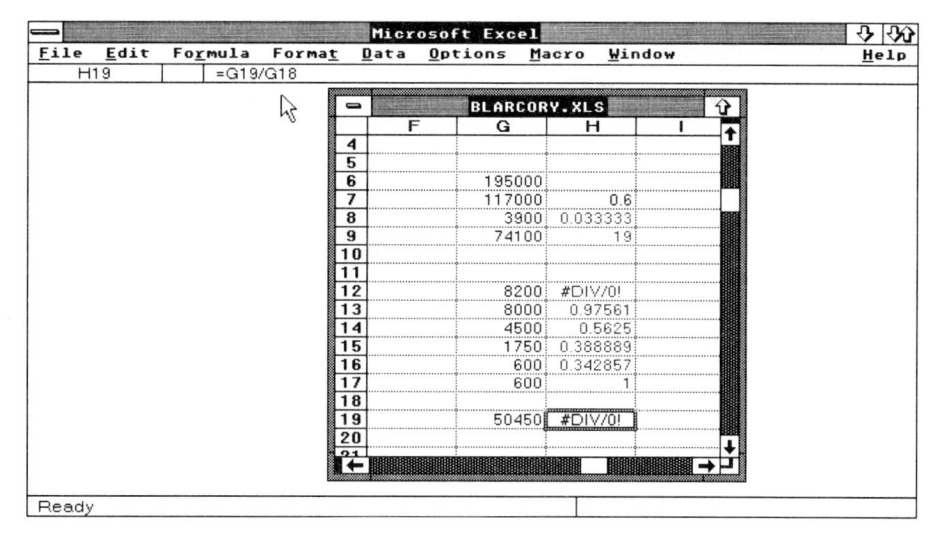

Fig. 2.9.
The results of using an incorrect reference format.

Step 18. Select the range G6:G19. From the Format menu, select Number; double-click the format option #,##0.

Step 19. Now select the range H7:H19. Reselect Number from the Format menu and double-click the format option 0.00%.

Step 20. To store the modified worksheet structure, choose Save from the File menu. (Remember, the first step in the exercise was to use the Save As command. Now it's okay to use Save to store the new worksheet.) The completed income statement looks like that in figure 2.10.

Fig. 2.10.
The completed income statement for Blaire & Cory's Wholesale Flowers.

Designing the Balance Sheet

When you create a balance sheet, you apply the same simple techniques that you use to build an income statement. In this section, you will develop a balance sheet for Blaire & Cory's Wholesale Flowers and, in doing so, gain better insight into creating comprehensive, one-company financial reports.

Whereas the income statement describes the revenues and expenses at one particular point in time, a balance sheet paints a cumulative picture of the firm's financial position—by summarizing assets, liabilities, and equity—at a given point in time.

As you recall, you prepared a fiscal year-end income statement for Blaire & Cory's Wholesale Flowers in the last exercise. After you complete the company's balance sheet, you will design a financial-ratio-analysis report. This report combines critical elements of the income statement and the balance sheet and displays the results as ratios, thereby providing the owner or manager the means to evaluate the firm's position in terms of its own historical performance and the performance of other members in the same industry.

Before building the balance sheet, though, you should review an important strategic issue: single versus multiple worksheets. It's okay to use separate worksheets for each of your financial statements. Excel's document-linking feature makes this setup possible. If you want to take full advantage of the power of the electronic spreadsheet, however, you ought to consider including all the financial facts and figures on one worksheet whenever possible.

Why? First, with only one worksheet, you can be sure that you'll always remember to do a complete update as new accounting numbers become available. Second, as you learn more complex techniques in the latter part of this chapter for accessing and storing your financial data, you'll discover that updating information in one report automatically updates statistics appearing in another part of the worksheet—and that's an important time-saving technique. Finally, a multireport worksheet presents you with the most efficient way to do "what if" analysis. For example, wouldn't you like to adjust the cost-of-goods-sold figure on your income statement and instantly see the resulting balance sheet and financial-ratio effect? With Excel, it's easy.

Now, to create the balance sheet for Blaire & Cory's Wholesale Flowers, follow these steps:

Step 1. Select row 1 and choose Insert from the Edit menu. The reason for this step will soon become clear.

Step 2. Highlight the range D22:D24. Type = and then enter **D2**. Notice that the text appearing in cell D2 now appears in cell D22. Press Return.

> Tip: When you place an equal sign in a cell, you are telling Excel to prepare to accept a formula or cell reference input. If you reproduce title information for other reports (such as the company name) on the same worksheet, use the original title's cell reference. Then you won't have to retype the same title over and over again.

Step 3. In cell D23, enter the title **Balance Sheet**. In cell D24, enter **D4** and press Return (see fig. 2.11).

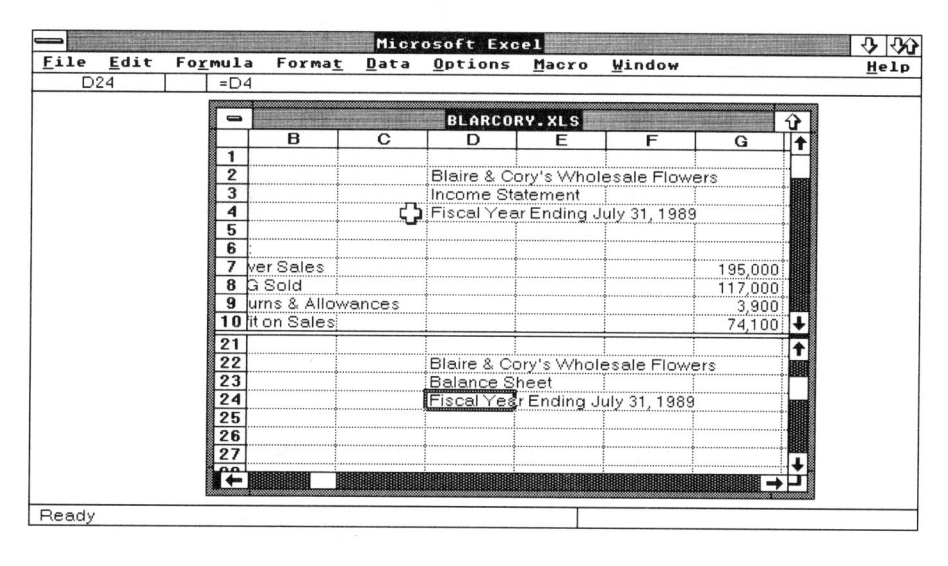

Fig. 2.11. A split-screen view of a cell formula that recalls text from another part of the worksheet.

Step 4. Select the range A25:A41 and enter the following account titles:

  A25: **Assets**
  A26: <space>**Cash**
  A27: <space>**Accounts Receivable**
  A28: <space>**Inventory**
  A29: <space>**Equipment & Automobile (net)**
  A30: **Total Assets:**
  A33: **Liabilities & Owners' Equity**
  A34: <space>**Notes Payable**

A35: <space>**Accounts Payable**
A36: <space><space>**Total Liabilities:**
A37: <space>**Blaire Courtney, Capital**
A38: <space>**Cory Lena, Capital**
A39: <space><space>**Total Owners' Equity**
A41: **Total Liabilities & OE:**

Step 5. Select the multiple range H26:H29, H34:H35, and H37:H38.

> Tip: To select a multiple range, simply highlight the first series in the range (H26:H29); then, while pressing the Ctrl key, click-select the second (H34:H35) and third (H37:H38) series in this range (see fig. 2.12).

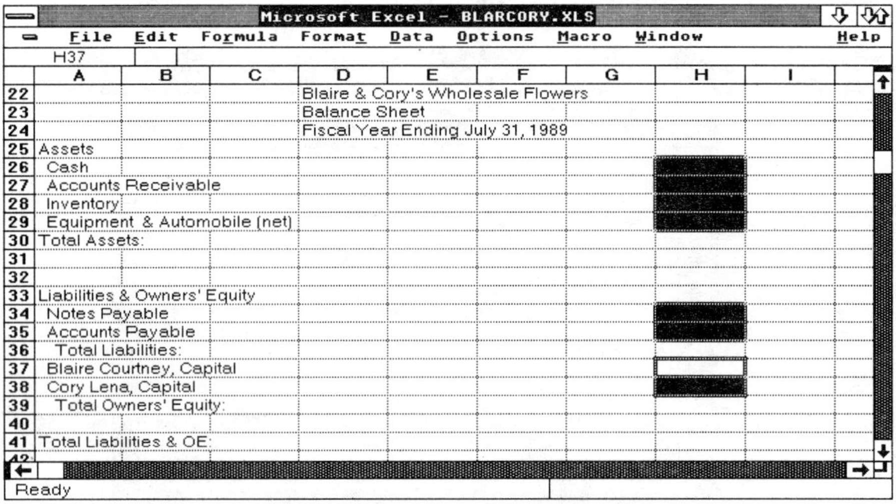

Fig. 2.12.
The highlighted multiple range.

When using this technique, be aware that not all of Excel's menu operations can be performed on a multiple range selection. For example, choosing Cut from the Edit menu invokes the warning message seen in figure 2.13.

Now enter the following account values (press Enter twice to get back to cell H26):

H26: **12709**
H27: **112000**
H28: **44756**
H29: **25540**
H34: **23450**

H35: **36555**

H37: **67500**

H38: **67500**

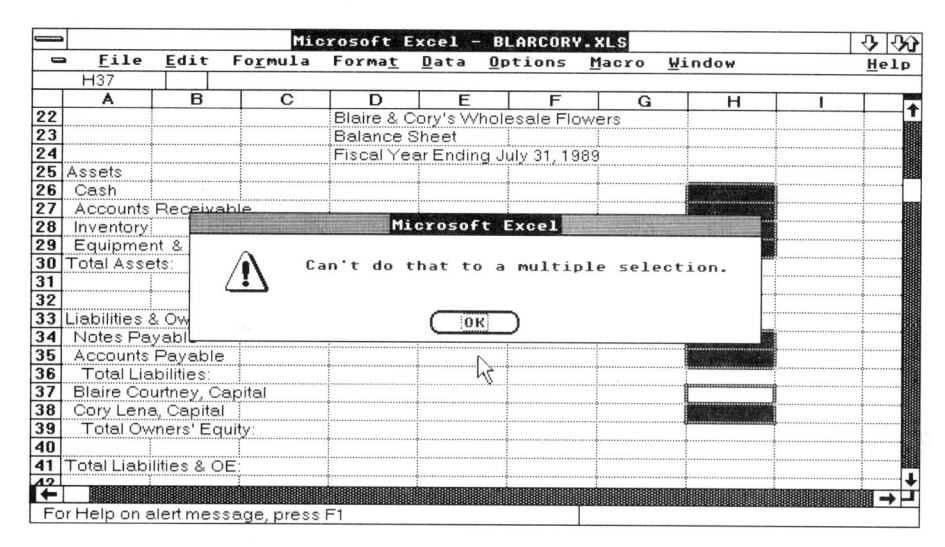

Fig. 2.13.
The warning message that appears if you try to use Cut on a multiple selection range.

Step 6. Select cells I30, I36, I39, and I41 by using the multiple-range-selection shortcut. Using the F4 key to designate an absolute-reference format, enter the following summation formulas for the account groupings:

I30: **=SUM($H$26:$H$30)**

I36: **=SUM($H$34:$H$36)**

I39: **=SUM($H$37:$H$39)**

I41: **$I$36+$I$39**

The reason that these formulas are entered in absolute-reference format should be obvious.

If you enter the total-assets formula in a relative-reference format (see fig. 2.14) and then copy the formula to cell I31, the outcome is incorrect. Why? Because the format adjusts in a *relative* fashion. The resulting error (that H26:H30 becomes H27:H31) appears in figure 2.15.

Fig. 2.14.
Using the relative-reference format.

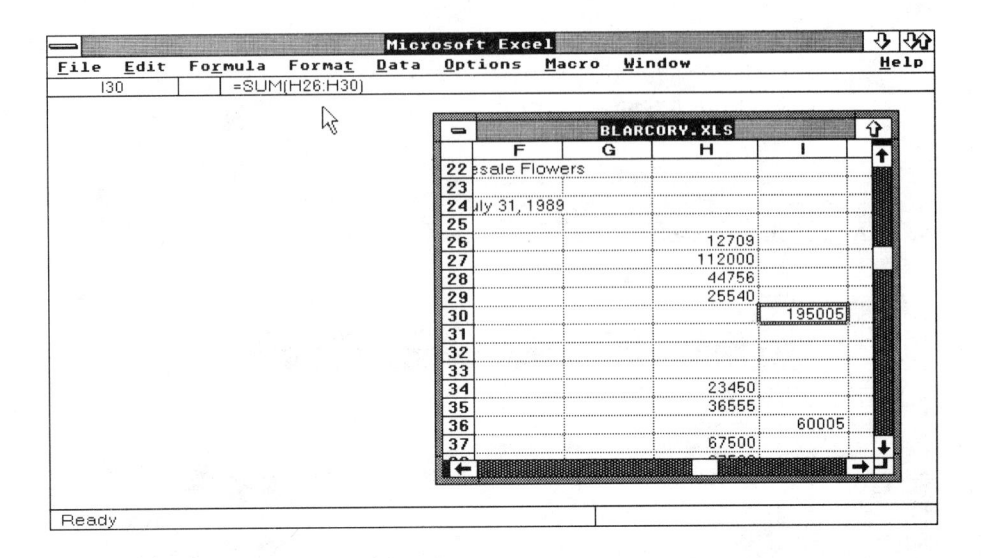

Fig. 2.15.
A formula entered in relative-reference format and adjusted in a relative fashion when copied to another location on the worksheet.

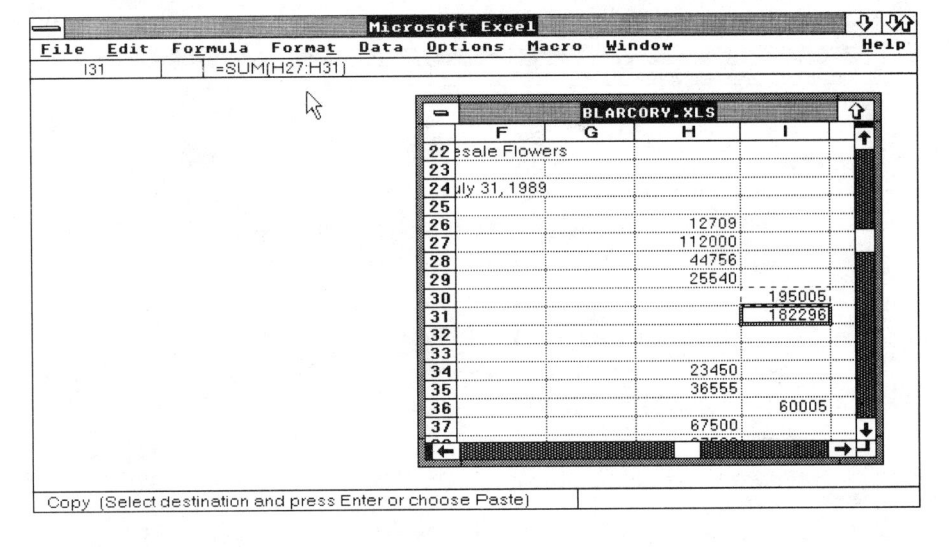

Step 7. Select the multiple range H26:H29 and H34:I39. From the Number menu, select the #,##0 format and click OK.

> Tip: Go ahead and format blank cells when they lie in a large selection range. This action has no consequences until you actually place text into the cell.

Step 8. Select cells I30 and I41. From the Number menu, select the #,#0 ;($#,##0) format and click OK.

Step 9. Select cells H29, H35, H38, I30:I31, and I41:I42. From the Format menu, choose Border; click the Bottom box.

Step 10. Select rows 31 and 42. Choose the Format menu, select Row Height, enter the value **3**, and click OK (see fig. 2.16).

> Tip: Use the Border option from the Format menu to enhance the layout of your worksheets.

Fig. 2.16. Changing the row height to create double-underlines.

	A	B	C	D	E	F	G	H	I
22				Blaire & Cory's Wholesale Flowers					
23				Balance Sheet					
24				Fiscal Year Ending July 31, 1989					
25	Assets								
26	Cash							12,709	
27	Accounts Receivable							112,000	
28	Inventory							44,756	
29	Equipment & Automobile (net)							25,540	
30	Total Assets:								$195,005
32									
33	Liabilities & Owners' Equity								
34	Notes Payable							23,450	
35	Accounts Payable							36,555	
36	Total Liabilities:								60,005
37	Blaire Courtney, Capital							67,500	
38	Cory Lena, Capital							67,500	
39	Total Owners' Equity:								135,000
40									
41	Total Liabilities & OE								$195,005
43									

Step 11. Select cell A1. Choose the Options menu, choose Display, and uncheck the box next to Gridlines.

Step 12. From the File menu, select Save. The completed balance sheet should look like that in figure 2.17.

The purpose of Step 1 in this exercise merits a closer look. Remember that you inserted one row above the income statement before even building the balance sheet. What benefit could this minor step possibly provide?

When you added that single line to the top of the worksheet, you provided a mechanism that will allow for a smooth transition from one financial statement to the next. How? Move your cursor to cell A1 and press the PgDn key once. Notice that the balance sheet now appears on-screen by itself, its title appearing in exactly the same worksheet location as it does on the income statement. Additionally, each statement begins on the second line of its own screen. Press the PgUp key once, and you return to the income statement.

Fig. 2.17.
The completed balance sheet for Blaire & Cory's Wholesale Flowers.

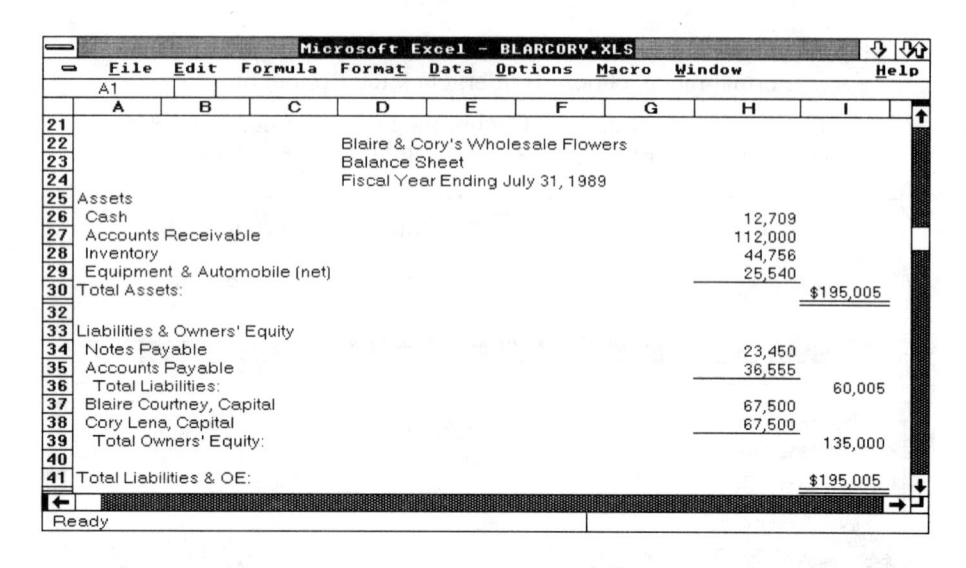

```
                   Microsoft Excel - BLARCORY.XLS
  File   Edit   Formula   Format   Data   Options   Macro   Window       Help
  A1
    A      B       C          D           E        F       G      H        I
21
22                      Blaire & Cory's Wholesale Flowers
23                      Balance Sheet
24                      Fiscal Year Ending July 31, 1989
25 Assets
26  Cash                                                         12,709
27  Accounts Receivable                                         112,000
28  Inventory                                                    44,756
29  Equipment & Automobile (net)                                 25,540
30 Total Assets:                                                        $195,005
31
32
33 Liabilities & Owners' Equity
34  Notes Payable                                                23,450
35  Accounts Payable                                             36,555
36   Total Liabilities:                                                   60,005
37  Blaire Courtney, Capital                                     67,500
38  Cory Lena, Capital                                           67,500
39   Total Owners' Equity:                                              135,000
40
41 Total Liabilities & OE:                                              $195,005

Ready
```

Note: On some displays, you will have to insert two lines to create this effect. The important point is that you can insert rows to "frame" your worksheet on your display.

This elementary technique improves your worksheet functionality dramatically. The notion of functionality is one that you must always address during the worksheet-planning stages, for if you design tools that are easy to operate, then you've created an instrument that everyone will want to use. As your worksheets grow in length, this book will place increasing emphasis on how Excel enables you to design worksheets, macros, and charts to meet this important goal. In fact, you'll even find it advantageous to split up lengthy statements into two or more screens, separating the report at a logical break point. In the case of the balance sheet, a logical break point occurs between the Assets section and the Liabilities & Owners' Equity section.

Designing the Financial-Ratio Report

There are several ways to gauge the financial well-being of your company. The income statement and balance sheet are two examples of a standard accounting report that examines a company's key operational concerns: revenues, expenses, assets, liabilities, and equity. Ratio analysis offers a slightly different approach for gauging the firm's financial health. The first two reports you built in this chapter provide you summarized data of your internal operations; ratio analysis does that and then goes one step further.

Ratios provide a relative measure of your firm's performance and condition. This relative measure enables the manager to evaluate a firm's continuing operations, and it also serves as a barometer for assessing how the firm measures up to competitors in the same industry.

The key inputs to ratio analysis are the income statement and the balance sheet. Financial ratios are divided into four basic categories: liquidity ratios, activity ratios, debt ratios, and profitability ratios. Liquidity, activity, and profitability ratios provide critical, short-term information about a firm's health. The debt ratios are elemental to long-range forecasting and capital budgeting.

There are undoubtedly hundreds of ways to create ratio comparisons between income-statement and balance-sheet figures. The following exercise uses only a few ratios from each category; you can always add more ratios to your firm's report later.

Remember the earlier recommendation to keep all the financial facts and figures on one worksheet whenever possible? Doing so makes the creation of the ratio report easy and provides a built-in forecasting tool.

To create the ratio-analysis report for Blaire & Cory's Wholesale Flowers, follow these steps:

Step 1. Select the range H44:H46. In H44 enter the cell reference **H2**, in H45 enter the title **Financial Ratio Report**, and in H46 enter the cell reference **H4**.

Step 2. Highlight the multiple range A48:A50, A52:A54, A56:A57, and A59:A62. Enter the following ratio descriptions (press Enter four times to get to cell A48):

    A48: **Liquidity**
    A49: <space>**Current ratio**
    A50: <space>**Quick ratio**
    A52: **Activity**
    A53: <space>**Inventory turnover**
    A54: <space>**Average collection period**
    A56: **Debt**
    A57: <space>**Debt ratio**
    A59: **Profitability**
    A60: <space>**Gross-profit margin**
    A61: <space>**Net-profit margin, after taxes**
    A62: <space>**Return on equity**

Step 3. Select the range E61:F61. In E61, enter the description **Tax rate:**, and in F61 enter the number **0.28**.

> Tip: In financial forecasting, two figures receive regular attention: the tax rate and the interest rate. By adding a variable block to your worksheet at E61:F61, you may easily manipulate ratios tied to this block by simply entering a new tax rate.

Step 4. Highlight the multiple range H49:H50, H53:H54, H57, and H60:H62. Enter the following formulas to compute each ratio (press Enter three times to get to cell H49):

    H49: =SUM($H$26:$H$28)/SUM($H$34:$H$35)
    H50: =SUM($H$26:$H$27)/SUM($H$34:$H$35)
    H53: =$G$8/$H$28
    H54: =$H$27/($G$7/365)
    H57: =$I$36/$I$30
    H60: =$G$10/$G$7
    H61: =$G$20*(1-$F$61)/$G$7
    H62: =$G$20*(1-$F$61)/$I$39

> Shortcut: If you're concerned about entering all of the ratio formulas by hand, good! There is a much easier (and more accurate) way to execute Step 4, one that uses your ability to click-select critical cell references that are to appear in a formula and that has you use the F4 key to enter values in the absolute-reference format.

Step 5. Figure 2.18 shows the initial step required to enter the debt-ratio formula. With the cursor resting in H55, scroll to the cell containing the firm's total debt: cell I36. When you click-select this cell, it appears as the first reference on the formula bar. Press F4 to invoke the absolute-reference format.

Type / to perform division, and select the second cell, I30. Press F4 once more and then press Return. The formula is now complete (see fig. 2.19). Use this procedure to enter all the ratio formulas (unless, of course, you've already typed them).

Step 6. Select the multiple range H49:H50 and H53:H54. Choose the Format menu, select Number, highlight the #,##0.00 option, and click OK.

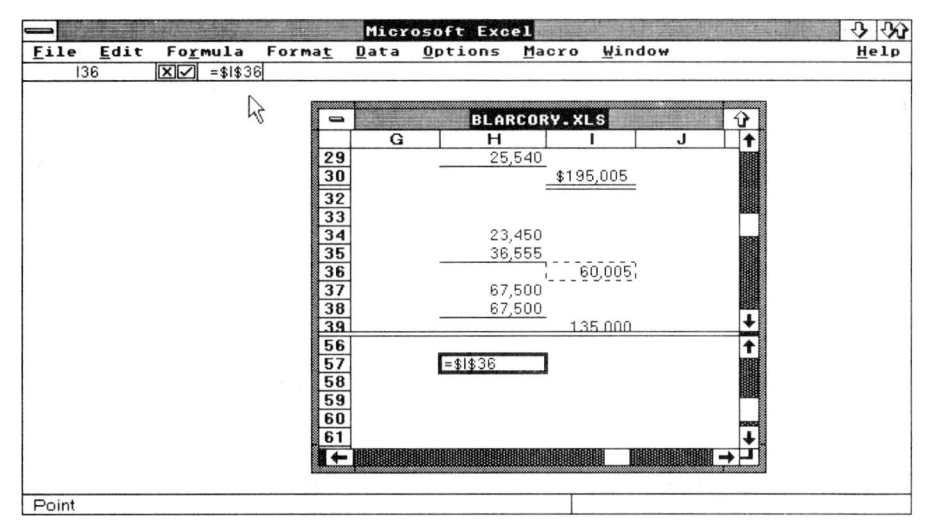

Fig. 2.18. Click-selecting the first cell reference to appear in the debt-ratio formula.

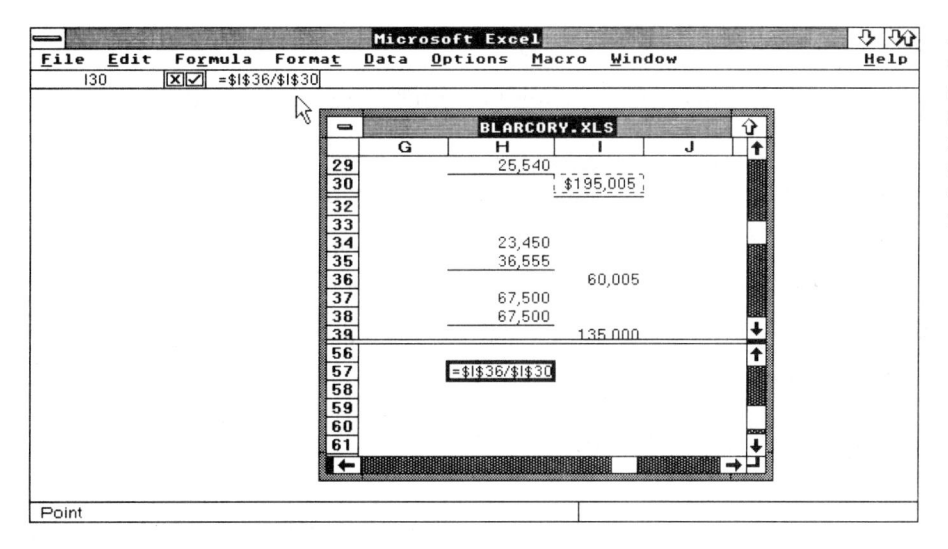

Fig. 2.19. Click-selecting the second cell reference to appear in the debt-ratio formula.

Step 7. Select the multiple range H57 and F60:H62. Choose the Format menu once more and again select Number. Highlight the 0.00% option and click OK.

Step 8. From the File menu, select Save. The completed financial-ratio report should look like that in figure 2.20.

Fig. 2.20.
Blaire & Cory's completed financial-ratio report.

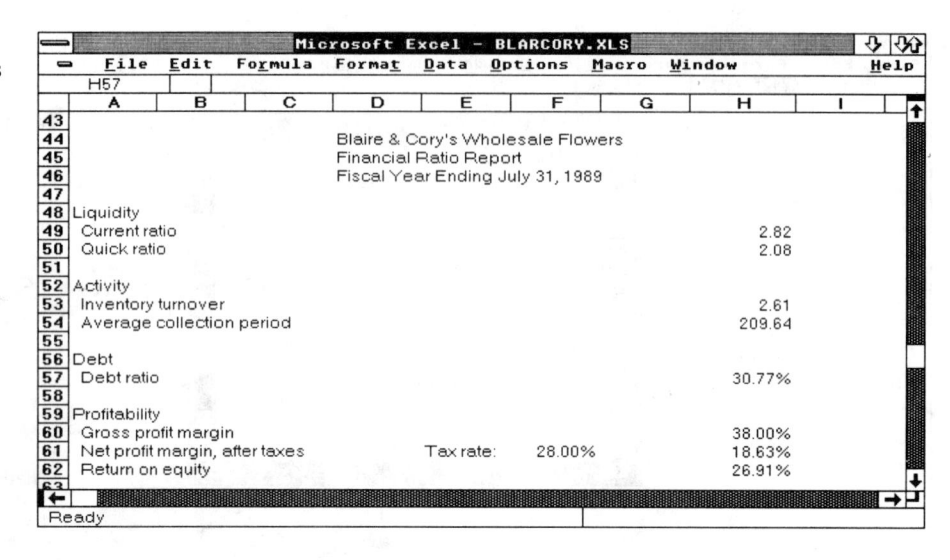

```
┌──────────────────── Microsoft Excel - BLARCORY.XLS ─────────────┬─┐
│  ═  File  Edit  Formula  Format  Data  Options  Macro  Window   Help │
│  H57                                                                  │
│      A       B         C          D           E        F      G       H        I   │
│ 43                                                                    │
│ 44                     Blaire & Cory's Wholesale Flowers              │
│ 45                     Financial Ratio Report                         │
│ 46                     Fiscal Year Ending July 31, 1989               │
│ 47                                                                    │
│ 48  Liquidity                                                         │
│ 49    Current ratio                                            2.82   │
│ 50    Quick ratio                                              2.08   │
│ 51                                                                    │
│ 52  Activity                                                          │
│ 53    Inventory turnover                                       2.61   │
│ 54    Average collection period                              209.64   │
│ 55                                                                    │
│ 56  Debt                                                              │
│ 57    Debt ratio                                             30.77%   │
│ 58                                                                    │
│ 59  Profitability                                                     │
│ 60    Gross profit margin                                    38.00%   │
│ 61    Net profit margin, after taxes    Tax rate:  28.00%    18.63%   │
│ 62    Return on equity                                       26.91%   │
│ Ready                                                                 │
└───────────────────────────────────────────────────────────────────────┘
```

Following are explanations of the ratios presented in the financial-ratio report.

Current ratio. This ratio compares the firm's current assets to its current liabilities, indicating the firm's capability to pay its current debts with its current assets. In the preceding example, the ratio 2.82 means that the firm's current assets are roughly three times the amount of its current liabilities.

Quick ratio. This ratio equals the current ratio, with inventory deducted from current assets. Why deduct inventory? Assuming that the firm cannot sell its inventory quickly enough to cover current debts, the ratio 2.08 in the preceding example indicates that the firm's current assets are still roughly two times the amount of its current debts. In other words, Blaire & Cory's Wholesale Flowers should have no problem meeting its immediate debt obligations.

Inventory turnover ratio. This ratio—2.61 in the preceding example—equals the cost of goods sold divided by inventory. What does this mean? The inventory turnover ratio is most meaningful when compared to industry standards. If the industry standard in this case is 25.7, should Blaire & Cory's be concerned?

Consider this ratio in a different light. If you divide the ratio into 365 (days per year), the result equals the average age of inventory. The average age of inventory for Blaire & Cory's is 139.8 days! For flowers? The industry standard is 14.0 days!

Average collection period. This ratio is equal to current accounts receivable divided by average daily sales (which is annual sales divided by 365). The result in the example is 209.64, indicating that on average, it takes the firm 209.64 days—almost seven months—to collect an account receivable!

Debt ratio. This ratio is equal to the firm's total liabilities divided by its total assets. The total debt of Blaire & Cory's is 30.77 percent of its total company value. Conversely, 30.77 percent of the company assets are provided for by their creditors.

Gross-profit margin. Although this percentage is already expressed on the income statement, it also has a place on the financial-ratio report.

Net-profit margin, after taxes. The income statement indicates that Blaire & Cory's has a 25.87 percent pretax net-profit margin. To compute the after-tax net-profit margin, multiply net profit by (1–0.28). (1–0.28) equals the amount of profit that the company gets to keep. Blaire & Cory's earned an 18.63 percent after-tax profit margin.

Return on equity. This ratio evaluates the return that owners Blaire Courtney and Cory Lena receive on their current company equity. In this example, the resulting 26.91 percent is derived by dividing after-tax profit by total equity.

Note: One of Excel's seldom used, seldom discussed menu features enables you to split your Excel window into independent panes. The Split option is available from the Control menu, which you activate by click-selecting the little hyphen that appears directly to the left of the File menu. After you select the Split option, use your mouse (or the arrow keys) to drag the split bar to divide your window in half or segment the window into quarters.

Large spreadsheets often contain a labyrinth of interconnected formulas. If you change data in A1 and want to evaluate that change's effect on the data in cell A355, split your window and scroll each pane so that A1 and A355 appear on the same worksheet. You can change data in the first pane and instantly view the result on the second. With a little practice, you will master this invaluable tool and quickly appreciate its time-saving benefits. Figures 2.11, 2.18, and 2.19 show the effect of choosing the Split option.

Imagine how much help this tool can be when you want to examine the effect on your equity ratio of an increase in the federal-income-tax rate. The process of changing formula variables and noting the results of such changes is the topic of this chapter's final section.

Using What-If Analysis

Contrary to television advertisements that extol what-if analysis as an ability unique to the employees of an obscure northern California computer company, *what-if analysis* is really just a phrase that describes natural inquisitiveness. The following are three pertinent examples of "what-iffing" in the discipline of business management. (Note: The borders appearing around particular cells in the following five figures highlight the ratios that are affected by a change in the balance-sheet and/or income-statement accounts.)

1. What if the federal-income-tax rate rises to 32 percent?

    If the income-tax rate increases to 32 percent, the after-tax net-profit margin and owners' return on equity decrease (see fig. 2.21, which shows lower percentages for these values than does fig. 2.20). The earlier sections on the income statement and balance sheet do not include income-tax liability; in reality, both statements would require adjustment for this liability.

Fig. 2.21.
The result of increasing the tax rate.

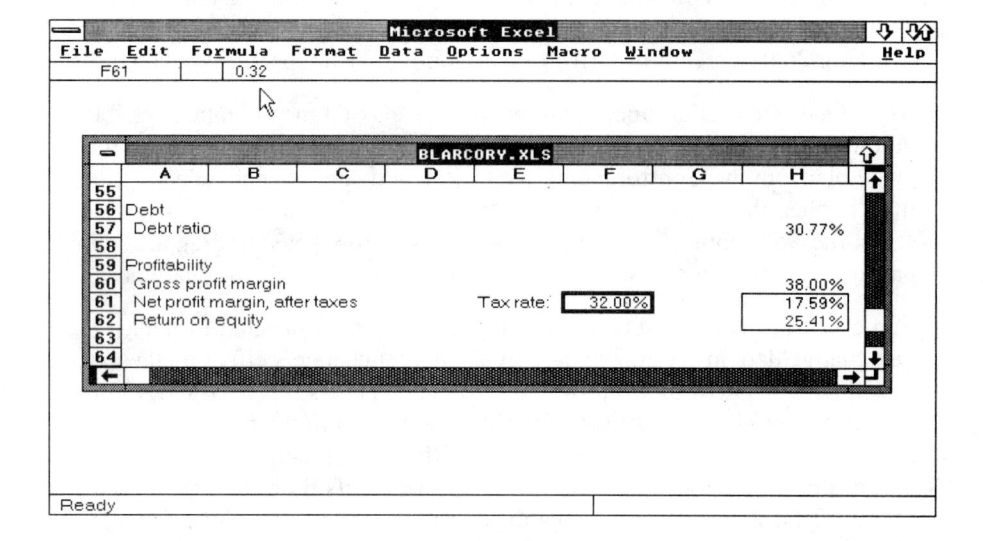

2. What if the cost of goods sold was understated by $13,000 on the original income statement?

    The cost-of-goods-sold figure flows through the income statement to the balance sheet and then to various financial ratios. The adjustment to correct this error causes net income to decrease by $13,000 to $37,450 (see fig. 2.22).

The decrease in net income on the income statement reduces the owners' capital on the balance sheet from $67,500 to $61,000 (see fig. 2.23). If the cost of goods sold is understated, then inventory must be overstated. The corrected inventory value appears in figure 2.23. The changes were entered manually because the balance sheet is not tied to the income statement through formulas.

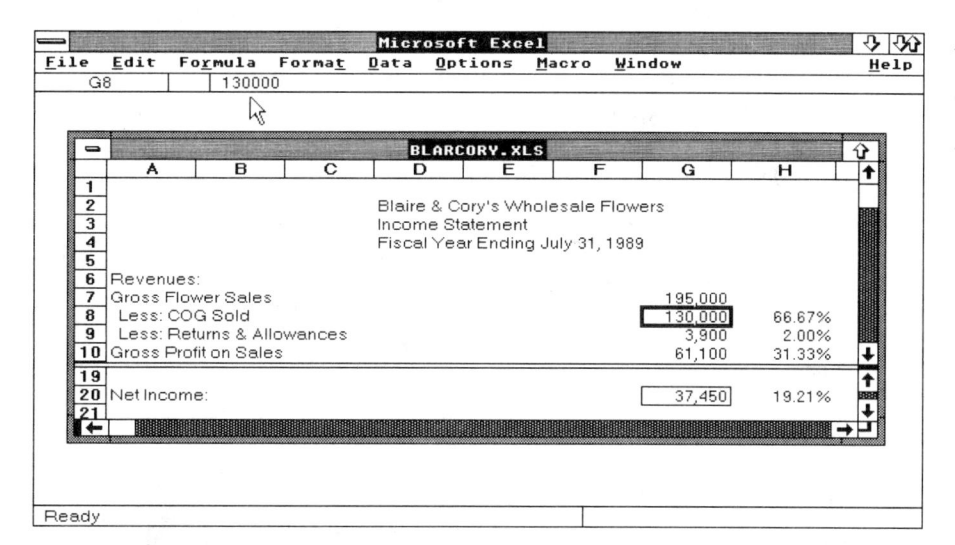

Fig. 2.22. The result of changing the reported cost of goods sold.

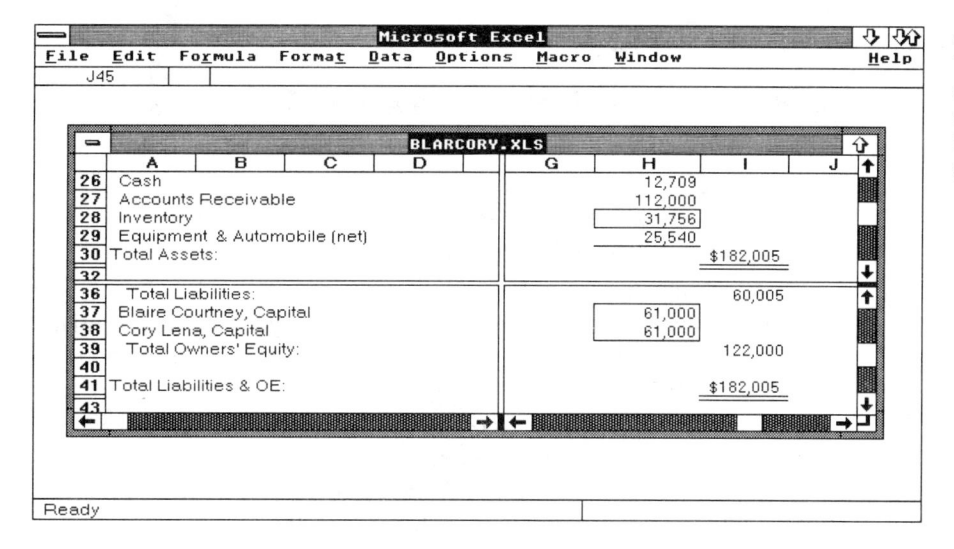

Fig. 2.23. The balance-sheet effect of understating the cost of goods sold.

In figure 2.24, six financial ratios change as a result of correcting this understatement. After you correct the values that appear on the income statement and balance sheet, the financial ratios are automatically updated.

Clearly, the current ratio, the inventory turnover ratio, and all the profitability ratios decrease with higher-than-reported costs (less inventory). The reason why the debt ratio increased may not be so obvious. If you think about it, the total firm debt did not change. Decreasing the firm's assets (inventory) and liabilities and equity (owner capital), however, lowers the total firm value. If debt remains constant and the firm value decreases, then debt is now a larger percentage of the firm's value.

Fig. 2.24.
The financial-ratio effect of correcting the understatement of the cost of goods sold.

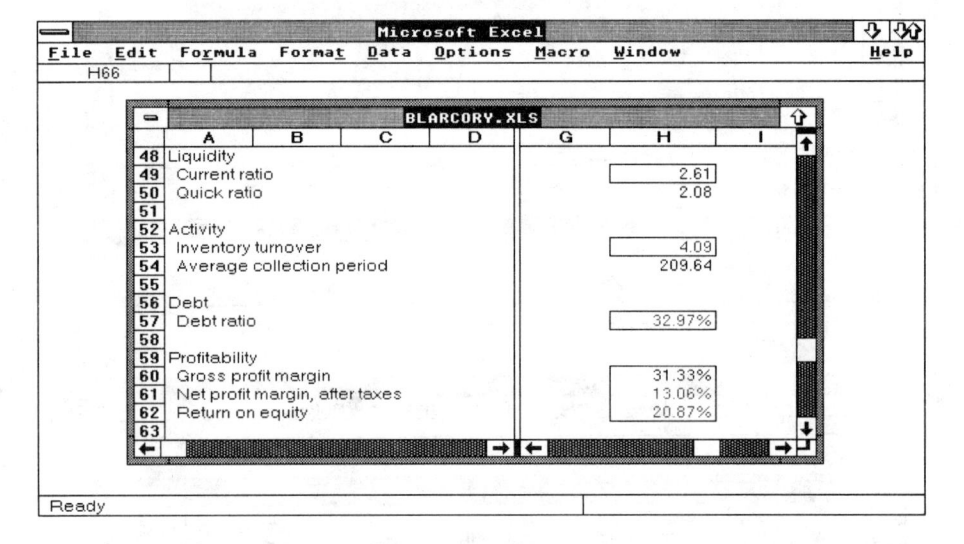

	A	H
48	Liquidity	
49	Current ratio	2.61
50	Quick ratio	2.08
51		
52	Activity	
53	Inventory turnover	4.09
54	Average collection period	209.64
55		
56	Debt	
57	Debt ratio	32.97%
58		
59	Profitability	
60	Gross profit margin	31.33%
61	Net profit margin, after taxes	13.06%
62	Return on equity	20.87%

3. What if the bookkeeper transposed the Cash and Accounts Receivable values on the original balance sheet?

   The adjusting entry to correct this mistake does not affect the income statement. In fact, the entry doesn't even affect the essential composition of the firm's balance sheet, because both current and total assets remain at the same level.

   In figure 2.25, notice the effect the adjustment has on the firm's average collection period. The average collection period drops from 209.6 to 23.79, a much more realistic estimation. If it took 210 days for Blaire & Cory's to collect its receivables, the company surely couldn't stay in business for long.

The previous two figures display the completed financial-statement worksheet for Blaire & Cory's Wholesale Flowers. To enhance the presentation impact of this report, choose the Options menu, select Display, uncheck Gridlines, and then click OK.

You can easily recall each report by pressing the PgDn and PgUp keys in succession until you arrive at the desired report. If you want to alter values that appear on any of the financial statements, use the Split window option on the Control menu.

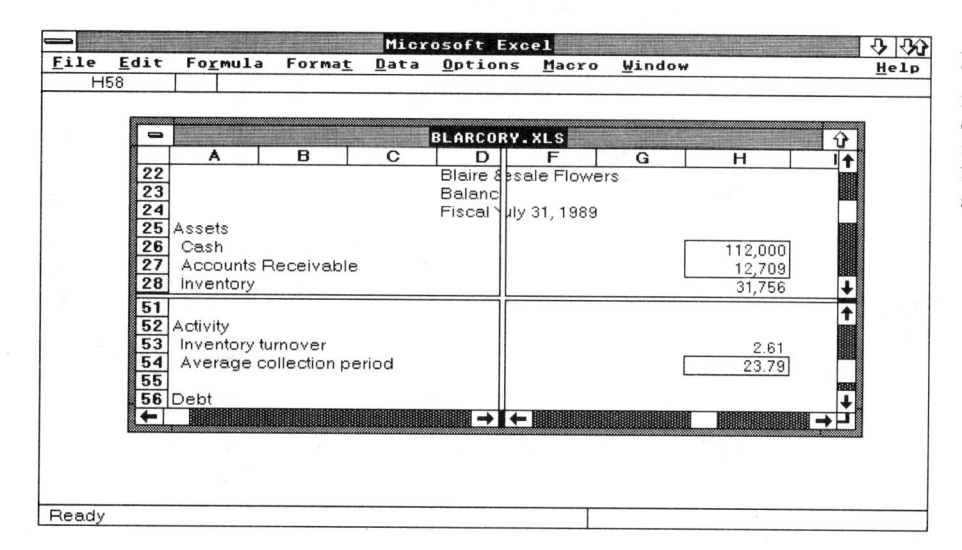

Fig. 2.25.
The financial-ratio effect of correcting two transposed balance-sheet accounts.

Enhancing the Financial Worksheet Model (INCBALRA.XLS)

The financial worksheet model that you just completed is a bit basic for nitty-gritty financial analysis. But now that you understand the basics of financial model-building, you can explore how to reshape the basic model into a full-blown, ready-to-use financial analysis tool.

On the disk that came with this book is the INCBALRA.XLS model, a fully operable, one-year financial-statement model that consists of three parts: the monthly income statement, the monthly balance sheet, and the financial-ratio report. This model, which helps you analyze one year's worth of financial data for your company, is an enhanced version of the one you designed and built in earlier sections of this chapter.

The Monthly Income Statement

Load INCBALRA.XLS into Excel. Notice that the first screen contains the first 6 months of a 12-month income-statement shell (see fig. 2.26). This model contains sample data for your evaluation.

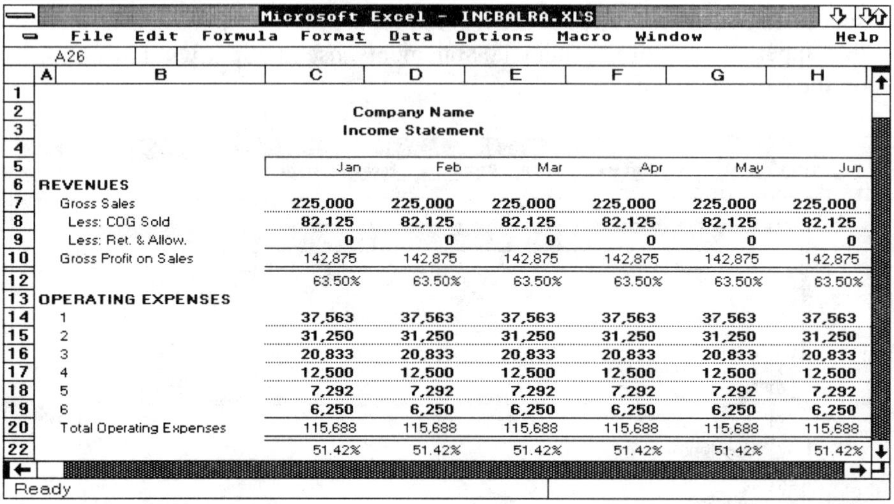
Microsoft Excel - INCBALRA.XLS
File Edit Formula Format Data Options Macro Window Help
A26

	A / B	C	D	E	F	G	H
1							
2			Company Name				
3			Income Statement				
4							
5		Jan	Feb	Mar	Apr	May	Jun
6	REVENUES						
7	Gross Sales	225,000	225,000	225,000	225,000	225,000	225,000
8	Less: COG Sold	82,125	82,125	82,125	82,125	82,125	82,125
9	Less: Ret. & Allow.	0	0	0	0	0	0
10	Gross Profit on Sales	142,875	142,875	142,875	142,875	142,875	142,875
12		63.50%	63.50%	63.50%	63.50%	63.50%	63.50%
13	OPERATING EXPENSES						
14	1	37,563	37,563	37,563	37,563	37,563	37,563
15	2	31,250	31,250	31,250	31,250	31,250	31,250
16	3	20,833	20,833	20,833	20,833	20,833	20,833
17	4	12,500	12,500	12,500	12,500	12,500	12,500
18	5	7,292	7,292	7,292	7,292	7,292	7,292
19	6	6,250	6,250	6,250	6,250	6,250	6,250
20	Total Operating Expenses	115,688	115,688	115,688	115,688	115,688	115,688
22		51.42%	51.42%	51.42%	51.42%	51.42%	51.42%

Ready

Fig. 2.26. The income-statement model, part 1 (January through June).

If you press Ctrl-PgDn to scroll one screen to the right, you can view the format for the remaining six months (see fig. 2.27). The YTD column provides you with an ongoing, year-to-date accounting of all the income-statement accounts.

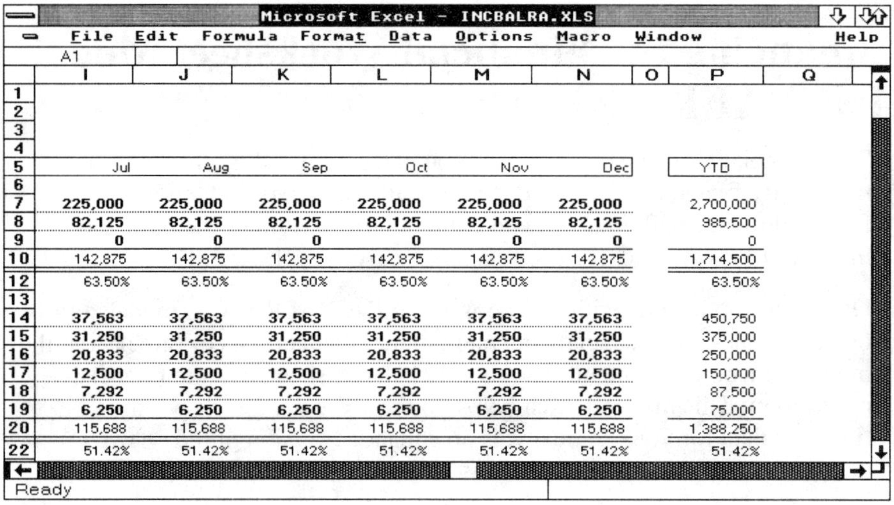
Microsoft Excel - INCBALRA.XLS
File Edit Formula Format Data Options Macro Window Help
A1

	I	J	K	L	M	N	O	P	Q
1									
2									
3									
4									
5	Jul	Aug	Sep	Oct	Nov	Dec		YTD	
6									
7	225,000	225,000	225,000	225,000	225,000	225,000		2,700,000	
8	82,125	82,125	82,125	82,125	82,125	82,125		985,500	
9	0	0	0	0	0	0		0	
10	142,875	142,875	142,875	142,875	142,875	142,875		1,714,500	
12	63.50%	63.50%	63.50%	63.50%	63.50%	63.50%		63.50%	
13									
14	37,563	37,563	37,563	37,563	37,563	37,563		450,750	
15	31,250	31,250	31,250	31,250	31,250	31,250		375,000	
16	20,833	20,833	20,833	20,833	20,833	20,833		250,000	
17	12,500	12,500	12,500	12,500	12,500	12,500		150,000	
18	7,292	7,292	7,292	7,292	7,292	7,292		87,500	
19	6,250	6,250	6,250	6,250	6,250	6,250		75,000	
20	115,688	115,688	115,688	115,688	115,688	115,688		1,388,250	
22	51.42%	51.42%	51.42%	51.42%	51.42%	51.42%		51.42%	

Ready

Fig. 2.27. The income-statement model, part 1 (July through YTD).

Now press Ctrl-PgUp to return to the first screen. Enter your company name into cell D2.

The most common account names are already entered into the model. For example, the REVENUES section is complete. You may enter up to six of your own expense-account names in the OPERATING EXPENSES section. As you already know, however, it's a simple task to select Edit Insert and add an extra row to this income-statement shell. But before you begin to make any changes, first review the rest of this model.

Press PgDn once to view the lower portion of the income-statement model (see fig. 2.28). The top of the second screen shows the calculated income from operations. Below this number, in the OTHER EXPENSES section, you'll find additional accounts such as Interest and Taxes. You will also find a blank expense account (between Interest and Taxes), should you want to add another expense account later.

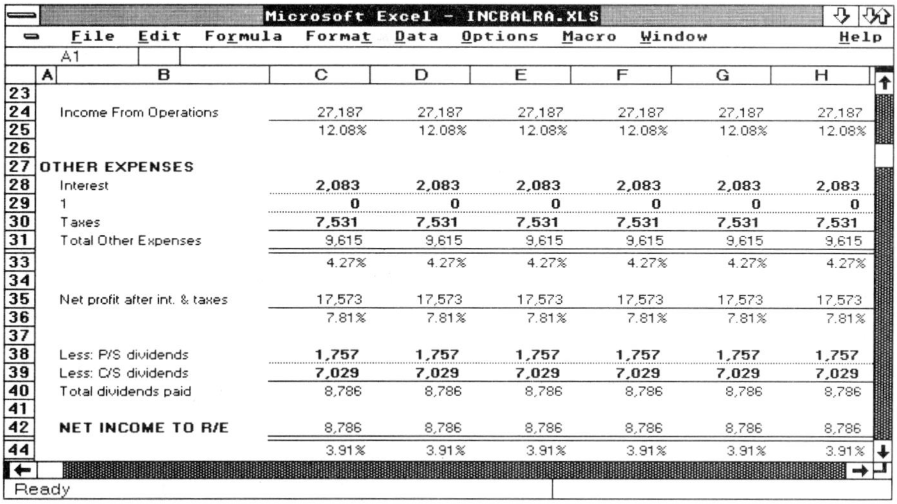

Row	A/B	C	D	E	F	G	H
23							
24	Income From Operations	27,187	27,187	27,187	27,187	27,187	27,187
25		12.08%	12.08%	12.08%	12.08%	12.08%	12.08%
26							
27	OTHER EXPENSES						
28	Interest	2,083	2,083	2,083	2,083	2,083	2,083
29	1	0	0	0	0	0	0
30	Taxes	7,531	7,531	7,531	7,531	7,531	7,531
31	Total Other Expenses	9,615	9,615	9,615	9,615	9,615	9,615
33		4.27%	4.27%	4.27%	4.27%	4.27%	4.27%
34							
35	Net profit after int. & taxes	17,573	17,573	17,573	17,573	17,573	17,573
36		7.81%	7.81%	7.81%	7.81%	7.81%	7.81%
37							
38	Less: P/S dividends	1,757	1,757	1,757	1,757	1,757	1,757
39	Less: C/S dividends	7,029	7,029	7,029	7,029	7,029	7,029
40	Total dividends paid	8,786	8,786	8,786	8,786	8,786	8,786
41							
42	NET INCOME TO R/E	8,786	8,786	8,786	8,786	8,786	8,786
44		3.91%	3.91%	3.91%	3.91%	3.91%	3.91%

Fig. 2.28. The income-statement model, part 2.

When INCBALRA.XLS contains no data, hyphens appear below each of the single- and double-underlined figures. These cells contain special formulas that calculate and display percentage values when the model contains information. To consider the syntax of one of these formulas, place your cursor in cell C25. The formula =IF(C$24=0,"---",C$24/C$7) tells Excel to do the following:

1. Check the contents of C24.
2. Display a hyphen if C24's value is zero.
3. If C24 doesn't equal zero, display the income from operations (C$24) as a percentage of gross sales (C$7).

This special IF() function prevents Excel from displaying divide-by-zero error messages.

Scroll through the formulas appearing in the monthly income-statement shell. Be sure that you understand the flow of information through this first part of the model.

The Monthly Balance Sheet

The third screen contains the ASSETS section of a monthly balance sheet (see fig. 2.29). Keep in mind that the balance sheet is a cumulative account of a firm's assets, liabilities, and equity at one point in time.

Fig. 2.29.
The balance-sheet model, part 1 (January through June).

	A	B	C	D	E	F	G	H
45								
46				Company Name				
47				Balance Sheet				
49				Jan	Feb	Mar	Apr	May	Jun
50	ASSETS							
51	Current Assets							
52		Cash		92,450	92,450	92,450	92,450	92,450	92,450
53		Accounts Receivable		225,000	225,000	225,000	225,000	225,000	225,000
54		Inventory		240,000	240,000	240,000	240,000	240,000	240,000
55		1		50,000	50,000	50,000	50,000	50,000	50,000
56		Total Current Assets:		607,450	607,450	607,450	607,450	607,450	607,450
58	Fixed Assets							
59		1		375,000	375,000	375,000	375,000	375,000	375,000
60		2		150,000	150,000	150,000	150,000	150,000	150,000
61		3		150,000	150,000	150,000	150,000	150,000	150,000
62		Less: Accumlated Dep.		(135,750)	(135,750)	(135,750)	(135,750)	(135,750)	(135,750)
63		Net Fixed Assets:		539,250	539,250	539,250	539,250	539,250	539,250
65		TOTAL ASSETS		1,146,700	1,146,700	1,146,700	1,146,700	1,146,700	1,146,700

Press Ctrl-PgDn once to scroll to the second half of the ASSETS section (see fig. 2.30). Column P, which presents the end-of-year balance-sheet standing, contains the exact same data that appears in column N—the last month of the calendar year. This model assumes that the calendar year is also the fiscal year, both ending on December 31.

The December 31 balance sheet is reproduced in column P because the year-to-date income-statement data also appears in column P. This format will make good sense to you when you explore the ratio-analysis report later in this section.

Press Ctrl-PgUp once and go back to the first screen of the ASSETS section. In this part of the model, you may enter descriptions for one extra current asset and three extra fixed assets.

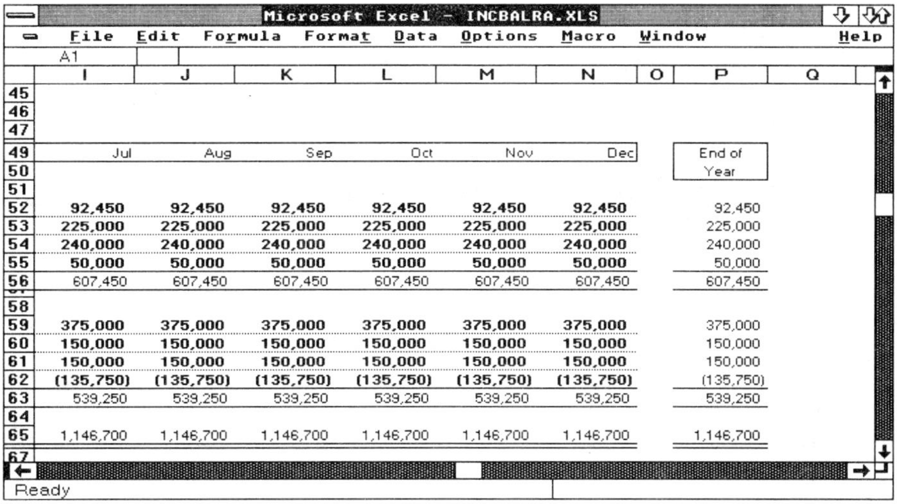

Microsoft Excel - INCBALRA.XLS

File Edit Formula Format Data Options Macro Window Help

A1

	I	J	K	L	M	N	O	P
45								
46								
47								
49	Jul	Aug	Sep	Oct	Nov	Dec		End of Year
50								
51								
52	92,450	92,450	92,450	92,450	92,450	92,450		92,450
53	225,000	225,000	225,000	225,000	225,000	225,000		225,000
54	240,000	240,000	240,000	240,000	240,000	240,000		240,000
55	50,000	50,000	50,000	50,000	50,000	50,000		50,000
56	607,450	607,450	607,450	607,450	607,450	607,450		607,450
58								
59	375,000	375,000	375,000	375,000	375,000	375,000		375,000
60	150,000	150,000	150,000	150,000	150,000	150,000		150,000
61	150,000	150,000	150,000	150,000	150,000	150,000		150,000
62	(135,750)	(135,750)	(135,750)	(135,750)	(135,750)	(135,750)		(135,750)
63	539,250	539,250	539,250	539,250	539,250	539,250		539,250
64								
65	1,146,700	1,146,700	1,146,700	1,146,700	1,146,700	1,146,700		1,146,700
67								

Ready

Fig. 2.30. The balance-sheet model, part 1 (June through End of Year).

Press PgDn once to view the LIABILITIES & OWNERS' EQUITY section (see fig. 2.31). The model displays preferred and common stock issues, as well as paid-in capital in excess of the common stock par value. If your company has no stock, simply enter zeros into these cells. Note in advance that the EQUITY section in the ratio report will be blank if your company has no stock issues.

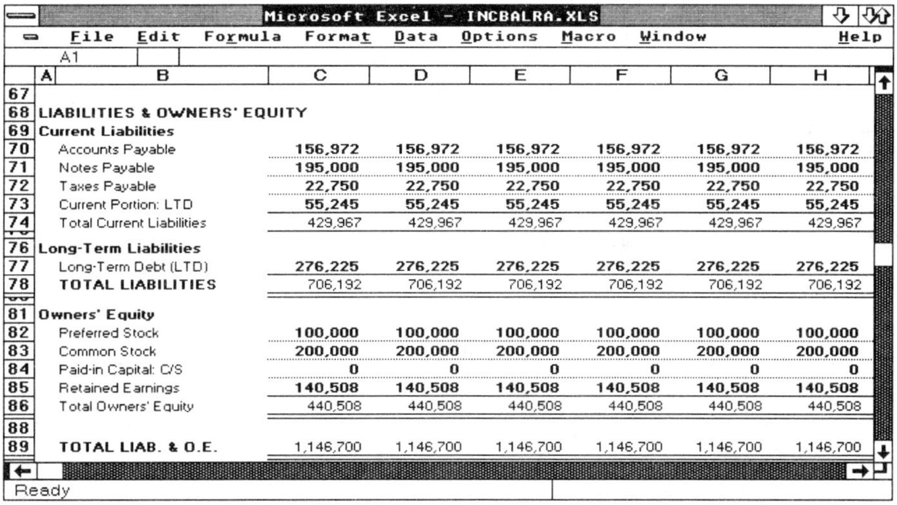

Microsoft Excel - INCBALRA.XLS

File Edit Formula Format Data Options Macro Window Help

A1

	A / B	C	D	E	F	G	H
67							
68	LIABILITIES & OWNERS' EQUITY						
69	Current Liabilities						
70	Accounts Payable	156,972	156,972	156,972	156,972	156,972	156,972
71	Notes Payable	195,000	195,000	195,000	195,000	195,000	195,000
72	Taxes Payable	22,750	22,750	22,750	22,750	22,750	22,750
73	Current Portion: LTD	55,245	55,245	55,245	55,245	55,245	55,245
74	Total Current Liabilities	429,967	429,967	429,967	429,967	429,967	429,967
76	Long-Term Liabilities						
77	Long-Term Debt (LTD)	276,225	276,225	276,225	276,225	276,225	276,225
78	TOTAL LIABILITIES	706,192	706,192	706,192	706,192	706,192	706,192
81	Owners' Equity						
82	Preferred Stock	100,000	100,000	100,000	100,000	100,000	100,000
83	Common Stock	200,000	200,000	200,000	200,000	200,000	200,000
84	Paid-in Capital: C/S	0	0	0	0	0	0
85	Retained Earnings	140,508	140,508	140,508	140,508	140,508	140,508
86	Total Owners' Equity	440,508	440,508	440,508	440,508	440,508	440,508
88							
89	TOTAL LIAB. & O.E.	1,146,700	1,146,700	1,146,700	1,146,700	1,146,700	1,146,700

Ready

Fig. 2.31. The balance-sheet model, part 2 (January through June).

The Financial-Ratio Report

Even with only one month's worth of financial data, you can review the financial-ratio report. To move to the ratio report from the LIABILITIES & OWNERS' EQUITY section, press PgDn once (see fig. 2.32).

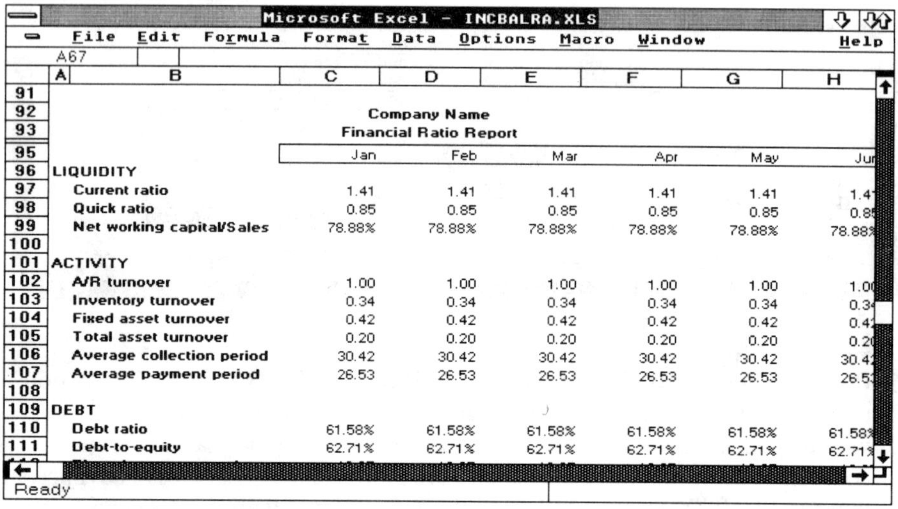

Microsoft Excel - INCBALRA.XLS

File Edit Formula Format Data Options Macro Window Help

A67

	A	B	C	D	E	F	G	H
91								
92				Company Name				
93				Financial Ratio Report				
95			Jan	Feb	Mar	Apr	May	Ju
96	LIQUIDITY							
97		Current ratio	1.41	1.41	1.41	1.41	1.41	1.4
98		Quick ratio	0.85	0.85	0.85	0.85	0.85	0.8
99		Net working capital/Sales	78.88%	78.88%	78.88%	78.88%	78.88%	78.88
100								
101	ACTIVITY							
102		A/R turnover	1.00	1.00	1.00	1.00	1.00	1.0
103		Inventory turnover	0.34	0.34	0.34	0.34	0.34	0.3
104		Fixed asset turnover	0.42	0.42	0.42	0.42	0.42	0.4
105		Total asset turnover	0.20	0.20	0.20	0.20	0.20	0.2
106		Average collection period	30.42	30.42	30.42	30.42	30.42	30.4
107		Average payment period	26.53	26.53	26.53	26.53	26.53	26.5
108								
109	DEBT							
110		Debt ratio	61.58%	61.58%	61.58%	61.58%	61.58%	61.58
111		Debt-to-equity	62.71%	62.71%	62.71%	62.71%	62.71%	62.71

Ready

Fig. 2.32. The financial-ratio report, part 1 (January through June).

You will recognize many of the ratios from the earlier model-building exercise. Now press PgDn again to move to the final screen in the model (see fig. 2.33).

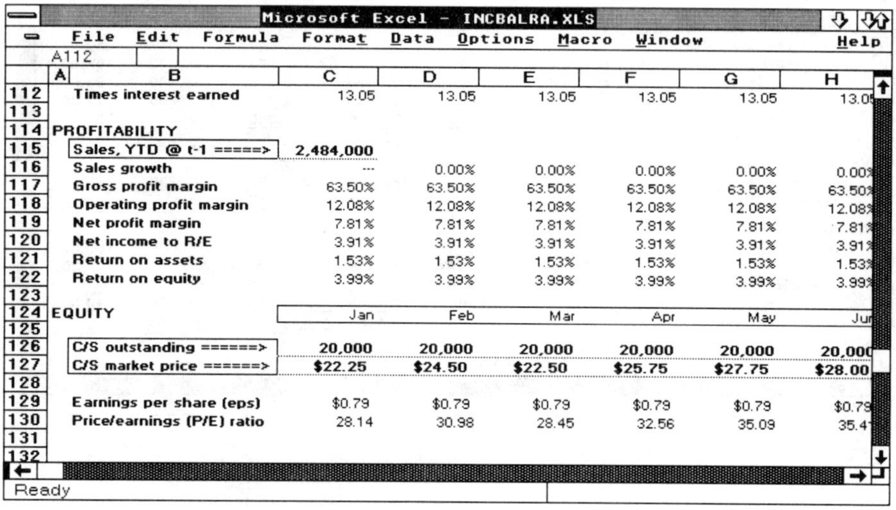

Microsoft Excel - INCBALRA.XLS

File Edit Formula Format Data Options Macro Window Help

A112

	A	B	C	D	E	F	G	H
112		Times interest earned	13.05	13.05	13.05	13.05	13.05	13.0
113								
114	PROFITABILITY							
115		Sales, YTD @ t-1 =====>	2,484,000					
116		Sales growth	---	0.00%	0.00%	0.00%	0.00%	0.00
117		Gross profit margin	63.50%	63.50%	63.50%	63.50%	63.50%	63.50
118		Operating profit margin	12.08%	12.08%	12.08%	12.08%	12.08%	12.08
119		Net profit margin	7.81%	7.81%	7.81%	7.81%	7.81%	7.81
120		Net income to R/E	3.91%	3.91%	3.91%	3.91%	3.91%	3.91
121		Return on assets	1.53%	1.53%	1.53%	1.53%	1.53%	1.53
122		Return on equity	3.99%	3.99%	3.99%	3.99%	3.99%	3.99
123								
124	EQUITY		Jan	Feb	Mar	Apr	May	Ju
125								
126		C/S outstanding ======>	20,000	20,000	20,000	20,000	20,000	20,00
127		C/S market price ======>	$22.25	$24.50	$22.50	$25.75	$27.75	$28.00
128								
129		Earnings per share (eps)	$0.79	$0.79	$0.79	$0.79	$0.79	$0.7
130		Price/earnings (P/E) ratio	28.14	30.98	28.45	32.56	35.09	35.4
131								
132								

Ready

Fig. 2.33. The financial-ratio report, part 2 (January through June).

If you have skipped directly to this part of the chapter, take a moment to review these ratios. The following abbreviations are used in the definitions of the ratios:

A/P	=	Accounts payableal	NWC	=	Net working capit
A/R	=	Accounts receivable	OE	=	Owners' equity
CA	=	Current assets	PAIT	=	Net profit after interest and taxes
CL	=	Current liabilities			
COGS	=	Cost of goods sold	PBIT	=	Net profit before interest and taxes
C/S	=	Common stock			
DIV	=	Dividends	P/S	=	Preferred stock
INV	=	Inventory	REV	=	Gross revenues
LTD	=	Long-term debt	TA	=	Total assets
m	=	Month(ly)	TL	=	Total liabilities
NFA	=	Net fixed assets	y	=	Year(ly)

Liquidity Ratios

Current ratio	=	CA / CL
Quick ratio	=	(CA–INV) / CL
NWC / Sales	=	(CA–CL) / REV

Activity Ratios

A/R turnover	=	REV / A/R
Inventory turnover	=	COGS / INV
Fixed asset turnover	=	REV / NFA
Total asset turnover	=	REV / TA
Average collection period	=	A/R / (REV/365)
Average payment period	=	A/P /((.8*(COG)/365)) DEBT

Note: In the average-payment-period calculation, the constant .8 is multiplied by the cost of goods sold. This operation estimates your firm's monthly purchases. If your firm has a different proportion of purchases to cost of goods sold, enter a new constant. Be sure to copy the edited formula through the range C107:N107. Because the formula in cell P107 is slightly different, you'll have to edit the formula manually.

Debt Ratios

Debt ratio	=	TL / TA
Long-term debt-to-equity ratio	=	LTD / OE
Times interest earned	=	PBIT / Interest

Profitability Ratios

Sales growth (m) $= \dfrac{REV(t=2) - REV(t=1)}{REV(t=1)}$

Sales growth (y) $= \dfrac{REV(t=12) - REV(t=1)}{REV(t=1)}$

Gross-profit margin	=	Gross profit / REV
Operating profit margin	=	Operating profit / REV
Net-profit margin	=	PBIT / REV
Net income to R/E	=	(PAIT–DIV) / REV
Return on assets	=	PAIT / TA
Return on equity	=	PAIT / OE

Equity Ratios

Earnings per share (eps) $= \dfrac{PAIT - DIV}{\text{\# of C/S shares outstanding}}$

Price/earnings ratio $= \dfrac{\text{Per share price of C/S}}{eps}$

Summary

The topics presented in this chapter represent the best of the Excel basics for building the perfect spreadsheet. You will discover many more intricate spreadsheet-building strategies as you delve into later chapters, so don't hesitate to return to this one for a quick review of the tips and shortcuts that make Excel all the more fun to use.

In the next chapter, you will have an opportunity to create an automated checkbook, the heart of every business.

3

Managing a Business Checkbook

Managing the company checkbook is a function that goes to the core of every business. From the simplest double-entry bookkeeping system to the most complex multidivision accounting software program, the checkbook functions as the firm's heart, responsible for regulating the flow of funds in and out of the company. In this chapter, you will build spreadsheet tools that correspond to each element of the business checkbook: the check register, the bank statement reconciliation sheet, and the general ledger distribution—also called the accounting summary worksheet.

So far, you've been exposed to several ways of creating spreadsheet tools that meet your business-reporting needs. Chapter 1 previewed a powerful and fully operative macro program that automatically generates chart graphics from a presentation-quality sales report. In Chapter 2 you concentrated on the development of a stand-alone financial-statement worksheet. The concept of worksheet chronology was introduced to show how easy it is to create one worksheet that controls three separate financial reports, each new report dependent on information presented in the preceding report.

Excel provides two other means for storing and retrieving data. The first enables you to file a series of Excel worksheets, charts, and macros by using one workspace file name. The next time you need to load these documents, enter the workspace file name; Excel automatically recalls the entire group. The second method is called linking worksheets. The last part of this chapter reviews the procedures for linking worksheets so that your checkbook can become a working model and so that the check register—complete with general ledger reference numbers—can be fully operative.

This chapter also introduces the practice of password protection and spreadsheet locking. And, as always, the tips and shortcuts included provide additional insight into the topics at hand.

Building the Check Register

Regardless of the type of bookkeeping system you use in your company, every business checkbook is composed of at least three elements: the register, the reconciliation sheet, and the accounting summary. In the register, you enter such information as the following:

- The check or deposit number
- The transaction date
- The name of the payee or a description of the transaction
- The general ledger account number(s) and the corresponding amount(s)

The check register should also contain an additional space for checking off each transaction when it clears your bank. This space is critical, because you will create formulas that automatically place the values of all deposits and outstanding checks into two special accumulator columns. The summed values of these special columns then become the input values for your checkbook reconciliation sheet. If you've ever had to reconcile a business checkbook against a bank statement, you will appreciate this feature—particularly if your business creates several hundred transactions per month.

Try building a check register for Taryn Hartley Cosmetics, a small, private corporation that markets its own men's cosmetics line. A review of the company's business checkbook indicates that the firm creates between 10 and 15 checkbook transactions a month. Knowing this, you can design a spreadsheet check register tailor-fit to the firm's level of business activity. If the number of transactions suddenly increases, the check register can easily be expanded.

To create the check register for Taryn Hartley Cosmetics, follow these steps:

Step 1. From the File menu, choose New Worksheet.

Step 2. From the Format menu, choose Column Width. Change column A to 5; B to 7.57; C to 23; D, F, I, and K to 8.57; E to 2; G to 0.58; and H and J to 3.

Step 3. Select the range C1:C3 and enter the report title as follows:

C1: **Taryn Hartley Cosmetics**
C2: **Check Register**
C3: **June, 1989**

Step 4. Select the range A4:K20. From the Format menu, select Border and choose the Outline option.

Step 5. Then select the multiple range A6:F6, A7:K18, H6:K6, A19:F19, and H19:K19: Again, select Border and choose Outline.

Step 6. Next select the multiple range A6:E6, H6:K6, B19:C19, E19:F19, H19, and J19. Click-select the Shade option in the Border dialog box.

Step 7. Finally, select the range A6:K19. Choose Border and then choose Right (see fig. 3.1).

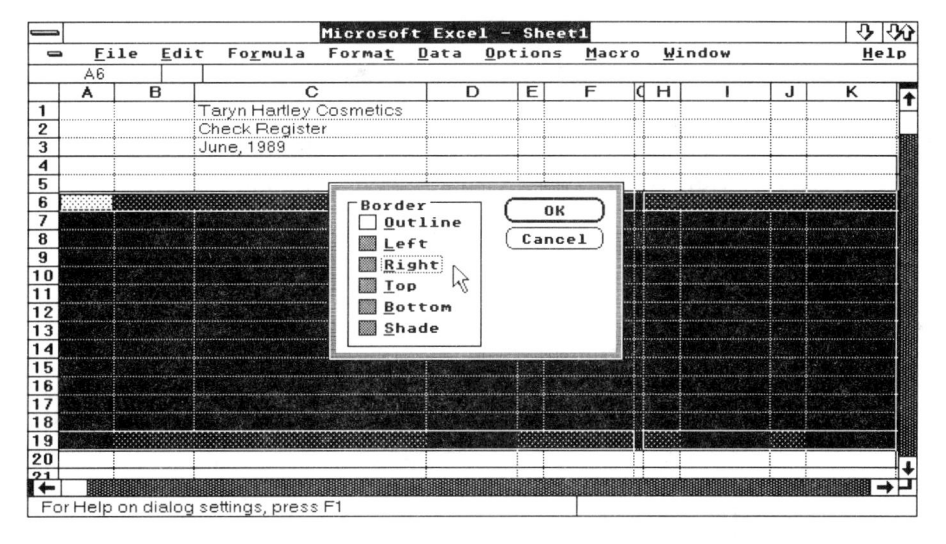

Fig. 3.1.
Entering the final border format for the check register.

Tip: If you happen to select a cell (or a range of cells) twice when formatting with Border, Excel shades the selection boxes for each format already occurring in the new range. In figure 3.1, for example, notice that all the Border options have been used in various areas of the new selection range. To choose a new Border format in this situation, just click the desired box twice. The box clears after the first click and then rechecks itself after the second.

Step 8. Choose Display from the Options menu and turn Gridlines off by click-selecting its box once. Your worksheet should resemble the one pictured in figure 3.2.

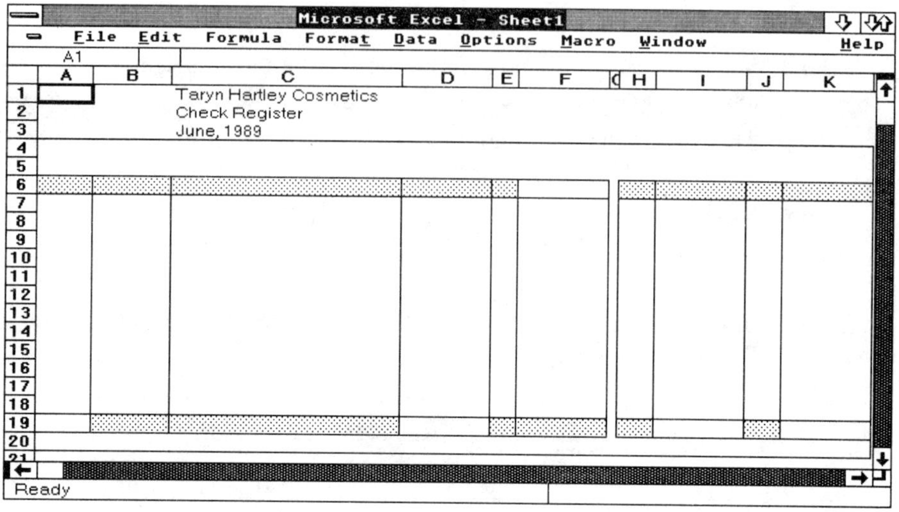

Fig. 3.2.
Turning off the worksheet gridlines.

Step 9. Select the ranges A4:K5 and A20:K20. (This order of selection places the active cell at cell A20.) Enter the following column descriptions and labels:

    A4: **Check**
    A5: **No.**
    B5: **Date**
    C5: **Description**
    D5: **Amount**
    E4: **IN**
    E5: **?**
    F5: **Balance**
    H4: **GL**
    H5: **#1**
    I5: **Amount**
    J4: **GL**
    J5: **#2**
    K5: **Amount**
    A20: **Items**
    C20: **Check Figure**
    E20: **=**
    F20: '------------------> (18 hyphens)
    I20: **#1**
    J20: **+**
    K20: **#2**

Managing a Business Checkbook **65**

> Tip: Excel reserves certain characters for mathematical operations. To enter in cell F20 a series of hyphens, which are normally reserved for subtraction, first enter an apostrophe (see fig. 3.3). Doing so tells Excel that the entry is text, not a mathematical operator.

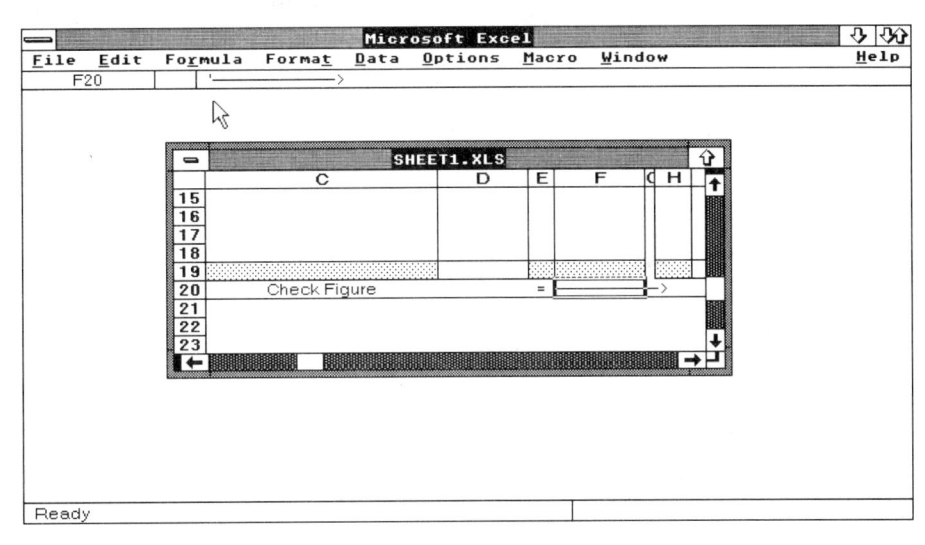

Fig. 3.3.
Precede a label with an apostrophe.

Step 10. Reselect C1:C3, the report title range. From the Format menu, select Font and click-select Helv-10, Bold.

Step 11. With C1:C3 still selected, select the multiple range A4:K5, A7:B18, E7:E18, H7:H18, J7:J18, A19, A20:C20, and E20:K20. From the Format menu, choose Alignment and click-select Center (see fig. 3.4).

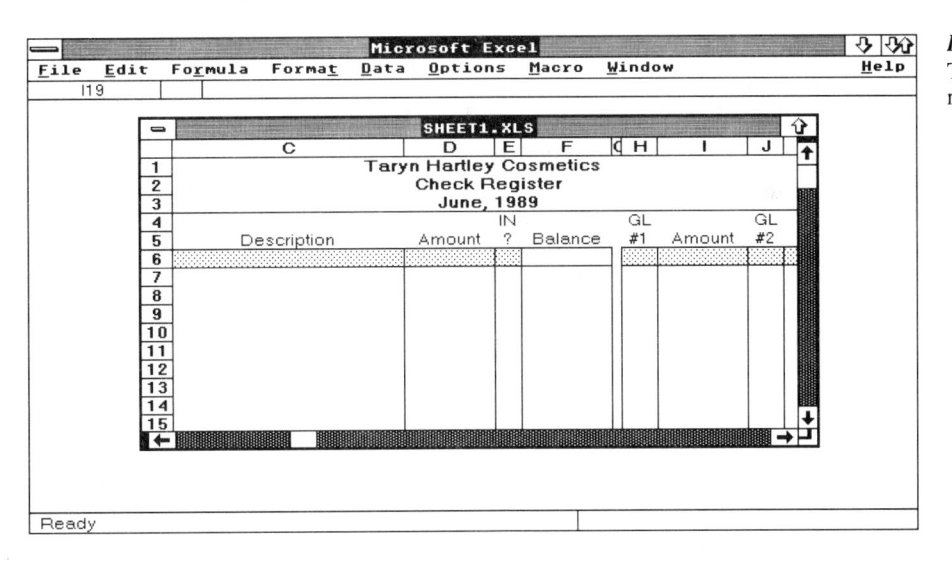

Fig. 3.4.
The centered report title.

> Tip: Sometimes it's necessary to insert spaces in front of text in order to position the text where you want it in the worksheet.

Step 12. Press F2 to edit cell C1 and then insert enough blank spaces so that the *T* in *Taryn* is positioned directly below the *t* in the word *Options* appearing on the menu bar. Using this same technique, center the contents of C2 and C3 below C1.

Step 13. Next, select the range C7:C18 and choose Left alignment from the Format menu.

Step 14. Finally, select the multiple range D7:D20, F6:F18, I7:I19, and K7:K19 and choose Right alignment.

Step 15. In cell A19, enter the formula **=COUNTA(A7:A18)**, shown in figure 3.5.

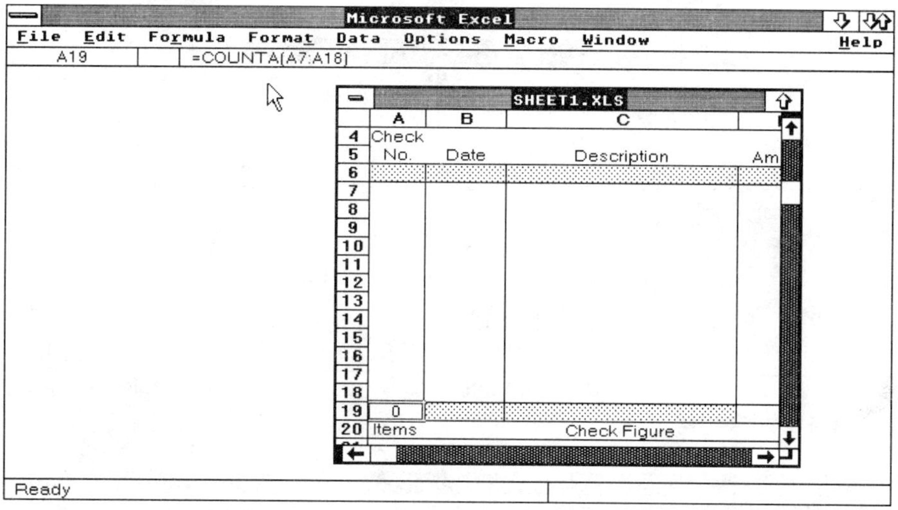

Fig. 3.5. Using the COUNTA() function to compute the number of entries in a column.

Step 16. In cell D19, enter the formula **=SUM(D7:D18)**, shown in figure 3.6. Then copy the formula to cells I19 and K19.

Step 17. In cell D20, enter the formula **=I19+K19**, shown in figure 3.7.

Step 18. In cell F7, enter the formula **=IF(A7="D",F6+D7,F6-D7)**, shown in figure 3.8. Copy this result to the range F8:F18.

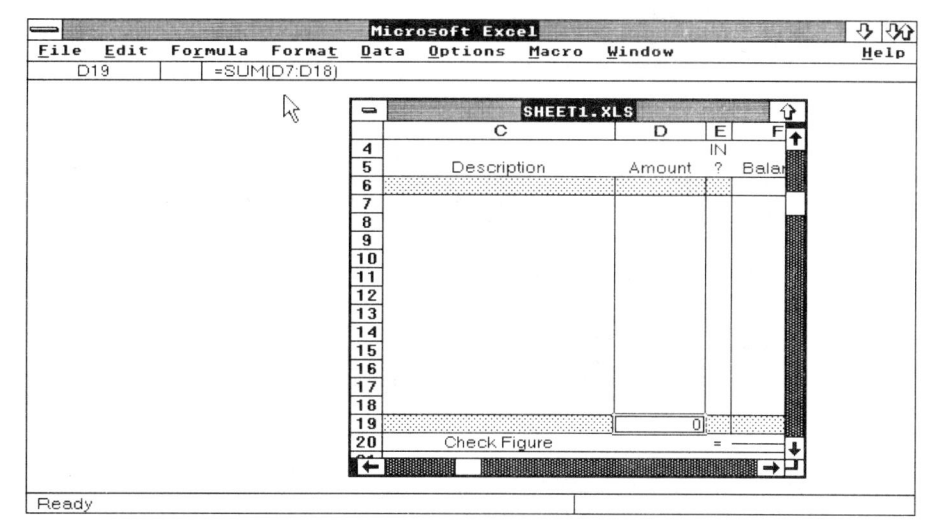

Fig. 3.6. Using the familiar SUM() function to total the values of the entries in a column.

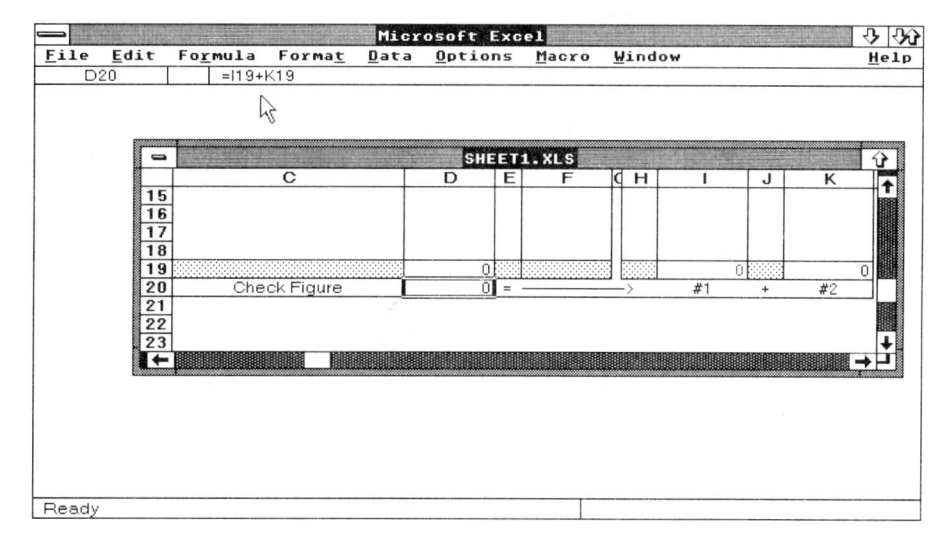

Fig. 3.7. Creating a check figure for the general ledger distribution columns.

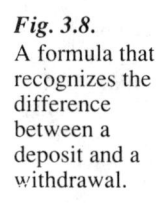

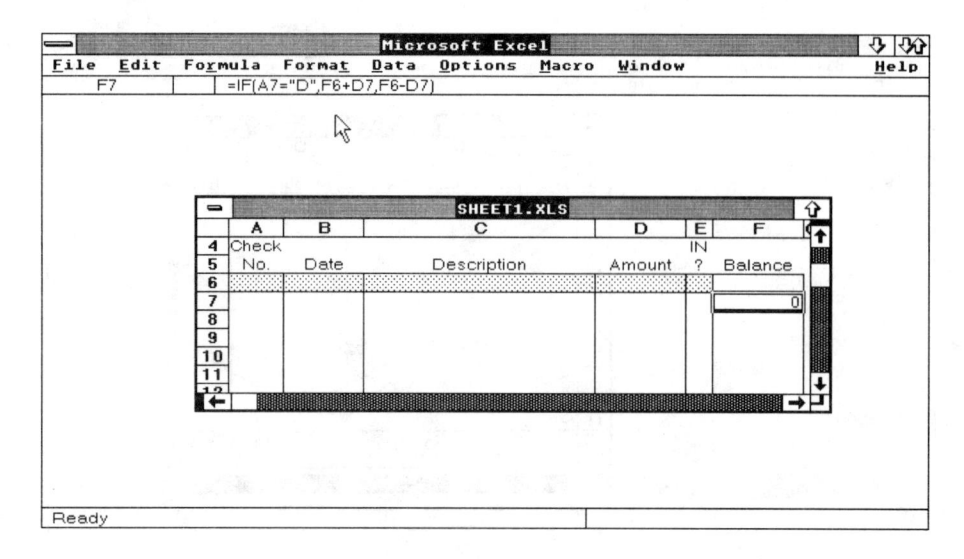

Fig. 3.8.
A formula that recognizes the difference between a deposit and a withdrawal.

The formula in figure 3.8 deserves closer scrutiny. This formula recognizes the difference between a deposit and a withdrawal when both are entered as positive numbers. How?

The formula accomplishes this task by first looking at the value appearing in cell A7. If the transaction is a check withdrawal, the data entry operator enters a check number; if the transaction is a deposit, the data entry operator enters the letter **D**. The syntax of this formula thus means the following:

"If the value in cell A7 indicates that the transaction is a deposit, add the value in cell F6 to the value in D7. If not, then subtract the value in D7 from the value in F6, because the transaction must be a check withdrawal."

Step 19. In cell K7, enter the formula =**IF(J7<>"",D7-I7,0)**, shown in figure 3.9.

The formula in figure 3.9 automatically distributes a compound transaction entry. Here, goods bought at McGregor's Pharmacy for $2,000 are equally divided between two expense accounts. The formula is designed to function only after the bookkeeper enters the second general ledger account number. Until then, a zero value remains in the second Amount column.

If the entry is left as it appears in figure 3.9, the Check Figure amount at the bottom of the register will not match the ending Balance amount. This is one way in which the formula identifies incorrect entries. The last part of the formula calculates the correct value of the second entry. This way, as long as the bookkeeper enters the first distribution value correctly, the second will always be correct. Need a third distribution? Just add a third column.

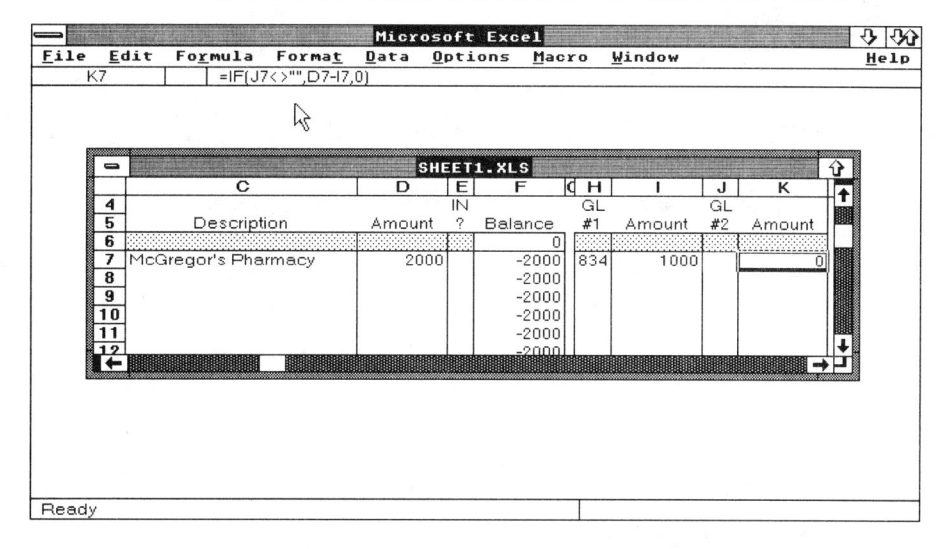

Fig. 3.9.
Using the IF() function to autodistribute a compound general ledger entry.

> Tip: Some managers prefer not to have columns of zeros appearing on their reports. To eliminate zeros, use this formula:
>
> =IF(J7<>"",D7-I7,"")
>
> In this equation, the quotation marks return an empty cell if the initial condition proves false. The new syntax thus means this:
>
> "If cell J7 is empty (isn't *not* empty), then leave cell K7 empty."
>
> If, however, J7 contains data, Excel autodistributes the balance of the check to the second GL number in column J, as shown in figure 3.10.

Step 20. Select the range B7:B18. From the Format menu, select Number and choose the "m/d/yy" option (see fig. 3.11). Before clicking OK, though, modify this option on the Format line so the final format is "mm-dd-yy." Then click OK.

> Tip: Enter any date into the newly formatted range. If you enter the date **06-28** without the year, Excel automatically places the current year in the cell for you. If you enter only the month, though, Excel misinterprets the date.

Excel Business Applications: IBM Version

Fig. 3.10.
Entering a general ledger number in column J so that Excel automatically calculates the distributed value.

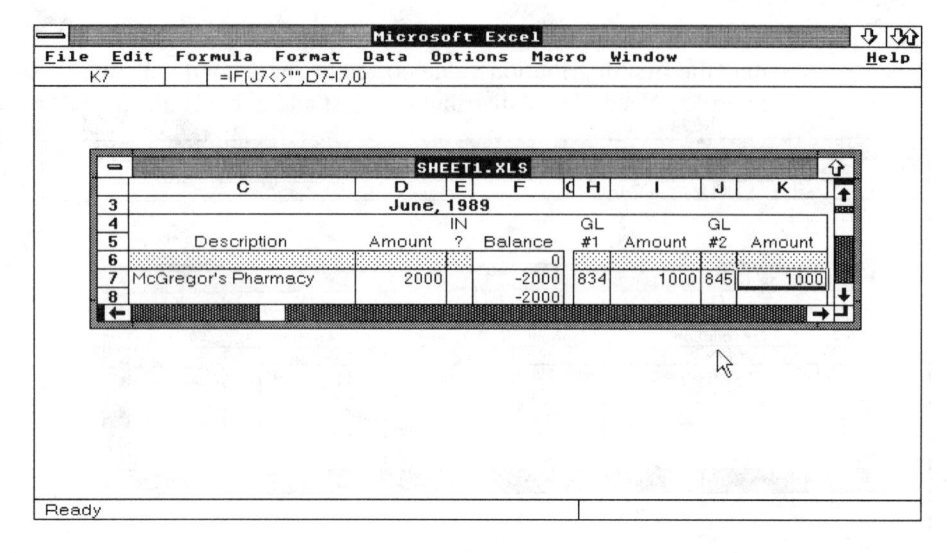

Fig. 3.11.
Selecting a format number.

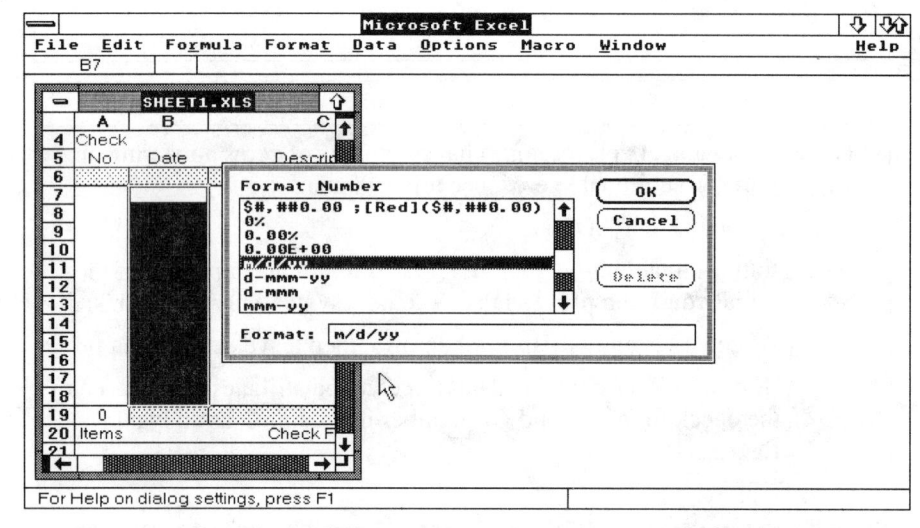

Step 21. Select the range D7:D20, F7:F18, I7:I19, and K7:K19. From the Format menu, select Number and choose $#,##0; ($#,##0), as in figure 3.12. Again, before clicking OK, modify the option on the Format line. Here, delete the dollar signs from the Format line—you don't want them. Click OK.

Managing a Business Checkbook 71

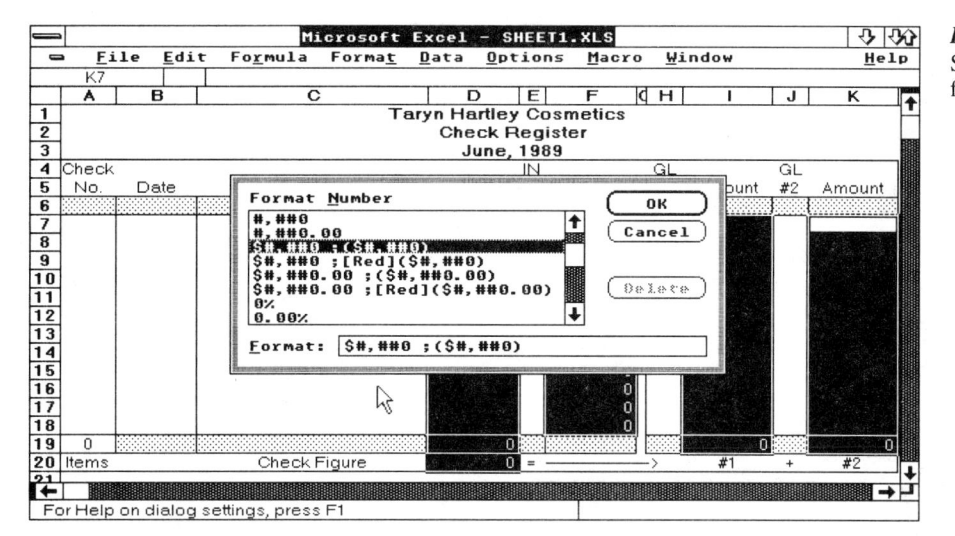

Fig. 3.12.
Selecting a format number.

> **Tip:** Whenever you modify one of Excel's default Format Number formats, the new format will appear as an option at the bottom of the Number menu, following all the default selections—but only for the active worksheet.

Step 22. Select the range H7:H18. From the Formula menu, select Define Name. When the dialog box appears, enter **num1** into the Name dialog box.

Step 23. Select the range I7:I18. Reselect Define Name from the Formula menu and enter **amt1** into the Name dialog box.

Step 24. Using the procedure described in Steps 22 and 23, give the range J7:J18 the name **num2**. Next, give the range K7:K18 the name **amt2**.

> **Tip:** These last three steps are critical to the creation and operation of the accounting summary model later on in this chapter.

Step 25. Save this worksheet, using the file name CHKBOOK.XLS.

At this time, you may enter your own data into the check register. Or you may want to enter and experiment with the data from Taryn Hartley Cosmetics' check register, shown in figure 3.13.

Fig. 3.13.
The completed check register for Taryn Hartley Cosmetics.

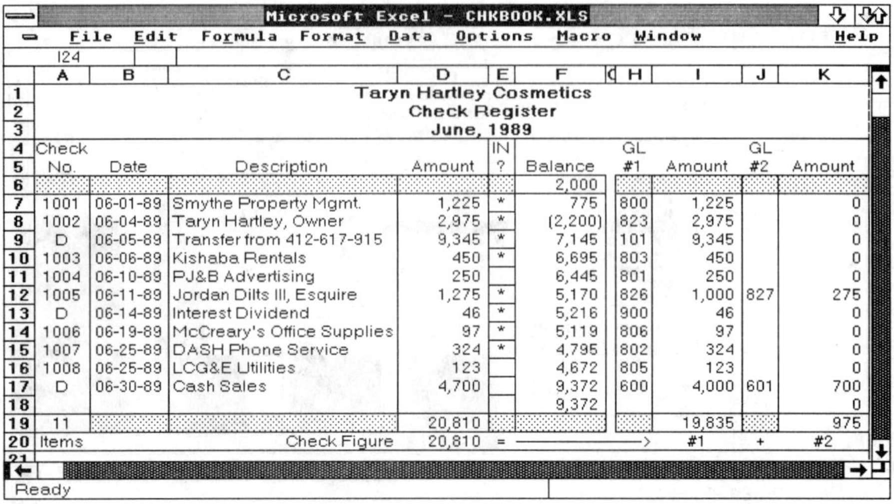

Check No.	Date	Description	Amount	IN ?	Balance	GL #1	Amount	GL #2	Amount
					2,000				
1001	06-01-89	Smythe Property Mgmt.	1,225	*	775	800	1,225		0
1002	06-04-89	Taryn Hartley, Owner	2,975	*	(2,200)	823	2,975		0
D	06-05-89	Transfer from 412-617-915	9,345	*	7,145	101	9,345		0
1003	06-06-89	Kishaba Rentals	450	*	6,695	803	450		0
1004	06-10-89	PJ&B Advertising	250		6,445	801	250		0
1005	06-11-89	Jordan Dilts III, Esquire	1,275	*	5,170	826	1,000	827	275
D	06-14-89	Interest Dividend	46	*	5,216	900	46		0
1006	06-19-89	McCreary's Office Supplies	97	*	5,119	806	97		0
1007	06-25-89	DASH Phone Service	324	*	4,795	802	324		0
1008	06-25-89	LCG&E Utilities	123		4,672	805	123		0
D	06-30-89	Cash Sales	4,700		9,372	600	4,000	601	700
					9,372				0
11			20,810				19,835		975
Items		Check Figure	20,810	=	——————>	#1	+	#2	

Building the Reconciliation Sheet

The second element of the checkbook system is the reconciliation sheet. Here, envision an automated spreadsheet model—one that continually updates itself as you enter new information into your check register.

There are two schools of thought on what constitutes proper cash-account reconciliation. The first method reconciles the ending balance in the check register to the ending bank statement balance. The second method reconciles the bank statement balance to the final balance in the check register. Both methods achieve the same end; the decision to use one or the other is completely yours. Therefore, in this next portion of the chapter, you will design a spreadsheet model that uses both methods. At the conclusion of this exercise, you'll learn the similarities between the two methods.

In the reconciliation sheet, you enter such information as the following:

- Your ending check-register balance
- The value of deposits outstanding
- The value of checks outstanding
- Any adjustments made by the bank to your account

Continuing with the sample company, Taryn Hartley Cosmetics, create the reconciliation sheet by following these simple steps:

Managing a Business Checkbook

Step 1. Enter the titles, descriptions, and worksheet formats as shown in figure 3.14. Be sure to boldface the report titles. Use the Helv-8 font for the text in cell B41. Change the height of rows 31 and 40 to 3.

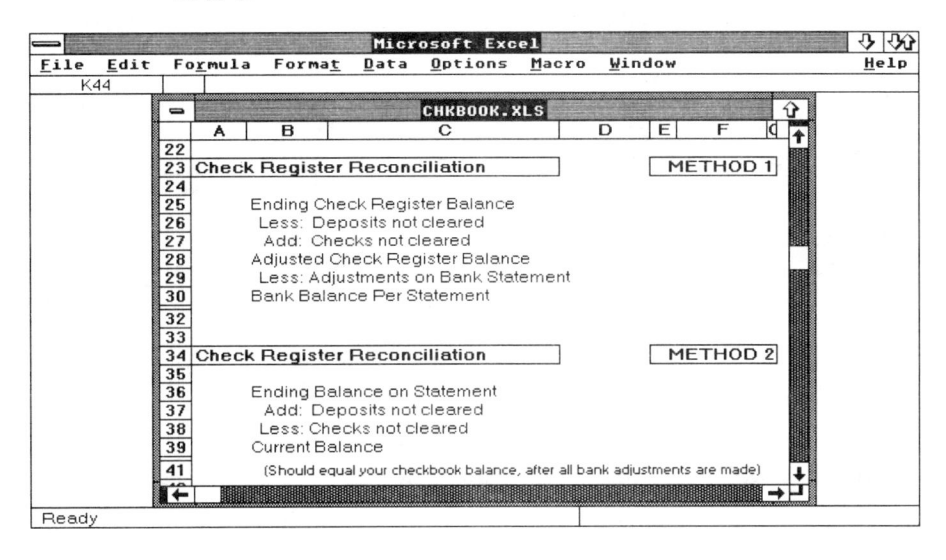

Fig. 3.14. Creating the worksheet format for the reconciliation sheet.

Step 2. In cell F25, enter **=D19**, as shown in the formula bar in figure 3.15. Cell F25 receives its value directly from cell D19 in the check register.

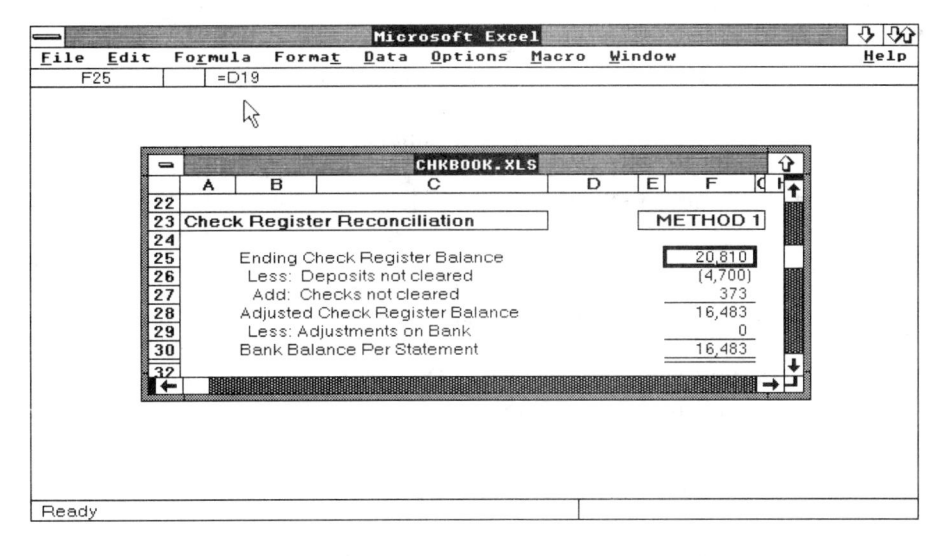

Fig. 3.15. When the ending balance in the check register changes, cell F25 automatically updates.

Step 3. Create the format for the two accumulator blocks shown in figure 3.16. Place the two blocks in the range M4:N19—directly opposite the check register. The summed values of these blocks (found in cells M19 and N19) feed to the second and third lines of the reconciliation sheet, as shown in the left-hand portion of figure 3.16.

Fig. 3.16. Two accumulator blocks transfer the values of the deposits and checks outstanding directly to the reconciliation sheet.

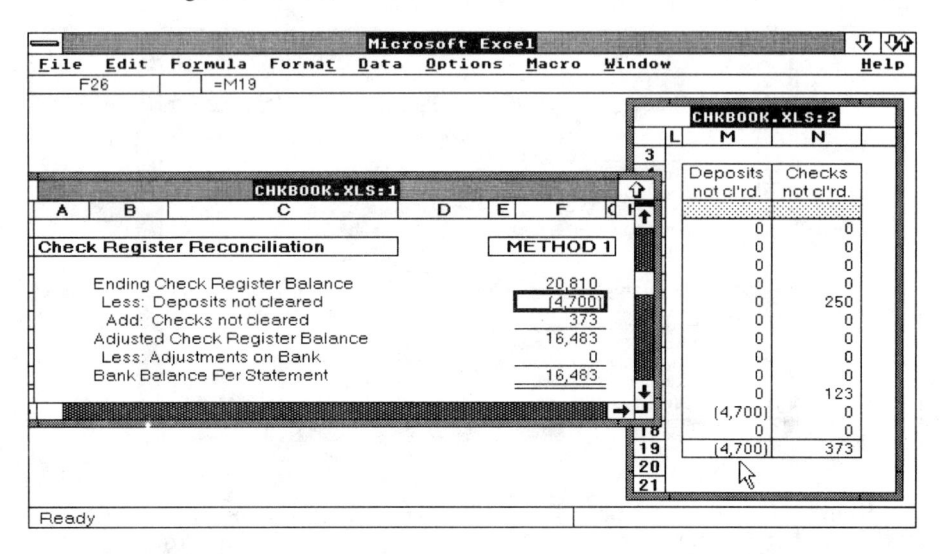

> Shortcut: The Deposits accumulator block stores each outstanding deposit as a negative value. Why? So that when this value is transferred to the reconciliation sheet, it is automatically subtracted from the ending check-register balance according to the format of method 1. Conversely, the Checks accumulator block stores each outstanding check as a positive value so that the summed value automatically adds to the ending check-register balance. The formulas that perform these tasks are shown in figures 3.17 and 3.18.

The syntax of the formula appearing in cell M7 in figure 3.17 means this: "If this entry has not cleared (if cell E7 is blank), and this transaction is a deposit (a D appears in cell A7), then enter the negative of the value appearing in cell D7."

The formula specifically states that both conditions must be true before a deposit is considered outstanding. If the value in cell A7 is a check number, then the second part of the formula is false, and Excel returns a zero. If A7 indicates that this transaction is, in fact, a deposit, but an asterisk appears in cell E7, then the first part of the formula is false, and Excel again returns a zero. After all, if the deposit has cleared the bank—as indicated by the asterisk—then you want cell M7 to equal zero.

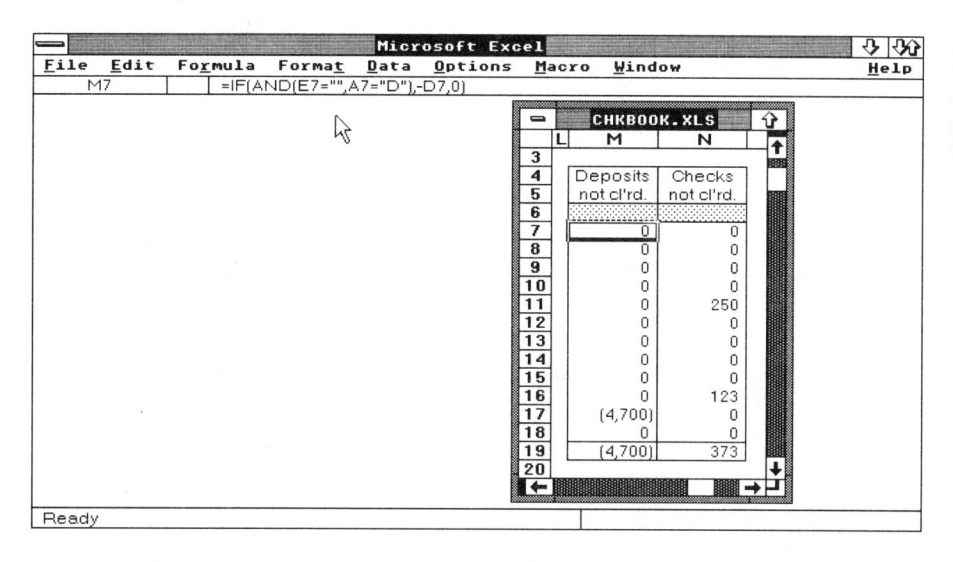

Fig. 3.17.
The outstanding deposits' accumulator block formula.

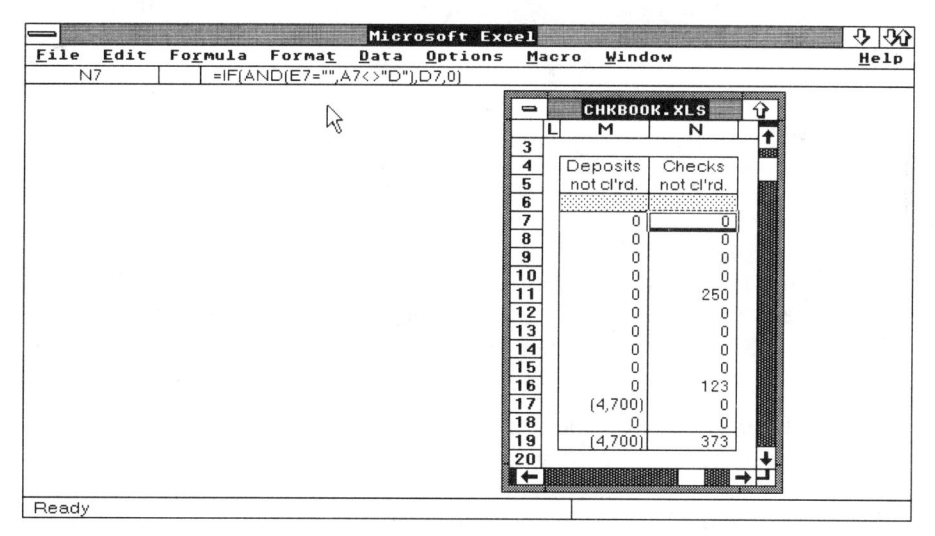

Fig. 3.18.
The outstanding checks' accumulator block formula.

The syntax of the formula appearing in cell N7 in figure 3.18 is identical, except that you want all outstanding values to appear as positive values. Therefore, the value D7 in the formula is positive.

A final note: The formulas in cells M19 and N19 use the familiar SUM() function to compute their respective totals.

Step 4. For the second reconciliation method, enter the formulas to calculate the values. Here, precede the formulas in cells F37 and F38 by a minus sign. This method is exactly opposite in sign from the first method (see fig. 3.19). The value appearing in cell F36 comes directly from your bank statement.

Fig. 3.19.
The values of method 2's outstanding checks and deposits are exactly opposite in sign from the values produced by method 1.

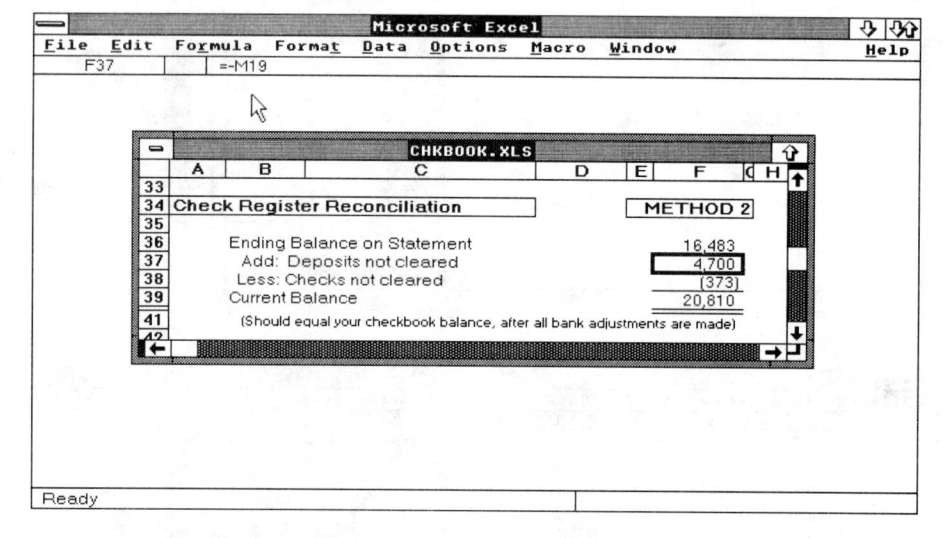

	METHOD 2
Ending Balance on Statement	16,483
Add: Deposits not cleared	4,700
Less: Checks not cleared	(373)
Current Balance	20,810

(Should equal your checkbook balance, after all bank adjustments are made)

> Tip: Turn Scroll Lock on and press PgUp and PgDn to shift back and forth between the two models—without affecting the currently selected cell or range of cells. To move one windowful left or right, press Ctrl-PgUp or Ctrl-PgDn, respectively.

Review Taryn Hartley Cosmetics' completed check-register reconciliation sheet, shown in figure 3.20. The arrows demonstrate that both methods accomplish the same task. The only difference between the methods is the perspective from which you prefer to look at this checkbook management function.

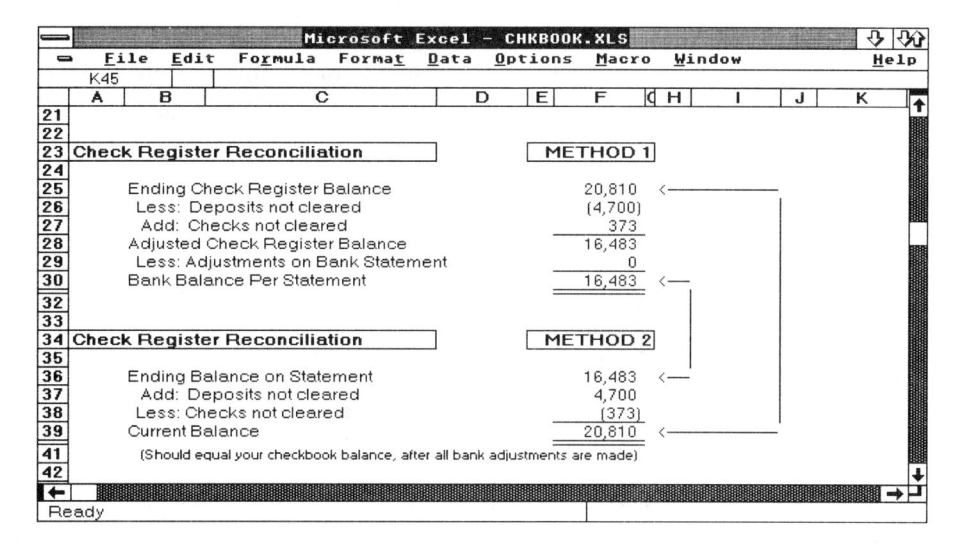

Fig. 3.20.
The completed check-register reconciliation sheet for Taryn Hartley Cosmetics.

The next section introduces the concept of linking Excel worksheets and has you develop the final element of the model, the check-register accounting summary.

Building the Check Register Accounting Summary: A Linked Worksheet Model

Have you ever wished that you could quickly summarize all the information in your checkbook into a simple report that organized your various transactions by general ledger account number?

In a manual bookkeeping system, this task generally takes place once at the end of each month, when a clerk posts the general journal entries. More sophisticated accounting packages can produce this kind of information instantaneously, and on a daily basis if necessary.

In Excel, linking spreadsheets combines the power of the canned accounting package with the simplicity of the manual system. When you link spreadsheets, several possibilities emerge:

- You can consolidate information from several worksheets, applications, or data sources.
- You can store several different report formats for the same spreadsheet.

- You can increase the efficiency of your computer's memory by breaking large, complicated models into several smaller models.
- Linking worksheets is flexible. You can link 2 or 200 worksheets, depending on your needs.

The next model links the check register to an accounting summary worksheet. Here, the information you enter into your check register is summed by general ledger account and organized in order of Taryn Hartley Cosmetics' chart of accounts.

Continuing with the sample company, Taryn Hartley Cosmetics, create an accounting summary by following these simple steps:

Step 1. Select the File menu and choose New Worksheet. The new worksheet will cover CHKBOOK.XLS.

Step 2. Save the new worksheet, using the file name CHKSUMMR.XLS.

Step 3. Change the column widths as follows: A to 5; B and J to 2; C to 6; D to 23; E, G, and I to 10; and F and H to 3.

Step 4. Enter the titles, descriptions, and worksheet formats as shown in figure 3.21. Be sure to boldface the report title, which appears in E1 and E2.

Fig. 3.21.
The check-register accounting summary, ready for formula input.

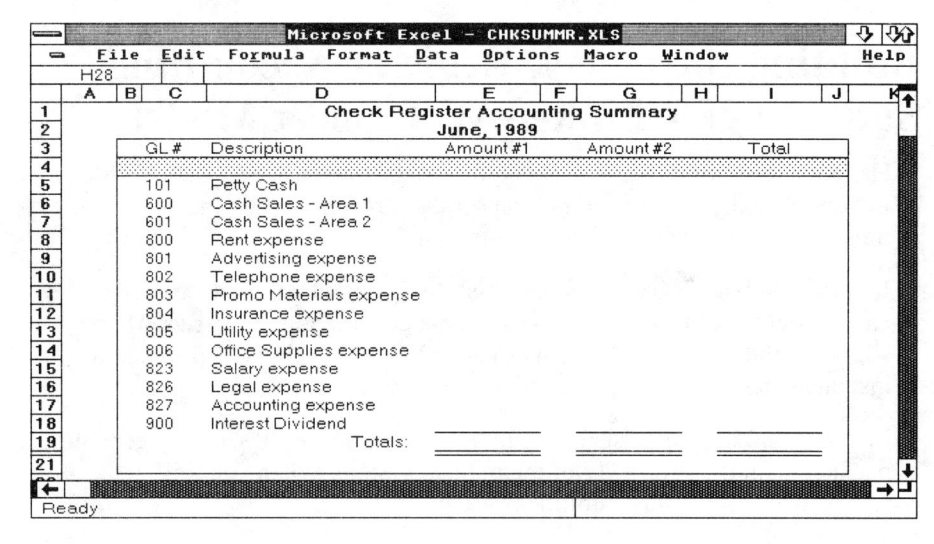

> Tip: When you use the Border command to underline the values in cells E18, G18, and I18, first highlight cells E19, G19, and I19. Then select the Border command from the Format menu and click Top. The other choice is to put a bottom border into these cells. If you enter your formulas through the Edit Copy command, however, you'll erase the Bottom Border format from the cells, unless the cell you are copying from already has a border.

Step 5. Select row 20 and change the height to 3.

Now that you've completed the screen format, it's time to analyze how to link the two worksheets.

Step 6. Enter the following two formulas as arrays. These arrays sum the values of each check-register transaction by general ledger account number:

E5: =SUM(IF($C5=CHKBOOK.XLS!num1,
CHKBOOK.XLS!amt1))
G5: =SUM(IF($C5=CHKBOOK.XLS!num2,
CHKBOOK.XLS!amt2))

> Shortcut: Instead of retyping this lengthy formula, copy cell E5 to G5 and modify the references as needed.

Reminder: You enter a formula as an array by simultaneously pressing Ctrl-Shift-Enter. When an array formula is entered correctly, braces surround the formula.

Step 7. Copy these two formulas to the respective ranges E6:E18 and G6:G18.

The syntax of these formulas is much simpler to understand than it may appear. First, recall that you want to organize all the check-register entries by general ledger account number. If in any month you use the same general ledger account twice, then this formula must sum the values of all applicable check-register entries.

The formula in figure 3.22 does just that. Notice that the check register contains two entries (in GL column 1) for account number 803, the Promo Materials expense account. The total of these two expenses is 795—the amount that appears next to account 803 on the accounting summary report.

Fig. 3.22.
An array formula that refers to a named range on another worksheet.

[Screenshot of Microsoft Excel showing CHKSUMMR.XLS and CHKBOOK.XLS worksheets. Formula bar at E11 shows: {=SUM(IF($C11=CHKBOOK.XLS!num1,CHKBOOK.XLS!amt1))}

CHKSUMMR.XLS:
	B	C	D	E
3		GL #	Description	Amount #1
5		101	Petty Cash	9,345
6		600	Cash Sales - Area 1	4,000
7		601	Cash Sales - Area 2	0
8		800	Rent expense	1,225
9		801	Advertising expense	250
10		802	Telephone expense	324
11		803	Promo Materials expense	795
12		804	Insurance expense	0

CHKBOOK.XLS:
	H	I	J	K
4		GL		GL
5		#1	Amount	#2	Amount
7		800	1,225		0
8		823	2,975		0
9		101	9,345		0
10		803	450		0
11		801	250		0
12		826	1,000	827	275
13		900	46		0
14		806	97		0
15		802	324		0
16		805	123		0
17		600	4,000	601	700
18		803	345		0
19			20,180		975 |]

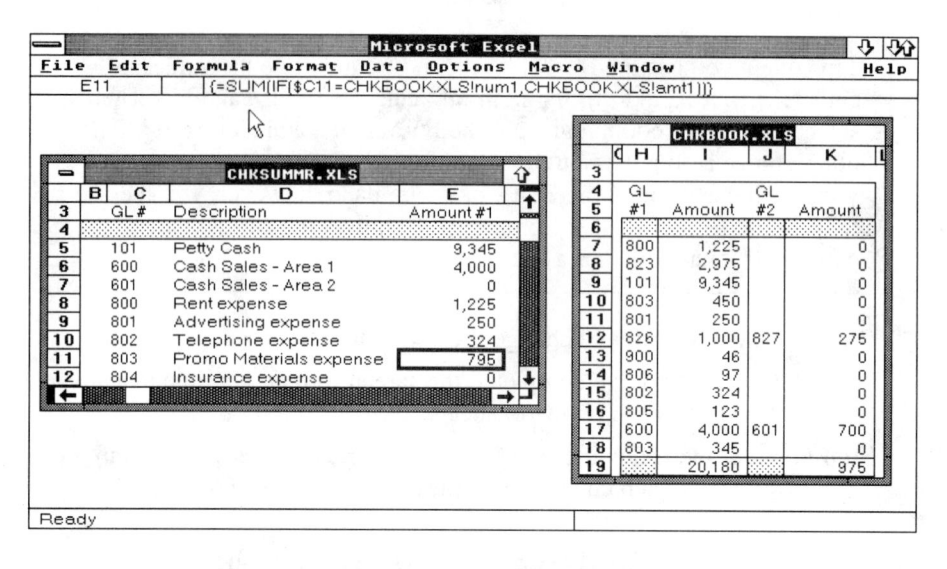

The formula in figure 3.23 is exactly the same, with the exception that the range names are "num2" and "amt2." This slight variation tells Excel to search the second general ledger distribution column rather than the first.

Fig. 3.23.
An array formula that refers to a named range on another worksheet.

[Screenshot of Microsoft Excel. Formula bar at G7 shows: {=SUM(IF($C7=CHKBOOK.XLS!num2,CHKBOOK.XLS!amt2))}

CHKSUMMR.XLS:
	B	C	D	G
6		600	Cash Sales - Area 1	0
7		601	Cash Sales - Area 2	700
8		800	Rent expense	0
9		801	Advertising expense	0
10		802	Telephone expense	0
11		803	Promo Materials expense	0
12		804	Insurance expense	0
13		805	Utility expense	0
14		806	Office Supplies expense	0
15		823	Salary expense	0
16		826	Legal expense	0
17		827	Accounting expense	275 |]

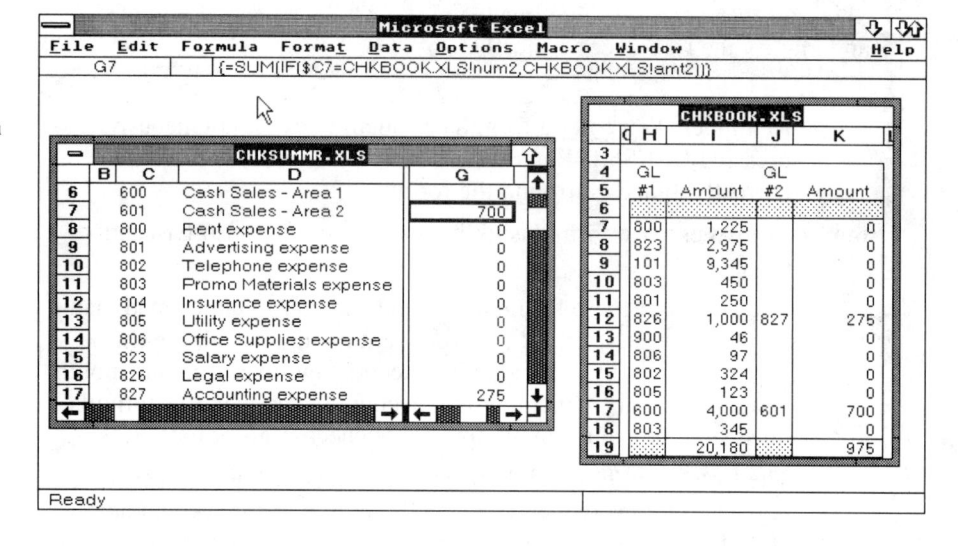

Step 8. Enter into cells E19 and G19 and into the range I5:I19 the summation formulas needed.

Step 9. To record the additions to the CHKSUMMR.XLS model, choose Save from the File menu.

Testing the Entire Checkbook Management System

To test the finished model, simply enter a new transaction into the last line of the check register. Follow along as each model updates its own values to account for the new entry.

To track the updates, first make sure that CHKBOOK.XLS is the active window. Then select New Window from the Window menu. When the new window appears, you can drag the window borders to create the screen format shown in figure 3.24. Now, when you enter new data into CHKBOOK.XLS, you can watch as Excel quickly updates the check register reconciliation section.

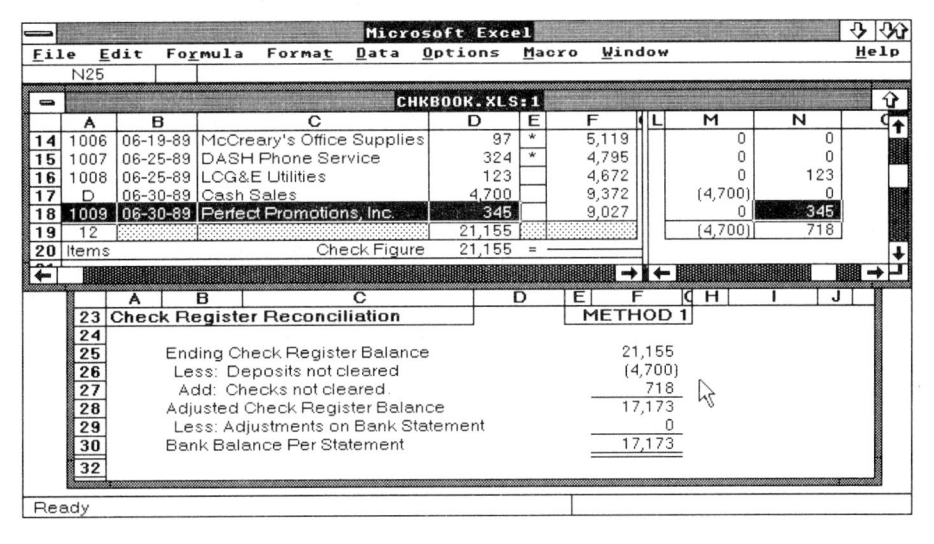

Fig. 3.24. Using New Window from the Window menu and Split from the Control menu to track the result of adding a new entry into the check register.

The new transaction appears highlighted in row 18. Using the Split option from the Control menu, scroll over to the check-register accumulator column and verify that the $345 check withdrawal appears in the correct column.

Now trace the path from the accumulator column totals to their location on the reconciliation sheet. Excel has correctly updated the value of the checks outstanding, as shown in figure 3.24.

Close CHKBOOK.XLS:2. Use the Split command once more and verify that the $345 check is properly distributed in the general ledger column. If so, then CHKSUMMR.XLS automatically updates the value of its Promo Materials expense account. Verify that the new summed total of this expense account is $795, as shown in figure 3.25. The completed accounting summary is shown in figure 3.26.

Fig. 3.25.
Verifying that Excel has properly passed the new checkbook entry to the accounting summary worksheet.

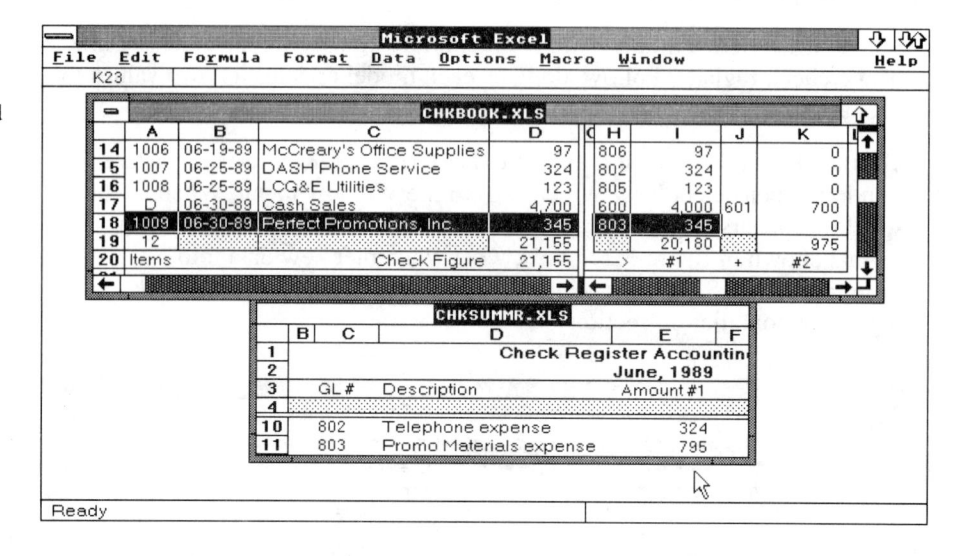

Fig. 3.26.
The completed check-register accounting summary for Taryn Hartley Cosmetics.

Automating the Checkbook Management System

So far, you have created three interdependent models on two separate worksheets. Imagine needing 10 or 20 or 30 worksheets to meet a similar, albeit larger, objective. It would take you a half-hour to open all the necessary worksheets!

Fortunately, Excel has a mechanism that "automates" the process of opening all your check-register files. With both CHKBOOK.XLS and CHKSUMMR.XLS open on your screen, choose the Save Workspace option from the File menu (see fig. 3.27).

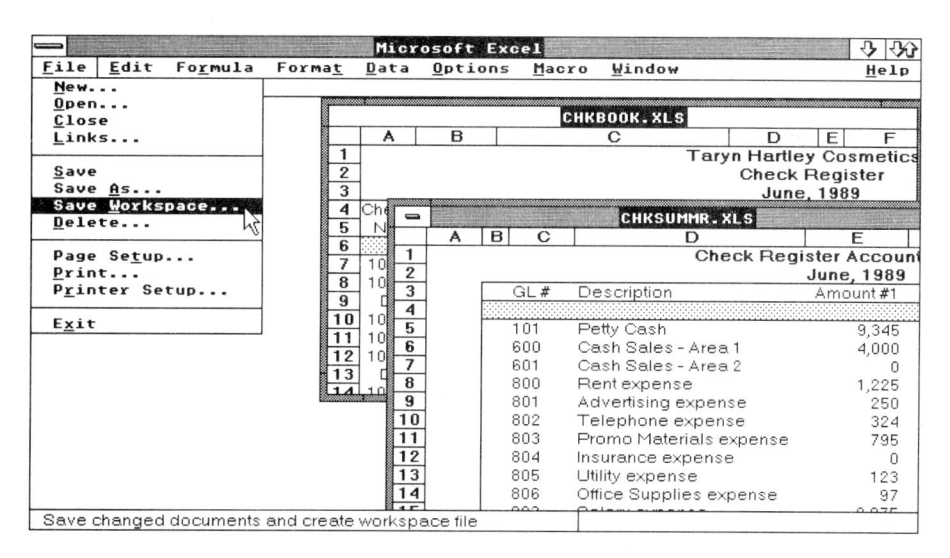

Fig. 3.27. Saving your workspace to automate your model.

Excel requests a new file name under which your open files may be stored. Enter the file name **CHKBOOK** and click OK (see fig. 3.28). Excel automatically supplies an XLW extension.

Now exit from Excel so that you can see how easy it is to autoload your entire applications library. At the command prompt, type **EXCEL CHKBOOK.XLW**; Excel automatically loads both spreadsheet models.

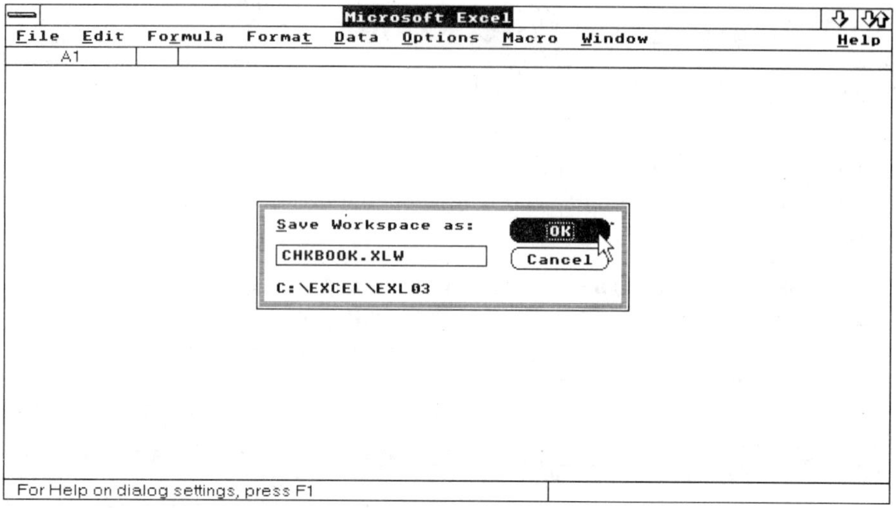

Fig. 3.28.
Naming your workspace.

Safeguarding Your Sensitive Data

All businesses have sensitive data that they prefer to conceal from employees, competitors, and sometimes even their professional advisers.

Excel provides several good ways to protect your data from prying eyes or fumbling fingers. You can even control the level of information that appears on a report. In other words, Excel enables you to decide what types of information may be viewed and/or changed on any given worksheet.

Protecting Cells in the Accounting Summary Worksheet

Taryn Hartley Cosmetics forwards a copy of the completed check-register accounting summary to its outside bookkeeper each month. The company is concerned about protecting the integrity of the formulas that lie at the heart of this report. Specifically, the company wants to prevent its data entry operator from accidentally altering any of the report titles or formulas, because the results would be disastrous.

Excel uses a default setting for cell protection for each of its worksheets. To review this default setting, highlight the entire worksheet and then select Cell Protection from the Format menu (see fig. 3.29).

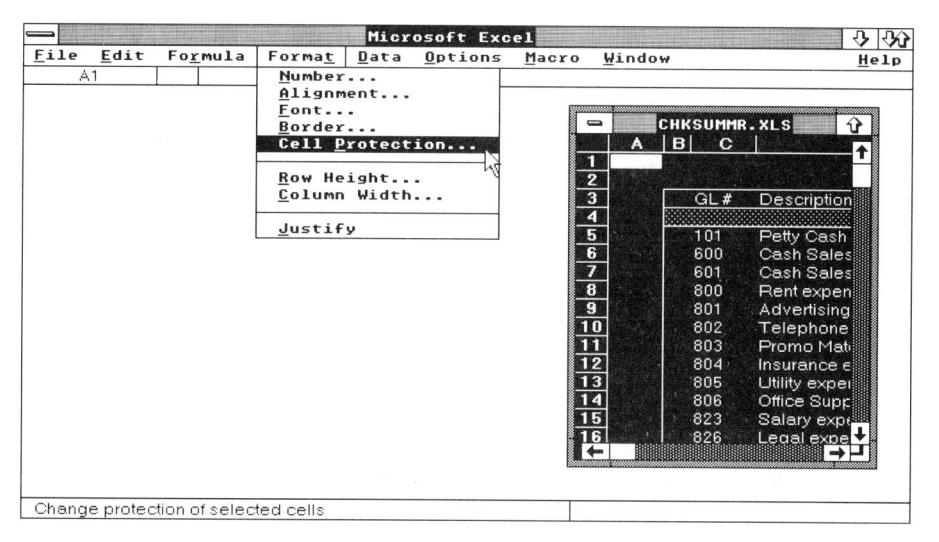

Fig. 3.29.
Reviewing the cell-protection setting for the accounting summary worksheet.

As expected, the Locked option is checked in the Cell Protection dialog box (see fig. 3.30). Once that option is invoked, locking your spreadsheet cells prevents users from altering any worksheet data. If you need to, check the Hidden option to turn off the formula bar. This action prevents users from viewing cell formulas on the formula bar; it does not, however, hide cell text and calculated results.

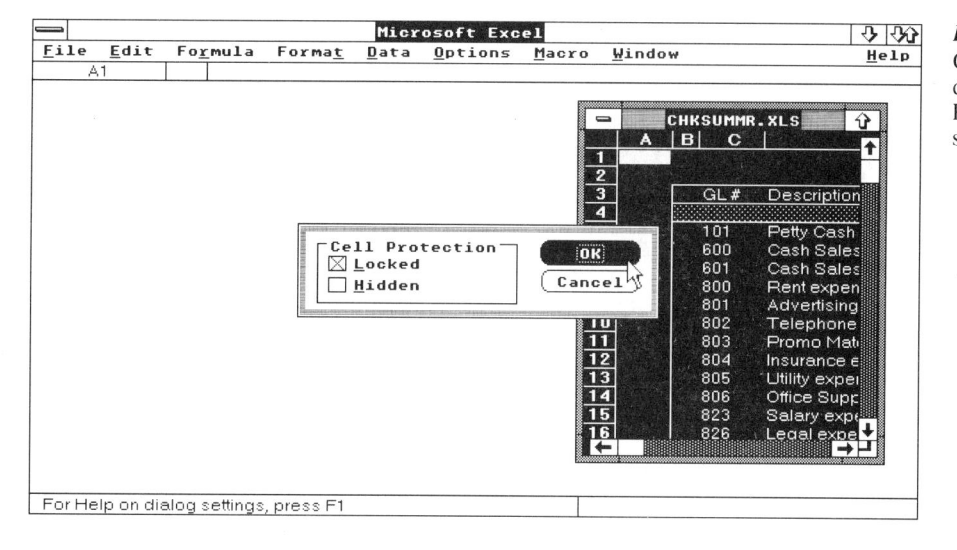

Fig. 3.30.
Confirming the default Cell Protection setting.

Designating the Cell Protection format does not in and of itself protect your worksheets. To protect your worksheets, choose the Options menu and select Protect Document. Figure 3.31 shows the dialog box that appears when you select Protect Document. You have several choices to make in this dialog box. The default setting protects the cell contents as specified in the Format Cell Protection command. If you like, enter a password to prevent prying eyes from gaining access to the document. Or simply select OK, and Excel will implement your Cell Protection scheme.

Fig. 3.31.
Using Options Protect Document to invoke the cell-protection settings.

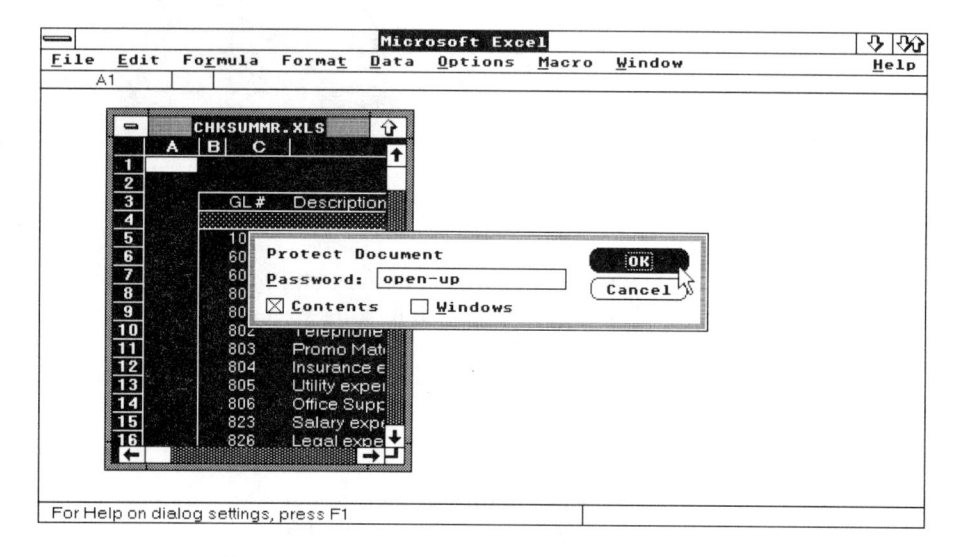

> Tip: When you use the Protect Document command, Excel turns off most of the options that appear in the menus. Pull down the Edit menu, for example. Notice that Excel does not permit you to cut, copy, or paste any data that appears in the protected document.

Now try to enter or change any of the cell contents in the check-register accounting summary worksheet. When you do, the alert box shown in figure 3.32 appears. To continue, you must select OK.

Turning off the document protection of your worksheets is easy. Pull down the Options menu once more and notice that the Unprotect Document command appears in place of the Protect Document command. Just select OK, and you again have the freedom to alter any worksheet data. If you initially designated a password, type the password here (see fig. 3.33) and select OK to unprotect the document.

Managing a Business Checkbook **87**

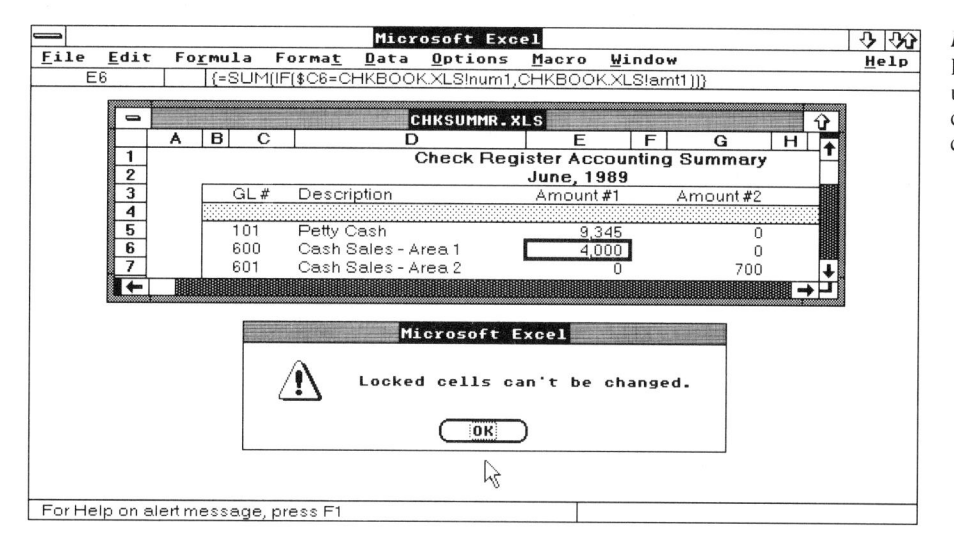

Fig. 3.32.
Excel alerts the user that locked cells can't be changed.

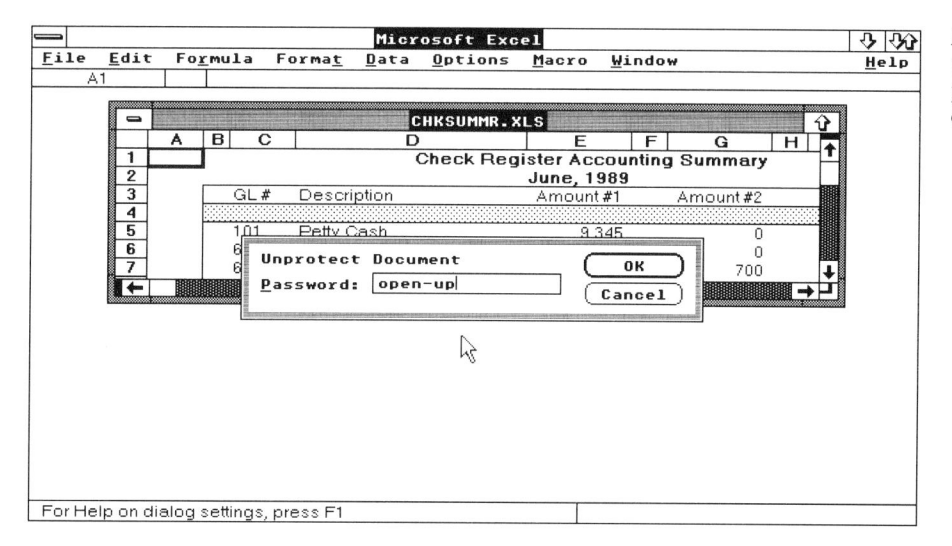

Fig. 3.33.
Unprotecting your Excel documents.

> Tip: Use discretion when choosing password protection in the Protect Document command from the Options menu. If you forget the password—and depending on the Cell Protection scheme you chose—Excel won't enable you access to worksheet cells. Without a password, you can't unprotect your document.

Password-Protecting the Accounting Summary Worksheet

Password protection through the Options Protect Document command is a low-level defense mechanism. High-level password protection is available from the File menu, through the Save Worksheet As Options command.

In figure 3.34, the password controls access to this document. Unlike choosing the password option in Protect Document from the Options menu, selecting a password here gives you ultimate control over who may and may not use this worksheet. When you try to open the document later, the dialog box shown in figure 3.35 appears.

Fig. 3.34. High-level password protection.

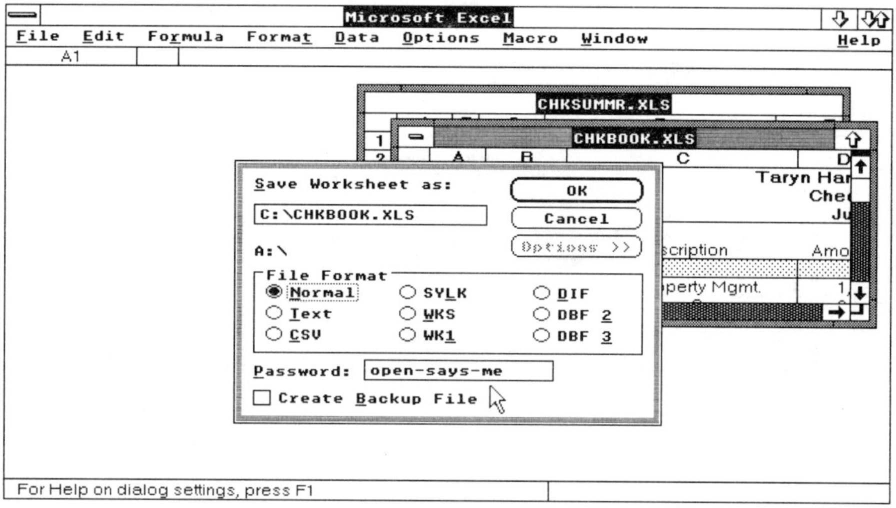

Fig. 3.35. Enter the password to open the document.

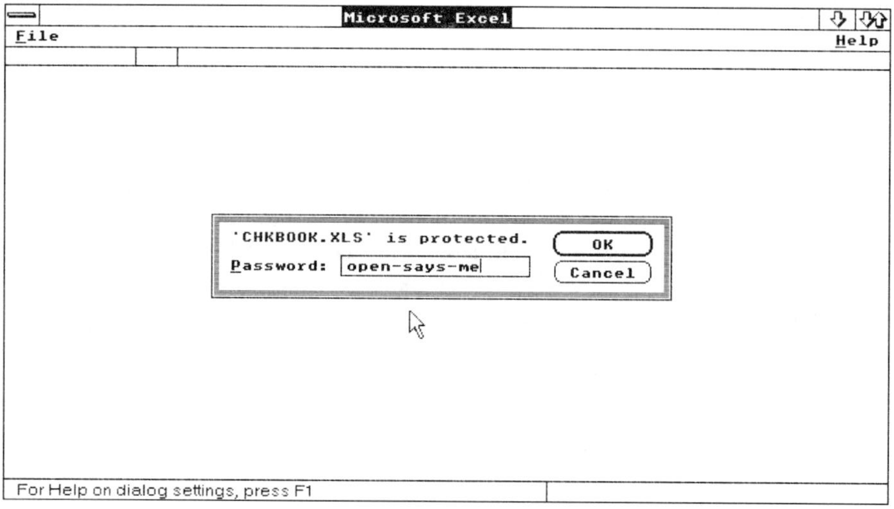

Don't forget the password, though, because Excel is unforgiving in this situation. Lose the password and you lose the document. It's as simple as that.

Summary

The completed checkbook management system for Taryn Hartley Cosmetics appears in figures 3.36 through 3.38.

Fig. 3.36. The check register.

	A	B	C	D	E	F	H	I	J	K
1						Taryn Hartley Cosmetics				
2						Check Register				
3						June, 1989				
4	Check				IN		GL		GL	
5	No.	Date	Description	Amount	?	Balance	#1	Amount	#2	Amount
6						2,000				
7	1001	06-01-89	Smythe Property Mgmt.	1,225	*	775	800	1,225		0
8	1002	06-04-89	Taryn Hartley, Owner	2,975	*	(2,200)	823	2,975		0
9	D	06-05-89	Transfer from 412-617-915	9,345	*	7,145	101	9,345		0
10	1003	06-06-89	Kishaba Rentals	450	*	6,695	803	450		0
11	1004	06-10-89	PJ&B Advertising	250		6,445	801	250		0
12	1005	06-11-89	Jordan Dilts III, Esquire	1,275	*	5,170	826	1,000	827	275
13	D	06-14-89	Interest Dividend	46	*	5,216	900	46		0
14	1006	06-19-89	McCreary's Office Supplies	97	*	5,119	806	97		0
15	1007	06-25-89	DASH Phone Service	324	*	4,795	802	324		0
16	1008	06-25-89	LCG&E Utilities	123		4,672	805	123		0
17	D	06-30-89	Cash Sales	4,700		9,372	600	4,000	601	700
18	1009	06-30-89	Perfect Promotions, Inc.	345		9,027	803	345		0
19	12			21,155				20,180		975
20	Items		Check Figure	21,155	=	---------------		#1	+	#2

	M	N
1		
2		
3		
4	Deposits	Checks
5	not cl'rd.	not cl'rd.
6		
7	0	0
8	0	0
9	0	0
10	0	0
11	0	250
12	0	0
13	0	0
14	0	0
15	0	0
16	0	123
17	(4,700)	0
18	0	345
19	(4,700)	718
20		

Fig. 3.37.
The check-register reconciliation.

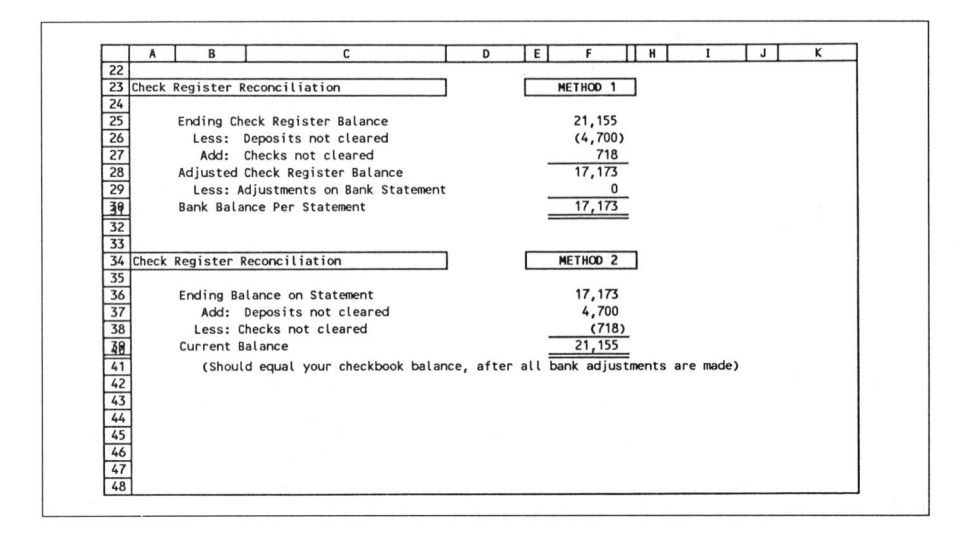

	A	B	C	D	E	F	H	I	J	K
22										
23	Check Register Reconciliation					METHOD 1				
24										
25		Ending Check Register Balance				21,155				
26		Less: Deposits not cleared				(4,700)				
27		Add: Checks not cleared				718				
28		Adjusted Check Register Balance				17,173				
29		Less: Adjustments on Bank Statement				0				
30		Bank Balance Per Statement				17,173				
32										
33										
34	Check Register Reconciliation					METHOD 2				
35										
36		Ending Balance on Statement				17,173				
37		Add: Deposits not cleared				4,700				
38		Less: Checks not cleared				(718)				
40		Current Balance				21,155				
41		(Should equal your checkbook balance, after all bank adjustments are made)								

Fig. 3.38.
The check-register accounting summary.

	A	B	C	D	E	F	G	H	I	J
1					Check Register Accounting Summary					
2					June, 1989					
3		GL #	Description		Amount #1		Amount #2		Total	
4										
5		101	Petty Cash		9,345		0		9,345	
6		600	Cash Sales - Area 1		4,000		0		4,000	
7		601	Cash Sales - Area 2		0		700		700	
8		800	Rent expense		1,225		0		1,225	
9		801	Advertising expense		250		0		250	
10		802	Telephone expense		324		0		324	
11		803	Promo Materials expense		795		0		795	
12		804	Insurance expense		0		0		0	
13		805	Utility expense		123		0		123	
14		806	Office Supplies expense		97		0		97	
15		823	Salary expense		2,975		0		2,975	
16		826	Legal expense		1,000		0		1,000	
17		827	Accounting expense		0		275		275	
18		900	Interest Dividend		46		0		46	
19				To	$20,180		$975		$21,155	

You may already have envisioned the changes required to make this three-part model a fully operative, working model for your own business. You will find it easy, for example, to extend the size of the model to account for an average of 40 transactions per month. Just insert the amount of lines necessary and copy the cell formulas throughout the newly inserted range; you're ready to go.

At the end of each month, save under a different file name a backup copy of the completed checkbook management system. Then simply clear the entries on the active check-register worksheet and enter the prior months' ending balance in cell F6 (to give you a cash balance forward for the new month). Then you're ready for the new month's transactions.

In the next chapter, you will concentrate on building specific financial spreadsheets to promote your standing; format and appearance are emphasized. With your growing knowledge of spreadsheet-building techniques, you can implement the automation techniques that you feel most comfortable with—whether they be macros, one worksheet that creates several reports, or a series of linked spreadsheets.

4
Using Financial Spreadsheets To Promote Your Standing

Chapter 2 illustrated how you can use Excel to present the financial standing of your company. You created formulas to add, subtract, and compute percentages and then successfully constructed a simple income statement and balance sheet—two standard accounting statements.

Chapter 3 demonstrated how to build a fully operative model for business checkbook management. This model uses the daily transactions from your business checkbook to create a monthly accounting summary report, complete with automatic checkbook reconciliation. Using Excel's formidable screen-formatting tools, you improved the look of your final reports, adding shaded bars and varying the font sizes to highlight all the significant data.

These types of presentations represent just two ways to use Excel as a financial productivity tool. After you build Excel models that meet your ongoing business-reporting needs, the next logical step is to invent models that will help you anticipate, or forecast, your future business standing.

In this chapter, you will learn how to use three complex forecasting models: a cash budget model, a pro forma financial-statements model, and a breakeven analysis model. These ready-to-use models appear on the disk that came with this book. Now that you have the worksheet-building experience of Chapters 2 and 3 behind you, you'll want to modify these generic models to fit your own business-forecasting needs. Once you personalize these automated forecasting tools, you'll find them an essential and invaluable addition to your Excel business library.

The following are items you should consider before using your *Excel Business Applications* spreadsheet models:

1. Make a backup copy of the models disk and store the backup in a safe place.
2. Save all your modified models under a unique file name so that you can quickly revert to the generic model if necessary. Don't ignore this recommendation! You'll need the original format if you accidentally erase a modified model file.
3. If you have a hard disk drive, create a new subdirectory in Excel and load the models into this subdirectory. Then store the disk.
4. Each model has been saved in Options Protect Document mode. You can thus enter data only into worksheet cells that have been previously unlocked with the Format Cell Protection command. When Protect Document mode is enabled, these cells appear boldfaced and, in certain cases, underlined.

If you want to modify CASHBUDG.XLS's structure, for example, first save the generic model under a new name. To unprotect the worksheet so that you can change descriptions and titles, select Options Unprotect Document.

Using the Cash Budget Forecast (CASHBUDG.XLS)

The cash budget approach to financial forecasting estimates a company's future cash needs by looking at the pattern of past cash receipts and cash disbursements. This way, the firm manager can better estimate how much cash will be needed to meet management's growth objectives. Simply put, if you want to buy, for example, a new truck next year, use your cash budget to forecast how much cash will be available to purchase that new truck.

When you use a cash budget forecast, you must determine the *forecast time period*—the time frame to be used in the forecast. Choosing a time period that coincides with your firm's reporting cycle is important, whether that cycle is monthly, quarterly, or yearly. Why forecast on an annual basis when you generate monthly financial statements?

If your firm experiences erratic cash flows, you may find it necessary to use weekly cash budgeting—even if you create monthly financial statements. This way, you can sum the values of the four weekly budgets to calculate your forecasted monthly cash requirements.

For the purposes of this chapter, the forecast time period will be monthly. But keep in mind that this model can be easily adapted to any time period; a yearly forecast is simply 12 monthly forecasts, 52 weekly forecasts, and so on.

A good rule of thumb in financial forecasting is this: the shorter the forecast time period, the greater the amount of detailed assumptions you'll need to provide. Why? When forecasting the cash receipts for your yearly cash budget, you can make an estimated guess based on last year's cash receipts and this year's forecasted increase in cash sales. If you need this same information in a weekly format, though, you must be prepared to validate the weekly cash sales forecast—that is, to determine who the cash customers are, how the terms will affect cash sales, what level of returns and allowances can be expected, and so on.

To consider this concern from a different angle, think about which of the following two forecasts you would have more faith in:

Forecast 1: Next year's sales will be 15 percent higher than this year's sales.

Forecast 2: Next year's sales during the third week of March will be 15 percent higher than this year's sales during the third week of March.

You can reduce the prediction error associated with any forecast by spreading the prediction error out over longer forecasted time periods. So the flip side of this issue is that when you reduce the forecast error by using a yearly versus weekly time period, you lose some of the report detail that ultimately could be valuable for management to have. The correct choice is the one that best meets your management team's forecasting needs.

In addition to the forecast time period, you must determine the *horizon time period*—how far into the future you want to forecast. You can forecast 10 years into the future if you want. Keep in mind, though, that you are preparing your cash budget forecast by using recent historical data. Ask yourself, "What is the likelihood that last year's cash needs will closely coincide with this year's, or next year's, or those of the year after?" When you feel confident with the answer to this question, you've selected a good forecast horizon for your firm.

After selecting the time period and the forecast horizon, you must consider all the different day-to-day activities in your business that affect your cash position. Then pick a variable that ties all these activities together. Many companies relate a change in their cash position to a growth or decrease in sales. The critical assumption in this chapter's models is that all changes in the financial makeup of the firm are tied to a change in sales.

To create a cash budget for the sample company Donnelly Manufacturing, use the CASHBUDG.XLS model provided on your disk. This model processes data through six separate minimodels:

- Base-period sales and sales forecast
- Charge vs. cash sales analysis
- Cash receipts forecast
- Base-period purchases
- Charge vs. cash purchases analysis
- Cash disbursements forecast

Donnelly is currently at the end of its fourth quarter of operations for fiscal year 1989. Management wants to prepare a 12-month cash budget forecast for fiscal 1990, using the following assumptions:

- The time period is monthly.
- The forecast horizon is 12 months.
- Sales will grow at a yearly rate of 8 percent, or .667 percent per month.

Figure 4.1 shows the first screen of the basic CASHBUDG.XLS model.

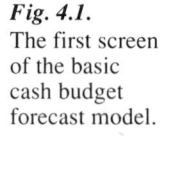

Fig. 4.1.
The first screen of the basic cash budget forecast model.

To add the appropriate titles and the forecast time line to the model, do the following:

Step 1. Open CASHBUDG.XLS.

Step 2. Enter **Donnelly Manufacturing** into cell F2.

Step 3. Select cells F5 and J5 and append **89** and **90** to the FY labels.

Step 4. Select the range E6:G6 and enter **10**, **11**, and **12** as the base-period months.

Step 5. Save the model under the file name DONNELLY.XLS, using the Save As command.

Note: Place your cursor in cell H6 and examine the formula =IF(G$6<12,G$6+1,1). If the value in G6 were 11 (for November), Excel would display 12 (G$6+1) in H6 as the first period to be forecasted.

Notice that the data you entered into F5, J5, and E6:G6 automatically updates the descriptions that appear in the rest of the model. The reason is that you used direct cell references and also appended one text label to another.

Consider how direct cell references work. Cell F15 contains the formula =$F$5 but displays a text label. Using a direct cell reference that tells Excel to display FY '89 in cell F15 results in the text-label display. You also can append a direct cell reference to an existing label, as shown in figure 4.2. Here, the direct cell reference appears as a string (it's surrounded by ampersands) attached to a label. This formula tells Excel to append the contents of F5 to the contents of B7.

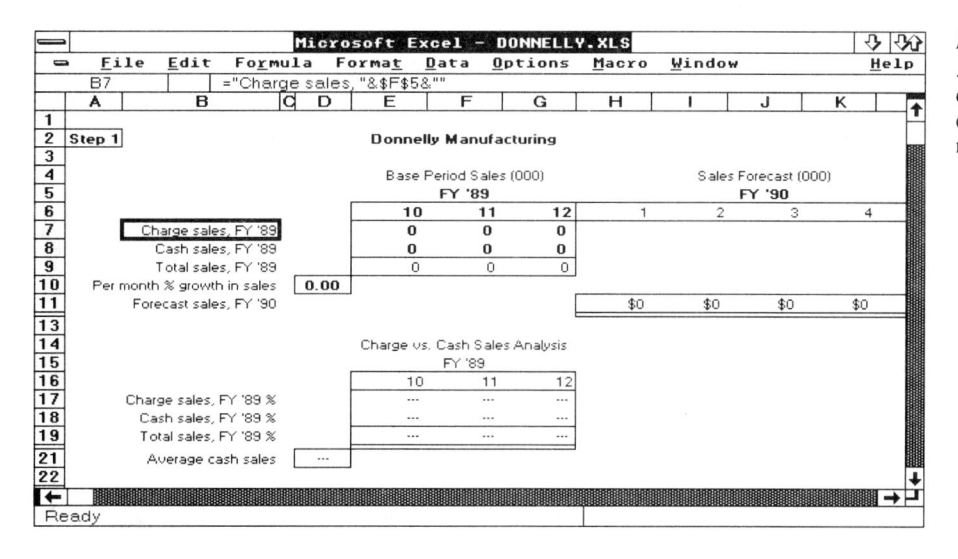

Fig. 4.2. Adding descriptions and designating the model time line.

Note: Examine the formulas used in column B for examples of how you can combine text on your worksheets.

The Sales Forecast

Before you can use the cash budget model for the sample company Donnelly Manufacturing, you must compile a history of Donnelly's charge and cash sales for fiscal year 1989. Enter these values only to the thousands place, because the model indicates that sales will be forecast to the thousands (000).

The monthly sales estimates for fiscal 1990 are calculated in this way: month 2 sales equal month 1 sales multiplied by the expected growth in monthly sales. To build this formula into the model, use cell D10 as a variable cell.

A variable cell's value changes as expectations in sales growth change. Altering the value of this variable causes the forecast of total sales to change. Follow these steps to complete the Base Period Sales input block:

Step 1. Select the range E7:G8. Enter the charge and cash sales for months 10, 11, and 12, shown in figure 4.3.

Step 2. Enter the value 0.667 into D10, the variable cell (see fig. 4.3). The value in this cell represents the expected percentage increase in monthly sales.

Note: Formatting conventions used in this model round off numbers to the tenth and hundredth places. So always enter a number in its entirety; let Excel do the rounding for you.

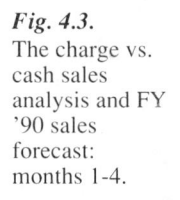

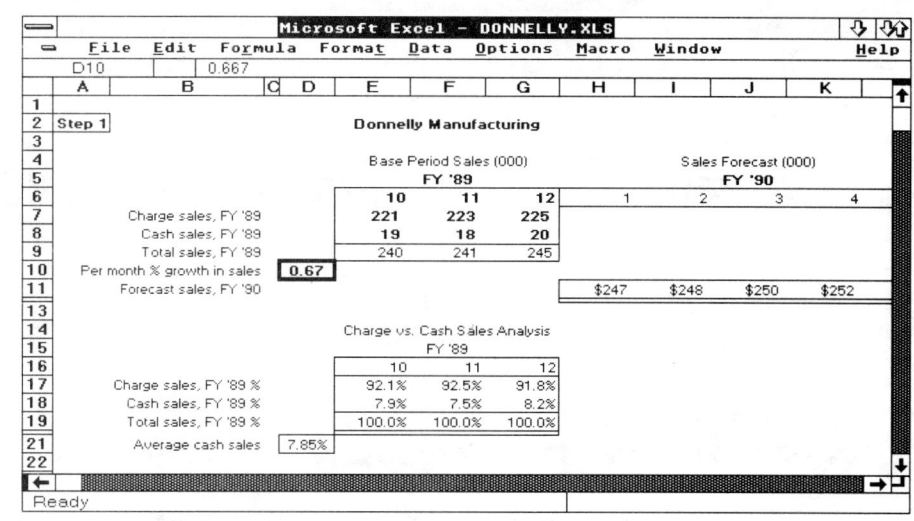

Fig. 4.3.
The charge vs. cash sales analysis and FY '90 sales forecast: months 1-4.

Note: Be sure to distinguish here between a monthly growth rate and a yearly growth rate. If the time horizon of this forecast were years, you would use a yearly growth rate of 8 percent.

> Tip: Using variable cells in your models gives you great flexibility when you want to rerun the model under a different set of assumptions. Otherwise, you must edit your cell formulas manually each time you want to create a new forecast scenario.

Press Ctrl-PgDn to scroll one window to the right and review the final eight months of the sales forecast (see fig. 4.4). Forecast sales range from $247,000 in forecast period 1 to $265,000 in forecast period 12; that's an annual growth of 8 percent, as expected.

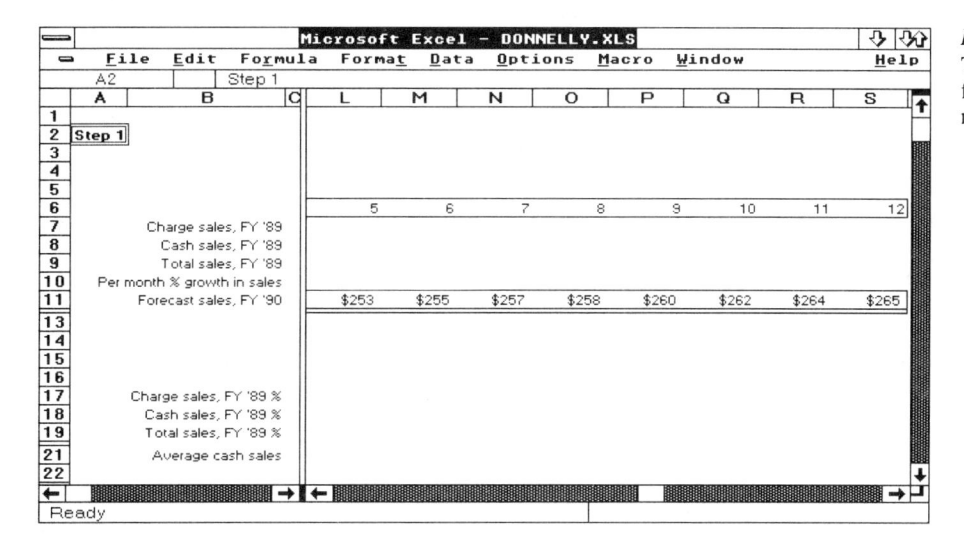

Fig. 4.4. The sales forecast: months 5-12.

The Charge vs. Cash Sales Analysis

The charge vs. cash sales analysis breaks down historical total sales into charge and cash sales. This important analysis computes the average cash sales for the base period, as shown in figure 4.5. Use this average to estimate your future cash sales receipts for fiscal 1990.

Fig. 4.5.
Calculating average cash sales for the base period.

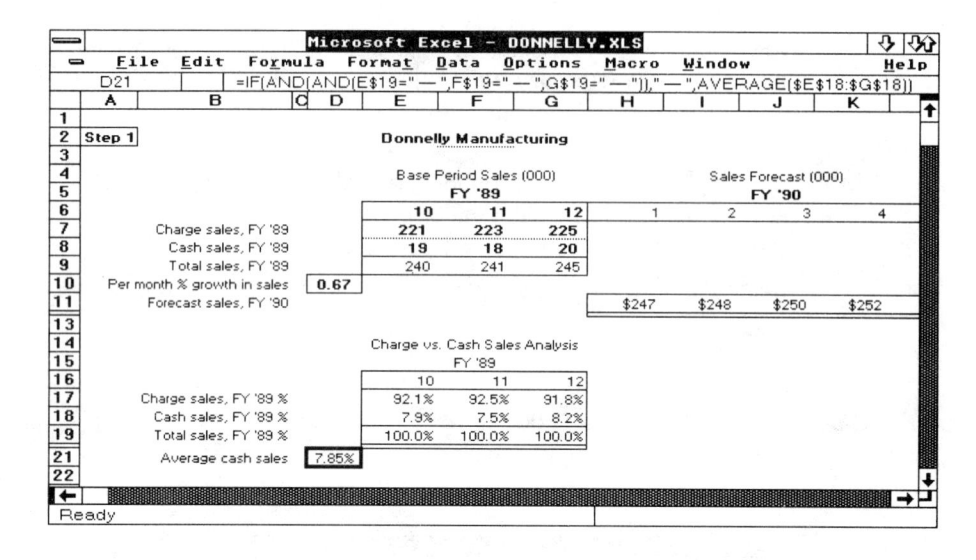

```
Microsoft Excel - DONNELLY.XLS
File  Edit  Formula  Format  Data  Options  Macro  Window                    Help
D21         =IF(AND(AND(E$19=" — ",F$19=" — ",G$19=" — ")," — ",AVERAGE($E$18:$G$18))
```

	A	B	C	D	E	F	G	H	I	J	K
1											
2	Step 1					Donnelly Manufacturing					
3											
4						Base Period Sales (000)			Sales Forecast (000)		
5						FY '89				FY '90	
6					10	11	12	1	2	3	4
7		Charge sales, FY '89			221	223	225				
8		Cash sales, FY '89			19	18	20				
9		Total sales, FY '89			240	241	245				
10	Per month % growth in sales			0.67							
11		Forecast sales, FY '90						$247	$248	$250	$252
13											
14						Charge vs. Cash Sales Analysis					
15						FY '89					
16					10	11	12				
17		Charge sales, FY '89 %			92.1%	92.5%	91.8%				
18		Cash sales, FY '89 %			7.9%	7.5%	8.2%				
19		Total sales, FY '89 %			100.0%	100.0%	100.0%				
21		Average cash sales			7.85%						
22											

Ready

Donnelly's average cash sales for the base period is 7.85 percent of total sales. What would happen if the company offered a discount to customers who pay with cash? Surely this average would increase, and Donnelly's would want to incorporate this expected change into its forecast.

The Cash Receipts Forecast

The cash receipts forecast assimilates the data from the preceding section into one model (see fig. 4.6). This forecast also enables you to estimate when cash will be received from charge sales and what the total value of all other cash receipts is. The sum of all these estimates equals the total expected cash receipts for your 12-month forecast horizon.

The data in cells E29:P30 comes directly from the estimated sales on the sales forecast model. Move your cursor through the cells in this range to examine the direct cell references used to create this display. Inspect the formulas in the "Charge sales" row. These formulas subtract cash sales from forecast sales. When the cash sales variable equals zero, then charge sales equal total sales.

For the coming fiscal year, Donnelly's management anticipates that average cash sales will remain at 7.85 percent of sales. Perform the following steps to complete the cash receipts forecast:

    Step 1. Enter **.0785** into cell D31 and watch as charge sales and total cash receipts update.

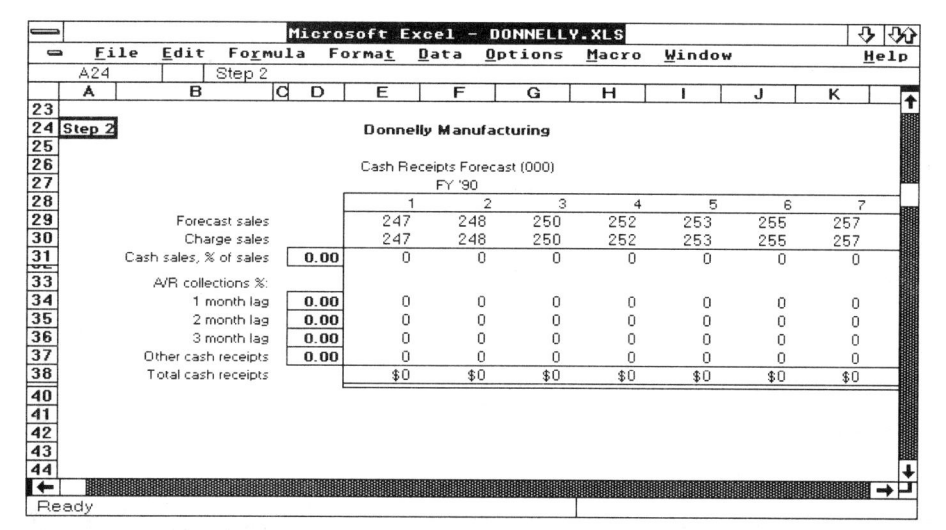

Fig. 4.6.
The cash receipts forecast model.

> **Tip:** Notice that you are to enter into cell D31 the value **.0785**, not a reference to the computed value in cell D21. If you were sure that the value in D21 would always represent the forecast of the cash sales percentage, then it would be okay to use a direct reference.

A/R cash receipts are normally lagged by 30, 60, and 90 days. From previous experience in collecting receivables, the sales manager believes that 80 percent, 10 percent, and 5 percent of all charge sales will be collected in the first, second, and third months after the sales. For example, 80 percent of period 1's charge sales will be collected in period 2. The remaining 5 percent (100–80–10–5) is uncollectible, reflecting the estimated bad debt expense for fiscal 1990.

Other receipts—cash dividends and interest from miscellaneous equity investments—average 1.5 percent of sales.

Step 2. Highlight cells D34:D36 and enter **.8**, **.1**, and **.05**.

Step 3. Enter **.015** into cell D37.

When you use lagged measurements, you risk restricting the amount of usable periods in a model. Generally, usable periods equal the forecast horizon less the total number of lagged periods. This model should have only 9 useful periods of data (a 12-month forecast horizon less 3 lagged periods), but in fact it has 12 useful periods. Why? By using 3 base periods, you have eliminated the "usable period" effect of lagged measurement on this model. Period 1, the first forecast month, is the first month having complete data for each of the three lagged periods. The forecast of A/R collections for FY '90 period 1 is complete because you have charge sales data for FY '89 periods 10, 11, and 12.

Figures 4.7 and 4.8 show the completed cash receipts forecast for months 1 through 7 and for months 8 through 12, respectively.

Fig. 4.7.
The completed cash receipts forecast: months 1-7.

Donnelly Manufacturing
Cash Receipts Forecast (000)
FY '90

			1	2	3	4	5	6	7
Forecast sales			247	248	250	252	253	255	257
Charge sales			228	229	230	232	233	235	237
Cash sales, % of sales		0.08	19	19	20	20	20	20	20
A/R collections %:									
1 month lag		0.80	180	182	183	184	185	187	188
2 month lag		0.10	22	23	23	23	23	23	23
3 month lag		0.05	11	11	11	11	11	11	12
Other cash receipts		0.02	4	4	4	4	4	4	4
Total cash receipts			$236	$239	$241	$242	$243	$245	$247

Fig. 4.8.
The completed cash receipts forecast: months 8-12.

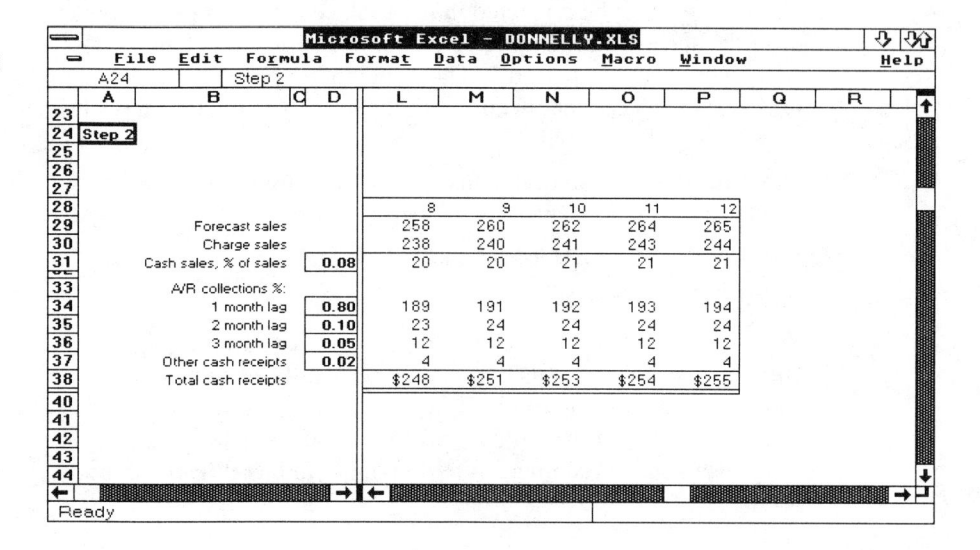

			8	9	10	11	12
Forecast sales			258	260	262	264	265
Charge sales			238	240	241	243	244
Cash sales, % of sales		0.08	20	20	21	21	21
A/R collections %:							
1 month lag		0.80	189	191	192	193	194
2 month lag		0.10	23	24	24	24	24
3 month lag		0.05	12	12	12	12	12
Other cash receipts		0.02	4	4	4	4	4
Total cash receipts			$248	$251	$253	$254	$255

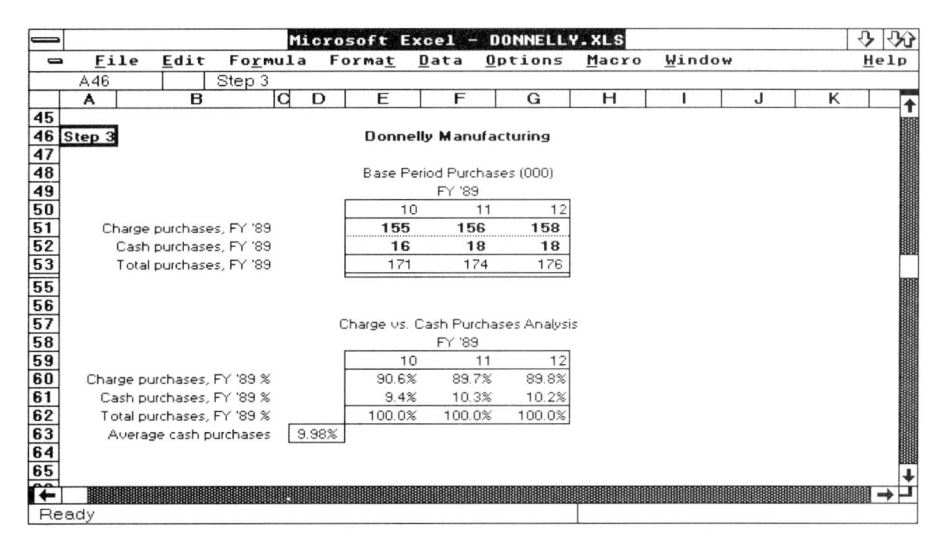

Base-Period Purchases and the Charge vs. Cash Purchases Analysis

The next model uses data gathered from Donnelly's purchasing manager. Precise purchase data is available for only the last three months of FY '89. Even so, the purchasing manager makes these estimates about the past few years:

- Purchases equal 72 percent of sales.
- 10 percent of all purchases are paid with cash.

The charge vs. cash purchases analysis breaks down historical total purchases into charge and cash purchases. This important analysis computes the average-cash-purchases percentage for the base period, as shown in figure 4.9. To estimate Donnelly's future cash purchase outlays for fiscal 1990, do the following: highlight the range E51:G52 and enter the purchases data shown in figure 4.9.

Fig. 4.9. Base-period purchases and the charge vs. cash purchases analysis.

	10	11	12
Charge purchases, FY '89	155	156	158
Cash purchases, FY '89	16	18	18
Total purchases, FY '89	171	174	176

Charge vs. Cash Purchases Analysis
FY '89

	10	11	12
Charge purchases, FY '89 %	90.6%	89.7%	89.8%
Cash purchases, FY '89 %	9.4%	10.3%	10.2%
Total purchases, FY '89 %	100.0%	100.0%	100.0%
Average cash purchases	9.98%		

This scenario uses an *estimate* of cash purchases to forecast future cash outlays. It sounds a bit fishy, doesn't it? The important thing to remember is to use actual accounting data when it is available. But when the actual figures aren't available, use good judgment in creating the estimate. Even though there were no precise accounting figures, Donnelly's purchasing manager was able to draw on experience and common sense to make an estimate.

The Cash Disbursements Forecast

This model enables you to link the estimate of future cash purchases to the sales forecast from the first model. Then, by judging when the on-account purchases will be paid and estimating miscellaneous cash disbursements, you will arrive at the total expected disbursements for the forecast horizon.

Donnelly pays 95 percent of all on-account purchases in the first month following all charge purchases, 3 percent in the second month, and 2 percent in the third month. Historically, other cash disbursements equal 25 percent of sales. Other cash disbursements account for company payroll, supplies, overhead expense payments, and so on.

Perform the following steps to complete the cash disbursements forecast:

Step 1. Enter **.72** into cell D72 and **.10** into cell D74.

Step 2. Highlight cells D77:D79 and enter the lag percentage values **.95**, **.03**, and **.02**.

> **Tip:** Recognize that although Donnelly predicts that it will collect only 95 percent of its accounts receivable due, the company intends to remit 100 percent of the money owed to vendors.

Step 3. Enter **.25** into cell D80.

Figures 4.10 and 4.11 show the completed cash disbursements forecast for months 1 through 7 and for months 8 through 12, respectively.

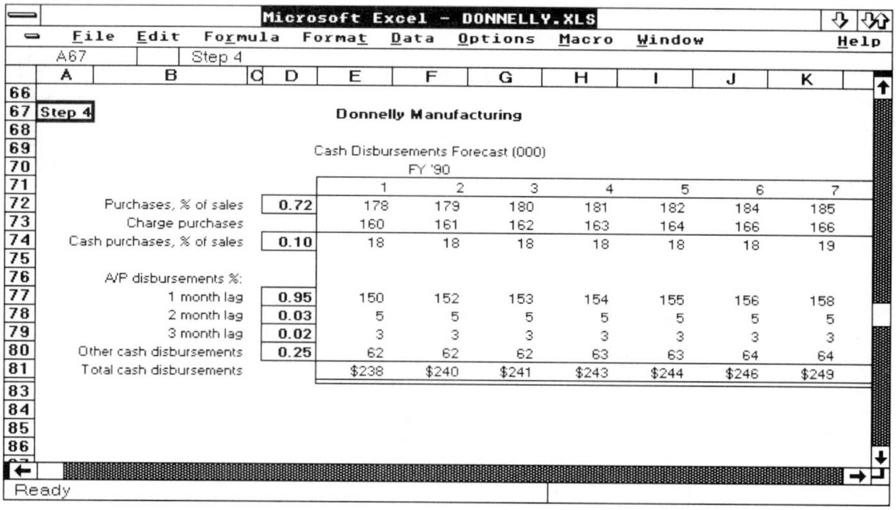

Fig. 4.10.
The completed cash disbursements forecast: months 1-7.

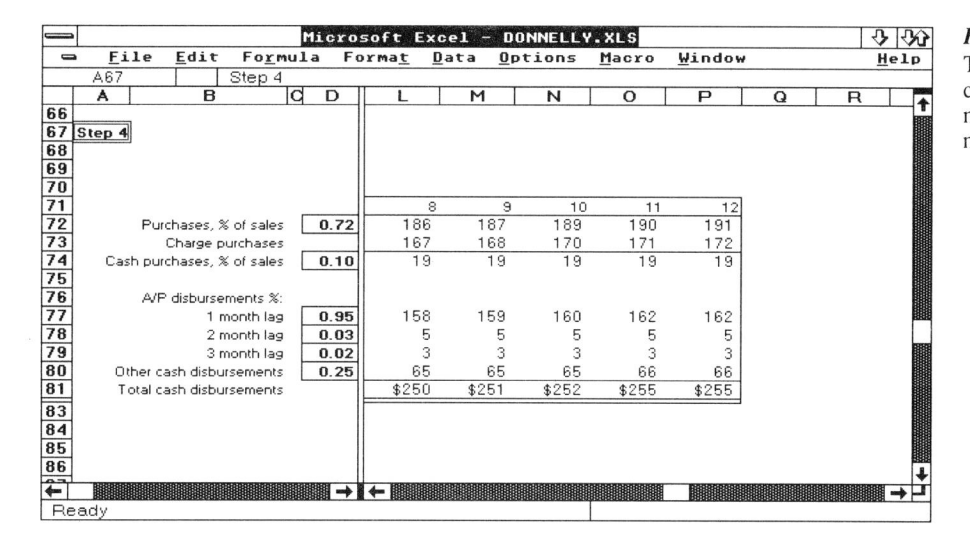

Fig. 4.11.
The completed cash disbursements forecast: months 8-12.

	8	9	10	11	12
Purchases, % of sales 0.72	186	187	189	190	191
Charge purchases	167	168	170	171	172
Cash purchases, % of sales 0.10	19	19	19	19	19
A/P disbursements %:					
1 month lag 0.95	158	159	160	162	162
2 month lag 0.03	5	5	5	5	5
3 month lag 0.02	3	3	3	3	3
Other cash disbursements 0.25	65	65	65	66	66
Total cash disbursements	$250	$251	$252	$255	$255

The Completion of the Cash Budget Model

The cash budget model merges the critical data from the sales forecast, the cash receipts forecast, and the cash disbursements forecast and reveals the impact of all previous model assumptions on your cash position. Most important, the cash budget model tells you whether you will need to finance your growth externally, and thus borrow needed funds from banks, or whether your firm has the cash on hand to finance its growth internally. When you enter the minimum acceptable cash level, the cash budget tells you the amount of extra funds or the required total financing.

Donnelly Manufacturing has an FY '89 end-of-year cash balance equal to $59,000. Management deems it necessary to keep at least $50,000 on hand at all times for emergencies. Perform the following steps to complete the cash budget model.

Step 1. Enter **59** into cell E96.

Step 2. Enter **50** into cell E98.

Step 3. Using Paste Special Values, copy the value in cell E98 through the range E98:P98.

Figures 4.12 and 4.13 show the completed cash budget model for months 1 through 7 and for months 8 through 12, respectively.

Fig. 4.12.
The completed cash budget model: months 1-7.

	A	B	C D	E	F	G	H	I	J	K
87										
88	Step 5									
89				Donnelly Manufacturing						
90					Cash Budget (000)					
91					FY '90					
92				1	2	3	4	5	6	7
93		Cash receipts		236	239	241	242	243	245	247
94		Less: Cash disbursements		238	240	241	243	244	246	249
95		Net cash flow		(2)	(1)	0	(1)	(1)	(1)	(2)
96		Add: Beginning cash		59	57	56	56	55	54	53
97		Ending cash		57	56	56	55	54	53	51
98		Less: Min. cash balance		50	50	50	50	50	50	50
100		Required total financing		0	0	0	0	0	0	0
101		Excess cash balance		7	6	6	5	4	3	1

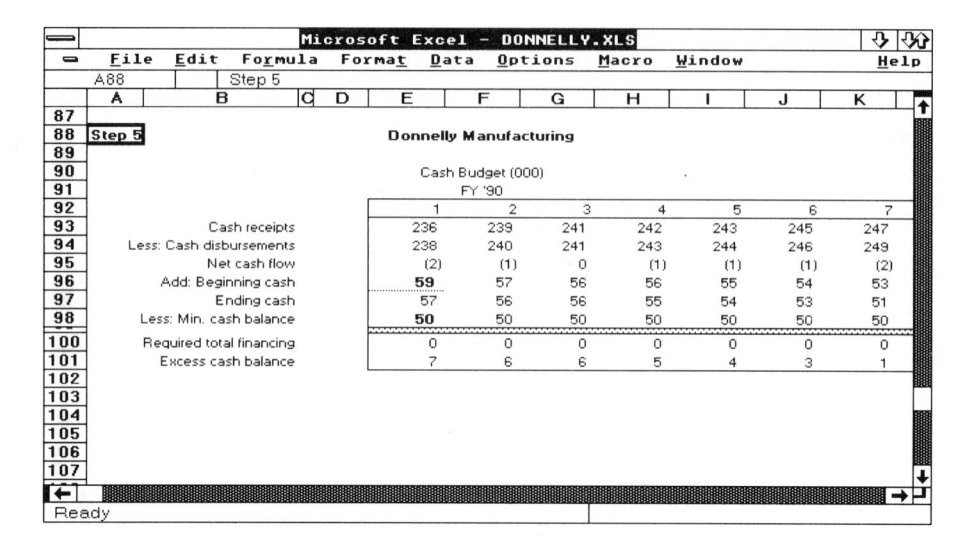

Fig. 4.13.
The completed cash budget model: months 8-12.

	A	B	C D	L	M	N	O	P	Q	R
87										
88	Step 5									
89										
90										
91										
92				8	9	10	11	12		
93		Cash receipts		248	251	253	254	255		
94		Less: Cash disbursements		250	251	252	255	255		
95		Net cash flow		(2)	0	1	(1)	0		
96		Add: Beginning cash		51	49	49	50	49		
97		Ending cash		49	49	50	49	49		
98		Less: Min. cash balance		50	50	50	50	50		
100		Required total financing		1	1	0	1	1		
101		Excess cash balance		0	0	0	0	0		

Review the logic of the required-total-financing formulas, found in the range E100:P100. The formula in cell E100 is as follows:

=IF(E$97<E$98,E$98-E$97,0)

This formula means "if the ending cash balance (E97) is less than the required minimum cash balance (E98), then needed financing equals their difference (E98–E97); otherwise, there is no need for financing (0)."

Now review the logic of the excess-cash-balance formulas, found in the range E101:P101. The formula in cell E101 is the following:

=IF(E$100=0,E$97-E$98,0)

This formula means "if required total financing (E100) is equal to zero, then calculate the value of the excess cash (E97–E98); otherwise, there is no excess cash (0)."

A Review of the Cash Budget

Using Excel to create a cash budget affords you tremendous flexibility. How else could you generate a large number of scenarios in just a matter of minutes?

Altering the value of one model variable ultimately affects the firm's forecasted cash position. The true power of this Excel business tool, therefore, lies in its capability to quickly evaluate the bottom-line effect of a change in cash management policy.

In general, people think in linear terms. This multivariable Excel forecasting tool enables you to react in a multidimensional fashion. How? Well, it's not too hard to gauge the effect on sales of a price decrease or to measure the impact on cash flow of purchasing all raw materials with cash. Every good manager has instinctive reactions to such events. But gut reactions are hardly trustworthy when the same information is accompanied by changes in company policy such as the following:

- Charge sales must be accompanied by a 10 percent cash deposit.
- All receivables older than 60 days will be turned over to a collection agency immediately.
- Management salaries will be increased by 5 percent.
- The minimum cash balance will be raised to $75,000.

Bottom-line analysis involves more than just cash budgeting, although the cash budget is a critical input to the process. No fiscal forecast is complete without pro forma financial statements, and building the models to create these statements is this chapter's next topic.

Using Pro Forma Financial Statements (PROFORMA.XLS)

Another effective way to forecast your future business standing is to build pro forma financial statements. When you create pro forma statements, you base a look into the future on today's financial position; pro formas are "forecasted replicas" of your current financial statements.

This forecast approach is based on the belief that historical financial relationships—as between sales and the cost of goods sold—will not change in the coming period. Consider a three-year historical trend in which the cost of goods sold equals 65 percent of sales. It's fair to assume, then, that the cost of goods sold will remain at 65 percent of sales in the coming period—regardless of whether sales rise or decline.

The two inputs for pro forma analysis are next year's sales forecast and this year's financial statements. Pro forma statements commonly use one year as both the forecast time period and horizon period. You will thus use 1989's year-end income statement to forecast 1990's year-end income statement. The file PROFORMA.XLS contains the basic model for building pro forma financial statements. As always, you are at liberty to modify a *copy* of this model.

In this section, you will create pro forma financial statements for the sample company Calkins Brothers, Inc., using the model PROFORMA.XLS. This model processes assumptions about the following (see fig. 4.14):

- Expected growth in yearly sales
- Expected tax rate
- Expected dividend payout ratio
- Expected relationship between sales and the income-statement and balance-sheet account values

In this model, base periods and forecast periods become the base fiscal year and the forecast fiscal year. Calkins Brothers, Inc., wants to forecast its 1990 financial position by using its 1989 year-end financial statements. Management anticipates that in fiscal 1990, the following will be the case:

- Sales will grow 25.0 percent.
- The income-tax rate will be 30 percent.
- The dividend payout ratio will be 10 percent for preferred stock and 40 percent for common stock.
- Long-term debt and equity will not change in the short term.

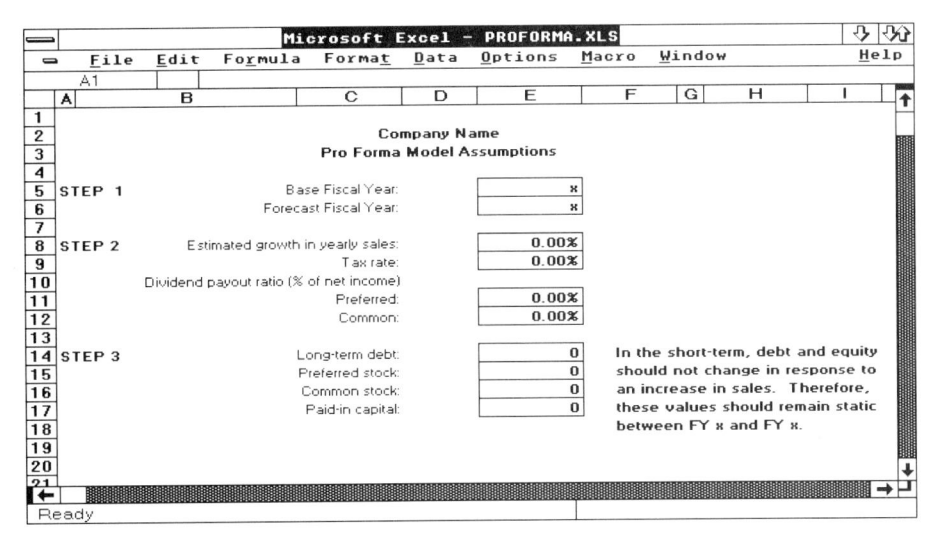

Fig. 4.14.
The assumptions screen of the pro forma model.

- In general, the relationships between FY '89 sales and the income-statement and balance-sheet accounts will hold for FY '90.

Perform the following steps to enter the pro forma model assumptions for Calkin Brothers, Inc.:

Step 1. Open PROFORMA.XLS.

Step 2. Enter **Calkins Brothers, Inc.** into cell D2.

Step 3. Select cells E5 and E6 and enter **1989** and **1990**.

Step 4. Select the range E8:E9 and enter **.25** and **.30** as the estimates for the annual sales growth and the tax rate.

Step 5. Select the range E11:E12 and enter **.10** and **.40** for the preferred and common stock payout ratios.

Tip: Taxes and common stock dividends are not generally forecast as a percentage of sales. The reason is that the tax rate remains fairly constant in the short term and that the dividend payout rate is set by management.

Step 6. Highlight the range E14:E17 and enter **276,225**, **100,000**, **200,000**, and **0**.

Tip: These numbers equal the FY 1989 values because management does not expect a short-term increased need for debt or equity.

Step 7. Save the model, using the file name CALKINS.XLS (see fig. 4.15).

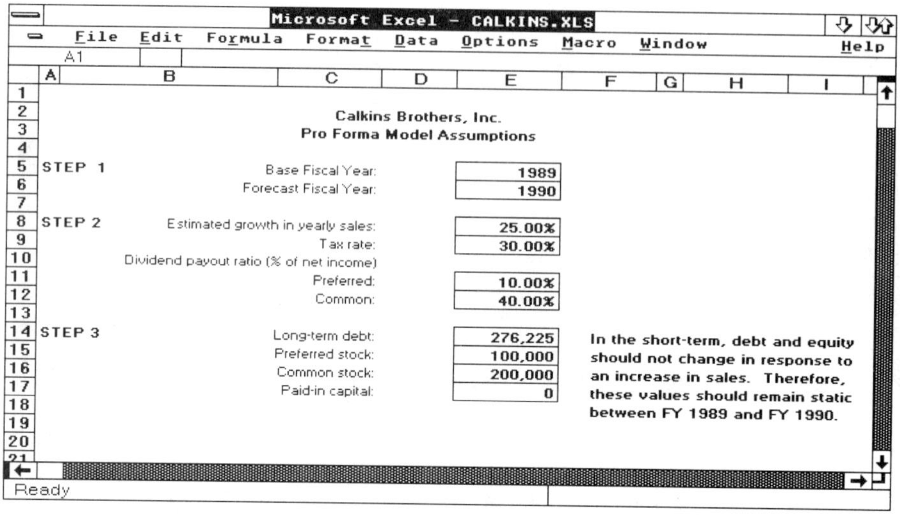

Fig. 4.15.
The completed assumptions section.

	A	B	C	D	E
2			Calkins Brothers, Inc.		
3			Pro Forma Model Assumptions		
5	STEP 1		Base Fiscal Year:		1989
6			Forecast Fiscal Year:		1990
8	STEP 2		Estimated growth in yearly sales:		25.00%
9			Tax rate:		30.00%
10			Dividend payout ratio (% of net income)		
11			Preferred:		10.00%
12			Common:		40.00%
14	STEP 3		Long-term debt:		276,225
15			Preferred stock:		100,000
16			Common stock:		200,000
17			Paid-in capital:		0

In the short-term, debt and equity should not change in response to an increase in sales. Therefore, these values should remain static between FY 1989 and FY 1990.

The Historical and Pro Forma Income Statement

Figure 4.16 shows how the pro forma model ties the present to the future. As you enter historical data into the left portion of the model, Excel displays the percent-of-sales values. Use these FY 1989 percentages to forecast the FY 1990 percentages.

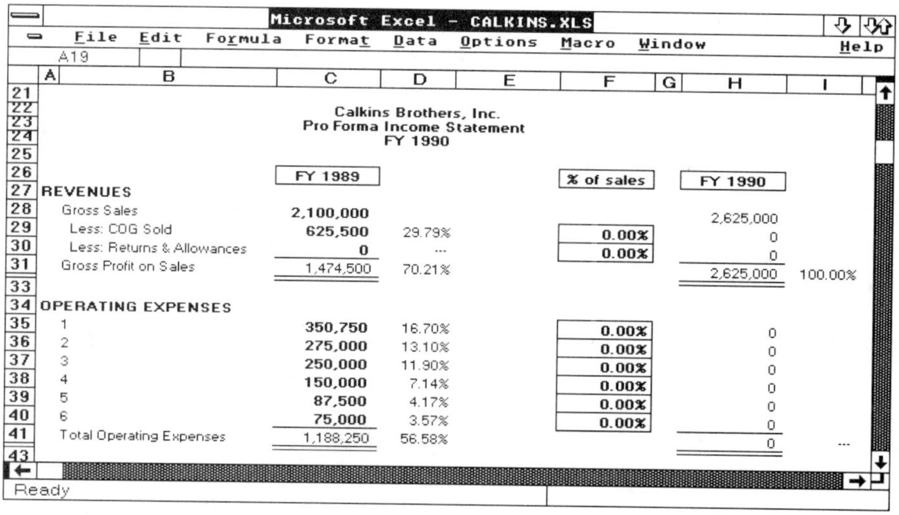

Fig. 4.16.
The historical income statement.

	B	C	D	E	F	G	H	I
22			Calkins Brothers, Inc.					
23			Pro Forma Income Statement					
24			FY 1990					
26		FY 1989			% of sales		FY 1990	
27	REVENUES							
28	Gross Sales	2,100,000					2,625,000	
29	Less: COG Sold	625,500	29.79%		0.00%		0	
30	Less: Returns & Allowances	0	...		0.00%		0	
31	Gross Profit on Sales	1,474,500	70.21%				2,625,000	100.00%
34	OPERATING EXPENSES							
35	1	350,750	16.70%		0.00%		0	
36	2	275,000	13.10%		0.00%		0	
37	3	250,000	11.90%		0.00%		0	
38	4	150,000	7.14%		0.00%		0	
39	5	87,500	4.17%		0.00%		0	
40	6	75,000	3.57%		0.00%		0	
41	Total Operating Expenses	1,188,250	56.58%				0	...

Although sales are expected to grow by 25 percent, Calkins Brothers management feels strongly that all other account values will stay at the same percent of sales.

Perform the following steps to enter the percent-of-sales forecast assumptions for the pro forma income statement model:

Step 1. Highlight the range F29:F30 and F35:F40. Reproduce FY 1989's percent values into the variable blocks in this range (see fig. 4.17).

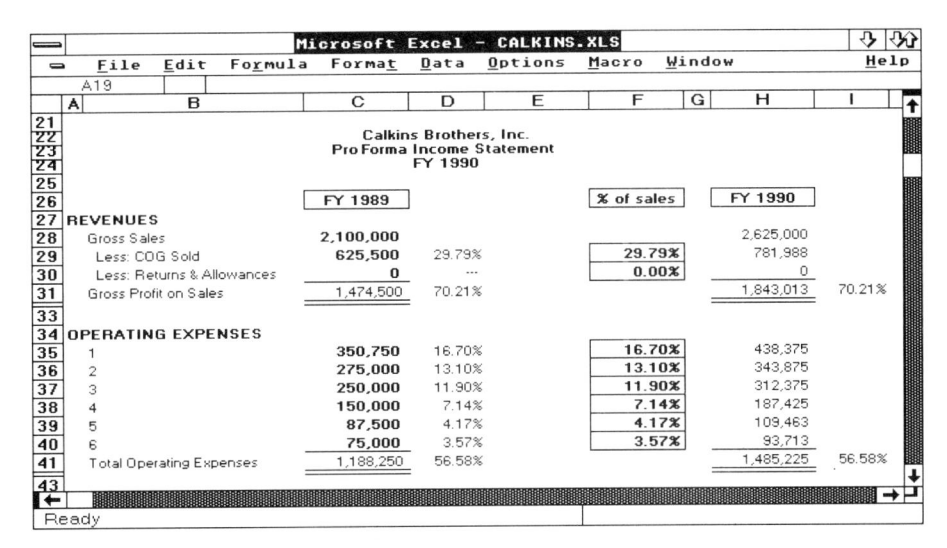

Fig. 4.17. The pro forma income statement, section 1.

	FY 1989		% of sales	FY 1990	
REVENUES					
Gross Sales	2,100,000			2,625,000	
Less: COG Sold	625,500	29.79%	29.79%	781,988	
Less: Returns & Allowances	0	...	0.00%	0	
Gross Profit on Sales	1,474,500	70.21%		1,843,013	70.21%
OPERATING EXPENSES					
1	350,750	16.70%	16.70%	438,375	
2	275,000	13.10%	13.10%	343,875	
3	250,000	11.90%	11.90%	312,375	
4	150,000	7.14%	7.14%	187,425	
5	87,500	4.17%	4.17%	109,463	
6	75,000	3.57%	3.57%	93,713	
Total Operating Expenses	1,188,250	56.58%		1,485,225	56.58%

Step 2. Press PgDn once to move to the lower portion of the pro forma income statement.

Step 3. Repeat Step 1 for the range F47:F48 (see fig. 4.18).

> **Tip:** If a firm pays 50 percent of after-tax profits as dividends, then dividends will always equal the net-income-to-retained-earnings ratio.

The pro forma income-statement model is complete. Now evaluate how the forecasted increase in sales affects the bottom-line financial position of Calkins Brothers, Inc.

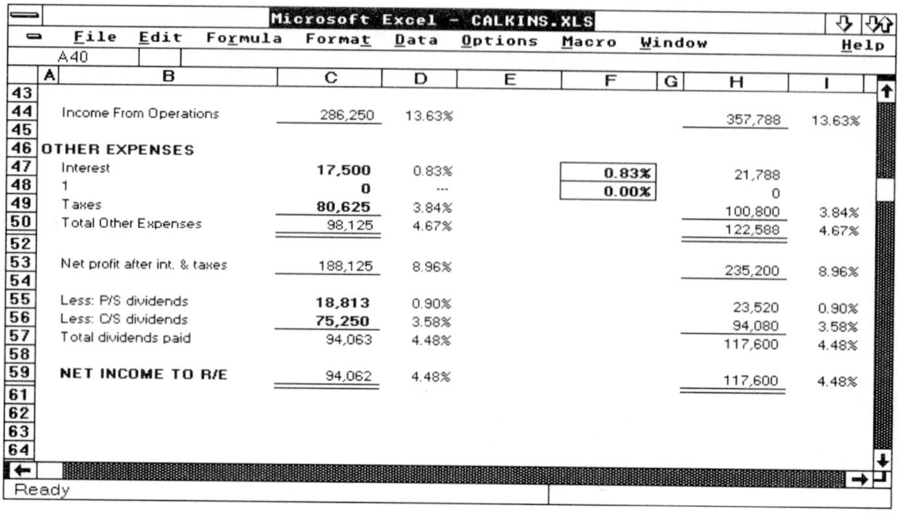

Fig. 4.18.
The pro forma income statement, section 2.

	B	C	D	E	F	G	H	I
43								
44	Income From Operations	286,250	13.63%				357,788	13.63%
45								
46	**OTHER EXPENSES**							
47	Interest	17,500	0.83%		0.83%		21,788	
48	1	0	...		0.00%		0	
49	Taxes	80,625	3.84%				100,800	3.84%
50	Total Other Expenses	98,125	4.67%				122,588	4.67%
52								
53	Net profit after int. & taxes	188,125	8.96%				235,200	8.96%
54								
55	Less: P/S dividends	18,813	0.90%				23,520	0.90%
56	Less: C/S dividends	75,250	3.58%				94,080	3.58%
57	Total dividends paid	94,063	4.48%				117,600	4.48%
58								
59	**NET INCOME TO R/E**	94,062	4.48%				117,600	4.48%

As expected, each pro forma account has remained at the same percentage of sales. This condition is expected because you assumed that the income-statement accounts would remain at the same percentage of sales. Although you increased sales by 25 percent—from $2,100,000 to $2,625,000—you maintained the percent-of-sales relationships for the rest of the income-statement accounts.

Because the pro forma sales are higher than the historical sales, the pro forma income-statement account values also are higher. In FY 1989, the net profit after interest and taxes is 8.96 percent of total sales, or $188,125. In FY 1990, this figure remains 8.96 percent of total sales but increases in value to $235,200!

It's easy to experiment with this powerful model by alternately changing the assumptions-block values and the percent-of-sales relationships among the different income-statement accounts and total forecast sales.

The Historical and Pro Forma Balance Sheet

The pro forma balance sheet also is created through the use of percent-of-sales estimates. Even though balance sheets are generally not reported in percentage terms, percent-of-sales values are included for forecast purposes. The expectation is that as sales increase, so does the need for additional assets and certain liabilities.

This pro forma model has one additional element, called an *external-funds-requirement calculation*. This value tells you the amount of cash needed to finance a growth in sales. When this amount is negative, the firm has excess cash (a negative financing need) that it may retain internally, distribute to its shareholders, or use to repay debt obligations. Figure 4.19 shows balance-sheet assets as a percentage of historical total sales.

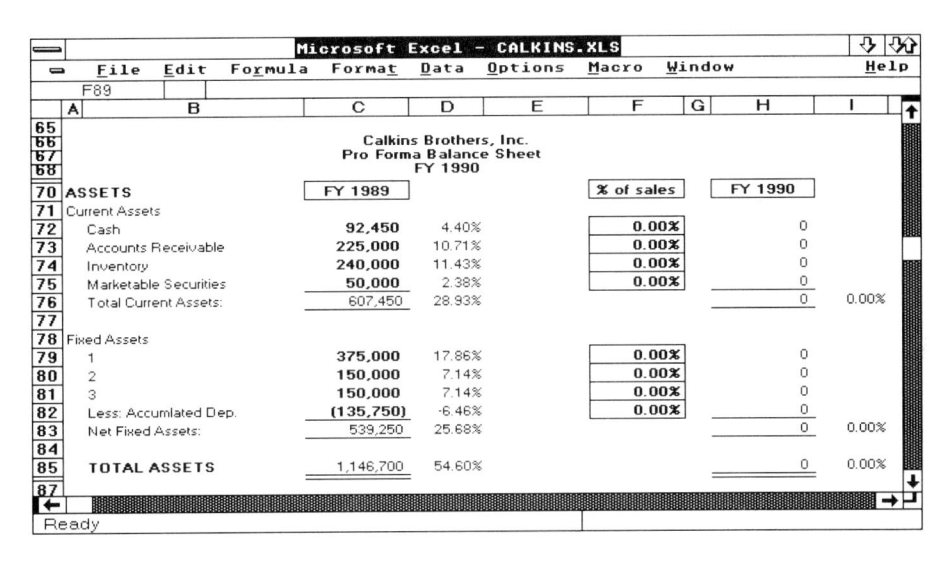

Fig. 4.19. The historical balance sheet.

> **Tip:** The values for long-term debt and common stock are recorded as constants because only Calkins' managers can change the level of the company's long-term financing.

Perform the following steps to enter the percent-of-sales forecast assumptions for the pro forma balance sheet model:

Step 1. Highlight the ranges F72:F75 and F79:F82. Reproduce FY 1989's percent values into the variable blocks in this range (see fig. 4.20).

Step 2. Press PgDn once to move to the lower portion of the pro forma balance sheet.

Step 3. Repeat Step 1 for the range F91:F94 (see fig. 4.21).

Note: Because the liabilities and owners' equity sections do not fit into one Excel window, you'll have to scroll down a few lines to view the last line of the balance sheet.

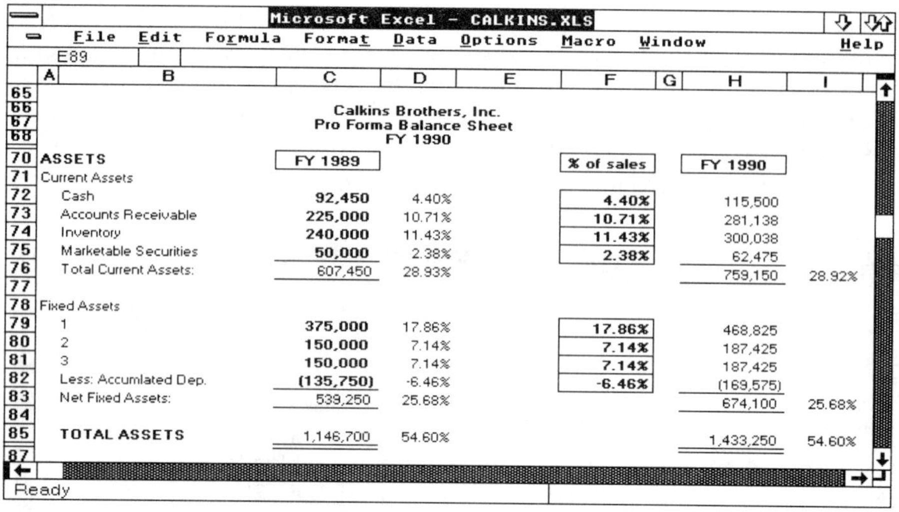

Microsoft Excel - CALKINS.XLS

File Edit Formula Format Data Options Macro Window Help

E89

Row	A/B	C	D	E	F	G	H	I
65								
66		Calkins Brothers, Inc.						
67		Pro Forma Balance Sheet						
68		FY 1990						
70	ASSETS	FY 1989			% of sales		FY 1990	
71	Current Assets							
72	Cash	92,450	4.40%		4.40%		115,500	
73	Accounts Receivable	225,000	10.71%		10.71%		281,138	
74	Inventory	240,000	11.43%		11.43%		300,038	
75	Marketable Securities	50,000	2.38%		2.38%		62,475	
76	Total Current Assets:	607,450	28.93%				759,150	28.92%
77								
78	Fixed Assets							
79	1	375,000	17.86%		17.86%		468,825	
80	2	150,000	7.14%		7.14%		187,425	
81	3	150,000	7.14%		7.14%		187,425	
82	Less: Accumlated Dep.	(135,750)	-6.46%		-6.46%		(169,575)	
83	Net Fixed Assets:	539,250	25.68%				674,100	25.68%
84								
85	TOTAL ASSETS	1,146,700	54.60%				1,433,250	54.60%
87								

Ready

Fig. 4.20. The pro forma balance sheet, section 1.

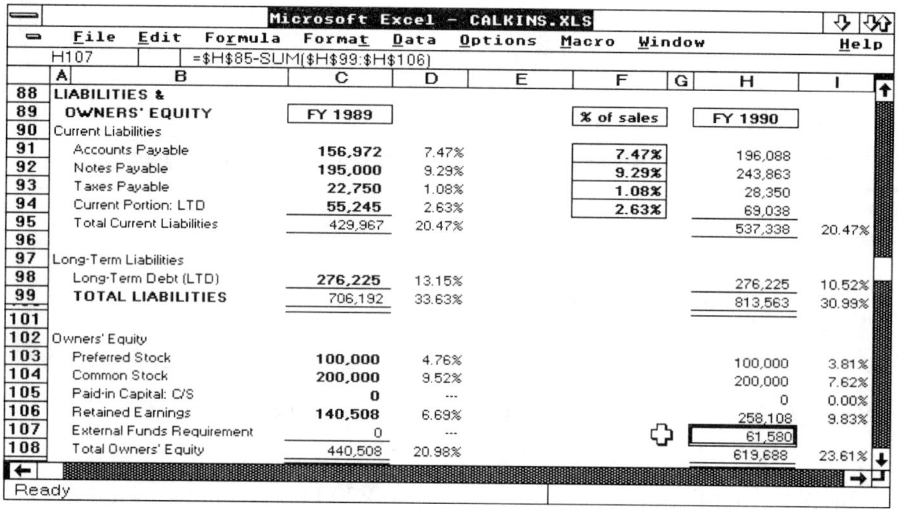

Microsoft Excel - CALKINS.XLS

File Edit Formula Format Data Options Macro Window Help

H107 =$H$85-SUM($H$99:$H$106)

Row	A/B	C	D	E	F	G	H	I
88	LIABILITIES &							
89	OWNERS' EQUITY	FY 1989			% of sales		FY 1990	
90	Current Liabilities							
91	Accounts Payable	156,972	7.47%		7.47%		196,088	
92	Notes Payable	195,000	9.29%		9.29%		243,863	
93	Taxes Payable	22,750	1.08%		1.08%		28,350	
94	Current Portion: LTD	55,245	2.63%		2.63%		69,038	
95	Total Current Liabilities	429,967	20.47%				537,338	20.47%
96								
97	Long-Term Liabilities							
98	Long-Term Debt (LTD)	276,225	13.15%				276,225	10.52%
99	TOTAL LIABILITIES	706,192	33.63%				813,563	30.99%
101								
102	Owners' Equity							
103	Preferred Stock	100,000	4.76%				100,000	3.81%
104	Common Stock	200,000	9.52%				200,000	7.62%
105	Paid-in Capital: C/S	0	---				0	0.00%
106	Retained Earnings	140,508	6.69%				258,108	9.83%
107	External Funds Requirement	0	---				61,580	
108	Total Owners' Equity	440,508	20.98%				619,688	23.61%

Ready

Fig. 4.21. The pro forma balance sheet, section 2.

Take a moment to review your work so far. As you well know, on a balance sheet, total assets must always equal total liabilities plus equity.

The pro forma balance-sheet model always proves this basic accounting equation because of the special external-funds-requirement calculation. This figure does not normally appear on a company's balance sheet; however, on a pro forma balance sheet, this figure indicates whether the firm requires additional funds to meet its growth objectives.

How do you know what these financing needs are? Remember the assumption that assets would grow with sales. The financing for this growth in assets can come from three sources: company cash, borrowed funds, and stockholder investment. When the firm uses all its cash (when the firm is at its minimum cash balance), it must look to banks and investors to help finance its growth.

Table 4.1 summarizes how you've tied the growth in total assets and current liabilities to the anticipated 25 percent growth in sales. Because sales grew by 25 percent, assets and the sum of liabilities and equity should also grow by 25 percent.

Table 4.1
The Effect of the Expected Increase in Sales on the Pro Forma Balance Sheet

	Historical FY 1989	*Pro Forma FY 1990*	*% growth*
Sales	2,100,000	2,625,000	25%
Total Assets	1,146,700	1,433,250	25%
Total CL	429,967	537,338	25%

So far, you have proved that assets and current liabilities have grown by 25 percent. Now review the formulas that balance total assets with total liabilities plus equity.

First of all, you may have noticed that long-term debt and the equity accounts do not have variable blocks. In the pro forma balance sheet, cell H98 and the cells in the range H103:H105 contain cell references to the range E14:E17 found in the assumptions section of the pro forma model. Remember, management must take definitive steps to alter these account values. If you want to raise debt or forecast an inflow of equity financing, enter the dollar values in the assumptions section of the pro forma model.

Cell H106 contains a formula that calculates FY 1990's retained earnings by adding FY 1990's pro forma net income to FY 1989's retained earnings.

Figure 4.21 displays the formula that determines the required total financing. The formula in cell H107 tells Excel to subtract the sum of total current liabilities, long-term debt, preferred stock, common stock, paid-in capital, and retained earnings from total assets.

If the resulting value is positive, the firm needs additional financing. Figure 4.21 illustrates that Calkins needs $61,580 to fund the growth in its assets. As previously mentioned, this cash can come from investors or lenders, or it can come from the company's own cash—as long as the company doesn't fall below management's established minimum cash balance.

If the value in cell H107 is negative, the firm has excess funds after paying for its growth in assets. The excess funds can be used to repay debt, repurchase stock, or pay the stockholders extra dividends.

The Historical and Pro Forma Ratio Analysis

Figures 4.22, 4.23, and 4.24 display the pro forma ratio-analysis report. Most of the data is automatically reproduced from the historical and pro forma income statements and balance sheets. This report requires four pieces of data from you for the completion of the EQUITY section:

- The beginning stock price
- The forecast ending stock price
- The beginning common stock shares outstanding
- The forecast ending common stock shares outstanding

Fig. 4.22.
Historical and pro forma financial ratios, section 1.

	FY 1989	FY 1990
LIQUIDITY		
Current ratio	1.41	1.41
Quick ratio	0.85	0.85
Net working capital/Sales	8.45%	8.45%
ACTIVITY		
A/R turnover	9.33	9.34
Inventory turnover	2.61	2.61
Fixed asset turnover	3.89	3.89
Total asset turnover	1.83	1.83
Average collection period	39.11	39.09
Average payment period	114.50	114.41

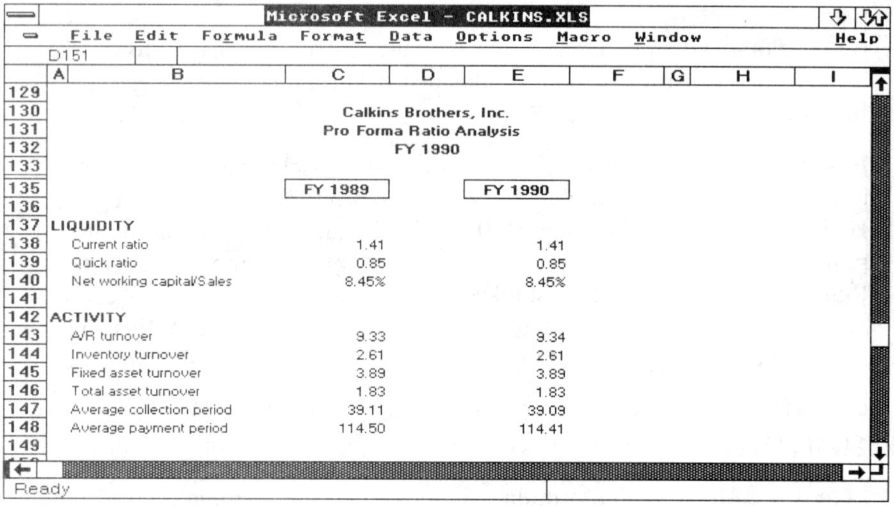

Calkins Brothers, Inc.
Pro Forma Ratio Analysis
FY 1990

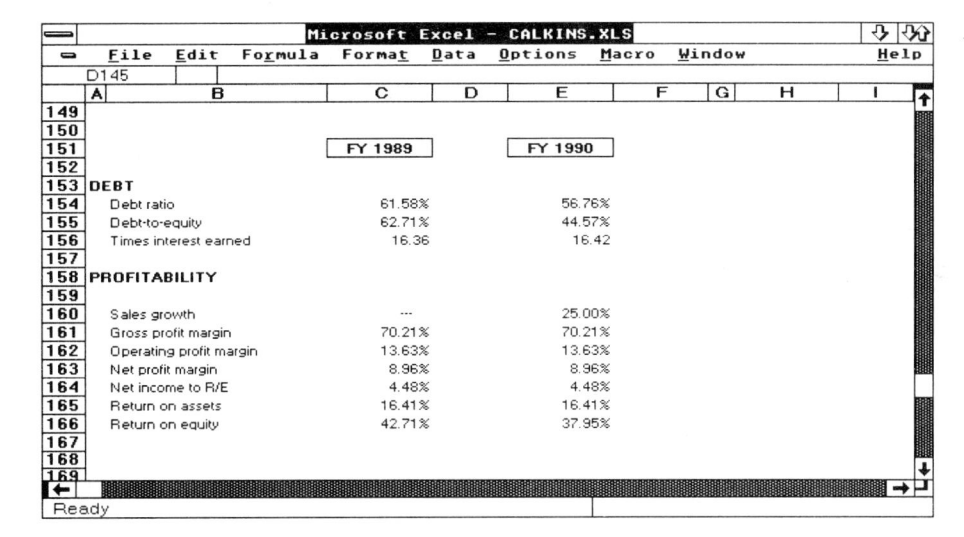

Fig. 4.23.
Historical and pro forma financial ratios, section 2.

	FY 1989	FY 1990
DEBT		
Debt ratio	61.58%	56.76%
Debt-to-equity	62.71%	44.57%
Times interest earned	16.36	16.42
PROFITABILITY		
Sales growth	...	25.00%
Gross profit margin	70.21%	70.21%
Operating profit margin	13.63%	13.63%
Net profit margin	8.96%	8.96%
Net income to R/E	4.48%	4.48%
Return on assets	16.41%	16.41%
Return on equity	42.71%	37.95%

Fig. 4.24.
Historical and pro forma financial ratios, section 3.

	FY 1989	FY 1990
EQUITY		
C/S outstanding ======>	100,000	100,000
C/S market price ======>	$32.25	$34.75
Earnings per share (eps)	$1.69	$2.12
Price/earnings (P/E) ratio	19.05	16.42

Maintaining Your Historical Records (HISTORY.XLS)

The next model illustrates how you can give your financial statements a polished, presentation-quality look. The sample statements shown in figures 4.25 through 4.28 are stored in a file called HISTORY.XLS.

Fig. 4.25.
Donnelly's 1989 income statement: sales and cost-of-goods-sold section.

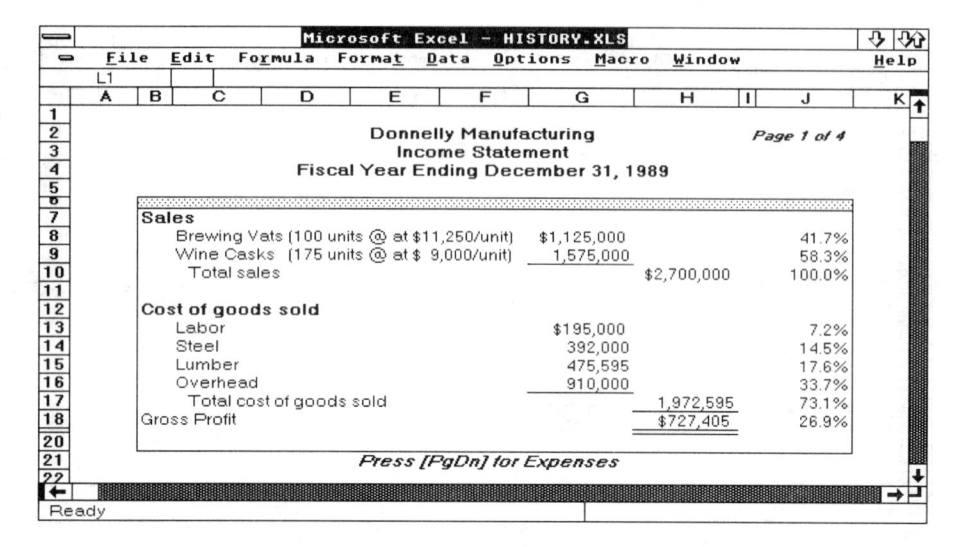

```
┌─────────────────────────────────────────────────────────────┐
│              Microsoft Excel - HISTORY.XLS                  │
│  File  Edit  Formula  Format  Data  Options  Macro  Window  Help │
│  L1                                                          │
│    A  B   C      D         E        F       G      H  I  J  K │
│  1                                                           │
│  2              Donnelly Manufacturing          Page 1 of 4  │
│  3                Income Statement                           │
│  4          Fiscal Year Ending December 31, 1989             │
│  5                                                           │
│  7   Sales                                                   │
│  8     Brewing Vats (100 units @ at $11,250/unit) $1,125,000  41.7% │
│  9     Wine Casks  (175 units @ at $ 9,000/unit)  1,575,000  58.3% │
│ 10       Total sales                             $2,700,000  100.0% │
│ 12   Cost of goods sold                                      │
│ 13     Labor                                      $195,000    7.2% │
│ 14     Steel                                       392,000   14.5% │
│ 15     Lumber                                      475,595   17.6% │
│ 16     Overhead                                    910,000   33.7% │
│ 17       Total cost of goods sold                1,972,595   73.1% │
│ 18   Gross Profit                                 $727,405   26.9% │
│ 20                                                           │
│ 21            Press [PgDn] for Expenses                      │
│  Ready                                                       │
└─────────────────────────────────────────────────────────────┘
```

Fig. 4.26.
Donnelly's 1989 income statement: expenses and net-income section.

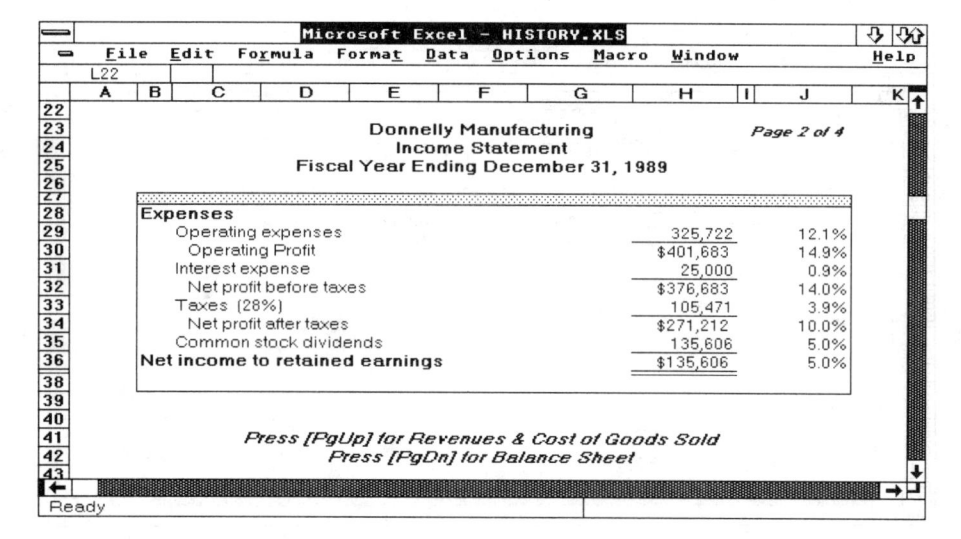

```
┌─────────────────────────────────────────────────────────────┐
│              Microsoft Excel - HISTORY.XLS                  │
│  File  Edit  Formula  Format  Data  Options  Macro  Window  Help │
│  L22                                                         │
│    A  B   C      D         E        F       G      H  I  J  K │
│ 22                                                           │
│ 23              Donnelly Manufacturing          Page 2 of 4  │
│ 24                Income Statement                           │
│ 25          Fiscal Year Ending December 31, 1989             │
│ 28   Expenses                                                │
│ 29     Operating expenses                         325,722   12.1% │
│ 30       Operating Profit                        $401,683   14.9% │
│ 31     Interest expense                            25,000    0.9% │
│ 32       Net profit before taxes                 $376,683   14.0% │
│ 33     Taxes (28%)                                105,471    3.9% │
│ 34       Net profit after taxes                  $271,212   10.0% │
│ 35     Common stock dividends                     135,606    5.0% │
│ 36   Net income to retained earnings             $135,606    5.0% │
│ 41       Press [PgUp] for Revenues & Cost of Goods Sold      │
│ 42             Press [PgDn] for Balance Sheet                │
│  Ready                                                       │
└─────────────────────────────────────────────────────────────┘
```

For this type of multiple-statement presentation, you can use three formatting tricks to make the viewer of the presentation feel that he is paging through an annual report:

1. When you create multiple window displays, always divide the display at a logical location. In this case, the income statement is separated into two major parts: a sales/cost-of-goods-sold section and an expenses/net-income section.

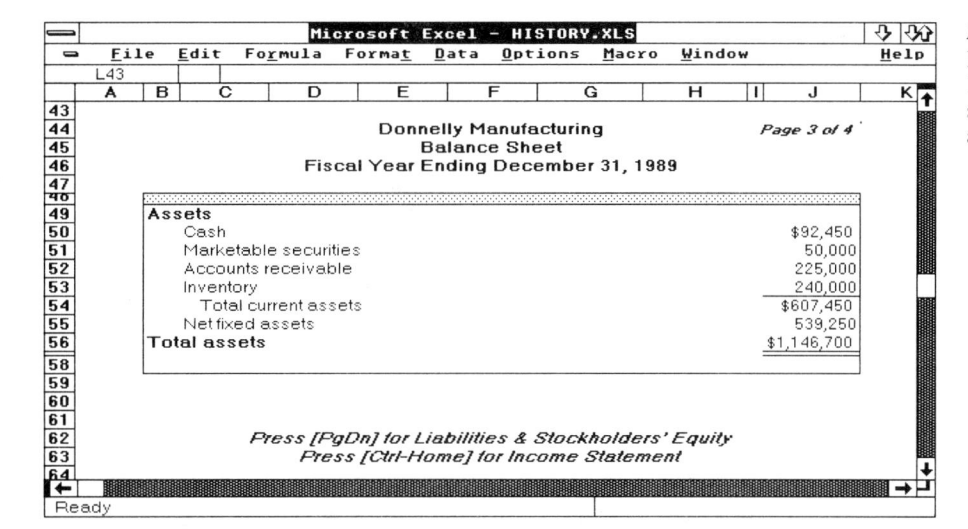

Fig. 4.27. Donnelly's 1989 balance sheet: total assets section.

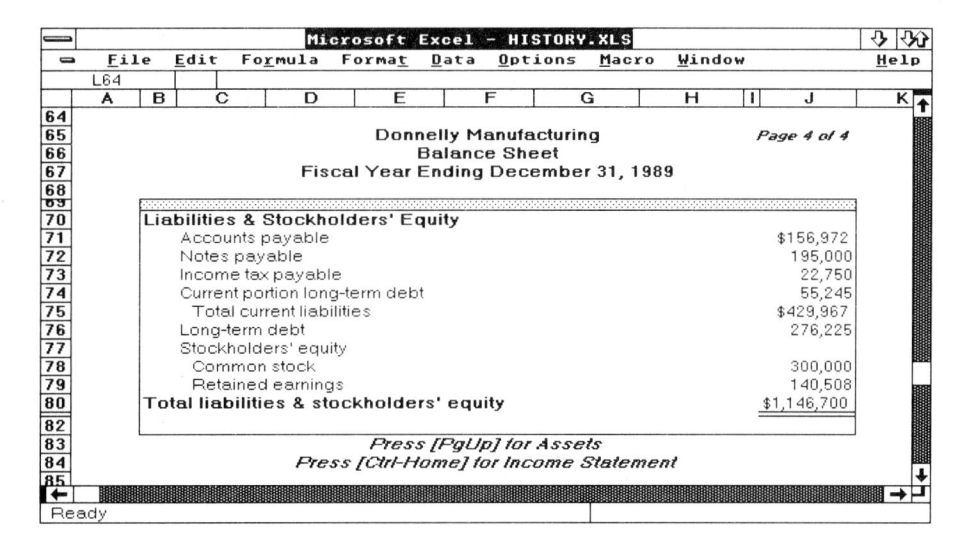

```
Donnelly Manufacturing                    Page 3 of 4
                Balance Sheet
        Fiscal Year Ending December 31, 1989

Assets
    Cash                                        $92,450
    Marketable securities                        50,000
    Accounts receivable                         225,000
    Inventory                                   240,000
       Total current assets                    $607,450
    Net fixed assets                            539,250
Total assets                                 $1,146,700


        Press [PgDn] for Liabilities & Stockholders' Equity
              Press [Ctrl-Home] for Income Statement
```

Fig. 4.28. Donnelly's 1989 balance sheet: total liabilities and stockholders' equity section.

```
Donnelly Manufacturing                    Page 4 of 4
                Balance Sheet
        Fiscal Year Ending December 31, 1989

Liabilities & Stockholders' Equity
    Accounts payable                           $156,972
    Notes payable                               195,000
    Income tax payable                           22,750
    Current portion long-term debt               55,245
       Total current liabilities               $429,967
    Long-term debt                              276,225
    Stockholders' equity
       Common stock                             300,000
       Retained earnings                        140,508
Total liabilities & stockholders' equity     $1,146,700

              Press [PgUp] for Assets
           Press [Ctrl-Home] for Income Statement
```

2. Add screen directions to show a viewer how to move through your report. The page number appears in the upper right portion of the screen. A screen direction in the bottom center portion of the screen tells the viewer how to move to the next part of the report.

3. Be creative when you format your report displays. Using border outlines and font enhancements and altering the row heights has created an effective presentation of Donnelly's financial statements.

Using Breakeven Analysis (BREAKEVN.XLW)

Companies in the business of manufacturing goods rely on forecasts to pinpoint how many units of product X they must sell in order to break even. This type of financial forecast is often used as one of several inputs to the sales-forecasting process. It also provides production management with valuable data that helps them schedule efficient production runs.

The final model in this chapter is an automated forecasting model that uses a worksheet, macro, and chart to produce a presentation-quality breakeven analysis report. To calculate a breakeven point for any manufactured product, you need to know the sales price per unit, the fixed operating costs per period, and the variable operating costs per unit.

The breakeven model is called BREAKEVN.XLW. Files with the XLW extension are called *workspace* files. You can store several documents in one workspace. To create an Excel workspace, load all the documents into Excel, select the File menu, and choose Save Workspace. When you open a workspace, Excel simultaneously loads all the workspace documents.

The BREAKEVN.XLW model follows the same procedural conventions as do the previous models in this chapter. Data input areas are identified by an outlined box and use a boldfaced font. The input screen for this model appears on the BREAKEVN.XLS worksheet. This document is protected through the use of Options Protect Document, so you may enter data only into the predesignated input cells.

The breakeven model requires four inputs (see fig. 4.29):

- Sales price per unit (P)
- Fixed operating cost per period (FC)
- Variable operating cost per unit (VC)
- Graph-scale variance factor (V)

To use this model, you need only enter the first three pieces of data. The fourth item—the graph-scale variance factor—uses your data to help control the way Excel creates a graph.

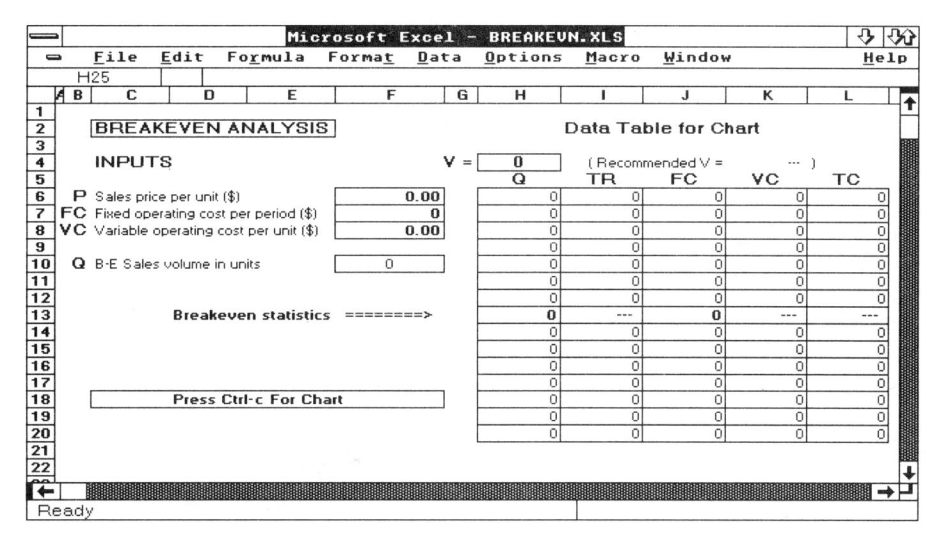

Fig. 4.29.
The breakeven
analysis model.

Creating a Data Table

The best way to analyze your firm's production potential is to display the results of your breakeven analysis as part of a whole set of production possibilities—a possibilities frontier, if you will.

You can easily use a data table to create a chart that displays a wide range of possible outcomes. The data table in figure 4.29 contains five elements:

- Quantity produced (Q)
- Total revenue (TR)
- Fixed cost (FC)
- Variable cost (VC)
- Total cost (TC)

This data table has room for 15 different production levels. The breakeven statistics appear in the eighth row (the middle row). The remaining numbers in this table come from Excel formulas residing in the individual cells. These formulas create a scenario of equivalently increasing and decreasing production quantities above and below your breakeven data.

Enter some sample data to see how this model works. Stefan E. Blackwell, GmbH (SEB), an international manufacturer of special memory chips for medical computer expansion boards, historically produces 125 percent of its breakeven quantity. Recently an accounting analysis revealed that SEB's fixed operating costs have risen by 5 percent since the last production run.

Before recalibrating the machinery, production management needs to establish a new breakeven production level.

To create a new breakeven analysis for SEB, complete the following steps:

Step 1. Load BREAKEVN.XLW into Excel.

Step 2. Highlight the range F6:F8 and enter the values **12.95**, **10000**, and **1.95** (see fig. 4.30).

> Tip: Remember that by definition, fixed costs remain the same during any single period, regardless of the production level.

Fig. 4.30.
Entering data into the model.

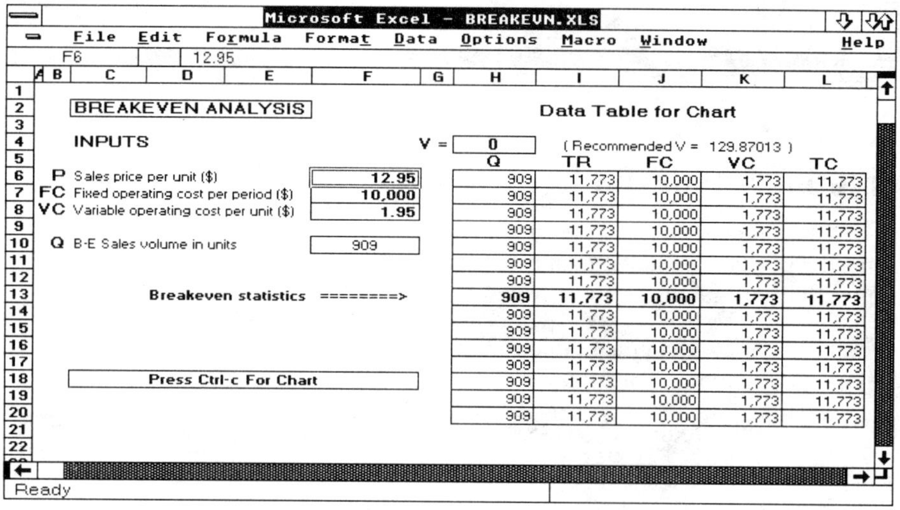

Excel calculates the new breakeven level at 909 units per period. Notice that the values within the breakeven production levels Q, TR, FC, VC, and FC are the same. The reason is that the graph-scaling variance factor (V) is 0. The model computes its own recommended V value, but you may enter any value you want. Remember, though, that the purpose of the variance factor is to create a production distribution that is ideal for graphing.

Step 3. Highlight cell H4 and enter the value **129.87013** (see fig. 4.31).

Note: The formatting conventions used in this model automatically round off data. Always enter the full number and let Excel round it for you.

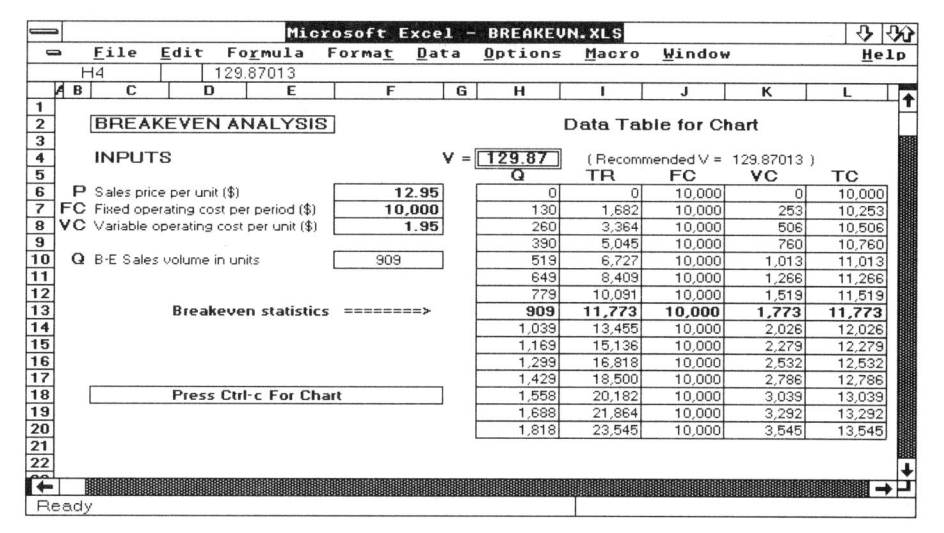

Using Financial Spreadsheets To Promote Your Standing **123**

Fig. 4.31.
Entering the recommended variance to create the ideal graphing distribution.

Looking at the data table, you will notice two things: The lowest value of Q is 0—an ideal starting point for any graph. More important, notice that when Q equals 0, TR and VC equal 0, and FC and TC equal 10,000. This makes sense, because a firm has fixed costs—and therefore total costs—even when it is not manufacturing anything.

Using a Chart-Creating Macro

Did you notice on the breakeven analysis worksheet the screen direction "Press Ctrl-c For Chart"? Pressing Ctrl-c activates a macro that automatically creates a chart of the breakeven statistics that appear in the data table. Excel loaded this macro when you selected BREAKEVN.XLW. Once Excel finishes building the chart, it automatically asks whether you want to save the chart. To create a breakeven analysis chart of the data shown in figure 4.31, simply press Ctrl-c. Figure 4.32 shows the chart.

Each time you enter new data into the model, press Ctrl-c; the breakeven macro will create a chart reflecting the new results from the data table.

This chart plots each of the variables appearing in the data table. Another useful chart would plot total revenues (TR) and total costs (TC) against quantity (Q). You can create such a chart by altering the selection criteria in the macro or by creating your own macro with Excel's Recorder. In either case, highlight only the TR, TC, and Q data ranges from the data table before creating the chart.

Excel Business Applications: IBM Version

Fig. 4.32.
The breakeven analysis chart.

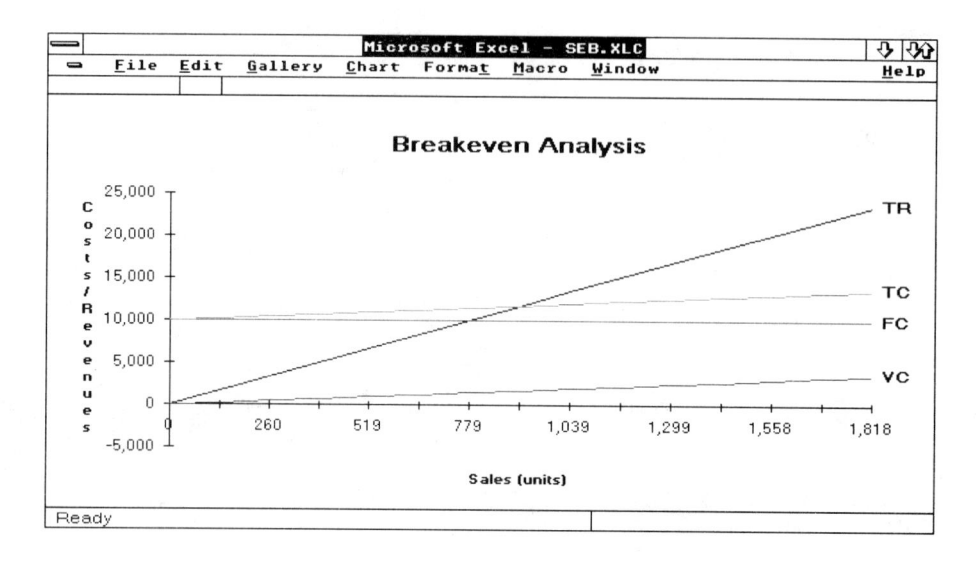

```
                  Microsoft Excel - SEB.XLC
  File   Edit   Gallery   Chart   Format   Macro   Window                Help

                         Breakeven Analysis

    25,000                                                          TR
  C
  o  20,000
  s
  t
  s  15,000                                                         TC
  /
  R  10,000                                                         FC
  e
  v   5,000
  e
  n      0                                                          VC
  u       0    260    519    779   1,039   1,299   1,558   1,818
  e   -5,000
  s
                              Sales (units)

Ready
```

The benefit of this type of presentation is that you can visually inspect where breakeven production occurs. In addition, you can get a better feel for the relationship between costs and revenues by looking at the chart (see fig. 4.33).

Fig. 4.33.
The breakeven analysis macro.

	A
1	Breakeven Chart Macro
2	=ACTIVATE("BREAKEVN.XLS")
3	=SELECT("R6C9:R20C12")
4	=NEW(2)
5	=SELECT("S1P12")
6	=FORMULA("=SERIES(,'BREAKEVN.XLS'!R6C8:R20C8,'BREAKEVN.XLS'!R6C9:R20C9,1)")
7	=SELECT("Axis 2")
8	=SCALE(1,1,21,FALSE,FALSE,FALSE)
9	=SCALE(1,2,1,FALSE,FALSE,FALSE)
10	=ATTACH.TEXT(1)
11	=FORMULA("=""Breakeven Analysis""")
12	=FORMAT.FONT(0,1,FALSE,"Helv",14,TRUE,FALSE,FALSE,FALSE)
13	=SELECT("Axis 1")
14	=ATTACH.TEXT(2)
15	=FORMULA("=""Costs/Revenues""")
16	=FORMAT.TEXT(2,2,TRUE,FALSE,TRUE,FALSE,FALSE)
17	=FORMAT.FONT(0,1,FALSE,"Helv",8,TRUE,FALSE,FALSE,FALSE)
18	=SELECT("Axis 2")
19	=ATTACH.TEXT(3)
20	=FORMULA("=""Sales (units)""")
21	=FORMAT.FONT(0,1,FALSE,"Helv",8,TRUE,FALSE,FALSE,FALSE)
22	=SELECT("S1P15")
23	=ATTACH.TEXT(4,1,15)
24	=FORMULA("=""TR""")
25	=FORMAT.FONT(0,1,FALSE,"Helv",10,TRUE,FALSE,FALSE,FALSE)
26	=SELECT("S4P15")
27	=ATTACH.TEXT(4,4,15)
28	=FORMULA("=""TC""")
29	=FORMAT.FONT(0,1,FALSE,"Helv",10,TRUE,FALSE,FALSE,FALSE)
30	=SELECT("")
31	=SELECT("S3P15")
32	=ATTACH.TEXT(4,3,15)
33	=FORMULA("=""VC""")
34	=FORMAT.FONT(0,1,FALSE,"Helv",10,TRUE,FALSE,FALSE,FALSE)
35	=SELECT("S2P15")
36	=ATTACH.TEXT(4,2,15)
37	=FORMULA("=""FC""")
38	=FORMAT.FONT(0,1,FALSE,"Helv",10,TRUE,FALSE,FALSE,FALSE)
39	=SELECT("")
40	=SAVE.AS?()
41	=RETURN()

Using Excel Workspaces

When you create several dependent documents—such as the worksheet, macro, and chart in this example—you can simplify the steps required to reload all three documents.

To do so, select the File menu and choose Save Workspace. It's a good idea to pick a workspace name that is similar to the workspace documents. The breakeven analysis documents are saved in a workspace called BREAKEVN.XLW.

To load all workspace documents at once, select Open from the File menu, highlight the workspace name, and click OK (see fig. 4.34).

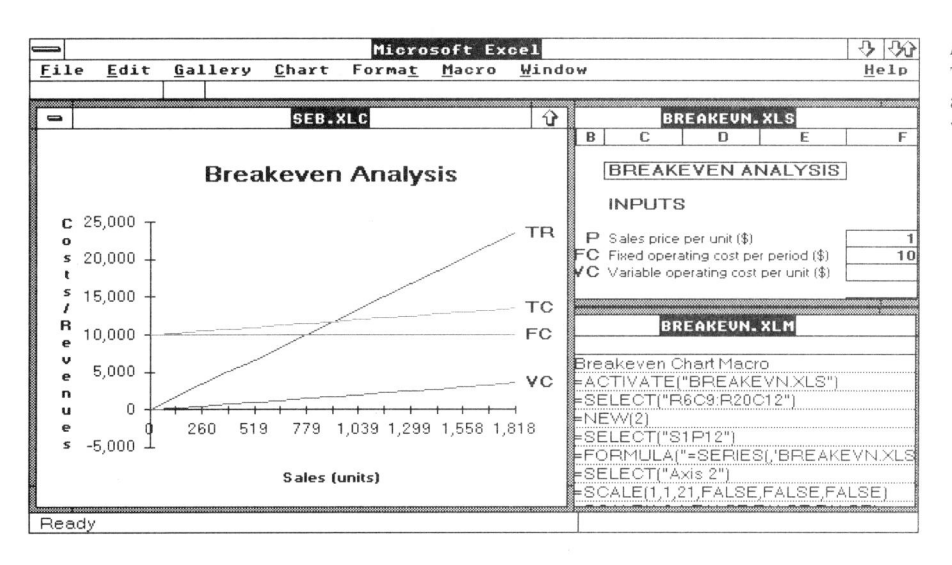

Fig. 4.34. The breakeven analysis workspace.

Summary

This chapter has set the tone of things to come: ready-to-run models that require only your data input. So far, the material covered has been of varying levels of complexity. If you are completely lost with regard to using Excel, you should probably refer to the reference manuals that come with the program.

At this point, you should be well versed in the following topics:

- Excel terminology
- The Excel concept
- Spreadsheet-building techniques
- Tips and tricks for enhancing the appearance of your models
- The use and modification of existing Excel models

The remainder of this book is dedicated to providing you with ready-to-use Excel business models. Use the same common-sense approach for modifying these models that was presented in this chapter.

In Chapter 5 you will learn how easy it is to manage your financial assets and investments by using Excel models. The topics covered are broad, ranging from the time value of money to examining the risk and return tradeoffs in the capital asset pricing of model (CAPM).

5

Performing Accurate Asset and Investment Analysis

So far, this book has taken a primarily broad approach in looking at your firm's financial position. The business-checkbook, income-statement, balance-sheet, and ratio-analysis reports are integral to the financial management of your firm. But note that each of these reports relies on your ability to gather specific accounting data. An income statement and balance sheet, for example, require data from subsidiary journals and ledgers in order to be complete. And the ratio report, of course, is utterly useless without completed summary data from the income statement and balance sheet. As you've seen, once you have all the specific numbers and figures together, you have many good ways to manipulate this data to create different presentations of your firm's financial standing.

But what happens when you put all this information together only to discover that you're operating at a loss, or that you're in a negative cash-flow position, or that you're earning only a 2 percent return on your firm's assets? All business managers face these issues at one time or another, but the best business managers do something about them on a daily basis. The important thing is to ensure that you're always in the position to respond before it's too late.

How? By regularly reviewing and evaluating the worth of your business assets and investments, a process that ensures that you plan, budget, save, and invest all your capital and reserves wisely. In this chapter you will discover that ongoing asset and investment analysis is a profitable exercise when you use Excel. This chapter is divided into four major sections: asset management, the time value of money, risk and return analysis, and techniques for cash-flow and investment valuation. As you review these major concepts, you will learn how to apply this chapter's models to your own business environment.

The following are items you should consider before using your *Excel Business Applications* spreadsheet models:

1. Make a backup copy of the models disk and store that backup in a safe place.
2. Save all your modified models under a unique file name so that you can quickly revert to the generic model if necessary. Don't ignore this recommendation! You'll need the original format if you accidentally erase a modified model file.
3. If you have a hard disk drive, create a new subdirectory in Excel and load the models into this subdirectory. Then store the disk.
4. Each model has been saved in Options Protect Document mode. This way, you can enter data only into worksheet cells that have been previously unlocked with the Format Cell Protection command. When Protect Document mode is enabled, these cells appear boldfaced and, in certain cases, underlined.

   If you want to modify DUPONT.XLS's structure, for example, first save the generic model under a new name. To unprotect the worksheet so that you can change descriptions and titles, select Options Unprotect Document.
5. The models in this chapter use macros containing commands that use the name of the spreadsheet file. If you want to rename any of the models in this chapter, you will also need to edit any references to the spreadsheet file found in the macro program code (more on this later).
6. Most of this chapter's models are saved in unique workspaces. A workspace contains the spreadsheet, a macro, and a chart. For example, the depreciation model is composed of the following files:

    DEPRECI8.XLS (spreadsheet)

    DEPRECI8.XLM (macro)

    DEPRECI8.XLC (chart)

    DEPRECI8.XLW (workspace file name)

If you want to follow the chapter examples, load a model by using the workspace file names. Otherwise, you can load the spreadsheet XLS and macro XLM files in order for each model to be operable.

Understanding Asset Management

The balance sheet of the typical business lists both liquid and fixed assets. Liquid assets such as marketable securities, inventory, and receivables can be quickly converted into cash, whereas fixed assets are usually employed to serve the firm's ongoing operations. Businesses have the right to depreciate fixed assets by using methods that are in accordance with current tax laws. Choosing a depreciation method is important both for small and large privately held firms, because to a certain extent, depreciation expenses enable you to control your firm's income-tax burden. Publicly traded firms often shape the look of their balance sheet by using one depreciation method for stockholder reporting (usually accelerated cost recovery) and another method for internal-management purposes.

Both models in this section help you manage and evaluate the performance of your fixed and liquid assets.

Model 1: The DuPont Method (DUPONT.XLS)

The DuPont method of analysis combines data from your income statement and balance sheet to produce two measures of profitability: return on investment in assets (ROI) and return on equity (ROE). These two figures also can be found on any good ratio-analysis report but usually are buried among several other ratios. The DuPont method emphasizes the ROI and ROE ratios because they clearly indicate your firm's capability to manage its assets.

The DuPont method establishes the relationship among assets, liabilities, and equity in the following manner:

Return on Investment in Assets (ROI)

$$\text{Net Profit Margin} = \frac{\text{Net Profit after Taxes}}{\text{Revenues}}$$

$$\text{Total Asset Turnover} = \frac{\text{Revenues}}{\text{Total Assets}}$$

ROI = Net Profit Margin * Total Asset Turnover

Return on Equity (ROE)

$$\text{Equity Multiplier} = \frac{\text{Total Assets}}{\text{Stockholders' Equity}}$$

ROE = ROI * Equity Multiplier

Using the DUPONT.XLS Model

The DuPont model has two separate input blocks. The first block, pictured in figure 5.1, retains summary data from your income statement and balance sheet for the first six months of an operating year. Press Ctrl-PgDn to move to the second input screen, where you enter the same summary data for the final six months of an operating year.

Fig. 5.1.
DuPont input screen #1.

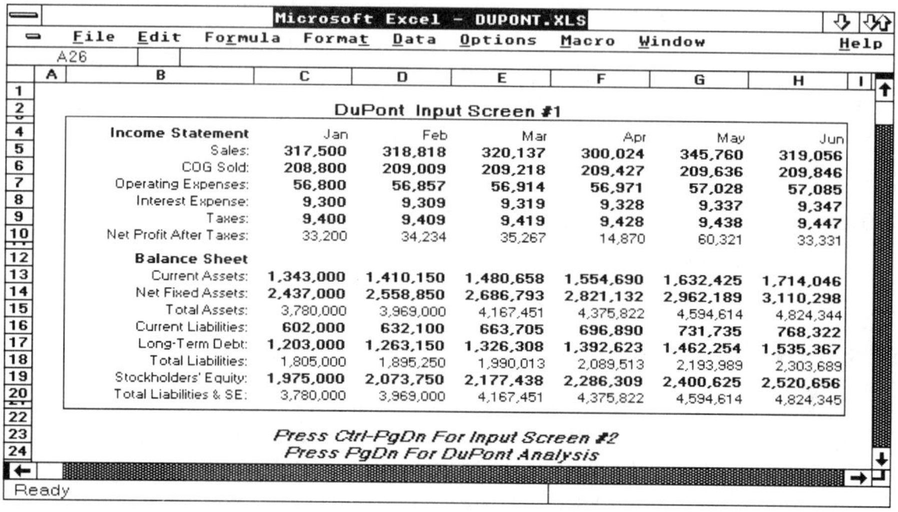

Income Statement	Jan	Feb	Mar	Apr	May	Jun
Sales:	317,500	318,818	320,137	300,024	345,760	319,056
COG Sold:	208,800	209,009	209,218	209,427	209,636	209,846
Operating Expenses:	56,800	56,857	56,914	56,971	57,028	57,085
Interest Expense:	9,300	9,309	9,319	9,328	9,337	9,347
Taxes:	9,400	9,409	9,419	9,428	9,438	9,447
Net Profit After Taxes:	33,200	34,234	35,267	14,870	60,321	33,331
Balance Sheet						
Current Assets:	1,343,000	1,410,150	1,480,658	1,554,690	1,632,425	1,714,046
Net Fixed Assets:	2,437,000	2,558,850	2,686,793	2,821,132	2,962,189	3,110,298
Total Assets:	3,780,000	3,969,000	4,167,451	4,375,822	4,594,614	4,824,344
Current Liabilities:	602,000	632,100	663,705	696,890	731,735	768,322
Long-Term Debt:	1,203,000	1,263,150	1,326,308	1,392,623	1,462,254	1,535,367
Total Liabilities:	1,805,000	1,895,250	1,990,013	2,089,513	2,193,989	2,303,689
Stockholders' Equity:	1,975,000	2,073,750	2,177,438	2,286,309	2,400,625	2,520,656
Total Liabilities & SE:	3,780,000	3,969,000	4,167,451	4,375,822	4,594,614	4,824,345

Press Ctrl-PgDn For Input Screen #2
Press PgDn For DuPont Analysis

When you are looking at input screen #1, press PgDn once to move to DuPont analysis screen #1. The analysis screen displays each of the five inputs to the DuPont analysis, as shown in figure 5.2. To move to DuPont analysis screen #2, just press Ctrl-PgDn once.

Fig. 5.2.
DuPont analysis screen #1.

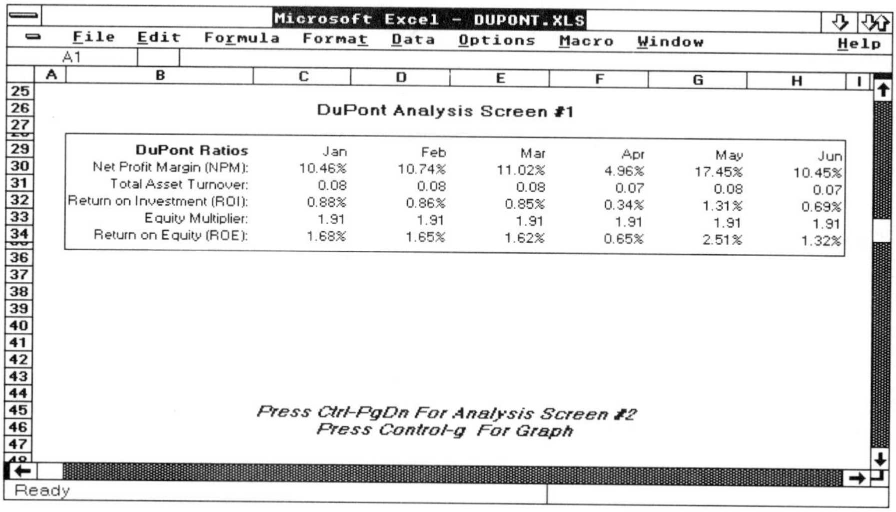

DuPont Analysis Screen #1

DuPont Ratios	Jan	Feb	Mar	Apr	May	Jun
Net Profit Margin (NPM):	10.46%	10.74%	11.02%	4.96%	17.45%	10.45%
Total Asset Turnover:	0.08	0.08	0.08	0.07	0.08	0.07
Return on Investment (ROI):	0.88%	0.86%	0.85%	0.34%	1.31%	0.69%
Equity Multiplier:	1.91	1.91	1.91	1.91	1.91	1.91
Return on Equity (ROE):	1.68%	1.65%	1.62%	0.65%	2.51%	1.32%

Press Ctrl-PgDn For Analysis Screen #2
Press Control-g For Graph

The model in figure 5.3 contains data for the final six months of an operating year. The YTD data in column R sums the data from both the input screens. Notice that only the input cell areas appear underlined and boldfaced. The remaining cells contain formulas that perform calculations on your financial-statement data.

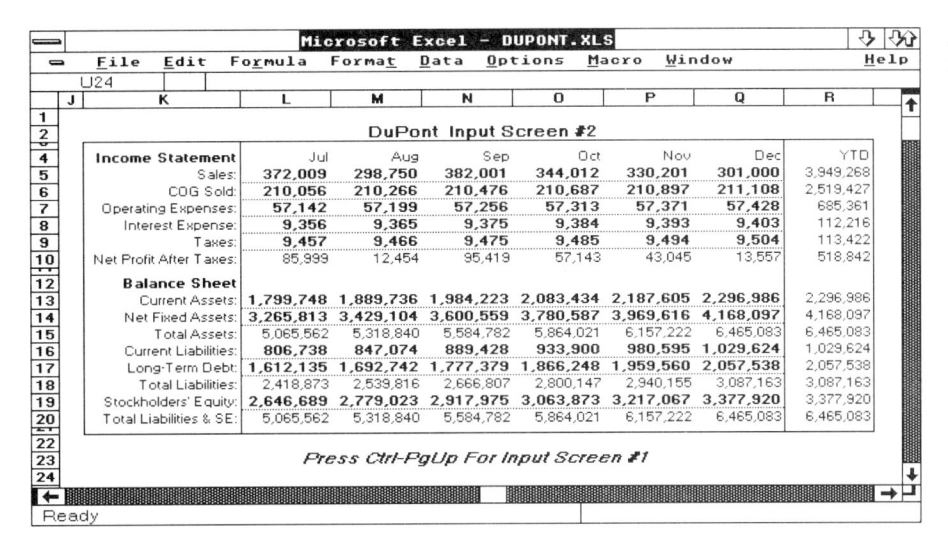

Fig. 5.3. Entering data into input screen #2.

This model automatically performs the DuPont analysis once you finish entering all the required financial data. Figure 5.4 shows the finished view of the second DuPont analysis screen. As you can see, at the end of the year ROI equals 8.03 percent, and ROE equals 15.36 percent.

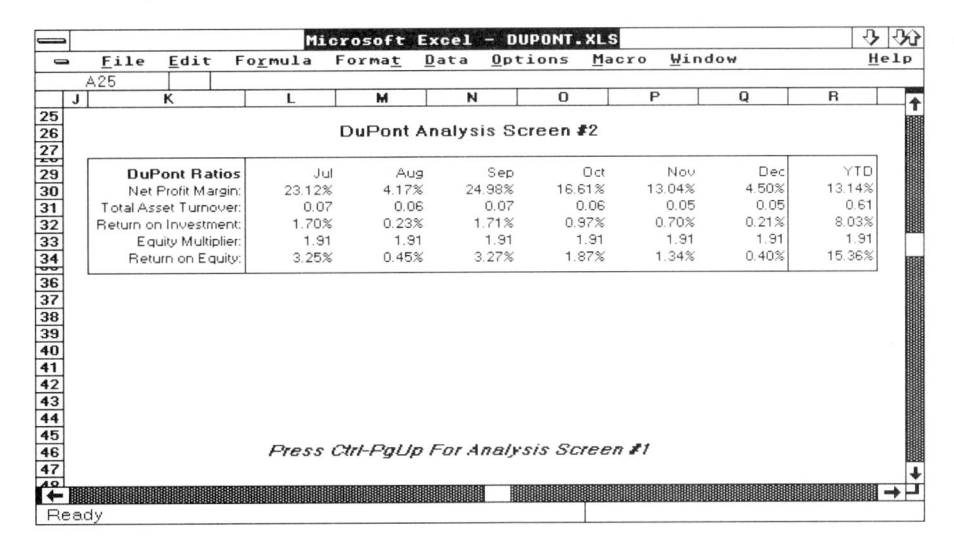

Fig. 5.4. DuPont analysis screen #2.

When you've finished reviewing the results of this analysis, press Ctrl-g; the model automatically generates a DuPont ratio-analysis graph. Figure 5.5 displays the NPM-ROI-ROE graph.

Fig. 5.5.
The DuPont ratio-analysis graph.

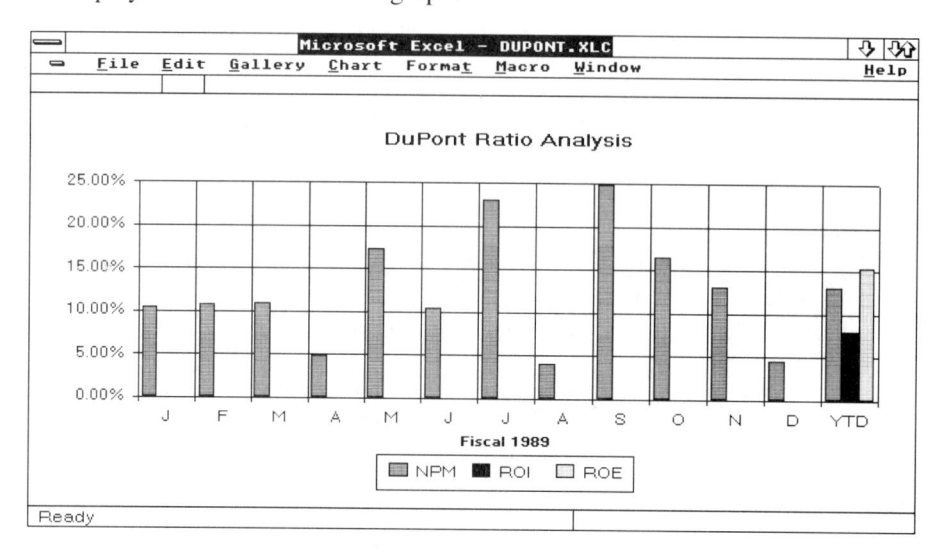

[Screenshot of Microsoft Excel - DUPONT.XLC showing a bar chart titled "DuPont Ratio Analysis" with NPM, ROI, and ROE values plotted monthly for Fiscal 1989 plus YTD, with y-axis from 0.00% to 25.00%.]

In this model, the net-profit margin is reviewed monthly, whereas the ROI and ROE ratios are evaluated at the end of the operating year. Why? An ROI of 0.23 percent for the month of August is not as illustrative as an end-of-year ROI equal to 8.03 percent. The YTD ROI reveals that during the course of the year, your firm's assets have provided you an 8.03 percent return.

Modifying the DUPONT.XLS Model

You can do several things to enhance this model:

- Change the account descriptions to match those appearing on your own financial statements.
- If you would like to know the annualized rate of growth of your monthly net profit, include the following formula, which calculates the annualized NPM as of the end of March:

    =SUM(C10:E10)/SUM(C5:E5):=10.737672%

- Using similar logic, develop the formulas that will display the annualized ROI and ROE on a monthly basis.
- To plot different items on the graph, edit the graph data-table range C53:F67. This range is referred to in the DUPONT.XLM macro (see fig. 5.6), so be sure to edit the macro if you insert or delete rows or columns in this model.

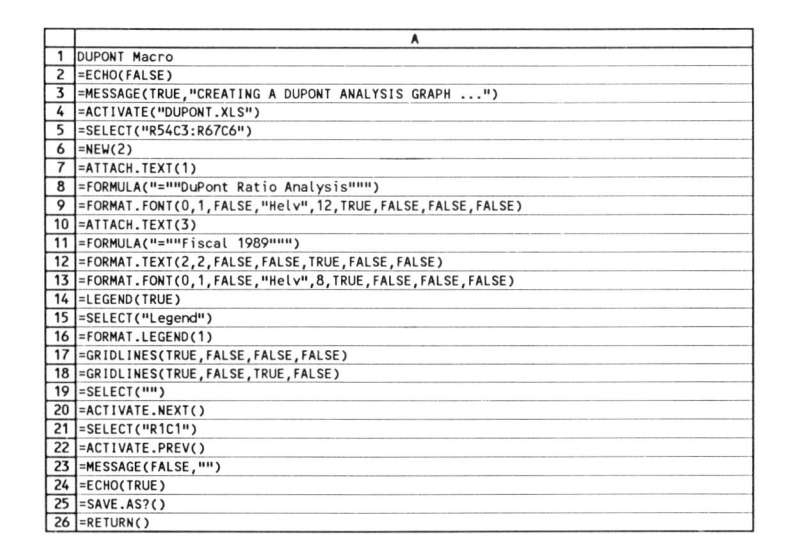

	A
1	DUPONT Macro
2	=ECHO(FALSE)
3	=MESSAGE(TRUE,"CREATING A DUPONT ANALYSIS GRAPH ...")
4	=ACTIVATE("DUPONT.XLS")
5	=SELECT("R54C3:R67C6")
6	=NEW(2)
7	=ATTACH.TEXT(1)
8	=FORMULA("=""DuPont Ratio Analysis""")
9	=FORMAT.FONT(0,1,FALSE,"Helv",12,TRUE,FALSE,FALSE,FALSE)
10	=ATTACH.TEXT(3)
11	=FORMULA("=""Fiscal 1989""")
12	=FORMAT.TEXT(2,2,FALSE,FALSE,TRUE,FALSE,FALSE)
13	=FORMAT.FONT(0,1,FALSE,"Helv",8,TRUE,FALSE,FALSE,FALSE)
14	=LEGEND(TRUE)
15	=SELECT("Legend")
16	=FORMAT.LEGEND(1)
17	=GRIDLINES(TRUE,FALSE,FALSE,FALSE)
18	=GRIDLINES(TRUE,FALSE,TRUE,FALSE)
19	=SELECT("")
20	=ACTIVATE.NEXT()
21	=SELECT("R1C1")
22	=ACTIVATE.PREV()
23	=MESSAGE(FALSE,"")
24	=ECHO(TRUE)
25	=SAVE.AS?()
26	=RETURN()

Fig. 5.6.
The DuPont chart-building macro.

Model 2: The Depreciation Analyzer (DEPRECI8.XLS)

DEPRECI8.XLS generates straight-line, declining-balance, and sum-of-the-years'-digits depreciation tables once you enter the appropriate data. The data-input area for this model is shown in figure 5.7.

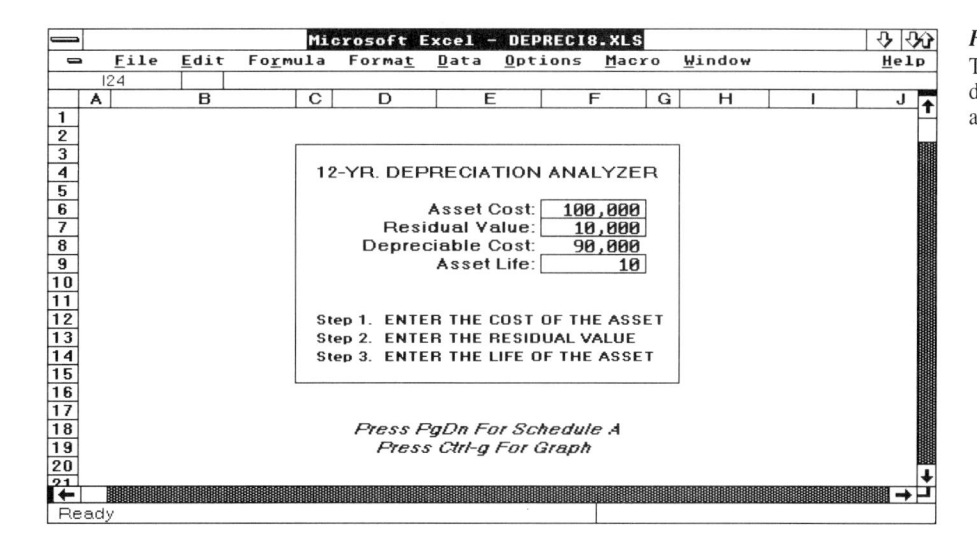

Fig. 5.7.
The 12-year depreciation analyzer.

Using the DEPRECI8.XLS Model

To use this model, enter the asset cost, the residual value, and the asset life. Excel automatically calculates the depreciable base for you when you enter the asset cost and residual value. Figure 5.7 illustrates a case in which a $100,000 asset with a $10,000 residual value has an estimated 10-year useful life.

To move to the first depreciation table, Schedule A, press PgDn once (see fig. 5.8). As expected, this method produces an equivalent yearly depreciation expense—in this case, equal to $9,000. After year 10, the asset's book value is equal to its residual value of $10,000.

Fig. 5.8.
Schedule A: straight-line method.

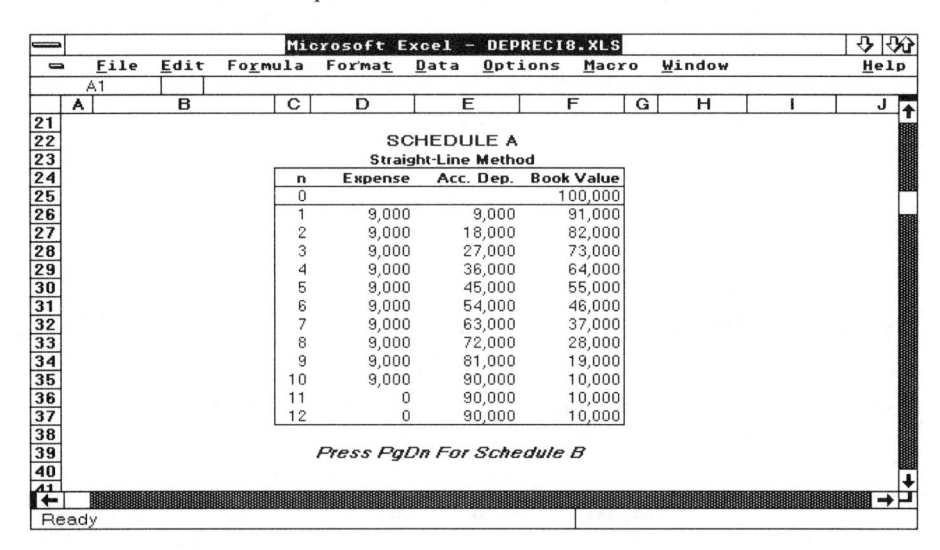

n	Expense	Acc. Dep.	Book Value
0			100,000
1	9,000	9,000	91,000
2	9,000	18,000	82,000
3	9,000	27,000	73,000
4	9,000	36,000	64,000
5	9,000	45,000	55,000
6	9,000	54,000	46,000
7	9,000	63,000	37,000
8	9,000	72,000	28,000
9	9,000	81,000	19,000
10	9,000	90,000	10,000
11	0	90,000	10,000
12	0	90,000	10,000

Press PgDn For Schedule B

To move to the second depreciation table, Schedule B, press PgDn once (see fig. 5.9). This table calculates the periodic depreciation expense as being equal to the current book value multiplied by twice the straight-line rate. Under the straight-line method, a 10-year asset is depreciated 10 percent per year. Here, the same asset is depreciated at a rate of 20 percent per year on the prior period's ending book value. The depreciation rate for a 5-year asset is therefore twice the straight-line rate of 20 percent per year—or 40 percent per year.

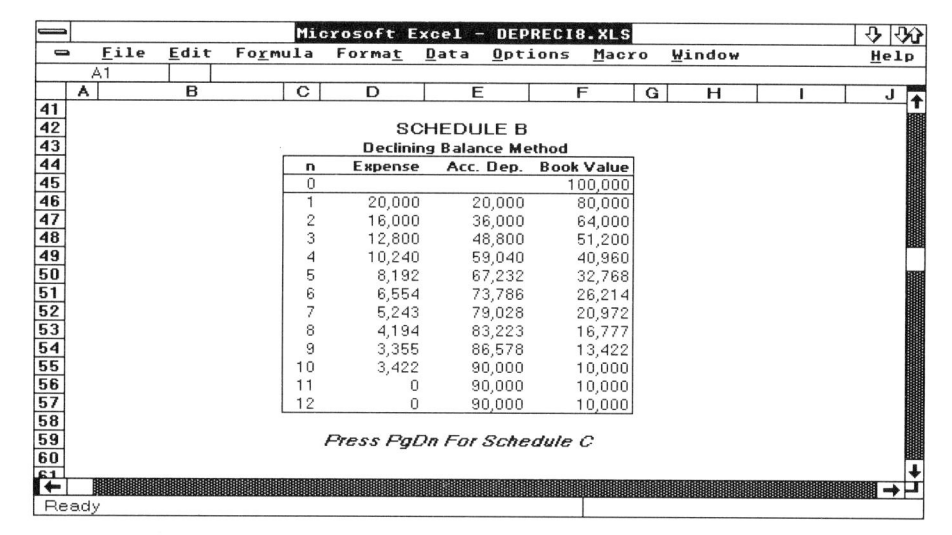

Fig. 5.9.
Schedule B: declining-balance method.

```
                    Microsoft Excel - DEPRECI8.XLS
    File   Edit   Formula   Format   Data   Options   Macro   Window       Help
    A1

         A      B      C      D          E          F       G    H    I     J
41
42                              SCHEDULE B
43                          Declining Balance Method
44                     n    Expense    Acc. Dep.  Book Value
45                     0                           100,000
46                     1    20,000     20,000      80,000
47                     2    16,000     36,000      64,000
48                     3    12,800     48,800      51,200
49                     4    10,240     59,040      40,960
50                     5     8,192     67,232      32,768
51                     6     6,554     73,786      26,214
52                     7     5,243     79,028      20,972
53                     8     4,194     83,223      16,777
54                     9     3,355     86,578      13,422
55                    10     3,422     90,000      10,000
56                    11         0     90,000      10,000
57                    12         0     90,000      10,000
58
59                      Press PgDn For Schedule C
60

 Ready
```

To move to the third depreciation table, Schedule C, press PgDn once more (see fig. 5.10). The sum-of-the-years'-digits method is a bit more complicated to explain than the previous two; the following example shows the formula used to create the periodic depreciation expense for this third method.

Fig. 5.10.
Schedule C: sum-of-the-years'-digits method.

```
                    Microsoft Excel - DEPRECI8.XLS
    File   Edit   Formula   Format   Data   Options   Macro   Window       Help
    A1

         A      B      C      D          E          F       G    H    I     J
61
62                              SCHEDULE C
63                       Sum-Of-The-Years'-Digits Method
64                     n    Expense    Acc. Dep.  Book Value
65                     0                           100,000
66                     1    16,364     16,364      83,636
67                     2    14,727     31,091      68,909
68                     3    13,091     44,182      55,818
69                     4    11,455     55,636      44,364
70                     5     9,818     65,455      34,545
71                     6     8,182     73,636      26,364
72                     7     6,545     80,182      19,818
73                     8     4,909     85,091      14,909
74                     9     3,273     88,364      11,636
75                    10     1,636     90,000      10,000
76                    11         0     90,000      10,000
77                    12         0     90,000      10,000
78
79                 Press Ctrl-Home to Return to Input Screen
80

 Ready
```

Example: A 4-year, $10 asset, no salvage value

Depreciation factor	=	sum-of-the-years'-digits
	=	1 + 2 + 3 + 4
	=	10

$$\text{Yearly expense} = \frac{\text{Year \#'s in reverse order}}{\text{Depreciation factor}} * \$10$$

Year #1	=	4/10 * $10	=	4.00
Year #2	=	3/10 * $10	=	3.00
Year #3	=	2/10 * $10	=	2.00
Year #4	=	1/10 * $10	=	1.00
Total periodic depreciation expenses			=	$10.00

When you've finished reviewing each of the three depreciation tables, press Ctrl-g; the model automatically generates a graph showing an analysis of the depreciation methods. This graph, shown in figure 5.11, plots book value over time.

Fig. 5.11.
A graph showing an analysis of the depreciation methods.

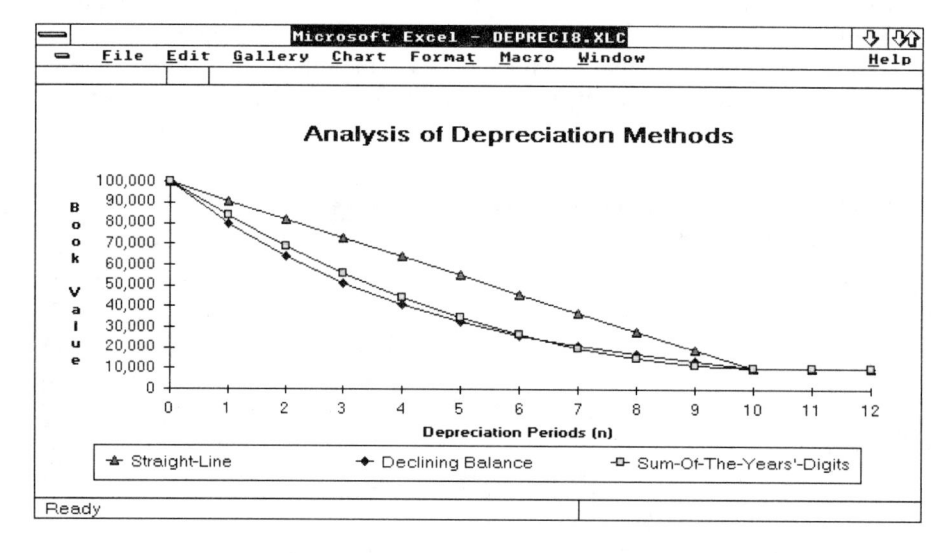

It's easy to identify the graph line that represents the straight-line method; however, the distinction between the declining-balance method and the sum-of-the-years'-digits method is more subtle. In this example, you can see that the declining-balance method produces larger depreciation expense write-offs in years 1 through 6, whereas the sum-of-the-years'-digits method lowers the book value more quickly in years 7 through 10. Check the schedules to verify that this is true.

Modifying the DEPRECI8.XLS Model

You can do several things to enhance this model:

- You can add other methods of depreciation—such as the modified-accelerated-cost-recovery-system (MACRS) method—to this model by copying an existing table range into an area just below Schedule C. Then simply adjust the cell formulas to reflect the desired method.

- A graph data table appears in the range C85:F97. This range is referred to in the DEPRECI8.XLM macro, so be sure to edit the macro if you insert or delete any rows or columns in the model (see fig. 5.12).

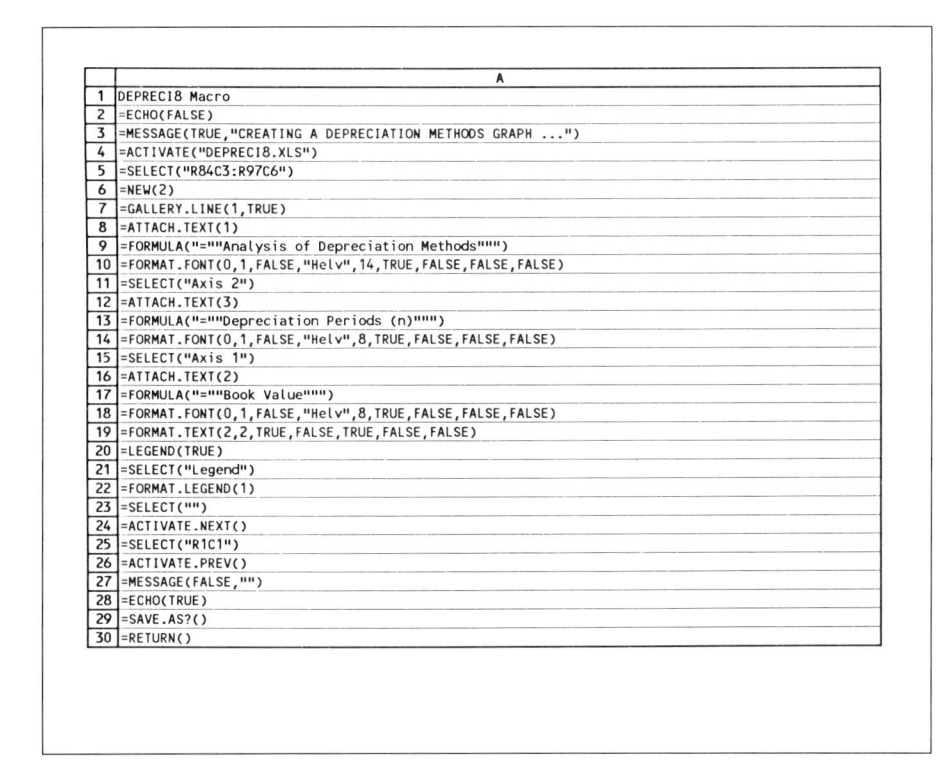

	A
1	DEPRECI8 Macro
2	=ECHO(FALSE)
3	=MESSAGE(TRUE,"CREATING A DEPRECIATION METHODS GRAPH ...")
4	=ACTIVATE("DEPRECI8.XLS")
5	=SELECT("R84C3:R97C6")
6	=NEW(2)
7	=GALLERY.LINE(1,TRUE)
8	=ATTACH.TEXT(1)
9	=FORMULA("=""Analysis of Depreciation Methods""")
10	=FORMAT.FONT(0,1,FALSE,"Helv",14,TRUE,FALSE,FALSE,FALSE)
11	=SELECT("Axis 2")
12	=ATTACH.TEXT(3)
13	=FORMULA("=""Depreciation Periods (n)""")
14	=FORMAT.FONT(0,1,FALSE,"Helv",8,TRUE,FALSE,FALSE,FALSE)
15	=SELECT("Axis 1")
16	=ATTACH.TEXT(2)
17	=FORMULA("=""Book Value""")
18	=FORMAT.FONT(0,1,FALSE,"Helv",8,TRUE,FALSE,FALSE,FALSE)
19	=FORMAT.TEXT(2,2,TRUE,FALSE,TRUE,FALSE,FALSE)
20	=LEGEND(TRUE)
21	=SELECT("Legend")
22	=FORMAT.LEGEND(1)
23	=SELECT("")
24	=ACTIVATE.NEXT()
25	=SELECT("R1C1")
26	=ACTIVATE.PREV()
27	=MESSAGE(FALSE,"")
28	=ECHO(TRUE)
29	=SAVE.AS?()
30	=RETURN()

Fig. 5.12. The depreciation analyzer chart-building macro.

Understanding the Time Value of Money

As a manager, you are constantly aware of your long-term business-growth objectives. Part of your planning process requires that you obtain and manage productive assets for your firm today and that you be able to evaluate the worth of those assets into the future. This managerial responsibility relies on the concept of the *time value of money*—one of the most important asset and investment management concepts. The two primary components of time value are future value and present value.

Future value is closely related to the concept of compounded interest. For example, if you deposit a sum of money into an interest-bearing account, you can easily determine its future value after five years if you know the rate of interest. You can also use future value analyses to calculate an interest or growth rate of a series of cash flows.

The *present value* of an asset is its worth today. This time-value technique is inversely related to future value and is a critical element in determining the worth of your business today.

Both models in this section help you manage and evaluate the performance of your money, potential investments, and company cash flows.

Model 1: Future Value Investment Analysis (FV.XLS)

This model does three different future value calculations: annual compounding, intrayear compounding, and determining the future value of an annuity.

Annual compounding is the most basic application of future value analysis. This analysis method tells you the future value of an investment made today at a fixed interest rate.

Intrayear compounding works just like annual compounding, except that this technique accounts for multiple compounding periods in any one year. Use this model to evaluate investment opportunities that compound interest semiannually, monthly, weekly, or daily.

An *annuity* is an asset that pays a series of equal payments. The annuity model will tell you the future value of, for example, a fixed-interest-bearing bank account into which you deposit $100 at the end of the month for 12 consecutive months.

Using the FV.XLS Model

Figure 5.13 shows the annual and intrayear compounding models. To use this model, highlight the range D5:D7 and enter the principal, annual interest rate, and number of periods for your investment.

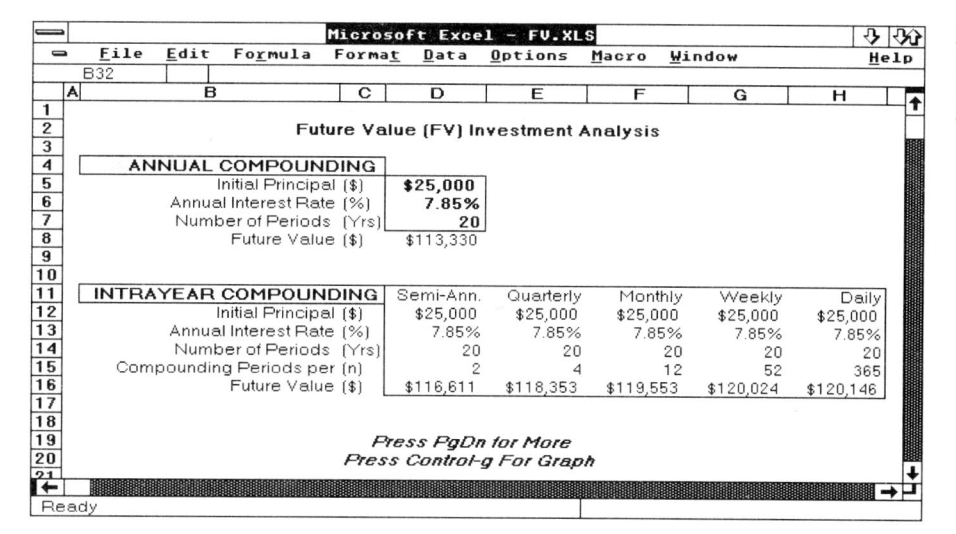

Fig. 5.13. Future value investment analysis.

Figure 5.13 shows that a $25,000 lump-sum investment earning 7.85 percent will be worth $113,330 in 20 years. The same investment will be worth $120,146 if the interest is compounded daily. That's an extra $6,816 in your pocket just for shopping around. To display a graph that illustrates the advantages of intrayear over annual compounding, press Ctrl-g (see fig. 5.14).

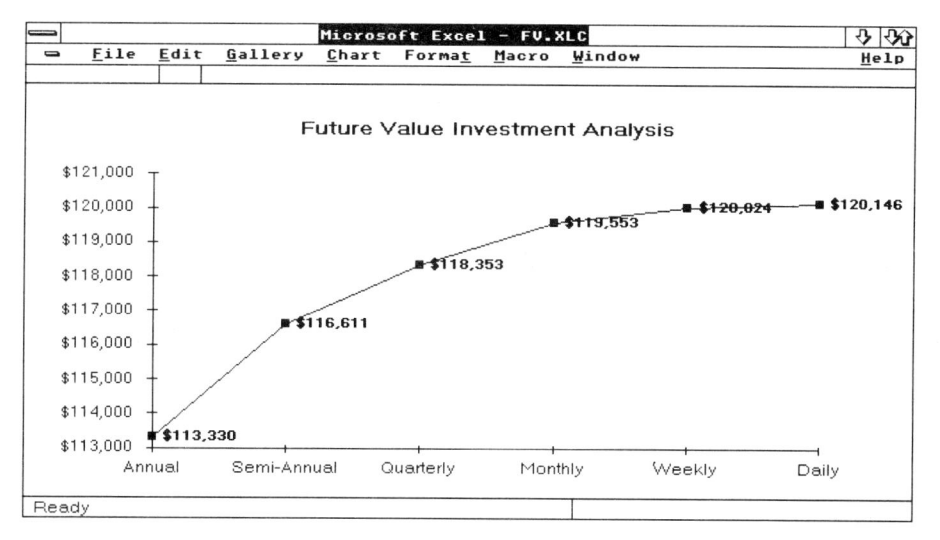

Fig. 5.14. A graph showing a future value investment analysis.

The final part of the future value model helps you evaluate the future worth of investing in an annuity. Figure 5.15 displays a completed data-input screen for an investment in an annuity. According to the model, you would have $5,751 at the end of five years if you made five equal payments of $1,000, at an annual interest rate of 7.0 percent. You are investing in an ordinary annuity when you make payments at the end of year 1, year 2, year 3, and so on. What would happen if you made the payments at the beginning of the period instead of at the end?

Fig. 5.15. Evaluating the future worth of an ordinary annuity.

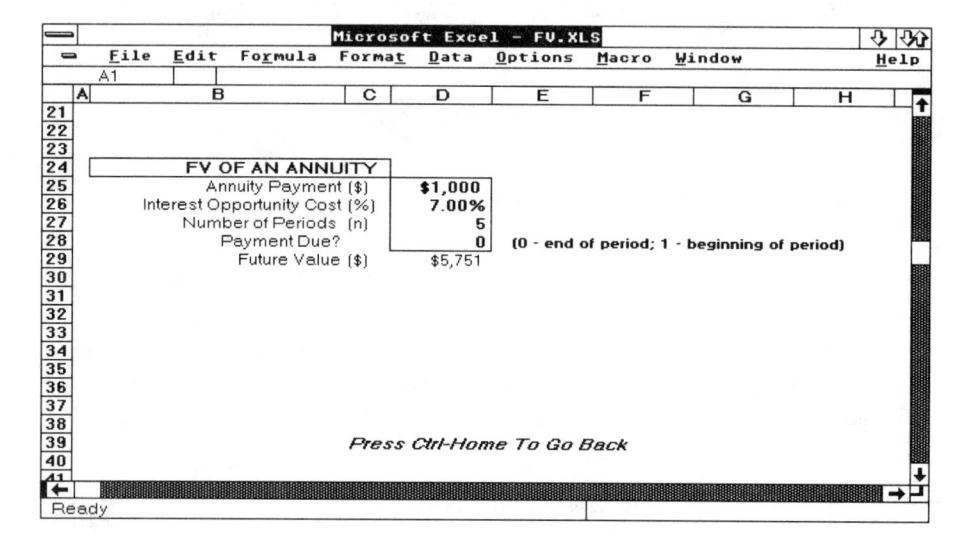

When you make payments at the beginning of a period, you are investing in an *annuity due*. Clearly, an annuity due provides a greater future value because your first payment accrues interest starting at day 1. You will earn an extra $402 by investing in an annuity due (see fig. 5.16).

Fig. 5.16. Evaluating the future worth of an annuity due.

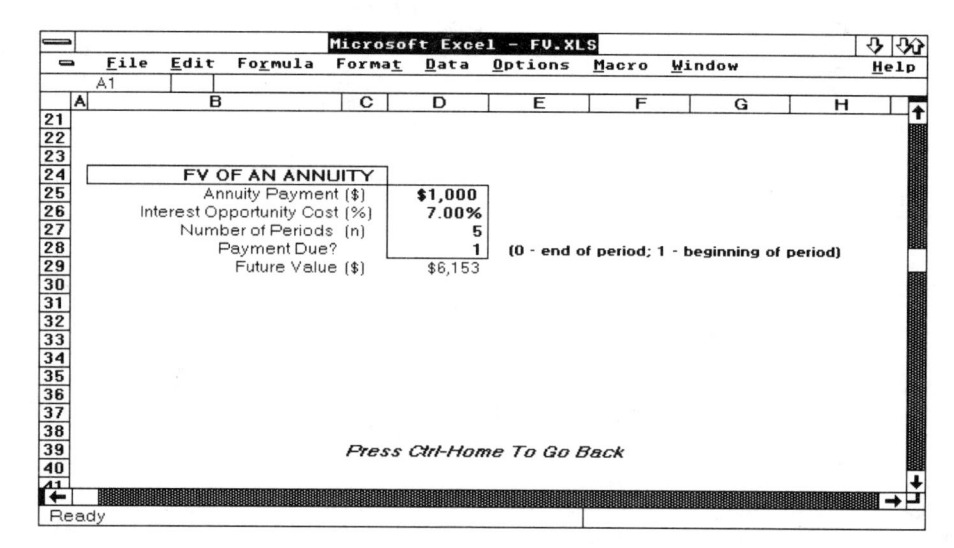

Modifying the FV.XLS Model

You can enhance this model in the following ways:

- If you would like to know the value of an investment that is compounded continuously, simply append another block onto the range I11:I16. Review the formulas in row 16 to get a feel for the calculations involved in intrayear compounding.

  Note: The formula that compounds on a continuous basis is somewhat more complex; it requires that you use e, the natural base for logarithms. A sum invested at a continuously compounded rate of r percent a year for t years is equal to the following:

  $$\text{sum} * e^{rt}$$

  The value of e is approximately 2.718, so this formula becomes the following:

  $$\text{sum} * (2.718)^{rt}$$

- A graph data table appears in the range D47:E53. This range is referred to in the FV.XLM macro, so be sure to edit the macro if you insert or delete any rows or columns in this model (see fig. 5.17).

	A
1	FV Macro
2	=ECHO(FALSE)
3	=MESSAGE(TRUE,"CREATING A FUTURE VALUE GRAPH ...")
4	=ACTIVATE("FV.XLS")
5	=SELECT("R48C4:R53C5")
6	=NEW(2)
7	=GALLERY.LINE(1,TRUE)
8	=ATTACH.TEXT(1)
9	=FORMULA("=""Future Value Investment Analysis""")
10	=FORMAT.FONT(0,1,FALSE,"Helv",12,TRUE,FALSE,FALSE,FALSE)
11	=SELECT("S1P1")
12	=ATTACH.TEXT(4,1,1)
13	=FORMAT.FONT(0,1,FALSE,"Helv",8,TRUE,FALSE,FALSE,FALSE)
14	=FORMAT.TEXT(3,2,FALSE,TRUE,TRUE,TRUE,FALSE)
15	=SELECT("S1P1")
16	=SELECT("S1P2")
17	=ATTACH.TEXT(4,1,2)
18	=FORMAT.FONT(0,1,FALSE,"Helv",8,TRUE,FALSE,FALSE,FALSE)
19	=FORMAT.TEXT(3,2,FALSE,TRUE,TRUE,TRUE,FALSE)
20	=SELECT("S1P3")
21	=ATTACH.TEXT(4,1,3)
22	=FORMAT.FONT(0,1,FALSE,"Helv",8,TRUE,FALSE,FALSE,FALSE)
23	=FORMAT.TEXT(3,2,FALSE,TRUE,TRUE,TRUE,FALSE)
24	=SELECT("S1P4")
25	=ATTACH.TEXT(4,1,4)
26	=FORMAT.FONT(0,1,FALSE,"Helv",8,TRUE,FALSE,FALSE,FALSE)
27	=FORMAT.TEXT(3,2,FALSE,TRUE,TRUE,TRUE,FALSE)
28	=SELECT("S1P5")
29	=ATTACH.TEXT(4,1,5)
30	=FORMAT.FONT(0,1,FALSE,"Helv",8,TRUE,FALSE,FALSE,FALSE)
31	=FORMAT.TEXT(3,2,FALSE,TRUE,TRUE,TRUE,FALSE)
32	=SELECT("S1P6")
33	=ATTACH.TEXT(4,1,6)
34	=FORMAT.FONT(0,1,FALSE,"Helv",8,TRUE,FALSE,FALSE,FALSE)
35	=FORMAT.TEXT(3,2,FALSE,TRUE,TRUE,TRUE,FALSE)
36	=SELECT("")
37	=ACTIVATE.NEXT()
38	=SELECT("R1C1")
39	=ACTIVATE.PREV()
40	=MESSAGE(FALSE,"")
41	=ECHO(TRUE)
42	=SAVE.AS?()
43	=RETURN()

Fig. 5.17. The future value investment analysis chart-building macro.

Model 2: The Present Value Investment Analysis Model (PV.XLS)

This model should remind you of the future value model just discussed. The present value model performs four separate calculations: present value of a future sum, present value of an annuity, present value of a perpetuity, and present value of a mixed cash-flow stream.

Present value analysis is the opposite of future value analysis. In present value analysis, you want to determine what a future payment or set of payments is worth today. Stated another way, the present value of an asset is the most that you'd want to pay today for the right to receive known benefits from that asset in the future.

Consider the opportunity of making an investment today that will enable you to pay the entire cost of your child's education (through college). In other words, how much will you have to deposit in your bank today so that you can withdraw an equal amount of payments over the next 20 years? This type of analysis tells you the present value of a series of annuity payments.

A close cousin to the annuity investment is the *perpetuity*. In a perpetuity the periodic payments continue forever (or as long as your bank remains in business). So here, the objective is to determine the amount that you'd have to deposit today to ensure that you could continue to withdraw a specific amount of money indefinitely.

The final part of the present value model enables you to determine the current worth of a series of uneven cash flows. Until now, all the present value models have assumed that you are receiving (or making) a fixed payment. This final section is essential to helping you value your business.

Using the PV.XLS Model

Figure 5.18 shows examples of calculating both the present value of a future sum and the present value of an annuity model. To use these models with your own data, highlight the data ranges D6:D8 or D13:D16 and enter the appropriate data.

The top portion of figure 5.18 shows that a $1,500,000 lump sum to be received in eight years is worth $810,403 today when your opportunity interest cost is 8 percent.

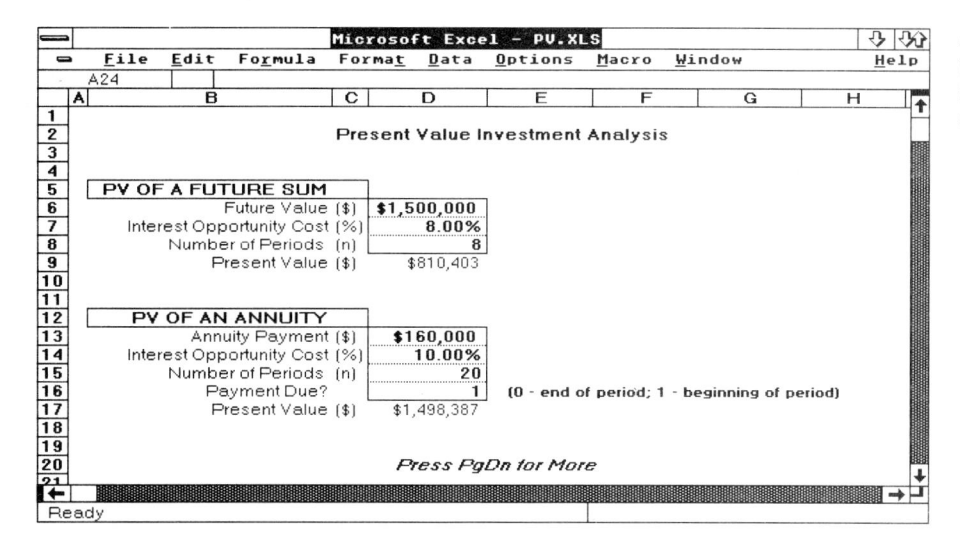

Fig. 5.18.
Present value investment analysis.

Think of it like this: if you demand an average return of 8 percent on all investments made over the next eight years, you'd expect an $810,403 investment made today to grow to $1,500,000 in eight years.

The second model works on a similar principle, only here you will be making (or receiving) a series of fixed payments over time. The 1 in cell D16 tells you that you are evaluating an annuity due. The present value of this 20-year, $160,000 annuity is $1,498,387 when your opportunity interest cost is 10 percent. Change the 1 in cell D16 to a 0 to assess the present value of an ordinary annuity.

So have you figured out how to invest today to plan for tomorrow's cost of raising your children and providing them an education? The perpetuity analysis shown in the top portion of figure 5.19 presents one solution to this monstrous financial hurdle. To launch an investment that would provide you with $15,000 per year forever, assuming that your interest opportunity cost is 10 percent, you would need $150,000 today.

The lower portion of this model values a mixed stream of 10 cash flows. One obvious use for such a model is to value your firm. After all, your business today is worth the present value of all future expected cash flows. Of course, you could bias this analysis by padding the cash flows or projecting that you will be in business for 150 years, but that doesn't do you any good. The main reason why anyone wants to value a business is that the owner is considering selling, and no buyer in his right mind would agree to such an inflated valuation.

Fig. 5.19.
The present value of a perpetuity and the present value of a mixed stream of cash flows: periods 1-5.

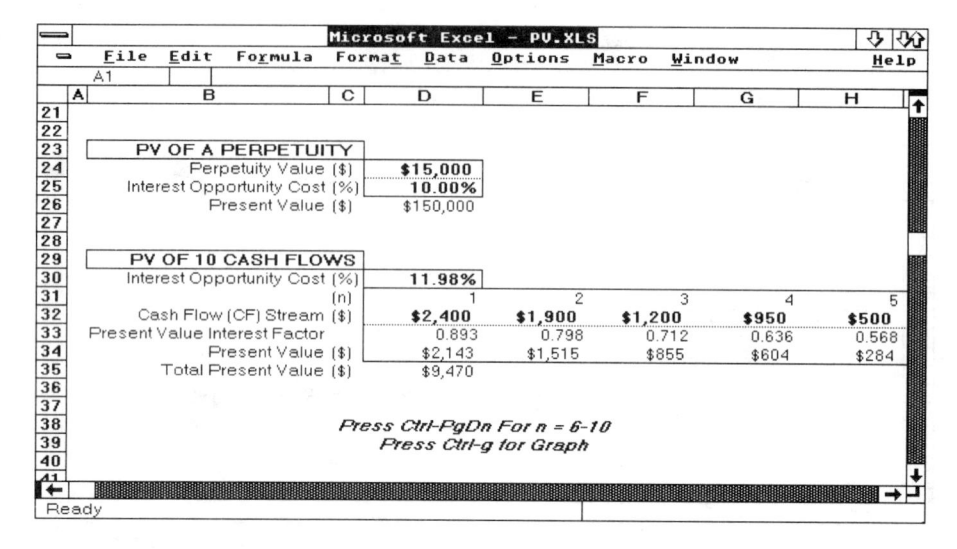

```
┌─────────────────────────────────── Microsoft Excel - PV.XLS ───────────────────┬─⇩─⇩⇩─┐
│  ⇨   File   Edit   Formula   Format   Data   Options   Macro   Window          │ Help │
│      A1                                                                        │      │
│    A │      B            │     C        │    D     │    E    │    F   │   G   │  H   │
│ 21   │                   │              │          │         │        │       │      │
│ 22   │                   │              │          │         │        │       │      │
│ 23   │ PV OF A PERPETUITY│              │          │         │        │       │      │
│ 24   │   Perpetuity Value ($)           │ $15,000  │         │        │       │      │
│ 25   │   Interest Opportunity Cost (%)  │  10.00%  │         │        │       │      │
│ 26   │   Present Value ($)              │ $150,000 │         │        │       │      │
│ 27   │                                                                                │
│ 28   │                                                                                │
│ 29   │ PV OF 10 CASH FLOWS                                                            │
│ 30   │   Interest Opportunity Cost (%)  │  11.98%  │                                  │
│ 31   │                         (n)      │     1    │    2    │   3    │   4   │  5   │
│ 32   │   Cash Flow (CF) Stream ($)      │  $2,400  │ $1,900  │ $1,200 │ $950  │ $500 │
│ 33   │   Present Value Interest Factor  │  0.893   │ 0.798   │ 0.712  │ 0.636 │ 0.568│
│ 34   │   Present Value ($)              │  $2,143  │ $1,515  │ $855   │ $604  │ $284 │
│ 35   │   Total Present Value ($)        │  $9,470  │                                  │
│ 36   │                                                                                │
│ 37   │                                                                                │
│ 38   │              Press Ctrl-PgDn For n = 6-10                                      │
│ 39   │              Press Ctrl-g for Graph                                            │
│ 40   │                                                                                │
│ Ready                                                                                 │
└───────────────────────────────────────────────────────────────────────────────────────┘
```

Consider a firm that has projected its cash flows for the next 10 years. The firm is currently in a product-maturity phase characterized by medium sales and relatively high profits. However, management expects to reap the benefits of new product innovations in three or four years. They anticipate that they will remain in this high-growth phase, characterized by high sales and low profits, for at least two years. At this time, they anticipate entering a product-maturity phase again as they reach economies of scale. The firm's interest opportunity cost is 11.98 percent.

The lower portions of figures 5.19 and 5.20 display the firm's cash flows for the 10-year period.

Fig. 5.20.
The present value of a mixed stream of cash flows: periods 6-10.

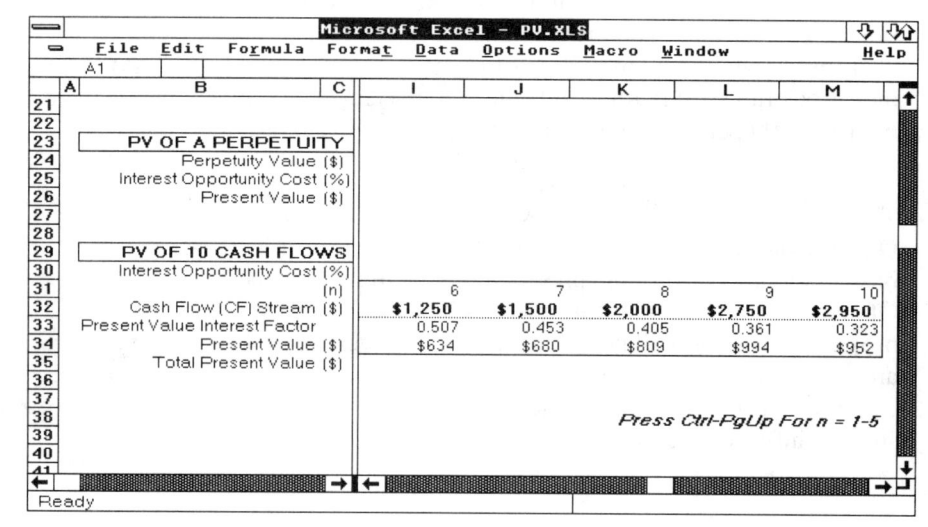

```
┌─────────────────────────────────── Microsoft Excel - PV.XLS ───────────────────┬─⇩─⇩⇩─┐
│  ⇨   File   Edit   Formula   Format   Data   Options   Macro   Window          │ Help │
│      A1                                                                        │      │
│    A │      B            │     C        │    I     │    J    │    K   │   L   │   M  │
│ 21   │                                                                                │
│ 22   │                                                                                │
│ 23   │ PV OF A PERPETUITY                                                             │
│ 24   │   Perpetuity Value ($)                                                         │
│ 25   │   Interest Opportunity Cost (%)                                                │
│ 26   │   Present Value ($)                                                            │
│ 27   │                                                                                │
│ 28   │                                                                                │
│ 29   │ PV OF 10 CASH FLOWS                                                            │
│ 30   │   Interest Opportunity Cost (%)                                                │
│ 31   │                         (n)      │    6     │    7    │   8    │   9   │  10  │
│ 32   │   Cash Flow (CF) Stream ($)      │ $1,250   │ $1,500  │ $2,000 │ $2,750│$2,950│
│ 33   │   Present Value Interest Factor  │  0.507   │ 0.453   │ 0.405  │ 0.361 │ 0.323│
│ 34   │   Present Value ($)              │  $634    │ $680    │ $809   │ $994  │ $952 │
│ 35   │   Total Present Value ($)                                                      │
│ 36   │                                                                                │
│ 37   │                                                                                │
│ 38   │                                 Press Ctrl-PgUp For n = 1-5                    │
│ 39   │                                                                                │
│ 40   │                                                                                │
│ Ready                                                                                 │
└───────────────────────────────────────────────────────────────────────────────────────┘
```

The present value interest factor appearing below each cash-flow value is calculated as

$$\text{PV Interest Factor}_t = \frac{1}{(1+i)^t}$$

where t is the period number and i is interest opportunity cost.

Multiplying this factor by each period's cash flows yields a present value of the cash flow for each period. By summing the individual present values, you arrive at the value of the firm today.

This process reflects the effect of time value on the worth of expected future cash flows. After all, the $500 cash flow in period 5 surely isn't worth $500 today. The analysis shows that you'd have to invest only $284 today at 11.98 percent to get $500 in five years. To see this, press Ctrl-g to view a graph that plots the cash flow against its present value (see fig. 5.21).

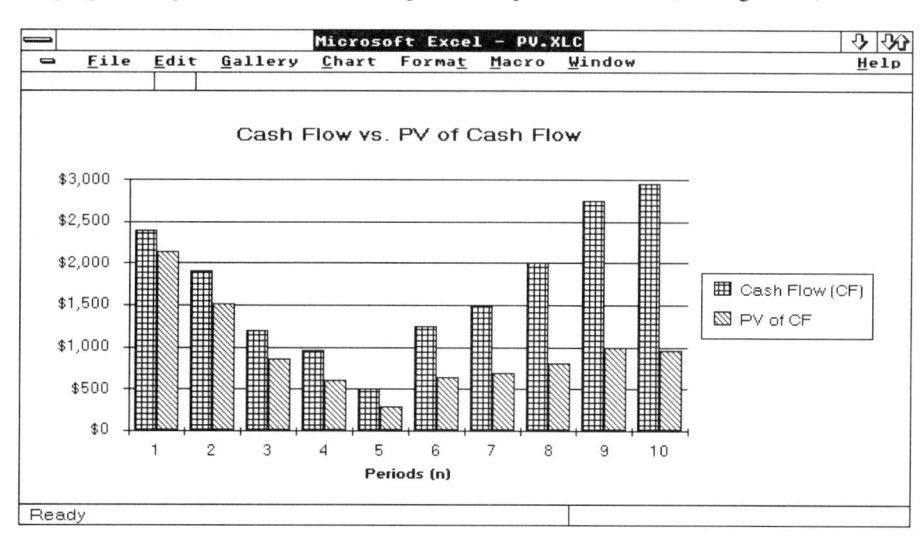

Fig. 5.21. A graph showing the cash flow plotted against the present value of the cash flow.

Notice in this graph that the time-value-of-money concept rears its head in periods 6 through 10, where quickly rising cash flows are matched by relatively stable present values.

Modifying the PV.XLS Model

You can enhance this model in ways similar to those suggested for the future value models. Just remember that a graph data table appears in the range D47:E53. This range is referred to in the PV.XLM macro, so be sure to edit the macro if you insert or delete any rows or columns in this model (see fig. 5.22).

Fig. 5.22.
The present value investment analysis chart-building macro.

	A
1	PV Macro
2	=ECHO(FALSE)
3	=MESSAGE(TRUE,"CREATING A PRESENT VALUE GRAPH ...")
4	=ACTIVATE("PV.XLS")
5	=SELECT("R47C3:R57C5")
6	=NEW(2)
7	=ATTACH.TEXT(1)
8	=FORMULA("=""""Cash Flow vs. PV of Cash Flow""""")
9	=FORMAT.FONT(0,1,FALSE,"Helv",12,TRUE,FALSE,FALSE,FALSE)
10	=ATTACH.TEXT(3)
11	=FORMULA("=""""Periods (n)""""")
12	=FORMAT.FONT(0,1,FALSE,"Helv",8,TRUE,FALSE,FALSE,FALSE)
13	=LEGEND(TRUE)
14	=SELECT("Legend")
15	=FORMAT.LEGEND(4)
16	=SELECT("")
17	=GALLERY.COLUMN(6,TRUE)
18	=SELECT("S1P7")
19	=PATTERNS(0,1,1,1,FALSE,0,15,1,6,FALSE,FALSE)
20	=SELECT("S2P7")
21	=PATTERNS(0,1,1,1,FALSE,0,13,1,8,FALSE,FALSE)
22	=SELECT("")
23	=ACTIVATE.NEXT()
24	=SELECT("R1C1")
25	=ACTIVATE.PREV()
26	=MESSAGE(FALSE,"")
27	=ECHO(TRUE)
28	=SAVE.AS?()
29	=RETURN()

Evaluating Risk and Return

Some risk-and-return-analysis models involve extremely complex financial calculations that rely on high-order calculus, multiple-regression analysis, and statistical correlations. The results produced by these complex models, however, seem to remain in roughly the same ballpark as those produced by simpler models. In fact, it's a good idea to evaluate the risks and returns of undertaking any Excel model-building exercise. If you can do it on a calculator, and you're used to using a calculator, why build it into a spreadsheet model?

Certain basic ways to look at risk and return are well suited for the electronic spreadsheet. In this next section, you will use two such techniques: the single-asset risk model and the capital-asset pricing model (CAPM).

Model 1: Single-Asset Risk Evaluation (RSK&RTN.XLS)

Figure 5.23 displays the single-asset risk model for asset A and asset B. Although this model's title suggests that it works with only one particular asset, you can in fact use the model to evaluate the risk of any asset. A limitation of this model is that it evaluates the risk of a single asset against itself, whereas more sophisticated models also calculate correlations among a group of similar-risk assets. Assets are grouped into risk classes according to their expected returns [E(R)], and as a rule, you shouldn't compare assets across risk classes. Read on to see why.

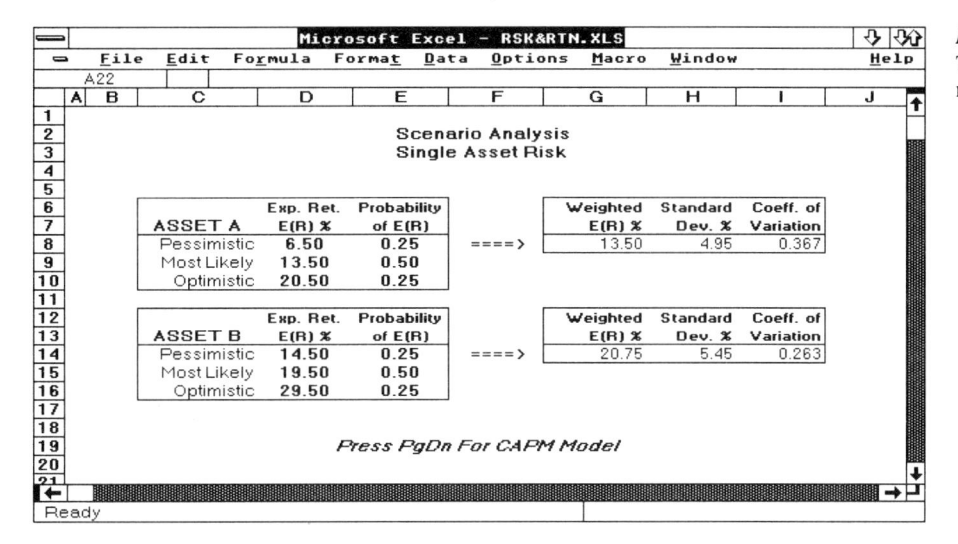

Fig. 5.23.
The single-asset risk scenario.

	Exp. Ret. E(R) %	Probability of E(R)		Weighted E(R) %	Standard Dev. %	Coeff. of Variation
ASSET A				13.50	4.95	0.367
Pessimistic	6.50	0.25	====>			
Most Likely	13.50	0.50				
Optimistic	20.50	0.25				
ASSET B				20.75	5.45	0.263
Pessimistic	14.50	0.25	====>			
Most Likely	19.50	0.50				
Optimistic	29.50	0.25				

Press PgDn For CAPM Model

Suppose that you are considering buying a new computer system for your business. IBM, DEC, Unisys, and AT&T all manufacture business PCs that provide similar benefits. Even though the price range of the systems may vary somewhat, you'd expect the higher-priced systems to have a higher salvage value and the lower-priced systems to have a correspondingly lower salvage value. Regardless, each system would do the same calculations, be susceptible to roughly the same types of malfunctions, and therefore have similar risk-return trade-offs.

Now suppose that J. Edgar Jobs, Inc., a start-up computer company, happens by with the deal of the century. The company has just completed production on its new mainframe computer system and will gladly sell it to you for the same price as that of the PCs you've been looking at.

Although similar products (business PCs) are being discussed, they are really "apples and oranges." The reason is the astronomical risk associated with buying an untested computer system that has no obvious track record. So even though the new computer system could be the buy of the century, you'd have as likely a chance of meeting your required return objectives as if you invested in penny stocks. In fact, it probably wouldn't be too far off base to suggest that these two items—the JEJ computer and penny stocks—are in the same risk class. But that analysis is the subject of another book.

The single-asset risk model combines two separate schools of thought about risk and return analysis. The first school of thought involves scenario analysis. As you can see in figure 5.23, the left-hand portion of this model offers three possible situations: pessimistic, most likely, and optimistic. Drawing on your managerial expertise, you can formulate an idea of the expected return associated with an investment opportunity. Then, by estimating the probability that each scenario will occur, you can produce a weighted expected return for the investment.

The weighted expected return is an input to the next part of the model, which belongs to the second school of thought—statistical analysis. In the right-hand portion of this model, you see the standard deviation and coefficient of correlation for each asset.

Standard deviation describes how much spread exists in the weighted expected return. The higher the standard deviation, the riskier the asset. When you compare assets that have different expected returns (but are still in the same risk class), use the correlation of variation to help you make a final decision about which asset is riskier. The higher the correlation of variation, the riskier the asset.

Consider the situation in figure 5.23 in which the following data is produced by the model:

	Asset A	Asset B
Weighted E(R)	13.50%	20.75%
Standard deviation	4.95%	5.45%
Coefficient of variation	0.367	0.263

Which asset would you choose? If you chose B, you selected the better asset.

Why? If you select assets solely on the basis of expected returns, you'd choose the right asset but for the wrong reason. When you compare standard deviations, it becomes apparent that even though asset B offers a higher return, asset A is more desirable because it has a lower standard deviation from its expected return. But can you compare the standard deviations of these two assets? No! Because the assets have different weighted expected returns, their standard deviations are not on the same scale.

What can you do? Compare the assets' coefficients of variation for the answer. This statistic is always on the same scale because it is derived from both of the first two measures. As you can see, asset B is the best choice because it has a lower coefficient than that of asset A. And, happily, it also offers a higher weighted expected return.

The following points recap the use of this model:

1. The single-asset model can be used to evaluate the risk and return trade-offs between two or more assets that lie in a similar risk class.
2. When the weighted expected returns are not equal—and they rarely are—choose the asset with the lowest standard deviation.
3. In the more likely case in which expected returns differ, always choose the asset with the lowest coefficient of variation.

Model 2: The Capital-Asset Pricing Model (RSK&RTN.XLS)

The capital-asset pricing model (CAPM) determines the expected return on an investment in an asset according to the formula

$$E(R)_a = R_f + \beta_a * (E(R)_m - R_f)$$

where $E(R)_a$ = expected return on $Asset_a$, R_f = risk-free rate of return, β_a = beta coefficient for $Asset_a$, and $E(R)_m$ = expected average rate of return on all assets.

If you are wondering how you will ever be able to come up with the expected returns for the single-asset risk model, you will be grateful to know that the CAPM calculates it for you. The CAPM requires the current three-month T-bill rate, a *Value Line* beta list, and the most recent S&P 500 stock composite index value. Most of the values are published in *The Wall Street Journal* (or in *Value Line*, in the case of beta values), but when they are unavailable, they are relatively easy to estimate. Once you have gathered and input the appropriate data, the CAPM will compute an expected return for an asset.

Figure 5.24 illustrates the case in which the risk-free rate is 7.0 percent, the *Value Line* asset beta is 1.5, and the expected return on the market portfolio of assets equals 11.0 percent.

As previously mentioned, you can use the three-month T-bill rate as the risk-free rate; the S&P 500 composite index serves as a good estimate of the expected return on the market portfolio of assets. Of the three values, though, the most difficult to find is the asset beta. If you fail to locate an asset beta in *Value Line*, choose a substitute beta. For example, pick a company from *Value Line* that is in a similar industry and has a similar capital structure (that is, the same relationship between debt and equity), because the assets of such a firm would most likely be in a similar risk class. If you find such a company, just substitute its asset beta into the CAPM equation.

Fig. 5.24.
The capital-asset pricing model.

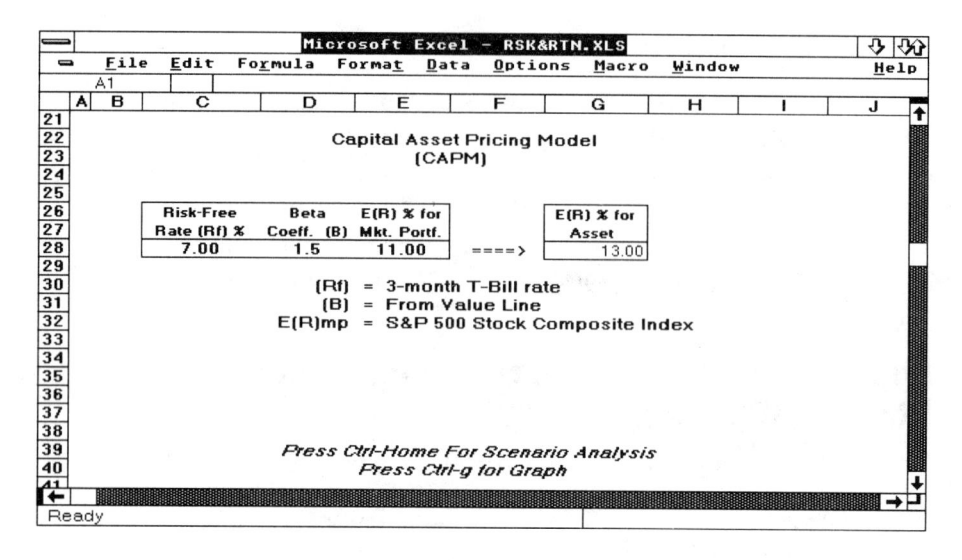

```
                 Microsoft Excel - RSK&RTN.XLS
   File   Edit   Formula   Format   Data   Options   Macro   Window        Help
   A1
   A  B      C          D         E           F        G        H      I    J
21
22                       Capital Asset Pricing Model
23                                (CAPM)
24
25
26          Risk-Free      Beta      E(R) % for                E(R) % for
27          Rate (Rf) %   Coeff. (B) Mkt. Portf.                  Asset
28             7.00         1.5        11.00       ====>          13.00
29
30                           (Rf) = 3-month T-Bill rate
31                            (B) = From Value Line
32                          E(R)mp = S&P 500 Stock Composite Index
33
...
39                     Press Ctrl-Home For Scenario Analysis
40                         Press Ctrl-g for Graph
Ready
```

Now press Ctrl-g to generate a graphic representation of the security market line (SML). The SML represents the range of possible returns for various beta values, given a risk-free rate (see fig. 5.25).

Fig. 5.25.
The security market line graph.

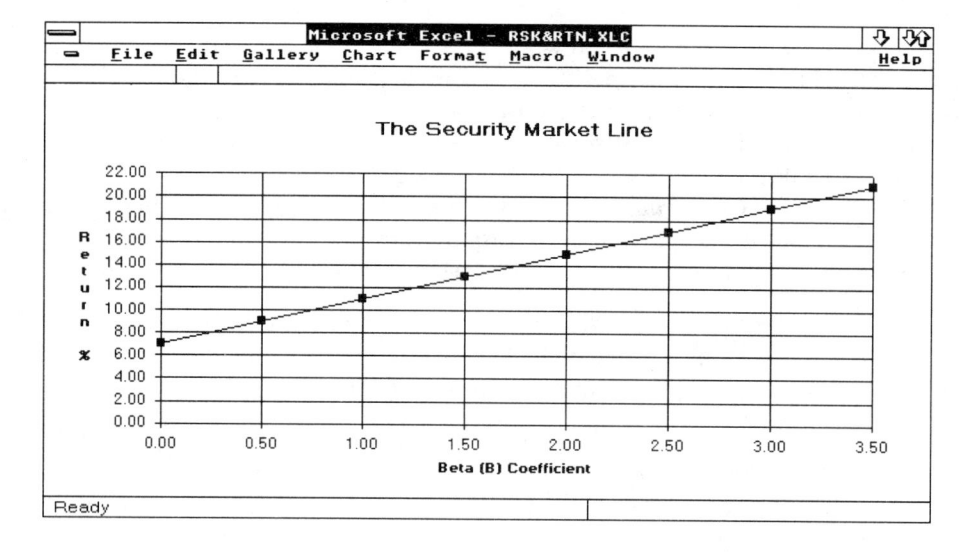

```
                 Microsoft Excel - RSK&RTN.XLC
   File   Edit   Gallery   Chart   Format   Macro   Window        Help

                        The Security Market Line

   22.00
   20.00
   18.00
R  16.00
e  14.00
t
u  12.00
r  10.00
n   8.00
%   6.00
    4.00
    2.00
    0.00
        0.00    0.50    1.00    1.50    2.00    2.50    3.00    3.50
                            Beta (B) Coefficient
Ready
```

The y-intercept in this graph lies at a beta value of zero and a return equal to 7.0 percent. The risk-free asset (B = 0) is of course the three-month T-bill. Also notice that the sample asset appears at the intersection of beta value 1.5 and return value 13.0 percent.

What would happen if you changed only the beta value in the CAPM? Figure 5.26 shows the effect of lowering the asset's beta from 1.5 to .5.

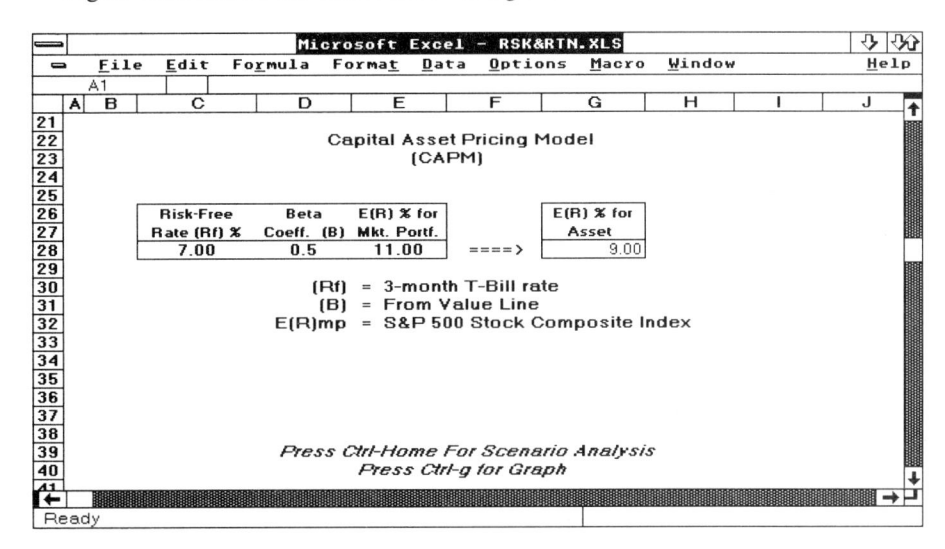

Fig. 5.26. Changing the CAPM assumptions.

The E(R) decreases from 13.0 percent to 9.0 percent. Now look back at figure 5.25 and locate the new beta and its return on the same SML. Remember, the SML represents the range of possible returns for all beta values when the risk-free rate and E(R) on the market portfolio are known. Because you changed only the value of the beta, you simply slid down the same SML. When either the risk-free rate or E(R) on the market portfolio changes, there will be a new SML. Figure 5.27 shows the macro code that creates the SML graph.

Fig. 5.27.
The CAPM
chart-building
macro.

	A
1	Risk and Return Macro
2	=ECHO(FALSE)
3	=MESSAGE(TRUE,"CREATING A SECURITY MARKET LINE GRAPH ...")
4	=ACTIVATE("RSK&RTN.XLS")
5	=SELECT("R48C5:R56C6")
6	=NEW(2)
7	=GALLERY.LINE(1,TRUE)
8	=ATTACH.TEXT(1)
9	=FORMULA("=""The Security Market Line""")
10	=FORMAT.FONT(0,1,FALSE,"Helv",12,TRUE,FALSE,FALSE,FALSE)
11	=FORMAT.TEXT(2,2,FALSE,FALSE,TRUE,FALSE,FALSE)
12	=SELECT("Axis 1")
13	=ATTACH.TEXT(2)
14	=FORMULA("=""Return %""")
15	=FORMAT.FONT(0,1,FALSE,"Helv",8,TRUE,FALSE,FALSE,FALSE)
16	=FORMAT.TEXT(2,2,TRUE,FALSE,TRUE,FALSE,FALSE)
17	=SELECT("Axis 2")
18	=ATTACH.TEXT(3)
19	=FORMULA("=""Beta (B) Coefficient""")
20	=FORMAT.FONT(0,1,FALSE,"Helv",8,TRUE,FALSE,FALSE,FALSE)
21	=SELECT("Axis 1")
22	=SCALE(TRUE,TRUE,2,TRUE,TRUE,FALSE,FALSE,FALSE)
23	=GRIDLINES(TRUE,FALSE,TRUE,FALSE)
24	=SELECT("")
25	=ACTIVATE.NEXT()
26	=SELECT("R1C1")
27	=ACTIVATE.PREV()
28	=MESSAGE(FALSE,"")
29	=ECHO(TRUE)
30	=SAVE.AS?()
31	=RETURN()

Using Valuation Techniques

When you value something, you determine its worth. As a business manager, you must understand how to value stocks, bonds, and assets that contribute to the worth of your firm. The valuation techniques presented in this last part of the chapter assimilate time-value-of-money concerns with risk and return trade-offs. Both these items have already been addressed in the earlier parts of the chapter.

Why do you need to be able to value assets, stocks, and bonds? Simply because it is important for you to be able to gauge how time-value and risk and return principles interact to create value for your firm. Creating value means much more than just generating accounting profits: when you can identify the proper mix of assets, debt, and equity for your firm, you not only generate substantial profits but also ensure that your assets earn you the highest return possible.

The three-part valuation model discussed here will let you determine the contribution to your firm's worth by stocks, bonds, and investments in assets. The necessary inputs to this valuation method are cash flows, the timing of the cash flows, and the discount rate. Cash flows and their timing incorporate time-value and return concepts into the valuation process, whereas the discount rate is used to incorporate risk.

Model 1: Stock Analyzer (STOCKS.XLS)

The stock-analyzer model uses three different approaches to valuing common stock. The first technique, called the *zero-growth model*, estimates the value of a share of common stock as being equal to the present value of all future expected dividends. As the title of this model suggests, dividends are expected to remain the same over time.

The second technique, called the *expected-return model*, lets you predict a stock's return when you know the original selling price, today's selling price, and the expected dividend.

The third technique is the well-known *Gordon constant growth model*. With it you can determine the worth of a share of stock when you know the dividends for five years and can estimate the sixth year's dividend.

Figure 5.28 shows the first two stock-valuation techniques. As always, the data-input areas appear boldfaced and underlined. In the top part of the screen, a stock that pays a dividend of $1.25 forever is worth $10.00 when you require a 12.5 percent return on your investment. But what if you want to calculate the return that a share of stock provides when you know the price of the stock? The lower part of this screen illustrates how to calculate the expected return. Suppose that you bought a stock last year for $97.50 and that the stock is worth $110.00 this year. If the stock pays a $5.00 dividend, you have earned a 17.95 percent return on your one-year investment.

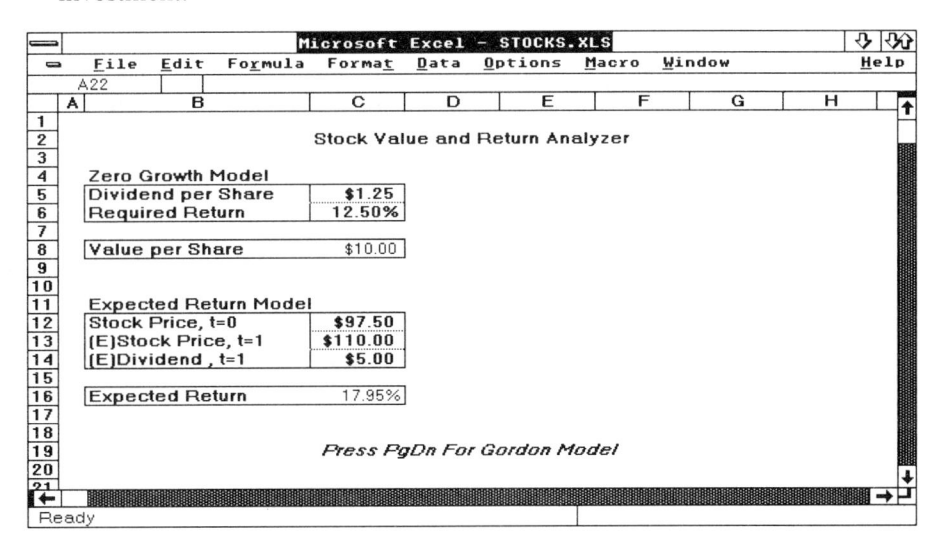

Fig. 5.28. The zero-growth model and the expected-return model.

When a company's financial position improves, management often decides to increase the dividends paid to shareholders. When dividends grow over time, use the Gordon growth model to evaluate the worth of your investment (see fig. 5.29).

Fig. 5.29.
The Gordon five-year constant growth model.

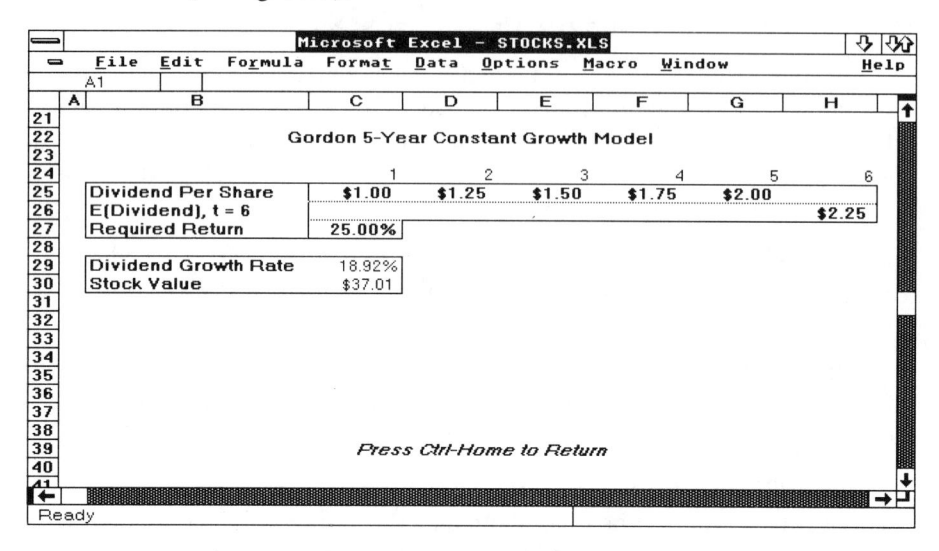

```
                    Microsoft Excel - STOCKS.XLS
    File  Edit  Formula  Format  Data  Options  Macro  Window      Help
    A1
   A│    B         │   C    │   D    │   E    │   F    │   G    │   H
21
22              Gordon 5-Year Constant Growth Model
23
24                    1         2         3         4         5         6
25   Dividend Per Share │ $1.00 │ $1.25 │ $1.50 │ $1.75 │ $2.00
26   E(Dividend), t = 6                                              $2.25
27   Required Return     25.00%
28
29   Dividend Growth Rate  18.92%
30   Stock Value          $37.01
31
...
39              Press Ctrl-Home to Return
40
Ready
```

Review the five-year dividend stream that appears in figure 5.29. When you enter a required return of 25 percent and an expected $2.25 sixth-year dividend, Excel computes a dividend growth rate of 18.92 percent and a stock value of $37.01.

The stock value produced by this model rarely matches the price currently listed in the stock-quote section of a newspaper. In fact, the stock's current price will be higher or lower, reflecting the public's perception about the worth of that company. This model tells you what the value *should* be, given its dividend flow stream and your anticipated return. Obviously, values will be different for different investors simply because everyone has different return requirements.

Look at it this way. If the stock is currently selling at $42, your stock is selling at a premium—a boon to you, given that your perception of its value is lower by roughly $5. If the stock were currently selling at $22, you'd want to reevaluate your investment in this particular company, especially given that public consensus suggests that the stock's value is $15 lower than you believe it to be. Of course, this type of analysis ignores the possibility that the stock could be overvalued or undervalued. Even so, using the Gordon model is a good starting point for stock valuation.

What do think would happen if you entered a $1 dividend for all six periods in the Gordon model? Figure 5.30 shows that if you require a 25 percent return on your investment, then the stock's value equals $4. Notice that the dividend growth rate is 0 percent, which suggests that this scenario would produce the same result as if you used the zero-growth model pictured in figure 5.28.

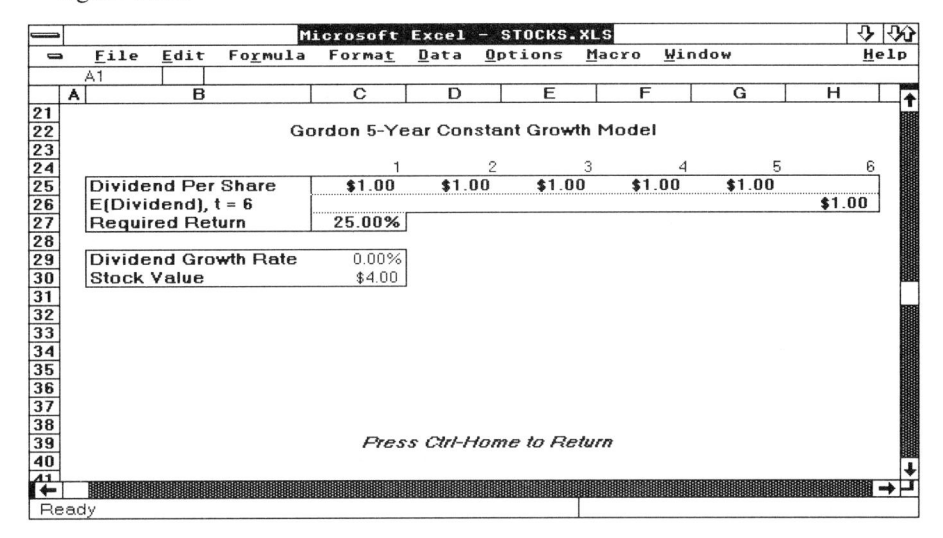

Fig. 5.30. The Gordon model revisited.

Model 2: Bond Analyzer (BONDS.XLS)

The bond-analyzer model uses two valuation techniques to help you value the worth of an investment. The first method uses data about a bond to determine its value and calculate its premium or discount price when applicable. The second technique uses similar bond data to calculate a bond's yield to maturity (YTM). Both methods enable you to factor in annual and semiannual interest payments.

What exactly happens when you buy a bond? When you buy a company's bond, you purchase some of its debt and in effect become a company creditor. As a creditor, you will receive payment (interest) before the company stockholders receive payment (dividends). So the risk associated with bond investments is lower on average than that associated with stocks; however, bonds on average offer a correspondingly lower return than stocks. The decision about investing in a stock or bond is an important one, and after you learn to use this next model, you'll be prepared to analyze the pros and cons of one investment over another.

The bond-analyzer model needs five pieces of data in order to function:

- The bond's par value (usually $1,000)
- The time to maturity
- The coupon interest rate
- The frequency with which interest is paid
- The required return for investing in bonds

When you complete the data-input table, Excel calculates the periodic interest payment, the annual interest payment, the value of the bond, and a premium or discount value when applicable.

Figure 5.31 shows the completed data table for a 10-year, 10 percent AT&T bond. The par value of this bond is $1,000, and interest is paid annually. When your required return is 9.5 percent, the bond is worth $1,031.39 to you. If this bond were currently available at this price, it would be selling at a $31.39 premium over par value. If the interest on this bond were paid semiannually instead of annually, the bond's premium value would increase to $31.83 (see fig. 5.32).

Fig. 5.31.
The bond value analyzer.

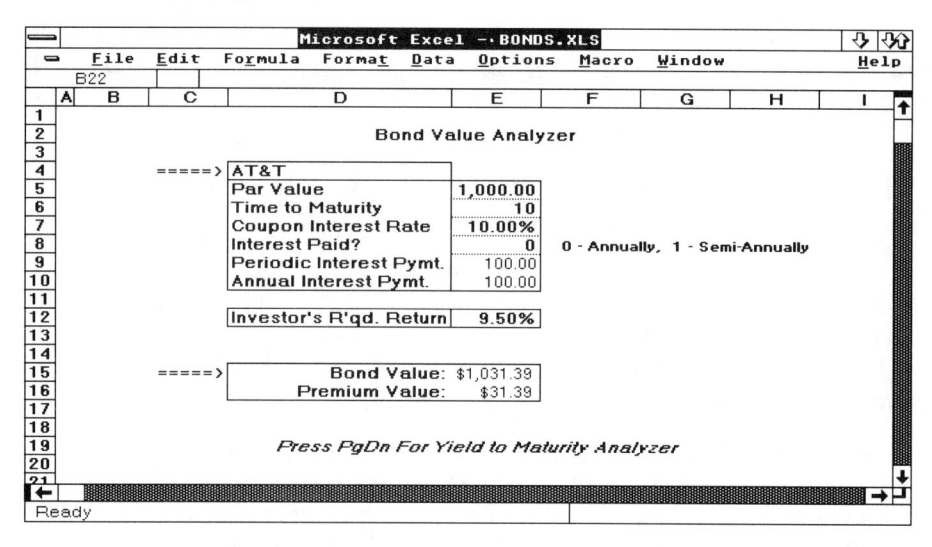

What if you raise your expected return from 9.5 percent to 10.75 percent? At the new level, the bond would be worth $955.36 to you (see fig. 5.33). If this bond were currently available at this price, it would be selling at a $44.64 discount under par value.

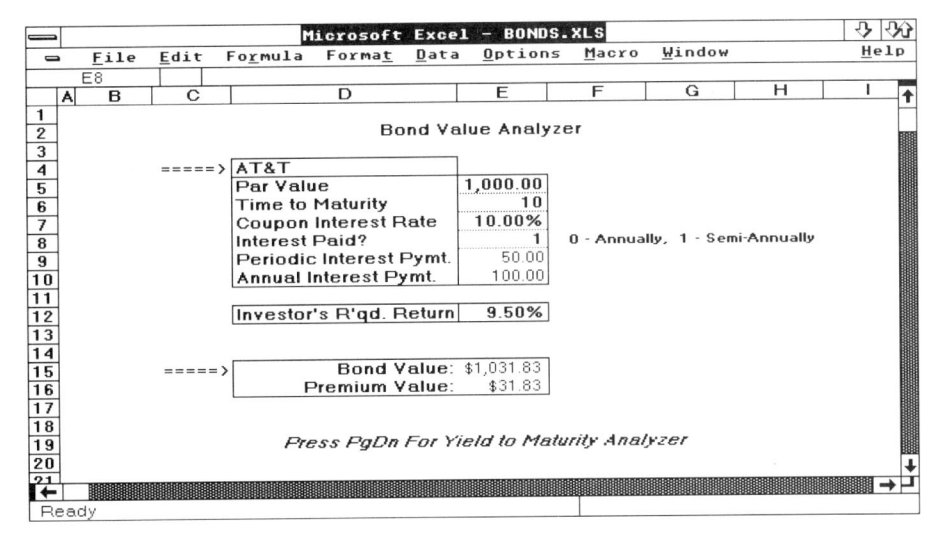

Fig. 5.32.
The bond value analyzer, computing the value of an AT&T bond that pays interest semiannually.

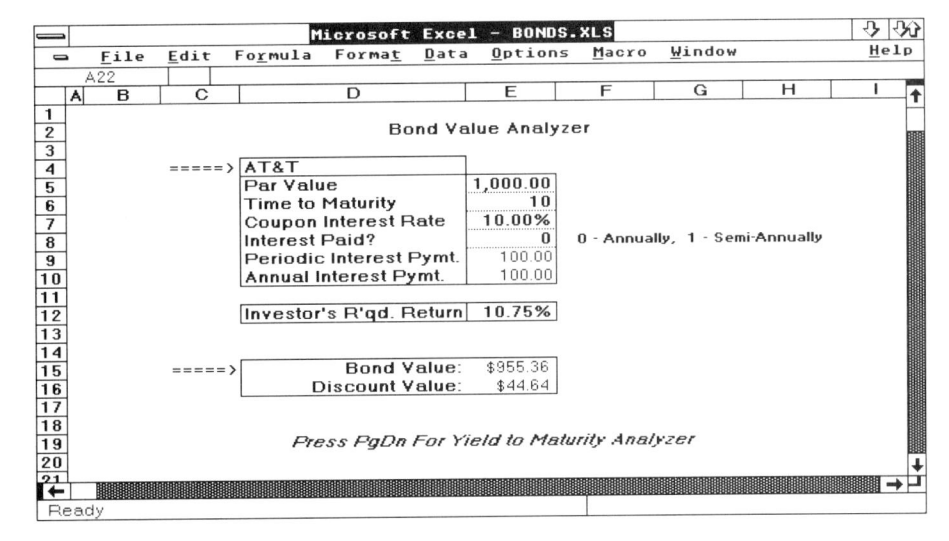

Fig. 5.33.
Changing your required return alters the bond's value to you.

So far you have considered situations in which your required return is higher and lower than the bond's coupon interest rate. What happens when these two values are exactly equal? Figure 5.34 demonstrates that when an investor's required return matches the bond's coupon interest rate, the bond's worth to the investor is equal to its par value.

Fig. 5.34.
A bond valued at its par value.

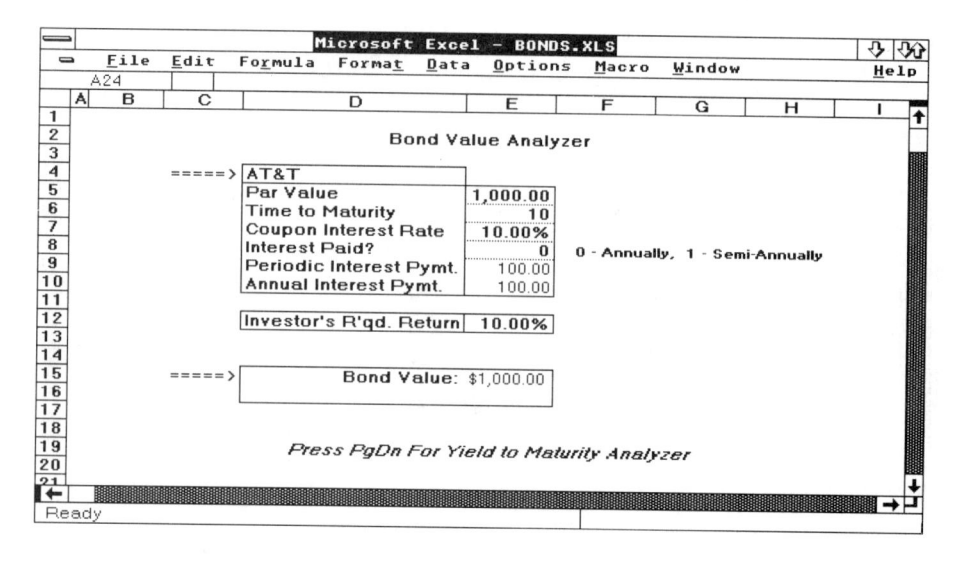

```
┌─────────────────── Microsoft Excel - BONDS.XLS ───────────────────┐
│  File   Edit   Formula   Format   Data   Options   Macro   Window    Help │
├───────────────────────────────────────────────────────────────────┤
│ A24                                                                │
│   A │ B │ C │     D     │     E     │     F     │  G  │  H  │ I  │
│  1                                                                 │
│  2              Bond Value Analyzer                                │
│  3                                                                 │
│  4         =====> AT&T                                             │
│  5                Par Value              1,000.00                  │
│  6                Time to Maturity            10                   │
│  7                Coupon Interest Rate    10.00%                   │
│  8                Interest Paid?               0   0 - Annually, 1 - Semi-Annually │
│  9                Periodic Interest Pymt. 100.00                   │
│ 10                Annual Interest Pymt.   100.00                   │
│ 11                                                                 │
│ 12                Investor's R'qd. Return  10.00%                  │
│ 13                                                                 │
│ 14                                                                 │
│ 15         =====>       Bond Value: $1,000.00                      │
│ 16                                                                 │
│ 17                                                                 │
│ 18                                                                 │
│ 19              Press PgDn For Yield to Maturity Analyzer          │
│ 20                                                                 │
│ Ready                                                              │
└───────────────────────────────────────────────────────────────────┘
```

The second valuation technique uses a different perspective. Suppose that you are interested in valuing a bond's expected return when you know its current selling price. Figure 5.35 depicts a 20-year, 12.5 percent bond that is currently selling for $1,450. The bond is selling at a premium of $450 over par value, so the yield to maturity (its return over the life of the bond) is lower than the coupon interest rate. If the same bond now sells for $975, it is selling at a $25 discount under par value (see fig. 5.36). Now that you can buy the bond below par value, you will earn a return higher than the bond's coupon interest rate (12.78 percent versus 12.5 percent).

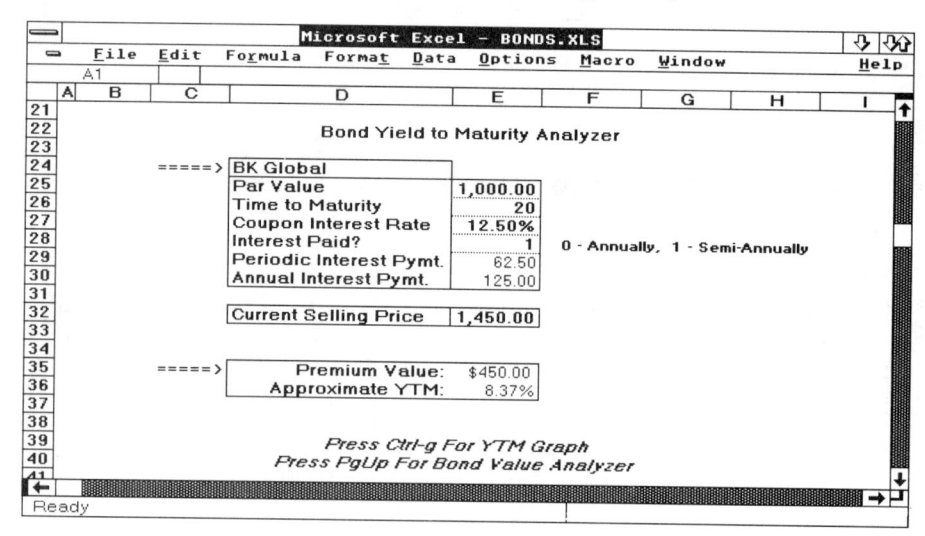

Fig. 5.35.
Calculating the YTM for a bond selling at a premium.

```
┌─────────────────── Microsoft Excel - BONDS.XLS ───────────────────┐
│  File   Edit   Formula   Format   Data   Options   Macro   Window    Help │
├───────────────────────────────────────────────────────────────────┤
│ A1                                                                 │
│   A │ B │ C │     D     │     E     │     F     │  G  │  H  │ I  │
│ 21                                                                 │
│ 22              Bond Yield to Maturity Analyzer                    │
│ 23                                                                 │
│ 24         =====> BK Global                                        │
│ 25                Par Value              1,000.00                  │
│ 26                Time to Maturity            20                   │
│ 27                Coupon Interest Rate    12.50%                   │
│ 28                Interest Paid?               1   0 - Annually, 1 - Semi-Annually │
│ 29                Periodic Interest Pymt.  62.50                   │
│ 30                Annual Interest Pymt.   125.00                   │
│ 31                                                                 │
│ 32                Current Selling Price  1,450.00                  │
│ 33                                                                 │
│ 34                                                                 │
│ 35         =====>    Premium Value:      $450.00                   │
│ 36                   Approximate YTM:      8.37%                   │
│ 37                                                                 │
│ 38                                                                 │
│ 39                    Press Ctrl-g For YTM Graph                   │
│ 40                  Press PgUp For Bond Value Analyzer             │
│ Ready                                                              │
└───────────────────────────────────────────────────────────────────┘
```

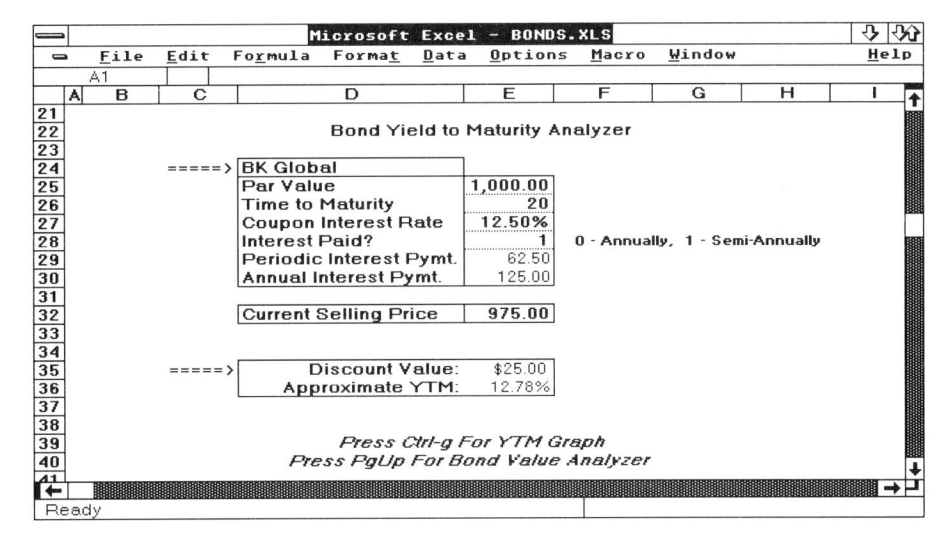

```
                Microsoft Excel - BONDS.XLS
   File   Edit   Formula  Format  Data  Options  Macro  Window        Help
   A1
 A  B    C         D              E        F         G        H     I
21
22                     Bond Yield to Maturity Analyzer
23
24        =====> BK Global
25                Par Value          1,000.00
26                Time to Maturity         20
27                Coupon Interest Rate  12.50%
28                Interest Paid?            1   0 - Annually,  1 - Semi-Annually
29                Periodic Interest Pymt.  62.50
30                Annual Interest Pymt.   125.00
31
32                Current Selling Price  975.00
33
34
35        =====>  Discount Value:      $25.00
36                Approximate YTM:      12.78%
37
38
39                   Press Ctrl-g For YTM Graph
40                 Press PgUp For Bond Value Analyzer
41
Ready
```

Fig. 5.36. Calculating the YTM for a bond selling at a discount.

Figure 5.37 shows that, as expected, when a bond sells at its par value, the coupon interest rate equals the yield to maturity. Now press Ctrl-g to create a yield-to-maturity graph for the 20-year BK Global bonds. This graph is shown in figure 5.38.

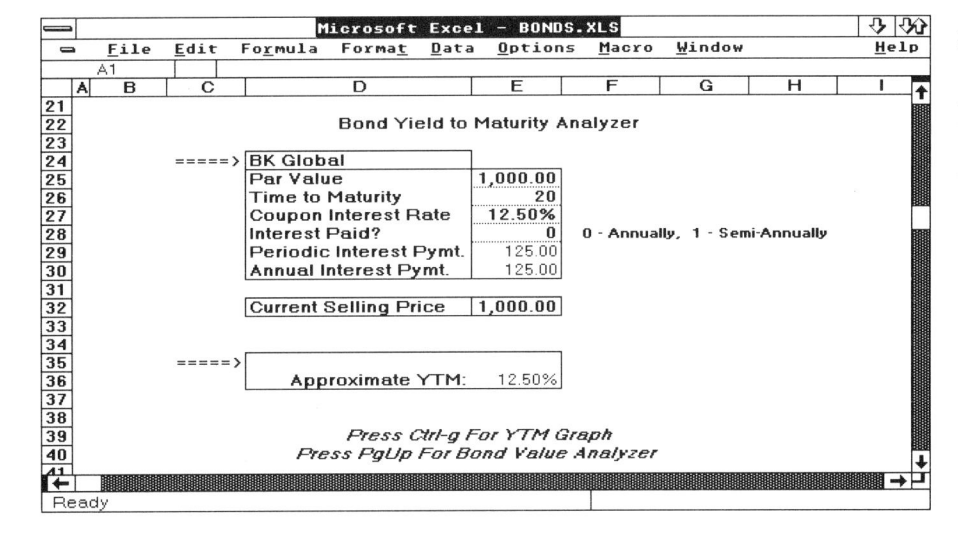

```
                Microsoft Excel - BONDS.XLS
   File   Edit   Formula  Format  Data  Options  Macro  Window        Help
   A1
 A  B    C         D              E        F         G        H     I
21
22                     Bond Yield to Maturity Analyzer
23
24        =====> BK Global
25                Par Value          1,000.00
26                Time to Maturity         20
27                Coupon Interest Rate  12.50%
28                Interest Paid?            0   0 - Annually,  1 - Semi-Annually
29                Periodic Interest Pymt. 125.00
30                Annual Interest Pymt.   125.00
31
32                Current Selling Price 1,000.00
33
34
35        =====>
36                Approximate YTM:      12.50%
37
38
39                   Press Ctrl-g For YTM Graph
40                 Press PgUp For Bond Value Analyzer
41
Ready
```

Fig. 5.37. The coupon interest rate equals the YTM when a bond sells at par value.

Fig. 5.38.
The BK Global 20-Year bond.

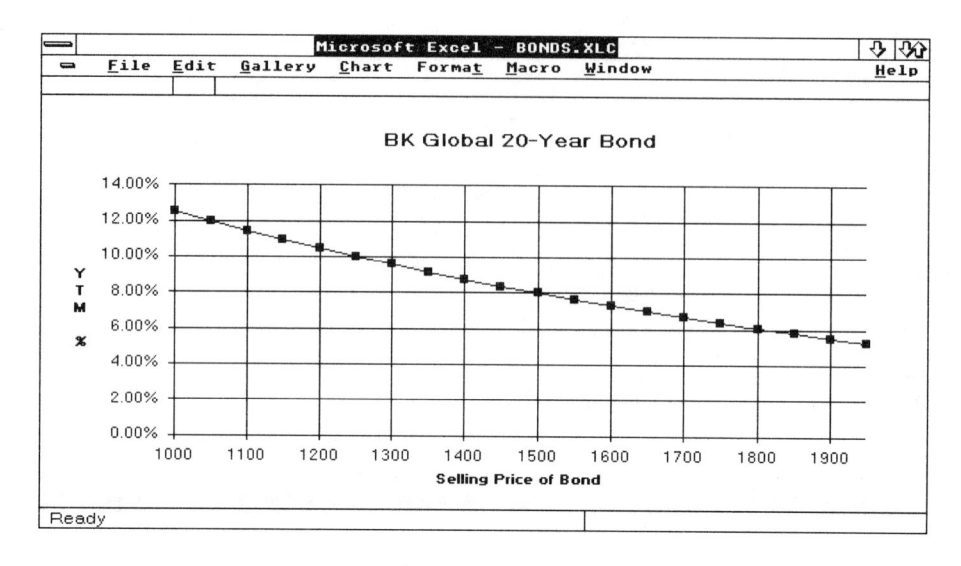

Figure 5.39 shows the macro code that creates the bond graph.

Fig. 5.39.
The bond investment analyzer chart-building macro.

	A
1	YTM Macro
2	=ECHO(FALSE)
3	=MESSAGE(TRUE,"CREATING A YIELD TO MATURITY GRAPH ...")
4	=ACTIVATE("BONDS.XLS")
5	=SELECT("R44C5:R64C6")
6	=NEW(2)
7	=GALLERY.LINE(1,TRUE)
8	=SELECT("Title")
9	=FORMAT.TEXT(2,2,FALSE,TRUE,TRUE,FALSE,FALSE)
10	=FORMAT.FONT(0,1,FALSE,"Helv",12,TRUE,FALSE,FALSE,FALSE)
11	=SELECT("Axis 1")
12	=ATTACH.TEXT(2)
13	=FORMULA("=""YTM %""")
14	=FORMAT.TEXT(2,2,TRUE,FALSE,TRUE,FALSE,FALSE)
15	=FORMAT.FONT(0,1,FALSE,"Helv",8,TRUE,FALSE,FALSE,FALSE)
16	=SELECT("Axis 2")
17	=ATTACH.TEXT(3)
18	=FORMULA("=""Selling Price of Bond""")
19	=FORMAT.FONT(0,1,FALSE,"Helv",8,TRUE,FALSE,FALSE,FALSE)
20	=SELECT("Axis 2")
21	=SCALE(1,2,2,FALSE,FALSE,FALSE)
22	=GRIDLINES(TRUE,FALSE,TRUE,FALSE)
23	=SELECT("")
24	=ACTIVATE.NEXT()
25	=SELECT("R1C1")
26	=ACTIVATE.PREV()
27	=MESSAGE(FALSE,"")
28	=ECHO(TRUE)
29	=SAVE.AS?()
30	=RETURN()

Model 3: Discounted-Cash-Flow Analyzer (DCFA.XLS)

The last model in this chapter uses discounted-cash-flow analysis to value a single asset or to value the incremental cash flows between two asset opportunities.

The measurements that produce this analysis are net present value (NPV), internal rate of return (IRR), and profitability index (PI). The net present value of an asset equals the cost of the asset less the sum of its discounted cash flows. In general, assets that produce an NPV greater than or equal to zero increase the value of the firm. The IRR measurement is closely related to NPV. The IRR tells you the discount rate (DR) that causes the NPV of an asset to equal zero exactly. In general, assets whose IRR is greater than or equal to the discount rate increase the value of the firm. Also known as the benefit-cost ratio, the PI value is useful for evaluating the incremental cash flows of two competing assets when NPV and IRR measurements offer conflicting data.

In the single-asset model, you supply a discount rate and the relevant cash flows to arrive at the asset's NPV and IRR values. When you want to value the cost of choosing one asset over another, you supply a single discount rate and the relevant cash flows for both assets.

Asset A produces the cash-flow stream shown in figure 5.40. When the cash flows are discounted at 10.0 percent, the NPV is equal to $12,499.79, and the IRR is equal to 12.97 percent.

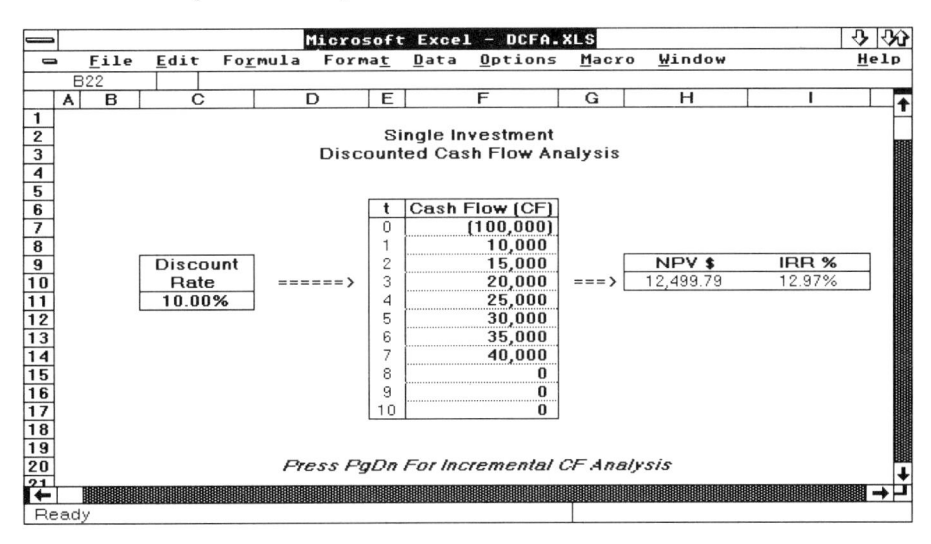

Fig. 5.40.
Single-asset analysis.

Because NPV is greater than or equal to zero and IRR is greater than or equal to the discount rate, the asset will add value to the firm and is thus desirable.

In figure 5.41, asset A is reevaluated through the use of a higher discount rate. When the cash flows are discounted at 15.0 percent, the NPV equals ($7,433.79), and the IRR equals 12.97 percent. Because NPV is less than zero and IRR is less than the discount rate, the asset would reduce the value of the firm and is thus undesirable.

Fig. 5.41.
Single-asset analysis revisited.

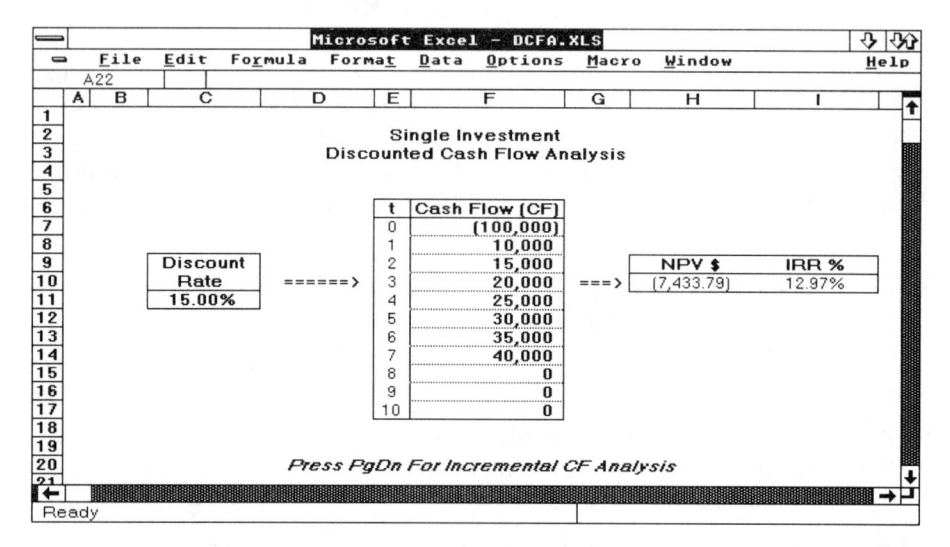

t	Cash Flow (CF)
0	(100,000)
1	10,000
2	15,000
3	20,000
4	25,000
5	30,000
6	35,000
7	40,000
8	0
9	0
10	0

Discount Rate: 15.00%

NPV $: (7,433.79)
IRR %: 12.97%

Press PgDn For Incremental CF Analysis

Now examine a situation in which you must choose between two competing assets, A and B. The left-hand portion of figure 5.42 shows the cash flows, NPVs, IRRs, and PIs for both assets.

If you evaluate each asset independently, you would have a difficult time deciding which one is the better choice, because both asset A and B have NPV greater than or equal to zero and IRR greater than or equal to DR. And whereas asset A's NPV is higher than B's, asset B's profitability index is higher than A's. Confused? This example demonstrates the need to perform incremental cash-flow analysis.

Consider the organization of the assets in the data tables. Your asset alternatives won't be called asset A and asset B. When you enter data into the table, make asset A the asset with the larger cash flows. In this analysis, you are always evaluating the incremental cost of choosing asset A over asset B.

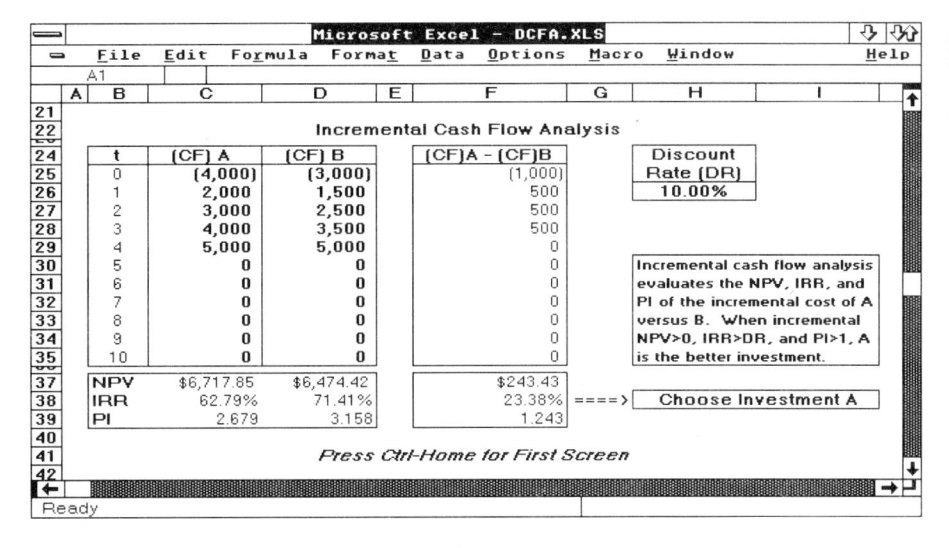

Fig. 5.42. Evaluating incremental cash flows.

	Incremental Cash Flow Analysis			
t	(CF) A	(CF) B	(CF)A - (CF)B	Discount Rate (DR) 10.00%
0	(4,000)	(3,000)	(1,000)	
1	2,000	1,500	500	
2	3,000	2,500	500	
3	4,000	3,500	500	
4	5,000	5,000	0	
5	0	0	0	
6	0	0	0	
7	0	0	0	
8	0	0	0	
9	0	0	0	
10	0	0	0	
NPV	$6,717.85	$6,474.42	$243.43	====> Choose Investment A
IRR	62.79%	71.41%	23.38%	
PI	2.679	3.158	1.243	

When (1) the incremental NPV is greater than or equal to zero, (2) the incremental IRR is greater than or equal to DR, and (3) the incremental PI is greater than 1, then asset A is the better choice.

Figure 5.43 shows an example of two assets, of which asset B is the preferable choice. Here, the tests of incremental NPV, IRR, and PI all fail, so asset B is preferred to asset A.

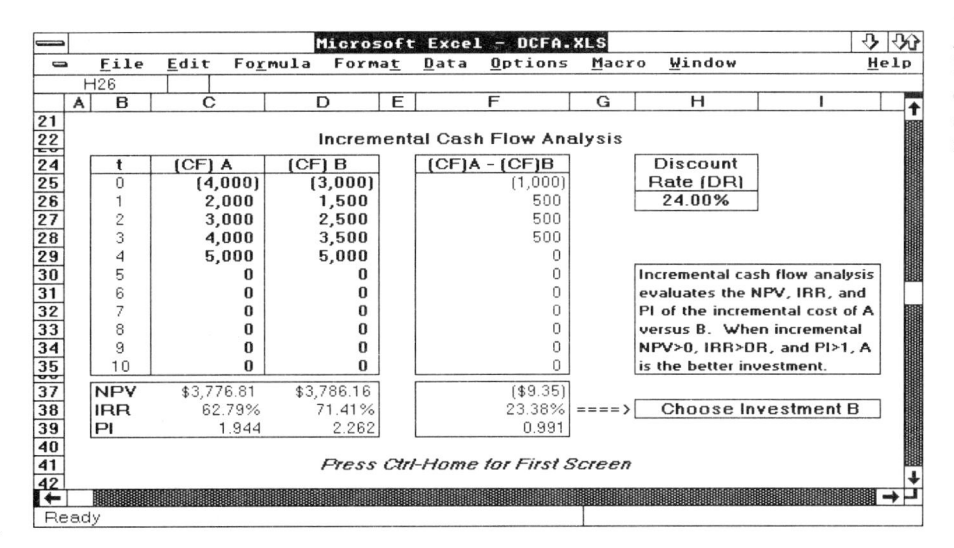

Fig. 5.43. Incremental-cash-flow analysis revisited.

	Incremental Cash Flow Analysis			
t	(CF) A	(CF) B	(CF)A - (CF)B	Discount Rate (DR) 24.00%
0	(4,000)	(3,000)	(1,000)	
1	2,000	1,500	500	
2	3,000	2,500	500	
3	4,000	3,500	500	
4	5,000	5,000	0	
5	0	0	0	
6	0	0	0	
7	0	0	0	
8	0	0	0	
9	0	0	0	
10	0	0	0	
NPV	$3,776.81	$3,786.16	($9.35)	====> Choose Investment B
IRR	62.79%	71.41%	23.38%	
PI	1.944	2.262	0.991	

Summary

This chapter presented specific coverage of the various financial-valuation tools you can use to manage your firm's assets and investments. As you can see, there appears to be a model or technique available to analyze just about every investment opportunity that might befall you.

As you continue to learn the nuances of using the models in this chapter, don't forget that much of the data you generate with these models can be used as input to the models presented in Chapter 4.

The major topics of this chapter—asset management, the time value of money, risk and return, and valuation—also have practical applications for the personal investor. Even if you can't find a use for some of these models in your own business, you can surely put them to use managing your own personal-investment portfolio. Theories and practices that help lead businesses into successful ventures can often guide you down the road to personal financial success. As you begin the journey, take the time to experiment with these models so that you will understand how they can help you make the right decisions.

In Chapter 6 you will learn how to use a fully automated Excel general ledger system. This powerful model will help you track the flow of your accounting data from the general journal through the preparation of summary financial statements.

6

Achieving General Ledger Accounting Success

In Chapter 3 you learned how easy it is to create a business checkbook system that summarizes your firm's cash-related accounting data. You also learned that this summarized accounting data is an important input to the process of creating accounting statements and financial forecasts. Later chapters showed how easy it is to use Excel models to track the productivity of your firm's investment in assets and liabilities. So that you could use each of these various models, one important assumption was made: that *all* the required summarized accounting data is readily available to you.

The checkbook system in Chapter 3 enabled you to record and summarize all your cash-related business expenses. Your firm's income statement and balance sheet, however, list more than just cash expenses. You also need to gather revenue data, record depreciation expenses, record credit purchases, and calculate the change in your firm's equity at the end of the accounting period. These extra accounting functions do not normally flow through a business checkbook system. To record and summarize this accounting data, you need a general ledger accounting system.

Chapter 6 introduces a powerful Excel application called the General Ledger Accounting System (GLAS) model. This application is made up of a workspace, two menu worksheets, a general ledger/journal worksheet, several user-friendly macros, and a report worksheet. Once the system is loaded into Excel, just follow the on-screen instructions that appear on the menus, and you're off. You'll undoubtedly enjoy using this application because, unlike any other model you've encountered so far in this book, the GLAS model is completely self-running.

This chapter begins by highlighting the best features of the GLAS model and defining each component. Next, you learn exactly what you need to do to prepare the model for first-time use. Then the discussion turns to how to use the model, emphasizing its "chronological" nature (you enter transactions before posting transactions before printing reports, and so on). To reinforce your understanding of the GLAS model's chronological nature, the discussion presents the main menu choices in the recommended order of operation (entering journal transactions precedes posting journal transactions, which precedes printing reports, and so on). Along the way, the rules of operation are highlighted, as well as potential pitfalls and macro-error traps that you might encounter. To conclude, the chapter demonstrates using the application with the model firm Protocol Services Int'l.

If in earlier chapters you have ignored this book's pleas to follow along with the examples, that's fine. You are urged to follow Chapter 6's step-by-step case study, however, because doing so will give you a feel for the proper use of the model. And even more important, following along with the case study will raise questions in your own mind about how to adapt GLAS to your firm's accounting environment.

The following are items you should consider before using the *Excel Business Application* models:

1. Make a backup copy of the models disk and store the backup in a safe place.
2. If you have a hard disk drive, create a new subdirectory in Excel and load the models into this subdirectory. Then store the disk.
3. Each model has been saved in Options Protect Document mode. You may enter data only into worksheet cells that have been previously unlocked with the Format Cell Protection command. When the Options Protect Document is enabled, these cells appear underlined.

An Overview of the GLAS Model

The GLAS model is indeed indicative of the power that Excel places at your fingertips. With GLAS, you can re-create your firm's chart of accounts. GLAS enables you to enter your general ledger account balances and per-period budget estimates.

Once you are in a new accounting period, GLAS uses Excel's Data Form command to simplify transaction entry into the general journal. When you make an entry into the general journal, GLAS automatically assigns a transaction number and verifies the validity of your debit and credit account selection. If a transaction is acceptable, GLAS gives you an okay to continue.

Posting a period's accounting transactions is as easy as pressing Ctrl-p. And GLAS never posts bad accounting data. If you forget to enter a transaction amount, or if you select a nonexistent ledger account, GLAS tells you so and won't post your transactions until you correct the error. If you're not sure *where* the error is, don't worry—GLAS highlights each transaction that it cannot post. If you're not sure *what* the nature of the error is, check the data form, because it has a Status field that describes exactly what's wrong with a bad entry. And unlike most other accounting systems, GLAS clears, reverifies, and then reposts both the current and prior transactions each time you post a set of transactions within the same period. You'll never have to make extra "correcting entries" again. At the end of an accounting period, post the general journal one last time, and you're ready to print the period-end reports.

GLAS has four built-in reports available on the Print Reports menu. You can print out your firm's chart of accounts, print a trial balance sheet, calculate and print a budget summary and variance analysis, and print a period-to-date ledger summary.

These valuable reports compile and present the critical summary accounting data that you'll need in order to prepare an income statement and a balance sheet for your firm.

When you have all the end-of-period reports in hand, it's time to back up and clear your general journal and update the general ledger account balances. This complex operation is completely automated, requiring only that you press Ctrl-c. But before GLAS closes the accounting documents, it automatically creates a backup file, using a unique name that you select. Now you have on file all the period's transactions, which constitute an important audit trail should you need to refer to it later.

Understanding the GLAS Model Components

In this section, you examine the individual components of the GLAS model. The model consists of seven files:

GL.XLW	(the GLAS workspace file)
GENMENU.XLS	(the main menu worksheet)
GL.XLM	(application macros)
GL.XLS	(the general ledger/journal worksheet)
REPMENU.XLS	(the Print Reports menu worksheet)
TEMP.XLS	(the report worksheet)
PROTOCOL.XLS	(the model company's general ledger/journal worksheet)

The files GENMENU.XLS, GL.XLM, GL.XLS, and REPMENU.XLS are part of the GL.XLW workspace and load in that order of precedence. The files TEMP.XLS and PROTOCOL.XLS are not part of the GL.XLW workspace.

GL.XLW: The GLAS Workspace File

This workspace file controls all the files (except TMP.XLS) that enable the GLAS model to operate. When you're at the operating system level, you can quickly load the application model into Excel by typing **GL.XLW** after **Excel** at the command prompt and by then pressing Enter. But don't load the model just yet; you first need to review the rest of the GLAS files.

GENMENU.XLS: The GLAS Main Menu Worksheet File

Once loaded, GLAS displays the main menu, shown in figure 6.1. This menu offers six choices, listed in the order in which you should execute them to properly use the GLAS model.

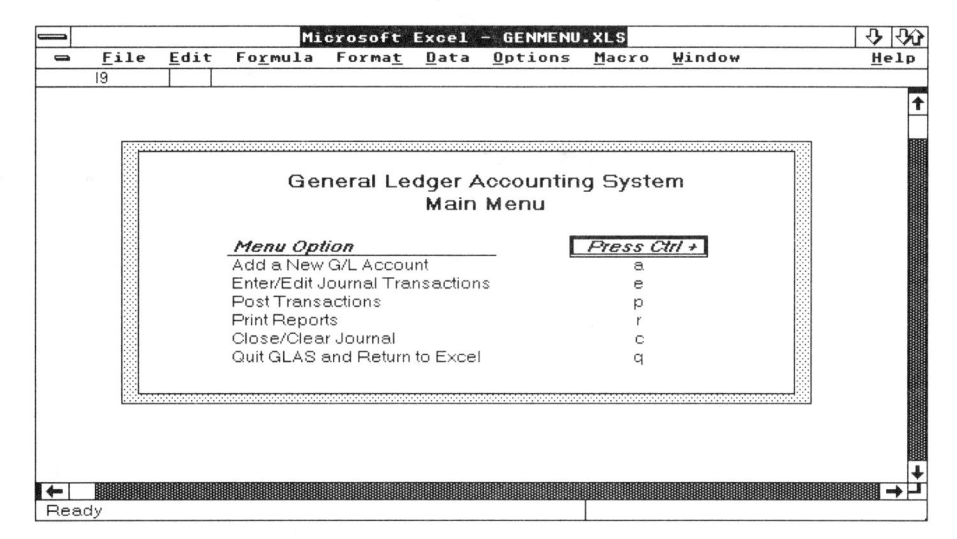

Fig. 6.1.
The GLAS main menu file.

GL.XLS: The GLAS General Ledger/Journal Worksheet File

The GL.XLS file stores the firm name, the chart of accounts, the ledger account balance and budget data, and the general journal. The general journal stores up to 50 transactions per period, expandable up to roughly the maximum amount of lines available on an Excel worksheet. Unlike most other accounting software packages, the GLAS model combines the general ledger and the general journal data into one document.

GL.XLM: The GLAS Application Macros File

This file contains 12 macros and 2 subroutines. Together these macros control almost all the data input and output to this application model. Later, you will explore the purpose of each macro and discover those instances when you'll be required to do a task that the macros do not control.

REPMENU.XLS: The GLAS Print Reports Menu File

When you select Ctrl-r from the main menu, Excel activates the Print Reports menu file, shown in figure 6.2. This menu displays four report choices and one exit-menu choice. In contrast to the choices found on the main menu, the report menu choices may be executed in any order you like. The assumption, of course, is that you have already posted your journal transactions by using the Ctrl-p macro.

Fig. 6.2.
The GLAS Print Reports menu file.

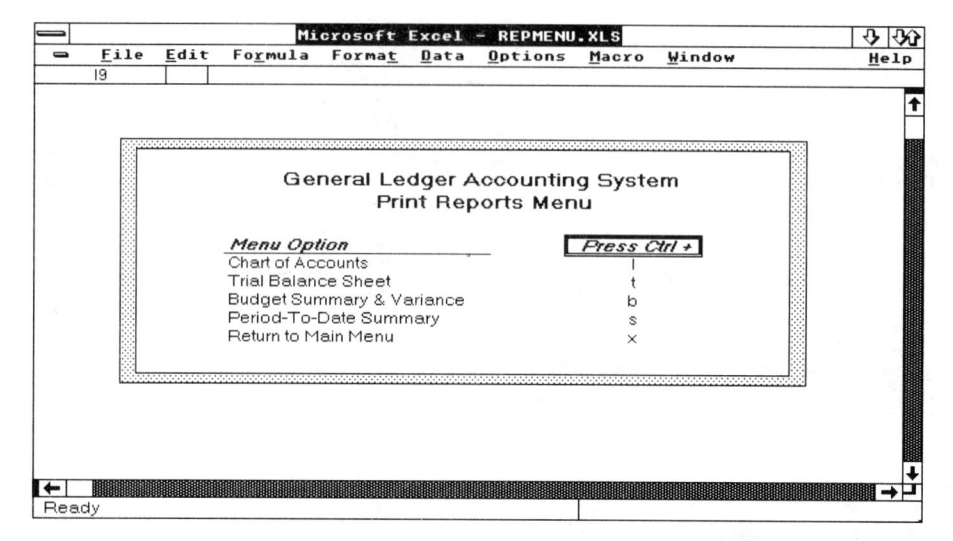

```
┌─────────────── Microsoft Excel - REPMENU.XLS ───────────────┐
  File  Edit  Formula  Format  Data  Options  Macro  Window        Help
  |9

              General Ledger Accounting System
                    Print Reports Menu

         Menu Option                    Press Ctrl +
         Chart of Accounts                   l
         Trial Balance Sheet                 t
         Budget Summary & Variance           b
         Period-To-Date Summary              s
         Return to Main Menu                 x

 Ready
```

TMP.XLS: The GLAS Report Worksheet File

The TMP.XLS file is not part of the GLAS workspace and so does not automatically load when you load GL.XLW. The purpose of this file is to act as a temporary repository for report data created by the report macros. The GLAS report macros contain commands that open and close this temporary file as needed.

PROTOCOL.XLS: The Model Company's General Ledger/Journal Worksheet File

Like TEMP.XLS, the PROTOCOL.XLS file is not part of the GLAS workspace and so does not automatically load when you load GL.XLW. After you are familiar with the GLAS application, you can use PROTOCOL.XLS to examine the results of an accounting cycle of a hypothetical company that uses GLAS in its accounting department.

One final note: All seven files must be present in the same directory on your floppy or hard disk drive. GLAS will not work without them.

Preparing the GLAS Model for First-Time Use

The GLAS model on your distribution disk contains no data and only a skeleton chart of accounts, so before configuring the GLAS model for the first time, you must do the following:

- Select a starting month for using the GLAS model.
- Gather your firm's current accounting records.
- Gather your firm's current fiscal budget.

Once you have all these records in hand, and once you are near the beginning of the designated starting accounting period, you are ready to prepare GLAS for first-time use. Do the following:

- Enter your firm's chart of accounts into the GLAS model.
- Enter your firm name.
- Enter the ledger account balances and budget estimates.

Entering the New Chart of Accounts

The GLAS model uses the following chart-of-accounts numbering system:

100-199	Assets	600-799	Revenues
200-499	Liabilities	800-999	Expenses
500-599	Equity		

The GLAS model also comes equipped with standard account descriptions from each major category:

100	Cash	600	Revenues, Net
120	Accounts Receivable, Net	605	Interest
150	Fixed Assets, Net	801	Rent
200	Notes Payable	802	Utilities
220	Accounts Payable	803	Telephone
500	Equity 1	804	Salaries
501	Drawing 1	805	Depreciation
505	Equity 2	806	Interest
506	Drawing 2		

If your firm's current general ledger contains contra accounts such as Accumulated Depreciation, Allowance for Doubtful Accounts, or Sales Returns & Allowances, you will have to make a slight adjustment when adding these accounts to your GLAS chart of accounts.

First, convert the dependent account into a "net" account. Next, subtract the contra account's balance from the dependent account's balance. Suppose, for example, that you have the following account balances at the end of your most recent fiscal year:

Fixed Assets   36,000
Acc. Depreciation   7,200

Convert them to the following GLAS account:

Fixed Assets, Net   28,800

To record the depreciation expense for the first month of the new fiscal year, make the general journal entry as follows:

Depreciation Expense 600
Fixed Assets, Net.   600

The reports generated by the GLAS model display and print ledger account data sorted by account number. All the report macros use Excel's built-in Data Sort function to sort the report data prior to printing. So if you elect to use your own numbering system, assign account numbers carefully, remembering that you can always go back and edit account numbers later as needed. The only numbering rule that you must adhere to is that every ledger account must have a unique account number.

It's a given that you will need to immediately add more accounts to the basic GLAS chart of accounts provided with the model. It's also likely that over time you will need to add extra ledger accounts. The procedure for accomplishing either task is the same, although the first-time chart-of-accounts setup takes a bit longer.

To add asset, liability, revenue, or expense accounts, first determine how many of each account type you want to add to the existing chart of accounts. With those numbers in mind, go to GLAS's main menu and select Ctrl-a.

Note: Every attempt has been made to assign mnemonic keys to the GLAS macros. Most of the macros correspond to mnemonic keys, but others don't. For example, whereas Ctrl-c invokes the (C)lose and Clear Journal macro, it's probably not as clear why Ctrl-l is used to (l)ist the Chart of Accounts. Simply put, because *C* had already been chosen for the former macro, and because the next logical key, *A*, was assigned to a different macro, *L* was selected by default. Makes sense, huh?

GLAS prompts you for the account type, as shown in figure 6.3. Next, GLAS asks you how many accounts to add. This number refers to the specific account type that you just selected. For example, you might add 10 asset accounts, then 5 liability accounts, then 2 equity accounts, and so on.

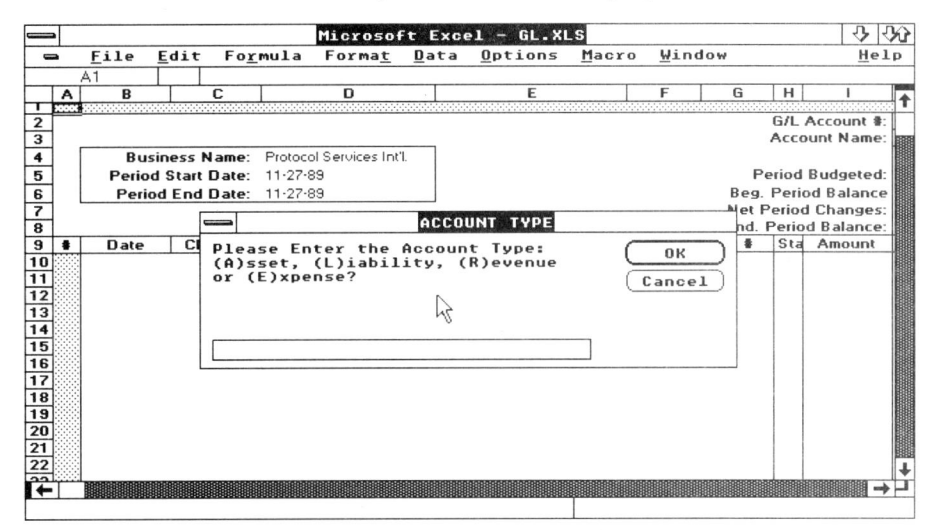

Fig. 6.3. Adding to GLAS's chart of accounts.

If you want to stop this operation for some reason, simply click on the Cancel button in the input box; GLAS returns you to the main menu.

> **Tip:** In general, you can cancel a GLAS macro operation in two ways. The better method is to click on an input box's Cancel button. When the input box requests a number, however, you can instead enter 0 to cancel the operation.

Entering invalid data or out-of-range data causes GLAS to display an error or caution message. Two such messages appear in figure 6.4.

After you are finished adding new ledger accounts, you will need to enter account descriptions, the starting account balances, and budget amounts (if available). This task is an example of one that is not controlled by a macro. You must enter this information manually—and that is the topic of the next section.

Fig. 6.4.
Error messages in the Ctrl-a macro.

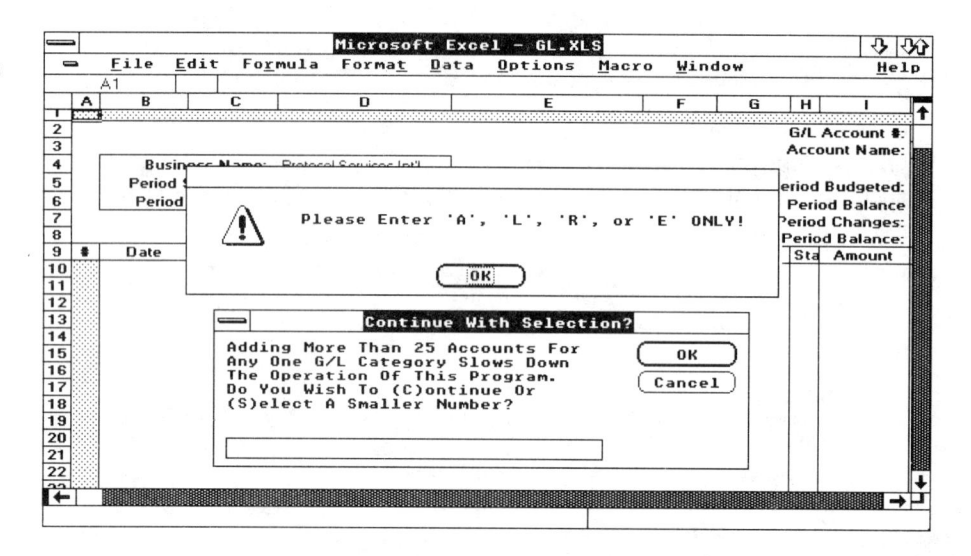

Manually Entering Account Descriptions and Balances

If you successfully added new ledger accounts by using the Ctrl-a macro, then you are now back on GLAS's main menu. To enter account descriptions and balances manually, select Window from Excel's menu bar and activate GL.XLS by clicking its name once.

You are now on the general ledger/journal worksheet. The first window of this worksheet is shown in figure 6.5.

Fig. 6.5.
The general ledger/journal worksheet, areas A and B.

Area A contains the name and date block. Enter your firm name into cell D4. The period-start and period-end dates are automatically displayed after you enter transactions into the journal. Until then, Excel displays your computer's system date in cells D5:D6. *Do not* enter dates into these cells.

Area B contains the general journal block. When you enter transactions by using the Ctrl-e macro, Excel gives you access to columns B:G and column I. When you have entered a valid transaction, GLAS assigns a transaction number in column A and displays the transaction status in column H. Don't worry about the fact that column H is so narrow: when you are using the Ctrl-e macro, Excel displays the full contents of this column on the data form (more about this in the next section).

Note: You should have noticed that with the exception of columns A and H, the general journal block in figure 6.5 is underlined. The underlining appears when Option Protect Document mode is on. When you are using the Ctrl-e macro, notice that Excel displays the contents of column H but doesn't permit you to change them.

Press Ctrl-PgDn once to move to the area shown in figure 6.6. (On your monitor, Excel may display a different amount of columns and rows.)

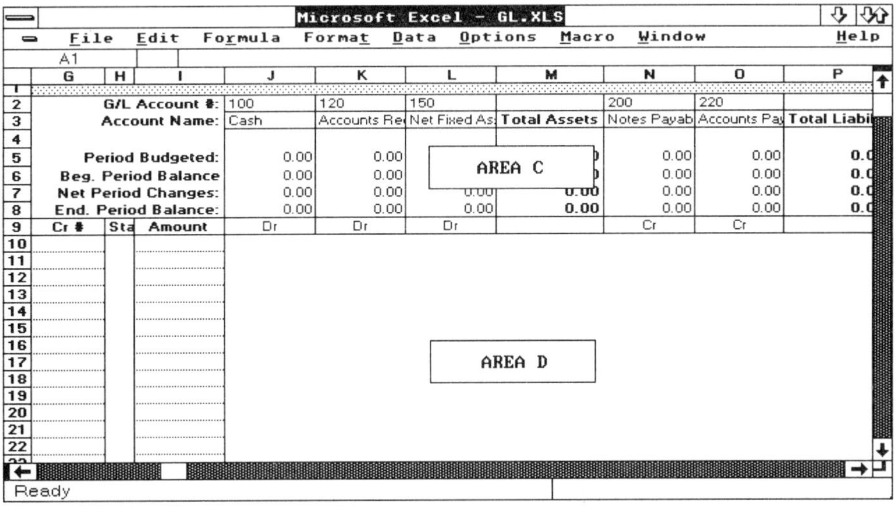

Fig. 6.6.
The general ledger/journal worksheet, areas C and D.

Area C in figure 6.6 shows the ledger titles and ledger accounts. New ledger accounts (if you've already added new accounts) are titled [New Acct]. For these accounts, enter an account number into row 2, a description into row 3, the period-budgeted value into row 5, and the beginning-period balance into row 6.

> Tip: To enter this data, you first must choose Option UnProtect Document. When you have finished entering the new ledger account data, be sure to select Option Protect Document and File Save to record the changes.

> Warning: *Never enter data in row 7 or 8.* These rows contain formulas critical to the successful operation of GLAS. Entering numerical values into these rows destroys the integrity of the GLAS model.

The terms "Dr" and "Cr" that appear in row 9 indicate the type of account when the account is in normal balance. For example, asset accounts are normally debit "Dr" accounts when they have normal balances.

Also notice that several boldfaced columns total the assets, liabilities, equity, revenues, expenses, net income, and net income to retained earnings. These columns also contain important formulas; feel free to look, but don't alter them in any way.

Valid journal transactions are posted into area D when you run the Ctrl-p macro. For the time being, this area remains completely blank.

When you have finished creating your new chart of accounts, return to the GLAS main menu by clicking the Window menu and selecting GENMENU.XLS.

At this time, the general journal/ledger worksheet is prepared to accept transactions for a new accounting period. The next section discusses in detail how to operate the GLAS model for the first time.

Using the Options on GLAS's Main Menu and Print Reports Menu

You can use GLAS on a daily basis in your business, or you can use the model just once at the end of each monthly accounting period: the choice is yours. In making this decision, consider the number of total accounting transactions that you make in an average month. If the number is small (10 to 50), it's easier to record all the transactions in one sitting. If your average transactions run in the hundreds, however, you should consider using GLAS on a regular basis—once per week, for example.

The following sections explain the six menu options on GLAS's main menu and then the five menu options on the Print Reports menu.

Adding a New G/L Account

You have already learned how to create a new chart of accounts before using GLAS for the first time. If you need to add an additional ledger account in the future, simply press Ctrl-a from the main menu and follow these simple steps:

Step 1. Select GL.XLS from the Window menu.

Step 2. Choose UnProtect Document from the Options menu.

Step 3. Manually edit the account descriptions.

Step 4. Enter the beginning account balance and budget estimate.

Step 5. Choose Protect Document from the Options menu.

Step 6. Choose Save from the File menu.

Step 7. Select GENMENU.XLS from the Windows menu.

Entering and Editing Journal Transactions

Once you have the proper chart of accounts in place, you are ready to enter transactions into GLAS's general journal. Pressing Ctrl-e once at the main menu activates GL.XLS and calls the data form shown in figure 6.7.

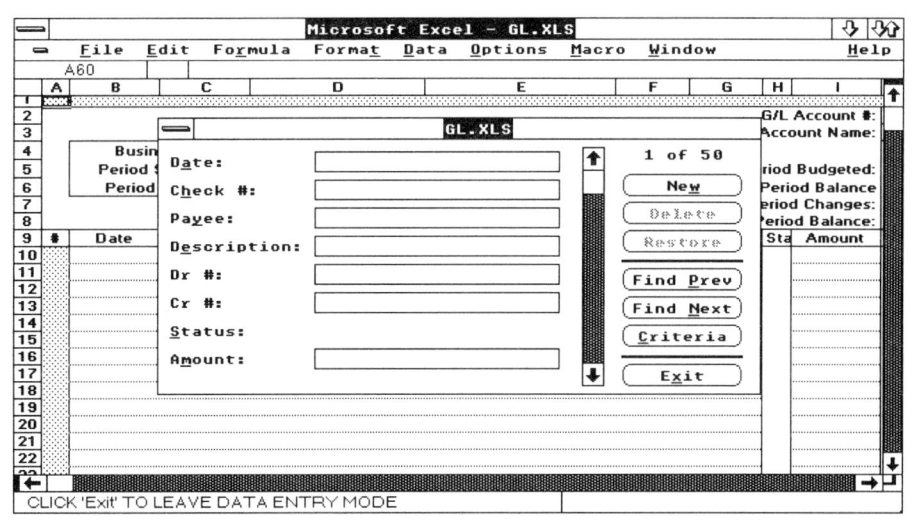

Fig. 6.7. The GLAS data form.

The data fields appearing on the left side of the data form mirror those found in the range B9:I9 on GL.XLS. The reason is that the data form acts as a data-entry medium between you and the database (the general ledger/journal worksheet). Use the Tab key to move from field to field within a record. To record a transaction entry, press Enter once after entering data into the amount field.

> Tip: Recall that although the column H field—the Status field—appears on the data form, the contents of this field are determined by the GLAS model. Use the Status field to visually check that you have entered a transaction correctly.

The items on the right side of the data form tell you the current record number and also enable you to perform actions on the database by clicking on an action button. Use the action buttons to restore a partially edited transaction; to scroll through the database, selecting previous and next records; to enter search criteria; and to exit from the data form.

> Tip: When you use an Excel database form, click the Criteria button to enter query mode. While in this mode, you can locate all database records that meet your specifications. For example, to find all records in the database that debit account 100, enter 100 in the "Dr#:" field and press the Find Next button. To leave query mode, click Exit; Excel returns you to the data form.

If you prefer, press the Alt-*letter* combination indicated by the single underlined letter in each action word. To exit, press Alt-X.

Note: Usually, the New action button is used to expand the number of records in a given database. Here, the New button is inoperative because the GLAS general journal is initially configured to accept only 50 transactions per period. Later, you will learn how to increase the size of this database.

You can move the data form around the GL.XLS worksheet by dragging the form's title bar. Moving the form around enables you to see the resulting transaction entries on GL.XLS. Although this feature is a nice one, the true power of the Ctrl-e macro lies in the skillful use of the data form itself.

You can use the data form to enter and edit general journal transactions—even posted ones. You should always ensure that the status of your transactions is "Ok" before posting them to the general ledger with the Ctrl-p macro.

> Tip: When you edit a bad transaction—for example, a transaction that uses a nonexistent ledger account—the Status field updates *after* the data form is closed. The next time you return to the data form, scroll to the edited transaction and look at the Status field; it should now display an "Ok."

When you want to enter or edit new general journal transactions in the future, simply press Ctrl-e from the main menu and follow these simple steps:

Step 1. Enter data into the first transaction field, Date.

Step 2. Use the Tab key to move to the next field, Check #, and enter data into it.

Step 3. Continue moving to the next field and entering data into it until every field within a record contains data.

Step 4. Use the action buttons to scroll through the general journal database, record by record.

Step 5. Click the Exit button when you have finished with the transaction-entry operation.

Step 6. GLAS asks whether you want to make additional entries, displaying the input box shown in figure 6.8.

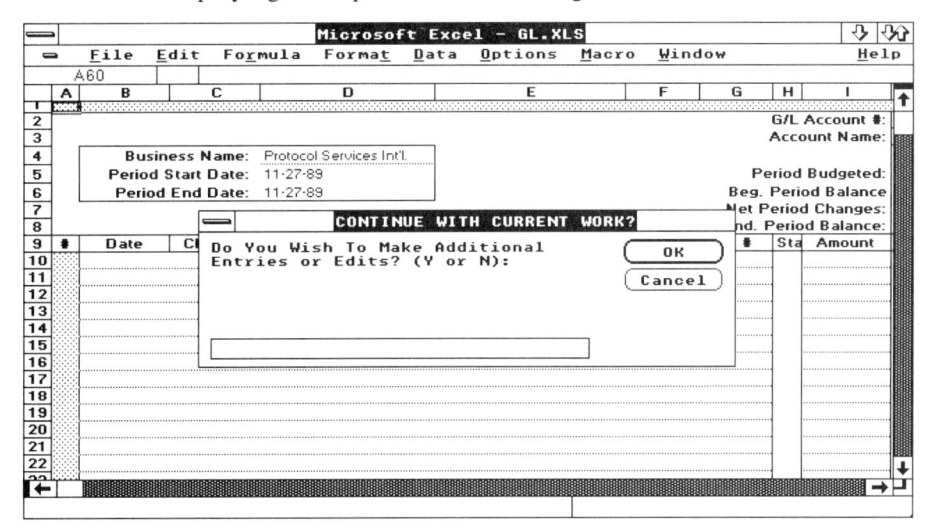

Fig. 6.8.
A prompt that enables you to continue the operation.

Posting Transactions

When you are at the main menu and press Ctrl-p, GLAS automatically posts your transactions from the general journal to the general ledger, updating the ledger account balances.

You *must* post the general journal transactions before printing reports and/or closing and clearing the general journal. You may use the posting macro as often as you like—at the end of each transaction day or at the end of each monthly accounting period; the results are the same.

The reason for this feature is to allow you the flexibility of printing reports at any time during the accounting period. For example, you may find it expedient to print a trial balance sheet at the end of each transaction day. This procedure lets you verify the equality of the debit and credit entries into your general journal on a daily basis. On the other hand, posting once a month may be sufficient for your reporting needs. The decision is yours.

In any case, when you select Ctrl-p from the main menu, GLAS activates the general ledger/journal worksheet. Although you won't see anything happening on-screen, GLAS is rapidly posting transactions behind the scenes.

GLAS will not execute the posting macro if either of two conditions exists. First, the model will not post a general journal transaction whose status is not "Ok." Second, the model will not post a journal whose first record is blank (the assumption is that the rest of the journal will also be empty). In these cases, GLAS displays one of the two error messages shown in figure 6.9.

Fig. 6.9.
Error messages in the Ctrl-p macro.

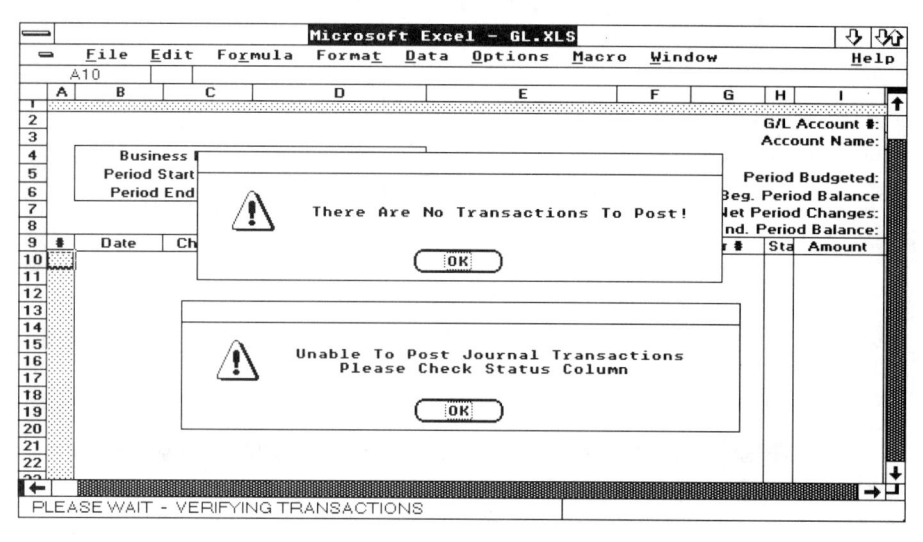

> **Tip:** In figure 6.9, notice that GLAS displays a message on Excel's status bar, in the lower left portion of the Excel worksheet window. Each macro displays status-bar messages during execution. Watch the status bar to track a macro's activity.

When GLAS halts the execution of the Ctrl-p macro, the model does two things. First, it displays one of the two error messages shown in figure 6.9.

To exit from the error-message mode, you must click the OK button in the alert box. Second—after you click the OK button—GLAS highlights the entire transaction line of the entry that caused the error. To determine and/or correct the entry error, select Ctrl-e; doing so recalls the data form.

When you want to post the general journal to the general ledger in the future, follow these simple steps:

Step 1. Use the Ctrl-e macro to verify that all transactions have an "Ok" status.

Step 2. Edit the transaction as needed.

Step 3. While on the main menu, select Ctrl-p.

Step 4. If the Ctrl-p macro halts, click the OK button in the alert box.

Step 5. Note the highlighted transaction and return to Step 1.

Step 6. If the Ctrl-p macro executes successfully, GLAS returns you to the main menu.

Printing Reports

While at the main menu, press Ctrl-r to call the Print Reports menu (described in detail later).

Closing and Clearing the Journal

After you have printed out all the accounting reports available in the GLAS system, you are ready for the final step in the accounting cycle. From the GLAS main menu, press Ctrl-c to back up, close, and clear the general journal and the general ledger; this step should be taken at the end of each monthly accounting period.

When you close and clear the general journal, GLAS automatically updates all balance-sheet accounts and zeros out all income-statement accounts. Although GLAS does not accumulate income-statement data for your firm, the model does provide the mechanism for you to store each end-of-period journal for future reference.

GLAS always leaves intact the initial budget values for each general ledger account. After you close the first accounting period, you have the option of keeping the Period 1 budget values or returning to the general ledger/journal worksheet to edit the values for Period 2.

If you choose to change the budget values on a period-to-period basis, be sure to adhere to the seven rules of operation outlined under the section heading "Adding a New G/L Account."

During macro execution, GLAS prompts you to select a unique name for the backup journal (see fig. 6.10).

Fig. 6.10.
Selecting a backup file name.

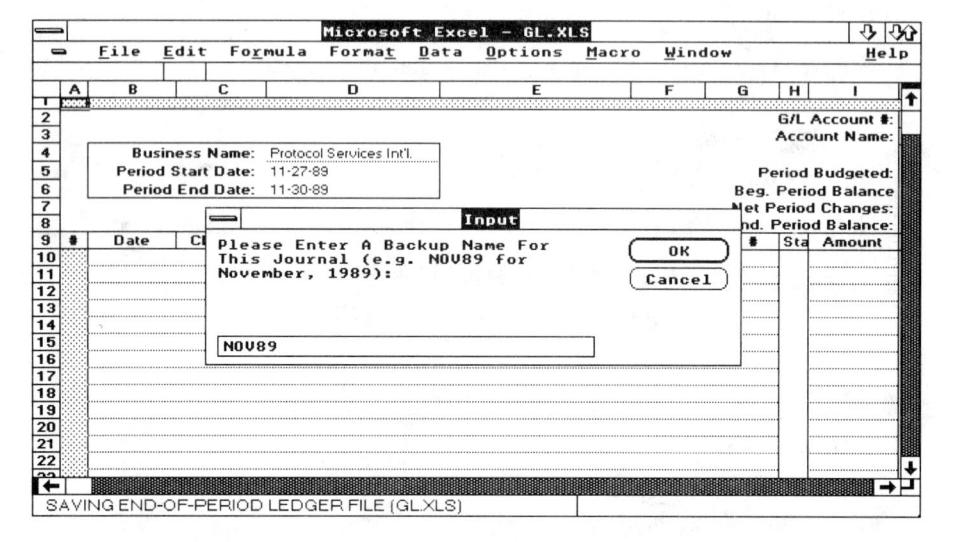

Choose your backup file names carefully. A good rule of thumb is to create file names that combine the name of the month with the accounting year. For example, if you are currently closing the November 1989 accounting period, choose NOV89 as the backup file name. At the end of December, choose DEC89, and so on.

> Tip: Enter the file name without an extension. Excel automatically assigns the XLS extension for you.

If you successfully post your general journal transactions, you will not encounter any errors during Ctrl-c macro execution. GLAS will not close and clear your general journal if it contains unposted transactions. In this situation, GLAS flashes the error message shown in figure 6.11.

When you want to close the general journal to the general ledger in the future, follow these simple steps:

Step 1. Make sure that you have successfully posted all the general journal transactions (see the section "Posting Transactions").

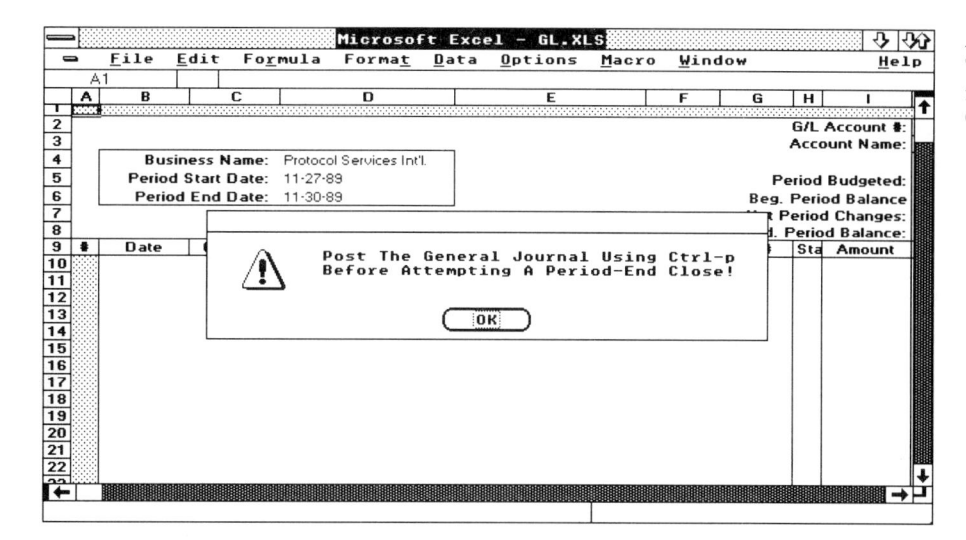

Fig. 6.11.
The error message in the Ctrl-c macro.

Step 2. Make sure that you have successfully printed out all the reports from the Print Reports menu.

Step 3. At the main menu, press Ctrl-c.

Step 4. If the Ctrl-c macro halts, click the OK button in the alert box. GLAS returns you to the main menu.

Step 5. Press Ctrl-p and follow the instructions outlined in the section "Posting Transactions."

Step 6. Return to Step 3.

Step 7. If the Ctrl-c macro executes successfully, GLAS returns you to the main menu.

Quitting GLAS and Returning to Excel

At the main menu, press Ctrl-q to back up (save) the files in your GLAS workspace, quit the GLAS model, and return to Excel.

GLAS prompts you with the alert box shown in figure 6.12. Click on the OK button; Excel will then prompt you to back up any files that have been altered during the course of your work session. Click on the OK button in response to each of the prompts. The saved files automatically reload the next time you use GLAS.

Fig. 6.12.
The Ctrl-q macro's alert box.

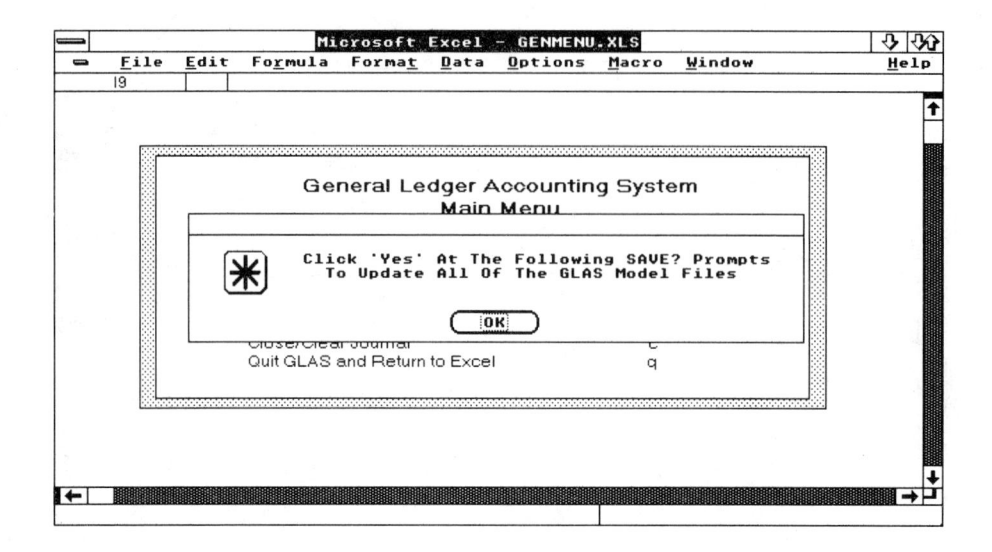

```
┌─────────────────────────────────────────────────────────────┐
│                  Microsoft Excel - GENMENU.XLS              │
│  File  Edit  Formula  Format  Data  Options  Macro  Window  Help │
│  19                                                         │
│                                                             │
│        ┌─────────────────────────────────────────────┐      │
│        │        General Ledger Accounting System      │      │
│        │                  Main Menu                   │      │
│        │   ┌──┐  Click 'Yes' At The Following SAVE? Prompts │
│        │   │✱ │  To Update All Of The GLAS Model Files      │
│        │   └──┘                                              │
│        │              ( OK )                          │      │
│        │        Quit GLAS and Return to Excel      q  │      │
│        └─────────────────────────────────────────────┘      │
└─────────────────────────────────────────────────────────────┘
```

Printing the Chart of Accounts

After successfully posting your general journal transactions, you may print out any of the four accounting reports. When you select a report to print, GLAS displays the dialog box shown in figure 6.13. Click OK after you have prepared your printer.

Fig. 6.13.
The ? dialog box.

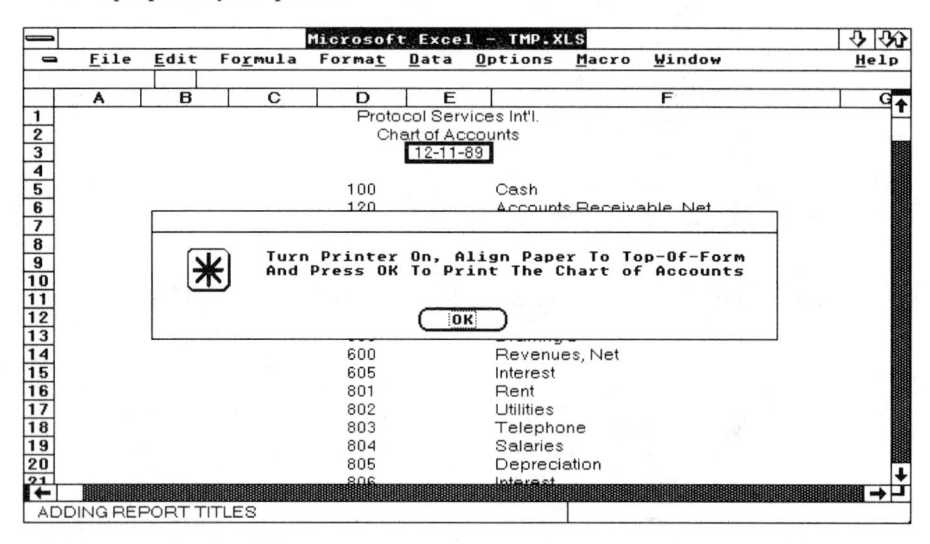

```
┌─────────────────────────────────────────────────────────────┐
│                  Microsoft Excel - TMP.XLS                  │
│  File  Edit  Formula  Format  Data  Options  Macro  Window  Help │
│    A     B     C     D       E                F          G │
│ 1                     Protocol Services Int'l.              │
│ 2                        Chart of Accounts                  │
│ 3                         12-11-89                          │
│ 4                                                           │
│ 5                  100          Cash                        │
│ 6                  120          Accounts Receivable, Net    │
│ 7                                                           │
│ 8   ┌──┐  Turn Printer On, Align Paper To Top-Of-Form       │
│ 9   │✱ │  And Press OK To Print The Chart of Accounts       │
│10   └──┘                                                    │
│11              ( OK )                                       │
│12                                                           │
│13                                                           │
│14                  600          Revenues, Net               │
│15                  605          Interest                    │
│16                  801          Rent                        │
│17                  802          Utilities                   │
│18                  803          Telephone                   │
│19                  804          Salaries                    │
│20                  805          Depreciation                │
│21                  806          Interest                    │
│ ADDING REPORT TITLES                                        │
└─────────────────────────────────────────────────────────────┘
```

Press Ctrl-l at the Print Reports menu to print a copy of your firm's chart of accounts, sorted by general ledger account number. Keep an eye on the messages that GLAS displays in the Excel worksheet window status line. These messages describe the general steps required to create this report.

Printing the Trial Balance Sheet

Press Ctrl-t at the Print Reports menu to print a copy of your firm's trial balance sheet, sorted by general ledger account number. Be sure to verify that the general ledger ending account balances are correct per your journal transactions.

Keep an eye on the messages that GLAS displays in the Excel worksheet window status line. These messages describe the general steps required to create this report.

Printing the Budget Summary and Variance

Press Ctrl-b at the Print Reports menu to calculate and print a budget summary and variance report, sorted by general ledger account number. The variance is equal to the difference between an account's ending balance and its budget estimate. The report also displays an over/under-budget percentage for each account.

Keep an eye on the messages that GLAS displays in the Excel worksheet window status line. These messages describe the general steps required to create this report.

Printing the Period-to-Date Summary

Press Ctrl-s at the Print Reports menu to print a period-to-date summary of the general ledger account values, sorted by account number. This report includes the period-budgeted value, the beginning-period account balance, the net-period changes, and the end-of-period account balance.

Keep an eye on the messages that GLAS displays in the Excel worksheet window status line. These messages describe the general steps required to create this report.

Returning to the Main Menu from the Print Reports Menu

While at the Print Reports menu, press Ctrl-x to return to the main menu.

Now turn to the case study and see how easy it is to put GLAS to work for you in your own company.

A GLAS Case Study: Protocol Services, Int'l

Protocol Services, Int'l (PSI), is a newly formed single proprietorship owned by John P. Michaels. PSI offers travel services to domestic corporations involved in international trade. PSI is staffed by three full-time consultants, including the owner.

Mr. Michaels began operations at the beginning of November 1989 with capitalization equal to $35,000 cash, $25,000 in fixed assets, and $75,000 in marketable securities. He also transferred into PSI's ledger a $35,000 personal note payable.

Figure 6.14 shows all of PSI's general journal entries for the month. Several items in the journal merit a closer look.

Fig. 6.14. PSI's November general journal.

#	Date	Check #	Payee	Description	Dr #	Cr #	Sta	Amount
1	11-01-89	1201	BLM Property Mgmt.	November rent	801	100	Ok	5,000.00
2	11-07-89	SJ		Charge sales	120	600	Ok	5,000.00
3	11-10-89	GJ	Stylish Furniture, Inc.	Office furniture	150	220	Ok	35,000.00
4	11-15-89	CR		Int. income: money mkt. acct.	100	605	Ok	750.00
5	11-15-89	SJ		Charge sales	120	600	Ok	2,700.00
6	11-15-89	SJ		Cash sales	100	600	Ok	12,750.00
7	11-20-89	1202	Bank of La Tosca	Loan #12003-5: Principal	200	100	Ok	240.50
8	11-20-89	same	same	Loan #12003-5: Interest	806	100	Ok	509.50
9	11-21-89	SJ		Charge sales	120	600	Ok	1,000.00
10	11-21-89	SJ		Cash sales	100	600	Ok	3,175.00
11	11-21-89	CR		On account payments	100	120	Ok	1,950.00
12	11-25-89	1203	SDE&G Utility	Electric & gas bill	802	100	Ok	142.50
13	11-27-89	1204	Atlantic Bell	Local phone service	803	100	Ok	297.43
14	11-28-89	1205	DASH, Inc.	Long distance phone srvc.	803	100	Ok	644.45
15	11-30-89	SJ		Charge sales	120	600	Ok	4,775.00
16	11-30-89	SJ		Cash sales	100	600	Ok	19,750.00
17	11-30-89	1206	Winston Z. Sterling	Monthly salary - November	804	100	Ok	5,000.00
18	11-30-89	1207	Catherine Leneuve	Monthly salary - November	804	100	Ok	6,500.00
19	11-30-89	GJ		Monthly depreciation	805	150	Ok	650.00
20	11-30-89	1208	Stylish Furniture, Inc.	33% Payment due	220	100	Ok	11,550.00
21	11-30-89	1209	John P. Michaels	Owner draw - November	501	100	Ok	7,500.00
22	11-30-89	GJ		Estimate of federal income ta	807	240	Ok	9,347.00

Area A is the transaction number (#) column and the Status column. When PSI entered each transaction, GLAS automatically assigned a transaction number and verified the accuracy of the entry with an "Ok" in the Status column.

Area B illustrates how PSI journalized its entries by using standard accounting references. In addition to recording check disbursements by using the check number, PSI recorded asset acquisitions (GJ = General Journal), sales (SJ = Sales Journal), and cash receipts (CR = Cash Receipts Journal). If PSI needs to allocate the amount of a single check among several accounts, the company enters "same" for the check number (#).

Area C demonstrates how PSI carefully documents the nature of each transaction. Here, PSI turned what would normally be a compound transaction (cash and charge sales) into two separate journal entries. Using this strategy, PSI recorded both the principal and interest portions of its loan payment as two entries.

Area D shows how Excel deals with a description that is longer than the width of the column. The full description is actually there; it's just obscured by the data appearing in the column to the right. Feel free to enter descriptions of any length. You can always go back to a particular entry with the data form and read the entire description.

Area E is the Amount column. When you record transactions in the general journal, using the data form, always enter a positive (+) value for Amount. GLAS automatically deals with the debits and the credits when you post the journal.

Figure 6.15 shows PSI's ledger accounts at the end of November. Below each account name, you'll find the period budget, beginning-period balance, net-period changes, and the ending-period balance. Notice that PSI started with the GLAS chart of accounts and then added three additional accounts: Marketable Securities, Taxes Payable, and Income Taxes expense.

100 Cash	120 Accounts Re	150 Fixed Assets	160 Marketable S	Total Assets	200 Notes Payab	220 Accounts Pa	240 Taxes Payab	Total Liabilit
35,000.00	10,000.00	55,000.00	75,000.00	175,000.00	34,500.00	25,000.00	7,024.50	66,524.50
35,000.00	0.00	25,000.00	75,000.00	135,000.00	35,000.00	0.00	0.00	35,000.00
990.62	11,525.00	34,350.00	0.00	46,865.62	(240.50)	23,450.00	9,347.00	32,556.50
35,990.62	11,525.00	59,350.00	75,000.00	181,865.62	34,759.50	23,450.00	9,347.00	67,556.50
Dr	Dr	Dr	Dr		Cr	Cr	Cr	

500 Equity 1	505 Equity 2	Total O.E.	600 Revenues, N	605 Interest	Total Revenu	801 Rent	802 Utilities	803 Telephone
108,475.50	0.00	108,475.50	40,000.00	700.00	40,700.00	5,000.00	125.00	1,000.00
100,000.00	0.00	100,000.00	0.00	0.00	0.00	0.00	0.00	0.00
14,309.12	0.00	14,309.12	49,150.00	750.00	49,900.00	5,000.00	142.50	941.88
114,309.12	0.00	114,309.12	49,150.00	750.00	49,900.00	5,000.00	142.50	941.88
Cr	Cr		Cr	Cr		Dr	Dr	Dr

804 Salaries	805 Depreciation	806 Interest	807 Income Taxe	Total Expens	Net Income	501 Drawing 1	506 Drawing 2	Net Income
10,000.00	650.00	510.00	7,024.50	24,309.50	16,390.50	0.00	0.00	16,390.50
0.00	0.00	0.00	0.00	0.00	0.00	0.00	0.00	0.00
11,500.00	650.00	509.50	9,347.00	28,090.88	21,809.12	7,500.00	0.00	14,309.12
11,500.00	650.00	509.50	9,347.00	28,090.88	21,809.12	7,500.00	0.00	14,309.12
Dr	Dr	Dr	Dr			Dr	Dr	

Fig. 6.15. PSI's general ledger accounts at the end of November.

Figures 6.16 through 6.19 display PSI's end-of-period reports. GLAS uses the computer's system date as the date heading in each report.

Figure 6.20 shows the entire worksheet.

Fig. 6.16.
PSI's chart of accounts.

```
          Protocol Services Int'l.
             Chart of Accounts
                 11-27-89

      100         Cash
      120         Accounts Receivable, Net
      150         Fixed Assets, Net
      160         Marketable Securities
      200         Notes Payable
      220         Accounts Payable
      240         Taxes Payable
      500         Equity 1
      501         Drawing 1
      505         Equity 2
      506         Drawing 2
      600         Revenues, Net
      605         Interest
      801         Rent
      802         Utilities
      803         Telephone
      804         Salaries
      805         Depreciation
      806         Interest
      807         Income Taxes
```

Fig. 6.17.
PSI's trial balance worksheet.

```
               Protocol Services Int'l
               Trial Balance Worksheet
                    11-27-89

   100  Cash                         35,990.62
   120  Accounts Receivable, Net     11,525.00
   150  Fixed Assets, Net            59,350.00
   160  Marketable Securities        75,000.00
   200  Notes Payable                              34,759.50
   220  Accounts Payable                           23,450.00
   240  Taxes Payable                               9,347.00
   500  Equity 1                                  100,000.00
   501  Drawing 1                     7,500.00
   505  Equity 2                                        0.00
   506  Drawing 2                         0.00
   600  Revenues, Net                              49,150.00
   605  Interest                                      750.00
   801  Rent                          5,000.00
   802  Utilities                       142.50
   803  Telephone                       941.88
   804  Salaries                     11,500.00
   805  Depreciation                    650.00
   806  Interest                        509.50
   807  Income Taxes                  9,347.00
                                    217,456.50  217,456.50
```

```
                 Protocol Services Int'l.
              Budget Summary and Variance Report
                         11-28-89

                            Budgeted      Actual     Variance         %

100   Cash                 35,000.00    35,990.62       990.62      2.83%
120   Accounts Receivable, Net 10,000.00 11,525.00    1,525.00     15.25%
150   Fixed Assets, Net    55,000.00    59,350.00     4,350.00      7.91%
160   Marketable Securities 75,000.00   75,000.00         0.00      0.00%
200   Notes Payable        34,500.00    34,759.50       259.50      0.75%
220   Accounts Payable     25,000.00    23,450.00    (1,550.00)    (6.20%)
240   Taxes Payable         7,024.50     9,347.00     2,322.50     33.06%
500   Equity 1            108,475.50   114,309.12     5,833.62      5.38%
501   Drawing 1                 0.00     7,500.00     7,500.00       n/a
505   Equity 2                  0.00         0.00         0.00       n/a
506   Drawing 2                 0.00         0.00         0.00       n/a
600   Revenues, Net        40,000.00    49,150.00     9,150.00     22.88%
605   Interest                700.00       750.00        50.00      7.14%
801   Rent                  5,000.00     5,000.00         0.00      0.00%
802   Utilities               125.00       142.50        17.50     14.00%
803   Telephone             1,000.00       941.88       (58.12)    (5.81%)
804   Salaries             10,000.00    11,500.00     1,500.00     15.00%
805   Depreciation            650.00       650.00         0.00      0.00%
806   Interest                510.00       509.50        (0.50)    (0.10%)
807   Income Taxes          7,024.50     9,347.00     2,322.50     33.06%
```

Fig. 6.18. PSI's budget summary and variance report.

```
                 Protocol Services Int'l.
                   Period to Date Summary
                         11-28-89

                          Period    Beg. Period  Net Period   End of
                         Budgeted     Balance      Change    Period Bal.

100   Cash               35,000.00   35,000.00       990.62   35,990.62
120   Accounts Receivable, Net 10,000.00   0.00   11,525.00   11,525.00
150   Fixed Assets, Net  55,000.00   25,000.00   34,350.00   59,350.00
160   Marketable Securities 75,000.00 75,000.00       0.00   75,000.00
200   Notes Payable      34,500.00   35,000.00    (240.50)   34,759.50
220   Accounts Payable   25,000.00        0.00   23,450.00   23,450.00
240   Taxes Payable       7,024.50        0.00    9,347.00    9,347.00
500   Equity 1          108,475.50  100,000.00   14,309.12  114,309.12
501   Drawing 1               0.00        0.00    7,500.00    7,500.00
505   Equity 2                0.00        0.00        0.00        0.00
506   Drawing 2               0.00        0.00        0.00        0.00
600   Revenues, Net      40,000.00        0.00   49,150.00   49,150.00
605   Interest              700.00        0.00      750.00      750.00
801   Rent                5,000.00        0.00    5,000.00    5,000.00
802   Utilities             125.00        0.00      142.50      142.50
803   Telephone           1,000.00        0.00      941.88      941.88
804   Salaries           10,000.00        0.00   11,500.00   11,500.00
805   Depreciation          650.00        0.00      650.00      650.00
806   Interest              510.00        0.00      509.50      509.50
807   Income Taxes        7,024.50        0.00    9,347.00    9,347.00
```

Fig. 6.19. PSI's period-to-date summary.

190 Excel Business Applications: IBM Version

	A	B	C	D	E	F	G	H	I
									G/L Account #:
									Account Name:
4			Business Name:	Protocol Services Int'l.					Period Budgeted:
5			Period Start Date:	11-01-89					Beg. Period Balance
6			Period End Date:	11-30-89					Net Period Changes:
									End. Period Balance:
#	Date	Check #	Payee	Description	Dr #	Cr #	Sta	Amount
1	11-01-89	1201	BLM Property Mgmt.	November rent	801	100	Ok	5,000.00
2	11-07-89	SJ		Charge sales	120	600	Ok	5,000.00
3	11-10-89	GJ	Stylish Furniture, Inc.	Office furniture	150	220	Ok	35,000.00
4	11-15-89	CR		Int. income: money mkt. a	100	605	Ok	750.00
5	11-15-89	SJ		Charge sales	120	600	Ok	2,700.00
6	11-15-89	SJ		Cash sales	100	600	Ok	12,750.00
7	11-20-89	1202	Bank of La Tosca	Loan #12003-5: Principal	200	100	Ok	240.50
8	11-20-89	same	same	Loan #12003-5: Interest	806	100	Ok	509.50
9	11-21-89	SJ		Charge sales	120	600	Ok	1,000.00
10	11-21-89	SJ		Cash sales	100	600	Ok	3,175.00
11	11-21-89	CR		On account payments	100	120	Ok	1,950.00
12	11-25-89	1203	SDE&G Utility	Electric & gas bill	802	100	Ok	142.50
13	11-27-89	1204	Atlantic Bell	Local phone service	803	100	Ok	297.43
14	11-28-89	1205	DASH, Inc.	Long distance phone srvc.	803	100	Ok	644.45
15	11-30-89	SJ		Charge sales	120	600	Ok	4,775.00
16	11-30-89	SJ		Cash sales	100	600	Ok	19,750.00
17	11-30-89	1206	Winston Z. Sterling	Monthly salary - November	804	100	Ok	5,000.00
18	11-30-89	1207	Catherine Leneuve	Monthly salary - November	804	100	Ok	6,500.00
19	11-30-89	GJ		Monthly depreciation	805	150	Ok	650.00
20	11-30-89	1208	Stylish Furniture, Inc.	33% Payment due	220	100	Ok	11,550.00
21	11-30-89	1209	John P. Michaels	Owner draw - November	501	100	Ok	7,500.00
	11-30-89	GJ		Estimate of federal income	807	240	Ok	9,347.00

Fig. 6.20a. The PROTOCOL.XLS worksheet, part 1.

Achieving General Ledger Accounting Success

	J	K	L	M	N	O	P	Q	R
	100	120	150	160		200	220	240	
	Cash	Accounts Re	Fixed Assets	Marketable	Total Assets	Notes Paya	Accounts Pa	Taxes Paya	Total Liabilitie
4									
5	35,000.00	10,000.00	55,000.00	75,000.00	175,000.00	34,500.00	25,000.00	7,024.50	66,524.50
6	35,000.00	0.00	25,000.00	75,000.00	135,000.00	35,000.00	0.00	0.00	35,000.00
	990.62	11,525.00	34,350.00	0.00	46,865.62	(240.50)	23,450.00	9,347.00	32,556.50
	35,990.62	11,525.00	59,350.00	75,000.00	181,865.62	34,759.50	23,450.00	9,347.00	67,556.50
	Dr	Dr	Dr	Dr		Cr	Cr	Cr	
	(5,000.00)								
		5,000.00							
	750.00		35,000.00				35,000.00		
		2,700.00							
	12,750.00								
	(240.50)					(240.50)			
	(509.50)	1,000.00							
	3,175.00								
	1,950.00	(1,950.00)							
	(142.50)								
	(297.43)								
	(644.45)	4,775.00							
	19,750.00								
	(5,000.00)								
	(6,500.00)		(650.00)						
	(11,550.00)						(11,550.00)		
	(7,500.00)							9,347.00	

Fig. 6.20b. The PROTOCOL.XLS worksheet, part 2.

	S	T	U	V	W	X	Y	Z	AA
	500	505		600	605		801	802	803
	Equity 1	Equity 2	Total O.E.	Revenues,	Interest	Total Revenu	Rent	Utilities	Telephone
4									
5	108,475.50	0.00	108,475.50	40,000.00	700.00	40,700.00	5,000.00	125.00	1,000.00
6	100,000.00	0.00	100,000.00	0.00	0.00	0.00	0.00	0.00	0.00
	14,309.12	0.00	14,309.12	49,150.00	750.00	49,900.00	5,000.00	142.50	941.88
	114,309.12	0.00	114,309.12	49,150.00	750.00	49,900.00	5,000.00	142.50	941.88
	Cr	Cr		Cr	Cr		Dr	Dr	Dr
							5,000.00		
				5,000.00					
					750.00				
				2,700.00					
				12,750.00					
				1,000.00					
				3,175.00					
								142.50	
				4,775.00					297.43
				19,750.00					644.45

Fig. 6.20c. The PROTOCOL.XLS worksheet, part 3.

Achieving General Ledger Accounting Success — 193

	AB	AC	AD	AE	AF	AG	AH	AI	AJ
	804	805	806	807			501	506	
	Salaries	Depreciatio	Interest	Income Tax	Total Expense	Net Income	Drawing 1	Drawing 2	Net Income to
4									
5	10,000.00	650.00	510.00	7,024.50	24,309.50	16,390.50	0.00	0.00	16,390.50
6	0.00	0.00	0.00	0.00	0.00	0.00	0.00	0.00	0.00
	11,500.00	650.00	509.50	9,347.00	28,090.88	21,809.12	7,500.00	0.00	14,309.12
	11,500.00	650.00	509.50	9,347.00	28,090.88	21,809.12	7,500.00	0.00	14,309.12
	Dr	Dr	Dr	Dr			Dr	Dr	
	5,000.00								
	6,500.00	650.00	509.50	9,347.00			7,500.00		

Fig. 6.20d. The PROTOCOL.XLS worksheet, part 4.

Expanding the GLAS Database

The GLAS application model is configured to accept 50 general journal transactions per month. If your firm has more entries than this each month, you will have to increase the size of the database. A GLAS worksheet can accommodate roughly 16,380 transactions—the number of rows on a worksheet, less the number of headings, blank rows, and so on. Having this many active database rows, though, is completely unrealistic. It would slow the operation of GLAS tremendously.

Remember Chapter 1's discussion of how Excel allocates memory for worksheets? If not, go back now for a quick review. Suffice it to say that the larger the GLAS database, the more memory Excel eats up; thus more time is required by GLAS to post the general journal transactions.

It is recommended that you increase the size of the database in increments of exactly 25—and that you do this at the start of an accounting period, before you enter data into the general journal/ledger worksheet. The reason is that you will use Excel's Insert, Copy, and Paste commands to do this operation. It is critical that you not duplicate existing general journal transactions while adding to the database!

To expand the general journal/ledger database, perform the following steps:

Step 1. Activate the blank GL.XLS worksheet.

Step 2. Select UnProtect Document from the Options menu.

Step 3. Click-select row 20 to row (19 + x), where x is the number of rows you want to add to the database.

Step 4. Select Insert from the Edit menu.

Step 5. Click-select row 19 and choose Copy from the Edit menu.

Step 6. Reselect row 20 to row (19 + x).

Step 7. Choose Paste Special from the Edit menu.

Step 8. Click the button next to All in the Paste Special dialog box and click OK.

Step 9. Select Protect Document from the Options menu and click OK on the Protect Document dialog box.

Step 10. Select Save from the File menu to record your changes.

Now you may run the Ctrl-e macro to enter new transactions for the month.

Summary

This chapter introduced you to a powerful, self-running macro application called the General Ledger Accounting System (GLAS). You can easily adapt the model to your specific accounting needs and put it to work for you in your own firm in a short period of time.

A review of the division of labor in the operation of the GLAS application model shows that your job is to do the following:

- Enter the descriptions and beginning balances of your general ledger accounts—just once!
- Enter the period budget for each of the general ledger accounts—just once each month!
- Enter your firm's accounting transactions for each accounting period.

GLAS's job is to do the following:

- Verify that debits equal credits in the general journal.
- Post all general journal transactions to the appropriate general ledger accounts.
- Print the summarized accounting data reports.
- Back up, close, and clear the general journal/ledger worksheet at the end of period$_t$.
- Create a new period general journal/ledger with worksheet for period$_{t+1}$.

Chapter 7 turns your attention to the many ways in which you can use Excel to control your payables and receivables.

7

Controlling Your Accounts Receivable and Accounts Payable

All the models you've used so far in this book contribute to your understanding of how to manage your business affairs. You learned in Chapter 5 about the present value of money as it pertains to a series of payments. In this chapter, you'll come to understand how the smart management of receivables and payables is critical to the continued financial health of any business, large or small.

Managing your accounts payable and accounts receivable is similar to managing the present value and future value of investments, but on a much smaller scale. Income statements, balance sheets, and even cash-flow statements give you a broad look at your company's financial health, but they don't tell you much about individual sources of income and expenses. Your accounts receivable, unless carefully monitored, can be a major source of financial problems: you may have already paid for the goods and labor necessary to create your product, and you may have already paid for transporting the goods to your customer, but unless your customer pays his bill promptly, you are in effect paying him to take your product off your hands. That's not the way business is supposed to work, and poorly managed accounts receivable can cause serious problems with your cash flow.

On the other hand, when you manage your accounts payable properly, you can create some short-term credit with your suppliers and thus shorten the time interval between your purchase of supplies and your collection of payment for the finished product.

This chapter offers several smart, efficient ways to organize your business data into reports that will tell you how to stretch your company dollar. To begin, you will learn how to use the credit-application generator. This model contains all the standard questions found on credit applications. You will more than likely want to tailor it to your own credit policy, however. Adding to or editing the credit-application generator is a simple operation, and after you make the modifications you want, you can store this important document away for future use.

Next, you will learn how to quickly develop and use an invoice-register model. The transactions that flow through this model will be used to create many of the specialized reports found in the chapter. For example, once your business comes to the end of a transaction cycle (a day, a week, or a month, for instance), you can immediately review and assess your total sales (in summary form) and your accounts receivable by date and by customer. Or you can process your transactions through the accounts receivable aging report to construct a 30/60/90-day analysis of your customer's purchases.

When necessary, you can also generate another report that flags all overdue accounts. Based on the information from the invoice register and the accounts receivables reports, this report summarizes the outstanding balances—by customer and as a percentage of the total company receivables. Before getting on the phone to call your overdue customers, you can print out a collections worksheet as well, which enables you to refer to specific invoices, dates, amounts, payments, and days past due.

Excel provides a way of sharing data between multiple files: *linking*. Linked files enable you to update data in one file and have the updated data and related calculations reflected in other files as well. By saving several linked files as a *workspace* file, you can subsequently open all the related files at once. This chapter will show you how to create and use linked files and workspace files.

Using the Credit-Application Generator (CREDAPP.XLS)

When your business extends credit, you need to know some basic information about the person or entity receiving credit. What are the names and phone numbers of other businesses where this entity has established credit? Where does this entity do its banking? Who handles the bill-paying in this company?

Included among the worksheet files that came with this book is CREDAPP.XLS, which produces a blank credit-application form, shown in figure 7.1.

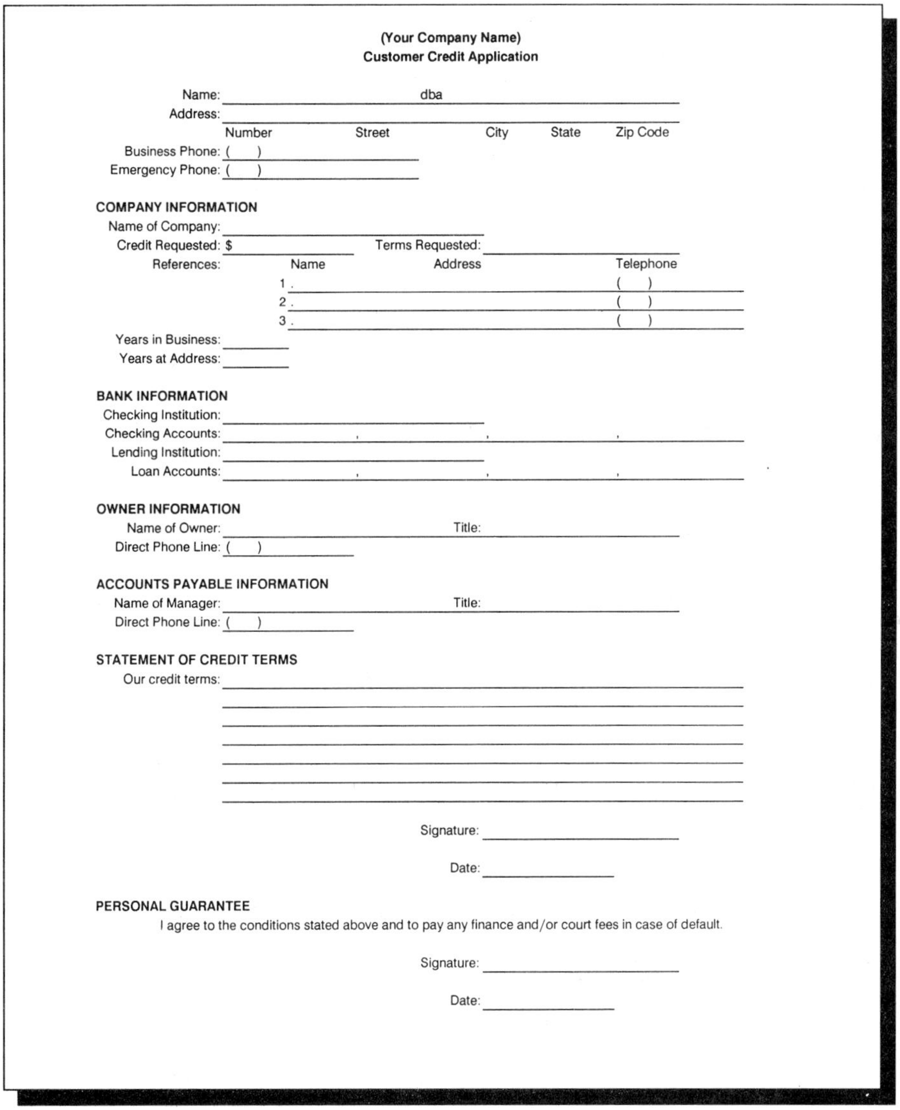
(Your Company Name)
Customer Credit Application

Name: ______ dba ______
Address: ______
Number Street City State Zip Code
Business Phone: ( ) ______
Emergency Phone: ( ) ______

COMPANY INFORMATION
Name of Company: ______
Credit Requested: $ ______ Terms Requested: ______
References: Name Address Telephone
1. ______ ( ) ______
2. ______ ( ) ______
3. ______ ( ) ______

Years in Business: ______
Years at Address: ______

BANK INFORMATION
Checking Institution: ______
Checking Accounts: ______ , ______ , ______ , ______
Lending Institution: ______
Loan Accounts: ______ , ______ , ______ , ______

OWNER INFORMATION
Name of Owner: ______ Title: ______
Direct Phone Line: ( ) ______

ACCOUNTS PAYABLE INFORMATION
Name of Manager: ______ Title: ______
Direct Phone Line: ( ) ______

STATEMENT OF CREDIT TERMS
Our credit terms: ______

Signature: ______

Date: ______

PERSONAL GUARANTEE
I agree to the conditions stated above and to pay any finance and/or court fees in case of default.

Signature: ______

Date: ______

Fig. 7.1. A blank credit application produced by CREDAPP.XLS.

With the blank stored on disk, you can print a form any time a new customer requests credit. Have the customer fill out the form; check the customer's references and keep the copy on hand in case problems arise.

Using Simple Accounts Receivable and Accounts Payable Worksheets (AR10_89.XLS, AP10_89.XLS, AR4_90.XLS, AP4_90.XLS)

Managing *accounts receivable* (money your customers owe you) and *accounts payable* (money you owe your suppliers) properly is the best way to be able to determine your future needs for cash. If several of your customers string out their payments 90 and 120 days after purchase, you'll probably have to use working capital or even do some short-term borrowing of your own to finance this short-term credit. If, on the other hand, you can offer incentives to get your customers to pay their bills promptly, you'll be able to pay your own bills within a reasonable time and not have to use up your working capital.

Consider this graphic, if somewhat limited, example of what the proper management of receivables and payables can achieve. Lydia's Bridal Fashions is the name of your next-door neighbor's small business, which specializes in making wedding dresses and accessories. Lydia's customers are the daughters of friends. When a customer comes to her, Lydia and the customer go over patterns and fabric samples and decide on style, fabric, and color as well as trims and accessories.

When ordering dresses for a bridal party, the customer pays 50 percent of the estimated cost as a down payment, with 25 percent due at the first fitting and the remaining 25 percent due when the dresses are picked up. With the money from the down payment, Lydia buys the fabric at a discount from a local retail fabric store, then cuts and assembles the dresses. If she has estimated her costs correctly, her supplies cost about what the customer pays as the down payment. But she hasn't been paid for her time; there is no margin for error in her calculations, nor is there any money for the overhead of her business. Even though she operates the business from her home, the business should pay its share of rent, utilities, phone, insurance, and other costs.

The second and third payments go on Lydia's records as accounts receivable. Her overhead costs go on the records as accounts payable. If

Lydia made no mistakes in her estimating, she is about even on her cost of goods. If there is even one error, however, she's got problems.

With this in mind, Lydia arranges for an account with the fabric store where she does most of her business. Because she does a lot of business with the fabric store, the store's management agrees to let her have a 30-day account. This arrangement means that Lydia can pay for her cost of goods within the 30-day period after she buys the material, and if she's managed to construct and fit the dresses for which she bought the material, she can probably pay both the bill at the fabric store and her overhead costs within this 30-day period. So far, so good.

Under this arrangement, however, Lydia has to wait until a customer's final payment before she gets paid for her time or makes any profit. And if her customers are slow in making the final payment, Lydia doesn't get any benefit for her work. By negotiating a new arrangement with the fabric store to extend credit for up to 60 days—an arrangement by which she makes at least partial payments every month—and by carefully managing the flow of payments for her overhead costs, Lydia can reserve money for herself and money to cover errors in estimating the cost of other projects.

As Lydia's business grows, she needs to keep track of which customers still owe her money and which payments have been made. Figure 7.2 shows a simple accounts receivable worksheet that helps her monitor her accounts.

Fig. 7.2. A simple accounts receivable worksheet (AR10_89.XLS).

	Customer Name	Order Amount	Order Date	Fitting Date	Date of Pickup	Total Amount Due
7	Anderson, Lori	$1,057.44	8/14/89	9/16/89	11/17/89	$264.36
8	Brenner, Jennifer	$2,553.75	9/7/89	9/29/89	10/27/89	$1,276.88
9	Crawley, Joan	$844.38	10/1/89	10/20/89	11/1/89	$422.19
10	Dunbar, Carolee	$1,198.32	8/29/89	9/22/89	11/3/89	$299.58
11	Edmondstone, Liza	$2,449.13	9/16/89	10/25/89	12/1/89	$1,224.57

Date: 1/3/90

The worksheet in figure 7.2 is included with the sample models as AR10_89.XLS. To have the worksheet on-screen as you follow the discussion, open the file AR10_89.XLS. Note that the worksheet includes, for each account, the customer's name, the full amount of the order, the date the down payment was made, the date Lydia expects to do the fitting and thus receive the second payment, and the amount and date of the expected final payment. Not all accounts receivable worksheets look like this one, because each should serve the needs of its user.

Most of the data on the worksheet in figure 7.2 requires no functions or formulas. Because of Lydia's 50/25/25 percent payment schedule, the formula used in column F to calculate the total amount due is either .25*B7 or .5*B7. To see these formulas, move the cursor to F7 and look in the formula bar. As you move the cursor down column F, you will see for each cell the formula in effect.

Lydia also needs to keep track of her bills for fabric, which are directly related to specific customers. Figure 7.3 shows a simple accounts payable worksheet that helps her monitor this part of her business. The worksheet in figure 7.3 is included with the sample models as AP10_89.XLS. Open this file.

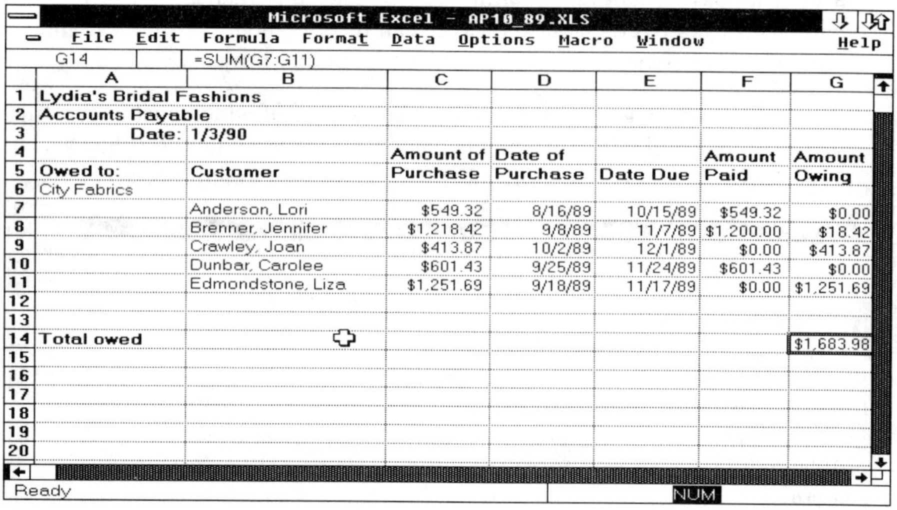

Fig. 7.3.
A simple accounts payable worksheet (AP10_89.XLS).

	A	B	C	D	E	F	G
1	Lydia's Bridal Fashions						
2	Accounts Payable						
3	Date:	1/3/90					
4			Amount of	Date of		Amount	Amount
5	Owed to:	Customer	Purchase	Purchase	Date Due	Paid	Owing
6	City Fabrics						
7		Anderson, Lori	$549.32	8/16/89	10/15/89	$549.32	$0.00
8		Brenner, Jennifer	$1,218.42	9/8/89	11/7/89	$1,200.00	$18.42
9		Crawley, Joan	$413.87	10/2/89	12/1/89	$0.00	$413.87
10		Dunbar, Carolee	$601.43	9/25/89	11/24/89	$601.43	$0.00
11		Edmondstone, Liza	$1,251.69	9/18/89	11/17/89	$0.00	$1,251.69
12							
13							
14	Total owed						$1,683.98

G14: =SUM(G7:G11)

Note that the common factor between the accounts receivable and accounts payable worksheets is the name of the customer. Lydia needs to know which customer is related to which fabric bill, although the store to which Lydia owes money—City Fabrics—is interested only in her total monthly purchases and payments. This accounts payable worksheet shows her the effect of any single customer on her total bill with the store, as well as her monthly status with the store.

Because Lydia has negotiated a 60-day payment plan with the store, the date shown in column E is a result of the formula =60+D7. This formula appears in the other cells in column G, with the row numbers adjusted. When Lydia pays for the fabric—a payment that may take place when she acquires the merchandise—she enters the amount in column F. Move the cursor to column G and notice that column G contains the simple formula C7-F7.

As her business grows, Lydia can add more customers' names to the accounts receivable worksheet by inserting them below the names of previous customers and by deleting the names of customers who have completely paid their accounts. She can also add her overhead costs to the accounts payable worksheet by inserting those figures below the fabric bills. Figures 7.4 and 7.5 show the accounts receivable and accounts payable worksheets six months later; both worksheets reflect these changes.

Fig. 7.4. Accounts receivable, Lydia's Bridal Fashions, six months later (AR4_90.XLS).

	A	B	C	D	E	F
1	Lydia's Bridal Fashions					
2	Accounts Receivable					
3		Date:	7/2/90			
4						Total
5	Customer	Order	Order	Fitting	Date of	Amount
6	Name	Amount	Date	Date	Pickup	Due
7	Larson, June	$1,132.54	2/15/90	4/4/90	5/18/90	$283.14
8	Matsuda, Janet	$2,943.42	1/29/90	3/30/90	6/1/90	$735.86
9	Noriega, Pamela	$1,014.05	3/2/90	4/6/90	4/27/90	$507.03
10	Okun, Marianne	$673.29	4/2/90	5/3/90	6/22/90	$336.65
11	Palestra, Louise	$893.24	3/16/90	3/29/90	4/20/90	$223.31
12	Quinn, Erin	$742.90	2/21/90	4/5/90	5/4/90	$185.73
13	Reinhold, Greta	$1,748.33	3/27/90	5/1/90	6/8/90	$874.17
14	Sakai, Amy	$3,541.22	3/8/90	5/16/90	6/29/90	$1,770.61
15	Terranova, Tammy	$2,218.38	4/4/90	4/24/90	5/18/90	$1,109.19
17					Total due:	$6,025.66

The worksheets in figures 7.4 and 7.5 are included with the sample models as AR4_90.XLS and AP4_90.XLS, respectively. If you want to use them for comparison with other worksheets covered later in this chapter, use the Print command from the File menu to print each worksheet. When you've printed the file, you can close it.

> Tip: Use any of the date formats to show the dates in columns C, D, and E on the accounts receivable worksheet and in columns D and E on the accounts payable worksheet. Because Excel carries dates as numbers, you can manipulate any date as if it were an ordinary number, adding to it and subtracting from it to determine other dates—in this case, due dates for payments to the store. Lydia's customers, however, make appointments for fittings—and thus make their second payments—according to their own calendars, so the dates for customers must be entered rather than calculated.

Fig. 7.5. Accounts payable, Lydia's Bridal Fashions, six months later (AP4_90.XLS).

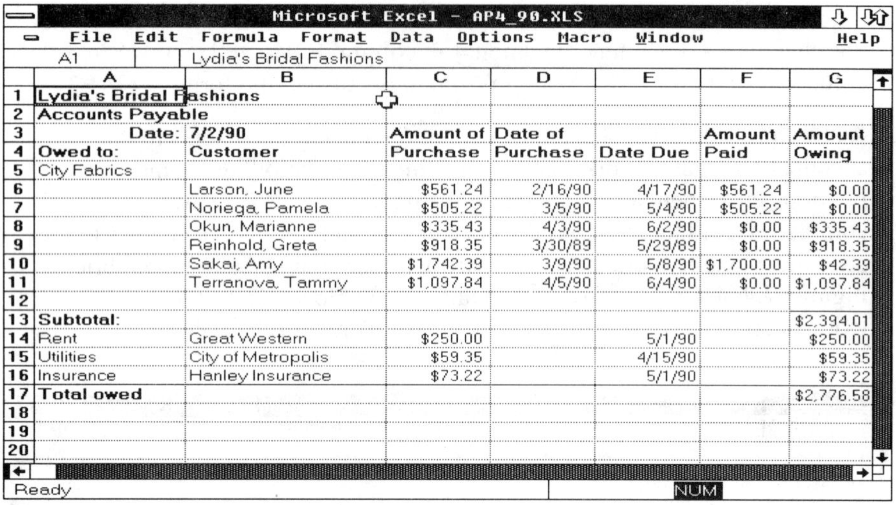

Microsoft Excel - AP4_90.XLS

File Edit Formula Format Data Options Macro Window Help

A1 Lydia's Bridal Fashions

	A	B	C	D	E	F	G
1	Lydia's Bridal Fashions						
2	Accounts Payable						
3	Date:	7/2/90	Amount of	Date of		Amount	Amount
4	Owed to:	Customer	Purchase	Purchase	Date Due	Paid	Owing
5	City Fabrics						
6		Larson, June	$561.24	2/16/90	4/17/90	$561.24	$0.00
7		Noriega, Pamela	$505.22	3/5/90	5/4/90	$505.22	$0.00
8		Okun, Marianne	$335.43	4/3/90	6/2/90	$0.00	$335.43
9		Reinhold, Greta	$918.35	3/30/89	5/29/89	$0.00	$918.35
10		Sakai, Amy	$1,742.39	3/9/90	5/8/90	$1,700.00	$42.39
11		Terranova, Tammy	$1,097.84	4/5/90	6/4/90	$0.00	$1,097.84
12							
13	Subtotal:						$2,394.01
14	Rent	Great Western	$250.00		5/1/90		$250.00
15	Utilities	City of Metropolis	$59.35		4/15/90		$59.35
16	Insurance	Hanley Insurance	$73.22		5/1/90		$73.22
17	Total owed						$2,776.58
18							
19							
20							

Ready NUM

Using an Invoice Register (INVCREG1.XLS)

Lydia's concerns about managing her accounts receivable and accounts payable are similar to the concerns of her major supplier, City Fabrics. City Fabrics is a retailer, but the company also sells to other small businesses that, like Lydia's, have problems tracking customers who pay for work in progress. Whereas Lydia needs to track a relatively small number of customers, City Fabrics needs to track perhaps 10 or more times that number. City Fabrics also needs to be able to keep track of more than one purchase by a single customer and to monitor which purchases have been paid for and which are still being carried as active accounts.

City Fabrics has other concerns that small operations don't normally see. Some of its transactions require the collection of sales tax, and some, such as transactions with Lydia, don't. (Lydia collects the sales tax from her customers, so City Fabrics doesn't charge Lydia sales tax for goods that Lydia will resell.) And some of City Fabrics' transactions incorporate shipping charges, whereas customers like Lydia walk out with their purchases.

Nonetheless, an invoice register worksheet for City Fabrics uses the same basic concepts as Lydia's financial worksheets, although the invoice register worksheet arranges the data differently and adds more details. For example, City Fabrics needs to be able to track not just individual customers, but multiple purchases by a single customer. And unlike Lydia, whose customers walk out the door with their purchases, City Fabrics has some customers whose total purchases reflect amounts for tax and freight charges.

With these concerns in mind, open the file INVCREG1.XLS, which is included with the sample models. On-screen you'll see the row and column labels, as shown in figure 7.6.

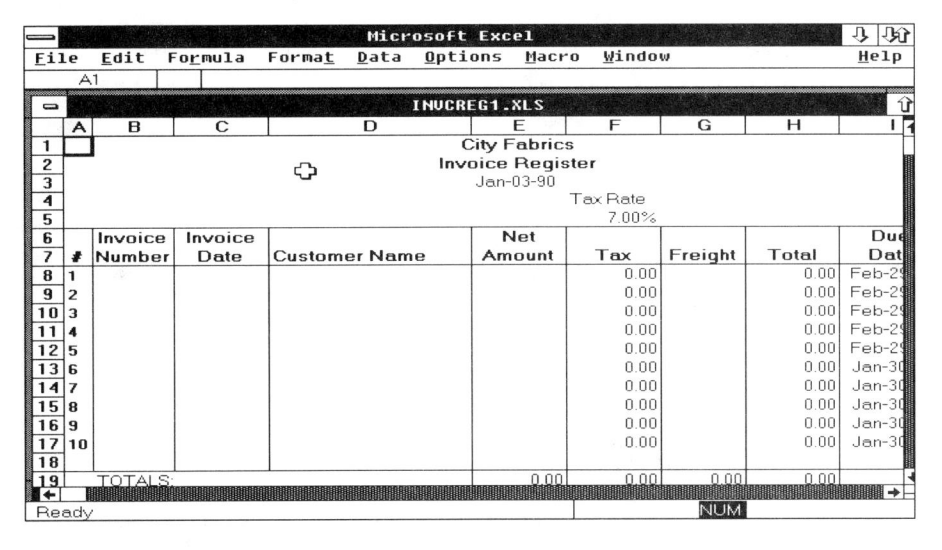

Fig. 7.6.
The headings for City Fabrics' invoice register.

Follow these steps to inspect the formulas that are in place and to add data to the worksheet:

Step 1. Make F5 the active cell. Notice that the decimal number 0.07 is entered here. You can change this number to whatever tax rate is appropriate for your location.

Step 2. Enter information for the four invoices for Lydia's Bridal Fashions, as shown in figure 7.7. Notice that column C has been formatted to accept date information and to display it in mmm-dd-yy format. For each of Lydia's purchases, enter 0's for the tax amount in column F. Because Lydia collects the tax on the finished product, she pays no tax on her supplies. Notice also that the formula in column H automatically sums the net amount, tax, and freight.

Step 3. Move the active cell to F12, which contains the formula $E12*$F$5.

This formula computes the tax on taxable purchases by multiplying the tax rate, which you entered in F5, by the net amount in column E.

Fig. 7.7.
City Fabrics'
invoice register,
showing data
for Lydia's
Bridal Fashions.

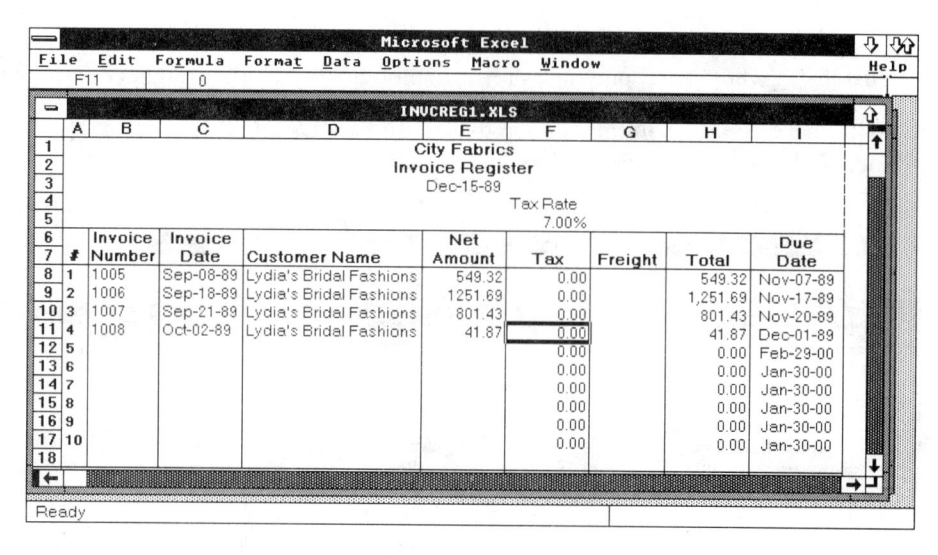

	A	B	C	D	E	F	G	H	I
1					City Fabrics				
2					Invoice Register				
3					Dec-15-89				
4						Tax Rate			
5						7.00%			
6		Invoice	Invoice		Net				Due
7	#	Number	Date	Customer Name	Amount	Tax	Freight	Total	Date
8	1	1005	Sep-08-89	Lydia's Bridal Fashions	549.32	0.00		549.32	Nov-07-89
9	2	1006	Sep-18-89	Lydia's Bridal Fashions	1251.69	0.00		1,251.69	Nov-17-89
10	3	1007	Sep-21-89	Lydia's Bridal Fashions	801.43	0.00		801.43	Nov-20-89
11	4	1008	Oct-02-89	Lydia's Bridal Fashions	41.87	0.00		41.87	Dec-01-89
12	5					0.00		0.00	Feb-29-00
13	6					0.00		0.00	Jan-30-00
14	7					0.00		0.00	Jan-30-00
15	8					0.00		0.00	Jan-30-00
16	9					0.00		0.00	Jan-30-00
17	10					0.00		0.00	Jan-30-00
18									

Step 4. Enter data (shown in fig. 7.8) for rows 12, 13, 14, and 15. Notice that the tax is automatically computed when you enter an amount in column E, as is the total amount in column H. When a customer such as Lydia pays no tax, you override the tax calculation by entering a 0. When there is a charge for freight, enter the amount in column G; the amount will be included in the calculation in column H.

Step 5. Notice the totals shown in row 19 on your screen. As you enter invoices for an accounting period, you can use these total amounts to reconcile freight bills or taxable transactions in other worksheets.

When you're finished entering data, save your worksheet, using the file name INVCREG2.XLS. Your worksheet should look like that shown in figure 7.8.

City Fabrics also needs to be able to track payments for any single purchase, in keeping with the agreements it has with its charge-account customers. You can set up this arrangement on the same invoice register worksheet so that any entry in the invoice section will set up a payment schedule, and so that any payment against an invoice will be tied to the original transaction.

Step 6. Assume that City Fabrics extends a flat 60-day credit period to selected customers. The formula that calculates the due date for such customers can use the invoice date—which, after all, is stored by Excel as a numeric value—in a simple calculation. For instance, cell I8 can contain the formula

=$C8+60

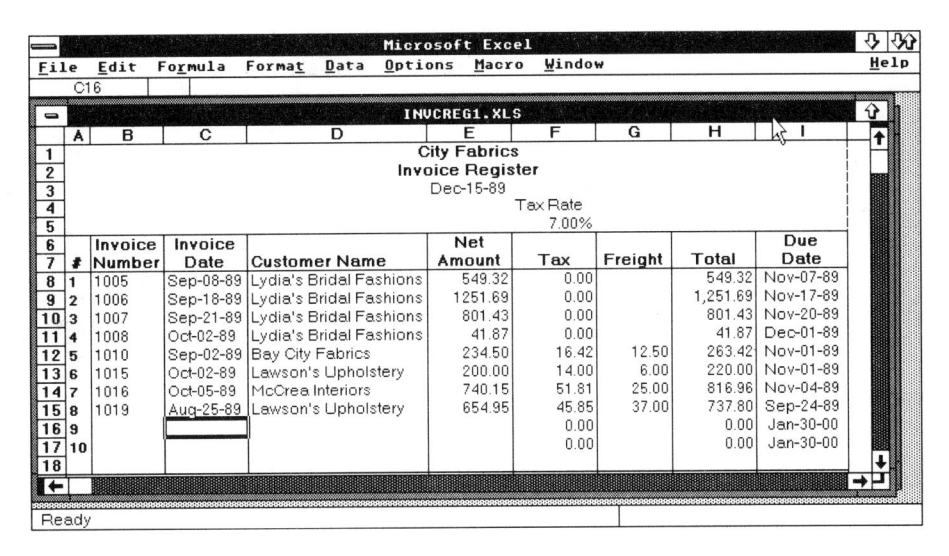

Fig. 7.8.
The finished invoice register.

```
                          Microsoft Excel
File  Edit  Formula  Format  Data  Options  Macro  Window              Help
      C16
                              INVCREG1.XLS
      A      B         C          D              E       F      G       H        I
 1                                        City Fabrics
 2                                       Invoice Register
 3                                          Dec-15-89
 4                                                    Tax Rate
 5                                                      7.00%
 6          Invoice   Invoice                    Net                            Due
 7      #   Number    Date     Customer Name   Amount    Tax   Freight  Total   Date
 8   1      1005      Sep-08-89 Lydia's Bridal Fashions  549.32   0.00           549.32  Nov-07-89
 9   2      1006      Sep-18-89 Lydia's Bridal Fashions 1251.69   0.00         1,251.69  Nov-17-89
10   3      1007      Sep-21-89 Lydia's Bridal Fashions  801.43   0.00           801.43  Nov-20-89
11   4      1008      Oct-02-89 Lydia's Bridal Fashions   41.87   0.00            41.87  Dec-01-89
12   5      1010      Sep-02-89 Bay City Fabrics         234.50  16.42   12.50   263.42  Nov-01-89
13   6      1015      Oct-02-89 Lawson's Upholstery      200.00  14.00    6.00   220.00  Nov-01-89
14   7      1016      Oct-05-89 McCrea Interiors         740.15  51.81   25.00   816.96  Nov-04-89
15   8      1019      Aug-25-89 Lawson's Upholstery      654.95  45.85   37.00   737.80  Sep-24-89
16   9                                                            0.00             0.00  Jan-30-00
17  10                                                            0.00             0.00  Jan-30-00
18
Ready
```

Using this assumption for all the invoices on this worksheet, enter this formula into I8. Then copy the formula down column I. Because the reference to the row number is relative, the formula is adjusted during the copy operation so that the formula refers to a cell in the same row.

If you want to change the formula to reflect different credit arrangements, simply change the number that is added to the invoice date.

Step 7. Adding data to this column filled up the screen if you kept columns the same width as they were when you started. To add the payment information, press Ctrl-right arrow three times so that the active cell is in column O.

Type the column headings and page description as shown in figure 7.9.

Step 8. Enter the following formulas into the indicated cells:

    L8: = **$C8+30**

    N8: = **$C8+60**

    O8: = **$H8-$K8-$M8**

Then copy the formulas into rows 9 through 18.

The formulas in columns L and N establish the 30-day period and 60-day period, based on the invoice date. (If you didn't use the file INVCREG1.XLS, which was on the disk that accompanies this book, these columns will need to be formatted to display the date. Choose the Format Number command; then select the mmm-dd-yy format for rows 8 through 18.)

Fig. 7.9.
Column headings for the payment schedule.

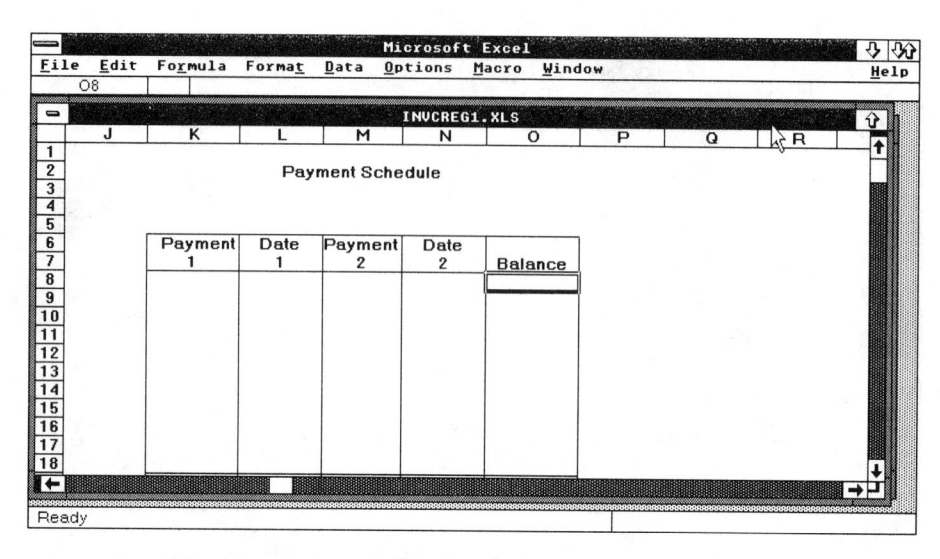

[Screenshot of Microsoft Excel worksheet INVCREG1.XLS showing columns J through R with "Payment Schedule" title and column headings "Payment 1", "Date 1", "Payment 2", "Date 2", "Balance"]

The formula in column O calculates the current balance on the assumption that any payments made are entered in column K or M, as appropriate.

Step 9. Enter the following into the indicated cells:

J19: **TOTALS:**

K19: **=SUM(K8:K18)**

M19: **=SUM(M8:M18)**

O19: **=SUM(O8:O18)**

These formulas produce running totals of the payments and outstanding balances, which are updated every time you open the worksheet.

Step 10. Now save the worksheet as INVCREG2.XLS. Your finished worksheet, complete with payment schedule, looks like the one in figure 7.10.

Notice the similarity between the completed invoice register and Lydia's accounts receivable worksheet (figs. 7.2 and 7.4). Whereas Lydia enters her fitting date and date of pickup manually, the invoice register worksheet for City Fabrics computes the payment dates based on the invoice dates and the credit agreement with the customer. Lydia's total amount due for each customer depends on the use of a formula; the balance in column O for City Fabrics also is calculated by a formula.

The data in columns E, F, G, and H shows the purchase amount, any sales tax and/or freight charges, and the total amount due. The formula in column H adds the amounts in columns E, F, and G.

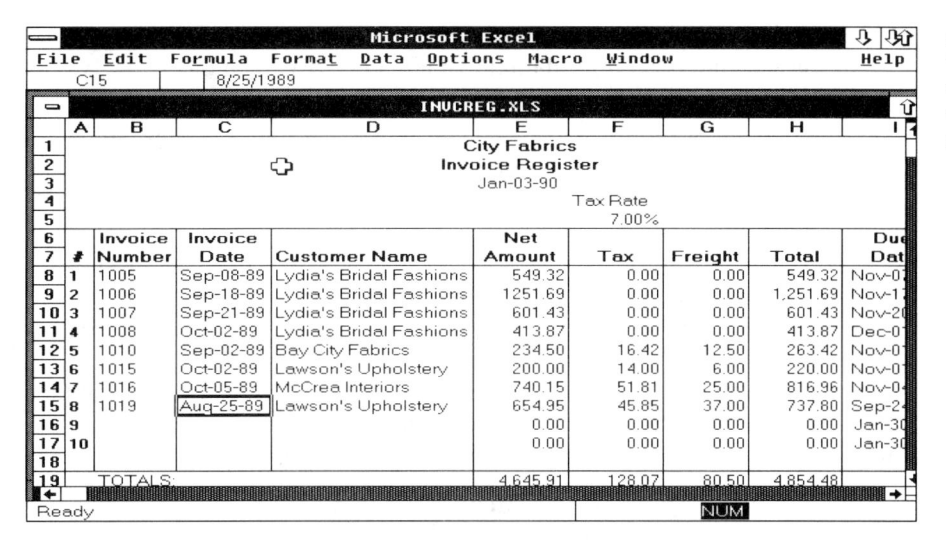

Fig. 7.10.
The invoice worksheet with payment schedule.

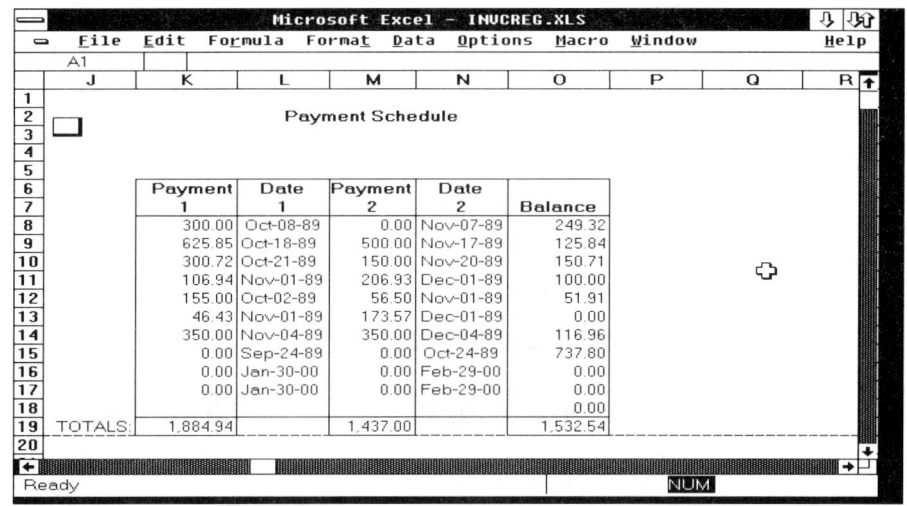

Sharing Information between Files (INVCREG.XLW)

The information in the invoice register can be used with other worksheets. Excel offers a way for you to use data from one worksheet in a totally separate worksheet without retyping the data. For instance, you can use in a sales summary the net amount, tax, freight, and total calculated in the invoice register. This section shows you how to do that.

When you create these linked worksheets, you can use an external reference in the current file to get information that already exists in another file. An external reference is created when you type the file name, followed by an exclamation mark, followed by the cell or range you want to use, as in this example:

INVCREG.XLS!D8

The file name must be a complete reference; that is, the file name must specify the drive, directory or other path information, file name, and extension. However, if the file you're after is on the current drive, current directory, or current path, you can eliminate that information in the reference. If, for instance, the file you're working with is on drive C, but the file you want to use is on drive A, the file name reference must point out this fact. Consider the external reference

A:\INVOICES\OCTOBER\INVCREG.XLS!D8

This reference tells Excel to use the information in cell D8 on the external file INVCREG.XLS, which is located in the subdirectory OCTOBER of the directory INVOICES on the disk in drive A.

What external references do is establish a link between two separate worksheets. Excel supports these links and offers you two different ways to use linked files. The Link command, when used with an open file in which there are external references to one or more files not already open, offers you a dialog box (see fig.7.11) that shows the file names involved in any external references in the current file.

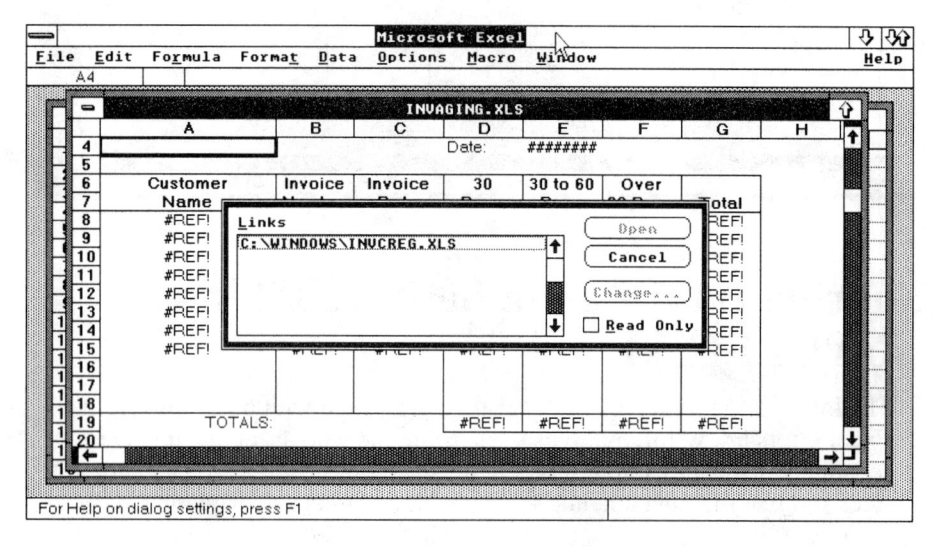

Fig. 7.11.
The Link dialog box.

The external file must be open in order for Excel to evaluate any formulas that contain an external reference to that file. When the dialog box appears, choose the file you want to open by pressing the Tab key to highlight the file name and by then pressing Enter or clicking on the Open button.

Note: Why have more than one file open at a time? Those cells that contain external references show the results of an attempt to evaluate those references. If your current worksheet refers to a file that isn't open, the cells containing or depending on those external references will contain either the error value #REF! or the value that was used the last time the external file was opened and used with this file. Only when the other file is open can Excel "reach over" into the other file and use the value found there.

The other method of using linked files is to declare a particular set of files a *workspace*. Like linking, a workspace enables data in one file to be automatically used by other files. When you have saved several open files as a workspace, you can then open all the related files at once. (Workspace files are saved with the command Save Workspace and bear the extension XLW, but individual files within the workspace are saved under the extension XLS, XLM, or XLC, as appropriate.)

Note: If you open one of the files declared to be part of a workspace without opening the related files, Excel prompts you about updating information in the other files (see fig. 7.12).

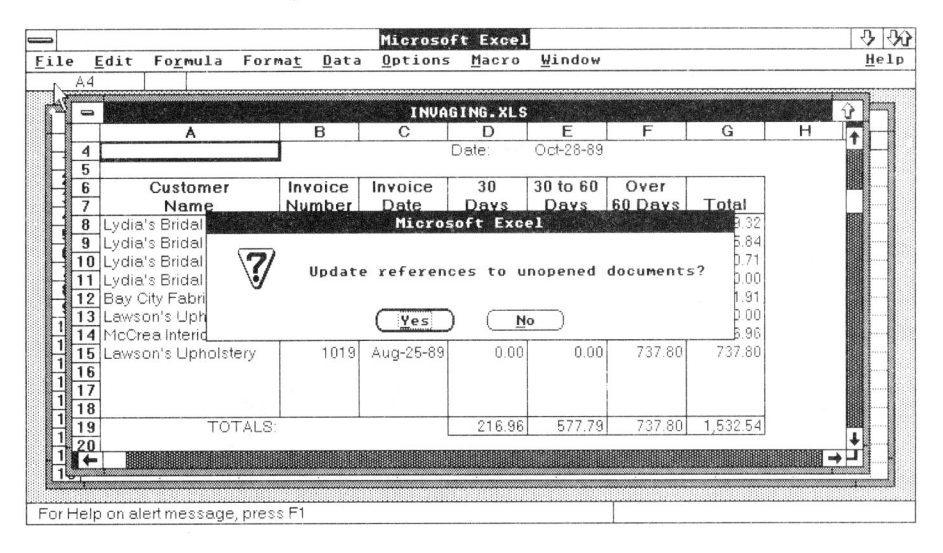

Fig. 7.12. The Excel message about updating information.

To sum up the difference between these two methods, you can open related files selectively or use the Save Workspace command so that the next time you use the files, you can open all the related files at once.

Back to City Fabrics' needs. The information generated by the invoice worksheet can be used for several accounting reports: a sales summary, an aging report to show which customers are paying bills slowly, an accounts receivable report sorted by date of invoice, and an accounts receivable report sorted by customer name. Because these worksheets use each other's data, it makes sense to save the set as a workspace so that updates to data in one worksheet will be automatically reflected in the others.

Note: The entire set of City Fabrics' related files is saved as a workspace. To see these files, open the file INVCREG.XLW.

For these new worksheets, very little new work needed to be done.

The Sales Summary (INVSALES.XLS)

The sales summary, shown in figure 7.13 and stored on disk as INVSALES.XLS, simply summarizes the sales information from the invoice register and presents that information as a single report.

Fig. 7.13. The sales summary.

	A	B	C	D	E
1		City Fabrics			
2		Sales Summary Report			
3			Jan-03-90		
4					
5		Tax Rate:	7.00%		
6	Customer	Net			
7	Name	Sales	Tax	Freight	Total
8	Lydia's Bridal Fashions	549.32	0.00	0.00	549.32
9	Lydia's Bridal Fashions	1,251.69	0.00	0.00	1,251.69
10	Lydia's Bridal Fashions	601.43	0.00	0.00	601.43
11	Lydia's Bridal Fashions	413.87	0.00	0.00	413.87
12	Bay City Fabrics	234.50	16.42	12.50	263.42
13	Lawson's Upholstery	200.00	14.00	6.00	220.00
14	McCrea Interiors	740.15	51.81	25.00	816.96
19	TOTALS:	3,990.96	82.23	43.50	4,116.69

Note that the Customer Name, Net Sales, Tax, Freight, and Total columns have the same information as was in columns D, E, F, G, and H of the invoice register (see figure 7.8). The sales summary worksheet uses external references to pick up the information in the invoice register and use it here. For instance, the formula in cell A8 of the sales summary contains the external reference

=INVCREG.XLS!D8

This reference tells Excel to "reach over" to the file INVCREG.XLS and use whatever it finds in cell D8 in that file. This arrangement is an especially efficient way of using data: when an item is added or changed on the invoice register, the new information is reflected on the related file.

The Aging Report (INVAGING.XLS)

The aging report, shown in figure 7.14 and stored on disk as INVAGING.XLS, uses the same approach, telling Excel to "reach over" to the invoice register, ascertain whether a payment is due, and put overdue payment information in the appropriate columns.

The aging report is based on the assumption that the following has been done with the payment schedule on the invoice register:

1. The first payment, either what is due or what has been paid, is entered under Payment 1, in column K, for each invoice.

2. The date due, or date paid, is entered under Date 1 in column L.

3. If a second payment is either due or paid, that information is entered in columns M and N.

Customer Name	Invoice Number	Invoice Date	30 Days	30 to 60 Days	Over 60 Days	Total
Lydia's Bridal Fashions	1005	Sep-08-89	0.00	0.00	249.32	249.32
Lydia's Bridal Fashions	1006	Sep-18-89	0.00	0.00	125.84	125.84
Lydia's Bridal Fashions	1007	Sep-21-89	0.00	0.00	150.71	150.71
Lydia's Bridal Fashions	1008	Oct-02-89	0.00	0.00	100.00	100.00
Bay City Fabrics	1010	Sep-02-89	0.00	0.00	51.91	51.91
Lawson's Upholstery	1015	Oct-02-89	0.00	0.00	0.00	0.00
McCrea Interiors	1016	Oct-05-89	0.00	0.00	116.96	116.96
Lawson's Upholstery	1019	Aug-25-89	0.00	0.00	737.80	737.80
TOTALS:			0.00	0.00	1,532.54	1,532.54

Fig. 7.14. The aging report.

4. The amount shown in column O, under Balance, shows the current balance. If the amount in column O for a particular invoice is 0, the balance has been paid. If the amount is greater than 0, there is an outstanding balance.

Now back to the aging report. The formulas in columns A, B, and C, row 8, of the aging report are the following, respectively:

=INVCREG.XLS!$A8
=INVCREG.XLS!$B8
=INVCREG.XLS!$C8

These formulas can be copied down the entire column.

Column D contains the formula

=IF(NOW()<(INVCREG.XLS!$C8+31),INVCREG.XLS!$O8,0)

This formula compares the current date with a value derived by the addition of 31 to the value in column C (the invoice date) of the invoice register. This comparison determines whether the current balance is a 30-day receivable. If the current date is less than the value it is compared with, the amount in column O of the invoice register is placed in the 30 Days column; otherwise, the formula puts a 0 in this column. The formula can be copied down the column.

The formula in column C uses a pair of IF statements to determine whether the balance should go in the 60-day-receivable category:

=IF(AND(NOW()>(INVCREG.XLS!$C8+30),NOW()<(INVCREG.XLS!$C8+61)),
    INVCREG.XLS!$O8,0)

This formula determines whether the current date is between 30 days and 61 days past the invoice date. The first part of the formula, NOW()>(INVCREG.XLS!$C8+30), determines whether the current date is greater than the invoice date plus 30.

The second part of the formula, NOW()<(INVCREG.XLS!$C8+61), determines whether the current date is less than the invoice date plus 61. Both parts of the formula must be true if the amount in column O is to be displayed. If either part is false (the date is outside these limits), the cell displays 0.

The formula in column D also uses the contents of column C to determine whether the balance is 0 or belongs in the past-due category:

=IF(NOW()>(INVCREG.XLS!$C8+61),INVCREG.XLS!$O8,0)

The figures determined in the aging report are important because they in turn are used by other files.

Accounts Receivable Summaries (INVARCUS.XLS, INVARDAT.XLS)

The accounts receivable summaries use information developed both in the invoice report and aging report. Both the Accounts Receivable by Customer report, shown in figure 7.15 and available on disk as INVARCUS.XLS, and the Accounts Receivable by Date report, shown in figure 7.16 and available on disk as INVARDAT.XLS, use information in columns D, C, B, and H on the invoice register and in column E on the aging report.

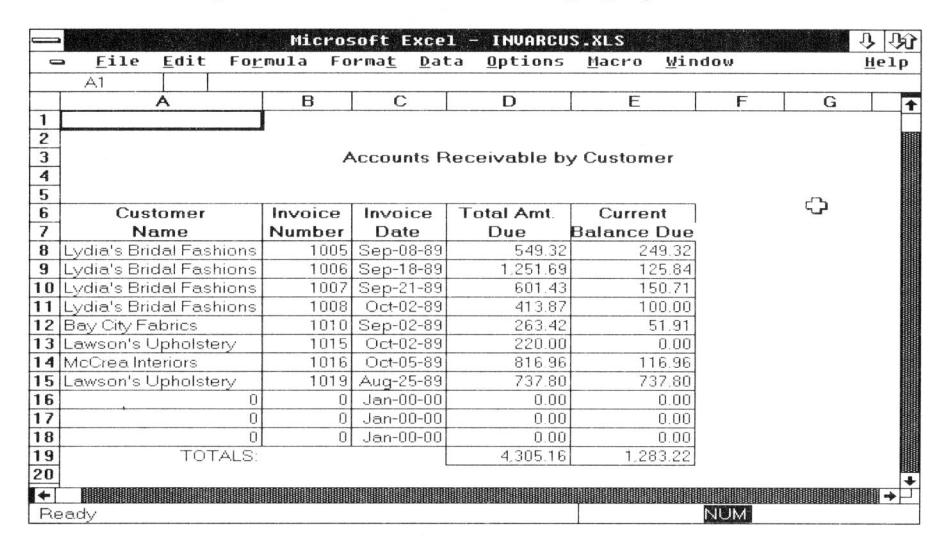

Fig. 7.15. The Accounts Receivable by Customer report.

Customer Name	Invoice Number	Invoice Date	Total Amt. Due	Current Balance Due
Lydia's Bridal Fashions	1005	Sep-08-89	549.32	249.32
Lydia's Bridal Fashions	1006	Sep-18-89	1,251.69	125.84
Lydia's Bridal Fashions	1007	Sep-21-89	601.43	150.71
Lydia's Bridal Fashions	1008	Oct-02-89	413.87	100.00
Bay City Fabrics	1010	Sep-02-89	263.42	51.91
Lawson's Upholstery	1015	Oct-02-89	220.00	0.00
McCrea Interiors	1016	Oct-05-89	816.96	116.96
Lawson's Upholstery	1019	Aug-25-89	737.80	737.80
0	0	Jan-00-00	0.00	0.00
0	0	Jan-00-00	0.00	0.00
0	0	Jan-00-00	0.00	0.00
TOTALS:			4,305.16	1,283.22

Fig. 7.16. The Accounts Receivable by Date report.

Invoice Date	Invoice Number	Customer Name	Total Amt. Due	Current Balance Due
Sep-08-89	1005	Lydia's Bridal Fashions	549.32	249.32
Sep-18-89	1006	Lydia's Bridal Fashions	1251.69	125.84
Sep-21-89	1007	Lydia's Bridal Fashions	601.43	150.71
Oct-02-89	1008	Lydia's Bridal Fashions	413.87	100
Sep-02-89	1010	Bay City Fabrics	263.415	51.915
Oct-02-89	1015	Lawson's Upholstery	220	0
Oct-05-89	1016	McCrea Interiors	816.9605	116.9605
Aug-25-89	1019	Lawson's Upholstery	737.7965	737.7965
Jan-00-00	0		0	0
Jan-00-00	0		0	0
Jan-00-00	0		0	0
			4,854.48	1,532.54

The Collections Worksheet (COLWKSHT.XLW, COLWKSHT.XLS)

You may want to use the data in the aging report to create a separate summary of delinquent accounts receivable, but you'll accomplish the same purpose with the collections worksheet, a sample of which is shown in figure 7.17.

Fig. 7.17.
An A/R collections worksheet.

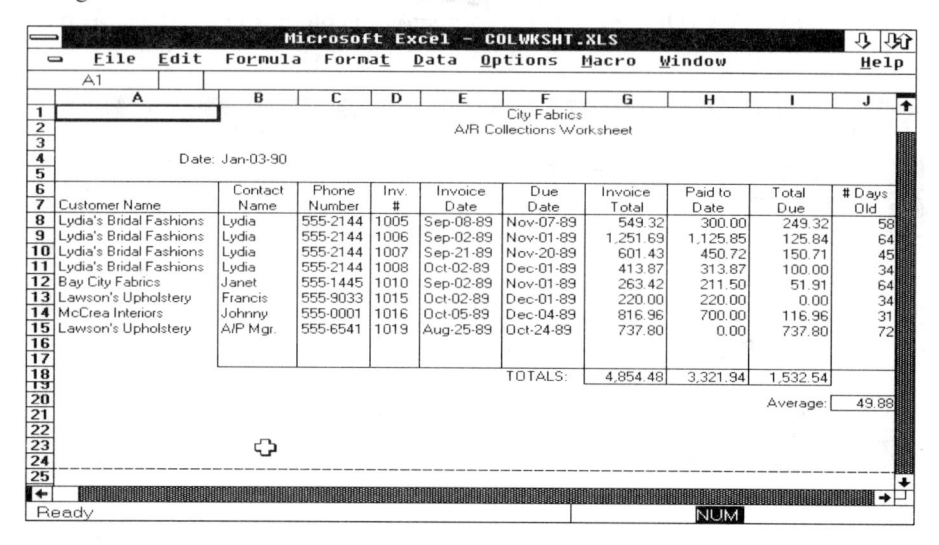

	A	B	C	D	E	F	G	H	I	J
1						City Fabrics				
2					A/R Collections Worksheet					
3										
4		Date: Jan-03-90								
5										
6			Contact	Phone	Inv.	Invoice	Due	Invoice	Paid to	Total	# Days
7	Customer Name	Name	Number	#	Date	Date	Total	Date	Due	Old
8	Lydia's Bridal Fashions	Lydia	555-2144	1005	Sep-08-89	Nov-07-89	549.32	300.00	249.32	58
9	Lydia's Bridal Fashions	Lydia	555-2144	1006	Sep-02-89	Nov-01-89	1,251.69	1,125.85	125.84	64
10	Lydia's Bridal Fashions	Lydia	555-2144	1007	Sep-21-89	Nov-20-89	601.43	450.72	150.71	45
11	Lydia's Bridal Fashions	Lydia	555-2144	1008	Oct-02-89	Dec-01-89	413.87	313.87	100.00	34
12	Bay City Fabrics	Janet	555-1445	1010	Sep-02-89	Nov-01-89	263.42	211.50	51.91	64
13	Lawson's Upholstery	Francis	555-9033	1015	Oct-02-89	Dec-01-89	220.00	220.00	0.00	34
14	McCrea Interiors	Johnny	555-0001	1016	Oct-05-89	Dec-04-89	816.96	700.00	116.96	31
15	Lawson's Upholstery	A/P Mgr.	555-6541	1019	Aug-25-89	Oct-24-89	737.80	0.00	737.80	72
						TOTALS:	4,854.48	3,321.94	1,532.54	
									Average:	49.88

Note: The A/R collections worksheet is included on the disk that accompanies this book, both as a workspace file (COLWKSHT.XLW) and as a separate worksheet file (COLWKSHT.XLS). When you open the worksheet file COLWKSHT.XLW, you automatically open the related files. You will be prompted about updating references; choose the Yes option. Don't cancel the process when you see several #REF error messages. These are replaced with data as the related worksheets are opened by the workspace file.

On the collections worksheet, the formula =NOW() in cell B4 means that whenever the worksheet is opened, the current date is placed in cell B4. However, information for most of the rest of this worksheet comes from other worksheets:

- The data in the columns labeled Customer Name, Inv. #., Invoice Date, and Invoice Total comes from the file INVAGING.XLS. The formulas are similar to the one in A8:

    =INVAGING.XLS!$A8

- The data in columns H and I, labeled Paid to Date and Total Due, comes from the file INVARCUS.XLS. Because the Accounts Receivable by Customer worksheet, INVARCUS.XLS, does not show the total amount paid to date, the formula in column H calculates that amount, using the values on the INVARCUS.XLS worksheet:

=INVARCUS.XLS!$D8-INVARCUS.XLS!$E8

The formula in column I subtracts the amount in column H from the amount in column G. The data in column F, the due date, is calculated by adding 60 to the invoice date in column E. The number of days delinquent, in column J, is determined by checking whether the difference between the current date (in B4) and the due date (in column F) is 0 or less. The formula in column J is this:

=IF((($B$4-$F8)<=0),0,($B$4-$F8))

The numbers that appear in column J depend on whether payments have been recorded on the aging report worksheet. If a payment has been made within the expected 60-day period and recorded in the payment schedule portion of the invoice register, this fact will show up in the aging report, which is used by this worksheet.

You'll want to add the contact name and phone number from the credit-application file you have for each account. As you're filling out this worksheet, you can open the appropriate credit-application worksheet for each client and use the Edit Copy command to copy the name and phone number from the Accounts Payable Information section onto this worksheet.

The Accounts Payable Tickler File (TICKLER.XLS)

You can use most of the same columns to set up your business's accounts payable tickler file, shown in figure 7.18 and included on the disk as the file TICKLER.XLS.

If you log your accounts payable in the same way that you log your sales on the invoice register, you can use workspace files to transfer information from one file to another automatically. For instance, the data in columns A, B, C, and E (the supplier name, invoice number, invoice date, and invoice total) could easily come from a payables register that looks very much like the invoice register.

As with other worksheets, the date in B4 is automatically updated every time you open the worksheet. As you use the worksheet, enter into column F the amount paid against each bill.

218 Excel Business Applications: IBM Version

Fig. 7.18.
The accounts payable tickler file.

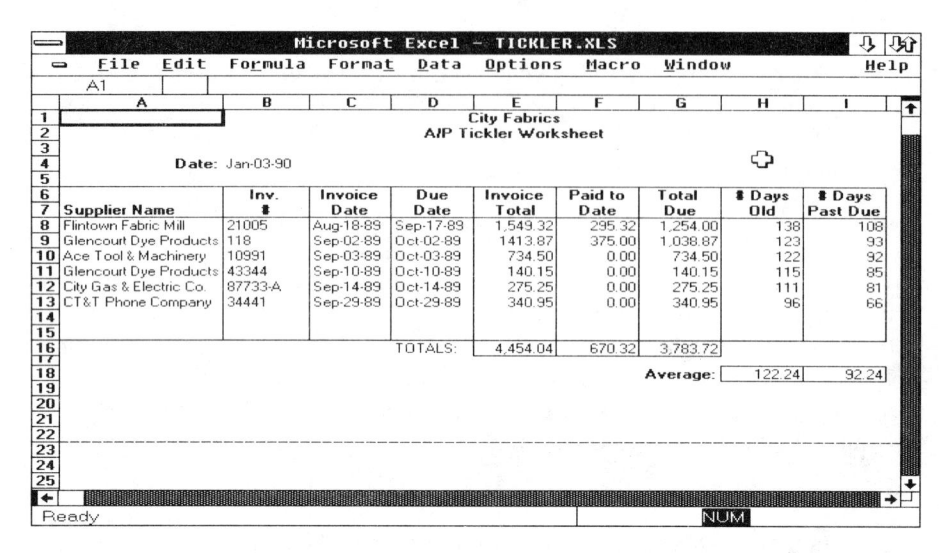

	A	B	C	D	E	F	G	H	I
1					City Fabrics				
2					A/P Tickler Worksheet				
3									
4		Date:	Jan-03-90						
5									
6			Inv.	Invoice	Due	Invoice	Paid to	Total	# Days	# Days
7	Supplier Name		#	Date	Date	Total	Date	Due	Old	Past Due
8	Flintown Fabric Mill	21005	Aug-18-89	Sep-17-89	1,549.32	295.32	1,254.00	138	108
9	Glencourt Dye Products	118	Sep-02-89	Oct-02-89	1413.87	375.00	1,038.87	123	93
10	Ace Tool & Machinery	10991	Sep-03-89	Oct-03-89	734.50	0.00	734.50	122	92
11	Glencourt Dye Products	43344	Sep-10-89	Oct-10-89	140.15	0.00	140.15	115	85
12	City Gas & Electric Co.	87733-A	Sep-14-89	Oct-14-89	275.25	0.00	275.25	111	81
13	CT&T Phone Company	34441	Sep-29-89	Oct-29-89	340.95	0.00	340.95	96	66
16				TOTALS:	4,454.04	670.32	3,783.72		
18							Average:	122.24	92.24

Columns D, G, H, and I are computed on this worksheet. If your company policy is to pay bills within 30 days, the formula in column D should be something like =C8+30, which is what the formula is on the disk. Column G computes the total due, using the formula =E8-F8.

Column H computes the number of days since the bill was received by subtracting the date in column C from the current day's date, which is in B4. Column H determines the number of days past due by subtracting the date in column D from the current day's date.

The totals, shown on line 16, sum the figures in the columns above. The average figure, in H18, determines the average number of days your bills go unpaid.

To use or modify the model, follow these steps:

Step 1. As each bill arrives, log it in this worksheet. Enter the name of the supplier, the invoice number, the date the bill arrived, and the invoice total. The rest of the information on each line is calculated automatically.

Step 2. If you need to add more lines, insert them above the line showing the totals. Highlight the entire line by clicking on the row number; then issue the Edit Insert command. Repeat this command for as many lines as you need.

Because of the SUM formulas at the end of each column, it's important to add new rows, which reflect new bills, by inserting new lines. If you insert a row, the range in the SUM formula is automatically adjusted to reflect the new row.

Step 3. As you pay a bill, enter into the Due Date column (column D) the date you paid it. Thus the date here reflects either the date by which the bill should be paid or the date it actually was paid.

Step 4. As you modify the contents during the month, save the file under the same file name. At the beginning of the next month, open the previous month's worksheet. Select the data areas of columns A, B, and C (A8:C15 in the file on disk). Then choose the Edit Clear command and the Formula option to clear the data in that area. Repeat the step for the data in columns E and F (E8:F15 in the file on disk). Then save the file under the name for the new month.

Note that you can use the same worksheet to include any payments due on notes on which your business is paying. You may want to add a column in which you compute the new balance after each month's payment. Once you've included the notes on the worksheet, along with the date due for each payment, you simply treat them the same as any other payable, except of course that you copy the item from one month's worksheet to the next month's until the note is paid off.

Creating Workspaces

As you get used to the concept of using linked files, you may find that you want to create your own workspace files so that you can open related files at once, rather than one at a time. If you want to create your own workspace files, follow these steps:

Step 1. Open a new file; create the headings, formula, and data you want on it; then save the file.

Step 2. Open any related files, with their headings and data, and any external references to the original or other open files. Remember that an external reference uses the form

filename.XLS!*location*

Step 3. Position the files, using the Size and Move commands (press Alt and choose the appropriate command; then use the arrow keys to move the window where you want it), or use your mouse to size and position the various windows. Be sure that the screen reflects what you want displayed when the entire workspace is opened.

Step 4. Using the Save Workspace command, save the entire set of opened files as a workspace, giving it a separate name. Note that you can use the same file name for the workspace as for an individual worksheet or macro file; Excel recognizes a workspace file by the XLW extension.

Modifying Existing Worksheets (INVFREG.XLS)

Most worksheet models in computer books can be run just as they are presented, but the authors usually intend them to serve as inspiration for other uses as well. The models in this book are examples of this kind of thinking.

The early portion of this chapter presented two simple versions of accounts receivable and accounts payable worksheets for Lydia's Bridal Fashions. You then learned how the concepts could be presented in more detail for City Fabrics. This section demonstrates some further changes to worksheets you've seen earlier. The intent is to show you how to use models as a tool so that you can take formulas or presentations that apply to your situation and change or delete what doesn't apply.

City Fabrics has a credit relationship with its suppliers, just as Lydia has a credit relationship with City Fabrics. In the same way that Lydia tries to use payments made by her customers to cover her costs of fabric ordered from City Fabrics, so City Fabrics tries to use its payments from customers like Lydia to cover its costs of fabric ordered from its suppliers.

Donaldson Fabric Supply sells to customers like City Fabrics, only it sells fabric by the bolt rather than by the yard. Donaldson's charges by the yard, however, but at a wholesale price. Because City Fabrics normally buys several bolts of fabric at a time, frequently in several colors of one style of fabric, Donaldson's must know what has been sold and what is still in stock in order to manage inventory. Thus the invoice register must show not only the price, tax, freight, and total cost information but also the style and color of the fabric, as well as the purchase-order number with which the fabric was ordered. Figure 7.19 shows a sample invoice register for Donaldson Fabric Supply.

Although this worksheet—INVFREG.XLS—is included on the disk that accompanies this book, you can construct a similar worksheet from an invoice register like the one in figure 7.8. Columns have been inserted into the Donaldson Fabric Supply invoice register for the purchase-order number, style, color, number of yards, and price per yard. The net amount in column J is a simple formula ($H8*$I8), not an amount you enter. The rest of the first part, through column N, is the same as columns F, G, H, and I in City Fabric's invoice register.

The calculations in the payment schedule are the same, too. Donaldson's can adjust them if other payment arrangements are in effect for selected customers.

Note that related files can use the same format, with formulas adjusted for the new file name and the new locations of the information. Figure 7.20 shows the aging report for Donaldson's, which, not surprisingly, looks much like the aging report for City Fabrics.

One of the benefits of using linked worksheets in situations like this one is that once you have entered the invoice information and any payments made, you can quickly see who's late in paying bills and who's still eligible for credit. For instance, the aging report shows that McMillan Distributors and Herald/Jackson may need a credit hold on their accounts, whereas City Fabrics has a clean record.

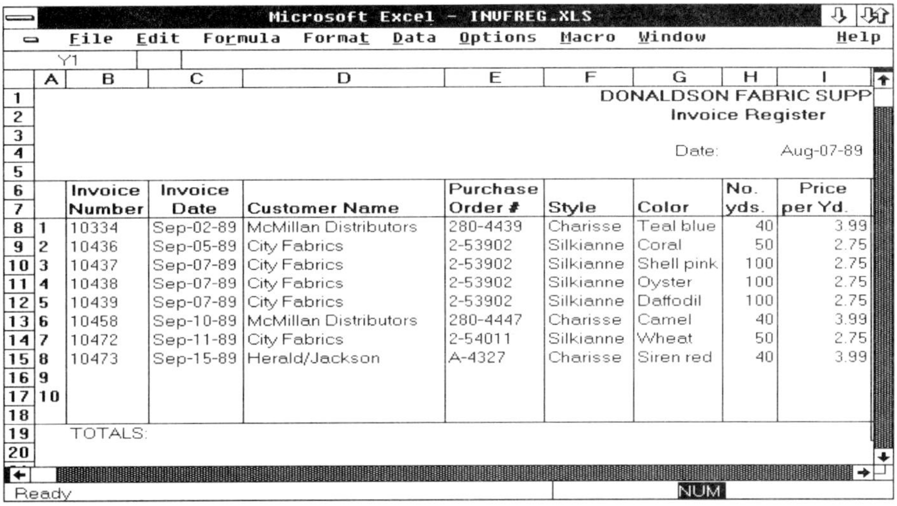

Microsoft Excel - INVFREG.XLS

File Edit Formula Format Data Options Macro Window Help

Y1

DONALDSON FABRIC SUPP

Invoice Register

Date: Aug-07-89

	Invoice Number	Invoice Date	Customer Name	Purchase Order #	Style	Color	No. yds.	Price per Yd.
1	10334	Sep-02-89	McMillan Distributors	280-4439	Charisse	Teal blue	40	3.99
2	10436	Sep-05-89	City Fabrics	2-53902	Silkianne	Coral	50	2.75
3	10437	Sep-07-89	City Fabrics	2-53902	Silkianne	Shell pink	100	2.75
4	10438	Sep-07-89	City Fabrics	2-53902	Silkianne	Oyster	100	2.75
5	10439	Sep-07-89	City Fabrics	2-53902	Silkianne	Daffodil	100	2.75
6	10458	Sep-10-89	McMillan Distributors	280-4447	Charisse	Camel	40	3.99
7	10472	Sep-11-89	City Fabrics	2-54011	Silkianne	Wheat	50	2.75
8	10473	Sep-15-89	Herald/Jackson	A-4327	Charisse	Siren red	40	3.99
9								
10								
	TOTALS:							

Ready NUM

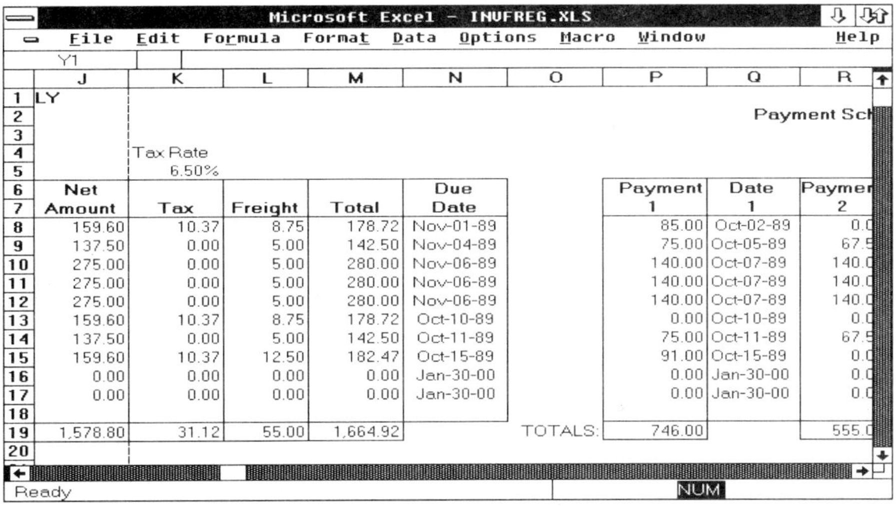

Microsoft Excel - INVFREG.XLS

File Edit Formula Format Data Options Macro Window Help

Y1

LY

Payment Sch

Tax Rate 6.50%

Net Amount	Tax	Freight	Total	Due Date		Payment 1	Date 1	Paymen 2
159.60	10.37	8.75	178.72	Nov-01-89		85.00	Oct-02-89	0.0
137.50	0.00	5.00	142.50	Nov-04-89		75.00	Oct-05-89	67.5
275.00	0.00	5.00	280.00	Nov-06-89		140.00	Oct-07-89	140.0
275.00	0.00	5.00	280.00	Nov-06-89		140.00	Oct-07-89	140.0
275.00	0.00	5.00	280.00	Nov-06-89		140.00	Oct-07-89	140.0
159.60	10.37	8.75	178.72	Oct-10-89		0.00	Oct-10-89	0.0
137.50	0.00	5.00	142.50	Oct-11-89		75.00	Oct-11-89	67.5
159.60	10.37	12.50	182.47	Oct-15-89		91.00	Oct-15-89	0.0
0.00	0.00	0.00	0.00	Jan-30-00		0.00	Jan-30-00	0.0
0.00	0.00	0.00	0.00	Jan-30-00		0.00	Jan-30-00	0.0
1,578.80	31.12	55.00	1,664.92		TOTALS:	746.00		555.0

Ready NUM

Fig. 7.19. Invoice register, Donaldson Fabric Supply.

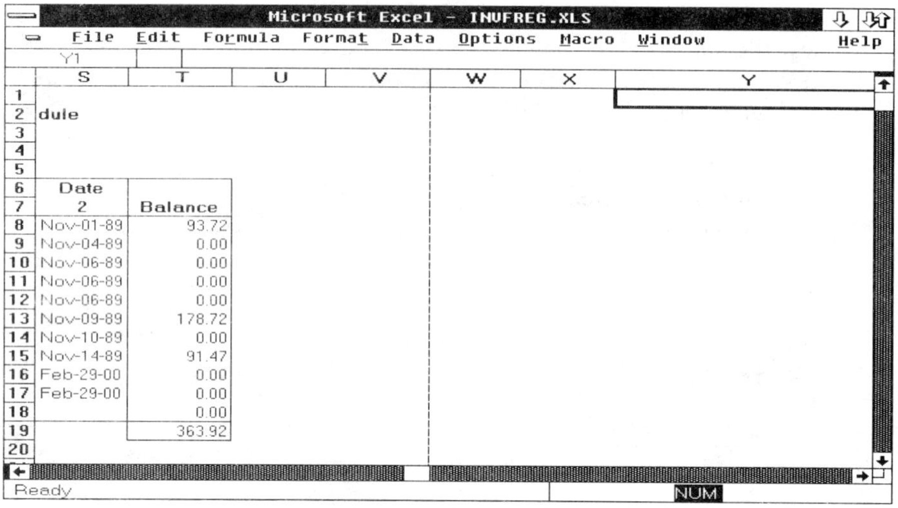

Microsoft Excel - INVFREG.XLS

File Edit Formula Format Data Options Macro Window Help

Y1

	S	T
1		
2	dule	
3		
4		
5		
6	Date	
7	2	Balance
8	Nov-01-89	93.72
9	Nov-04-89	0.00
10	Nov-06-89	0.00
11	Nov-06-89	0.00
12	Nov-06-89	0.00
13	Nov-09-89	178.72
14	Nov-10-89	0.00
15	Nov-14-89	91.47
16	Feb-29-00	0.00
17	Feb-29-00	0.00
18		0.00
19		363.92
20		

Ready NUM

Fig. 7.19, continued.

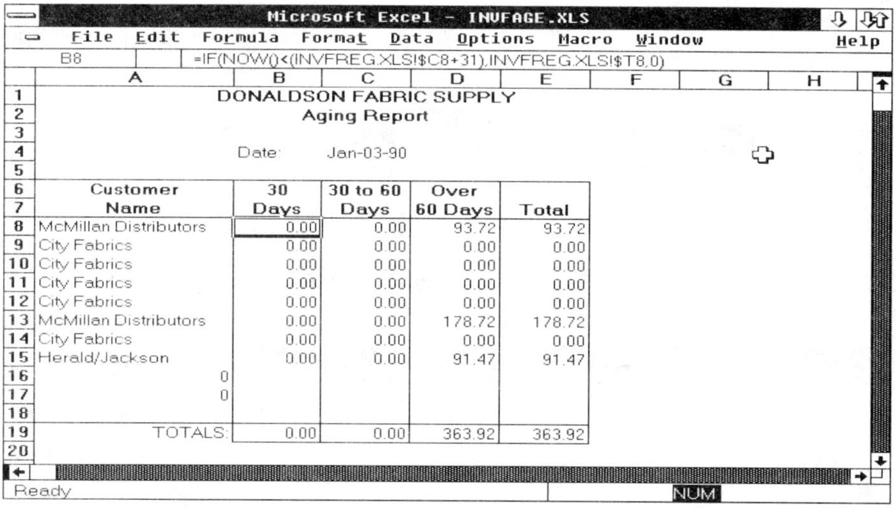

Microsoft Excel - INVFAGE.XLS

File Edit Formula Format Data Options Macro Window Help

B8 =IF(NOW()<(INVFREG.XLS!$C8+31),INVFREG.XLS!$T8,0)

DONALDSON FABRIC SUPPLY

Aging Report

Date: Jan-03-90

	Customer Name	30 Days	30 to 60 Days	Over 60 Days	Total
8	McMillan Distributors	0.00	0.00	93.72	93.72
9	City Fabrics	0.00	0.00	0.00	0.00
10	City Fabrics	0.00	0.00	0.00	0.00
11	City Fabrics	0.00	0.00	0.00	0.00
12	City Fabrics	0.00	0.00	0.00	0.00
13	McMillan Distributors	0.00	0.00	178.72	178.72
14	City Fabrics	0.00	0.00	0.00	0.00
15	Herald/Jackson	0.00	0.00	91.47	91.47
16	0				
17	0				
18					
19	TOTALS:	0.00	0.00	363.92	363.92

Ready NUM

Fig. 7.20. Aging report, Donaldson Fabric Supply.

Summary

In this chapter, you learned that the principles of controlling accounts receivable and payable apply to small, medium-sized, and large businesses, and you have become familiar with the following points:

- An accurate picture of your accounts receivable and accounts payable helps you maintain accurate budgets and cash-flow projections.

- Staying abreast of your accounts receivable helps you collect payments due you and helps you identify problem accounts quickly.
- Entering invoice information for each sale helps you track overall sales and accounts receivable.
- You can include identical information in separate reports, either by linking or by saving the reports as a workspace.
- Linking worksheets through external references enables Excel to "reach over" into a separate file and use a value from that file as a value in the current file.
- Reports saved as a workspace can be opened at the same time.
- You can modify an existing Excel worksheet to fit a new purpose.

In Chapter 8 you will learn how to use Excel to build easy-to-use worksheets for marketing, sales, and lending. Chapter 9 will show you how to use Excel's database capabilities in many business situations.

8

Using Marketing, Sales, and Financing Applications

Excel is superb at presenting the kinds of information necessary to predict marketing, sales, and financing success. This chapter establishes an important link among these three business disciplines, a link that ultimately can help you plan—rather than pray—for business success.

In this chapter you will discover how easy it is to use Excel to analyze and arrange your firm's marketing data into a pro forma sales presentation for a lender when you need to arrange for financing—or how easy it is to use the data to develop an investor prospectus if you seek venture capital. The result is the same.

To learn about and benefit from the marketing-sales-financing link, consider the following two statements:

1. You need to raise cash for your firm.

    To earn financial backing—whether you need to finance short-term liabilities or prepare for future growth by acquiring new assets—you must be able to demonstrate to a potential lender that your firm can support additional debt. In general, lenders like to see an increase in a firm's costs offset by an expected growth in sales. To maintain or increase your firm's current level of profitability, sales must grow faster than costs. Remember, it's unlikely that a bank will lend you cash if the burden of the new debt causes your firm to become less profitable.

2. You can gather (or forecast) your firm's marketing and sales data.

   To demonstrate that your firm can support additional debt, you must develop a series of reports that outline your firm's cost structure, expected sales, and expected profits. These reports tell a lender about the relative risk of loaning your firm cash. If you can talk intelligently and convincingly about how your firm will grow, you can put a lender at ease.

Once you feel comfortable with these two presumptions (and who wouldn't feel better about having some extra cash on hand?), you are ready to begin.

In the chapter's first section you will develop market projections by evaluating your firm's product-cost structure. This evaluation entails creating an equivalent-units conversion worksheet that lets you record the quantity of each raw material that goes into the manufacture of one unit of your product.

The next worksheet retains forecasted costs and sales. After you enter raw-material unit costs into a unit-costing matrix, you record your estimated monthly unit sales. This data is integral to the process of determining the exact dollar cost of one unit of your firm's product.

The data that you've gathered so far is next used to create the final report: a pro forma costs and sales report. This report shows the per-unit sales price, total monthly dollar sales, total monthly dollar costs, and total monthly dollar profits. Also included in this report is a year-end summary of sales, costs, and profits, as well as a costs-as-a-percentage-of-sales analysis.

In the final section of this chapter you will learn how to use Excel to analyze various financing plans. The concepts covered here include short-term borrowing, long-term borrowing, amortization modeling, and investor financing.

Each of the models presented in this chapter was created with the same Excel model-building skills that you have learned in the previous seven chapters. So feel free to modify the models to meet your own firm's reporting needs.

Here are several items to consider before using or modifying the *Excel Business Applications: IBM Version* models:

1. Make a backup copy of the models disk and store the backup in a safe place.

2. Save all your modified models under a unique file name so that you can quickly revert to the generic model if necessary. Don't ignore this recommendation! You'll need the original format if you accidentally erase a modified model file.

3. If you have a hard disk drive, create a new subdirectory on the hard disk and copy the models into this subdirectory. Then store the disk.

4. Each model has been saved in Options Protect Document mode. You can thus enter data only into worksheet cells that have been previously unlocked with the Format Cell Protection command. When Protect Document mode is enabled, these cells appear boldfaced and, in certain cases, underlined.

If you want to modify MN-CNVRT.XLS's structure, for example, first save the generic model under a new name. To protect the worksheet so that you can change descriptions and titles, select Options Unprotect Document.

> **Tip:** Arrange linked worksheets in an Excel workspace in the order in which they are used. To do this, simply order the file names according to how you want Excel to load the worksheets.

Developing Market Projections

As any business textbook will tell you, the following equation defines the relationship among sales, costs, and profits:

Sales – Costs = Profits

In maintaining acceptable profit levels, your challenge is to generate enough income from sales to cover your costs and have some left over to put in the bank. Specifically, your firm's success depends on your ability to keep tight control of your raw-material costs and establish prices that enable you to earn a profit. This section helps you to understand the effects of pricing and cost-control strategy on firm profits, emphasizing how good strategies help make your firm attractive to investors and lenders. Figure 8.1 illustrates the chronology of this process. On the left is a description of the actions that you might take if you want to prepare reports manually. On the right is an illustration of the data flow when you prepare the same reports with Excel.

Fig. 8.1.
The manual steps and worksheet data flow in the report-creation process.

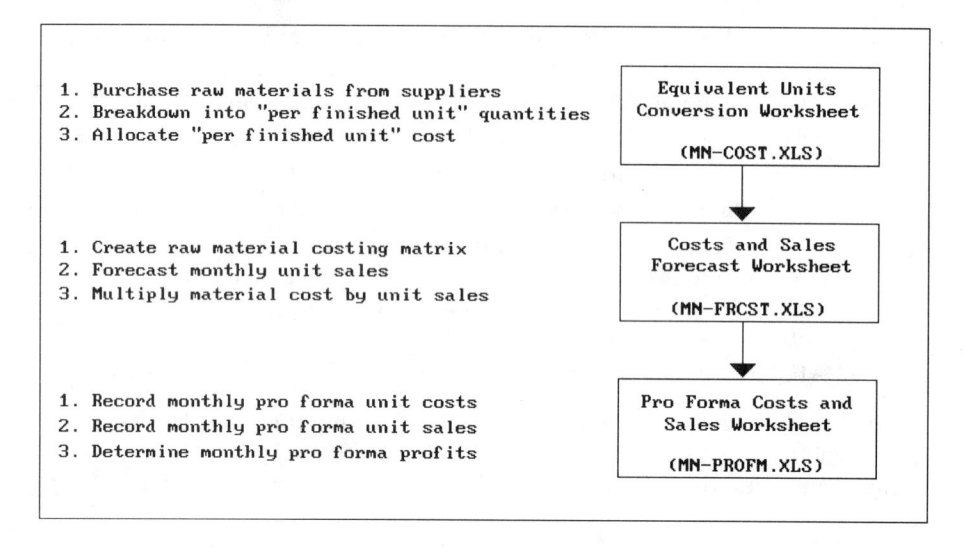

```
1. Purchase raw materials from suppliers         ┌─────────────────────┐
2. Breakdown into "per finished unit" quantities │  Equivalent Units   │
3. Allocate "per finished unit" cost             │ Conversion Worksheet│
                                                 │    (MN-COST.XLS)    │
                                                 └──────────┬──────────┘
                                                            ▼
1. Create raw material costing matrix            ┌─────────────────────┐
2. Forecast monthly unit sales                   │  Costs and Sales    │
3. Multiply material cost by unit sales          │ Forecast Worksheet  │
                                                 │   (MN-FRCST.XLS)    │
                                                 └──────────┬──────────┘
                                                            ▼
1. Record monthly pro forma unit costs           ┌─────────────────────┐
2. Record monthly pro forma unit sales           │ Pro Forma Costs and │
3. Determine monthly pro forma profits           │   Sales Worksheet   │
                                                 │   (MN-PROFM.XLS)    │
                                                 └─────────────────────┘
```

Understanding Unit Costs

The sales-costs-profits formula proves that profit depends directly on the income derived from the sales of products and the costs associated with the production of these goods. When you manage your product, or *unit*, costs effectively, you maximize the contribution to firm profits and, therefore, to your business's overall health.

Suppose, for example, that your company produces an item at a unit cost of $2.50 and sells it for $4.95. By the equation given earlier, you would earn $2.45 in profits. Now suppose that you have an opportunity to reduce your unit cost by 10 percent, or 25 cents. If you sell 10,000 units annually, you've generated an extra $2,500 in profits on that item alone.

Whether your business manufactures computer boards, serves fast-food burgers, or builds ocean liners, controlling unit costs is a fundamental responsibility of every business manager. The manager must react quickly to an unexpected increase in the cost of manufacturing a finished good. Why? Because there are only two ways to deal with unexpected, extra costs: increase the product's price, or accept a decrease in the product's profit contribution when price remains constant. Obviously, the smart manager will not settle for either alternative when cost-control solutions exist. As you can see, analyzing unit costs goes to the heart of predicting your firm's profits for the coming months.

In the restaurant industry, for example, fluctuations in the availability and cost of fresh produce dictate what can be offered on a menu as "fresh fruit" for a reasonable price. Similarly, seasonal fishing conditions or storms can profoundly affect the cost of offering a "fresh fish of the day." Obviously, it's difficult to make accurate cost projections when prices can jump or tumble wildly over the period of a few days or weeks.

Gathering Unit Costs

The most accurate sales and costs estimates come from two sources: detailed historical data from your own firm, and data from firms within the same industry. If you develop a business strategy to deal with unpredictable events such as storms or probable seasonal changes, you can reasonably predict how your restaurant will do in the future.

As mentioned in Chapter 4, nitty-gritty historical data helps to produce better detail in your sales forecasts. The more contributing factors you consider in making your forecasts, the more believable you will be to lenders and investors. Although you may not be able to predict how many people will walk into your restaurant, you can devise an estimate based on the numbers of customers patronizing other restaurants in the area. Using as a basis those figures and your own knowledge of what percentage of your patrons is expected to order which dishes, you will be able to come up with a good estimate of total food sales for a day.

Here lies the value of being able to predict the unit cost of anything. If you can reasonably predict the number of people who will buy your products, and if you have a good handle on the cost composition of each product, your forecasts will be reasonably accurate.

The value of having this detailed data goes well beyond management cost-control responsibilities. Bankers love this kind of detail, as do investors, property lessors, people who make equipment loans, management consultants, accountants, and suppliers with whom you hope to establish credit. And one benefit of storing such information in Excel worksheets is that the data can be shared with other files, as demonstrated in Chapter 7. You can use some of the information developed in a unit-cost worksheet, for example, to help you determine appropriate prices for your products. Those prices, when combined with your anticipated ordering patterns, can be used to produce monthly cash-flow projections.

Analyzing Unit Costs

The key to determining a product's total cost lies in finding the exact cost of each of the product's components. This means adding up all the raw-material and/or production costs associated with putting this product into the marketplace.

In the case of a manufactured product, components can include materials such as sheet metal, screws or bolts, the cost of machining the sheet metal, and associated labor. In the case of an assembled product, components can include parts, associated labor, and packaging. In the case of a food product, components can include the ingredients that go directly into the item and any packaging that is used to serve the item.

Consider the following discussion about a prospective restaurant operator. As you read, envision the structure of the worksheets that you can use to convince your own investors and lenders that your business-growth ideas are sound.

Creating a Market Projection for Ford's Pan-Galactic Bar & Grill

Increasingly, those who have capital at risk in your business (whether they are investors, lenders, or suppliers) want to know how you are prepared to handle the unexpected. As owner and operator of the hypothetical restaurant Ford's Pan-Galactic Bar & Grill, you are financially and contractually responsible to your lenders and investors. How, then, the lenders might ask, will your overall profitability suffer in the face of a strike among California's lettuce pickers? You can find lettuce and salad greens elsewhere, but probably at a higher cost. How many of your menu items use lettuce, your investors may ask, and can substitutions be made for costly ingredients? What if beef prices suddenly go up by 10 cents per pound? What will this cost increase do to your profit margin?

These questions can best be answered by a demonstration that uses the Equivalent Units Conversion (MN-CNVRT.XLS) worksheet, the Costs and Sales Forecast (MN-FRCST.XLS) worksheet, and the Pro Forma Costs and Sales (MN-PROFM.XLS) worksheet. Figures 8.2, 8.3, and 8.4 show the initial screen of each of these worksheets.

Note: To load these three worksheets simultaneously, use the MN.XLW workspace file. You do not need to load these files yet. Later, the text will guide you through the process of opening them and entering data.

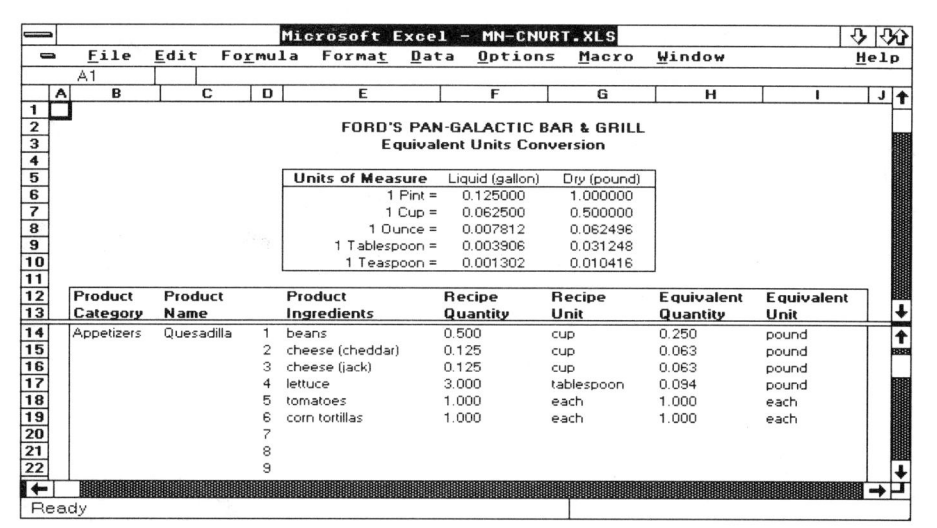

Fig. 8.2. The Equivalent Units Conversion worksheet.

Fig. 8.3. The Costs and Sales Forecast worksheet.

The worksheets in this example are abbreviated; they are pared down so that you can work with them quickly and easily. After you learn how to use the sample worksheets as they are, feel free to expand or modify them to suit your own needs. Further, although this text uses a restaurant as an example, remember that many kinds of businesses create products from separate components.

Fig. 8.4.
The Pro Forma Costs and Sales worksheet.

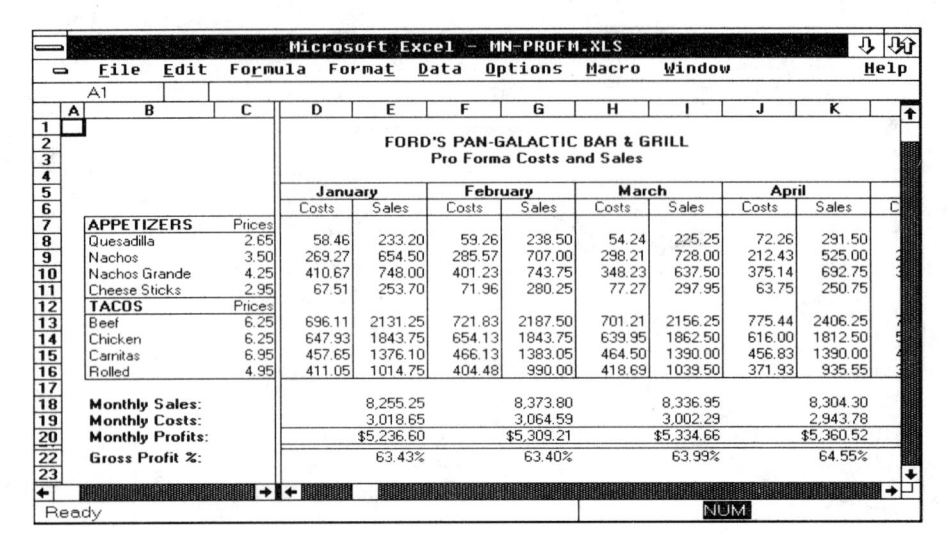

	January		February		March		April	
	Costs	Sales	Costs	Sales	Costs	Sales	Costs	Sales
APPETIZERS Prices								
Quesadilla 2.65	58.46	233.20	59.26	238.50	54.24	225.25	72.26	291.50
Nachos 3.50	269.27	654.50	285.57	707.00	298.21	728.00	212.43	525.00
Nachos Grande 4.25	410.67	748.00	401.23	743.75	348.23	637.50	375.14	692.75
Cheese Sticks 2.95	67.51	253.70	71.96	280.25	77.27	297.95	63.75	250.75
TACOS Prices								
Beef 6.25	696.11	2131.25	721.83	2187.50	701.21	2156.25	775.44	2406.25
Chicken 6.25	647.93	1843.75	654.13	1843.75	639.95	1862.50	616.00	1812.50
Carnitas 6.95	457.65	1376.10	466.13	1383.05	464.50	1390.00	456.83	1390.00
Rolled 4.95	411.05	1014.75	404.48	990.00	418.69	1039.50	371.93	935.55
Monthly Sales:		8,255.25		8,373.80		8,336.95		8,304.30
Monthly Costs:		3,018.65		3,064.59		3,002.29		2,943.78
Monthly Profits:		$5,236.60		$5,309.21		$5,334.66		$5,360.52
Gross Profit %:		63.43%		63.40%		63.99%		64.55%

FORD'S PAN-GALACTIC BAR & GRILL
Pro Forma Costs and Sales

These worksheets are designed to work together. You can thus enter changing ingredient uses into the Equivalent Units Conversion worksheet and increasing ingredient costs into the Costs and Sales Forecast worksheet to predict again your unit costs. To reflect seasonal patronage patterns, just fine-tune your forecast of the number of units (dishes) sold per month on the Costs and Sales Forecast worksheet.

The Equivalent Units Conversion Worksheet (MN-CNVRT.XLS)

The worksheet in figure 8.2 is outfitted for a Mexican restaurant and lists some of the common ingredients used in Mexican recipes. You can modify the worksheet to include any kind of raw materials; the worksheet will work just as it does in this example.

This extensive worksheet enables you to enter the recipe for each dish found on your menu. The conversion chart, which begins in cell E5, shows the relationship between measurements commonly used in food preparation and quantities commonly used when you buy ingredients in bulk. You can include any type of measure in such a conversion chart.

> Tip: For example, you could create a chart to convert English measurements to metric measurements, a tool that would surely interest the production manager of a bolt manufacturing company.

If you purchase goods "by the gross" and use them in quantities of two or four, or if you buy "by the carton" and use "by the piece," you can record the relationship in this portion of the worksheet.

The conversion chart contains measurements for both dry and liquid measure. So that the two are differentiated, each measurement is also an Excel named variable. In F7, the value 0.062500 is named *lcup* for a liquid cup; in G7, the value 0.50000 is named *dcup* for a dry cup. The same naming convention is used for the remaining measures. For example, in cell G9, Excel stores the name *dtbsp* to represent a dry tablespoon.

The conversion table in figure 8.2 reflects values as relative portions of either liquid gallons or dry pounds, whichever is the unit in which ingredients are purchased. Thus a liquid cup, the value in F7, is equal to 1/16 of a liquid gallon, whereas a dry cup, the value in G7, is 1/2 of a dry pound. You may need to set up your table to reflect different units of measurement. If so, be sure to name the variables so that they can be referenced by name when you list the components (in this case, individual ingredients for a food product, as shown in the recipes for each dish).

When you enter a recipe in the Equivalent Units Conversion worksheet, such as the beef tacos recipe shown in figure 8.5, enter only the ingredients required for an individual serving. If you alter the worksheet so that you enter, for example, raw materials used in the production of a printer ribbon, enter only the amounts used to produce a single ribbon, not a carton or whatever measurement you use for packaging or shipping your product.

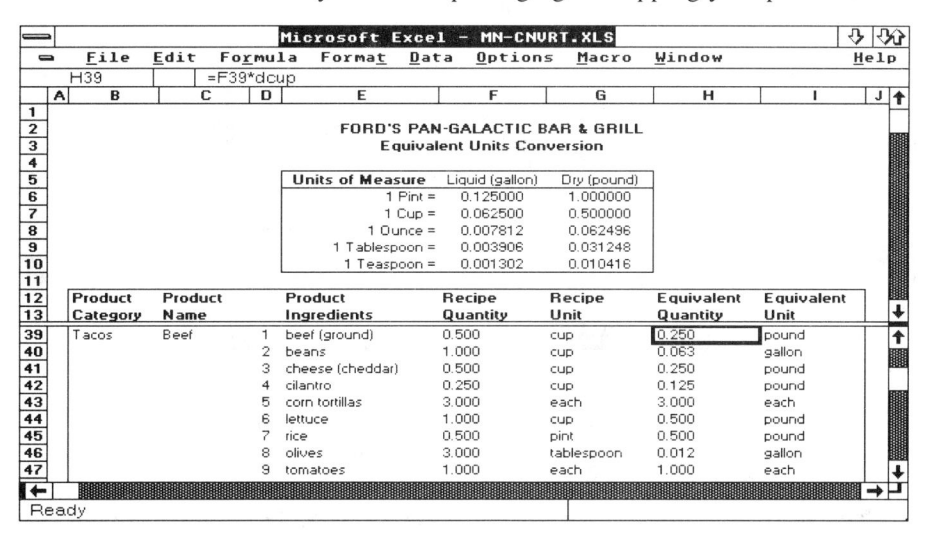

Fig. 8.5.
The beef taco recipe, showing the formula in cell H39 that calculates the equivalent quantity of ground beef used in the recipe.

The Costs and Sales Forecast Worksheet (MN-FRCST.XLS)

This second worksheet serves a dual purpose. First, it stores forecasted ingredient costs in the unit and value of purchase. In the costing matrix pictured in the top portion of figure 8.3, for example, you can see that beans are expected to cost from $1.15 to $1.20 per pound during the current year. Second, this worksheet stores the monthly sales forecast and calculates the per-dish cost of each menu item. The per-dish cost forecast is developed from data stored in MN-CNVRT.XLS as well as from the cost data in the costing matrix in MN-FRCST.XLS.

To calculate the total cost of preparing a single serving of each dish, this worksheet contains formulas that multiply the cost of each ingredient in a dish by the corresponding equivalent-quantity value stored in the MN-CNVRT.XLS worksheet.

The formula in figure 8.6, for example, calculates the cost of an individual serving of beef tacos for the month of January. Although this cost-calculating formula is long, it really is nothing more than a simple addition formula involving external references.

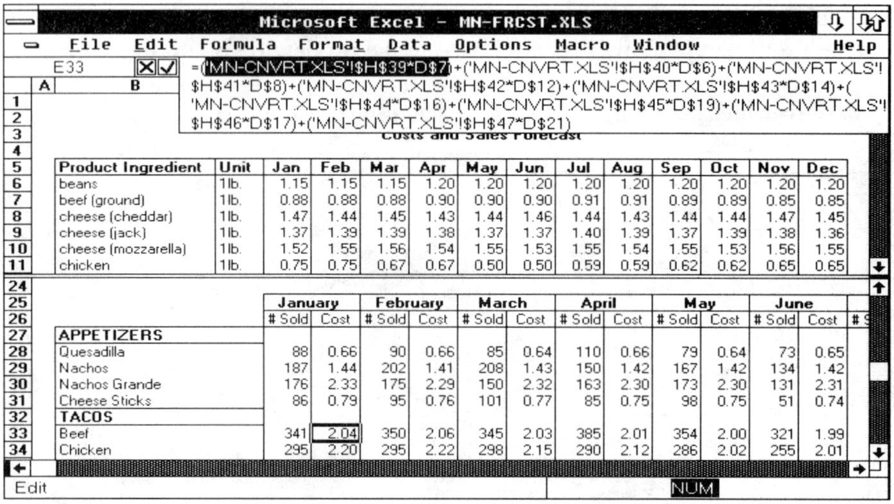

	Product Ingredient	Unit	Jan	Feb	Mar	Apr	May	Jun	Jul	Aug	Sep	Oct	Nov	Dec
6	beans	1lb.	1.15	1.15	1.15	1.20	1.20	1.20	1.20	1.20	1.20	1.20	1.20	1.20
7	beef (ground)	1lb.	0.88	0.88	0.88	0.90	0.90	0.90	0.91	0.91	0.89	0.89	0.85	0.85
8	cheese (cheddar)	1lb.	1.47	1.44	1.45	1.43	1.44	1.46	1.44	1.43	1.44	1.44	1.47	1.45
9	cheese (jack)	1lb.	1.37	1.39	1.39	1.38	1.37	1.37	1.40	1.39	1.37	1.39	1.38	1.36
10	cheese (mozzarella)	1lb.	1.52	1.55	1.56	1.54	1.55	1.53	1.55	1.54	1.55	1.53	1.56	1.55
11	chicken	1lb.	0.75	0.75	0.67	0.67	0.50	0.50	0.59	0.59	0.62	0.62	0.65	0.65

		January		February		March		April		May		June	
26		# Sold	Cost	# Sold	Cost	# Sold	Cost	# Sold	Cost	# Sold	Cost	# Sold	Cost
27	APPETIZERS												
28	Quesadilla	88	0.66	90	0.66	85	0.64	110	0.66	79	0.64	73	0.65
29	Nachos	187	1.44	202	1.41	208	1.43	150	1.42	167	1.42	134	1.42
30	Nachos Grande	176	2.33	175	2.29	150	2.32	163	2.30	173	2.30	131	2.31
31	Cheese Sticks	86	0.79	95	0.76	101	0.77	85	0.75	98	0.75	51	0.74
32	TACOS												
33	Beef	341	2.04	350	2.06	345	2.03	385	2.01	354	2.00	321	1.99
34	Chicken	295	2.20	295	2.22	298	2.15	290	2.12	286	2.02	255	2.01

Fig. 8.6. The formula in cell E33 calculates the total ingredients cost of a single serving of beef tacos.

This formula multiplies equivalent-quantity data found in the MN-CNVRT.XLS worksheet by data stored in the unit-costing matrix found in the MN-FRCST.XLS worksheet. The formula is long because most of its elements refer to the external file MN-CNVRT.XLS. The first part of the formula in figure 8.6 is this:

('MN-CNVRT.XLS'!$H$39*D$7)

This formula means, "Multiply 0.250 pounds, the amount of beef called for in the beef taco recipe ('MN-CNVRT.XLS'!$H$39), by the $0.88-per-pound cost of beef indicated in the costing matrix (D$7) on the current worksheet." When the cost of each ingredient is determined in this way, and then all costs are added together, the resulting value, $2.04, is stored in cell E33.

The Pro Forma Monthly Sales Worksheet (MN-PROFM.XLS)

This last worksheet uses values from MN-CNVRT.XLS and MN-FRCST.XLS to create an estimate of monthly costs, sales, and profits, by menu item, for the restaurant. You store the retail price of each menu item on this worksheet in column C. Let's see how the worksheet operates.

Remember the cost figure for beef tacos, $2.04, stored in the MN-FRCST.XLS worksheet in cell E33? The value adjacent to this amount is 341. This "# Sold" value represents the number of beef taco dishes that you expect to sell in January. These two figures are multiplied together to calculate the total ingredient costs associated with beef taco sales in January. This summary cost figure appears in cell D13 under the Costs column in the MN-PROFM.XLS worksheet. Figure 8.7 illustrates the syntax of the formula that creates the $696.11 value.

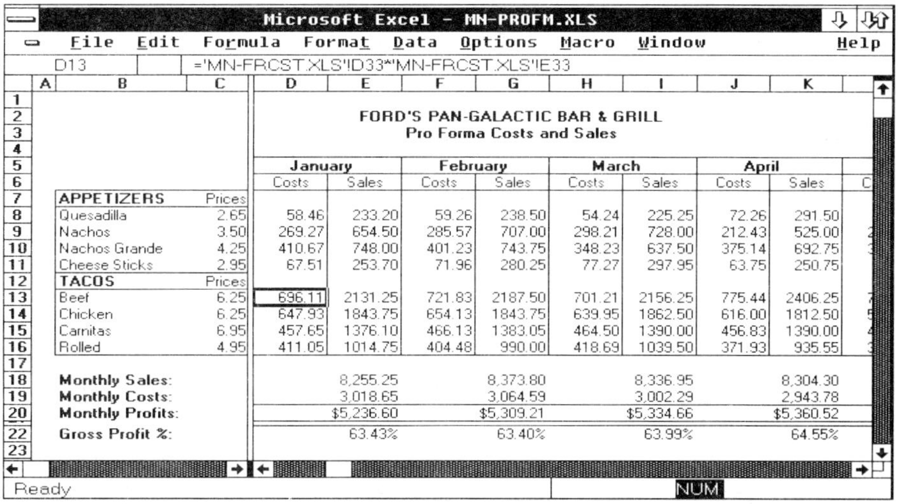

Fig. 8.7. Calculating the total ingredients cost for beef taco sales in January.

Remember the "# Sold" forecast of 341 from MN-FRCST.XLS? This figure is multiplied by the retail price found in column C in MN-PROFM.XLS. The resulting value, $2,131.25, appears in cell E13 under the Sales column on the same worksheet. The formula bar in figure 8.8 illustrates the syntax of the formula that creates January's pro forma beef taco sales.

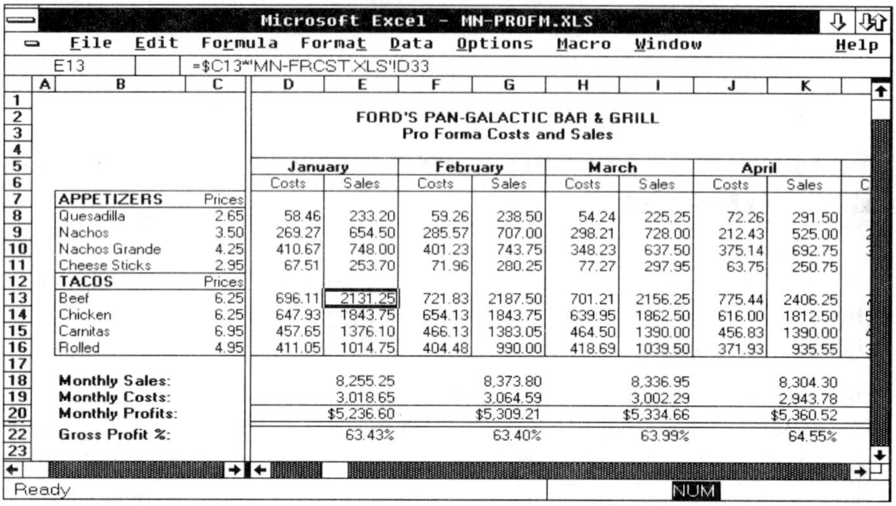

Fig. 8.8.
Calculating pro forma sales for beef tacos in January.

	A	B	C	D	E	F	G	H	I	J	K
					January		February		March		April
					Costs	Sales	Costs	Sales	Costs	Sales	Costs	Sales
7	APPETIZERS		Prices									
8	Quesadilla		2.65		58.46	233.20	59.26	238.50	54.24	225.25	72.26	291.50
9	Nachos		3.50		269.27	654.50	285.57	707.00	298.21	728.00	212.43	525.00
10	Nachos Grande		4.25		410.67	748.00	401.23	743.75	348.23	637.50	375.14	692.75
11	Cheese Sticks		2.95		67.51	253.70	71.96	280.25	77.27	297.95	63.75	250.75
12	TACOS		Prices									
13	Beef		6.25		696.11	2131.25	721.83	2187.50	701.21	2156.25	775.44	2406.25
14	Chicken		6.25		647.93	1843.75	654.13	1843.75	639.95	1862.50	616.00	1812.50
15	Carnitas		6.95		457.65	1376.10	466.13	1383.05	464.50	1390.00	456.83	1390.00
16	Rolled		4.95		411.05	1014.75	404.48	990.00	418.69	1039.50	371.93	935.55
18	Monthly Sales:					8,255.25		8,373.80		8,336.95		8,304.30
19	Monthly Costs:					3,018.65		3,064.59		3,002.29		2,943.78
20	Monthly Profits:					$5,236.60		$5,309.21		$5,334.66		$5,360.52
22	Gross Profit %:					63.43%		63.40%		63.99%		64.55%

Formula bar: =$C13*'MN-FRCST.XLS'!D33

You should now be familiar with the structure and use of the worksheets in this model. The following section turns to several likely scenarios that test your knowledge of this model and challenge your mettle as a manager.

What-Iffing under Different Scenarios

The following scenarios demonstrate how to use these worksheets under changing economic conditions. Before you begin, here's a quick review of Excel techniques that will help you get the most out of each exercise:

1. When necessary, select the Window menu and use your mouse to pull different open files "forward" onto the screen.

2. On worksheets with split screens, press F6 to toggle between screens. Use the PgUp, PgDn, and arrow keys to move around the worksheet.

3. On each worksheet, pause at the columns that contain formulas. Note that most of the worksheet values are derived through formulas that use data stored elsewhere. A few columns on these worksheets (specifically, the # Sold and Price columns) contain raw data that has been manually entered into the worksheet.

4. Now comes the fun part. Notice the summary figures in rows 18, 19, 20, and 22 on the Pro Forma Costs and Sales worksheet, MN-PROFM.XLS. You can perform what-if analyses with this

worksheet by changing the composition of a recipe, altering the cost of an ingredient, updating forecasted sales, and increasing or decreasing the retail price of a menu item.

What-if scenario #1: Your meat supplier tells you that beginning in March, the price of ground beef will increase by 10 cents per pound.

On MN-FRCST.XLS, move the active cell to F7 (column F holds the cost figures for March; row 7 contains the cost of ground beef) and change the value to 0.98. Assume that the cost of ground beef will remain constant for the rest of the year, and copy the value $0.98 into the range G7:O7.

Because the cost of ground beef affects the total ingredient cost of beef tacos and several other dishes, the following changes become immediately apparent in the worksheets:

- In the Costs and Sales Forecast, located in the bottom portion of MN-FRCST.XLS, the "Cost" values change for the remainder of the year for each dish containing ground beef.

- In the Pro Forma Costs and Sales, located in a linked but separate file (MN-PROFM.XLS), the "Costs" values change for the remainder of the year for each dish containing ground beef.

- The percentage and summary values in MN-PROFM.XLS, located in column AC and columns AE:AG, also change. The "Monthly Costs," "Monthly Profits," and "Gross Profits" figures in rows 19, 20, and 22 change as well.

You can make changes like those shown in figure 8.9 to the data in your worksheets to reflect seasonal price fluctuations, changes in demand, or changes in your costs.

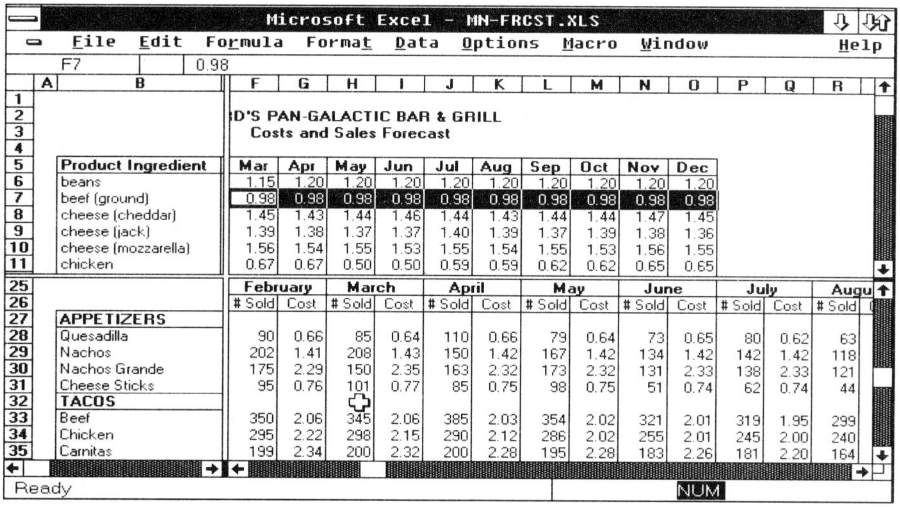

Fig. 8.9. Increasing the price of ground beef affects both costs and profits.

Remember the following two important things, however, as you incorporate new information into your worksheets. First, save each version of the worksheet as a separate file. You can then compare the worksheets to see how different assumptions affect your monthly profits. Second, make a written record of your assumptions by using the Formula Note command and then attaching the note to the first changed cell. Worksheet notes enable someone who is reviewing your Excel worksheets to understand how they differ and which assumptions are in effect for each worksheet.

The notes appear on-screen when you execute the Formula Note command. You also can show the note by making the note cell the active cell and selecting Info from the Window menu. You can add notes about the number of dishes sold, seasonal effects, the impact of special advertising promotions, and so on. Figure 8.10 shows an example of a worksheet note.

Fig. 8.10.
The Formula Note dialog box and a formula note that indicates a change in the cost of ground beef.

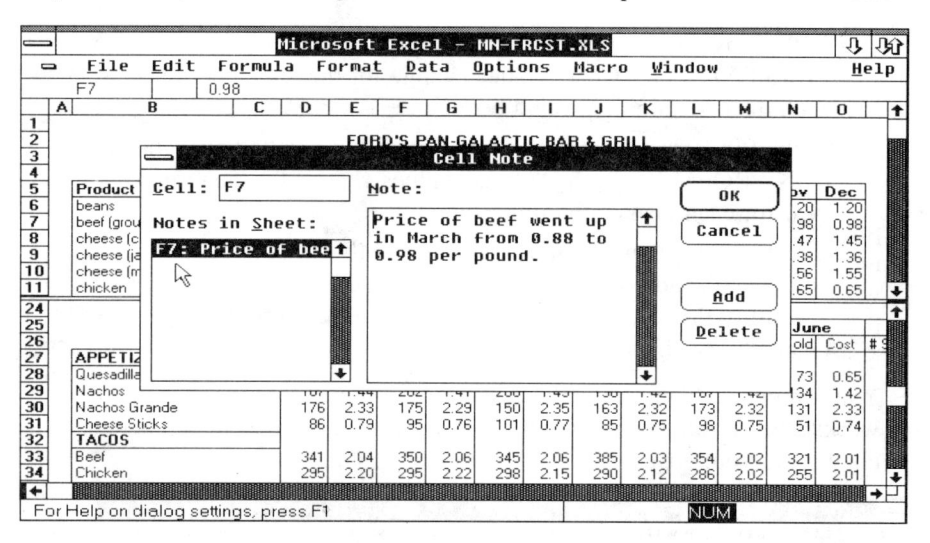

Note: Before you look at the next scenario, be sure to close your changed files, if necessary, after you have stored them under a different name and to open the versions that apply to the new scenario. Save the worksheet in scenario #1 as MN-FRCS1.XLS. Use MN-FRCST.XLS as the forecast worksheet for scenario #2.

What-if scenario #2: You decide to raise the price of all of the taco entrees by 25 cents.

This change is easy to accomplish. Activate MN-PROFM.XLS and move to cell C13, the first of four cell values in the range C13:C16 that store the retail price of each type of taco on the menu. Increase each value by 25 cents. The result of this what-if scenario is shown in figure 8.11.

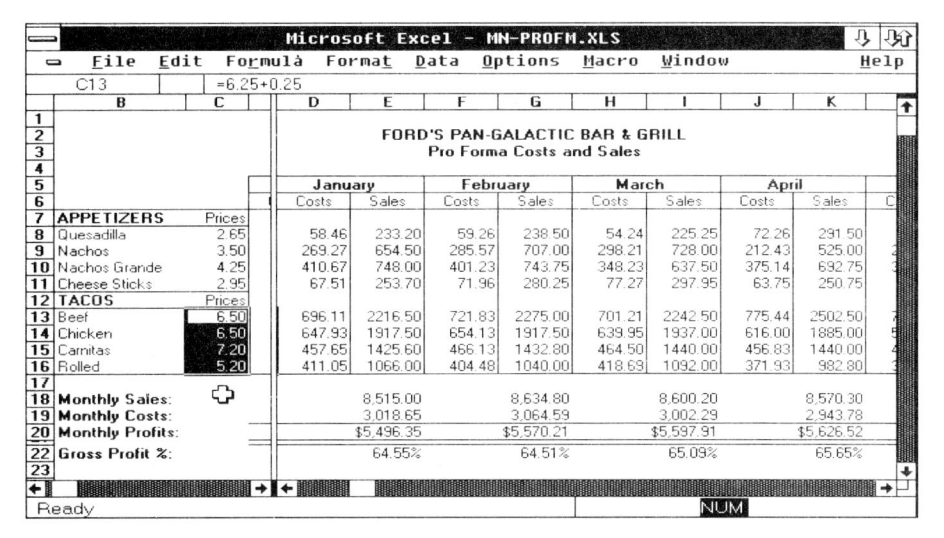

Using Marketing, Sales, and Financing Applications

Fig. 8.11.
The new formula in cell C13 increases the price of a beef taco by 25 cents.

What-if scenario #3: You decide to raise the price of beef and chicken tacos by 25 cents, starting in September.

Solving this scenario requires an approach different from the one used in the preceding example. To change the price of a menu item for an individual month, or for several months, move to the first cell in the range that you want to edit. Here, the first cell in the range is U13. To change the formula in cell U13 to reflect a 25-cent price increase, press F2 to enter Edit mode. Now alter the formula so that it reads as follows:

    ($C13+0.25)*'MN-FRCST'!T33

Press Enter to record the change.

Now revise the formula in cell U14 to reflect this increase for chicken tacos, and then revise the sales formulas for the months of October, November, and December in columns W, Y, and AA in the same way. The result of the price increase is shown in figure 8.12.

Now look at the summary figures in rows 20 and 22, shown in figure 8.12; these figures have changed substantially. Next, scroll the data over so that columns AC, AE, and AG appear on-screen. These columns contain totals for the year. Note that these totals also have changed from those shown in scenario #1.

Note: Save the file containing the changed price information and rename the file, using the unique file name MN-PROF1.XLS.

Fig. 8.12. Sales, profits, and gross-profit percentages change when you increase the price of tacos.

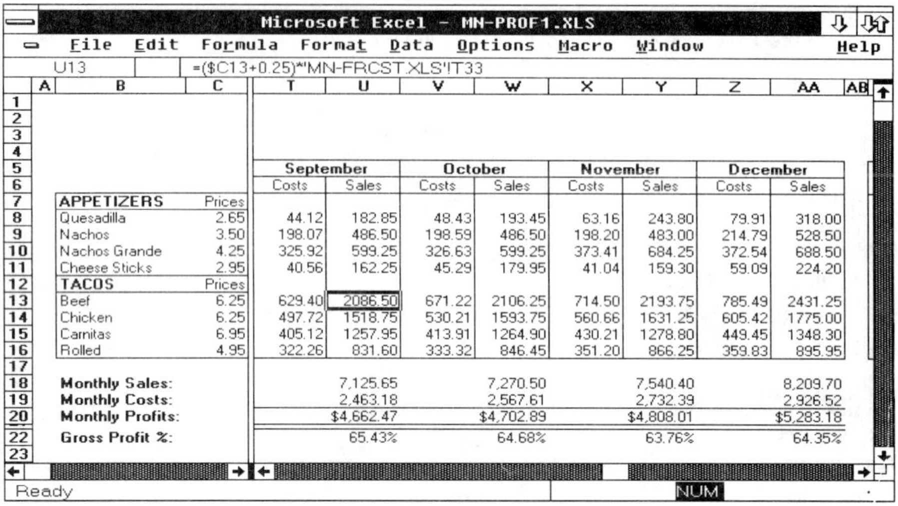
Microsoft Excel - MN-PROF1.XLS

File Edit Formula Format Data Options Macro Window Help

U13 =($C13+0.25)*'MN-FRCST.XLS'!T33

	B	C	T	U	V	W	X	Y	Z	AA
5			September		October		November		December	
6			Costs	Sales	Costs	Sales	Costs	Sales	Costs	Sales
7	APPETIZERS	Prices								
8	Quesadilla	2.65	44.12	182.85	48.43	193.45	63.16	243.80	79.91	318.00
9	Nachos	3.50	198.07	486.50	198.59	486.50	198.20	483.00	214.79	528.50
10	Nachos Grande	4.25	325.92	599.25	326.63	599.25	373.41	684.25	372.54	688.50
11	Cheese Sticks	2.95	40.56	162.25	45.29	179.95	41.04	159.30	59.09	224.20
12	TACOS	Prices								
13	Beef	6.25	629.40	2086.50	671.22	2106.25	714.50	2193.75	785.49	2431.25
14	Chicken	6.25	497.72	1518.75	530.21	1593.75	560.66	1631.25	605.42	1775.00
15	Carnitas	6.95	405.12	1257.95	413.91	1264.90	430.21	1278.80	449.45	1348.30
16	Rolled	4.95	322.26	831.60	333.32	846.45	351.20	866.25	359.83	895.95
18	Monthly Sales:			7,125.65		7,270.50		7,540.40		8,209.70
19	Monthly Costs:			2,463.18		2,567.61		2,732.39		2,926.52
20	Monthly Profits:			$4,662.47		$4,702.89		$4,808.01		$5,283.18
22	Gross Profit %:			65.43%		64.68%		63.76%		64.35%

Ready NUM

Next you will consider a case in which a lender wants proof of your ability to deal with changes in your initial assumptions about costs and sales. If costs go up, how can you keep net profits from declining? If sales drop, where can you cut costs? The next set of detailed worksheets will show a lender or investor that you are considering all the possibilities.

Using the Cost Data Elsewhere (MN-INCST.XLS)

The preceding section taught you how to fine-tune and analyze your unit-cost data to make your cost and sales projections look realistic to a prospective investor or lender. In and of itself, the ability to perform such detailed what-if analyses should impress lenders; it demonstrates that you know how to calculate the impact of changing conditions on your business.

This section illustrates how to use this data, in summary form, on the worksheet titled MN-INCST.XLS. This new worksheet uses your pro forma costs and sales forecast to paint a broader financial picture of your business. The models in Chapter 4 enabled you to make financial projections based on historical percentage relationships. The models in Chapter 8 enable you to create a more concrete forecast of your costs and sales, using known information (such as raw-materials costs and product pricing) as a basis. The MN-INCST.XLS worksheet uses both techniques for gathering data to create a pro forma income statement for the sample company Ford's Pan-Galactic Bar & Grill. Let's briefly examine the structure of this worksheet.

Using Marketing, Sales, and Financing Applications **241**

The portion of the pro forma income statement shown in figure 8.13 highlights the formula relationship between MN-INCST.XLS and MN-PROFM.XLS for the sales data.

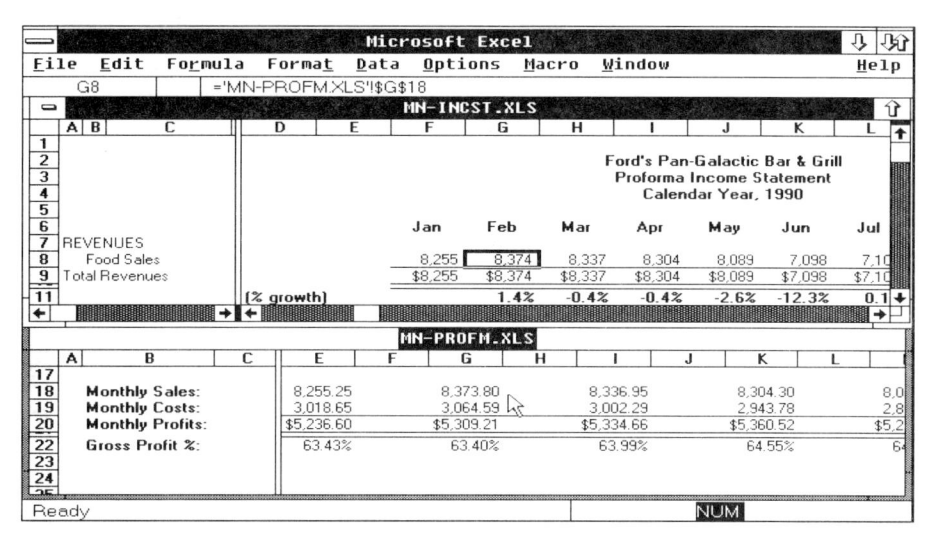

Fig. 8.13. Pro forma sales from MN-PROFM.XLS appear on the income statement in MN-INCST.XLS.

The portion of the pro forma income statement shown in figure 8.14 highlights the formula relationship between MN-INCST.XLS and MN-PROFM.XLS for the costs data.

Fig. 8.14. Pro forma costs from MN-PROFM.XLS appear on the income statement in MN-INCST.XLS.

The portion of the pro forma income statement shown in figure 8.15 illustrates that it is perfectly acceptable to integrate a percentage-of-sales forecast into this type of analysis. Here, labor expenses are estimated as a percentage of the current month's sales. A percentage-of-sales-expenses forecast based on a detailed costs and sales forecast will be much more accurate than one based solely on an assumption about how sales will grow in the future.

Fig. 8.15.
The firm's labor expenses are forecast as a percentage of firm sales.

	A	B	C	D	E	F Jan	G Feb	H Mar	I Apr	J May	K Jun	L Jul
6												
7	REVENUES											
8		Food Sales				8,255	8,374	8,337	8,304	8,089	7,098	7,103
9		Total Revenues				$8,255	$8,374	$8,337	$8,304	$8,089	$7,098	$7,103
11				(% growth)			1.4%	-0.4%	-0.4%	-2.6%	-12.3%	0.1%
12	COG SOLD											
13		Appetizers		25.1%		806	818	778	724	759	577	617
14		Tacos		74.9%		2,213	2,247	2,224	2,220	2,089	1,902	1,825
15	Total COG Sold			100.0%		$3,019	$3,065	$3,002	$2,944	$2,848	$2,479	$2,442
16	Gross Profit on Sales					$5,237	$5,309	$5,335	$5,361	$5,241	$4,619	$4,661
18				% Margin		63.4%	63.4%	64.0%	64.6%	64.8%	65.1%	65.6%
20	EXPENSES											
21		Labor Expense										
22			Management	$1,500	per mo.	1,500	1,500	1,500	1,500	1,500	1,500	1,500
23			Counter	8.0%	of sales	660	670	667	664	647	568	568
24			Cooks	8.0%	of sales	660	670	667	664	647	568	568
25			Workman's Comp.	10.0%	of labor	132	134	133	133	129	114	114
26			FICA Matching	7.5%	of labor	99	100	100	100	97	85	85
27			Miscellaneous	5.0%	of labor	66	67	66	66	65	57	57
28		Total Labor Expense:				$3,118	$3,141	$3,134	$3,128	$3,085	$2,891	$2,892

Cell F23: `=F9*$D$23`

Dealing with the Impact of Financing

All the work involved in justifying your costs and performing sales analyses pays off when you apply for a loan. Only rarely does a business survive without the active participation of a bank or other financial institution, which usually provides long- or short-term financing to cover cycles of business activity. The interest charged by the financial institution has to be considered a normal business expense, and paying back borrowed principal should be factored into overall projections.

The following sections examine the effects of financing on a cash-flow projection.

Building In the Effects of Financing

Besides earning proceeds from the sale of products or services, you can can raise money for a business in two ways:

- Borrowing, which involves loans from an entity that expects to be paid back, with interest

- Investor financing, usually called *equity*, which represents partial ownership of the company

Another way to raise money is through *business borrowing*, which is a normal business activity designed to cover the need to acquire assets while maximizing the uses of capital. Money can be borrowed over a long term or a short term. Long-term borrowing is usually required when a business buys some tangible asset, such as a building or a large piece of capital equipment. Short-term borrowing is usually arranged to help a business deal with the peaks and valleys of income. Through short-term borrowing, a business can continue to pay its bills while it waits a relatively short period for earned income to arrive.

Business Borrowing (AMORTIZE.XLS, DAILYINT.XLS)

Part of the justification for *long-term borrowing* usually involves the kinds of analyses discussed in Chapter 5, which examined annuities, return on assets, and depreciation. This section considers the payment structure from the lender's point of view. Because you, the business borrower, need to make payments, and the amount of those payments depends on the amount of interest you are charged, you need to be able to know the exact breakdown between interest and principal on your business loans.

Long-term borrowing usually involves some sort of down payment and a *credit instrument*, such as a note and deed of trust or a mortgage. The credit instrument spells out the length of the loan, the rate of interest, and the repayment schedule. Payments are considered an ordinary business expense, but because they are related to capitalized property, they are shown on the balance sheet rather than the income statement. Sometimes the payments are even divided into interest payments, which often can be deducted from income taxes, and payments against principal, which are nondeductible.

Suppose that a restaurateur needs to arrange long-term financing in order to buy heavy-duty commercial kitchen equipment. Because the equipment's total cost is $35,000, a long-term loan is more appropriate than using cash on hand, which otherwise is used to meet the firm's short-term liabilities.

Assume that the restaurateur gets a fixed-rate loan so that his payments will be steady. If he puts up 20 percent of the total cost as a down payment, what will his payments be, and how will the loan be amortized?

The file AMORTIZE.XLS, which is included on the disk accompanying this book, displays a loan amortization worksheet for a loan with fixed payments, with payments computed at the top (see figs. 8.16 and 8.17). You enter the amount of principal, the term in months, and the annual interest rate. The worksheet converts the annual interest rate to a monthly rate, computes the monthly payment, and sets up a loan amortization schedule.

Fig. 8.16.
A loan amortization worksheet showing the calculation of payment #1.

Fig. 8.17.
A loan amortization worksheet showing the calculation of the final interest payment.

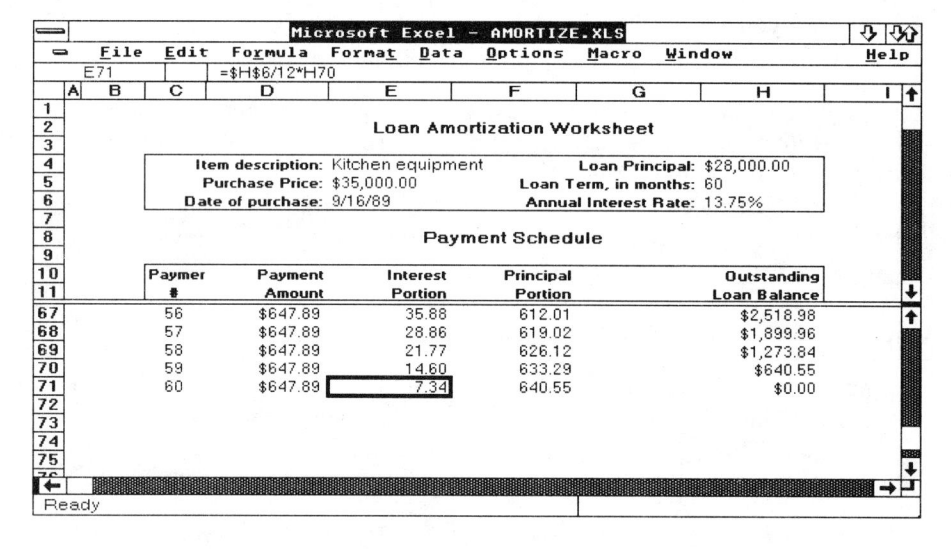

Notice that the same procedure can be used for any loan with a fixed interest rate—you can create one for a real estate loan, a personal loan, or any loan that has a fixed principal, term, and interest rate.

Short-term business borrowing is usually arranged to help a business cope when income does not arrive before bills come due or when a payroll needs to be met. Normally, a business owner establishes a line of credit with a bank or other lender and borrows against that line according to a predefined set of terms.

Interest on business borrowing is usually computed on the basis of the amount financed and the length of time the borrowed principal is needed. Interest rates are normally based on a commonly recognized index, such as the "prime plus 2" index (the current prime interest rate plus 2 percent) or another index related to the bank's cost of borrowing the money, plus a margin. In monitoring your real interest costs, you should keep daily or weekly track of your borrowing, repaying your debt as soon as cash is available and borrowing only when borrowing is prudent.

A worksheet like the one shown in figures 8.18 and 8.19 lets you keep daily track of your business borrowing.

Fig. 8.18. A daily interest worksheet showing the calculation of total interest paid for the current month.

Day #	Today's Int. Rate	Previous Balance	New Credit	Payments	Interest Cost	Current Blalance
1	13.75%	25,000.00	0.00	0.00	9.42	25,000.00
2	13.75%	25,000.00	0.00	5,000.00	7.53	20,000.00
3	13.75%	20,000.00	0.00	0.00	7.53	20,000.00
4	13.75%	20,000.00	0.00	0.00	7.53	20,000.00
5	13.75%	20,000.00	0.00	0.00	7.53	20,000.00
6	13.75%	20,000.00	0.00	0.00	7.53	20,000.00
7	13.75%	20,000.00	0.00	0.00	7.53	20,000.00
8	13.75%	20,000.00	0.00	0.00	7.53	20,000.00
9	13.75%	20,000.00	0.00	5,000.00	5.65	15,000.00
10	13.75%	15,000.00	0.00	0.00	5.65	15,000.00
11	13.75%	15,000.00	0.00	0.00	5.65	15,000.00
12	13.75%	15,000.00	0.00	0.00	5.65	15,000.00
13	13.75%	15,000.00	0.00	0.00	5.65	15,000.00

Date: Jan-18-90   Total Interest This Month: $193.50

This worksheet is included on the disk that accompanies this book, in the file DAILYINT.XLS. Before you move on to the following instructions, open this file and get the worksheet on-screen.

You can enter each day's interest rate in the worksheet, as well as any payments or amounts you borrow against the specified credit line. Enter the maximum credit line and then begin the month's activity by entering the balance for the last day of the previous month. After the first day, each day's opening balance is the same as the previous day's closing balance.

Fig. 8.19.
A daily interest worksheet showing the calculation of the interest cost for the last day in the month.

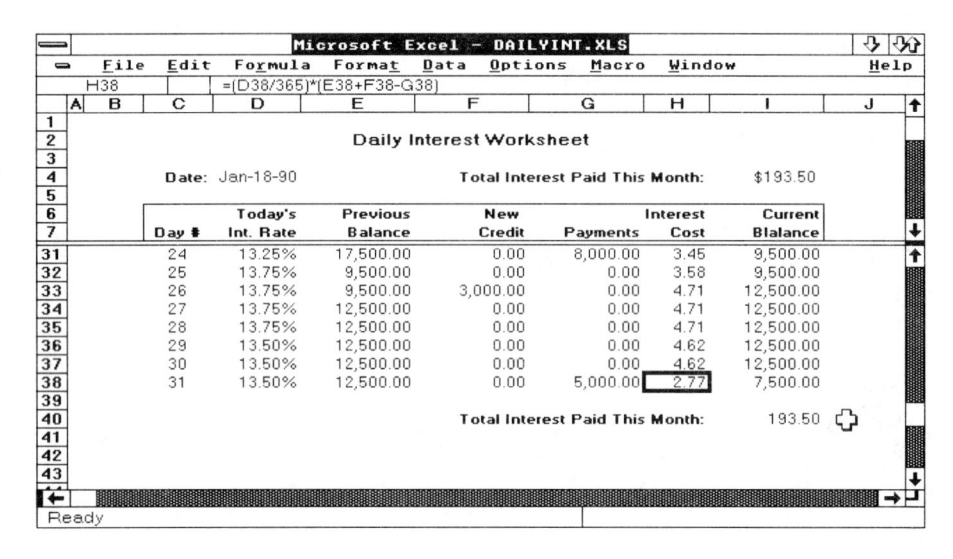

	A	B	C	D	E	F	G	H	I	J
	H38			=(D38/365)*(E38+F38-G38)						
1										
2					Daily Interest Worksheet					
3										
4				Date:	Jan-18-90		Total Interest Paid This Month:		$193.50	
5										
6					Today's	Previous	New		Interest	Current
7				Day #	Int. Rate	Balance	Credit	Payments	Cost	Blalance
31				24	13.25%	17,500.00	0.00	8,000.00	3.45	9,500.00
32				25	13.75%	9,500.00	0.00	0.00	3.58	9,500.00
33				26	13.75%	9,500.00	3,000.00	0.00	4.71	12,500.00
34				27	13.75%	12,500.00	0.00	0.00	4.71	12,500.00
35				28	13.75%	12,500.00	0.00	0.00	4.71	12,500.00
36				29	13.50%	12,500.00	0.00	0.00	4.62	12,500.00
37				30	13.50%	12,500.00	0.00	0.00	4.62	12,500.00
38				31	13.50%	12,500.00	0.00	5,000.00	2.77	7,500.00
39										
40							Total Interest Paid This Month:		193.50	

Each day, you enter any newly borrowed amounts in the New Credit column; if you make a payment on a given day, enter the amount of the payment in the Payments column. You also enter the current interest rate charged on the amount you borrow. The worksheet calculates the interest cost for the day, as well as the loan's current balance. The total interest for the month is calculated at the end of the worksheet; you can use this total in the appropriate cell in your monthly income statement.

The disk's worksheet contains sample entries for an entire month. To reuse the worksheet, just open it, change the data, and save the changed version under a different file name. If you want to change the interest rates shown for the last week of the month, for example, move the cursor to cell D32 and highlight the range D32:D38. Select the Edit Clear command and then the Formulas option; doing so clears the existing data from the specified cells.

With the same range selected, enter the following new interest rates:

.1375
.1375
.1375
.1375
.135
.135
.135

The worksheet automatically computes the amount of interest for that day, and the total for the month is adjusted to reflect the new data. This monthly total can be transferred to a monthly income statement so that interest expense is shown as a monthly expense item.

Investor Financing

Investor financing means that someone (or several people) puts money into a business entity. As a rule, investors expect some sort of return on their money. This return can come in the form of dividends, which represent a literal division of the business's net profits. Most investors like to receive some dividends each year, or even each quarter, but they also like to see a reasonable portion of the profits reinvested in the business, as *retained earnings*.

However you decide to divide the net profits of a given year, that decision must be factored into a cash-flow projection that looks three to five years ahead. Will you be able to pay your investors enough to warrant their risking their money in your business? Will their investment grow sufficiently in value over time so that they can expect to sell their shares at a profit?

The Pro Forma Financial Statement worksheet (CALKINS.XLS) in Chapter 4 used the concept of paying 50 percent of after-tax profits as dividends (see fig. 8.20).

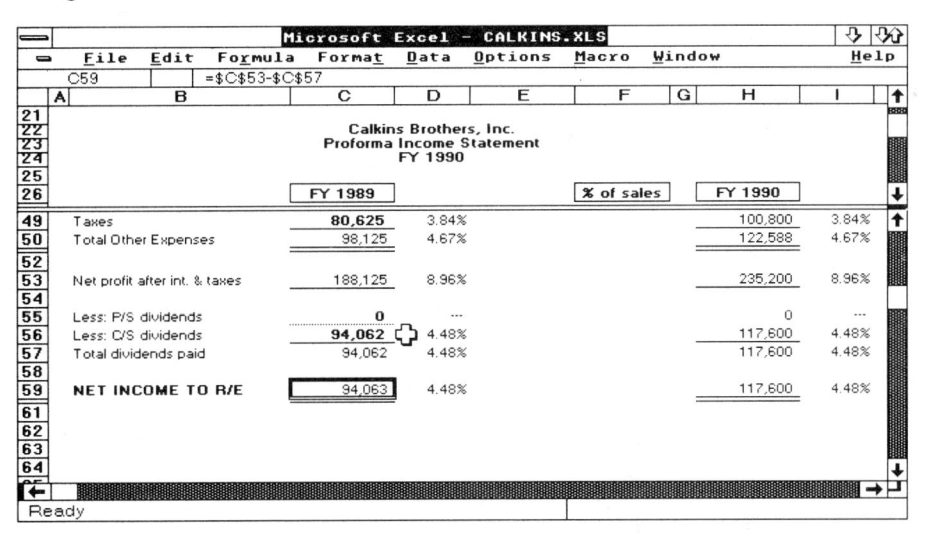

Fig. 8.20. A pro forma financial statement, including dividends for preferred and common stock.

Suppose that you decide to retain more profits within your business by paying out lower dividends. You can play "what if" with this portion of the worksheet by modifying the formula that computes dividends so that it reflects the desired apportioning. The restaurateur, for example, decides that he wants to keep 65 percent of the profits as retained earnings and pay only 35 percent as dividends. Figure 8.21 shows the modified worksheet.

Fig. 8.21.
The pro forma financial statement, reflecting a modified distribution of dividends.

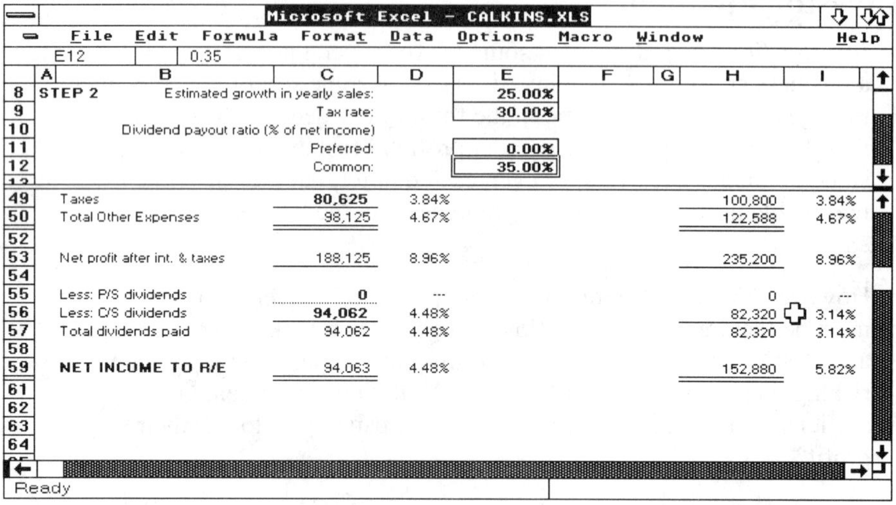

Summary

This chapter explained the detailed calculations you can use to justify your assumptions about your business's income and expenses. You learned how a small change in the price of a single component—such as ground beef—can affect the cost of a series of products—in this case, appetizers and main dishes on a menu. You then learned how to fine-tune your assumptions about prices (and, therefore, the sales) of your products.

Although such detailed forecasting may seem, at best, an exercise in wishful thinking, such detail tends to impress lenders and investors. If you show them that you can fine-tune your income and expense assumptions, they will know that you have the tools to adjust to changes in the marketplace and that you are therefore likely to be a sound investment risk.

The second portion of the chapter dealt with the results of collecting that fine detail. You learned how to use your forecasts to create a pro forma income statement and reviewed worksheets that let you analyze different forms of financing. All these exercises served to solidify in your mind the important relationship among marketing, sales, and lending.

In Chapter 9, you will examine the many uses of Excel's built-in database feature to further compile and analyze your firm's financial data.

9

Managing Databases

One of the benefits of using a full-function spreadsheet program like Excel is that it lends itself to sharing data with other functional organizations, such as databases. You can manipulate and sort data collected and stored on an Excel spreadsheet as if the data were on a database; this arrangement enables you to prepare sorted lists, search for specific information, extract records according to particular criteria, and perform calculations on data in selected records.

This chapter shows you several ways to use Excel's database abilities to manipulate data.

Setting Up the Database

Before setting up the database, you should review some basic terms:

- A *database* is the entire file where your information is stored, such as a prospect file for a sales office.
- A *database range* is the area of the worksheet where database information is stored. You will be using the Database Set Range command to define the database range area on the worksheet.
- A *record* is a single entry in the database range that contains all the data related to a specific item. Excel assumes that a single record occupies one row in the database. In a prospect file, a single record might contain the information for Pillar Books and Records.

- A *field* is a specific category of information stored on the database. Each record has several fields. The prospect file may have such fields as the name, address, and phone number of a potential client; the name of the person to contact; the salesperson responsible for the account; and so on.
- A *computed field* is just like a normal field, except that it is computed by Excel from information entered elsewhere, rather than being entered by a user.
- A *field name* is the name used to identify data stored in a particular field. Excel assumes that the top row of the database contains field names.
- *Criteria* tell Excel which records to manipulate. The criteria are contained in a separate *criteria range*, which tells Excel how to compare or compute information. Comparison criteria tell Excel which records to find, extract, or delete. Computed criteria tell Excel the formula against which data is tested.
- The *extract range* is a separate area where retrieved data is copied.

Figure 9.1 shows a sample database.

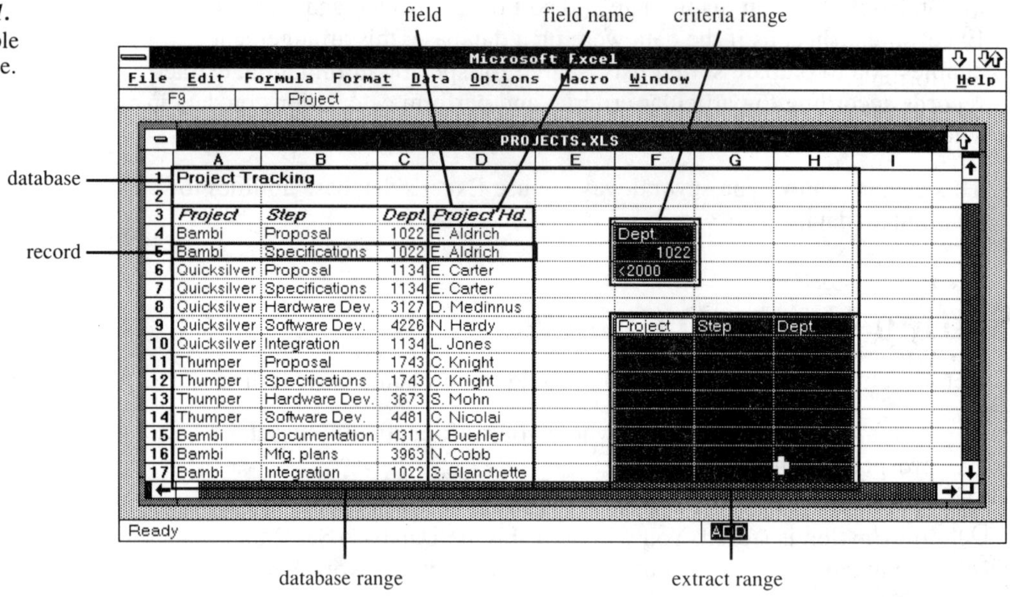

Fig. 9.1.
A sample database.

As you think through what kind of database you want to create, define exactly what you want to store. Are you after specific part-ordering information? Are you after a history of payroll records? Do you want client information?

When you create your database with Excel, keep in mind several tips that help you deal with the limitations of the program:

- Use the Data Form command to add new records to your database. When you define the database, you define the beginning and ending cells. When you use the Data Form command to add a new record, you automatically expand the size of the defined database. If you use another method to add a record after what was previously the last record, you will probably need to redefine the database.

- Keep in mind Excel's limits for database size. You can have no more than 256 fields and 16,383 records. Some applications can create huge databases, which become cumbersome to manipulate. If you find that your processing becomes bogged down by the sheer size of the database, consider how else you may define the database so that you work with less data.

- Excel allows only text constants to be used for field names. This arrangement means that you can't use numbers, logical values, formulas, error values, or empty cells as field names, even temporarily. However, if your database contains information of these types, consider naming the field a text version of the type you're showing: for example, ">50" instead of >50, "True?" instead of True, or "Error?" instead of #ERR.

- Field names can't be more than 255 characters long.

- Every record of your database must have the same number of fields, even if some records don't have data in each field.

- When working with a database, Excel ignores capitalization, which means that *Pear* and *pear*, for example, are seen as identical. For most sorting operations, this setup may not be a problem. String operations involving comparison, however, may pose some problems.

The area where you'll manipulate data by using the Data commands and the Database functions must be defined as a database range. You can use data from a worksheet as your database data, too, but you need to define a specific range as your database range, and that requirement may not coincide with the way you've organized your spreadsheet data.

The way Excel works with a database means that the database must be set up in a particular way:

1. You must declare the database range as such by selecting the range and using the Data Set Database command. You can also define the range with the Format Define Name command and name the range "database."

    If you know how big your database is going to be, define the range first. If you are the least bit unsure, wait until you've entered all your records, add a few more blank records to make sure you will have room to insert more, and then select the entire range and define it as a database with the Data Set Database command. When you add new records with the Data Form command, the database range will expand automatically.

2. Enter the field names into the first row of the database range. You can change the width of the fields if you need to accommodate lots of information, or you can keep the fields at the standard width, with extra information being stored in each cell but not displayed.

3. Enter records, one per row, using the Tab key to move from column to column. If you already have data in a worksheet, consider copying the data, column by column, to the separate database range. Copying the data in this way stores it in the form that the database commands can use.

Once you've defined the database, complete with field names, you can use the Data Form command to enter more records. Figure 9.2 shows the Data Form dialog box, in which the field names from the database are used.

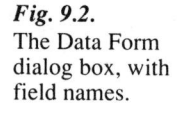

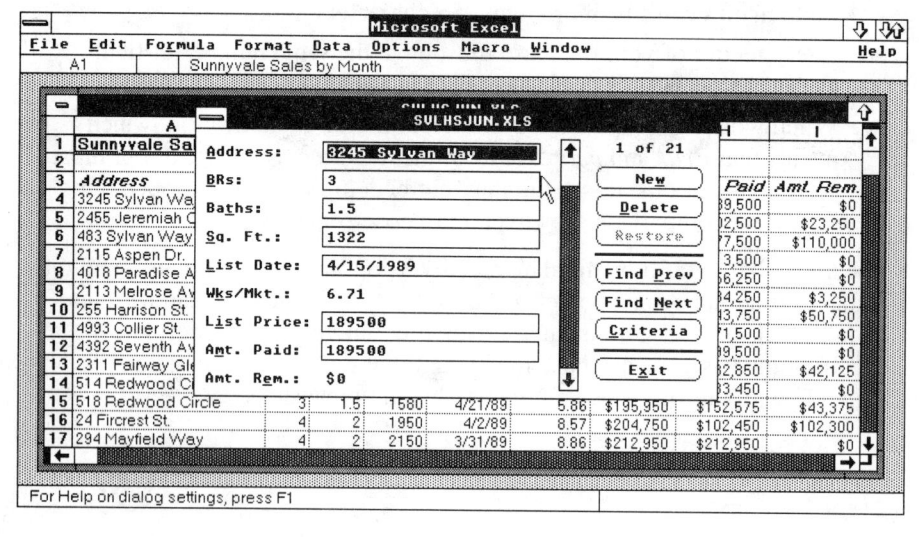

Fig. 9.2.
The Data Form dialog box, with field names.

The field names are the labels to the left of each bar. For each new record, you enter into each bar the data for that particular field. You can move from field to field by using the Tab key.

Notice that in this record, the amount paid on the account is entered, but the amount remaining is computed. Although you can edit information in any of the other fields in a record, you can't edit information in a computed field. Such information is, however, stored as part of the record.

The buttons in the column on the right indicate the actions you can take with the record. The first button is the New button, which you choose when the information you've entered is for a new record. The other buttons are explained in the next section.

Conducting a Search (SLSCONTC.XLS)

You can use the Data Form command to search for specific information. This section will show you how to search for data—data that can be as specific as a phone extension or a particular name. Your database can thus help you answer a number of questions:

- Who is the contact person at a particular company, and what is that person's phone number?
- Which of your client companies are in a particular city that is on your travel itinerary?
- Does one company with whom you do business have offices in several locations?

Use the Data Form command to display the form that helps you enter data by field for each record in your database. To search for specific data, type in the appropriate field the information for which you want to search; then choose either the Find Prev button or the Find Next button, depending on which direction (from the current record) you want to search.

You can also use the Data Form command to specify the criteria for a search. For instance, suppose that you want to find a record for a company that has the character string *flex* in its name, and you know that the contact person is somebody named Jones, but you can't remember the full company name, nor can you remember Mr. Jones's first name.

254   Excel Business Applications: IBM Version

To find the record, use the SLSCONTC.XLS file, which is on the disk that accompanies this book, and complete the following steps (SLSCONTC.XLS contains a sample database file):

Step 1. Open SLSCONTC.XLS. Declare it a database by selecting the entire range (A3:H13) and choosing the Data Set Database command.

Step 2. Choose the Data Form command. You'll see the first record, in Data Form format, on your screen (see fig. 9.3).

Fig. 9.3.
The first record, in Data Form format.

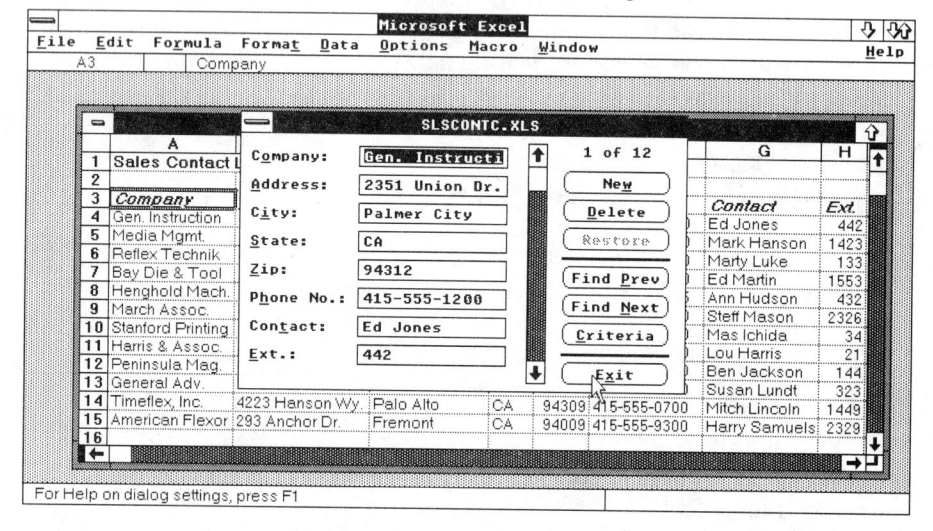

Note: If you have 16 or more fields for your records, you won't see all of them listed in the Data Form dialog box. Excel will list as many as will fit on your window and will provide a slide bar so that you can scroll down the dialog box and see the other fields and the current data within them.

Step 3. Choose the Criteria button. The form changes so that blanks are in the fields that, in figure 9.3, contained record data. Some of the options in the buttons also change.

Step 4. Use the Tab key or the mouse to position the blinking vertical line in the Company field, and type the characters ***flex**.

Note that you're using the asterisk as a wild-card specification. Excel allows two kinds of wild cards: The *asterisk* (*) instructs Excel to find, in this field, data that has any number of characters in the same position as the asterisk. In this case, company names like Reflex Technik, Timeflex Inc., and American Flexor would be selected.

The *question mark* (?) instructs Excel to find data that has any single character in the same position as the question mark. For example, specifying the criterion **f?r** finds records with the character string *far*, *fir*, and *for*.

If you want to change the criteria specified, use the Clear and Restore buttons.

Specifying ***flex** as the company name makes the Data Form dialog box look like that in figure 9.4.

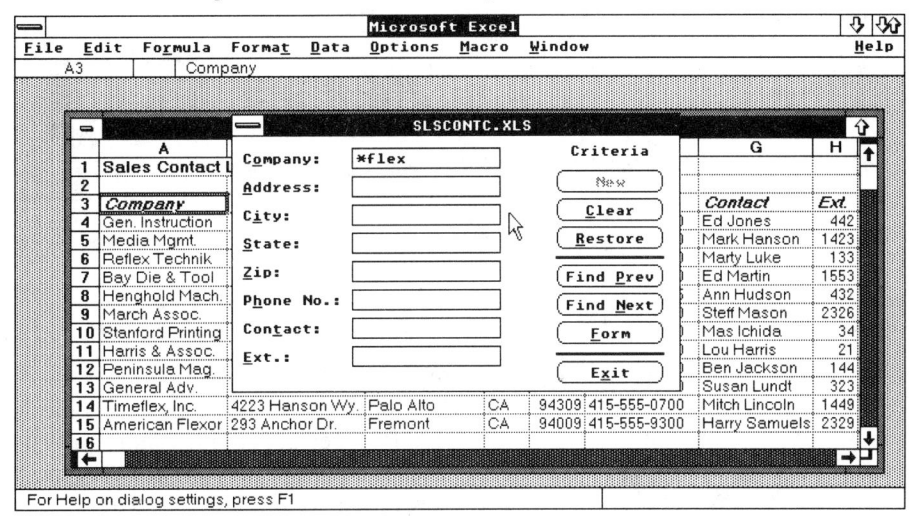

Fig. 9.4.
The Data Form box used to specify search criteria.

Step 5. Press the Enter key or choose the Exit button. This action sets the search in motion, and Excel selects all records meeting your criteria. These selected records are then reported to you on the Data Form dialog box. The retrieved record should look like figure 9.5.

You can also search for records that match computed criteria by using the standard comparison operators:

= < > >= <= <>

These can be used either separately or in combination with the character criteria to specify such records as those in which the company is within a certain ZIP code range and has not made a payment for over 90 days.

What else can you do with a database? If you keep in mind that a database is nothing more than another way of looking at spreadsheet data, you'll begin to see that you can sort, query, compare, and rearrange just about any set of data on a spreadsheet.

Fig. 9.5.
A record retrieved with search criteria.

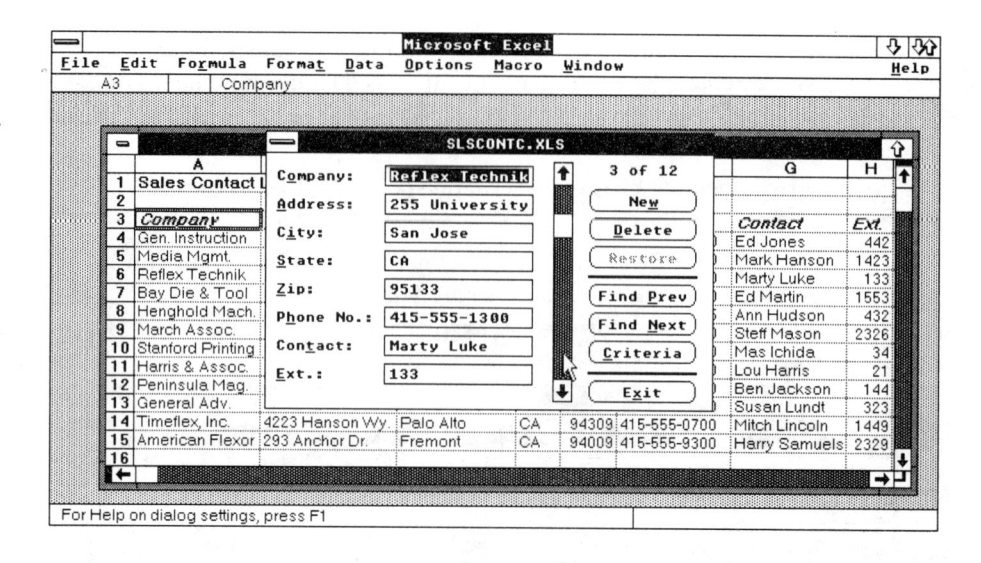

Extracting Records (EMPPHONE.XLS)

The policies of the hypothetical company General Training support the active participation of employees in a number of professional groups, some of which have working committees. The employees get compensatory time off for the work they do on these professional committees, so it makes sense for the company to keep track of who's on which committees.

Figure 9.6 shows the database from which this committee list can be generated. (This is the file EMPPHONE.XLS, available on the disk that accompanies this book.)

Fig. 9.6.
An employee database.

Suppose that you want to quickly create a mailing list of people who serve on the X.15 Policies committee and who work at Site 43 (their phone extensions start with *43*). You *could* scan the list and individually copy the appropriate records to a separate place on a worksheet. A simpler approach is to set up a separate area of your worksheet and use the Data Extract command to extract all those records fitting the criteria you specify—in this case, the records of employees who are on the X.15 Policies committee and who work at Site 43. To do so, complete the following steps:

Step 1. Open the EMPPHONE.XLS file and specify the range A5:E17 as a database, using the Data Set Database command.

Step 2. On row 20, in columns D and E, type **Extension** and **Committee** as the field names of the information you want. On row 21, in the same columns, type **43*** and **X.15 Policies**—the comparison data. The rows will look like those in figure 9.7.

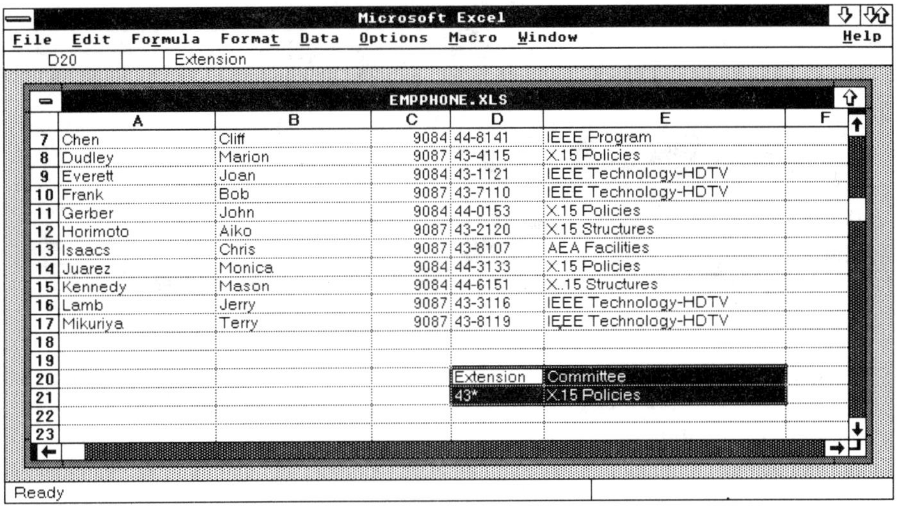

Fig. 9.7.
A criteria range.

Step 3. Specify the two rows as your criteria range, selecting D20:E21 and choosing the Data Set Criteria command.

Step 4. Set up the extract range—the area where Excel will copy the records matching the criteria you specify. The extract range is usually below the criteria range. The top row must contain the names of the fields where Excel is to look for the data specified by the criteria. Subsequent rows will contain the copies of the extracted records.

The criteria have specified the people who are on the X.15 Policies committee and who work at Site 43. On row 25, type the field names **Last Name**, **First Name**, and **Extension**.

Step 5. The extract range must be big enough to hold all the extracted records. Estimate how many records will be copied here and add a buffer zone of 5 to 10 more rows. (If there are more rows of extracted records than can fit in the extract range, you'll see an error message.)

In this example, you can safely use an extract range of 15 rows, so select A26:E41 and choose the Data Extract command.

The extracted record appears in the extract range and should look like figure 9.8.

Fig. 9.8. Extracting records by using criteria.

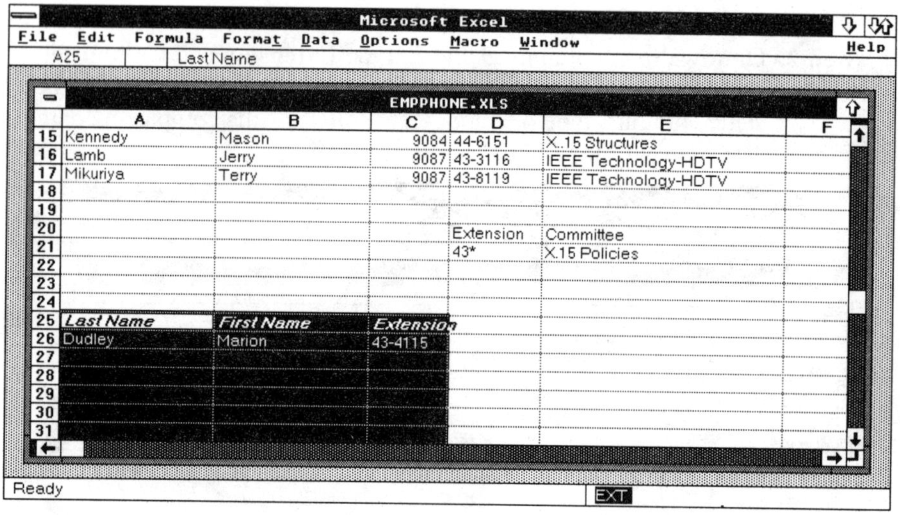

Step 6. To print just the extracted record, select the range again, choose the Options Set Print Area, and then choose the File Print command.

Plotting Trends with a Database (PR89COND.XLC, PR89HOME.XLC, SLSPR89.XLS)

You can use your Excel database to plot trends and see overall indicators of where sales or expenses are headed. You can use this data to produce a trend-analysis report, or if you're plotting data against time, you can create a seasonal index or an economic-cycle report.

Suppose that you've been keeping track of data for the local residential real estate market, and you'd like to know where the market is headed. Your monthly worksheet might look like the one shown in figure 9.9.

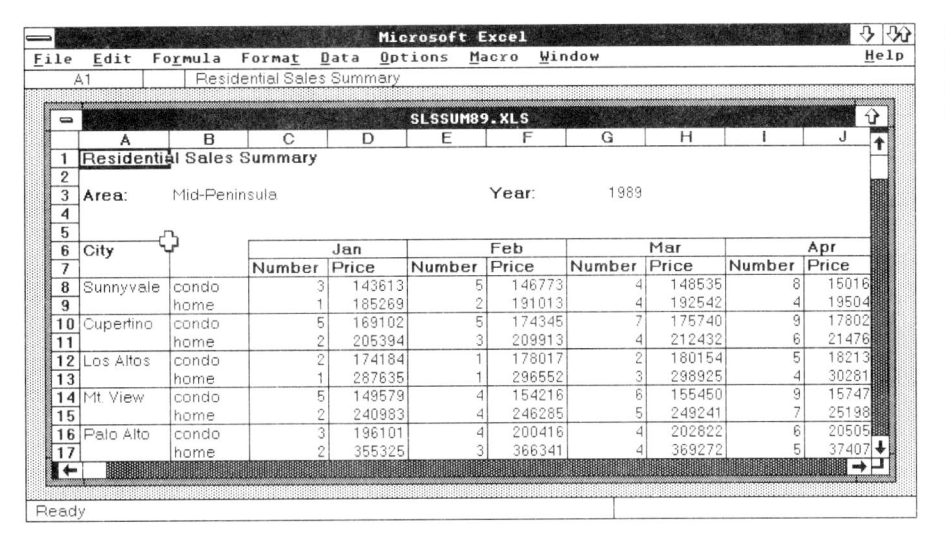

Fig. 9.9.
Residential sales by month.

Fig. 9.9 — Microsoft Excel screen showing SLSSUM89.XLS:

	A	B	C	D	E	F	G	H	I	J
1	Residential Sales Summary									
2										
3	Area:	Mid-Peninsula			Year:	1989				
4										
5										
6	City			Jan		Feb		Mar		Apr
7			Number	Price	Number	Price	Number	Price	Number	Price
8	Sunnyvale	condo	3	143613	5	146773	4	148535	8	15016
9		home	1	185269	2	191013	4	192542	4	19504
10	Cupertino	condo	5	169102	5	174345	7	175740	9	17802
11		home	2	205394	3	209913	4	212432	6	21476
12	Los Altos	condo	2	174184	1	178017	2	180154	5	18213
13		home	1	287635	1	296552	3	298925	4	30281
14	Mt. View	condo	5	149579	4	154216	6	155450	9	15747
15		home	2	240983	4	246285	5	249241	7	25198
16	Palo Alto	condo	3	196101	4	200416	4	202822	6	20505
17		home	2	355325	3	366341	4	369272	5	37407

Each month, for both condos and houses in each community, you enter the number of units sold and the average price; the average number of weeks listed is calculated. You create a new worksheet, using the same headings, each month. Your annual reports are created for each type of property and show both the average price for each month and the number of properties sold in each community. One such report is shown in figure 9.10.

Fig. 9.10.
The annual residential sales report for houses.

Fig. 9.10 — Microsoft Excel screen showing HOUSESUM.XLS:

	A	B	C	D	E	F	G	H	I	J
1	Residential Sales Summary									
2										
3	Area:	Mid-Peninsula			Year:	1989				
4										
5										
6	City			Jan		Feb		Mar		Apr
7			Number	Price	Number	Price	Number	Price	Number	Price
8	Sunnyvale	home	1	185269	2	191013	4	192542	4	19504
9	Cupertino	home	2	205394	3	209913	4	212432	6	21476
10	Los Altos	home	1	287635	1	296552	3	298925	4	30281
11	Mt. View	home	2	240983	4	246285	5	249241	7	25198
12	Palo Alto	home	2	355325	3	366341	4	369272	5	37407
13	Menlo Pk.	home	1	351640	2	359377	2	363690	4	36769
14	Portola Vly	home	1	487833	1	502956	2	506980	3	51357
15	Woodside	home	1	603290	2	616563	1	623962	4	63082

Is there a trend here? If so, what kind of trend, and where are sales headed?

Excel provides four functions that let you plot trends, as well as several database functions that are applicable to this analysis. The trend functions are GROWTH, LINEST, LOGEST, and TREND. LINEST and TREND deal with linear (straight line) projections; GROWTH and LOGEST deal with logarithmic (exponential curve) projections.

Linear projections use a set of data to plot a straight line. Suppose that you have the following set of monthly sales data:

January	5,000
February	6,000
March	7,000
April	8,000
May	9,000
June	10,000
July	11,000
August	12,000
September	13,000
October	14,000
November	15,000
December	16,000

When you plot this data on a graph (see fig. 9.11), it's pretty obvious that there is a linear relationship:

Fig. 9.11.
A linear graph.

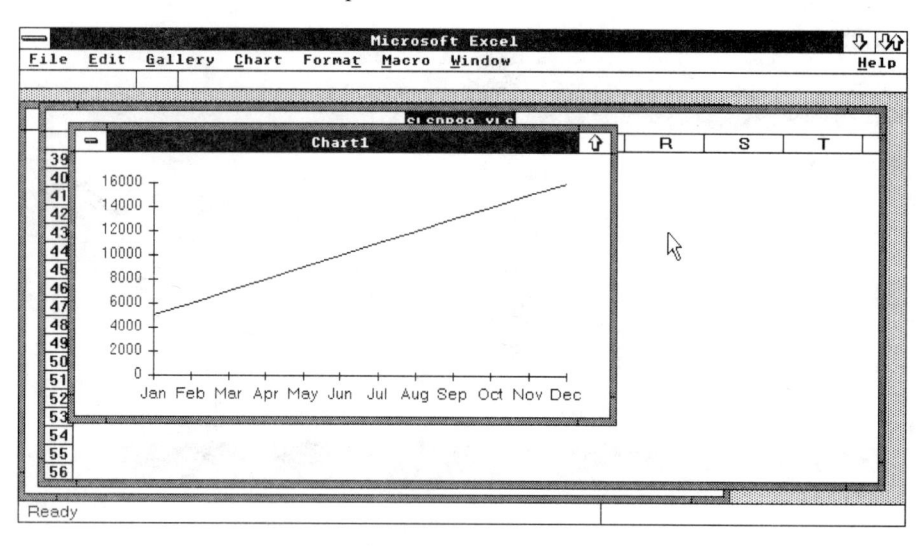

If you were to project data, using the existing data as a basis, you'd have a continuation of that straight line. Straight-line projections use the basic formula

$$y = ax + b$$

where *a* is the slope of the line, or the rate by which the line will change from one data point to the next, and *b* is the y-intercept of the line, or the point at which the line crosses the y-axis. In the data shown above, $a = 1,000$ and $b = 4,000$.

The LINEST and TREND functions let you work with linear projections. LINEST returns the slope and intercept values for any linear projection involving a set of data, and TREND determines the values for future points along that line.

Logarithmic projections (exponential curves) use a similar approach, but depend on the formula

$$y = (b*(a_1{\wedge}x_1)*(a_2{\wedge}x_2))$$

and look at data in arrays of *x* and *y* values. LOGEST returns the slope and intercept parameters that describe an exponential curve; GROWTH returns an array of *y* values, given the future values of *x*.

Note: If you want just the slope or intercept value, use the INDEX function with the LOGEST function. For instance, if in a particular worksheet you have *x* values in F5:F9 and *y* values in G5:G9, and you want only the slope value, the INDEX formula might look like this:

INDEX(LOGEST(G5:G9,F5:F9),1) = 45.33

Suppose that in columns D and E you have the following sales data for the year:

Row	Column D Month	Column E Sales
25	1	6,500
26	2	13,000
27	3	26,000
28	4	52,000
29	5	104,000
30	6	208,000
31	7	416,000
32	8	832,000
33	9	1,664,000
34	10	3,328,000
35	11	6,656,000
36	12	13,312,000

You have, of course, something approximating a Sales VP's wildest dreams come true: an exponential curve (see fig. 9.12).

Fig. 9.12.
An exponential curve.

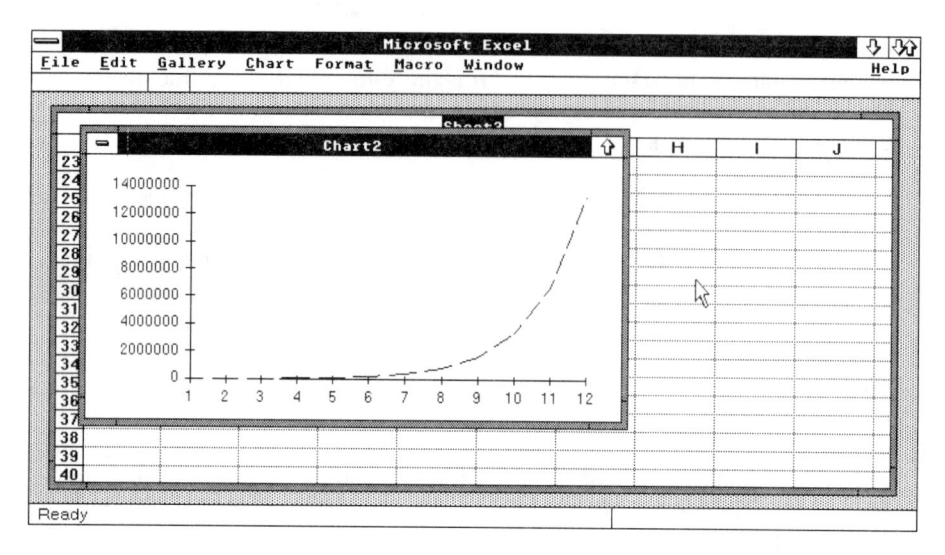

Using these data points as a basis, you could project the sales figures for the next few months with the GROWTH function.

Other curves, perhaps not as optimistic, can be generated with the LOGEST and GROWTH functions.

How do you know which kind of projection—linear or exponential—is applicable to data in your database? Take a look at the real estate example.

One approach is to graph the data to see what kind of trend appears. Figure 9.13 shows a graph of the average sales prices of condos for 1989, for all six communities (these prices are included on the disk as the file PR89COND.XLC).

Fig. 9.13.
The condo sales price summary for 1989.

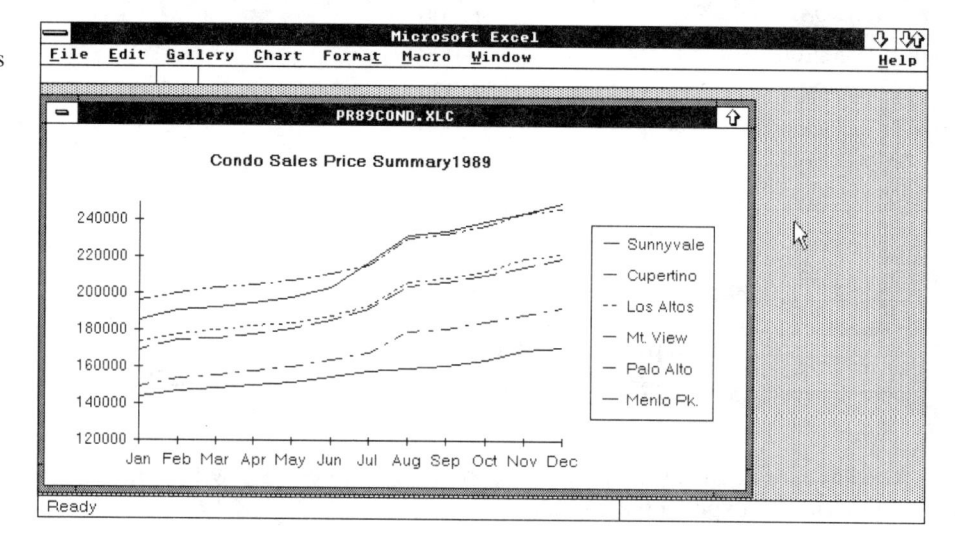

Figure 9.14 shows a graph of the average sales prices of houses in 1989 in the same six communities (these prices are included on the disk as the file PR89HOME.XLC).

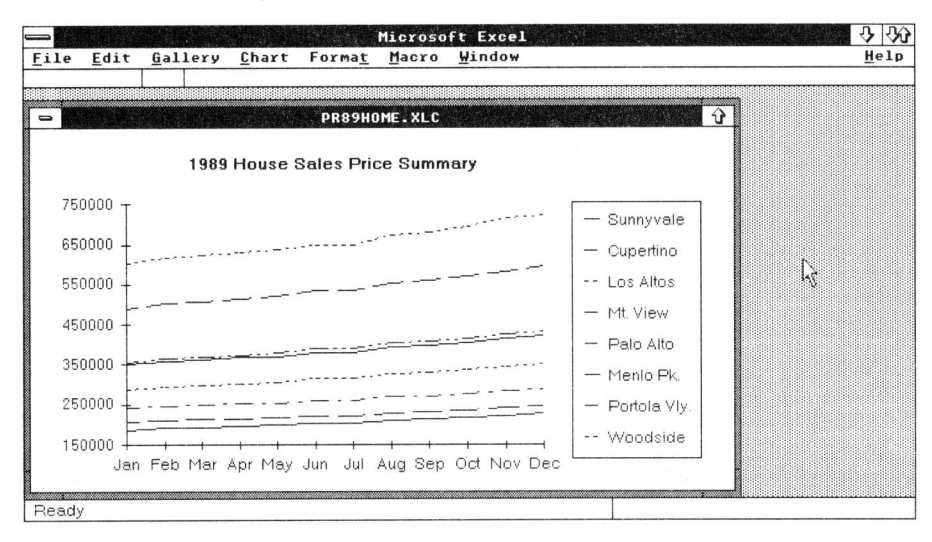

Fig. 9.14. The house sales price summary for 1989.

The trends appear to be generally up, but they're irregular. Are there linear relationships, or are these data points part of a curve?

Consider the Sunnyvale data on houses as an example. Figure 9.15 shows a linear graph, created by applying the LINEST function to the data for Sunnyvale houses. The actual data points are also shown.

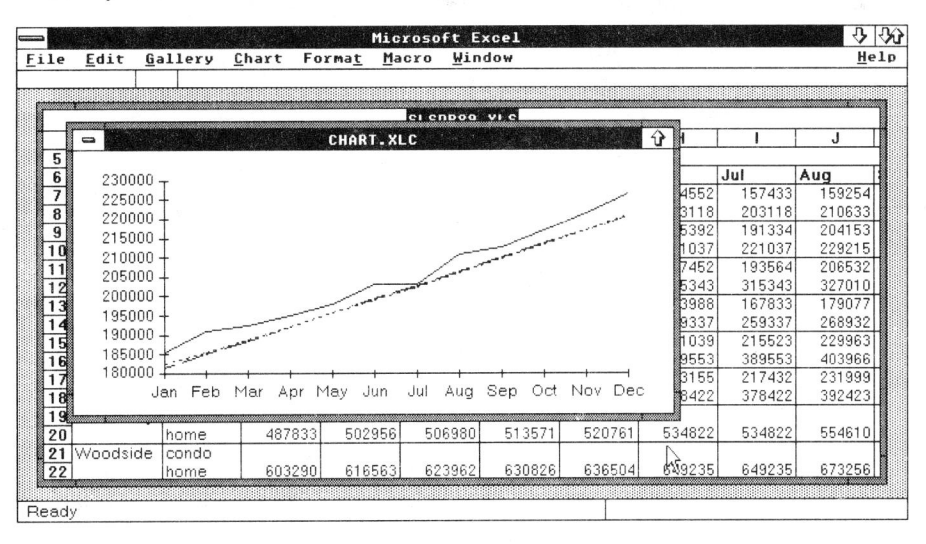

Fig. 9.15. A LINEST projection for Sunnyvale houses.

To create this projection, start with the file SLSPR89.XLS, which contains in spreadsheet form the data on house sales for 1989 (see fig. 9.16). Do the following:

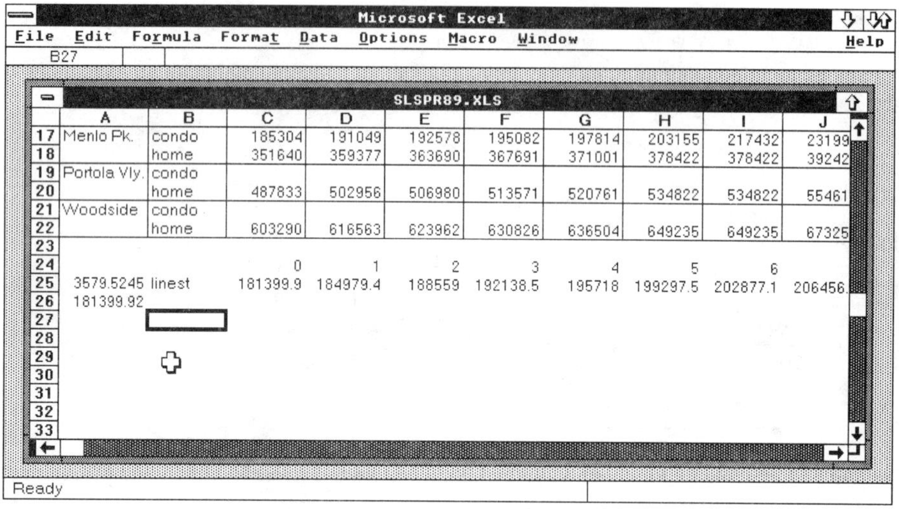
Microsoft Excel
File Edit Formula Format Data Options Macro Window Help
B27
SLSPR89.XLS
A B C D E F G H I J
17 Menlo Pk. condo 185304 191049 192578 195082 197814 203155 217432 23199
18 home 351640 359377 363690 367691 371001 378422 378422 39242
19 Portola Vly. condo
20 home 487833 502956 506980 513571 520761 534822 534822 55461
21 Woodside condo
22 home 603290 616563 623962 630826 636504 649235 649235 67325
23
24 0 1 2 3 4 5 6
25 3579.5245 linest 181399.9 184979.4 188559 192138.5 195718 199297.5 202877.1 206456
26 181399.92
27
28
29
30
31
32
33
Ready

Fig. 9.16. The house-sales data.

Step 1. In cell A25, enter the formula

=INDEX(LINEST(C8:N8),1)

This formula produces the slope for a linear estimate.

Step 2. In cell A26, enter the formula

=INDEX(LINEST(C8:N8),2)

This formula produces the y-intercept.

Step 3. Enter the numbers **0** through **11** in C24:N24. These are the index numbers you'll use in drawing the graph.

Step 4. In cell C25, enter the formula

=C24*$A$25+$A$26

Select cells C25:N25; then choose the Edit Fill Right command. Doing so generates a set of data points from the linear parameters in A25 and A26.

Step 5. Select C8:N8. This action selects the real Sunnyvale data. Choose the File New command and then the Chart option. Select the Gallery Line command; then choose one of the options to create the basic graph.

Step 6. Choose the Chart Select Chart command, which selects the chart area.

Step 7. Using the Window menu, return to the SLSPR89.XLS file, and on it select cells C25:N25. Choose the Edit Copy command, and use the Window menu to return to the chart. Choose the Edit Paste command, which pastes the linear-projection data into the chart as a new data series.

Step 8. Select either of the series on the chart. On the formula bar, select the portion of the formula that reads

SLSPR89.XLS!$C$25:$N$25

(See fig. 9.17.)

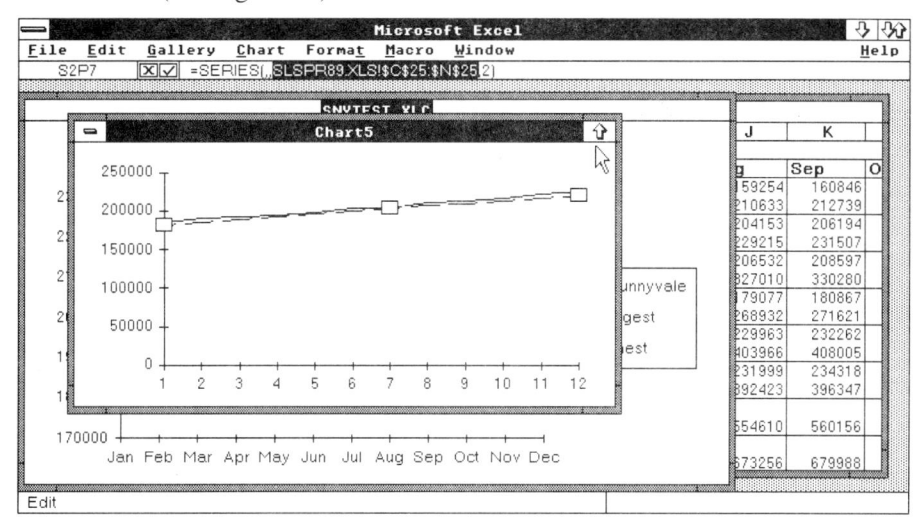

Fig. 9.17.
Editing series formula.

Move the cursor so that it is between the first two commas; choose the Edit Paste command. Doing so inserts the portion of the formula, which is incorrect as inserted. Change the $C$25:$N$25 to read $C$6:$N$6; press Enter.

Step 9. Perform the actions in Step 8 for the other series. Once you've done that, the series names at the bottom of the chart will reflect the month names.

Step 10. Select the real Sunnyvale data line on the chart and choose the Format Pattern command. In the Line box in the top half of the dialog box, click the Invisible button, and in the Marker box in the bottom half of the dialog box, click the Automatic button; then press Enter. These actions change the Sunnyvale data line into a series of boxes.

Step 11. If any of the month names appear to be truncated, resize the chart window so that it's appropriate for your screen.

Step 12. Save the chart and print it. Your finished chart should look like figure 9.15.

So much for a linear estimate. Is the data on a curve? To find out, do the following (keep both the worksheet and chart files on your workspace):

Step 1. In cell A27 on the worksheet, enter the formula

=INDEX(LOGEST(C8:N8),1)

This formula produces the first parameter of the exponential-curve formula—the derivative (rate of increase) of the curve.

Step 2. In cell A28, enter the formula

=INDEX(LOGEST(C8:N8),2)

This formula produces the y-intercept of the curve.

Step 3. In cell C26, enter the formula

=$A$28

This formula is the value for the first position in the series.

Step 4. In cell D26, enter the formula

=C26*$A$27

This formula uses the rate of increase to generate the second value in the series.

Step 5. Select D26:N26 and choose the Edit Fill Right command. This command copies the formula into the adjacent cells in the range and adjusts the references to fill the remaining data points in the series.

Step 6. Return to the chart, using the Window menu. Choose the Chart Select Chart command. Return to the worksheet by using the Window menu and select C26:N26. Choose the Edit Copy command. Again, use the Window menu to return to the chart; choose the Edit Paste command. Doing so pastes the logarithmic values into the chart and adds a third line to it. After adding a title and a legend and adjusting the values on the y-axis (select the y-axis, choose the Format Scale command, and change the minimum and maximum values on the axis), you should see a chart like that shown in figure 9.18.

It's hard to see the difference between the linear and logarithmic lines, isn't it? Both lines are fairly straight. What that tells you is that the increases are pretty close to linear.

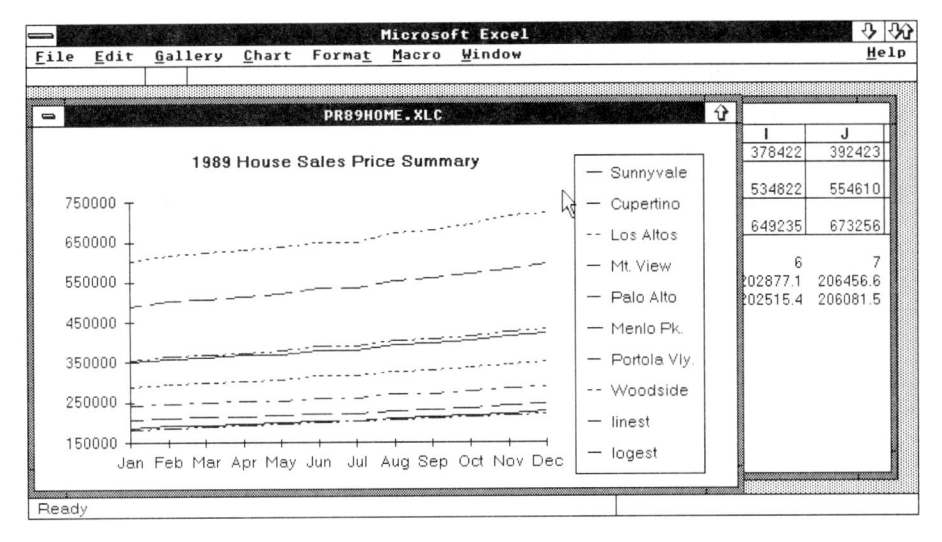

Fig. 9.18. Sunnyvale house prices, with linear and exponential projections.

Back to the big question: What kinds of price increases can you expect for this area, assuming that the linear projection is correct? To find out, do the following:

Step 1. On the spreadsheet, enter the numbers **12** through **17** in cells O24:T24. Doing so gives you room for a six-month projection.

Step 2. Select N25:T25. Choose the Edit Fill Right command, which puts the projected sales prices into the subsequent months, using the linear-projection formula as a basis.

The projection is that the average price in this community in June 1990 will be $242,252.

Using Database Functions To Verify Reliability (SVLHSJUN.XLS)

Now that you've done a linear projection and an exponential curve to look at your data, how reliable are the projections? One statistical measure is the *standard deviation*, which measures how much each data point deviates from the mean of the values in the database as selected by the criteria. The closer to 0, the more predictable (and therefore the more reliable) is each data point.

The monthly summary figures for each community that you looked at earlier are based on a more detailed database—presumably kept by the community board of realtors—which shows details about each piece of property that is available at the moment. A portion of such a database might look that in figure 9.19.

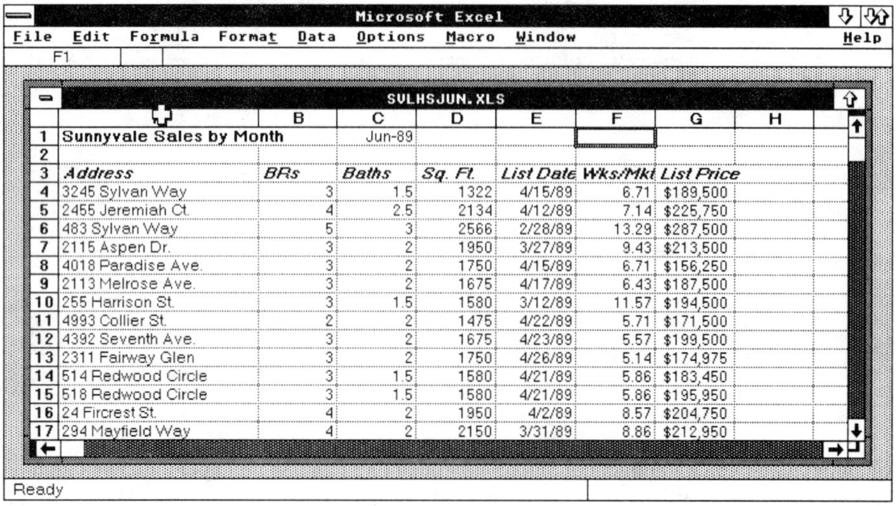

Fig. 9.19.
A portion of the Sunnyvale database, June 1989.

	Address	BRs	Baths	Sq. Ft.	List Date	Wks/Mkt	List Price
4	3245 Sylvan Way	3	1.5	1322	4/15/89	6.71	$189,500
5	2455 Jeremiah Ct.	4	2.5	2134	4/12/89	7.14	$225,750
6	483 Sylvan Way	5	3	2566	2/28/89	13.29	$287,500
7	2115 Aspen Dr.	3	2	1950	3/27/89	9.43	$213,500
8	4018 Paradise Ave.	3	2	1750	4/15/89	6.71	$156,250
9	2113 Melrose Ave.	3	2	1675	4/17/89	6.43	$187,500
10	255 Harrison St.	3	1.5	1580	3/12/89	11.57	$194,500
11	4993 Collier St.	2	2	1475	4/22/89	5.71	$171,500
12	4392 Seventh Ave.	3	2	1675	4/23/89	5.57	$199,500
13	2311 Fairway Glen	3	2	1750	4/26/89	5.14	$174,975
14	514 Redwood Circle	3	1.5	1580	4/21/89	5.86	$183,450
15	518 Redwood Circle	3	1.5	1580	4/21/89	5.86	$195,950
16	24 Fircrest St.	4	2	1950	4/2/89	8.57	$204,750
17	294 Mayfield Way	4	2	2150	3/31/89	8.86	$212,950

If the list price for each house is in line with trends in the community—for example, if the price is directly related to the number of bedrooms—the standard deviation will be low. If there are large fluctuations in price for houses in this category, the standard deviation will be relatively large. A large standard deviation indicates that factors other than the number of bedrooms are at work in determining price.

What's the standard deviation for the list price of three-bedroom houses that have been on the market for more than five weeks? If houses priced "reasonably" for the market generally sell within the first month they're listed, a buyer may be able to get the seller to lower the asking price of a house that's been on the market for more than five weeks. The greater the standard deviation for houses like the one the buyer is interested in, the more likely the buyer is to find room for negotiation.

The standard-deviation function that applies to a database like the one you are considering has the following syntax:

DSTDEV(*database,fieldname,criteria*)

This function, which applies to a sampling of the database, is used because the assumption is that the houses shown are only some of the 116 available for June. (The DSTDEVP function applies when the entire population is represented in the database.)

In this case, assume that the database has been defined through the Data Set Database command as the range A4:G24 and that the criteria range has been defined through the Data Set Criteria command as A26:G27. This setup enables you to use the words *Database* and *Criteria* (without enclosing them in quotes) as range names, because Excel automatically names the ranges when the respective commands are used.

That leaves the criteria to be specified and the field name argument to be defined in the DSTDEV function. The criteria you want to specify in this search are three-bedroom houses that have been on the market for more than five weeks. The data you want to measure is in the List Price field.

Note that the data in the Wks/Mkt field is computed. The formula in column F subtracts the list data in column E from the date of the report—in this case, June 1, 1989—and divides the result by seven.

To specify the criteria and define the field name argument, do the following:

Step 1. Open the file SVLHSJUN.XLS and inspect the data, which should look like that in figure 9.19.

Step 2. Use the Data Set Database command to specify the range A3:G24 as the database.

Step 3. Use the Data Set Criteria command to specify the range A26:G27 as the criteria range.

Step 4. Copy the field names BRs and Wks/Mkt into cells B26 and F26, respectively. These field names are needed to identify the fields that will contain criteria. In B27 enter the number **3** (for three bedrooms); in F27 enter **>5** (for more than five weeks on the market).

Step 5. In F28, type the formula

   =DSTDEV(Database,"List Price",Criteria)

As an alternative, you could type the argument as (**A3:G24**,"**List Price**",**A26:G27**), but because the database range and the criteria range are already defined, you can use the terms *Database* and *Criteria* instead of the actual range coordinates.

When you press the Enter key, you'll see the number

   17182.61

in F28, the cell containing the formula. This number is the actual standard deviation for the list prices of the houses selected by the criteria you've specified. Thus the prices of three-bedroom houses in the Sunnyvale area that have been on the market for more than five weeks have a standard deviation of $17,182.61—a relatively large number. This standard deviation may mean that you as a buyer have negotiating room, or it may mean that other factors—such as location or proximity to schools—are at work in determining the list price.

Sorting Records (PROJECTS.XLS)

One of the most frequently used database techniques is the sorting of records and of fields within records. Excel lets you sort by rows or columns and by keys that you specify. This capability enables you to go through your worksheets, select and reorganize the information, and present the sorted list as a variety of reports.

Suppose that you have a database in which you track projects as they progress through various development and marketing stages. The database is kept by project name, but when you do a status report, you need to present it by marketing stage, because the stage is related to available funding and thus budget categories.

Figure 9.20 shows the database for the month of October.

Fig. 9.20. A project-tracking worksheet.

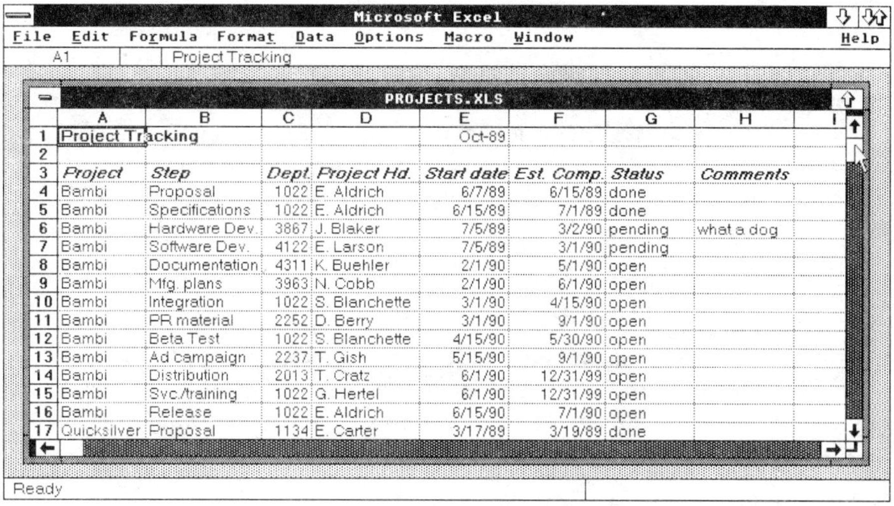

Microsoft Excel
File Edit Formula Format Data Options Macro Window Help
A1 | Project Tracking
PROJECTS.XLS

	A	B	C	D	E	F	G	H
1	Project Tracking				Oct-89			
2								
3	*Project*	*Step*	*Dept.*	*Project Hd.*	*Start date*	*Est. Comp.*	*Status*	*Comments*
4	Bambi	Proposal	1022	E. Aldrich	6/7/89	6/15/89	done	
5	Bambi	Specifications	1022	E. Aldrich	6/15/89	7/1/89	done	
6	Bambi	Hardware Dev.	3867	J. Blaker	7/5/89	3/2/90	pending	what a dog
7	Bambi	Software Dev.	4122	E. Larson	7/5/89	3/1/90	pending	
8	Bambi	Documentation	4311	K. Buehler	2/1/90	5/1/90	open	
9	Bambi	Mfg. plans	3963	N. Cobb	2/1/90	6/1/90	open	
10	Bambi	Integration	1022	S. Blanchette	3/1/90	4/15/90	open	
11	Bambi	PR material	2252	D. Berry	3/1/90	9/1/90	open	
12	Bambi	Beta Test	1022	S. Blanchette	4/15/90	5/30/90	open	
13	Bambi	Ad campaign	2237	T. Gish	5/15/90	9/1/90	open	
14	Bambi	Distribution	2013	T. Cratz	6/1/90	12/31/99	open	
15	Bambi	Svc./training	1022	G. Hertel	6/1/90	12/31/99	open	
16	Bambi	Release	1022	E. Aldrich	6/15/90	7/1/90	open	
17	Quicksilver	Proposal	1134	E. Carter	3/17/89	3/19/89	done	

Ready

The status report uses the Status field to do its initial sort and then organizes by the fields Project and Start date. The report is produced through the use of a simple sort. To produce the report, follow these steps:

Step 1. Open the file PROJECTS.XLS and specify the sort range by selecting A4:H42.

Step 2. Choose the Data Sort command. Because the records you are after are arranged as rows, choose the Row option.

Step 3. In the 1st Key box, enter the reference **G4**. Note that this procedure differs from the way you specify criteria, in which you use the field name. When you're sorting, if you specify a field name as a sort key, the field name will be sorted along with the rest of the records. In this step, you could specify any cell in column G (except the cell containing the field name), because you're going to be sorting by rows.

Step 4. In the 2nd Key box, type the reference **A4** to identify the project name.

Step 5. In the 3rd Key box, type the reference **E4** to identify the start date.

Step 6. Select the Ascending button to sort records by sequential date. Then choose the OK button.

The database is sorted and appears as shown in figure 9.21.

Fig. 9.21.
The sorted database, from which the status report is printed.

	A	B	C	D	E	F	G	H
1	Project Tracking				Oct-89			
2								
3	*Project*	*Step*	*Dept*	*Project Hd.*	*Start date*	*Est. Comp.*	*Status*	*Comments*
4	Bambi	Proposal	1022	E. Aldrich	6/7/89	6/15/89	done	
5	Bambi	Specifications	1022	E. Aldrich	6/15/89	7/1/89	done	
6	Quicksilver	Proposal	1134	E. Carter	3/17/89	3/19/89	done	
7	Quicksilver	Specifications	1134	E. Carter	3/19/89	4/5/89	done	
8	Quicksilver	Hardware Dev.	3127	D. Medinnus	4/11/89	7/27/89	done	
9	Quicksilver	Software Dev.	4226	N. Hardy	4/12/89	7/30/89	done	
10	Quicksilver	Integration	1134	L. Jones	7/27/89	8/19/89	done	
11	Thumper	Proposal	1743	C. Knight	10/13/89	10/16/89	done	
12	Thumper	Specifications	1743	C. Knight	10/17/89	10/22/89	done	
13	Thumper	Hardware Dev.	3673	S. Mohn	10/22/89	10/30/89	done	wow!
14	Thumper	Software Dev.	4481	C. Nicolai	10/22/89	10/29/89	done	
15	Bambi	Documentation	4311	K. Buehler	2/1/90	5/1/90	open	
16	Bambi	Mfg. plans	3963	N. Cobb	2/1/90	6/1/90	open	
17	Bambi	Integration	1022	S. Blanchette	3/1/90	4/15/90	open	

You may also want to sort the same report by department or by project head to determine whether particular staff members are overloaded with work. You can use the preceding steps to reorder a sort into any order you need.

When you save the file, the information will be stored in the order in which it was last sorted.

Making It Pretty: Formatting Hints for Your Reports (PROJECTS.XLS)

In creating your reports, it's sometimes important to add explanatory information as headers and footers or to add other information to the format of your pages.

To add the title *Status Report* to the top of the page, to remove the gridlines and the row and column identifiers, and to add the date to the bottom of the status report, complete these steps:

Step 1. With the PROJECTS.XLS file still on your screen, choose the File Page Setup command.

Step 2. When the dialog box appears, notice that the Header bar already contains the characters *&f*, followed by *Status Report*. If you want to change the header, move the cursor to the Header bar position—the vertical blinking line to the right of the *&f* characters—and type the new header. Delete the characters you no longer want.

A number of options are available for headers and footers, as shown in table 9.1.

Step 3. Move the cursor to the Footer bar, where you see the characters *Page &p*. These cause the page number to be automatically printed at the bottom of the page, on the left side, after the word *Page*. To add the date in boldface, add the characters **&D** to those in the footer box. (The characters have already been added on this file.) To clean up the report, turn off the Row & Column Headings box and the Gridlines box and then choose the OK button.

If you want a preview of what your printed page will look like, choose the File Print command and click the Preview box. You'll see a miniature version of the layout of the finished report, with headers and footers centered over the page. (When the report is printed, you'll have the headers and footers located appropriately on your page.) If you want to read anything on the tiny page, choose the Zoom button, which changes the scale of the page. When you're through inspecting the preview, choose the Cancel button.

**Table 9.1
Header and Footer Options**

Option	Effect
&L	Left-aligns the subsequent characters
&C	Centers the subsequent characters
&R	Right-aligns the subsequent characters
&B	Prints the subsequent characters in boldface
&I	Prints the subsequent characters in italics
&D	Prints the current date
&T	Prints the current time
&F	Prints the name of the document
&P	Prints the page number
&P+*number*	Adds the designated number to the page number and prints the resulting number (use this option for changing the starting page number)
&P-*number*	Subtracts the designated number from the page number and prints the resulting number

Printing Your Report (PROJB89.XLS, PROJECTS.XLS)

Normally, your report will be sent to the default printer for your system. You can change this setup by selecting the File Select Printer command and specifying the printer for each job. Once a printer is assigned to each print job, the spooler takes care of parceling out the printing assignments to the appropriate printer.

To print your report, choose the File Print command. This action puts your print job into the spooler, which enables you to line up a number of print jobs into a printing queue, managed by a program that sends them to the printer as a background task. You can thus return to the screen and continue to work on other worksheet projects while your job is running. As your print jobs are being printed, you'll see messages on-screen indicating their status.

This report, complete with headers and footers, is shown in figure 9.22.

Fig. 9.22.
The project report, with headers and footers.

PROJECTS.XLS Status Report

Project Tracking   Oct-89

Project	Step	Dept.	Project Hd.	Start date	Est. Comp.	Status	Comments
Bambi	Proposal	1022	E. Aldrich	6/7/89	6/15/89	done	
Bambi	Specifications	1022	E. Aldrich	6/15/89	7/1/89	done	
Bambi	Hardware Dev.	3867	J. Blaker	7/5/89	3/2/90	pending	what a dog
Bambi	Software Dev.	4122	E. Larson	7/5/89	3/1/90	pending	
Bambi	Documentation	4311	K. Buehler	2/1/90	5/1/90	open	
Bambi	Mfg. plans	3963	N. Cobb	2/1/90	6/1/90	open	
Bambi	Integration	1022	S. Blanchette	3/1/90	4/15/90	open	
Bambi	PR material	2252	D. Berry	3/1/90	9/1/90	open	
Bambi	Beta Test	1022	S. Blanchette	4/15/90	5/30/90	open	
Bambi	Ad campaign	2237	T. Gish	5/15/90	9/1/90	open	
Bambi	Distribution	2013	T. Cratz	6/1/90	12/31/99	open	
Bambi	Svc./training	1022	G. Hertel	6/1/90	12/31/99	open	
Bambi	Release	1022	E. Aldrich	6/15/90	7/1/90	open	
Quicksilver	Proposal	1134	E. Carter	3/17/89	3/19/89	done	
Quicksilver	Specifications	1134	E. Carter	3/19/89	4/5/89	done	
Quicksilver	Hardware Dev.	3127	D. Medinnus	4/11/89	7/27/89	done	
Quicksilver	Software Dev.	4226	N. Hardy	4/12/89	7/30/89	done	
Quicksilver	Integration	1134	L. Jones	7/27/89	8/19/89	done	
Quicksilver	Beta Test	1134	L. Jones	8/19/89	11/15/89	pending	
Quicksilver	Ad campaign	2248	W. Meier	10/22/89	6/5/90	pending	
Quicksilver	PR material	2249	S. Miller	10/22/89	12/31/89	pending	
Quicksilver	Documentation	4316	Von Rospach	10/22/89	12/20/89	pending	
Quicksilver	Mfg. plans	3977	L. Sefton	11/17/89	12/1/89	open	
Quicksilver	Svc./training	1134	D. Dougherty	12/15/89	12/31/99	open	
Quicksilver	Release	1134	E. Carter	12/20/89	12/31/89	open	
Quicksilver	Distribution	2066	L. Levy	1/1/90	12/31/99	open	
Thumper	Proposal	1743	C. Knight	10/13/89	10/16/89	done	
Thumper	Specifications	1743	C. Knight	10/17/89	10/22/89	done	
Thumper	Hardware Dev.	3673	S. Mohn	10/22/89	10/30/89	done	wow!
Thumper	Software Dev.	4481	C. Nicolai	10/22/89	10/29/89	done	
Thumper	Documentation	4382	J. Martin	10/23/89	11/25/89	pending	
Thumper	Mfg. plans	3951	L. Westberry	10/24/89	12/1/89	pending	
Thumper	Integration	1743	R. Parker	11/1/89	12/15/89	pending	already?!?
Thumper	Beta Test	1743	R. Parker	11/1/89	12/15/89	pending	
Thumper	Ad campaign	2014	T. Poetzl	11/1/89	12/15/89	pending	
Thumper	PR material	2331	R. Ramirez	11/1/89	12/15/89	pending	
Thumper	Release	1743	C. Knight	1/1/90	2/1/90	open	
Thumper	Distribution	2065	J. Bynum	1/1/90	12/31/99	open	
Thumper	Svc./training	1743	M. Wallis	1/1/90	12/31/99	open	

Page 1 1/3/90

You can do more with your data on this project. A business of this size will, logically, have budget reports associated with status reports. The file PROJB89.XLS shows the budgeted and actual figures for the same projects and steps so that the financial people can see what's going on, too. Figure 9.23 shows you what the Project Budgets file looks like.

Fig. 9.23. The budget report.

PROJB89.XLS

Oct-89

Project	Step	Status	Budget	Actual
Bambi	Proposal	done	$12,500	$17,263
Bambi	Specifications	done	$21,250	$34,264
Bambi	Hardware Dev.	pending	$104,500	$258,153
Bambi	Software Dev.	pending	$175,000	$214,521
Bambi		open	$45,000	$1,352
Bambi	Mfg. plans	open	$42,000	$677
Bambi	Integration	open	$46,500	$12,763
Bambi	PR material	open	$37,500	$0
Bambi	Beta Test	open	$12,000	$0
Bambi	Ad campaign	open	$140,000	$0
Bambi	Distribution	open	$450,000	$0
Bambi	Svc./training	open	$55,000	$0
Bambi	Release	open	$18,500	$0
Quicksilver	Proposal	done	$11,000	$1,558
Quicksilver	Specifications	done	$12,500	$7,411
Quicksilver	Hardware Dev.	done	$110,000	$100,599
Quicksilver	Software Dev.	done	$108,000	$78,855
Quicksilver	Integration	done	$15,000	$14,753
Quicksilver	Beta Test	pending	$11,000	$12,867
Quicksilver	Ad campaign	pending	$35,000	$42,543
Quicksilver	PR material	pending	$12,500	$9,437
Quicksilver		pending	$32,000	$25,856
Quicksilver	Mfg. plans	open	$6,000	$583
Quicksilver	Svc./training	open	$39,000	$632
Quicksilver	Release	open	$11,500	$214
Quicksilver	Distribution	open	$192,000	$0
Thumper	Proposal	done	$4,500	$1,689
Thumper	Specifications	done	$4,500	$2,253
Thumper	Hardware Dev.	done	$35,000	$10,533
Thumper	Software Dev.	done	$12,000	$7,034
Thumper		pending	$15,000	$17,207
Thumper	Mfg. plans	pending	$5,000	$5,625
Thumper	Integration	pending	$19,000	$374
Thumper	Beta Test	pending	$6,000	$0
Thumper	Ad campaign	pending	$48,000	$2,000
Thumper	PR material	pending	$11,000	$375
Thumper	Release	open	$13,200	$0
Thumper	Distribution	open	$292,000	$0

The final report that you want to hand to management should include both tracking data and budget data. Yet that's probably more information than will fit on one page, and some of that information isn't really necessary for an overview. The solution is to merge the files and see what can then be eliminated from the final report.

To merge the data from two files, copy data from one open file into another open file by completing the following steps:

Step 1. Open both the PROJECTS.XLS and PROJB89.XLS files.

Step 2. On the Budget file (PROJB89.XLS), highlight columns D and E and then choose the Edit Copy command.

Step 3. On the Windows menu, choose the PROJECTS.XLS file. Doing so makes it the active window.

Step 4. Move the cursor to column I and choose the Edit Paste command. Doing so pastes the budgeted and actual figures onto the worksheet with the Project Tracking data.

Step 5. The entire report won't fit on-screen and thus won't fit on a single page. You can do several things to change this situation:

- Change the font size from 10 point to something smaller, such as 8 point. You can do so by choosing the Format Font command and the Fonts >> option and by then picking the size and typeface you want. Reducing the font size means that more characters (and hence more information) can fit on a page.
- Make your report a two-page report. If the report *must* fit on one page, you could use a reducing copier to reduce the two pages so that they fit on a single sheet of paper.
- Hide some of the information on the merged file so that the remaining data fits on a single page. Hiding data enables you to print the page as displayed, although the file itself retains the original information.

If you choose to hide data on the existing file, what data could be hidden?

The department number shown on the status report (see figure 9.22) is important because it shows which group is responsible for that particular step; different individuals within that department, however, may be responsible for different steps. Thus the names of the project heads, in column D, can probably be removed from the page with the final report. You can also hide the comments shown in column H. Hiding these two columns of data would provide enough room on the screen for the budget data.

How do you hide data? Complete the following steps to find out:

Step 1. With the data on your screen the way you left it in Step 4, move the screen pointer to column D and do either of these:

- If you have a mouse, move the screen pointer to the left edge of the column label (containing the D). The screen pointer changes to a two-sided arrow when it's right over the column border between columns D and E. Drag the column edge to the left so that it overlaps the column border between columns C and D. Doing so effectively erases column D, although the data is still there.
- With the active cell anywhere in column D, choose the Format Column Width command and type the number **0** in the Column Width box. Doing so makes column D disappear.

(To restore a column that has been hidden, choose the Formula Goto command and type the address of any cell in the column. Excel selects the cell. Then choose the Format Column Width command and type any number greater than 0, or choose the Standard Width box. The column reappears on your screen.)

Step 2. Repeat the process with the comments in column H. When you've finished hiding column H, the data should fit on the screen and should thus fit on a page.

Step 3. To further enhance the page, you can separate the projects visually, and you can add some border effects that will make the whole report more professional-looking.

The report is already sorted by project, so to separate the projects, select the entire last row of the Bambi project, row 16 (click on the row number to select the entire row). Then choose the Edit Insert command to put a blank row below row 16.

Repeat this process with the last row (now row 30) of the Quicksilver project.

Step 4. Add borders to the columns. Select all the data in A3:A31 and choose the Format Border command. Then choose the Left and Right buttons to display borders on the column. Repeat the process with all the other data.

Step 5. Select A3:I3 and choose the Format Border command again. Leave the Left and Right buttons selected, but add the Outline buttons. Doing so encloses each of your column labels in an outline.

Step 6: Select row 2 and choose the Format Border command; then choose the Shade option. Doing so shades the entire row. Repeat this step for rows 18, 32, and 46.

Step 7: To enclose the entire report in a shaded border, you must insert a new column of shading on the left and shade the equivalent column on the left. Select all of column A and choose the Edit Insert command. This action creates a new column A and moves everything to the right. Now choose the Format Column Width command and type a **2** in the Column Width box. The column is now narrower but is still selected. Choose the Format Border command and select the Shade box, which shades the entire column.

Step 8: Move the cursor to column K, select it, and use the Format Column Width command to make it two characters wide. Then use the Format Border command and the Shade box to shade column K.

When you're finished, your report can be printed and should look like the one in figure 9.24.

Summary

This chapter has shown you ways to apply database-manipulation techniques to data stored in an Excel worksheet. You have learned how to construct a database from Excel data, to set up search criteria, to extract data, sort it, and report it. You have also learned some ways to apply database functions to the analysis of your data.

Using the Data Form command, you have entered data and searched for specific information. You've seen ways in which you can combine data from separate files into one report. You have also seen how to use the Page Setup command to add headers, footers, borders, and shading to create a more professional-looking product and how to use the Preview option to see how your page will look before it's printed.

Status Report

Project Tracking Oct-89

Project	Step	Dept.	Start date	Est. Comp.	Status	Budget	Actual
Bambi	Proposal	1022	6/7/89	6/15/89	done	$12,500	$17,263
Bambi	Specifications	1022	6/15/89	7/1/89	done	$21,250	$34,264
Bambi	Hardware Dev.	3867	7/5/89	3/2/90	pending	$104,500	$258,153
Bambi	Software Dev.	4122	7/5/89	3/1/90	pending	$175,000	$214,521
Bambi	Documentation	4311	2/1/90	5/1/90	open	$45,000	$1,352
Bambi	Mfg. plans	3963	2/1/90	6/1/90	open	$42,000	$677
Bambi	Integration	1022	3/1/90	4/15/90	open	$46,500	$12,763
Bambi	PR material	2252	3/1/90	9/1/90	open	$37,500	$0
Bambi	Beta Test	1022	4/15/90	5/30/90	open	$12,000	$0
Bambi	Ad campaign	2237	5/15/90	9/1/90	open	$140,000	$0
Bambi	Distribution	2013	6/1/90	12/31/99	open	$450,000	$0
Bambi	Svc./training	1022	6/1/90	12/31/99	open	$55,000	$0
Bambi	Release	1022	6/15/90	7/1/90	open	$18,500	$0
Quicksilver	Proposal	1134	3/17/89	3/19/89	done	$11,000	$1,558
Quicksilver	Specifications	1134	3/19/89	4/5/89	done	$12,500	$7,411
Quicksilver	Hardware Dev.	3127	4/11/89	7/27/89	done	$110,000	$100,599
Quicksilver	Software Dev.	4226	4/12/89	7/30/89	done	$108,000	$78,855
Quicksilver	Integration	1134	7/27/89	8/19/89	done	$15,000	$14,753
Quicksilver	Beta Test	1134	8/19/89	11/15/89	pending	$11,000	$12,867
Quicksilver	Ad campaign	2248	10/22/89	6/5/90	pending	$35,000	$42,543
Quicksilver	PR material	2249	10/22/89	12/31/89	pending	$12,500	$9,437
Quicksilver	Documentation	4316	10/22/89	12/20/89	pending	$32,000	$25,856
Quicksilver	Mfg. plans	3977	11/17/89	12/1/89	open	$6,000	$583
Quicksilver	Svc./training	1134	12/15/89	12/31/99	open	$39,000	$632
Quicksilver	Release	1134	12/20/89	12/31/89	open	$11,500	$214
Quicksilver	Distribution	2066	1/1/90	12/31/99	open	$192,000	$0
Thumper	Proposal	1743	10/13/89	10/16/89	done	$4,500	$1,689
Thumper	Specifications	1743	10/17/89	10/22/89	done	$4,500	$2,253
Thumper	Hardware Dev.	3673	10/22/89	10/30/89	done	$35,000	$10,533
Thumper	Software Dev.	4481	10/22/89	10/29/89	done	$12,000	$7,034
Thumper	Documentation	4382	10/23/89	11/25/89	pending	$15,000	$17,207
Thumper	Mfg. plans	3951	10/24/89	12/1/89	pending	$5,000	$5,625
Thumper	Integration	1743	11/1/89	12/15/89	pending	$19,000	$374
Thumper	Beta Test	1743	11/1/89	12/15/89	pending	$6,000	$0
Thumper	Ad campaign	2014	11/1/89	12/15/89	pending	$48,000	$2,000
Thumper	PR material	2331	11/1/89	12/15/89	pending	$11,000	$375
Thumper	Release	1743	1/1/90	2/1/90	open	$13,200	$0
Thumper	Distribution	2065	1/1/90	12/31/99	open	$292,000	$0
Thumper	Svc./training	1743	1/1/90	12/31/99	open	$34,000	$0

Fig. 9.24. The final report, with budget data.

10

Creating Business-Presentation Charts

This text has presented a wide range of Excel models that you can use in reporting and analyzing your firm's ongoing business activities. Along the way, you also have learned how to envision and create models of your own. As a result, this book has affirmed the principal advantage of electronic spreadsheets over hand-held calculators—that is, increased memory and a greater capacity to process numbers and complex, interdependent formulas.

So what does this principal advantage really mean to you? To answer, think about how much time it would take you to execute the following tasks manually, before your firm's year-end board meeting:

- Record all accounting transactions.
- Create period-end financial statements.
- Use the financial statements to create an estimated cost-of-production budget for the next period.
- Use the cost-of-production forecast and a sales history to compile a sales forecast for the coming period.
- Create pro forma financial statements.
- Compare actual data with forecast data and analyze the variance effects on profitability.
- Design and create pictorial representations of your firm's summary financial reports.

Up to now, this text has concentrated on numbers and formulas and has only alluded to Excel's graphics capability. In fact, Excel can turn any numerical analysis into an attractive, colorful graphic presentation. Calculators—and, in fact, many other spreadsheet programs—just can't do this.

This final chapter, therefore, turns its attention to the matter of aesthetics, or the idea that a financial report can be enhanced through the use of a chart graphic. Drawing from models presented in previous chapters, you will learn how to use Excel to create this important and effective type of report. In this chapter, you will discover the wonders of creating charts with Excel.

Note: Excel uses the word *chart* to describe what most of us call a graph. In this chapter, you will see that it sounds better to talk about "chart graphics" than "graph graphics."

This chapter begins with an overview of Excel's seven chart categories and the 44 chart types available in Excel's extensive graphics library. This overview will help you select the type of chart that most appropriately represents your data.

Once you are familiar with the different chart types, you will learn ways to select and organize your numerical data so that Excel can automatically generate attractive chart graphics. Further, you will examine the idea of using graph data tables, a concept that was introduced in Chapter 5.

This chapter also shows you how to create fully formatted charts containing data from models presented earlier. You will enhance the sample charts by using many of the stylistic tools found on Excel's chart menus. These tools enable you to add chart and axis titles; copy and paste extra data series; affix legends; choose fonts, patterns, and series markers; and print your charts.

The final section of this chapter offers tips for enhancing and modifying your Excel charts. With the help of fully formatted charts, you will learn when to enhance fonts, titles, and legends. You also will learn how to add an arrow for emphasis and how to modify a data series from a noncontinuous data range selection. All these skills will help you give your charts the perfect look. The chapter ends by showing you how to create a special type of graph data block.

Understanding Excel's Chart Types

You can use Excel's graphics capabilities to create 44 different types of charts. These chart types are divided among the following seven chart categories:

- Area
- Bar
- Column
- Line
- Pie
- Scatter
- Combination

If you select New Chart from the File menu when the active worksheet contains a highlighted data range, Excel automatically creates a chart for you. How? Excel starts the process by evaluating the data range you have specified. Using its evaluation of the data range as a basis, Excel chooses one of the 44 preformatted chart types and constructs a graphic representation of the data. If Excel doesn't create the type of chart you envisioned, you can select another type of chart that more clearly illustrates your worksheet data.

Now, examine each of the seven chart categories and the 44 chart types available in each category. These charts reside in Excel's Gallery menu.

> Tip: You can transform an existing chart by selecting the Gallery menu and choosing a new chart category, style, or both. Excel automatically reconstructs the chart for you, using on the newly selected chart style.

Area Charts

When you want to illustrate a change in volume over time, use an *area chart*. An area chart is basically similar to a line chart. The area chart gives a distinct impression about the magnitude of volume changes, however, because Excel fills in the area under the line. You can use an area chart, for example, to show a change in sales or production volume over time. Figure 10.1 shows the five types of charts available in the area chart gallery.

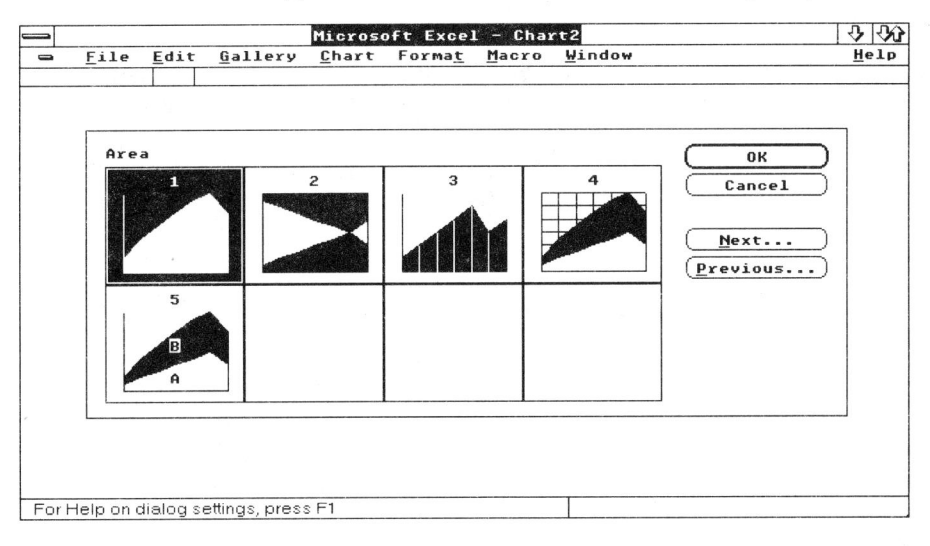

Fig. 10.1.
The area chart gallery.

Bar Charts

A *bar chart* compares the relative value or size of several similar items, such as expenses, to a standard performance value, such as zero. Bar charts describe relationships among variables rather than over time. A bar chart can be used to illustrate both positive and negative numeric relationships. For example, you can use a bar chart to compare the variance between actual and budgeted expenses. Figure 10.2 shows the seven types of charts available in the bar chart gallery.

Fig. 10.2.
The bar chart gallery.

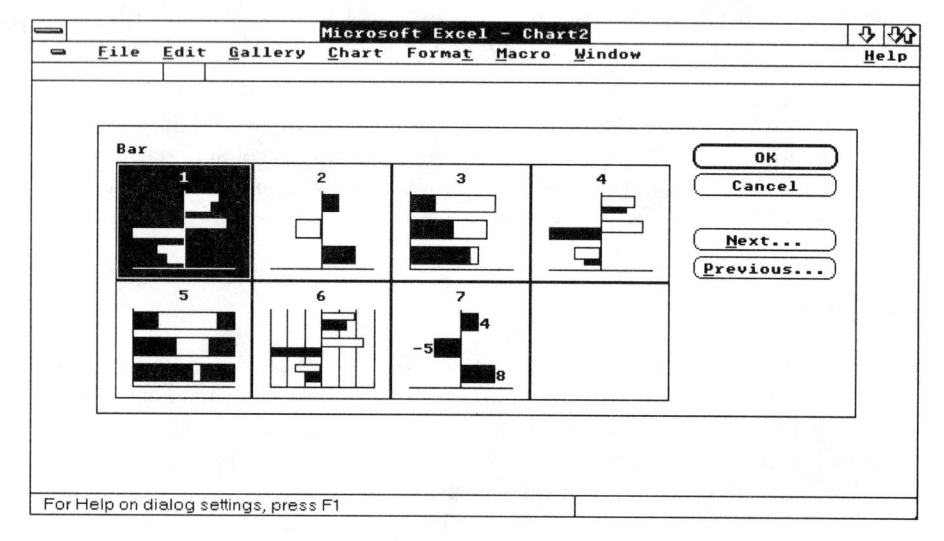

Column Charts

A *column chart*, also called a *vertical bar chart*, is simply a bar chart turned on its head. Like a bar chart, the column chart compares the relative value or size of several similar items, such as quarterly sales, to a standard measure of performance, such as zero. Figure 10.3 shows the eight types of charts available in the column chart gallery.

Line Charts

Line charts show trends or changes in data over time. Unlike area charts, line charts emphasize the rate of change over time rather than the magnitude of the change itself. The most commonly recognized use of the line chart is to illustrate sales that shoot through the ceiling, a stock market that has plunged through the floor, or the high-low-close-open statistics for an investment. Figure 10.4 shows the eight types of charts available in the line chart gallery.

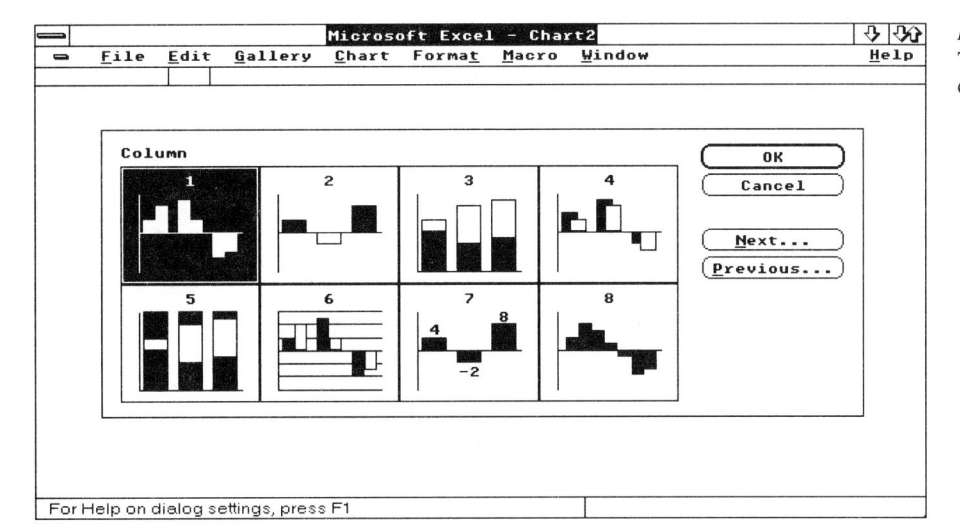

Fig. 10.3.
The column chart gallery.

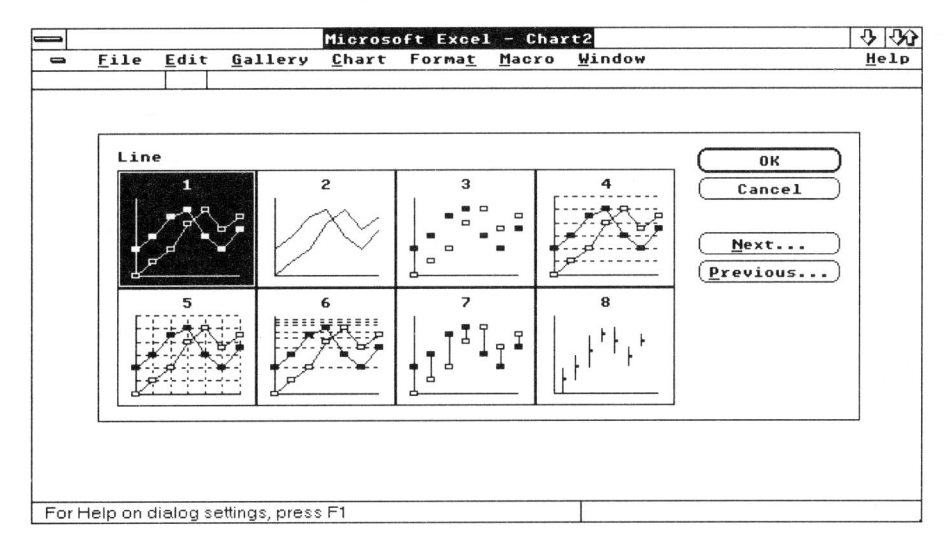

Fig. 10.4.
The line chart gallery.

Pie Charts

Pie charts undoubtedly are the most easily recognized type of chart graphic. Pie charts are used to illustrate and compare the relative sizes of the parts that make up a whole entity (such as a budget or a population). You can use a pie chart, for example, to illustrate the composition of total labor expenses by assigning one pie slice to each labor category. Because each slice represents an individual percentage (*x* percent) of the whole (100 percent), you can use the chart to compare the sizes of the whole's components. Excel pie charts can be *exploded*, meaning that you can cause one, several, or all of the slices to appear slightly pulled away from the pie. Figure 10.5 shows the six types of charts available in the pie chart gallery.

Fig. 10.5.
The pie chart gallery.

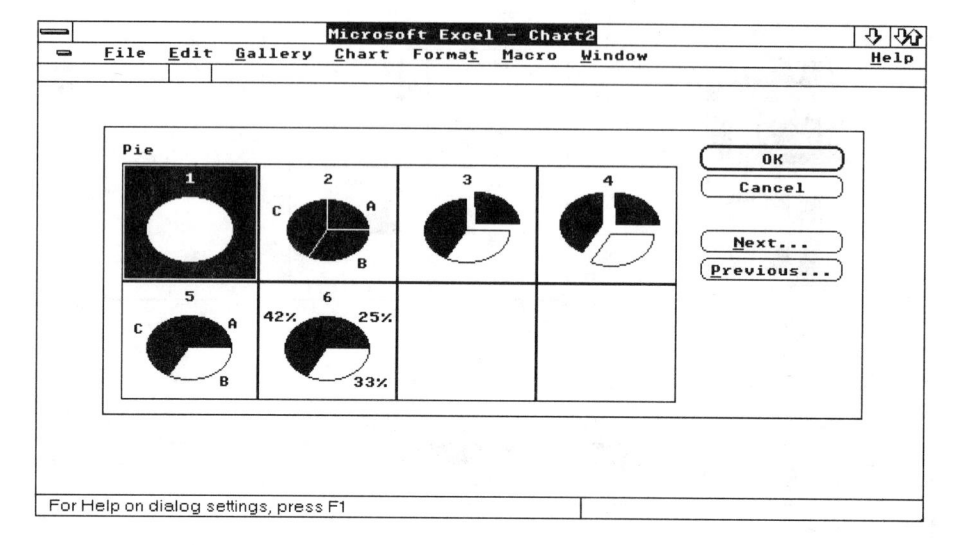

Scatter Charts

The *scatter chart* describes the relationship between two discrete variables, x and y. Scatter charts are commonly used in economics to illustrate correlations, for example, among heart disease and number of smokers per thousand people in 10 U.S. cities. Unlike line charts, scatter charts do not expose relationships over time. Figure 10.6 shows the five types of charts available in the scatter chart gallery.

Fig. 10.6.
The scatter chart gallery.

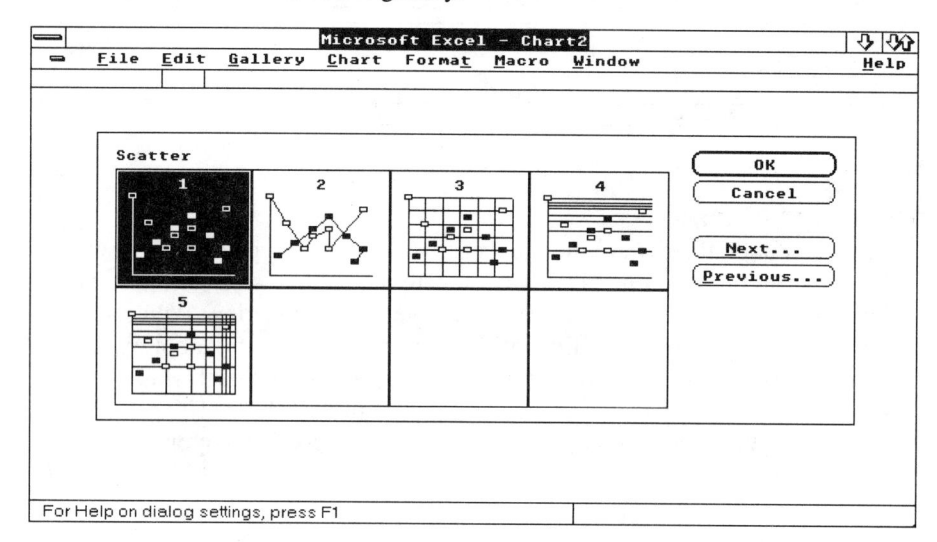

Combination Charts

Combination charts are exactly what they sound like: combinations of several types of charts. Combination charts enable you to illustrate and compare two variables over time, such as net profit margins and sales, while using separate scaling systems, such as dollars and percentages. A combination chart might use a line chart to represent sales and a column chart to depict net profit margin percentages. Or a combination chart might use an area chart to represent production volume and a column chart to show revenues. Figure 10.7 shows the five types of charts available in the combination gallery.

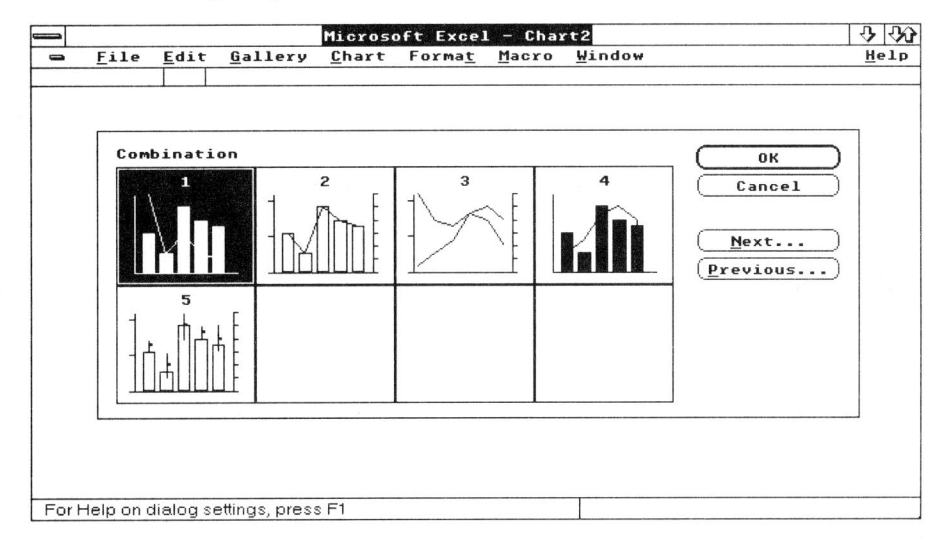

Fig. 10.7.
The combination chart gallery.

Now that you are familiar with the seven chart categories, you must learn why your numerical data's organization is so critical to the construction of a worthwhile chart.

Selecting and Organizing Your Numerical Data

It's a pleasure to watch Excel automatically create charts when you properly organize and select your worksheet data. Imagine highlighting numbers on a worksheet, selecting New Chart from the File menu, and then watching as Excel creates a perfect chart. You need only attach a legend and add axes and chart titles, and in minutes you have a presentation-quality report at your fingertips.

Once in a while, of course, Excel displays a graph that makes absolutely no sense, and this can be a headache. Nine times out of 10, however, this problem is easily corrected because it occurs for one of two reasons.

First, your selected numerical data may be organized in such a way that it does not lend itself well to Excel charts. In this case, you should either reorganize or summarize your worksheet data or create a graph data block.

Second, you may have tried to use a type of chart that is incompatible with the selected numerical data. You should not, for example, select a scatter chart to graph production volumes over a five-year period. If the chart category doesn't match the data, the illustration has no meaning. When this happens, select a chart style from a different chart category.

When you have problems creating a chart, you can usually resolve the dilemma by reselecting or reorganizing your numerical data. Figures 10.8 and 10.9 show the Fixed-Variable Expense worksheet from Chapter 1. These figures illustrate two different ways of grouping and charting the same data. Notice that both charts are believable (an important quality in a good chart!); the superior chart is simply the one that provides the greater visual impact.

Fig. 10.8.
A chart of fixed and variable expenses, showing expenses on the category axis.

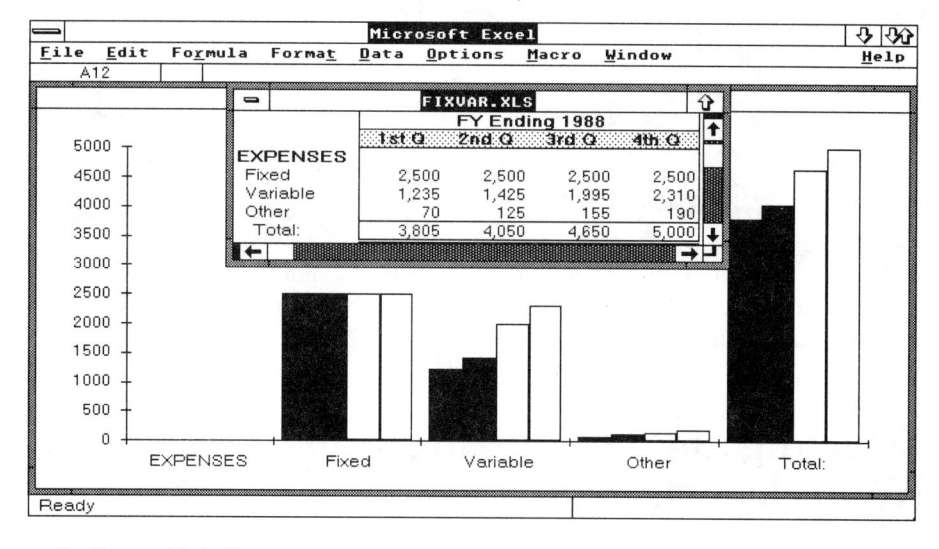

In figure 10.8, Excel groups the data points by expense category. This graph highlights the contribution that each expense category makes to total annual expenses. In figure 10.9, Excel groups the data points by quarter. This graph highlights the four expense categories' relationship on a quarterly basis.

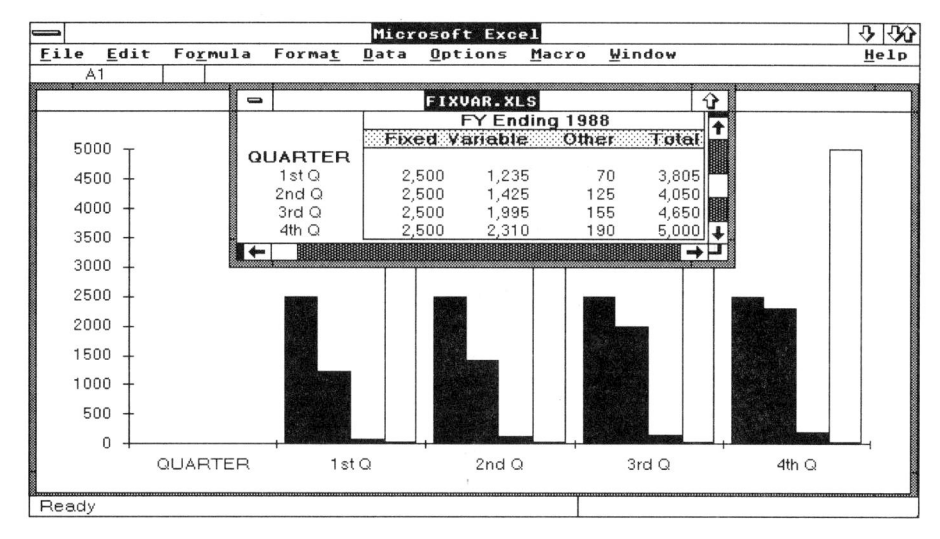

Fig. 10.9.
A chart of fixed and variable expenses, showing the yearly quarters on the category axis.

> **Tip:** When you group a worksheet and a chart in the same Excel window, the chart instantly reflects any change you make to the data in the selected range on the worksheet. To do this, select Arrange All from the Excel worksheet Window menu.

These two charts show that you can reorganize numerical data without affecting a chart's impact or meaning. In fact, reorganizing numerical data often helps you pinpoint the presentation with the most effective visual impact.

Proper data range selection is part of the process of organizing your numerical data. Once you understand how Excel evaluates a selected data range, you will always be able to create that best, most attractive look on the first try.

Understanding the Evolution of the Excel Chart

Figure 10.10 shows an example of a selected data range, B5:C9, and the data arranged in a bar chart. When you select a data range, you should find it helpful to know the basic process Excel follows in creating a new chart. This process is most easily understood as the following series of questions and answers, which you would ask yourself when you select a worksheet data range to chart:

Q: What is the data series?

A: The *data series* is the data that appears in the selected range. In figure 10.10, B5:C9 is the selected range; therefore, C5:C9 is the data series.

Q: What is the data series name?

A: When a chart contains more than one data series, Excel assigns a name to each series. Excel assigns the name by looking at the top of the data series range. The range used to define the category axis must be blank at the top cell. These names can appear in a legend box to help you visually match a data series with its name. The series name is coded with a specific color, pattern, or symbol. For example, in figure 10.10, "%" is the data series name because it describes the elements found in the data series, C5:C9.

Q: Which part of the selected data range becomes the value axis?

A: Excel displays the value-axis data (the percentage values that appear on the y-axis) according to the labels that appear along the short side of the selected data range. In figure 10.10, the short side is columns B:C, so Excel creates a value axis that includes percentage values ranging from 0.00 percent to 50.00 percent.

Q: Which part of the selected data range becomes the category axis?

A: Excel displays the category-axis names (the letters that appear under the x-axis) according to the labels that appear along the long side of the selected data range. In figure 10.10, the long side is rows 5:9, so Excel creates a category axis using the letters A through E from cells B5:B9 in the selected data range.

Fig. 10.10.
An example of a selected data range and its accompanying chart.

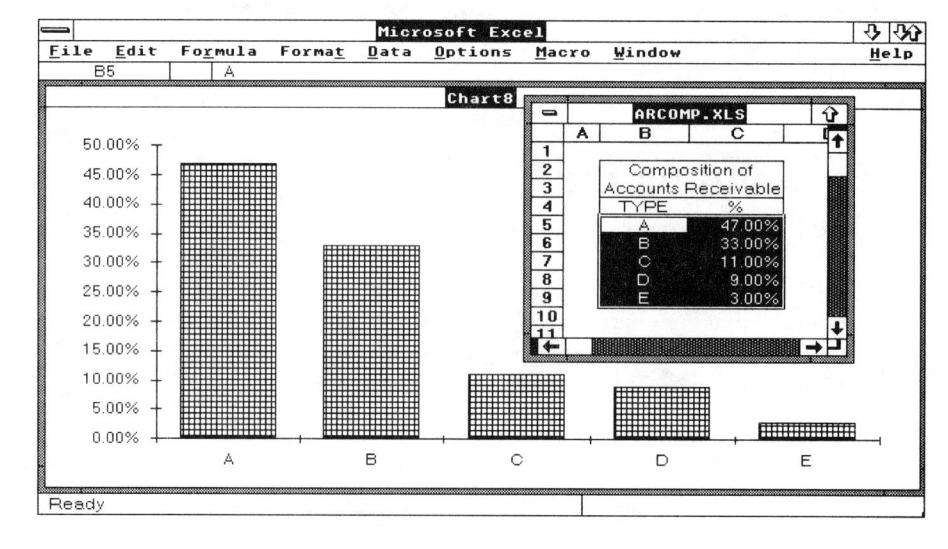

The range B5:C9 is an example of a *continuous data range* selection. If you are new to Excel chart-making, stick to charts that use this type of data range selection. Why? If you select *noncontinuous data ranges*, such as the one pictured in figure 10.11, you can cause problems for yourself. As shown, the data points in a noncontinuous data series can appear detached, leaving gaping holes along your chart's x-axis.

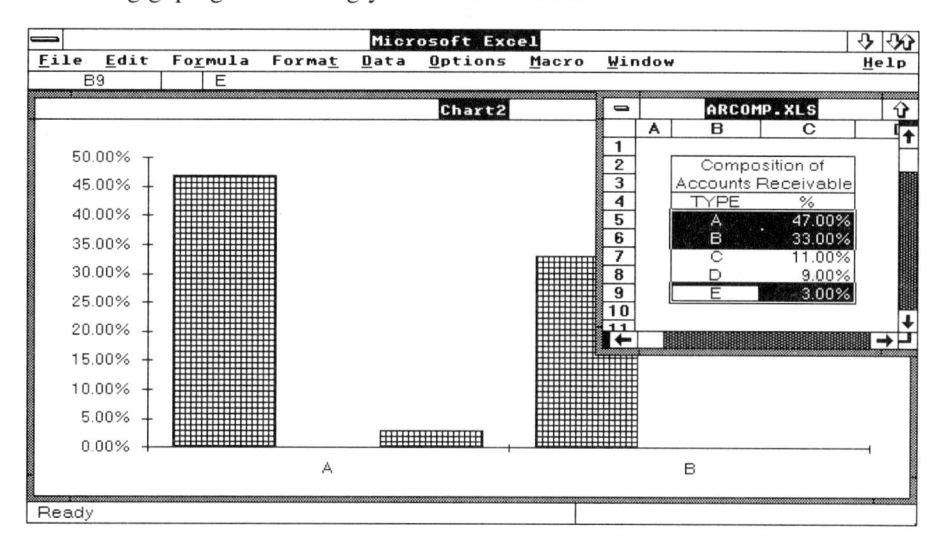

Fig. 10.11. Noncontinuous data range selections can cause chart-creation problems.

When you are comfortable with continuous data range selection, try creating charts by making noncontinuous data range selections. If you make your selections properly, you will be able to design more specialized and creative charts, as described in greater detail later in this chapter.

Graph data blocks, used in the models in Chapter 5, provide another useful means of creating Excel charts. You can use these special tables to reorganize the data in the active worksheet. Figure 10.12 shows a typical graph data block. This block summarizes key data from various parts of the active worksheet and organizes the data into adjacent rows and columns.

> Tip: A graph data block is made up of cell-referencing formulas, such as "=C5" or "=A22". These formulas call data from other parts of the active worksheet. When you create a graph data block, use the Paste Special command, which enables you to transpose data ranges.

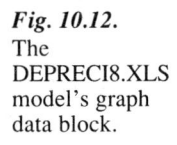

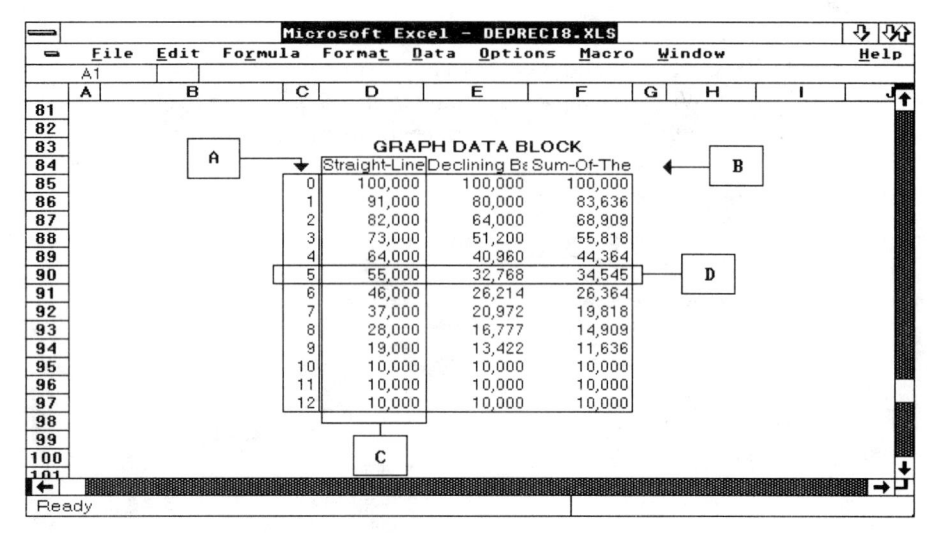

Fig. 10.12.
The DEPRECI8.XLS model's graph data block.

	A	B	C	D	E	F
83				GRAPH DATA BLOCK		
84				Straight-Line	Declining Ba	Sum-Of-The
85			0	100,000	100,000	100,000
86			1	91,000	80,000	83,636
87			2	82,000	64,000	68,909
88			3	73,000	51,200	55,818
89			4	64,000	40,960	44,364
90			5	55,000	32,768	34,545
91			6	46,000	26,214	26,364
92			7	37,000	20,972	19,818
93			8	28,000	16,777	14,909
94			9	19,000	13,422	11,636
95			10	10,000	10,000	10,000
96			11	10,000	10,000	10,000
97			12	10,000	10,000	10,000

When data appears in adjacent rows and columns, you can easily select a continuous data range. Now, simply select the range C84:F97, and Excel automatically creates a perfect chart for you.

The graph data block shown in figure 10.12 contains four major sections. Area A tells Excel how to define the category axis names. Here, the numbers 0 through 12 represent "years." Area B tells Excel how to define the data series names that appear in the legend box. The graph data contains three depreciation methods, so Excel uses three different legend patterns to differentiate the methods. The numbers appearing in Area C define the first of three data series. The numbers appearing in Area D define one of the 13 data points.

When should you reorganize worksheet data, build a graph data block, or select noncontinuous data ranges? Consider the merits and inconveniences of each of these options.

If you do not mind reorganizing your worksheet into continuous data blocks, go ahead and do it. This choice is the most practical one because it will teach you how to organize your data properly in future worksheets. Unfortunately, choosing this option also means that you must do your work twice.

If, however, you have designed a complex model such as DEPRECI8.XLS and you simply do not want to tackle the task of recreating complicated formula relationships, you should create a graph data block. This method requires you to spend some extra time creating cell-referencing formulas.

These formulas, which appear in the graph data block, exist to call and reorganize data from around the active worksheet. Once you create the formulas in the data block, though, the formulas will already exist, ready for the next time you create a chart.

If neither solution seems practical, you must learn how to create an Excel chart by using noncontinuous data range selections. If you like, skip ahead to the section "Building Charts from Noncontinuous Ranges," where this topic is covered.

Using Existing Models To Create Fully Formatted Charts

As promised, this section shows you how to create fully formatted report-quality charts by using *Excel Business Applications: IBM Version* models. In most cases, you will be able to create charts directly from data appearing in the models. In other cases, you may have to use an existing—or create a new—graph data block. In either case, this section offers a comprehensive survey of all of Excel's chart-formatting tools. Have fun.

Reviewing the Basics of Chart-Making

Figure 10.13 shows that constructing an Excel chart is as easy as highlighting the data range B7:H7 and selecting New Chart from the File menu. This chart uses the worksheet model INCBALRA.XLS from Chapter 2. This model appears in the next few figures and contains sample data for the first six months of fiscal year 1989.

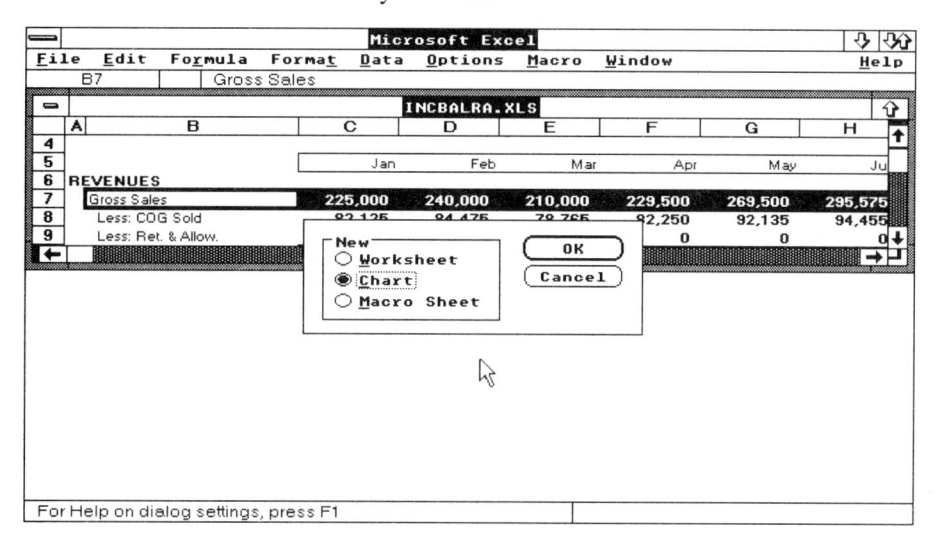

Fig. 10.13. Opening a new chart file.

Figure 10.14 shows a basic column chart that was automatically created by Excel. The chart contains scaled x- and y-axis labels and a chart title.

Fig. 10.14.
A basic column chart, automatically created by Excel.

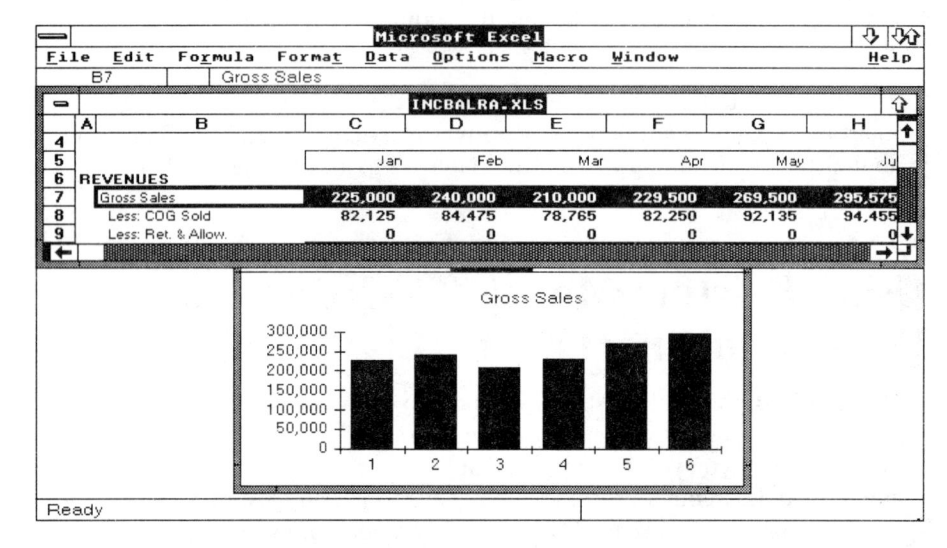

> Tip: When you chart a single data series, Excel uses text appearing at the short end of the specified data range as the chart title. In figure 10.14, Excel selected "Gross Sales" in cell B7 as the chart title.

Excel graphed this data as a column chart because Column was checked as the preferred setting on the Gallery menu. If you want to change the preferred setting, click-select another type of chart from the Gallery menu and then click-select Set Preferred. Afterward, Excel uses the new preferred chart setting whenever it automatically creates a new chart.

Figure 10.14 shows a chart of the worksheet data range B7:H7. The quickest way to add a second data range to such a chart is to use the Edit menu's Copy and Paste commands.

To expand the chart, specify the second data range on the active worksheet. Next, select Copy from the Edit menu and activate the chart. Click your mouse once anywhere on the chart to select the entire chart area. From the Edit menu, select Paste.

(You can always discard the first chart, specify a new data range, and select New Chart from the File menu. This method achieves the same result but takes too much time.)

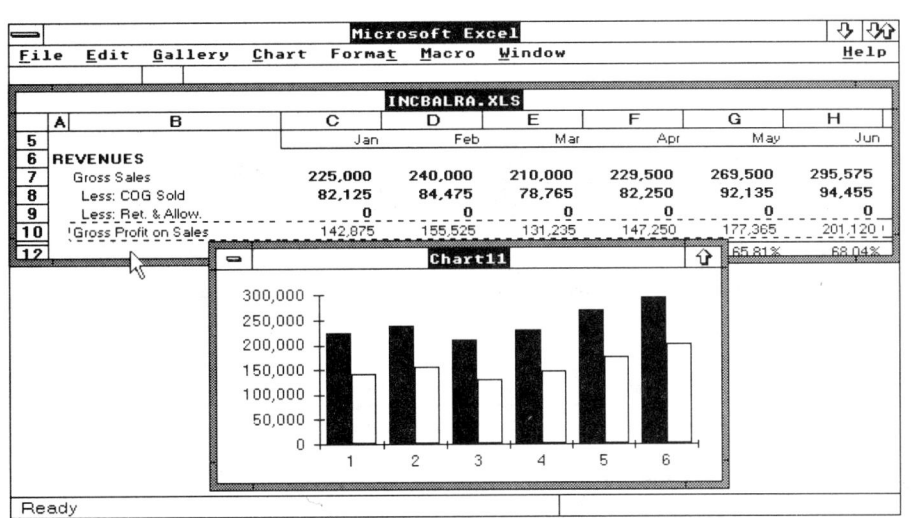

Figure 10.15 shows the result of copying the data range B10:H10 to the chart in figure 10.14.

Fig. 10.15. Using the Copy and Paste commands to add a second data range to an existing chart.

At this point, you may wonder why you must learn to select noncontinuous data ranges, when you can simply copy and paste new data to a chart as you go.

Both methods work, of course, but depending on the circumstances, one method can be more practical than the other. When you need to add one or two extra data ranges to a chart, go ahead and use the Copy and Paste commands. But if Excel must automatically create a chart that depends on three or more noncontinuous data ranges, you will find it quicker and easier to select the multiple ranges before making a new chart (see the section "Building Charts from Noncontinuous Ranges").

Once Excel has created the basic chart, you will no doubt want to enhance the chart's clarity and impact. Figure 10.16 shows a fully formatted version of the chart from figure 10.15.

The chart display in figure 10.16 was created with the help of commands from the Chart and Format menus. To create this chart, take the following steps:

Step 1. Create the chart shown in figure 10.15.

Step 2. Select Chart Attach Text Chart Title and click OK. Type **Gross Sales vs. Gross Profits** and press Enter.

Step 3. Select Format Font, choose Helv-12-Bold, and click OK.

Fig. 10.16.
A fully formatted chart based on income-statement data from INCBALRA.XLS.

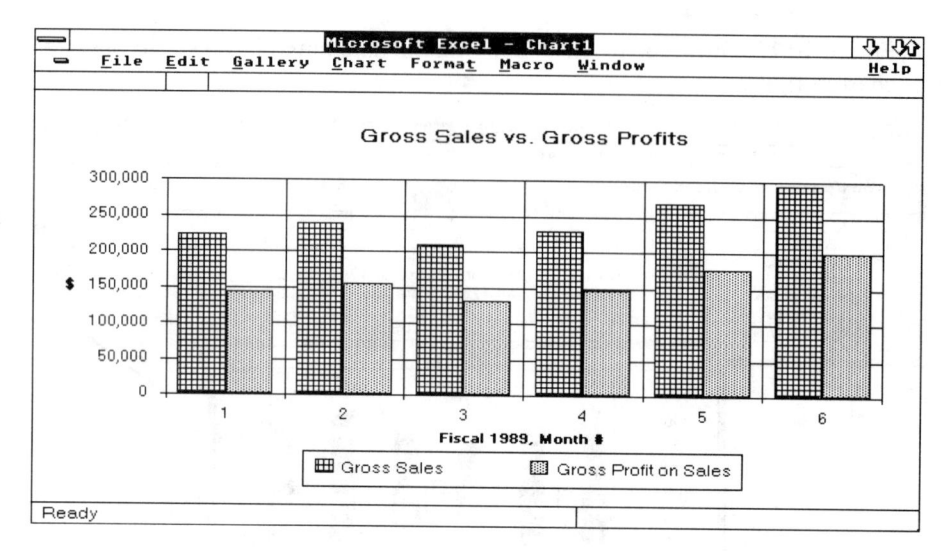

Step 4. Select Chart Attach Text Value Axis and click OK. Type **$** and press Enter.

Step 5. Select Format Font, choose Helv-8-Bold, and click OK.

Step 6. Select Chart Attach Text Category Axis and click OK. Type **Fiscal 1989, Month #** and press Enter.

Step 7. Select Format Font, choose Helv-8-Bold, and click OK.

Step 8. Select Chart Add Legend. Place your cursor inside the legend box and click once.

Step 9. Select Format Legend Bottom and click OK.

Step 10. Select Chart Gridlines. Check Major Gridlines for the Category and Value Axis and click OK.

Step 11. Select the first data series on the chart (Gross Sales) by clicking inside one of the columns. Choose Format Patterns and select the matching design from the Patterns box.

Step 12. Repeat Step 7 for the second data series (Gross Profits).

The Chart and Format menu commands used here are the most commonly used chart-formatting tools. Still, you can enhance your chart in many other ways.

This book's worksheet models give you an opportunity to experiment with just about every style of Excel chart. Some models analyze more than one type of financial data, which means that you can even create two or three charts for a single model. For example, the data from the ratio-analysis report (in INCBALRA.XLS) is perfect for a line chart. Figure 10.17 pictures one way to chart this data. You can duplicate most of the preceding 12 steps to create this chart.

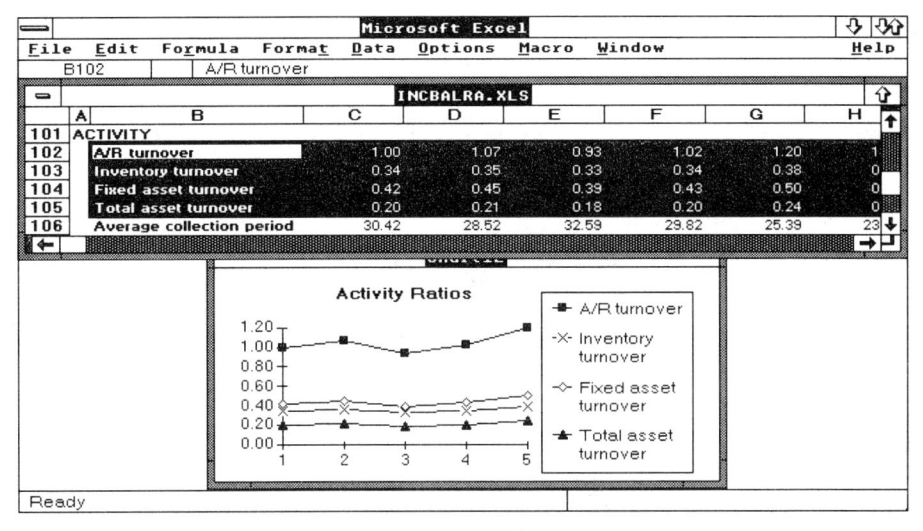

Fig. 10.17.
A fully formatted chart of the ratio-analysis data from INCBALRA.XLS.

You can use many of the same chart commands to format different styles of charts. With a few exceptions, all Excel charts should have a main title, axis titles, and a legend. But because each Excel chart style is unique in some way, you will always need to perform an extra formatting step or two to achieve the desired finished look.

When you created the chart shown in figure 10.16, for example, you selected special patterns for each data series. Notice that in figure 10.17 each of the four data series has a distinct series marker rather than a hatch pattern. A *series marker* helps distinguish one line from another on a chart. To edit a series marker, select the first data series in the chart, which in this case is A/R turnover. Next, select Format Patterns, pick the matching marker style from the Patterns box, and select matching foreground and background colors. Repeat these steps for each of the remaining three markers used in the chart.

This concludes the review of basic chart-making. Now look at some finished, formatted charts that you can create quickly and easily, using the models found in this book.

Using Models To Create Charts

Figures 10.18 through 10.21 show the different types of charts you can create by using data from the models in Chapter 3, 4, and 6. This chapter's final section enlists some of the charts already created for the Chapter 5 models to demonstrate special chart modification and enhancement techniques.

The chart in figure 10.18 graphs the data in cells D8:I7 and I8:I17 of CHKSUMMR.XLS, the checkbook accounting summary model from Chapter 3.

Fig. 10.18.
A pie chart showing a percentage breakdown of expenses from CHKSUMMR.XLS.

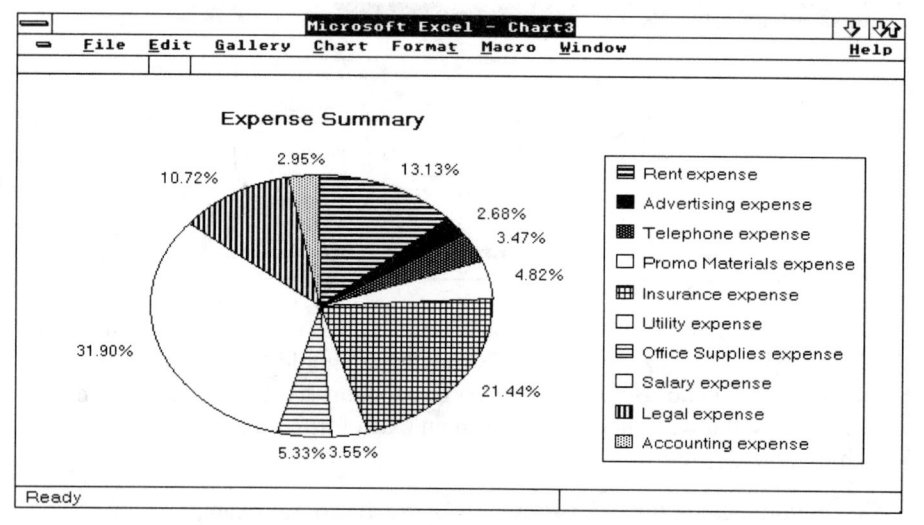

> Tip: To create this chart, specify the first data range, select New Chart from the File menu, and then use the Copy and Paste commands to place the second data range in the chart.

The chart pictured in figure 10.19 graphs the data in cells E34:P36 of CASHBUDG.XLS, the cash budget forecasting model from Chapter 4.

> Tip: To add text to this chart's legend, you need to edit the data series formulas for each legend box marker (this technique is demonstrated in the last section of the chapter).

The chart pictured in figure 10.20 graphs data in the range J5:K20 from BREAKEVN.XLS, the production breakeven analysis model from Chapter 4.

Creating Business-Presentation Charts **299**

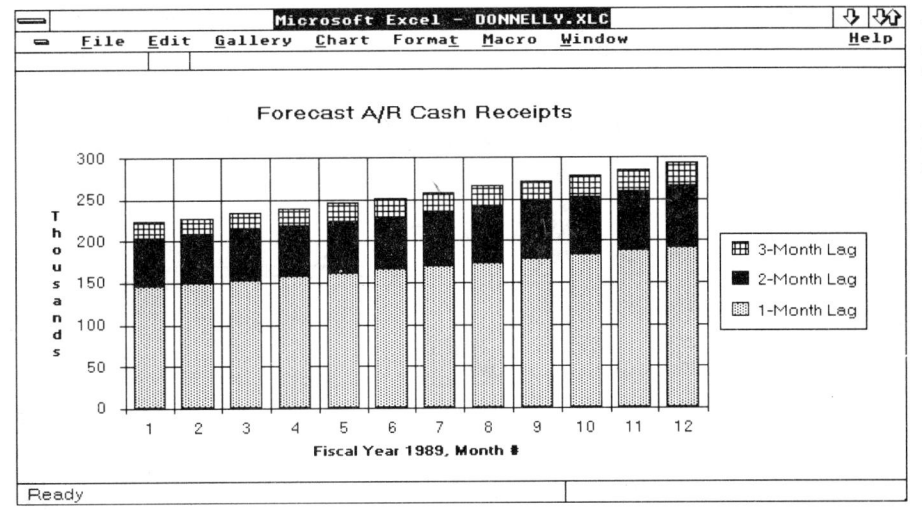

Fig. 10.19.
A stacked column chart showing lagged A/R cash receipts from CASHBUDG.XLS.

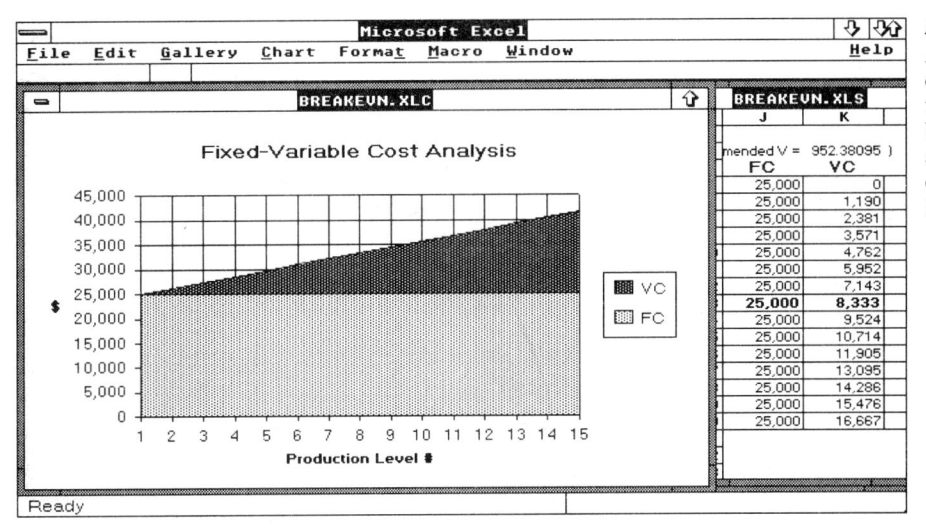

Fig. 10.20.
A stacked area chart showing the relationship between fixed and variable costs from BREAKEVN.XLS.

Tip: An area chart presents data in a special way. Because data appears stacked in an area chart, cumulative values are easily identifiable. The chart in figure 10.20, for example, illustrates data on variable costs (VC) and fixed costs (FC). Even though the chart does not include total costs, you can track the increase in total costs by tracing the upper line of the variable-cost triangle.

The chart pictured in figure 10.21 graphs the data in cells B19:D25 and F19:F25 of TMP.XLS, the general ledger accounting system (GLAS) model from Chapter 6.

Fig. 10.21.
A bar chart showing budget variance for TMP.XLS.

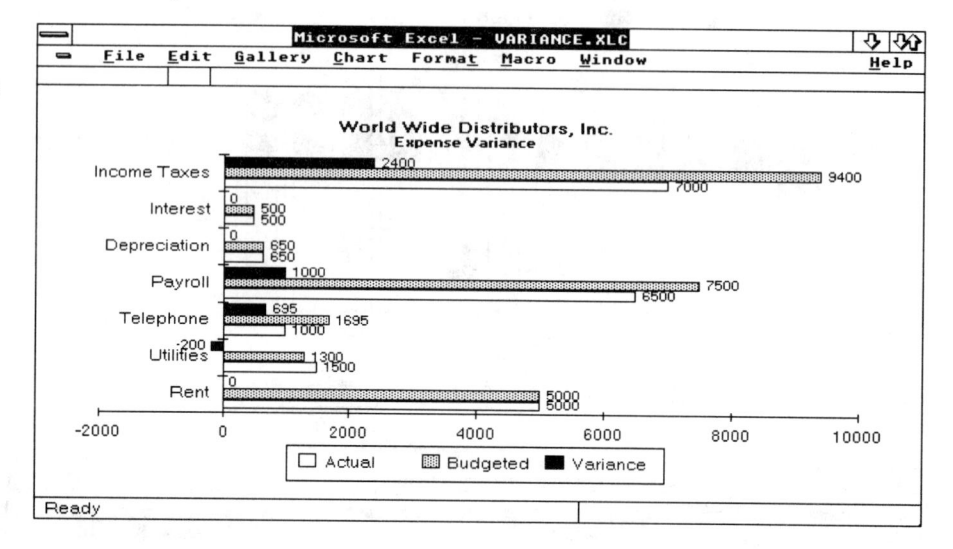

Chapter 6 introduced report macros that use the file TMP.XLS as a temporary repository for the data in the printed reports. After Excel prints a report, the program clears and closes TMP.XLS, discarding the report data. If you want to use the report data to create charts, you must modify cell A628 in the Close_TMP.XLS_Sub_Routine found in the worksheet GL.XLM. To modify cell A628, take the following steps:

Step 1. Activate GL.XLM and scroll to cell A628. This cell contains the command =CLOSE(FALSE).

Step 2. Choose Unprotect Document from the Options menu.

Step 3. Press F2 to edit the entry, and press the Home key to move the cursor to the beginning of the edit line.

Step 4. Type two periods (..) and press Enter.

These steps deactivate the macro subroutine that automatically clears and closes TMP.XLS. Afterward, when you run a report macro, Excel leaves the report data and report format in the TMP.XLS file. You may now create charts based on the data in this file.

When you are finished, be sure to reactivate the macro subroutine by removing the two periods (..) from cell A628.

> Tip: If you are going to create charts that draw data from more than one GLAS report, you must manually close TMP.XLS—without saving any changes—before you run a second report.

Printing Excel Charts

You print an Excel chart in much the same way that you print a worksheet. The main difference between the two is that when you select Page Setup while on a chart, the dialog box is slightly different (see fig. 10.22).

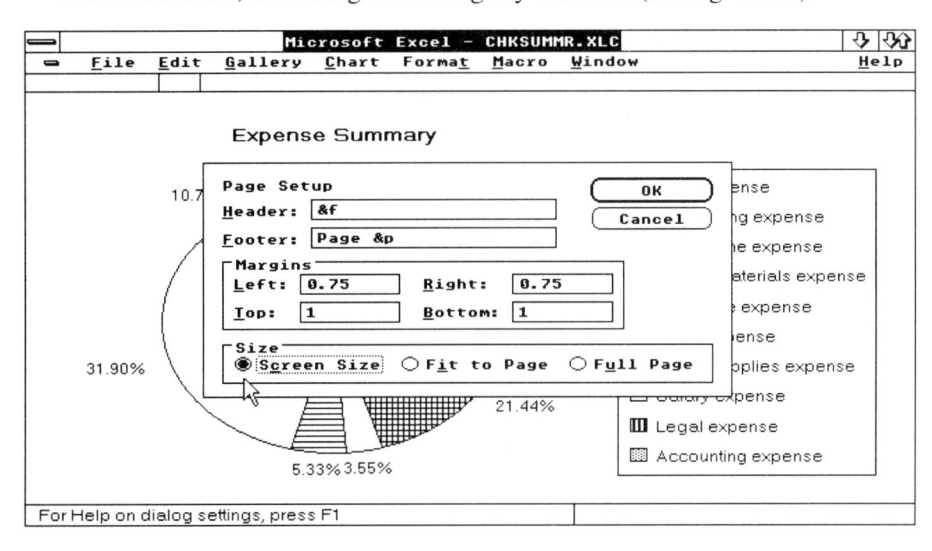

Fig. 10.22. The Page Setup command's dialog box.

Notice that you can specify headers, footers, and margins for your chart, just as you can with a worksheet. Further, you can control the chart's printed size by selecting one of the following options from the Size box:

Option	Description
Screen Size	Prints your chart the same size as it appears on your screen.
Fit to Page	Prints your chart to fit the page, while maintaining the chart's width-to-height relationship.
Full Page	Prints your chart as large as possible for the page.

> Tip: The term *page*, as used in the Page Setup Size options, is defined in your Printer Setup configuration. To change the default page size, select Printer Setup from the File menu and edit the page width and height.

Because Excel provides such flexibility in printing charts, you can conceivably print a chart within a page of text or on a worksheet printout. Use the Print command's Preview option to experiment with each of the three Size definitions. With practice, you'll discover how easy it is to include Excel charts in your printed reports—without ever having to cut and paste.

The preceding figures illustrate some of the charts you can create by using data from the model worksheets. Use these sample charts as a starting point for envisioning and creating your own Excel charts.

Enhancing and Modifying Charts

A chart is effective only if it conveys a message clearly. Whenever you design a chart, remember what you are trying to emphasize. A chart filled with numbers and graphics is useless unless your intended audience spots a trend, identifies a problem area, or confirms a management decision. Fortunately, Excel can help you fine-tune your charts until you achieve the exact desired graphic impact.

Figure 10.23 shows a yield-to-maturity chart you can create from the BONDS.XLS model in Chapter 5. By adding an arrow and a message, you make sure that the viewer quickly finds the chart's most important elements. Without these extra graphics, the chart is just another pretty figure.

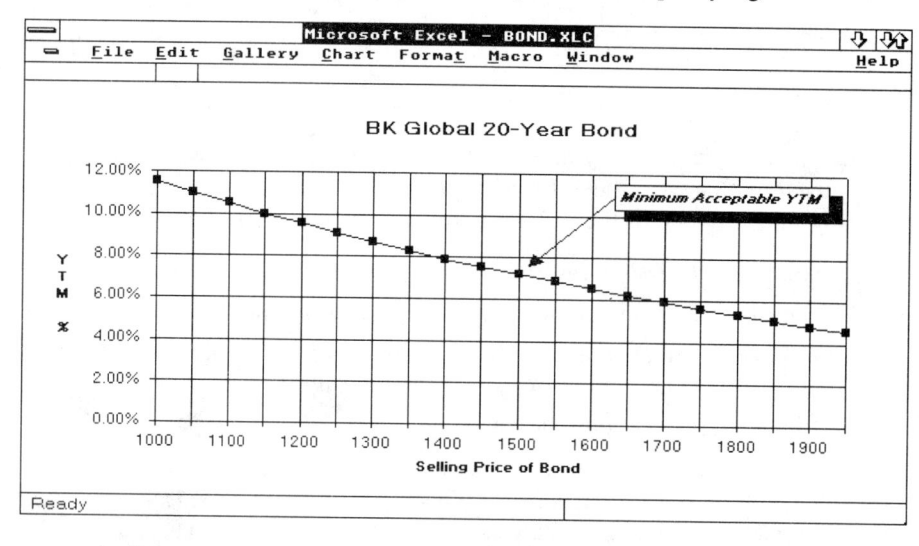

Fig. 10.23.
A yield-to-maturity chart that includes an arrow and a message.

To add an arrow to a chart, take the following steps:

Step 1. Select Chart Add Arrow.

Step 2. To relocate, enlarge, or reduce the arrow, drag the black squares appearing at either end of the arrow, as shown in figure 10.24.

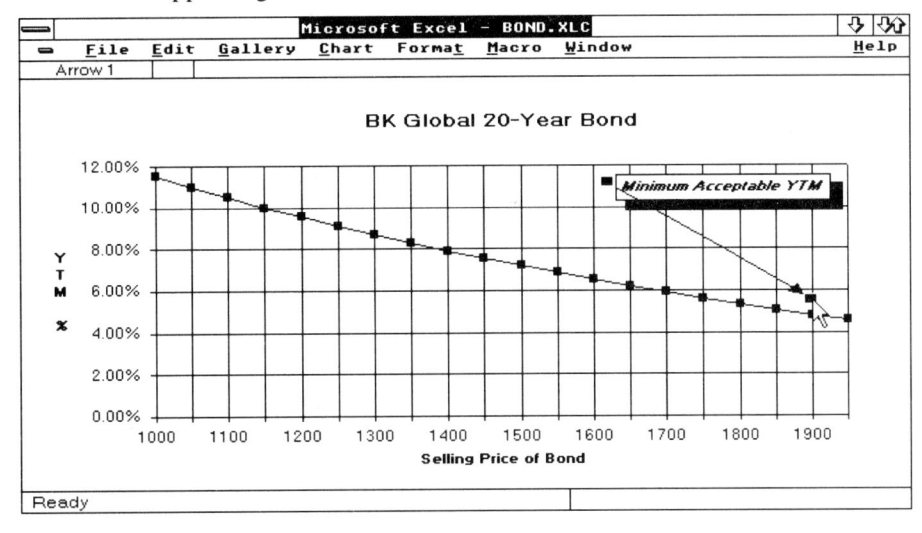

Fig. 10.24. Moving an arrow by dragging the black square at the tip of the arrow.

Step 3. Press Enter when the arrow is complete.

As indicated in figure 10.23, Excel enables you to add extra descriptions to your charts—descriptions beyond axis labels and a chart title. Such text is called "unattached" text. To add unattached text to the chart, follow these steps:

Step 1. Select the chart title. Excel surrounds the specified title with white squares.

Step 2. Press the down-arrow key once.

Step 3. Type the message text and press Enter.

Step 4. To position the message text in the chart, click inside the message text box, as shown in figure 10.25. Drag it to the desired area on the chart and press Enter.

Figure 10.26 shows the Analysis of Depreciation Methods chart you can create from the DEPRECI8.XLS model in Chapter 5. By shading and shadowing the legend box, you emphasize the three depreciation methods. This underscoring draws the legend to the reader's attention, clearly defining this chart's most important element.

Fig. 10.25.
Positioning the message text on a chart.

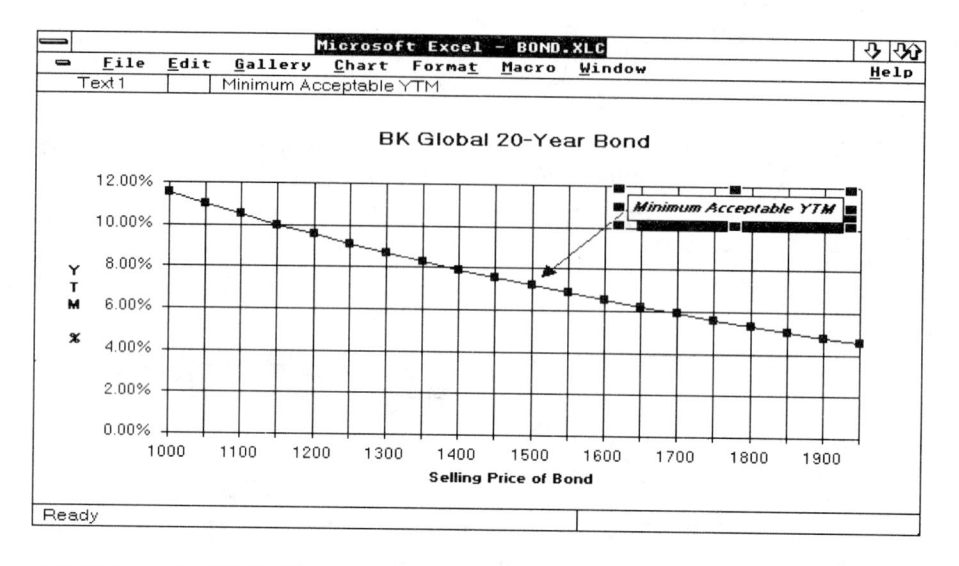

Fig. 10.26.
Enhancing a chart legend through shading and shadowing.

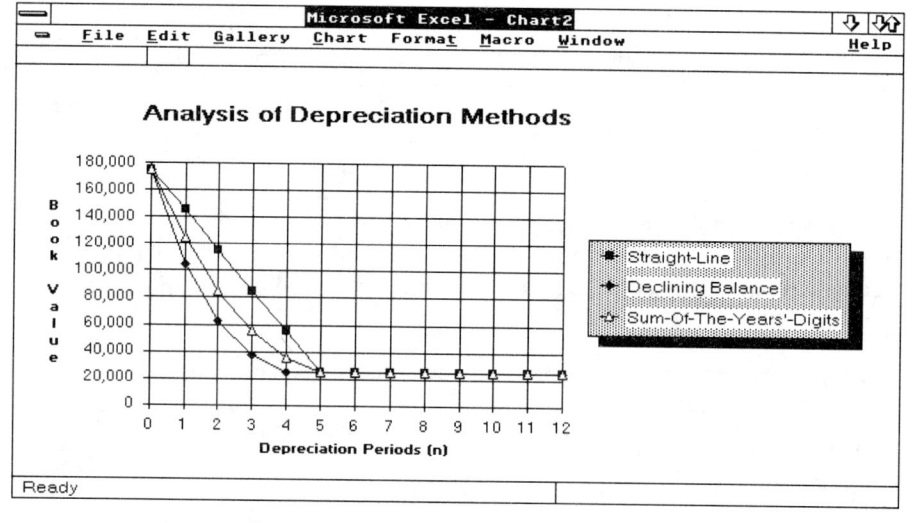

If you want to emphasize a chart legend through shading and shadowing, take the following steps:

Step 1. Click anywhere inside the legend box to select it.

Step 2. Select Legend from the Format menu and click-select Vertical, as shown in figure 10.27.

Step 3. Click the Patterns button to proceed to the Patterns dialog box.

Step 4. Click-select a pattern from the Pattern box.

Step 5. Click-select background and foreground colors.

Step 6. Click-select Shadow and press Return (see fig. 10.28).

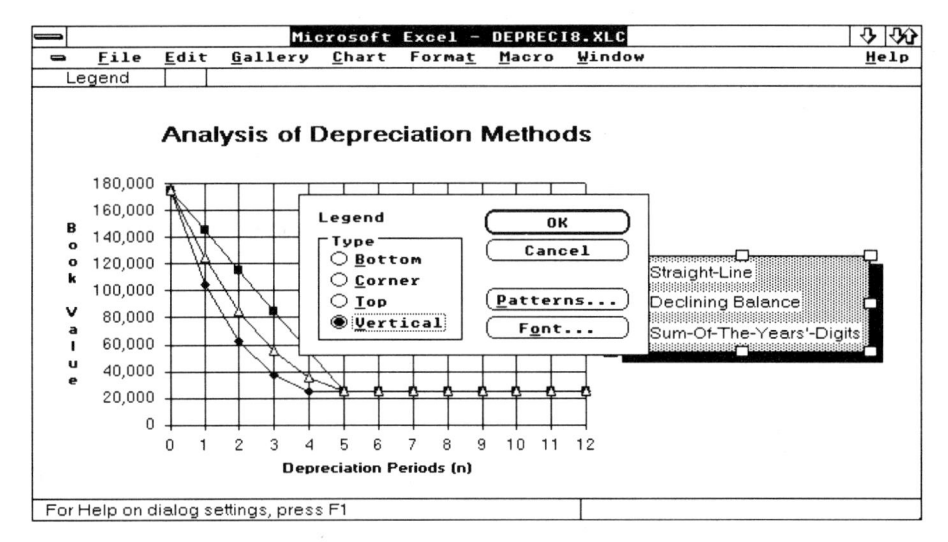

Fig. 10.27.
Positioning the legend on the chart by using the Format Legend command.

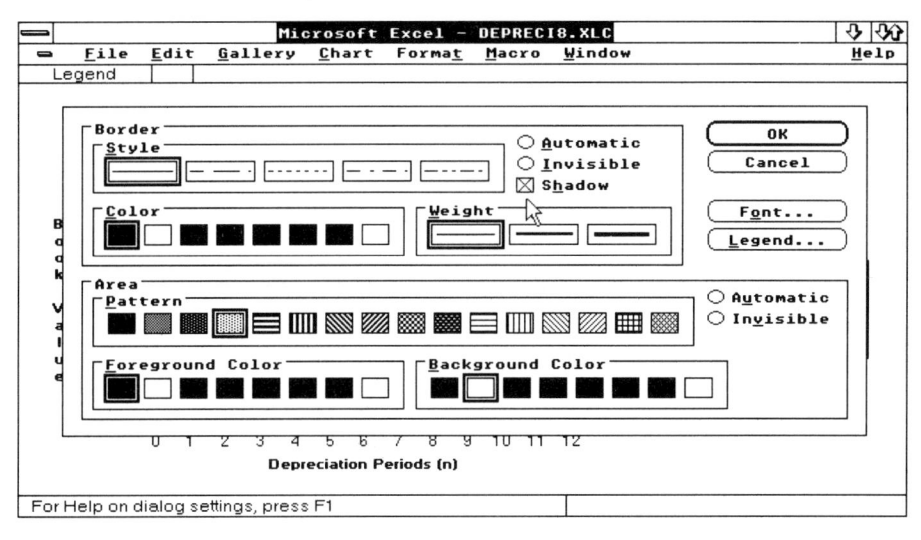

Fig. 10.28.
Selecting colors, patterns, and shading with the Format Patterns commands.

Building Charts from Noncontinuous Ranges

The following text demonstrates the proper selection and charting of data from noncontinuous ranges. The worksheet in the top half of figure 10.29 is part of the DUPONT.XLS model in Chapter 5. Using this model, Excel can automatically create a basic version of the combination chart shown in the lower half of the figure.

Fig. 10.29.
Selecting a noncontinuous data range to create a combination chart.

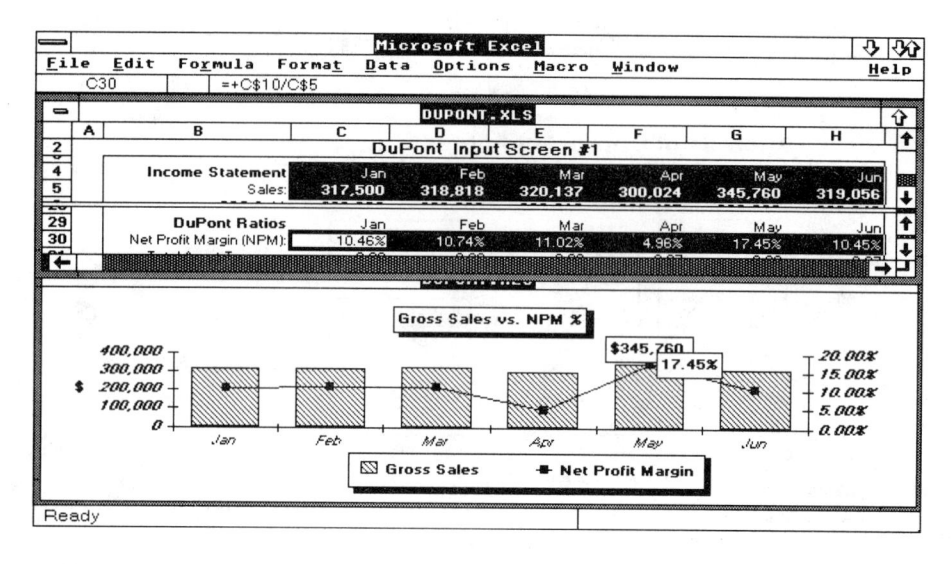

To create the chart shown in figure 10.29, follow these steps:

Step 1. Select C4:H5 as the first data range. While pressing the Ctrl key, select C30:H30 as the second data range.

Step 2. Select New Chart from the File menu.

Step 3. Select chart 2 from the Gallery Combination box and click OK.

Step 4. Select Add Legend from the Chart menu.

Step 5. Select Legend Bottom from the Format menu.

Step 6. To add text to the first label marker in the legend box, click-select the column in the first data series (the Jan column).

The following formula appears on the formula bar:

=SERIES(,DUPONT.XLS!$C$4:$H$4, DUPONT.XLS!$C$5:$H$5,1)

Press F2 and edit this formula so that it reads as follows:

=SERIES("Gross Sales",DUPONT.XLS!$C$4:$H$4, DUPONT.XLS!$C$5:$H$5,1)

Step 7. To add text to the second label marker in the legend box, click-select the small box marker in the first data series (inside the Jan column).

The following formula appears in the formula bar:

=SERIES(,DUPONT.XLS!$C$4:$H$4, DUPONT.XLS!$C$30:$H$30,2)

Press F2 and edit this formula so that it reads as follows:

=SERIES("Net Profit Margin",DUPONT.XLS!$C$4:$H$4, DUPONT.XLS!$C$30:$H$30,1)

Step 8. Click-select the first y-axis. Select Helv-8-Bold-Italics from the Format menu.

Step 9. Click-select the second y-axis. Select Helv-8-Bold-Italics from the Format menu.

Step 10. Click-select the x-axis. Select Helv-8-Italics from the Format menu.

Step 11. To add text to the first data series, click-select the fifth column in the series (the May column).

Step 12. Select Chart Attach Text. Click the Series or Data Point button in the dialog box. The Series Number is 1 and the Point Number is 5.

Step 13. To add text to the second data series, click-select the fifth box marker in the series (on the line at the top of the May column). Click OK.

Step 14. Select Chart Attach Text. Click the Series or Data Point button in the dialog box. The Series Number is 2 and the Point Number is 5. Click OK.

Step 15. To place a border around the text, click-select the first number. Select Format Patterns and click the desired color.

Now you can use your chart-enhancement experience to shadow the title and legend, boldface the remaining items, and choose a pattern for the column series.

Many of Excel's formatting tools were used to enhance the chart in figure 10.29. As a result, the chart achieves the desired impact—that is, it emphasizes the month with the top sales and net profit margin performance.

Figure 10.30 shows the original version of the Future Value Investment Analysis chart that you created from the FV.XLS model in Chapter 5. Figure 10.31 shows a modified version of the same chart. This second figure introduces four techniques you can use to improve the look of your charts.

The original chart produced from the FV.XLS model in Chapter 5 was too basic to leave a lasting impression. To enhance the chart, simply perform the following steps:

Step 1. Create the basic chart from the FV.XLS model.

Step 2. Choose Gallery Area and select option 1.

Fig. 10.30.
The original
FV.XLS chart.

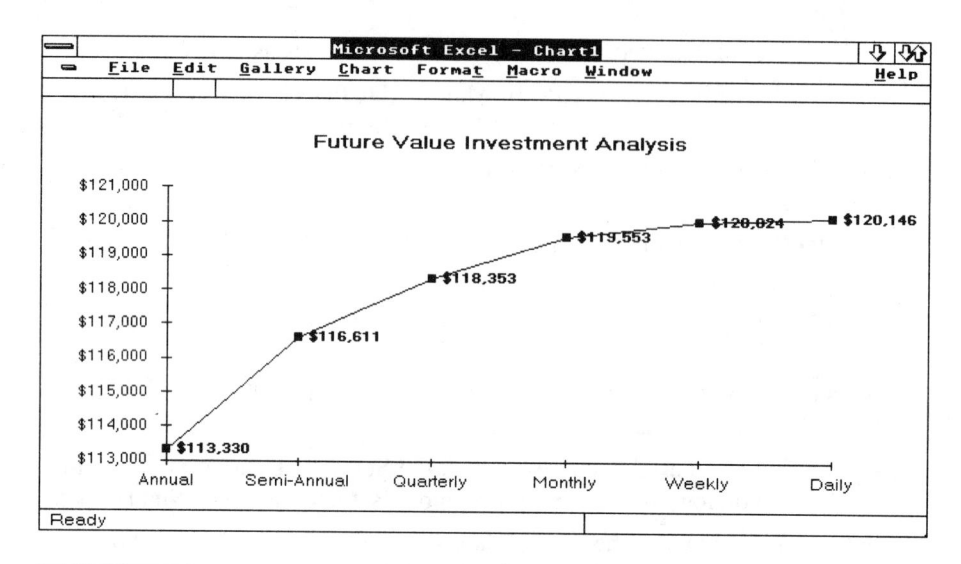

Fig. 10.31.
Modifying and
enhancing a line
chart.

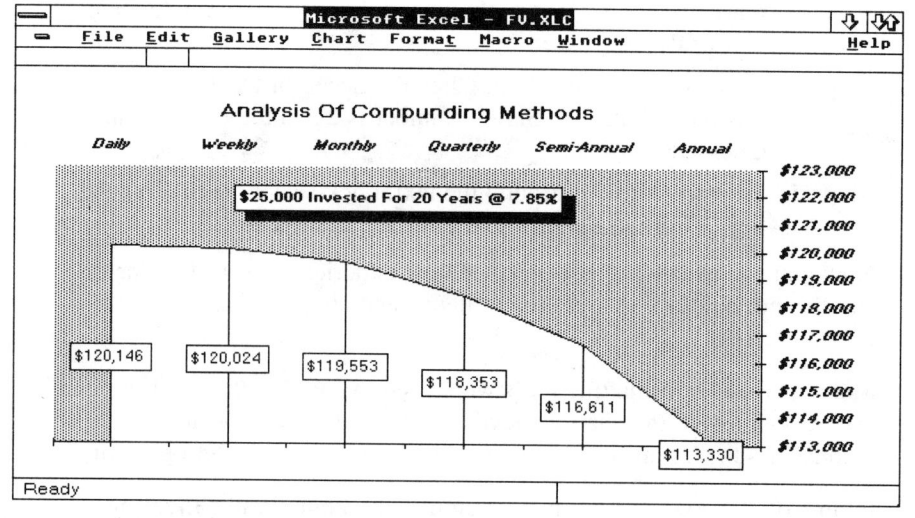

Step 3. Select the x-axis by clicking your mouse anywhere on the axis.

Step 4. Select Format Scale. Click the Value Axis Crosses Between Categories box.

Step 5. Now click the Categories in Reverse Order box.

Step 6. Choose Format Patterns and click the High button in the Tick Labels box. This selection relocates the x-axis labels to the top of the plot area.

Step 7. Select the y-axis. Select Format Scale and enter **113000** for the minimum value; then enter **123000** for the maximum value.

Step 8. Select Format Main Chart. Check the Drop Lines box.

Step 9. Choose Chart Select Plot Area.

Step 10. Select Format Patterns and pick a background pattern for the plot area.

Step 11. Click inside the area containing the drop lines. Select Format Patterns and pick a background pattern and color for this area.

Step 12. Use whatever formatting tools you like to complete the chart.

The chart in figure 10.31 is extremely effective for several reasons.

First, this area chart conveys a strong impression of the fact that you earn more money when there are more compounding periods per year. As an illustration of this fact, the area underneath the line grows larger the more often money is compounded.

Second, two purposes are served when the x-axis tick labels are moved to the top of the chart. The labels now act as a minor title, reinforcing the chart's main title. Further, notice that when you add text to each data series, the Annual method's text ($113,330) appears in the exact spot where the tick mark label (Annual) would normally appear.

Third, the unattached text confirms that when you invest $25,000 for 20 years at 7.85%, your money can grow to anywhere from $113,300 to $120,146, depending on which compounding method is employed.

Adding Enhancements to Graph Data Blocks

Figure 10.32 illustrates an enhanced version of the graph data block found in the RSK&RTN.XLS model from Chapter 5.

A previous definition described a graph data block as a series of cell-referencing formulas. By organizing these formulas in adjacent rows and columns, you can easily select the data when you want Excel to create a new chart.

Notice, however, that the graph data block in figure 10.32 is slightly different from the one shown in figure 10.12. Cells E46:F47 contain two pairs of known x and y coordinates. The paired values (0.00,7.00) are the x,y coordinates of the risk-free portfolio, and the paired values (1.00,11.00) are the x,y coordinates of the market portfolio. As you know, a line is always formed when you connect two points on the same plane. These two paired coordinate values also are used to determine the slope (m) and y-intercept (b) of the line. With this data in hand, you can extrapolate new coordinates. Together, all these coordinates form the Security Market Line graph.

Fig. 10.32.
The enhanced graph data block.

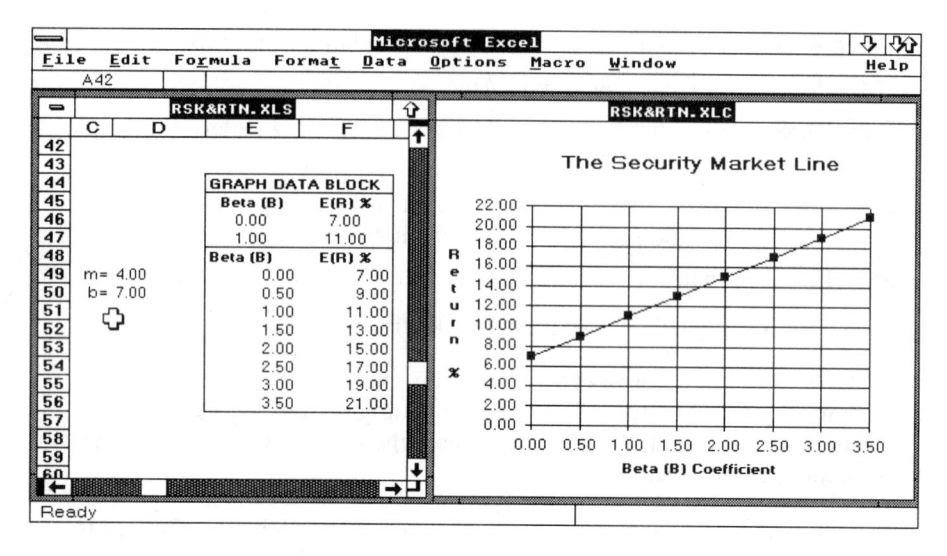

The purpose of this short exercise is to show you that the function of a graph data block is not limited to maintaining cell-referencing formulas. With a little creative thinking, you can calculate new data not available on a worksheet, scale the data to your desired specifications, and create the exact chart look that you are seeking. Figures 10.33 through 10.35 show an example of another use for a graph data block.

Fig. 10.33.
A worksheet that lets you selectively graph stocks in your portfolio.

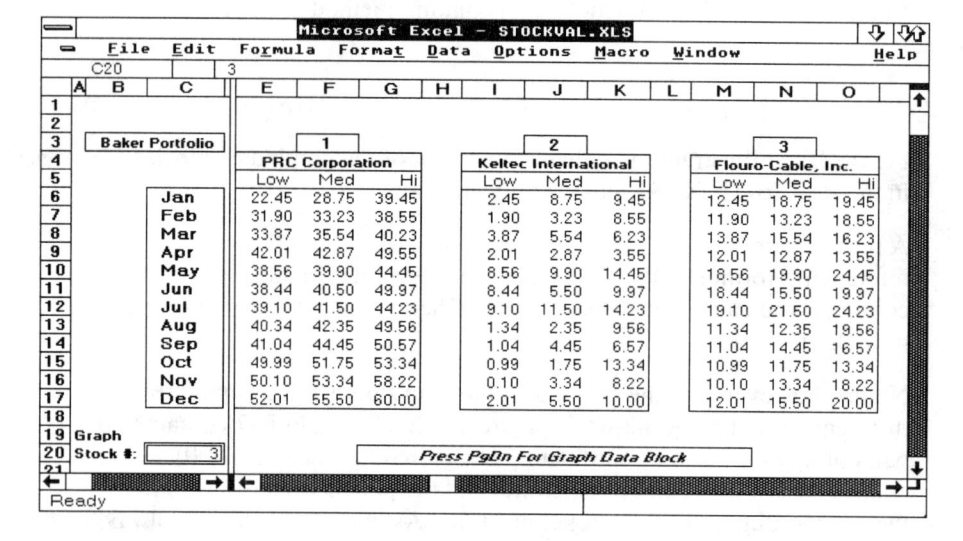

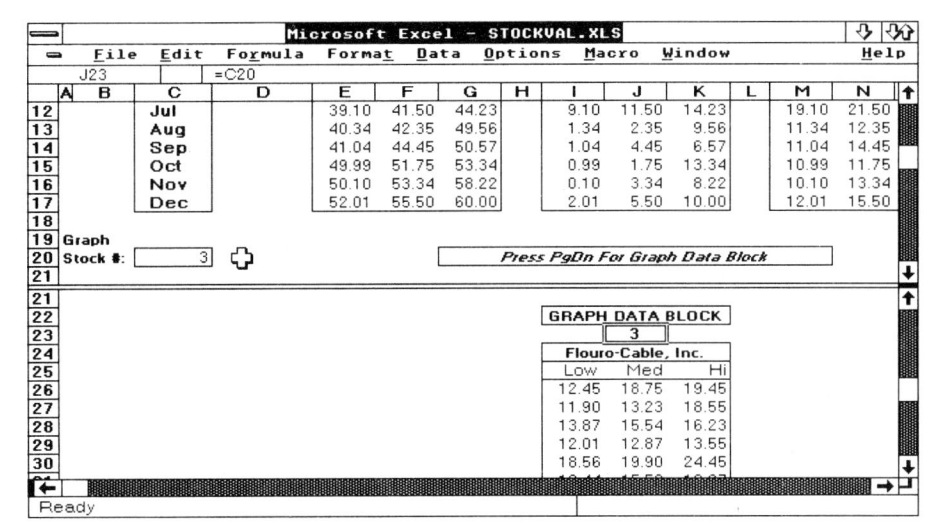

Fig. 10.34.
Cell J23 in the graph data block records the stock number you want to graph.

Fig. 10.35.
The formulas in the graph data block determine which stock prices to graph.

Summary

This chapter's primary goal was to reintroduce you to the basic techniques used in making charts. It is hoped that the text and examples also opened your mind to innovative uses for Excel charts, worksheets, and macros.

After completing Chapter 10, you should be very familiar with the 44 chart types available in Excel's seven chart categories. The figures and examples in this chapter demonstrated that you have many ways to enhance the look of your charts, using the many formatting tools found in Excel's chart menus. More important, you now have the experience to decide quickly when it's best to let Excel autocreate a chart, when it's best to create the chart yourself, and when it's best to employ graph data blocks to achieve the desired look.

The chapter also showed you how to create charts from the models included with this book. You are by no means limited to using the charts covered here in Chapter 10; rather, think of them as a stepping stone to envisioning and building charts just the way you like to see them.

Finally, continue to use and revise the models presented in the book as your business-reporting needs change. Ideally, as your business grows and as your demand for more detailed data increases, you can simply fine-tune the models that you've designed and used throughout this text.

A

How To Use the Applications Disk

This guide contains information to help you use the disk that accompanies *Excel Business Applications: IBM Version*. In addition to offering general information about the applications, this guide covers the procedures necessary for making working copies of the applications and provides a table of contents for the files on the applications disk. Please read the guide carefully before you start to use the disk.

The disk contains the files that implement the applications described in *Excel Business Applications: IBM Version*. The disk is specifically designed for use with the book; the book serves as the primary documentation for these applications.

What You Need To Get Started

The minimum requirements for using the applications are determined by the Excel program and the operating system you use. Representative requirements include the following:

- A PC or compatible computer based on the 80286, 80386, or similar microprocessor (including the IBM Personal Computer AT, IBM PS/2, COMPAQ, AT&T, and other compatible machines) with at least one double-sided 5 1/4-inch or 3 1/2-inch floppy disk drive and a hard disk drive that has at least 5M of free storage.

- Excel 2.0 or a later version.
- MS-DOS 3.0 or a later version, or OS/2 Standard Edition 1.1 or a later version.
- 640K of RAM for DOS; 3M of RAM for OS/2.
- A graphics card and monitor.
- A printer.

To obtain the applications on a 3 1/2-inch disk, use the order form in this book.

In addition to the proper equipment and software, you need to have some familiarity with Excel. To learn more about basic Excel operations, refer to Que's *Using Excel: IBM Version*.

How To Make Backup and Working Copies

The original *Excel Business Applications: IBM Version* disk is not copy-protected. We suggest that you never place this disk in your computer except to make copies for your use. You should make at least one complete copy of the disk in case you lose or damage the original disk.

You can use either the COPY or the DISKCOPY command to make the backup and working copies. Using the DISKCOPY command is preferable. The COPY command enables you to copy one file or a group of files. The DISKCOPY command makes an exact duplicate of an entire source disk.

To use the applications, you must copy the files from the applications disk to your hard disk. A few of the models must be in the same directory in order to operate properly.

To aid you in copying the models from the applications disk to your hard disk, we have included an installation program on the applications disk. The installation program is easy to use. The syntax is

INSTALL *d1: d2*

d1: is the floppy disk drive containing the applications disk. *d2:* is the drive on which you create a subdirectory and copy the files. To copy the files from your floppy disk drive A to your hard disk drive C, for example, type the following at the C> prompt:

A:INSTALL A: C:

Press Enter. The installation program creates the subdirectory \EXCELBA on drive C. Within the \EXCELBA directory are additional directories for each chapter of the book that contains models. For example, models for Chapter 8 are in the directory C:\EXCELBA\08. The installation program then copies from the applications disk to the hard disk the Excel business applications, each file in its appropriate directory.

How To Use the Applications

This section of the guide explains how to load and run the Excel business applications software.

Start Excel. Issue the command File Open. From the Open dialog box, select the subdirectory containing working copies of the files—C:\EXCELBA\08, for example—from Directories. To view or work with any of the applications, select the desired file from Files.

The following are the file names for each of the applications:

Chapter	File	Chapter	File
2	BLARCORY.XLS	5 (cont.)	DEPRECI8.XLW
	INCBALRA.XLS		DUPONT.XLM
	WHITNEY.XLS		DUPONT.XLS
3	CHKBOOK.XLS		DUPONT.XLW
	CHKBOOK.XLW		FV.XLM
	CHKSUMMR.XLS		FV.XLS
			FV.XLW
4	BREAKEVN.XLM		PV.XLM
	BREAKEVN.XLS		PV.XLS
	BREAKEVN.XLW		PV.XLW
	CALKINS.XLS		RSK&RTN.XLM
	CASHBUDG.XLS		RSK&RTN.XLS
	DONNELLY.XLS		RSK&RTN.XLW
	HISTORY.XLS		STOCKS.XLS
	PROFORMA.XLS	6	GENMENU.XLS
5	BONDS.XLM		GL.XLM
	BONDS.XLS		GL.XLS
	BONDS.XLW		GL.XLW
	DCFA.XLS		PROTOCOL.XLS
	DEPRECI8.XLM		REPMENU.XLS
	DEPRECI8.XLS		TMP.XLS

316 Excel Business Applications: IBM Version

Chapter	File	Chapter	File
7	AP10_89.XLS	8	AMORTIZE.XLS
	AP4_90.XLS		DAILYINT.XLS
	AR10_89.XLS		MN.XLW
	AR4_90.XLS		MN-CNVRT.XLS
	COLWKSHT.XLW		MN-FRCS1.XLS
	COLWKSHT.XLS		MN-FRCST.XLS
	CREDAPP.XLS		MN-INCST.XLS
	INVAGING.XLS		MN-PROF1.XLS
	INVARCUS.XLS		MN-PROFM.XLS
	INVARDAT.XLS	9	EMPPHONE.XLS
	INVCREG.XLS		PROJB89.XLS
	INVCREG.XLW		PROJECTS.XLS
	INVCREG1.XLS		PR89COND.XLC
	INVFREG.XLS		PR89HOME.XLC
	INVSALES.XLS		SLSCONTC.XLS
	TICKLER.XLS		SLSPR89.XLS
			SVLHSJUN.XLS

How To Troubleshoot Problems

If you have trouble using the Excel business applications disk, refer to the following troubleshooting guide.

You can avoid many problems by making complete backup copies of your disk. If your master disk is damaged or your files are lost accidentally, backup disks protect both your investment and your work. The following are examples of problems you may experience:

Symptom	Probable Cause	Solution
The application files won't copy to disk.	You did not specify the drive containing the disk.	Type, for example, **A:INSTALL A: C:**
	The drive door is not shut.	Close the door.
	The disk is in backwards.	Reinsert the disk.
Excel will not load the application.	The applications are not in the current Excel directory	Use the File Open command. Select the correct directory from the Open dialog box.

How To Get Help

If you have a problem, and the answer is not supplied in this appendix, look elsewhere in this book for the solution. Together with the rest of the book, this guide should provide the answers to most of your questions. If you still need help, feel free to call our technical-support office at (317)573-2500 (between 11 a.m. and 1 p.m. Eastern Standard Time). But please note that because you can customize the models in *Excel Business Applications: IBM Version*, we cannot answer questions related to your modifications of the applications.

Copy Restrictions

Under the terms of the license agreement, you can make an unlimited number of backup copies of the Excel business application files, as long as the copies are only for your use on a single computer. Please respect the license agreement by not making or distributing unauthorized copies.

By opening this package, you are agreeing to be bound by the following agreement.

These applications are copyrighted works, and all rights are reserved by Que Corporation. You are licensed to use these software applications on a single computer. You may copy and/or modify the applications as needed to facilitate your use of them on a single computer. Making copies of the applications for any other purpose is a violation of the United States copyright laws.

These applications are sold *as is* without warranty of any kind, either expressed or implied, including but not limited to the implied warranties of merchantability and fitness for a particular purpose. Neither Que nor its dealers or distributors assume any liability for any alleged or actual damages arising from the use of this program. (Some states do not allow the exclusion of implied warranties, so the exclusion may not apply to you.)

B

Using Excel's Worksheet Functions and Macro Language Library

This appendix lists and defines Excel's worksheet functions and the commands that constitute Excel's Macro Language Library, providing for each command the operational syntax used in written procedures. When these commands are combined with operators, Excel will perform the operations according to a predetermined order called the *level of precedence*.

The levels of operational precedence can be interrupted and restructured. Simply enclose within parentheses the operations to be evaluated first. Parentheses can be nested, or used in groups, to cause Excel to evaluate a larger string of expressions first. Within parenthetically enclosed expressions—or when no parentheses are used—operators at the same level of precedence will be executed in a left-to-right order. If the operators are not at the same level, the precedence outlined in table A.1 is enacted.

Note: In the following sections, the names of arguments in the function syntax are printed in roman type if the argument is mandatory; italic type is used if the argument is optional. However, all arguments (whether mandatory or optional) that are discussed in the macro function definition appear in italic type for easy identification.

Table A.1
Excel's Operational Order of Precedence

Level of Precedence	Operator	Explanation
1	:	All range evaluations
2	space	All intersection evaluations
3	,	All union evaluations
4	–	All negative numbers
5	%	All percent evaluations
6	^	All exponentiation
7	* or /	Multiplication and division for mathematical and Excel procedural expressions
8	+ or –	Addition and subtraction in all expressions
9	&	All text operator evaluations
10	=, <, <=, >, >=, <>	Comparison-expression conversions of equal, less than, less than or equal to, greater than, greater than or equal to, and not equal

Worksheet Functions

Excel's worksheet functions fall into these categories (and are discussed in this order):

- Database functions
- Date and time functions
- Financial functions
- Information functions
- Logical functions
- Lookup functions
- Mathematical functions
- Matrix functions
- Statistical functions
- Text functions
- Trigonometric functions

Database Functions

DAVERAGE(database,*field-name*,criteria)

This function calculates the mathematical average of the values that are supplied to numbers in a specific field of the *database* and that meet user-defined *criteria*. The calculation is performed on the contents of a user-defined *field-name*, or alternatively, a user-defined *field-index*.

DCOUNT(database,*field-name*,criteria)

This function returns the count of all the numbers that are located in a specific field of a *database* and that meet user-defined *criteria*.

DCOUNTA(database,*field-name*,criteria)

This function returns the count of all the nonblank numbers that are located in a specific field of a *database* and that meet user-defined *criteria*.

DMAX(database,field-name,criteria)

This function returns the value of the largest number in a *database* for all the records that meet user-defined *criteria*.

DMIN(database,field-name,criteria)

This function returns the minimum value of the smallest numbers in a *database* for all the records that meet user-defined *criteria*.

DPRODUCT(database,field-name,criteria)

This function calculates the product of the values in a specific field of a *database* for all the records that meet user-defined *criteria*.

DSTDEV(database,field-name,criteria)

This function calculates the standard deviation of the values in a specific field of a *database* for all the records that meet user-defined *criteria*. The assumption is that the numbers specified are of sample size.

DSTDEVP(database,field-name,criteria)

This function is the same as DSTDEV, except that for DSTDEVP, the assumption is that the numbers specified are representative of the population.

DSUM(database,field-name,criteria)

This function returns the summed value of a group of numbers in a specific field of a *database* for all the records that meet user-defined *criteria*.

DVAR(database,field-name,criteria)

This function calculates the variance of the values in a specified field of a *database* for all the records that meet user-defined *criteria*. The assumption is that the numbers specified are of sample size.

DVARP(database,field-name,criteria)

This function calculates the variance of the values in a specified field of a *database* for all the records that meet user-defined *criteria*. The assumption is that the numbers specified are representative of the population.

Date and Time Functions

DATE(year,month,day)

This function returns the serial-number equivalent of the date values that are input to the arguments.

DATEVALUE(date-text)

This function returns the serial-number equivalent of the date values that are input to the arguments.

DAY(serial-number)

This function converts a serial-number value into the day of the month. The possible values range from 1 to 31.

HOUR(serial-number)

This function converts a serial-number value into a time-of-day equivalent. The possible values range from 0 to 23.

MINUTE(serial-number)

This function converts a serial-number value into a minute-of-the-day equivalent. The possible values range from 0 to 59.

MONTH(serial-number)

This function converts a serial-number value into a month-of-the-year equivalent. The possible values range from 1 to 12.

NOW()

This function returns the serial-number equivalent of the current day and time of day. This function is updated after each recalculation.

SECOND(serial-number)

This function converts a serial-number value into a second-of-the-minute equivalent. The possible values range from 0 to 59.

TIME(hour,minute,second)

This function returns the serial-number equivalent of *hour*, *minute*, and *second*.

TIMEVALUE(time-text)

This function returns the serial-number equivalent of *time-text*. All the Excel time formats are acceptable.

WEEKDAY(serial-number)

This function converts a date (a month, day, and year, for example) into the day-of-the-week equivalent value. The possible values range from 1 to 7.

YEAR(serial-number)

This function converts a serial-number value into its year equivalent. The possible values range from 1904 to 2040.

Financial Functions

DDB(cost,salvage,life,period)

This function computes the depreciation of an asset by using the double-declining-balance method. Argument inputs must be positive numbers.

FV(rate,nper,pmt,*pv,type*)

This function calculates the future value of an investment that has equal cash flows. All cash outflows are preceded by a negative sign.

IPMT(rate,per,nper,pv,*fv,type*)

This function calculates the per-period interest payment of an investment involving both a constant payment and an interest rate. All cash outflows are preceded by a negative sign.

IRR(values,*guess*)

This function determines the internal rate of return for *values*—a user-defined series of cash flows. Using the *guess* argument, the user may specify a probable IRR value. All cash outflows are preceded by a negative sign.

MIRR(values,safe,risk)

This function computes the internal rate of return of an investment involving a series of cash flows. Using the *safe* and *risk* arguments, the user may define a negative and positive cash-flow financing rate. All cash outflows are preceded by a negative sign.

NPER(rate,pmt,pv,fv,type)

This function determines the number of periods required to provide constant cash flows, given user-specified criteria. All cash outflows are preceded by a negative sign.

NPV(rate,value1,*value2*,...)

This function computes the net present value of an investment, given user-specified criteria. All cash outflows are preceded by a negative sign.

PMT(rate,nper,pv,fv,type)

This function calculates the amount of a periodic payment for an investment, given user-specified criteria. All cash outflows are preceded by a negative sign.

PPMT(rate,per,nper,pv,fv,type)

This function computes the principal portion of a payment due for an investment, given user-specified criteria. All cash outflows are preceded by a negative sign.

PV(rate,nper,pmt,fv,type)

This function computes the present value of an investment, given user-specified criteria. All cash outflows are preceded by a negative sign.

RATE(nper,pmt,pv,fv,type,guess)

This function computes the per-period interest rate for an investment that has constant cash flows. All cash outflows are preceded by a negative sign.

SLN(cost,salvage,life)

This function computes a one-period depreciation value of an asset by using the straight-line method. Argument inputs must be positive numbers.

SYD(cost,salvage,life,per)

This function computes the depreciation value of an asset, using the sum-of-years'-digits method. Argument inputs must be positive numbers.

Information Functions

AREAS(reference)

This function returns the number of areas found in *reference*. An area can be a single cell, a range of continuous cells, or a range of noncontinuous cells.

CELL(type,*reference*)

This function supplies the coding information about a cell reference and its format, contents, and location.

COLUMN(*ref*)

This function returns the column-location number indicated by *ref*, where *ref* is a reference to one specific cell in that column.

COLUMNS(array)

This function is exactly like COLUMN, with the exception that COLUMNS(array) references an array rather than a single cell.

ISBLANK(value)

If *value* references a blank cell, this function returns the value TRUE; otherwise, the function returns the value FALSE.

ISERR(value)

If *value* is any of the Excel error values (with the exception of #N/A), this function returns the logical value TRUE. If *value* is #N/A, Excel returns the logical value FALSE.

ISERROR(value)

If *value* is any of the Excel error values, this function returns the logical value TRUE. If *value* is not an Excel error value, this function returns the logical value FALSE.

ISLOGICAL(value)

This function determines whether *value* is a logical value. If *value* is a logical value, TRUE is returned; otherwise, the value FALSE is returned.

ISNA(value)

When *value* is the error value #N/A, this function returns the value TRUE; otherwise, the function returns the value FALSE.

ISNONTEXT(value)

This function determines whether *value* is not text, in which case a TRUE value is returned. Otherwise, the logical value FALSE is returned.

ISNUMBER(value)

If *value* is a number, this function returns the value TRUE; otherwise, the function returns the value FALSE.

ISREF(value)

If *value* is a cell reference or a cell reference formula, this function returns the value TRUE; otherwise, the function returns the value FALSE.

ISTEXT(value)

This function determines whether *value* is text, in which case a TRUE value is returned. Otherwise, the value FALSE is returned.

N(value)

This function evaluates *value* and returns a number. If *value* is a number, it returns that number. If *value* is TRUE, it returns 1. If *value* is anything else, it returns 0.

NA()

The NA function returns the error value #N/A.

ROW(*ref*)

The ROW function returns the specific row number called by *ref* when *ref* is one cell reference. When *ref* is a range of cells, ROW returns the specific row numbers in a vertical array.

ROWS(array)

This function gives the number of rows in *array*.

T(value)

This function returns the text value of *value*, enclosed in quotation marks. If *value* is numerical, it is returned as one set of quotation marks.

TYPE(value)

The TYPE function returns the type of value code for *value*, where 1 is a number, 2 is text, 4 is a logical value, 16 is an error value, and 64 is an array.

Logical Functions

AND(logical1,*logical2*,...)

This function returns the logical value TRUE if all the elements in a group of arguments are TRUE; the function returns the logical value FALSE if any of the elements are FALSE. As many as 14 arguments may be used.

FALSE()

This function returns the logical value FALSE.

IF(logical,value-if-true,*value-if-false*)

This function returns *value-if-true* when *logical* is TRUE; the function returns *value-if-false* when *logical* is FALSE.

NOT(logical)

This function returns the logical value FALSE when *logical* equals TRUE; the function returns the logical value TRUE when *logical* is FALSE.

OR(logical1,*logical2*,...)

This function returns the logical value TRUE when any of the values returned to a group of arguments are TRUE; the function returns the logical value FALSE when all the values returned to a group of arguments are FALSE.

TRUE()

This function returns the logical value TRUE.

Lookup Functions

CHOOSE(number,value1,*value2*,...)

This function locates and chooses a value from the list of values (*value1, value2,...*), given a user-defined number. If *number* is 2, CHOOSE returns *value2*.

HLOOKUP(lookup-value,compare-array,index-number)

The HLOOKUP function looks for the largest value in the starting row of *compare-array* that is greater than or equal to *lookup-value*. Use *index-number* to step the search across the length of the row. Use VLOOKUP to perform the same comparison search down the length of a column.

INDEX(ref,row,column,*area*)

This function returns the reference of one particular cell within *ref*, given user-defined indices for *row*, *column*, and *area*. Use the following, optional syntax to return a value from a particular cell within *array*, again according to user-defined indexes:

    INDEX(array,row,column)

LOOKUP(lookup-value,compare-vector,result-vector)

This function examines *compare-vector* for the greatest value that is less than or equal to *lookup-value*. The value is returned in a *result-vector*.

MATCH(lookup-value,lookup-array,*type*)

This function returns the relative location of the items in *lookup-array* that match a *lookup-value*, given a user-specified match *type*.

VLOOKUP(lookup-value,compare-array,col-index)

This function looks for a row in *compare-array* in which the first column contains the user-specified *lookup-value*; the function returns the value of the cell. Use *col-index* to designate which column value in *compare-array* to use VLOOKUP on.

Mathematical Functions

ABS(number)

This function returns the absolute value of *number*.

EXP(number)

This function returns *e* to the specified power.

FACT(number)

This function returns the factorial of the value specified in *number*. When *number* is not an integer, Excel truncates *number*.

INT(number)

The INT function returns the largest integer less than or equal to *number*.

LN(number)

This function returns the natural, base *e*, logarithm of *number*.

LOG(number,*base*)

This function calculates the logarithm of a number, using a user-specified *base*.

LOG10(number)

This function returns the base 10 logarithm of a number.

MOD(number,divisor-number)

This function returns the remainder after *number* is divided by *divisor-number*. The resulting sign is the same as that of *divisor-number*.

PI()

This function gives returns the mathematical value of pi, 3.14159.

PRODUCT(number1,*number2*,...)

This function multiplies the values returned to all the arguments supplied by the user. As many as 14 arguments may be used.

RAND()

This function supplies a random number that is less than 1 and greater than or equal to 0. To return a new random number, recalculate the active worksheet.

ROUND(number,number-of-digits)

This function rounds to the nearest *number*, given a user-defined number of decimal places.

SIGN(number)

This function determines the sign of *number*. If the value 1 is returned, *number* is positive. A returned value of 0 indicates that *number* is 0. A -1 value indicates that *number* is negative.

SQRT(number)

This function calculates the positive square root of *number*.

TRUNC(number)

This function converts a decimal into integer form by truncating the decimal value.

Matrix Functions

MDETERM(array)

This function provides the matrix determinant of the value of *array*. In this case, *array* must be a numeric array containing an equal number of rows and columns.

MINVERSE(array)

This function provides the inverse matrix for the matrix defined by *array*. When *array* is not a continuous range of cells, Excel returns the error value #VALUE!.

MMULT(array-1,array-2)

This function calculates the matrix product of *array-1* and *array-2*. In this case, the arrays must contain an equal number of rows and columns.

TRANSPOSE(array)

This function returns the transposed values of an *array*.

Statistical Functions

AVERAGE(number1,*number2*,...)

This function computes the mathematical average specified in numbers. As many as 14 arguments may be used.

COUNT(number1,*number2*,...)

This function supplies the counted value of numbers given in numbers. As many as 14 arguments may be used.

COUNTA(value1,*value2*,...)

This function counts the number of values supplied in a group of arguments. As many as 14 argument values may be used. Blanks are ignored.

GROWTH(known-y's,*known-x's,new-x's*)

This function returns the values on an exponential trend, given a user-defined size and shape: *new-x's*. The function has the form $y = b * m^x$. The values are returned in an array for two variables, Y and X, which correspond to the array values in *known-y's* and *known-x's*.

LINEST(known-y's,*known-x's*)

The LINEST function computes the least-squares regression of *known-y's* and *known-x's*, using the functional form $y = mx + b$. The values of x and y are random.

LOGEST(known-y's,*known-x's*)

This function calculates the exact parameters of m and b in the functional form $y = b * m^x$ and returns the values as a horizontal array.

MAX(number1,*number2*,...)

This functions return the maximum value found in a list of numbers. As many as 14 arguments may be used.

MIN(number1,*number2*,...)

This function returns the minimum value found in a list of numbers. As many as 14 arguments may be used.

STDEV(number1,*number2,...*)

This function calculates the standard deviation of a group of user-input numbers. The assumption is that the numbers specified are of sample size. As many as 14 arguments may be used.

STDEVP(number1,*number2,...*)

This function calculates the standard deviation of a group of user-input numbers. The assumption is that the numbers specified are representative of the entire population of numbers. As many as 14 arguments may be used.

SUM(number1,*number2,...*)

This function returns the summed value of a group of numbers. As many as 14 arguments may be used.

TREND(known-y's,*known-x's,new-x's*)

The TREND function supplies the y values regressed on a line of equation $y = m * x + b$. The trended values are returned in an array.

VAR(number1,*number2,...*)

This function calculates the sample variance of a group of numbers supplied in a list of arguments. As many as 14 arguments may be used.

VARP(number1,*number2,...*)

This function calculates the population variance of a group of numbers supplied in a list of arguments. As many as 14 arguments may be used.

Text Functions

CHAR(number)

This function returns the ASCII-equivalent value of *number*, which can be in the range 1 to 255.

CLEAN(text)

This function extracts all nonprintable characters from text.

CODE(text)

This function looks at the first character in text and returns its corresponding ASCII-equivalent value.

DOLLAR(number,*number-of-digits*)

This function rounds *number* according to the user-defined *number-of-digits* and then returns the value as text with a currency format.

EXACT(text-1,text-2)

This function determines whether the values of *text-1* and *text-2* are equal. If the values are equal, the logical value TRUE is returned; otherwise, the logical value FALSE is returned.

FIND(find-text,within-text,*start-at-number*)

This function pinpoints *find-text* in a *within-text* string. The user defines where to begin the search by inputting *start-at-number*—a number that corresponds to the order in which characters in the string appear.

FIXED(number,*number-of-digits*)

This function rounds *number* according to the user-defined *number-of-digits* and then returns the value as text with a decimal format, including commas.

LEFT(text,*number-of-characters*)

This function returns the leftmost *number-of-characters* in a text string.

LEN(text)

This function returns the total number of characters in *text*.

LOWER(text)

This function changes all uppercase characters in *text* to lowercase characters. Nonletter characters are unaffected.

MID(text,start-position,number-of-characters)

This function removes a user-defined *number-of-characters* from a text string, beginning at a user-defined *start-position*.

PROPER(text)

This function converts the first letter in *text* from lowercase to uppercase and converts all other letters to lowercase format.

REPLACE(old-text,start-num,num-chars,new-text)

This function substitutes *new-text* for *old-text*, beginning at a user-defined starting number. The REPLACE procedure continues for a user-specified number of characters.

REPT(text,number-of-times)

This function duplicates *text* a user-specified *number-of-times*.

RIGHT(text,*number-of-characters*)

This function returns the rightmost *number-of-characters* in a text string.

SEARCH(search-text,text,*start-number*)

This function looks for *search-text* within a text string. The search begins at a user-specified starting character (*start-number*).

SUBSTITUTE(text,old-text,new-text,*number*)

This function replaces *old-text* with *new-text* in every occurrence of *text*. Use *number* to specify the occurrence of text on which to perform this operation.

TEXT(value,format-text)

This function formats *value* into a user-defined style. The value is returned as text.

TRIM(text)

This function eliminates all the blank spaces that are in front of and behind a text string. TRIM leaves one blank space between words in the text string.

UPPER(text)

This function changes all lowercase characters in *text* to uppercase characters. Nonletter characters are unaffected.

VALUE(text)

This function replaces a numerical value stored as *text* with the original numerical value.

Trigonometric Functions

ACOS(number)

This function returns the arccosine value of *number*. The argument *number* must be in the range -1 to 1.

ASIN(number)

This function returns the arcsine value of *number*. The argument *number* must be in the range -1 to 1.

ATAN(number)

This function returns the arctangent value of *number*.

ATAN2(x-value,y-value)

This function returns the arctangent radian value of the coordinates specified in *x-value* and *y-value*. To display the arctangent value in degrees, multiply the radian result by 180/PI().

COS(radians)

This function returns the cosine value of *radians*, where the argument *radians* is input as an angle in radian value.

SIN(radians)

This function returns the sine value of *radians*, where the argument *radians* is input as an angle in radian value.

TAN(radians)

This function returns the tangent value of *radians*, where the argument *radians* is input as an angle in radian value.

Macro Language Library

Commands in the Macro Language Library fall into these categories (and are discussed in this order):

- Command-equivalent functions
- Action-equivalent functions
- Customizing functions
- Control functions
- Value-returning functions

Command-Equivalent Functions

ACTIVATE(*window-text,pane-number*)

This function corresponds to the action of clicking on a file name in the Window menu.

ADD.ARROW()

This function corresponds to the Add Arrow command in the Chart menu.

ADD.OVERLAY()

This function corresponds to the Add Overlay command in the Chart menu.

ALIGNMENT(type)

This function corresponds to the Alignment command in the Format menu.

APPLY.NAMES()

This function corresponds to the Apply Names command in the Formula menu.

APP.MAXIMIZE()

This function, which corresponds to the Maximize command in the Control menu for the application window, fully enlarges the application window.

APP.MINIMIZE()

This function, which corresponds to the Minimize command in the Control menu for the application window, minimizes the size of the application window.

APP.MOVE(x-num,y-num)

This function corresponds to the Move command in the Control menu for the application window.

APP.RESTORE()

This function corresponds to the Restore command in the Control menu for the application window.

APP.SIZE(x-num,y-num)

This function corresponds to the Size command in the Control menu for the application window.

ARRANGE.ALL()

This function corresponds to the Arrange All command in the Window menu.

ATTACH.TEXT(attach-to-num,*series-num,point-num*)

This function corresponds to the Attach Text command in the Chart menu.

AXES(*main-cat,main-value,over-cat,over-value*)

This function corresponds to the Axes command in the Chart menu.

BORDER(outline,left,right,top,bottom,shade)

This function corresponds to the Border command in the Format menu.

CALCULATE.DOCUMENT()

This function corresponds to the Calculate Document command in the Options menu. The function also is equivalent to the Calculate Document command in the Chart menu. Both functions calculate an active document.

CALCULATE.NOW()

This function corresponds to the Calculate Now command in the Options menu. The function also is equivalent to the Calculate Now command in the Chart menu. CALCULATE.NOW() calculates all open documents.

CALCULATION()

This function is equivalent to the Calculation command in the Options menu.

CELL.PROTECTION(*locked,hidden*)

This function corresponds to the Cell Protection command in the Format menu.

CLEAR(parts)

This function corresponds to the Clear command in the Edit menu.

CLOSE(*save-logical*)

This function corresponds to the Close command in the Control application menu.

CLOSE.ALL()

This function closes all open Excel files.

COLUMN.WIDTH(width,*ref*)

This function corresponds to the Column Width command in the Format menu. This function also is identical to the action of dragging the column border to a specified width. In this syntax, *ref* may be either an external reference to an active worksheet or an R1C1 type of reference in the form of text.

COMBINATION(number)

This function corresponds to the Combination command found in the Gallery menu when a chart is the active document.

COPY()

This function corresponds to the Copy command in the Edit menu.

COPY.PICTURE(appearance,size)

This function corresponds to the Copy command in the Edit menu. The Shift key is pressed simultaneously (while you choose the Edit menu) to invoke the command.

CREATE.NAMES(*top,left,bottom,right*)

This function corresponds to the Create Names command in the Formula menu.

CUT()

This function corresponds to the Cut command in the Edit menu.

DATA.DELETE()

This function corresponds to the Delete command in the Data menu.

DATA.FIND(logical)

This function corresponds to the Find and Exit Find commands in the Data menu.

DATA.FORM()

This function corresponds to the Form command in the Data menu.

DATA.SERIES(series-in,type,unit,step,stop)

This function corresponds to the Series command in the Data menu.

DEFINE.NAME(name,refers-to,*type*,*key*)

This function corresponds to the Define Name command in the Formula menu. The argument *name* must be text.

DELETE.ARROW()

This function corresponds to the Delete Arrow command in the Chart menu. The function deletes a chosen arrow or returns the value FALSE.

DELETE.NAME(name)

This function corresponds to the Delete Name action available with the Define Name command in the Formula menu.

DELETE.OVERLAY()

This function corresponds to the Delete Overlay command in the Chart menu.

DISPLAY(*formula,gridline,heading,zero,color*)

This function corresponds to the Display command found in both the Options and Info menus.

EDIT.DELETE(direction)

This function corresponds to the Delete command in the Edit menu.

EXTRACT(unique-log)

This function corresponds to the Extract command in the Data menu.

FILE.CLOSE()

This function corresponds to the Close command in the File menu. This function also corresponds to the File Close command in the Control menu.

FILE.DELETE(document)

This function corresponds to the Delete command in the File menu.

FILL.DOWN()

This function corresponds to the Fill Down command in the Edit menu.

FILL.LEFT()

This function corresponds to the Fill Left command in the Edit menu.

FILL.RIGHT()

This function corresponds to the Fill Right command in the Edit menu.

FILL.UP()

This function corresponds to the Fill Up command in the Edit menu.

FORMAT.FONT(name-text,size-num,bold,italic,underline,strike)

This function corresponds to the Font command in the Format menu.

FORMAT.LEGEND(pos-num)

This function corresponds to the Legend command in the Format menu.

FORMAT.MOVE(x-pos,y-pos)

This function corresponds to the Move command in the Format menu.

FORMAT.NUMBER(format)

This function corresponds to the Format Number command in the Format menu.

FORMAT.SIZE(width,height)

This function corresponds to the Size command in the Format menu.

FORMAT.TEXT(x-align,y-align,vert-text,auto-text,auto-size,*show-key,show-value*)

This function corresponds to the Text command in the Format menu.

FORMULA.FIND(text,look-in,look-at,look-by)

This function corresponds to the Find command in the Formula menu.

FORMULA.GOTO(ref)

This function corresponds to the Goto command in the Formula menu or to pressing F5.

FORMULA.REPLACE(find-text,replace-text,*look-at,look-by,current-cell*)

This function corresponds to the Replace command in the Formula menu.

FREEZE.PANES(logical)

This function corresponds to the Freeze Panes command in the Options menu.

FULL(logical)

Using this function is identical to double-clicking the title bar to fully enlarge—or to reduce to normal—the worksheet size. Specifying TRUE expands the active window to the maximum size; specifying FALSE restores the original size.

GALLERY.AREA(number,*delete-overlay*)

This function corresponds to the Area command in the Gallery menu. In this syntax, *number* must equal a number that agrees with a specific format in the gallery.

GALLERY.BAR(number,*delete-overlay*)

This function corresponds to the Bar command in the Gallery menu. In this syntax, *number* must equal a number that agrees with a specific format in the gallery.

GALLERY.COLUMN(number,*delete-overlay*)

This function corresponds to the Column command in the Gallery menu. In this syntax, *number* must equal a number that agrees with a specific format in the gallery.

GALLERY.LINE(number,*delete-overlay*)

This function corresponds to the Line command in the Gallery menu. In this syntax, *number* must equal a number that agrees with a specific format in the gallery.

GALLERY.PIE(number,*delete-overlay*)

This function corresponds to the Pie command in the Gallery menu. In this syntax, *number* must equal a number that agrees with a specific format in the gallery.

GALLERY.SCATTER(number,*delete-overlay*)

This function corresponds to the Scatter command in the Gallery menu. In this syntax, *number* must equal a number that agrees with a specific format in the gallery.

GRIDLINES(cat-major,cat-minor,value-major,value-minor)

This function corresponds to the Gridlines command in the Chart menu.

HIDE()

This function corresponds to the Hide command in the Window menu.

INSERT(direction)

This function corresponds to the Insert command in the Edit menu.

JUSTIFY()

This function corresponds to the Justify command in the Format menu.

LEGEND(*logical*)

This function corresponds to the Add and Delete Legend commands in the Chart menu.

LIST.NAMES()

Using this function corresponds to selecting the Paste Name command from the Formula menu and pressing Paste List.

MAIN.CHART(type,stack,100,vary,overlap,drop,hilo,overlap%,cluster,angle)

This function corresponds to the Main Chart command in the Chart Format menu.

MAIN.CHART.TYPE(type)

This function corresponds to the Main Chart Type command in the Chart menu in Microsoft Excel for the Apple Macintosh.

MOVE(x-pos,y-pos,*window*)

This function corresponds to the Move command in the Control menu.

NEW(type)

This function corresponds to the New command in the File menu.

NEW.WINDOW()

This command corresponds to the New Window command in the Window menu.

OPEN(document,update,read-only)

This function corresponds to the Open command in the File menu.

OPEN.LINKS(document1,*document2*,...)

This function corresponds to the Links command in the File menu and supports 1 to 14 arguments.

OVERLAY(type,stack,100,vary,overlap,drop,hilo,overlap%, cluster,angle,series,auto)

This function corresponds to the Overlay command in the Format menu.

OVERLAY.CHART.TYPE(type)

This function corresponds to the Overlay Chart Type command in the Chart menu in Microsoft Excel for the Apple Macintosh.

PAGE.SETUP(header,footer,left,right,top,bot,headings,grid)

This function corresponds to the Page Setup command in the File menu. The syntax is appropriate when the active document is a worksheet or a macro.

PARSE(parse-text)

This function corresponds to the Parse command in the Data menu.

PASTE()

This function corresponds to the Paste command in the Edit menu.

PASTE.LINK()

This function corresponds to the Link command in the Paste menu.

PASTE.SPECIAL(parts,operation,skip-blanks,transpose)

This function corresponds to the Paste Special command in the Edit menu. The syntax is appropriate when you are pasting into a worksheet or macro.

PATTERNS

This function corresponds to the Patterns command in the Format menu. This command has five separate syntax forms, depending on which pattern is selected.

PRECISION(logical)

This function corresponds to the Calculation command found in the Data menu when the Precision as Displayed box is selected.

PREFERRED()

This function corresponds to the Preferred command in the Gallery menu.

PRINT(range,from,to,copies,draft,preview,parts)

This function corresponds to the Print command in the File menu.

PRINTER.SETUP(printer-text)

This function corresponds to the Printer Setup command in the File menu.

PROTECT.DOCUMENT(*contents,windows*)

This function corresponds to the Protect and Unprotect Document commands in both the Options and Chart menus. Use the question-mark form of this function to protect or unprotect a document that has a password.

QUIT()

This function corresponds to the Exit command in the File menu.

REMOVE.PAGE.BREAK()

This function corresponds to the Remove Page Break command in the Options menu.

REPLACE.FONT(font,name-text,size-num,bold,italic, underline,strike)

Using this function corresponds to selecting the Font command from the Format menu and then click-selecting the Replace button after a new font has been selected.

ROW.HEIGHT(height-num,*ref,standard-height*)

This function corresponds to the Row Height command in the Format menu. Using this function also is identical to dragging the row border to a specified width. In this syntax, *ref* may be either an external reference to an active worksheet or an R1C1 type of reference in the form of text.

RUN(ref)

This function corresponds to the Run command in the Macro menu. In this syntax, *ref* may either be an R1C1 type of reference or directly call to an external reference such as a macro—for example, RUN(Monthly!Quota).

SAVE()

This function corresponds to the Save command in the File menu.

SAVE.AS(document,type,password,backup)

This function corresponds to the Save As command in the File menu.

SAVE.WORKSPACE(*document*)

This function corresponds to the Save Workspace command in the File menu.

SCALE(min,max,major,minor,cross,logarithmic,reverse,max)

This function corresponds to the Scale command found in the Format menu when a chart is the active document.

SELECT.CHART()

This function corresponds to the Select Chart command in the Chart menu.

SELECT.PLOT.AREA()

This function corresponds to the Select Plot Area command in the Chart menu and is an Apple Macintosh macro-compatible function.

SELECT.SPECIAL(type-number,*value-types*,*levels*)

This function corresponds to the Select Special command in the Formula menu.

SET.CRITERIA()

This function corresponds to the Set Criteria command in the Data menu.

SET.DATABASE()

This function corresponds to the Set Database command in the Data menu.

SET.PAGE.BREAK()

This function corresponds to the Set Page Break command in the Options menu.

SET.PREFERRED()

This function corresponds to the Set Preferred command in the Gallery menu.

SET.PRINT.AREA()

This function corresponds to the Set Print Area command in the Options menu.

SET.PRINT.TITLES()

This function corresponds to the Set Print Titles command in the Options menu.

SHORT.MENUS(logical)

This function corresponds to the Short Menus command in the Options menu. This function is also equivalent to the Short Menus command in the Chart menu.

SHOW.INFO(enable-log)

This function corresponds to the Show Info command in the Windows menu.

SIZE(width,height,*window*)

Using this function is identical to resizing an active window by dragging the size box. In this syntax, *window* calls a specific worksheet. If you don't use the *window* argument, the active worksheet is called as the default.

SORT(sort-by,1st-key,order[1],2nd-key,order[2],3rd-key,order[3])

This function corresponds to the Sort command in the Data menu. In this syntax, both *sort-by* and *order* must be numbers, and *key* should be an external reference.

SPLIT(column-split,row-split)

Using this function is identical to dragging the split marker in the scroll bar of the active window.

TABLE(row-input,column-input)

This function corresponds to the Table command in the Data menu.

UNDO()

This function corresponds to the Undo command in the Edit menu.

UNHIDE(window-text)

This function corresponds to the Unhide command in the Window menu and also to the Unhide Window command in the File menu.

WORKSPACE(fixed,decimals,r1c1,scroll,formula,status,menu,remote)

This function corresponds to the Workspace command in the Options menu.

Action-Equivalent Functions

A1.R1C1(r1c1)

This function corresponds to the Workspace command in the Options menu.

ACTIVATE(*window,pane-number*)

Using this function is identical to activating a window and a pane in that window.

ACTIVATE.NEXT()

Using this function is identical to pressing Ctrl-F6, which activates the next window.

ACTIVATE.PREV()

Using this function is identical to pressing Ctrl-Shift-F6, which activates the previous window.

CANCEL.COPY()

Using this function is identical to pressing the Esc key after a cell or range selection is cut or copied; this function cancels the surrounding marquee.

COPY.CHART(as-shown)

This function corresponds to the Copy Chart command in the Edit menu when a chart is the active document. The Shift key is pressed simultaneously (while you choose the Edit menu) to invoke the command.

DATA.FIND.NEXT()

Using this function corresponds to pressing the down-arrow key, which locates the next record in a database.

DATA.FIND.PREV()

Using this function is identical to pressing the up-arrow key, which locates the previous record in a database.

DELETE.FORMAT(format)

This function is equivalent to deleting a format created with the Number command in the Format menu.

DIRECTORY(*path-name-text*)

This function assigns the current drive and path name active as specified in *path-name-text*.

FORMULA(formula-text,*ref*)

Using this function is identical to entering a formula into a worksheet cell.

FORMULA.ARRAY(formula-text,*ref*)

Using this function is identical to entering an array formula into a worksheet cell. The argument *ref* is the cell into which the formula will be placed; if the specified cell is blank, *ref* puts the formula into the active cell. You enter a formula array by simultaneously pressing Ctrl-Shift-Enter.

FORMULA.FILL(formula-text,*ref*)

Using this function is identical to entering a formula into a worksheet cell while pressing the Shift key—an action that copies the formula into all the cells indicated by *ref*.

FORMULA.FIND.NEXT()

Using this function is identical to pressing F7, which locates the next cell on the active worksheet. The user specifies the worksheet area to be searched by defining a Find criterion in the Formula menu.

FORMULA.FIND.PREV()

Using this function is identical to pressing Shift-F7, which locates the previous cell on the active worksheet. The user specifies the worksheet area to be searched by defining a Find criterion in the Formula menu.

HLINE(number)

Using this function is identical to scrolling through an active document horizontally by clicking the horizontal-scroll arrow. In this syntax, *number* is a positive or negative integer that specifies the number of columns to scroll.

HPAGE(number)

Using this function is identical to scrolling through an active document horizontally, one windowful at a time, by clicking in the gray area of the scroll bar. In this syntax, *number* is a positive or negative integer that specifies the number of windowfuls to scroll right or left, respectively.

HSCROLL(column-number,column-log)

Using this function is identical to scrolling through an active document horizontally by dragging the horizontal-scroll box.

SELECT(selection-ref,active-cell-ref)

Using this function is identical to click-selecting a new active cell on the active worksheet. In this syntax, *selection-ref* may be either a reference to the active worksheet or a cell reference in the R1C1 style. The argument *active-cell-ref* becomes the new active cell reference.

SELECT.END(direction-number)

This function relocates the active cell to the edge of the next block in the direction indicated by *direction-number*. The direction numbers are 1 for left, 2 for right, 3 for up, and 4 for down.

SELECT.LAST.CELL()

This function selects the cell at the intersection of the last row and column that has something in it.

SHOW.ACTIVE.CELL()

Using this function corresponds to pressing Ctrl-Backspace, which scrolls the active window to reveal the active cell.

SHOW.CLIPBOARD()

This command corresponds to the Run Clipboard command in Excel's Control menu.

STYLE(bold,italic)

This function corresponds to the Style command in the Format menu with Microsoft Excel for the Apple Macintosh.

UNLOCKED.NEXT()

Using this function is identical to pressing the Tab key to relocate the active cell to the next unlocked cell on a protected worksheet.

UNLOCKED.PREV()

Using this function is identical to simultaneously pressing the Shift and Tab keys to relocate the active cell to the previous unlocked cell on a protected worksheet.

VLINE(number)

Using this function is identical to scrolling through an active document vertically by clicking the vertical-scroll arrow. In this syntax, *number* is a positive or negative integer that specifies the number of lines to scroll.

VPAGE(number)

Using this function is identical to scrolling through an active document vertically, one windowful at a time, by clicking in the gray area of the scroll bar. In this syntax, *number* is a positive or negative integer that specifies the number of windowfuls to scroll.

VSCROLL(column-number,column-log)

Using this function is identical to scrolling through an active document vertically by dragging the vertical-scroll box.

Customizing Functions

ADD.BAR()

This function generates a new menu bar for the Excel menu display and returns the new menu bar ID number.

ADD.COMMAND(bar-number,menu-pos,menu-ref)

This function adds all user-created commands to a new menu bar. In this syntax, *menu-ref* is the range where the list of new commands resides on the worksheet, and *menu-pos* specifies to which menu the commands should be appended. The value, *bar-number*, indicates the specific number of the menu bar.

ADD.MENU(bar-number,menu-ref)

This function appends the new commands specified by *menu-ref* to the menu specified by *bar-number*.

ALERT(text,type)

This function invokes an Alert box. The Alert box displays the message that is specified in text.

APP.ACTIVATE(*title-text,wait-log*)

This function executes the Excel application specified in *title-text*, which is an Excel application title bar.

BEEP(*number*)

This function chimes the internal bell in the PC. The argument *number* refers to the loudness of the tone, which increases on a scale from 1 to 4.

CANCEL.KEY(enable,macro-ref)

This function disables the user's ability to interrupt macro execution and also tells Excel to run a macro if macro execution is interrupted.

CHECK.COMMAND(bar-number,menu-pos,command-pos,check)

This function enables the custom-menu designer to place a check mark next to a command specified by *command-pos*.

DELETE.BAR(bar-number)

This function deletes the custom-menu bar indicated by *bar-number*.

DELETE.COMMAND(bar-number,menu-pos,command-pos)

This function deletes the menu command indicated by *command-pos* from the menu specified by *menu-pos*.

DELETE.MENU(bar-number,menu-pos)

This function deletes the menu indicated by *menu-pos* from the menu bar indicated by *bar-number*.

DIALOG.BOX(dialog-ref)

This function tells Excel to create a dialog box by using user-specified criteria found in *dialog-ref* on the active macro sheet.

DISABLE.INPUT(logical)

When *logical* is TRUE, this function suspends all the keyboard and mouse input to Excel—except the input to the display boxes. When *logical* is FALSE, this function reenables all input to Excel.

ECHO(*logical*)

This function turns screen updating on when *logical* is TRUE and turns screen updating off when *logical* is FALSE.

ENABLE.COMMAND(bar-number,menu-pos,command-pos,enable)

This function commands Excel to enable the command specified by *command-pos* when *enable* is TRUE. When *enable* is FALSE, the command is disabled.

ERROR(logical,*ref*)

This function turns error checking on when *logical* is TRUE and turns error checking off when *logical* is FALSE.

EXEC(program-text,*window-number*)

This function executes the application specified by *program-text*, when the application is running under Microsoft Windows 2.0 or higher. The argument *window-number* specifies the window size (*maximize,minimize,normal*) of *program-text* when this function is executed.

EXECUTE(channel-number,execute-text)

This function executes the command specified by *execute-text*, when the application is running under Microsoft Windows 2.0 or higher. The argument *channel-number* directs Microsoft Windows to the selected application.

FCLOSE(file-number)

This function closes the file specified by *file-number*. The argument *file-number* must previously have been opened through the FOPEN function.

FOPEN(file-text,access-number)

This function opens the file specified by *file-text*. The argument *access-number* indicates how *file-text* may be accessed according to its read/write attributes.

FPOS(file-number,*pos-number*)

This function relocates the document specified by *file-number* to the position specified in *pos-number*.

FREAD(file-number,num-chars)

This function looks at a document file number specified in *file-number* and reads the number of characters (*num-chars*).

FREADLN(file-number)

This function reads a current document from the location in *file-number* to the end of the line.

FSIZE(file-number)

This function gives the total number of characters in the document specified by *file-number*.

FWRITE(file-number,text)

This function copies data specified in *text* to the document specified by *file-number*, beginning at the current position in *file-number*.

FWRITELN(file-number,text)

This function copies data specified in *text*—followed by a carriage return and a line feed—to the document specified by *file-number*, beginning at the current position in *file-number*.

HELP(*help-ref*)

This function initiates Excel's built-in Help feature, showing the topic indicated by *help-ref*.

INITIATE(app-text,topic-text)

This function opens a DDE (dynamic data exchange) channel to an application specified by *app-text*. The application must be running under Microsoft Windows 2.0 or higher.

INPUT(prompt,type,*title,default,x-pos,y-pos*)

This function invokes a user-defined dialog box. The dialog box contains a user-specified question (*prompt*) and a title. In this syntax, *type* designates the format for the data to be input.

MESSAGE(logical,*text*)

This function displays and deletes user-specified text messages from a worksheet status bar. When *logical* is TRUE, Excel displays the message indicated in text; when *logical* is FALSE, Excel deletes the message.

ON.DATA(document-text,macro-text)

This function executes the macro indicated by *macro-text* whenever an application sends new data to the document indicated by *document-text*. In this syntax, *document-text* describes one or more remote references, and *macro-text* is an R1C1-style reference in text form.

ON.KEY(key-text,macro-text)

This function executes the macro indicated by *macro-text* whenever the key indicated by *key-text* is pressed. In this syntax, *key-text* describes any single key or any key combined with Shift and/or Ctrl and/or Alt.

ON.TIME(time,macro-text,*tolerance,insert-log*)

This function executes the macro indicated by *macro-text* at a time specified by *time*. In this syntax, *tolerance* is the amount of time, in serial-number form, that should pass before the execution of the macro. When *insert-log* is TRUE, Excel executes the macro; when *insert-log* is FALSE, Excel ignores prior requests to execute *macro-text* at a specified time.

ON.WINDOW(*window-text,macro-text*)

This function tells Excel to execute the macro indicated by *macro-text* whenever the window indicated by *window-text* is activated.

POKE(channel-num,item-text,data-ref)

This function transmits—through the channel called by *channel-num*—the information specified in *data-ref* to the text specified in *item-text*.

RENAME.COMMAND(bar-number,menu-pos,command-pos,name-text)

This function renames the command name specified by *command-pos* as the name indicated in *name-text*.

REQUEST(channel-num,item-text)

This function requests the data defined as *item-text* from the specific application attached to the channel specified by *channel-num*. The application must be running under Microsoft Windows 2.0 or higher.

SEND.KEYS(key-text,*wait-log*)

This function relays the keystroke equivalent of *key-text* to the active application. When *wait-log* is TRUE, Excel processes the keystrokes before returning to macro control; when *wait-log* is FALSE, Excel continues macro execution without waiting for the keystrokes to be processed.

SET.NAME(name-text,*value*)

This function assigns the name *name-text* to *value* on the active macro sheet.

SET.VALUE(ref,values)

This function assigns the value *values* to the cells referenced in *ref* on the active macro sheet.

SHOW.BAR(bar-number)

This function shows the menu bar indicated in *bar-number*.

STEP()

This function displays a dialog box indicating the cell in which a STEP function was encountered. Then the active macro continues its calculation, one cell at a time, as the user clicks the Step bubble in the dialog box.

TERMINATE(channel-num)

This function closes the channel specified in *channel-num*.

WAIT(serial-number)

This function delays the execution of the current macro for the length of time specified in *serial-number*. To resume the execution of the macro, simultaneously press the Esc key and the period key.

Macro Language Control Functions

ARGUMENT(name,*type*)

This function permits arguments to be passed to another macro. The second macro may be called from a function on a worksheet or from another macro.

BREAK()

This function "breaks," or interrupts, the execution of a FOR-NEXT or a WHILE-NEXT loop and continues execution at the first statement following the end of the loop.

FOR(counter-name,start-number,end-number,*step-number*)

This function begins a FOR-NEXT or WHILE-NEXT loop.

GOTO(ref)

This function causes the execution and/or calculation of a macro to branch to *ref*. The argument *ref* may refer to either the active worksheet or any other open worksheet.

HALT()

This function halts, or stops, the execution of a macro.

NEXT()

This function ends a FOR-NEXT or WHILE-NEXT loop.

RESULT(type)

This function returns a user-defined value, specified by *type*. In a macro, the RESULT function must always precede all other formulas.

RETURN(*values*)

This function designates the end of a macro program and terminates the execution of the macro. In this syntax, if *values* are specified, RETURN gives values as a result of the calling function.

WHILE(logical-test)

This function initiates a WHILE-NEXT loop. The execution of the loop continues for as long as *logical-test* remains TRUE. When *logical-test* becomes FALSE, execution is passed to the NEXT loop.

Value-Returning Functions

ABSREF(ref-text,ref)

This function supplies the reference of the cells that have the relative relationship to *ref* that is indicated by *ref-text*. In this syntax, *ref-text* is an R1C1-style relative reference in text form, and *ref* is a cell reference or an external reference.

ACTIVE.CELL()

This function returns the external reference and cell location of the active cell.

DEREF(ref)

This function returns the value of the cell indicated by *ref*, either as a single value or, when *ref* is a range of cells, as an array.

DOCUMENTS()

This function displays in an alphabetized array the names of all documents open on the desktop.

FILES(*directory-text*)

This function displays the files residing in the directory specified by *directory-text*. The files are displayed in a horizontal array.

GET.BAR()

This function displays the ID number for the active menu bar.

GET.CELL(type-of-info,*ref*)

This function returns the format style, location, and contents of the cell indicated by *ref*. The argument *type-of-info* describes the information to be retrieved.

GET.CHART.ITEM(x-y-index,*point-index,item-text*)

This function gives the horizontal or vertical position of a specific point on a chart selection specified by *point-index*.

GET.DEF(*def-text,document*)

This function returns as text the name of *def-text*, which resides in *document*.

GET.DOCUMENT(type-of-info,*name-text*)

This function displays document information about *name-text*. In this syntax, *type-of-info* is a number from 1 to 26 that corresponds to the information to be retrieved.

GET.FORMULA(*ref*)

This function returns the contents of the cell described by *ref*. The contents are displayed as they would be on the formula bar.

GET.NAME(name-text)

This function displays the definition of *name-text* as it appears in the Define Name command in the Formula menu.

GET.NOTE(*cell-ref,start-char,count-char*)

This function counts the number of characters specified in *count-char*, starting at *start-char* in the note specified by *cell-ref*.

GET.WINDOW(type-of-info,*name-text*)

This function supplies information about the window described in *name-text*.

GET.WORKSPACE(type-of-info)

This function supplies information about the workspace described in *name-text*.

LINKS(*document*)

This function returns the names of all the worksheets called by outside references in a particular document. The names are returned as a text array.

NAMES(*doc-text*)

This function returns a horizontal text array of the defined names on the document specified by *doc-text*.

OFFSET(ref,row-offset,column-offset,*height,width*)

This function returns the new cell location of *ref*, where *ref* is offset by the number of rows and columns specified in *row-offset* and *column-offset*.

REFTEXT(ref,*a1*)

This function converts the value in *ref* to an absolute text reference. The text reference is in A1 style when *a1* is TRUE and is in R1C1 style when *a1* is FALSE.

RELREF(ref-1,ref-2)

This function describes the relative position of *ref-1* to *ref-2* and returns the text in R1C1-style relative form.

SELECTION()

This function returns the active document name and cell selection as an external reference. The cell selection may be one cell or a range of cells.

TEXTREF(text,*a1*)

This function converts into a cell reference the name described by *text*. The cell reference is displayed in A1 style when *a1* is TRUE and is displayed in R1C1 style when *a1* is FALSE.

WINDOWS()

This function returns the names of all active windows on the screen as an array of text values. The array of text values lists the windows in the order in which they appear on screen.

INDEX

#REF! error value, 216
10 cash flows calculation, 143-145

A

absolute reference
   format, 35-36, 41-42
   key (F4), 36
account
   balances
      adding, 174
      general ledger, 166
   descriptions
      adding, 174
   numbers, assigning, 171-173
accounting
   summary worksheet, 61, 77-79
   transactions, posting, 167
accounts, adding, 177
accounts payable
   managing, 197-222
   tickler file, 217-219
   worksheets, 200-203
accounts receivable
   delinquent accounts, 216-217
   managing, 197-222
   summaries, 215
   worksheets, 200-203
activity ratio, 45
add accounts (Ctrl-a) macro, 172-174, 177
adding
   account balances, 174
   account descriptions, 174
   accounts, 177
aging report, 213-214
   sharing information between files, 213-214
ALERT() function, 20
AMORTIZE.XLS file, 244-245, 316

annual compounding calculation, 138-139
annuity calculation, 138, 140, 142-143
AP10_89.XLS file, 200-203, 316
AP4_90.XLS file, 200-203, 316
apostrophe ('), 65
applications disk
   backing up, 314
   copying, 314
   hardware requirements, 313-314
AR10_89.XLS file, 200-203, 316
AR4_90.XLS file, 200-203, 316
area charts, 282-283, 299
array formula, 18
asset analysis, 127
   depreciation analyzer, 133-137
   DuPont method, 129-133
assigning account numbers, 171-173
asterisk (*) wild card, 254-255
AUTOEXEC.BAT file, 24-25
average collection period ratio, 49

B

backing up
   disks, 94
   applications disk, 314
   models, 94, 128
balance sheet, 38-44, 56-57
   designing, 38-44
   DuPont model, 130-131
   historical data, 112-116
   monthly, 56-57
   pro forma, 112-116
bar charts, 282, 284, 300
BLARCORY.XLS file, 315
bond analyzer, 155-160
   value analyzer, 155-157
   yield to maturity (YTM) analyzer, 155, 158-160

357

BONDS.XLM file, 315
BONDS.XLS file, 155-160, 315
    creating charts, 302-304
BONDS.XLW file, 315
Border option, 63
borrowing
    long term, 244-245
    short term, 246
breakeven analysis model, 93, 120-125
BREAKEVN.XLM file, 315
BREAKEVN.XLS file, 298-299, 315
BREAKEVN.XLW file, 120-125, 315
budget
    estimates, period, 166
    summary, 167
    summary and variance, printing, 185
business borrowing, 244-248

C

calculations
    dividends 247-248
    external-funds-requirement, 113
CALKINS.XLS file, 247, 248, 315
canceling, macros, 173
capital-asset pricing (CAPM) method, 146, 149-152
case study, General Ledger Accounting System (GLAS) model, 186-193
cash
    budget model, 93-107
    disbursements forecast, 104
    level minimum, 105
    receipts forecast, 100-102
CASHBUDG.XLS file, 94-107, 298-299, 315
Cell Protection dialog box, 85
cells
    formats, default, 71
    protecting, 84-86
    variable, 99
charge vs cash
    sales analysis, 99-100
    purchase analysis, 103
Chart menu, 295-296

chart of accounts
    General Ledger Accounting System (GLAS) model, 171-173
    printing, 184
charts, 281-287
    adding descriptions, 303-304
    conversion, 232-233
    creating, 287-295
        from worksheet models, 295-310
    data organization, 287-293
    emphasizing legends, 304
    enhancing, 302-304
    expanding, 295
    macro, 123-124
    modifying, 302-304
    printing, 301-302
    types
        area, 282-283, 299
        bar, 282-284, 300
        column, 282-285, 299
        combination, 282, 287
        line, 282, 284-285, 297, 302-304
        pie, 282, 285-286, 298
        scatter, 282, 286
check register, 61-71
checkbook managing, 61
    automating the system, 83
    testing the system, 80-82
CHKBOOK.XLS file, 78, 81, 83, 315
CHKBOOK.XLW file, 315
CHKSUMMR.XLS file, 78, 83, 315
    creating charts, 298
chronology, worksheet, 19
clear journal (Ctrl-c) macro, 167, 172-173, 181-83
closing general ledger/journal worksheet, 181-183
collections worksheet, 216-217
column charts, 282, 284-285, 299
COLWKSHT.XLS file, 216-217, 316
COLWKSHT.XLW file, 216-217, 316
combination charts, 282, 287
commands
    COPY (DOS), 314
    Data Extract, 257-258
    Data Form, 251-255

Index 359

Data Set Criteria, 257-258, 269-270
Data Set Database, 252, 269-270
Data Sort, 271
Database Set Range, 249
DISKCOPY (DOS), 314
Edit Fill Right, 267
Edit Paste, 276-277
File Page Setup, 272
File Print, 272-279
Format Define Name, 252
Link, 210-211
New Chart, 293-295
Save Workspace, 211
compounding interest, continuous basis, 141
computed
    criteria, 250
    field, 250
CONFIG.SYS file, 24
continuous
    compounding calculation, 141
    data range, 291-293
conversion chart, 232-233
COPY (DOS) command, 314
copying applications disk, 314
Cost Data Elsewhere worksheet, 240-243
Costs and Sales Forecast worksheet, 230-231, 234-235
costs estimate, monthly 235
creating
    charts from worksheet models, 295-310
    workspaces, 219
CREDAPP.XLS file, 198-200, 316
credit
    application
        form, 199-200
        generator, 198-200
    instrument, 244-245
criteria, 250
    comparison, 250
    computed, 250
    search, 253-255
Ctrl-a (add accounts) key, 172-174, 177
Ctrl-b (print Budget Summary and Variance) key, 185
Ctrl-c (clear journal) key, 167, 172-173, 181-183
Ctrl-c (create chart) macro, 123-124

Ctrl-e (enter transactions) key, 175, 177-179, 181
Ctrl-g (graph) key, 132, 136, 138-141, 145, 150-152, 159-160
Ctrl-l (list Chart of Accounts) key, 172-173, 184-185
Ctrl-p (post transactions) key, 167, 176, 179-181, 183
Ctrl-q (quit and save files) key, 183
Ctrl-r (print reports) key, 181
Ctrl-s (print Period-to-Date Summary) key, 185
Ctrl-t (print Trial Balance Sheet) key, 185
Ctrl-x (return to main menu) key, 185
current ratio, 48

D

DAILYINT.XLS file, 244, 246, 316
data
    blocks, graph, 291-293, 309-310
    hiding, 277
    organization charts, 287-293
    range, 294-295
        continuous, 291-293
        noncontinuous, 291-293, 295, 305-309
Data Extract command, 257-258
Data Form command, 251-255
Data Form dialog box, 252
Data Set Criteria command, 257-258, 269-270
Data Set Database command, 252, 269-270
Data Sort command, 271
DATA.SERIES() function, 20
Database Set Range command, 249
databases
    computed field, 250
    criteria, 250
    expanding GLAS model file, 194
    extracting records, 256-258
    field, 250
        name, 250, 253-254
        size, 251
        valid entries, 251

functions, 320-322
hiding data, 277
managing, 249-279
plotting trends, 258-267
range, 249, 251-254
    extract, 250
record, 249
searching for information, 253-255
setting up, 249-253
size limitation, 251
sorting records, 270-271
verifying reliability, 267-270
date and time functions, 320, 322-323
date format, updating, 203
DCFA.XLS file, 161-163, 315
debt ratio, 45, 49
declining-balance depreciation, 133-136
default formats, 71
delinquent accounts, 216-217
DEPRECI8.XLM file, 137, 315
DEPRECI8.XLS file, 133-136, 315
    creating charts, 303, 304
    modifying, 137
DEPRECI8.XLW file, 315
depreciation
    analyzer (asset analysis), 133-137
    declining-balance, 133-136
    modified-accelerated-cost-recovery-
        system (MACRS), 137
    straight-line, 133-134, 136
    sum-of-the-years'-digits, 133, 135-136
descriptions, adding to charts, 303-304
deviation functions
    DSTDEV, 268-270
    DSTDEVP, 268
dialog boxes
    Cell Protection, 85
    Protect Document, 86, 88-89
difference between deposits and
    withdrawals formula, 68
disbursements, cash, 104
discount rate (DR), 161-163
discounted-cash-flow analyzer
    incremental cash flow analysis, 161-163
    single investment method, 161-163

disk
    applications
        backing up, 314
        copying, 314
        hardware requirements, 313-314
    hard, 21
DISKCOPY (DOS) command, 314
dividend calculations, 247-248
DONNELLY.XLS file, 315
DR *see* discount rate
DSTDEV function, 268-270, 321
DSTDEVP function, 268, 321
DuPont method (asset analysis), 129-133
DUPONT.XLM file, 315
DUPONT.XLS file, 129-133, 315
    creating charts, 305-307
    modifying, 132
DUPONT.XLW file, 315

E

Edit (F2) key, 33
Edit Fill Right command, 267
Edit Paste command, 276-277
editing journal transactions, 177-179, 181
eliminate zeros formula, 69
EMPPHONE.XLS file, 256-258, 316
enter transactions (Ctrl-e) macro, 175, 177-179, 181
entering journal transactions, 177-179
equal (=) sign, 39
Equivalent Units Conversion worksheet, 230-233
Excel, requirements for using business applications, 313-314
excess cash balancing formula, 107
expanding
    charts, 295
    database, GLAS model, 194
expected return
    investment formula, 149
    method, 153
external-funds-requirement calculation, 113
extract range, 250
extracting records, databases, 256-258

F

F2 (Edit) key, 33
F4 (Absolute reference) key, 36
field, 250
    names, 250, 253-254
    size, 251
    valid entries, 251
file
    extensions
        XLC, 211
        XLM (macros), 128, 211
        XLS (spreadsheets), 128, 211
        XLW (worksheets), 128, 211
    linking methods
        Link command, 211
        Save Workspace command, 211
File Page Setup command, 272
File Print command, 272-279
files
    AMORTIZE.XLS, 244-245, 316
    AP10_89.XLS, 200-203, 316
    AP4_90.XLS, 200-203, 316
    AR10_89.XLS, 200-203, 316
    AR4_90.XLS, 200-203, 316
    AUTOEXEC.BAT, 24-25
    BLARCORY.XLS, 315
    BONDS.XLM, 315
    BONDS.XLS, 155-160, 315
        creating charts, 302-304
    BONDS.XLW, 315
    BREAKEVN.XLM, 315
    BREAKEVN.XLS, 315
        creating charts, 298-299
    BREAKEVN.XLW, 315
    BREAKEVN.XLW, 120-125
    CALKINS.XLS, 247-248, 315
    CASHBUDG.XLS, 94-107, 315
        creating charts, 298-299
    CHKBOOK.XLS, 315
    CHKBOOK.XLW, 315
    CHKSUMMR.XLS, 315
        creating charts, 298
    COLWKSHT.XLS, 216-217, 316
    COLWKSHT.XLW, 216-217, 316
    CONFIG.SYS, 24
    CREDAPP.XLS, 198-200, 316

DAILYINT.XLS, 244, 246, 316
DCFA.XLS, 161-163, 315
DEPRECI8.XLM, 137, 315
DEPRECI8.XLS, 133-137, 315
    creating charts, 303-304
DEPRECI8.XLW, 315
DONNELLY.XLS, 315
DUPONT.XLM, 315
DUPONT.XLS, 129-133, 315
    creating charts, 305-307
DUPONT.XLW, 315
EMPPHONE.XLS, 256-258, 316
FV.XLM, 315
FV.XLS, 138-141, 315
    creating charts, 307-309
FV.XLW, 315
GENMENU.XLS, 168, 176-177, 315
GL.XLM, 168-169, 300, 315
GL.XLS, 168-169, 174-183, 194, 315
GL.XLW, 168, 315
HISTORY.XLS, 117-119, 315
INCBALRA.XLS, 315
    creating charts, 297
INVAGING.XLS, 213-214, 316
INVARCUS.XLS, 215, 316
INVARDAT.XLS, 215, 316
INVCREG.XLS, 210-211, 214, 316
INVCREG.XLW, 209, 211-212, 316
INVCREG1.XLS, 204-208, 316
INVFREG.XLS, 220-222, 316
INVSALES.XLS, 212-213, 316
linking, 198, 219
merging for reports, 276-277
MN.XLW, 230, 316
MN_CNVRT.XLS, 230, 232-233, 316
MN_FRCS1.XLS, 316
MN_FRCST.XLS, 230, 234-235, 316
MN_INCST.XLS, 240-243, 316
MN_PROF1.XLS, 316
MN_PROFM.XLS, 230, 235-236, 241-243, 316
PR89COND.XLC, 258-267, 316
PR89HOME.XLC, 258-267, 316
PROFORMA.XLS, 108-116, 315
PROJB89.XLS, 273-279, 316
PROJECTS.XLS, 270-279, 316
PROTOCOL.XLS, 168, 170, 186-193, 315

PV.XLM, 315
PV.XLS, 142-146, 315
PV.XLW, 315
REPMENU.XLS, 168-170, 315
RSK&RTN.XLM, 315
RSK&RTN.XLS, 146-152, 315
    creating charts, 309-310
RSK&RTN.XLW, 315
SBLHSJUN.XLS, 316
SLSCONTC.XLS, 253-255, 316
SLSPR89.XLS, 258-267, 316
STOCKS.XLS, 153-155, 315
SVLHSJUN.XLS, 267-270
TEMP.XLS, 168, 170
TICKLER.XLS, 217-219, 316
TMP.XLS, 315
    creating charts, 300
WHITNEY.XLS, 315
financial
    functions, 320, 323-324
    ratio report, 44-52, 58
        designing, 44-52
        monthly, 58
    statements, 28-60
        pro forma, 108-109, 111-119
financing
    applications, 225-248
    impact, 242-248
footers, 272-273
forecasting, 93-125
    breakeven analysis, 93, 120-125
    cash budget, 93-107
        disbursements, 104
        charge vs cash
            sales analysis, 99-100
            purchase analysis, 103
        receipts, 100-102
        sales, 98-99
    pro forma financial statements, 93, 108-119
Format Define Name command, 252
Format menu, 295-296
formats
    absolute reference, 35-36, 41-42
    relative reference, 35-36, 41-42
formatting reports, 272-273
forms, credit application, 199-200

formulas
    difference between deposits and withdrawals, 68
    eliminate zeros, 69
    excess cash balancing, 107
    invoice register, 205-208
    ratio, 59-60
    required total financing, 106, 115-116
functions
    ALERT(), 20
    DATA.SERIES(), 20
    database, 320-322
    date and time, 320, 322-323
    financial, 320, 323-324
    information, 320, 324-326
    INPUT(), 20
    logical, 320, 326-327
    lookup, 320, 327-328
    macro language library, 334-355
    mathematical, 320, 328-329
    matrix, 320, 329-330
    Paste, 31
    standard deviation, 268-270
    statistical, 320, 330-331
    SUM(), 30-32
    text, 320-321, 332-333
    trend, 259-267
    trigonometric, 320, 333-334
future sum (present value) calculation, 142-143
future value, 138-141
    annual compounding, 138-139
    annuity, 138, 140
    continuous compounding, 141
    intrayear compounding, 138-139
FV.XLM file, 315
FV.XLS file, 138-140, 315
    creating charts, 307-309
    modifying, 141
FV.XLW file, 315

G

general ledger account
    balances, 166
    transactions, posting, 167

General Ledger Accounting System (GLAS)
    model, 165-167, 177-185
    case study, 186-193
    chart of accounts, 171-173
    components, 168-170
    expanding database, 194
    macros, 172-173
    preparation, 171-176
general ledger/journal worksheet, 174-183
    closing, 181-183
GENMENU.XLS file, 168, 176-177, 315
GL.XLM file, 168-169, 300, 315
GL.XLS file, 168-169, 174-183, 194, 315
GL.XLW file, 168, 315
GLAS *see* General Ledger Accounting System model
Gordon constant growth method, 153-155
graph data blocks, 291-293, 309-310
graphics, 281-282
    card, requirements, 21
    library, 282
graphing
    BONDS.XLS, 159-160
    depreciation analyzer, 136
    DuPont method, 132
    FV.XLS, 138-141
    PV.XLS, 145
    RSK&RTN.XLS, 150-152
graphs *see* charts
gross profit margin, 49
GROWTH trend function, 260-262

H

hard disk requirements, 21
hardware requirements, 21, 313-324
headers, 272-373
help, getting, 317
hiding data, 277
HISTORY.XLS file, 117-119, 315

I

impact of financing, 242-248
INCBALRA.XLS file, 315
    creating charts, 297
    worksheet, 53-58
income statements, 28-37, 54-56
    monthly, 55-56
    designing
        product-oriented statement, 32-37
        service-oriented statement, 28-32
    DuPont model, 130-131
    historical data, 110-112
    pro forma, 110-112
incremental cash flow analysis, 161-163
information functions, 320, 324-326
INPUT() function, 20
interest costs, real, 246
internal rate of return (IRR), 161-163
intrayear compounding calculation, 138-139
INVAGING.XLS file, 213-214, 316
INVARCUS.XLS file, 215, 316
INVARDAT.XLS file, 215, 316
INVCREG.XLS file, 210-211, 214, 316
INVCREG.XLW file, 209, 211-212, 316
INVCREG1.XLS file, 204-208, 316
inventory turnover ratio, 48
investment analysis, 127, 137-146
investor financing, 247-248
INVFREG.XLS file, 220-222, 316
invoice register, 198, 204-212
    formulas, 205-208
    sharing information between files, 209-212
INVSALES.XLS file, 212-213, 316
IRR *see* internal rate of return

J

journal transactions
    editing, 177-179, 181
    entering, 177-179
    posting, 179-181, 183
    quitting, 183

K

keys
- Ctrl-a (add accounts), 172-174, 177
- Ctrl-b (print Budget Summary and Variance), 185
- Ctrl-c (clear journal), 167, 172-173, 181-183
- Ctrl-c (create chart) macro, 123-124
- Ctrl-e (enter transactions), 175, 177-179, 181
- Ctrl-g (graph), 132, 136, 138-141, 145, 150-152, 159-160
- Ctrl-l (list Chart of Accounts), 172-173, 184-185
- Ctrl-p (post transactions), 167, 176, 179-181, 183
- Ctrl-q (quit and save files), 183
- Ctrl-r (print reports), 181
- Ctrl-s (print Period-to-Date Summary), 185
- Ctrl-t (print Trial Balance Sheet), 185
- Ctrl-x (return to main menu), 185
- F2 (Edit), 33
- F4 (Absolute ref), 36

L

level of precedence, 319
line charts, 282, 284-285, 297, 302-304
linear (straight line) projections, 260-267
LINEST trend function, 260-261, 263-265
Link command, 210-211
linked worksheets, 227
linking
- files, 198, 219
- methods, save workspace command, 211
- worksheets, 77-80, 210-213, 219

liquidity ratio, 45
list Chart of Accounts (Ctrl-l) macro, 172-173, 184-185
loading
- macros, 128
- spreadsheets, 128
- workspaces, 128
loan amortization schedule, 245

Locked option, 85
logarithmic (exponential curve) projections, 260-267
LOGEST trend function, 260-261, 266-267
logical functions, 320, 326-327
long-term borrowing, 244-245

M

macro language
- control functions, 352-353
- library functions
    - action-equivalent functions, 344-347
    - command-equivalent functions, 334-344
    - customizing functions, 347-352
    - macro language control functions, 352-353
    - value-returning functions, 353-355
macros
- add accounts (Ctrl-a), 172-174, 177
- array formula, 18
- building, 12
- canceling, 173
- clear journal (Ctrl-c), 167, 172-173, 181-183
- create chart (Ctrl-c), 123-124
- development, 14-15
- enter transactions (Ctrl-e), 175, 177-179, 181
- General Ledger Accounting System (GLAS) model, 172-173
- list Chart of Accounts (Ctrl-l), 172-173, 184-185
- loading, 128
- planning, 12
- post transactions (Ctrl-p), 176, 179-181, 183
- print
    - Budget Summary and Variance (Ctrl-b), 185
    - Period-to-Date Summary (Ctrl-s), 185
    - reports (Ctrl-r), 181
    - Trial Balance Sheet (Ctrl-t), 185
- quit and save files (Ctrl-q), 183
- return to main menu (Ctrl-x), 185
- transaction posting (Ctrl-p), 167

Index

managing
    accounts payable, 197-222
    accounts receivable, 197-222
    databases, 249-279
market projections, developing, 227-241
marketing applications, 225-248
mathematical
    functions, 320, 328-329
    operator override, 65
matrix functions, 320, 329-330
menus
    Chart, 295-296
    Format, 295-296
merging files for reports, 276-277
microprocessor chips, 23
Microsoft Windows, 22
MN.XLW file, 230, 316
MN-CNVRT.XLS file, 230, 232-233, 316
MN-FRCS1.XLS file, 316
MN-FRCST.XLS file, 230, 234-235, 316
MN-INCST.XLS file, 240-243, 316
MN-PROF1.XLS file, 316
MN-PROFM.XLS file, 230, 235-236, 241-243, 316
models, backing up, 94, 128
modified-accelerated-cost-recovery system (MACRS) depreciation, 137
modifying
    charts, 302-304
    DEPRECI8.XLS, 137
    DUPONT.XLS file, 132
    FV.XLS, 141
    spreadsheets, 32-33
    worksheets, 220-222
monthly
    costs estimate, 235
    profits estimate, 235
    sales estimate, 235

N

net
    present value (NPV), 161-163
    profit margin (NPM), 132
    profit margin after taxes, 49

New Chart command, 293-295
noncontinuous data range, 291-293, 295, 305-309
NOW() formula, 216
NPM *see* net profit margin
NPV *see* net present value

O

operating system requirements, 21
operational order of precedence, 320
options
    Border, 63
    Locked, 85
    Protect Document, 86
    Split, 49
Options Protection Document mode, 175-176
override mathematical operators, 65

P

password protecting, 86-89
Paste function, 31
percent of sales forecast, 113
period budget estimates, 166
period-to-date
    ledger summary, 167
    summary, printing, 185
perpetuity, 142
    calculation, 143-144
PI *see* profitability index
pie charts, 282, 285-286, 298
plotting trends, database, 258-267
post transactions (Ctrl-p) macro, 176, 179-181, 183
posting
    accounting transactions, 167
    journal transactions, 179-181, 183
PR89COND.XLC file, 258-267, 316
PR89HOME.XLC file, 258-267, 316
precedence, order of, 319-320

present value, 138, 142-146
    calculations
        10 cash flows, 143-145
        annuity, 142-143
        future sum, 142-143
        perpetuity, 143-144
previewing the printed page, 272
print
    Budget Summary and Variance (Ctrl-b) macro, 185
    Period-to-Date Summary (Ctrl-s) macro, 185
    reports (Ctrl-r) macro, 181
    Trial Balance Sheet (Ctrl-t) macro, 185
Printer Setup configuration, 301-302
printers
    dot matrix, 23
    LaserJet, 23
    LaserWriter, 23
printing
    chart of accounts, 185
    charts, 301-302
    reports, 181, 273-279
        Budget Summary and Variance, 185
        Chart of Accounts, 184-185
        Period-to-Date Summary, 185
        Trial Balance Sheet, 185
pro forma
    balance sheet, 112-116
    financial statements, 110
        model, 93, 108-119
    income statements, 110-112
    ratio analysis, 116-119
Pro Forma Costs and Sales worksheet, 230-231, 235-236, 241-243
problems, troubleshooting, 316
profitability
    ratio, 45
    index (PI), 161-163
profits estimate, monthly, 235
PROFORMA.XLS file, 108-116, 315
programming, 11
PROJB89.XLS file, 273-279, 316
projections
    linear (straight line), 260-267
    logarithmic (exponential curve), 260-267

PROJECTS.XLS file, 270-316
Protect Document
    dialog box, 86, 88-89
    option, 86
protecting
    cells, 84-86
    password, 86-89
    worksheets, 86-89
Protocol Services, Int'l case study, 186-193
PROTOCOL.XLS file, 168, 170, 186-193, 315
PV.XLM file, 315
PV.XLS file, 142-144, 315
    modifying, 145-146
PV.XLW file, 315

Q

query mode, 179
question mark (?) wild card, 255
quick ratio, 48
quit and save files (Ctrl-q) macro, 183
quitting, journal transactions, 183

R

random access memory (RAM)
    optimizing, 23, 24
    requirements, 21
ranges, selecting multiple, 40
ratio
    activity, 45
    analysis
        historical data, 116-119
        pro forma, 116-119
    average collection period, 49
    current, 48
    debt, 45, 49
    formulas, 59-60
    inventory turnover, 48
    liquidity, 45
    profitability, 45
    quick, 48
    return on equity, 49
reach over, 213

Index **367**

real interests costs, 246
reconciliation sheet, 61, 72-76
record, 249
relative reference format, 35-36, 41-42
REPMENU.XLS file, 168-170, 315
reports
    footers, 272-273
    formatting, 272-273
    headers, 272-273
    merging files, 276-277
    printing, 181, 273-279
        Budget Summary and Variance, 185
        Chart of Accounts, 184-185
        Period-to-Date Summary, 185
        Trial Balance Sheet, 185
required total financing formula, 106, 115-116
retained earnings, 247-248
return on equity (ROE), 129-132
    ratio, 49
return on investment in assets (ROI), 129-132
return to main menu (Ctrl-x) macro, 185
risk and return analysis, 146-152
    capital-asset pricing (CAPM) method, 146, 149-152
    single-asset risk method, 146-149
ROE *see* return on equity
ROI *see* return on investment, 132
rounding, 122
RSK&RTN.XLM file, 315
RSK&RTN.XLS file, 146-152, 315
    creating charts, 309-310
RSK&RTN.XLW file, 315

S

sales
    applications, 225-248
    estimate, monthly, 235
    forecast, 98-99
    summary, 212-213
        sharing information between files, 212-213
Save Workspace command, 211
SBLHSJUN.XLS file, 316

scatter charts, 282, 286
schedules, load amortization, 245
search criteria, databases, 253-255
series marker, 297
sharing information between files
    aging report, 213-214
    invoice register, 209-212
    sales summary, 212-213
short term borrowing, 246
single
    investment method, 161-163
    asset risk method, 146-149
size, database limitation, 251
SLSCONTC.XLS file, 253-255, 316
SLSPR89.XLS file, 258-267, 316
sorting records, database, 270-271
Split option, 49
spreadsheets
    backing up, 94, 128
    modifying, 32-33
    loading, 128
standard deviation, 267-270
    function, 268-270
statistical functions, 320, 330-331
stock analyzer, 153-155
    expected-return method, 153
    Gordon constant growth method, 153-155
    zero growth method, 153
STOCK.XLS file, 315
STOCKS.XLS file, 153-155
straight-line depreciation, 133-134, 136
SUM() function, 30-32
sum-of-the years'-digits depreciation, 133, 135-136
SVLHSJUN.XLS file, 267-270

T

tables, 121-124
TEMP.XLS file, 168, 170
text functions, 320, 331-333
tickler file, 217-219
TICKLER.XLS file, 217-219, 316
time value of money, 137-146

TMP.XLS file, 315
    creating charts, 300
transaction posting (Ctrl-p) macro, 167
trend functions, 259-267
    GROWTH, 260-262
    LINEST, 260-261, 263-265
    LOGEST, 260-262, 266-267
    TREND, 260-261
trial balance sheet, 167
    printing, 185
trigonometric functions, 320, 333-334
troubleshooting problems, 316

U

unit costs, 228
    analyzing, 230-233
    gathering, 229

V

valuation techniques, 152-163
    bond analyzer, 155-160
    discounted-cash-flow analyzer, 161-163
    stock analyzer, 153-155
value-returning functions (macro language library), 353-355
variable cells, 99
variance analysis, 167
vertical bar chart *see* column charts
video displays, EGA/VGA compatible, 23

W

What if
    scenarios, 236-240
    analysis, 50-52
WHITNEY.XLS file, 315
wild cards, 254-255
windows
    Microsoft, 22
worksheet chronology, 19

worksheets
    accounts payable, 200-203
    accounts receivable, 200-203
    backing up, 94, 128
    CHKBOOK.XLS, 78, 81, 83
    CHKSUMMR.XLS, 78, 83
    Cost Data Elsewhere, 240-243
    Costs and Sales Forecast, 230-231, 234-235
    Equivalent Units Conversion, 230-233
    INCBALRA.XLS, 53-58
    linked, 227
    linking, 77-80, 210-213, 219
    modifying, 220-222
    Pro Forma Costs and Sales, 230-231, 235-236, 241-243
    protecting, 86-89
workspaces
    creating, 219
    files, 120, 198, 230
    loading, 128
    saving, 125

Y

yield to maturity (YTM), 155, 158-160

Z

zero growth method, 153

More Computer Knowledge from Que

Lotus Software Titles

1-2-3 Database Techniques	24.95
1-2-3 Release 2.2 Business Applications	39.95
1-2-3 Release 2.2 Quick Reference	7.95
1-2-3 Release 2.2 QuickStart	19.95
1-2-3 Release 2.2 Workbook and Disk	29.95
1-2-3 Release 3 Business Applications	39.95
1-2-3 Release 3 Quick Reference	7.95
1-2-3 Release 3 QuickStart	19.95
1-2-3 Release 3 Workbook and Disk	29.95
1-2-3 Tips, Tricks, and Traps, 3rd Edition	22.95
Upgrading to 1-2-3 Release 3	14.95
Using 1-2-3, Special Edition	24.95
Using 1-2-3 Release 2.2, Special Edition	24.95
Using 1-2-3 Release 3	24.95
Using Lotus Magellan	21.95
Using Symphony, 2nd Edition	26.95

Database Titles

dBASE III Plus Applications Library	24.95
dBASE III Plus Handbook, 2nd Edition	24.95
dBASE III Plus Tips, Tricks, and Traps	21.95
dBASE III Plus Workbook and Disk	29.95
dBASE IV Applications Library, 2nd Edition	39.95
dBASE IV Handbook, 3rd Edition	23.95
dBASE IV Programming Techniques	24.95
dBASE IV QueCards	21.95
dBASE IV Quick Reference	7.95
dBASE IV QuickStart	19.95
dBASE IV Tips, Tricks, and Traps, 2nd Edition	21.95
dBASE IV Workbook and Disk	29.95
dBXL and Quicksilver Programming: Beyond dBASE	24.95
R:BASE User's Guide, 3rd Edition	22.95
Using Clipper	24.95
Using DataEase	22.95
Using Reflex	19.95
Using Paradox 3	24.95

Applications Software Titles

AutoCAD Advanced Techniques	34.95
AutoCAD Quick Reference	7.95
AutoCAD Sourcebook	24.95
Excel Business Applications: IBM Version	39.95
Introduction to Business Software	14.95
PC Tools Quick Reference	7.95
Smart Tips, Tricks, and Traps	24.95
Using AutoCAD, 2nd Edition	29.95
Using Computers in Business	24.95
Using DacEasy	21.95
Using Dollars and Sense: IBM Version, 2nd Edition	19.95
Using Enable/OA	23.95
Using Excel: IBM Version	24.95
Using Generic CADD	24.95
Using Harvard Project Manager	24.95
Using Managing Your Money, 2nd Edition	19.95
Using Microsoft Works: IBM Version	21.95
Using PROCOMM PLUS	19.95
Using Q&A, 2nd Edition	21.95
Using Quattro	21.95
Using Quicken	19.95
Using Smart	22.95
Using SmartWare II	24.95
Using SuperCalc5, 2nd Edition	22.95

Word Processing and Desktop Publishing Titles

DisplayWrite QuickStart	19.95
Harvard Graphics Quick Reference	7.95
Microsoft Word 5 Quick Reference	7.95
Microsoft Word 5 Tips, Tricks, and Traps: IBM Version	19.95
Using DisplayWrite 4, 2nd Edition	19.95
Using Freelance Plus	24.95
Using Harvard Graphics	24.95
Using Microsoft Word 5: IBM Version	21.95
Using MultiMate Advantage, 2nd Edition	19.95
Using PageMaker: IBM Version, 2nd Edition	24.95
Using PFS: First Choice	22.95
Using PFS: First Publisher	22.95
Using Professional Write	19.95
Using Sprint	21.95
Using Ventura Publisher, 2nd Edition	24.95
Using WordPerfect, 3rd Edition	21.95
Using WordPerfect 5	24.95
Using WordStar, 2nd Edition	21.95
Ventura Publisher Techniques and Applications	22.95
Ventura Publisher Tips, Tricks, and Traps	24.95
WordPerfect Macro Library	21.95
WordPerfect Power Techniques	21.95
WordPerfect QueCards	21.95
WordPerfect Quick Reference	7.95
WordPerfect QuickStart	21.95
WordPerfect Tips, Tricks, and Traps, 2nd Edition	21.95
WordPerfect 5 Workbook and Disk	29.95

Macintosh/Apple II Titles

The Big Mac Book	27.95
Excel QuickStart	19.95
Excel Tips, Tricks, and Traps	22.95
Using AppleWorks, 3rd Edition	21.95
Using AppleWorks GS	21.95
Using dBASE Mac	19.95
Using Dollars and Sense: Macintosh Version	19.95
Using Excel: Macintosh Verson	22.95
Using FullWrite Professional	21.95
Using HyperCard	24.95
Using Microsoft Word 4: Macintosh Version	21.95
Using Microsoft Works: Macintosh Version, 2nd Edition	21.95
Using PageMaker: Macintosh Version	24.95
Using WordPerfect: Macintosh Version	19.95

Hardware and Systems Titles

DOS Tips, Tricks, and Traps	22.95
DOS Workbook and Disk	29.95
Hard Disk Quick Reference	7.95
IBM PS/2 Handbook	21.95
Managing Your Hard Disk, 2nd Edition	22.95
MS-DOS Quick Reference	7.95
MS-DOS QuickStart	21.95
MS-DOS User's Guide, Special Edition	29.95
Networking Personal Computers, 3rd Edition	22.95
Norton Utilities Quick Reference	7.95
The Printer Bible	24.95
Understanding UNIX: A Conceptual Guide, 2nd Edition	21.95
Upgrading and Repairing PCs	27.95
Using DOS	22.95
Using Microsoft Windows	19.95
Using Novell NetWare	24.95
Using OS/2	23.95
Using PC DOS, 3rd Edition	22.95

Programming and Technical Titles

Assembly Language Quick Reference	7.95
C Programmer's Toolkit	39.95
C Programming Guide, 3rd Edition	24.95
C Quick Reference	7.95
DOS and BIOS Functions Quick Reference	7.95
DOS Programmer's Reference, 2nd Edition	27.95
Power Graphics Programming	24.95
QuickBASIC Advanced Techniques	21.95
QuickBASIC Programmer's Toolkit	39.95
QuickBASIC Quick Reference	7.95
SQL Programmer's Guide	29.95
Turbo C Programming	22.95
Turbo Pascal Advanced Techniques	22.95
Turbo Pascal Programmer's Toolkit	39.95
Turbo Pascal Quick Reference	7.95
Using Assembly Language	24.95
Using QuickBASIC 4	19.95
Using Turbo Pascal	21.95

For more information, call

1-800-428-5331

All prices subject to change without notice. Prices and charges are for domestic orders only. Non-U.S. prices might be higher.

Excel QuickStart
Developed by Que Corporation

Excel QuickStart takes readers step-by-step through basic Excel operations—including spreadsheets, databases, and graphs—with more than 100 two-page illustrations. Covers both IBM and Macintosh.

Order #957
$19.95 USA
0-88022-423-1, 400 pp.

Using Excel: IBM Version
by Ron Person and Mary Campbell

Que's *Using Excel: IBM Version* helps users master Excel. Includes **Quick Start** tutorials plus tips and tricks to help improve efficiency and troubleshoot problems. Also includes a special section for 1-2-3 users making the switch to Excel.

Order #87
$24.95 USA
0-88022-284-0, 804 pp.

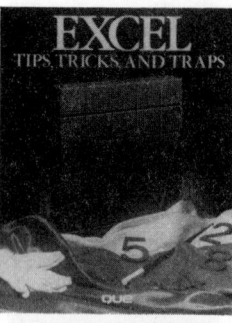

Excel Tips, Tricks, and Traps
by Ron Person

A collection of tips and techniques for using Excel in both the IBM and Macintosh environments. Includes information on manipulating charts, customizing fonts, and programming high-level macros.

Order #959
$22.95 USA
0-88022-421-5, 500 pp.

Using Microsoft Windows
by Ron Person

An easy-to-follow guide to Windows/286 and Windows/386! This powerful text incorporates a series of hands-on practice sessions to help you learn Windows Write, Windows Paint, and desktop applications. A practical resource for greater understanding of Windows.

Order #804
$19.95 USA
0-88022-336-7

Que Order Line: **1-800-428-5331**

All prices subject to change without notice. Prices and charges are for domestic orders only. Non-U.S. prices might be higher.

If your computer uses 3 1/2-inch disks . . .

If your computer uses 3 1/2-inch disks, you can return this form to Que to obtain a 3 1/2-inch disk to use with this book. Simply fill out the address label and mail to:

Excel Business Applications: IBM Version Disk Exchange

Que Corporation
11711 N. College Ave.
Carmel, IN 46032

Name _____ Phone _____
Company _____ Title _____
Address _____
City _____ St ____ ZIP ____